JOURNALS OF TRAVELS

JOURNALS OF TRAVELS

In

Assam, Burma, Bootan, Affghanistan and the Neighbouring Countries.

BY THE LATE

WILLIAM GRIFFITH, ESQ. F.L.S.

GYAN

Published by

GYAN

Gyan Publishing House
5, Ansari Road
Daryaganj, New Delhi-110002
Phone: 011-47034999, 9811692060
E-mail: books@gyanbooks.com

Distribution Network
gyanbooks.com
India, USA, Canada, UK, Australia, France

ISBN : 978-81-212-1220-5 (PB)
First Published, 1847

2nd Impression 2021

Printed at: Gyan Press, Delhi.

Journals of Travels
Author: William Griffith

POSTHUMOUS PAPERS

BEQUEATHED TO

THE HONORABLE THE EAST INDIA COMPANY,

AND

PRINTED BY ORDER OF THE GOVERNMENT OF BENGAL.

JOURNALS OF TRAVELS

IN

ASSAM, BURMA, BOOTAN, AFFGHANISTAN AND THE NEIGHBOURING COUNTRIES.

BY THE LATE

WILLIAM GRIFFITH, Esq., F.L.S.,

MEMBER OF THE IMPERIAL ACADEMY NATURÆ CURIOSORUM AT BONN: CORRESPONDING MEMBER OF THE ROYAL BOTANICAL SOCIETY OF RATISBON, OF THE ROYAL ACADEMIES OF SCIENCE AT TURIN AND CHRISTIANA, HORTICULTURAL AND ENTOMOLOGICAL SOCIETIES, AND SOCIETY OF ARTS, LONDON: MEMBER AND FOR SOMETIME VICE-PRESIDENT OF THE AGRI-HORTICULTURAL SOCIETY OF INDIA.

Assistant Surgeon on the Madras Establishment; and a short time Officiating Superintendent of the Honorable Company's Botanic Garden, Calcutta, and subsequently Civil Assistant Surgeon, Malacca.

ARRANGED

BY JOHN M'CLELLAND, F.L.S.,

Surgeon, Bengal Service.

Calcutta:

BISHOP'S COLLEGE PRESS.

1847.

At 33

Drawn on Stone by Edward Morton from a Daguerreotype.

Contents.

Page

List of Plates and Directions for the Binder.

ERRATA.

Page 3 line 18 from top, for *Palomogeton*, read Potamogeton.
” 3 ” 21 from top, for *Aryza*, read Oryza.
” 7 ” 9 from bottom, for *Terustræmiaceæ*, read Ternstrœmiaceæ.
” 8 ” 8 from top, for *Crawfordia*, read Crawfurdia.
” 11 ” 22 from bottom, for *Byonifolia*, read Begonifolia.
” 21 ” 7 from bottom, for *Lyriodendron*, read Liriodendron.
” 24 ” 5 from bottom, for *carpulis*, read carpellis.
” 31 ” 17 from bottom, for *Ireia*, read Zea.
” 36 ” 8 from top, for *Eupolanisia*, read Eupatorium.
, 42 ” { 13 from bottom, for *Mucnna*, read Mucuna.
11 from bottom, for *Liegesbeckia*, read Siegesbeckia.
” 47 ” 2 from bottom, after aculeata insert a comma.
” 58 and 59 { in the Table, read Modeccoideæ, Zanthoxyleæ, Begoniaceæ, Araliaceæ, and Orchideæ.
” 60 ” 3 from bottom, for *Corica*, read Carica.
” 62 ” { 11 from top, for *Epiptytes*, read Epiphytes.
19 from bottom, for *laceneæ*, read laciniæ.
6 from bottom, for *Bauheniæ*, read Bauhiniæ.
” 63 ” 16 from top, for *Callicarpæ*, read Callicarpa.
” 72 ” 20 from top, read *Podomolee* in italics.
” 80 ” 8 from bottom, for *Coladiun*, read Caladiam.
” 82 ” 16 from bottom, for *spinioenio*, read spinivenio.
” 89 ” 21 from bottom, for *Leriodendron*, Liriodendron.
” 99 ” 16 from bottom, for *processubus*, read processibus.
” 107 ” { 4 from top, for *Boerhaevia*, read Boerhaavia.
12 from top, for *Lemonea*, read Limonia.
7 from bottom, for *Melitotus*, read Melilotus.
” 108 ” 6 from top, for *pulcherrimea*, read pulcherrima.
” 112 ” 13 from top, *omit* Pl. 3, Fig. 4.
” 114 ” 2 from bottom, *omit* Pl. 1, Fig. 4.
” 153 ” 13 from bottom, after Areca omit and.
” 161 ” 15 from top, for *Myrtifolim*, read Myrtifolium.
” 165 ” 12 from bottom, for *cunescens*, read canescens.
” 167 ” 7 from top, for Pl. 10, read the annexed Landscape.
” 219 ” 18 from bottom, for *Veridiflorium*, read Viridiflorum.

Errata—(Continued.)

Page 220 „ 12 from bottom, for *ruscordeus*, read ruscoideus.
„ 220 „ 6 from bottom, } for *ilicifolium*, read ilecifolium.
„ 221 „ 3 from top, } for *ilicifolium*, read ilecifolium.
„ 225 „ 20 from bottom, after Clematis omit the comma.
„ 237 „ 2 from top, for *elicifolia*, read ilecifolia.
„ 238 „ 6 from top, for *digittatis*, read digitatis.
„ 245 „ 5 from top, for *Antymenium*, read Anhymenium.
„ 281 „ 13 from bottom, for *Hyperia*, read Hypericum.
„ 287 „ 9 from top, } for *Cycnium*, read Cycnia.
„ 288 „ 16 from bottom, } for *Cycnium*, read Cycnia.
„ 288 „ 11 from bottom, } for *Lantonica*, read Santonica.*
„ 294 „ 7 from bottom, } for *Lantonica*, read Santonica.*
„ 293 „ 3 from top, } for *Taxaxacum*, read Taraxacum.
„ 288 „ 9 from bottom, } for *Taxaxacum*, read Taraxacum.
„ 299 „ 7 from top, for *avalis*, read ovalis, for *Gortnera*, read Gœrtnera.
„ 299 „ 1 from top, for *Conbreta*, read Combretum.
„ 302 „ 10 from top, for *Lemicarpus*, read Semecarpus.
„ 343 „ 9 from top, } for *Hydogee*, read Hydozee.
„ 343 „ 17 from top, } for *Hydogee*, read Hydozee.
„ 392 „ 2 from bottom, for *black tents*, read black teal.

Doubtful.

Page 347 line 11 from top, } *Santonia*.*
„ 348 line 8 from bottom, } *Santonia*.*
„ 351 line 9 from bottom, } *Santonia*.*
„ 297 line 15 from top, for *Peloria*, read Petunia ?

Heading, Pages 453 and 454, for *Macrogens*, read In Acrogens.

Addenda, Page 444 line 7 from bottom, insert *a*, indusium.

* As in original.

NOTICE

OF

WILLIAM GRIFFITH,

From the Proceedings of the Linnæan Society,

WITH

A FEW EXTRACTS FROM HIS PRIVATE CORRESPONDENCE.

"WILLIAM GRIFFITH, Esq., the youngest son of the late Thomas Griffith, was born on the 4th of March 1810, at his father's residence at Ham Common, near Kingston-upon-Thames, in the county of Surrey.

"He was educated for the Medical profession, and completed his studies at the London University, where he became a pupil of Prof. Lindley, under whose able instructions, assisted by the zealous friendship of Mr. R. H. Solly, and in conjunction with two fellow pupils of great scientific promise, Mr. Slack and Mr. Valentine, he made rapid progress in the acquisition of botanical knowledge. The first public proofs that he gave of his abilities are contained in a microscopic delineation of the structure of the wood and an analysis of the flower of *Phytocrene gigantea*, in the third volume of Dr. Wallich's 'Plantæ Asiaticæ Rariores'; and in a note on the development and structure of *Targionia hypophylla*, appended to M. de Mirbel's Dissertation on *Marchantia polymorpha*, both published in 1832. So highly were his talents as an observer appreciated at this early period, that Dr. Wallich speaks of him as one " whose extraordinary talents and knowledge as a botanist, entitle him to the respect of all lovers of the science;" and M. de Mirbel characterizes him as "jeune Anglois, très instruit, très zélé et fort bon observateur."

"His note on *Targionia* is dated Paris, April 2nd, 1832, and in the month of May of the same year, having finished his studies at the London University with great distinction, he sailed from England for India, which was destined to be the scene of his future labours. He arrived at Madras on the 24th of September, and immediately received his appointment as Assistant-Surgeon in the service of the East India Company.

"His first appointment in India was to the coast of Tenasserim; but in the year 1835 he was attached to the Bengal Presidency, and was selected to form one of a deputation, consisting of Dr. Wallich and himself as botanists, and Mr. MacClelland as geologist, to visit and inspect the Tea-forests (as they were called) of Assam, and to make researches in the natural history of that almost unexplored district.

"This mission was for Mr. Griffith the commencement of a series of journeys in pursuit of botanical knowledge, embracing nearly the whole extent of the East India Company's extra-peninsular possessions, and adding large collections, in every branch of natural history, but especially botany, to those which, under the auspices of the Indian Government, had previously been formed. He next, under the directions of Capt. Jenkins, the Commissioner, pushed his investigations to the utmost eastern limit of the Company's territory, traversing the hitherto unexplored tracts in the neighbourhood of the Mishmee mountains which lie between Suddiya and Ava. Of the splendid collection of insects formed during this part of his tour some account has been given by Mr. Hope in the Transactions of the Entomological Society and in the eighteenth volume of our own Transactions.

"His collection of plants was also largely increased on this remarkable journey, which was followed by a still more perilous expedition, commenced in February of the following year, from Assam through the Burmese dominions to Ava, and down the Irrawadi to Rangoon, in the course of which he was reported to have been assassinated. The hardships through which he passed during the journey and his excessive application produced, soon after his arrival in Calcutta, a severe attack of fever: on his recovery from which he was appointed Surgeon to the Embassy to Bootan, then about to depart under the charge of the late Major Pemberton. He took this opportunity of revisiting the Khasiya Hills, among which he formed a most extensive collection; and having joined Major Pemberton at Goalpara, traversed with him above 400 miles of the Bootan country, from which he returned to Calcutta about the end of June 1839. In November of the same year he joined the army of the Indus in a scientific capacity, and penetrated, after the subjugation of Cabool, beyond the Hindoo Khoosh into Khorassan, from whence, as well as from Affghanistan, he brought collections of great value and extent. During these arduous journeys his health had several times suffered most severely, and he was more than once reduced by fever to a state of extreme exhaustion; but up to this time the strength of his constitution enabled him to triumph over the attacks of disease, and the energy of his mind was so great, that the first days of convalescence found him again as actively employed as ever.

"On his return to Calcutta in August 1841, after visiting Simla and the Nerbudda, he was appointed to the medical duties at Malacca: but Dr. Wallich having proceeded to the Cape for the re-establishment of his health, Mr. Griffith was recalled in August 1842 to take, during his absence, the superintendence of the Botanic Garden near Calcutta, in conjunction with which he also discharged the duties of Botanical Professor in the Medical College to the great advantage of the students. Towards the end of 1844 Dr. Wallich resumed his functions at the Botanic Garden. In September Mr. Griffith married Miss Henderson, the sister of the wife of his brother, Captain Griffith, and on the 11th of December he quitted Calcutta to return to Malacca, where he arrived on the 9th of January in the present year. On the 31st of the same month he was attacked by hepatitis, and notwithstanding every attention on the part of the medical officer who had officiated during his absence, and who fortunately still remained, he gradually sunk under the attack, which terminated fatally on the 9th of February. "His constitution," says his attached friend, Mr. MacClelland, in a letter to Dr. Horsfield, "seemed for the last two or three years greatly shattered, his energies alone remaining unchanged. Exposure during his former journeys and travels laid the seeds of his fatal malady in his constitution, while his anxiety about his pursuits and his zeal increased. He became care-worn and haggard in his looks, often complaining of anomalous symptoms, marked by an extreme rapidity of pulse, in consequence of which he had left off wine for some years past, and was obliged to observe great care and attention in his diet. In Affghanistan he was very nearly carried off by fever, to which he had been subject in his former travels in Assam. No government ever had a more devoted or zealous servant, and I impute much of the evil consequences to his health to his attempting more than the means at his disposal enabled him to accomplish with justice to himself."

"The most important of Mr. Griffith's published memoirs are contained in the Transactions of the Linnæan Society. Previous to starting on his mission to Assam, he communicated to the Society the first two of a series of valuable papers on the development of the vegetable ovulum in *Santalum, Loranthus, Viscum*, and some other plants, the anomalous structure of which appeared calculated to throw light on this still obscure and difficult subject. These papers are entitled as follows :—

1. On the Ovulum of *Santalum album*. Linn. Trans. xviii. p. 57.
2. Notes on the Development of the Ovulum of *Loranthus* and *Viscum;* and on the mode of Parasitism of these two genera. Linn. Trans. xviii. p. 71.
3. On the Ovulum of *Santalum, Osyris, Loranthus* and *Viscum*. Linn. Trans. xix. p. 171.

"Another memoir, or rather series of memoirs, "On the Root-Parasites, referred by authors to *Rhizantheæ*, and on various plants related to them," occupies the first place in the Part of our Transactions which is now in the press, with the exception of the portion relating to *Balanophoreæ*, unavoidably deferred to the next following Part. In this memoir, as in those which preceded it, Mr. Griffith deals with some of the most obscure and difficult questions of vegetable physiology, on which his minute and elaborate researches into the singularly anomalous structure of the curious plants referred to will be found to have thrown much new and valuable light.

"In India, on his return from his Assamese journey, he published in the 'Transactions of the Agricultural Society of Calcutta,' a 'Report on the Tea-plant of Upper Assam,' which, although for reasons stated avowedly incomplete, contains a large amount of useful information on a subject which was then considered of great practical importance. He also published in the 'Asiatic Researches,' in the 'Journal of the Asiatic Society of Bengal,' and in the 'Transactions of the Medical and Physical Society of Calcutta,' numerous valuable botanical papers; but the most important of his Indian publications are contained in the 'Calcutta Journal of Natural History,' edited jointly by Mr. MacClelland and himself. Of these it may be sufficient at present to refer to his memoir "On *Azolla* and *Salvinia*," two very remarkable plants which he has most elaborately illustrated, and in relation to which he has entered into some very curious speculations; and his still unfinished monograph of "The Palms of British India," which promises to be a highly important contribution to our knowledge of a group hitherto almost a sealed book to European Botanists.

"But the great object of his life, that for which all his other labours were but a preparation, was the publication of a General Scientific Flora of India, a task of immense extent, labour and importance. To the acquisition of materials for this task, in the shape of collections, dissections, drawings and descriptions, made under the most favourable circumstances, he had devoted twelve years of unremitted exertion. His own collections, (not including those formed in Cabool and the neighbouring countries) he estimated at 2500 species from the Khasiya Hills, 2000 from the Tenasserim provinces, 1000 from the province of Assam, 1200 from the Himalaya range in the Mishmee country, 1700 from the same great range in the country of Bootan, 1000 from the neighbourhood of Calcutta, and 1200 from the Naga Hills at the extreme east of Upper Assam, from the valley of Hookhoong, the district of Mogam, and from the tract of the Irrawadi between Mogam and Ava. Even after making large deductions from the sum-total of these numbers on account of the forms common to two or more of the collections, the amount of materials thus brought together by one man must be regarded as enormous. The time was approaching when he believed that he could render these vast collections subservient to the great end which he had in view. He had some time since issued an invitation to many eminent botanists in Europe to co-operate with him in the elaboration of particular families; and he purposed after a few years' additional residence in India to return to England with all his materials, and to occupy himself in giving to the world the results of his unwearied labours. But this purpose was not destined to be fulfilled, his collections have passed by his directions into the hands of the East India Company, and there can be no doubt, from the well-known liberality of the Directors, which this Society in particular has so often experienced, that they will be so disposed of by that enlightened body as to fulfil at once the demands of science and the last wishes of the faithful and devoted servant by whom they were formed. It is hoped too, that the most important of his unpublished materials, both in drawings and manuscripts, will be given to the world in a manner worthy of the author and of the rank in science which he filled."—*Proceedings of the Linnæan Society*, No. xxv, 1845.

To the foregoing brief sketch which was read before the Linnæan Society at the Anniversary Meeting 24th May 1845, it is scarcely necessary to make any addition. It is worthy of remark however, as showing how talents sometimes run in families, that Mr. Griffith was great grandson of Jeremiah Meyer, Historical Painter to George the Second, and one of the founders of the Royal Academy. It is also but fair to state on the present occasion, that he was not himself the only member of the family who would appear to have inherited something of his grandfather's peculiar art, as we owe the transfer of the landscapes to stone, which add so much to the appearance of the following volume, to the talent and kindness of his sister.

It may perhaps be acceptable in this place to afford a few extracts from the private letters of Mr. Griffith, especially those in which he adverts with a liberality of feeling to his contemporaries, no less honourable to himself than to the persons mentioned.

The following notes addressed to his uncle, at various periods, exhibit the sentiments with which he regarded the late Mr. Bauer not merely as an artist, but original observer.

From letters of Mr. Griffith, *to Mr.* Meyer.

Mergui: January 17th, 1835.

"My last accounts of Mr. Bauer state him to have been in excellent health: he had just completed some more of his unrivalled drawings."

Suddya: December 30th, 1836.

"Pray give the compliments of the season to Mr. Bauer, to whom I look up with the greatest admiration: what a pity it is for science that such a life as his is not renewable *ad libitum*. Tell him that I have a beautiful new genus allied to Rafflesia, the flowers of which are about a span across, it is diœcious and icosandrous, and has an abominable smell. How I look back occasionally on my frequent and delightful visits to Kew."

To Mrs. H——. *Serampore, Calcutta: July 22nd*, 1841.

"I was aware of the departure of Mr. Bauer through the *Athenæum*, in which an excellent notice of him appeared. He certainly was a man to whom I looked up with constant admiration: he was incomparable in several respects, and I am happy to find, that his death was so characteristic of his most inoffensive and meritorious life. It is also very pleasing to me to find that he continued to think well of me. How I should have been able to delight him had he lived a few years longer."

Calcutta: June, 1843.

"Poor Mr. Bauer, we never shall see his like again, I have seen but few notices of his life, which assuredly is worthy of study. There is not a place I shall visit with better feelings than Kew, it has so many pleasant associations even from my school-days."

Calcutta: December 31st, 1843.

"Mr. Bauer is not half appreciated yet; he is conisdered a very great artist, but what is that to what he was? But he did not fight for his own hand, though he worked hard enough in all conscience. Mr. Bauer in fact preceded all in the train of discovery: he saw in 1797, what others did not see till 30 years after. For instance, the elongation of the pollens' inner membrane into a tube, the first step towards the *complete* knowledge we now have of vegetable embryogeny. Unfortunately, Mr. Bauer drew, but did not write, and when I recall to mind a remark of Mr. Brown, that it was a disadvantage to be able to draw, I always fancy he had Bauer in his mind's eye; for had he been a writer and not a drawer, before 1800, in great probability we should have known nearly as much of embryogeny as we do now. But he shut his portfolio, and folks went on believing the old fovivillose doctrine and bursting of the pollen, which, his observations of the pollens' inner membrane, would have destroyed at once. Then with regard to Orchideæ and Asclepiadeæ, he was equally in advance: it would be a rich treat if some one would come forward and publish a selection from his drawings, without a word of letterpress."

Calcutta : February 11*th*, 1844.

"Mr. Bauer's light is not yet set on the hill. Really when I look back at his works I am lost in admiration, and always regret that he worked more for others than for himself, and that he did not use his pen as freely as he did his brush. When, in the name of all that is generous, will great men think that true greatness consist in endeavouring to make others more prominent than themselves?"

For some years before his death, Mr Griffith would appear to have had a presentiment that he would not be spared to complete the description of all his collections. On one occasion, when enumerating those who might contribute most efficiently to this object, in the event of its not being permitted to himself, he writes:—

"I cannot however refrain from paying my tribute of respect to Mr. George Bentham, the most industrious, perspicuous, and philosophical Botanist who has systematically contributed to lessen the difficulties under which Indian Botanists have generally suffered.

"There are a few others from whom the sincerity of friendship fully warrants me in expecting every possible assistance: of these Dr. Wight is already well known, and others are rising rapidly to fill, I hope, the highest Botanical stations when these shall have been vacated by the leviathans who now occupy them. Let not the cynic accuse me of partiality when I mention the names of William Valentine, of Decaisne, and C. M. Lemann."

He also delighted to speak and write in terms of the warmest regard of those to whom he was indebted for facilities in his pursuits. To Lord Auckland he invariably alluded in terms of the deepest gratitude—"Under his Lordship's patronage" he remarks on one occasion, "I have received such advantages as make me ashamed of the little I have done, and which are constantly holding up before me my deficiencies in many branches of enquiry connected with the physiology and distribution of plants."

The following letters are quoted chiefly for the additional information they afford on the subject of his travels and pursuits. His letters to Botanists would of course be more important and interesting.

Suddyah: 16th September, 1836.

"I am anxiously awaiting the arrival of the cold weather, as on the 1st of November I hope to accompany ——— to Ava, but in the meantime, I intend proceeding in search of the tea plant to the Mishmee Hills, especially about Bramakoond, where it is reported to grow. If I find it there, I will endeavour to trace it up into the mountains, which form due east of this an amphitheatre of high rugged peaks."

November 1st, 1836.

"I here write from the foot of the 'dreaded' Mishmee Hills. I left Suddyah on the 15th October, and have already been to Bramakoond, where I spent three days. I miss you much; you would have been delighted with the place, which is nothing but rocks and hills. I am recruiting my resources for a movement into the interior of the hills, in which I shall follow Wilcox's route, taking with me 15 coolies, for whom I am collecting grain. I have already made considerable collections, chiefly however in Botany, with a few stones and birds. I hope before my return to have seen Coptis teeta in flower, and to have proved that the Beese is different from that of Nepal. I have already seen numbers of the Mishmees who are civil people. I have however had great difficulties with the Chief of the Khond, who though apparently friendly, will, I fear, do all he can to hinder me from getting to Ghaloom, with the Gham of which place I wish to have a conference."

Noa Dihing Mookh: January 20th, 1837.

"I have just returned from the trip to the Lohit much sooner than I expected. I saw nothing of any consequence except rapids which are horrid things, and make one quite nervous. I made a beautiful collection on the Mishmee mountains, of which more anon. Many of the plants are very interesting. I was however worked very hard, all my people being sick: I had even to wash my own clothes, but I fear you will think I am grumbling: so good-bye."

Loodianah: 11*th December*, 1838.

"I arrived here in 14½ days, notwithstanding some delays on the road, and have put up with Cornet Robinson, Acting Political Agent. I am not pleased with the up-country, and would rather live in Bengal, for I cannot abide sandy plains and a deficiency of vegetation. Loodianah is a curious place, very striking to a stranger, the town is large, built under official direction, and consequently well arranged in comparison with native towns: there is much trade carried on in it, and it has the usual bustle of a large town.

"Capt. Wade's house is well situated on a rising ground, and the demesne is a pretty one. Otherwise the country is ugly enough, and very bare, yet it is here well wooded, in comparison with what I hear of Ferozepore. Along the face of the hill near the town, a nullah flows, abounding in fish, of which more anon. The rock pigeons, or grouse, are very abundant, and there are two species, one remarkable for the elongated side-feathers of the tail. Both are beautiful birds, but very difficult of access. Crows, kites, vultures, adjutants, herons, Drongoles, sparrows, parrots, etc. remain as before, but most of the less common birds are different from those to the south; the most European are genuine starlings; and, to my memory of eight years back, identical with those of Europe. I have already got thirty to forty species of fish. Cyprinidæ, are by far the most common; one loach, and one of Macrognathus.

"But as they are all from one water, viz. the neighbouring nullah, and the Sutledge being five miles off, I shall put them all into bottles, and send them off before I leave this. The most edible fish, and one of the most common is the Roh, but it is not the Roh of Bengal, and might well be called Cyprinus ruber. Burnes has given I think a drawing of it, which is faithful as to colour. All the forms will be familiar to you, but I hope there will be some new species.

"I have made further arrangements, and such as will give you a good insight into the fish of the Sutledge, as to the number of duplicates!—it is the safest plan for an ignoramus not to discriminate too nicely. I am to-day to get large specimens of the Kalabans, Rohi, etc. what a splendid fish the Rohi is, both to look at and to eat. There are two or three species of the transparent *Chandas*, and three or four Perilamps, six or eight Siluridæ, besides the Gwali, which is too large; of Ophiocephalus two or three, exclusive of the Sowli, but all ought to be examined, as there is no relying on native discrimination. There is a curious animal here burrowing like a mole, but more like a rat: of this I have not yet got a specimen, although they are very common.

"I commence with a list of the fish of this place. I have only to mention that several species are confounded under the name Bhoor, all the Chandras under Chunda Begla, Loaches under Pote, all the Perilamps except the Chulwa, which may be from its flavour a *Clupeia*, etc. The fact is, that the fishermen are aware of genera, but not of species, excepting when the distinctive marks are very strong. The fisherman enumerates forty species, but I have only twenty-six, I have promised him one rupee when he completes the list:

Native Name.	*Family.*	*General size.*
1. Khaila, ..	Cyprins, ..	6.
2. Bhoor, ..		mature.
3. Rewa, ..		mature.
4. Bangun, ..		18 inches, called also Kala Bhans.
5. Chund Bigla,	.. .. ..	mature.
6. Ditto ditto,	.. .. ..	ditto.
7. Ditto ditto,	.. .. ..	ditto.
8. Pote, ..	Loach, ..	ditto.
9. Mailoa, ..	Perilamps,	ditto.
10. Khurda, ..	.. .. ..	ditto Trichopterus ?
11. Puttra, ..	Salurida, ..	20 seers.
12. Kuttoa, ..	Ditto, ..	6 inches.
13. Ghichila, ..	Macrognathus,	7 ditto.
14. Bham, ..		3 feet.
15. Nunghree,	Cyprins, ..	6 inches.
16. Nowhan, ..		ditto.
17. Pootea, ..		12 inches.
18. Seengh, ..	Silurida, ..	8 inches.
19. Bugarlea,..	.. .. ..	ditto.
20. Mootunna,	.. .. ..	nearly mature.
21. Bardul, ..	.. .. ..	6 inches.
22. Chilwa, ..	Perilamp, ?	mature.
23. Nuwha, ..	Esox, ..	ditto.
24. Gwalee, ..	Silurus,	2 maunds,
25. Ruttgull,..		nearly mature.
26. Chundee,..	Clupeia,	ditto ditto.

Candahar: May the 2nd, 1839.

"We have seen three changes in the geological structure of the country.

"The Khojah Omrah was chiefly clay slate, and we are now in another formation, which no one seems to know; but it must be different as the outlines of the hills are completely changed. We are now 3,500 feet above the sea. The climate is good, and would be delightful in a good house, but in tents the thermometer varies from 60° to 98° and even 105°.

"I have got a decent collection of plants, only amounting however to 650 species. The flora continues quite European. I have some of singular interest. Compositæ, Cruciferæ, and Gramineæ form the bulk of the vegetation. All fish are very different from those below the Ghats. I have five or six species of Cyprinidæ. One very inimitable fuscous loach. There are few birds, and fewer quadrupeds; in fact the country is at a minimum in both these respects."

Ghuzni: July 25th, 1839.

"We have been gradually ascending since leaving Candahar, and are here at an elevation of 7,600 feet. The same features continue. I have as yet not more than 850 species. The mountains on every side, and indeed the whole face of the country, is still bare. Mookloor, a district through which we passed, about seventy miles from this, is well cultivated and inhabited. There are few birds to be seen, and scarcely any insects, but there are numerous lizards. The thermometer varies in tents from 60° to 90°."

Cabul: August 11th, 1839.

"I am encamped close to Baber's tomb, lulled by the sound of falling water, and cooled with the shade of poplar and sycamore trees, with abundance of delicious fruit, and altogether quite happy for the nonce. I have not yet seen the town which is a strange place, buried in gardens: but nothing can exceed the rich cultivation of the valley in which we are encamped. Beautiful fields on every side, with streamlets, rich verdure, poplars, willows, and bold mountain scenery, which contrasts most favourably with the dreary barren tracts to which we have been accustomed. I go with the Engineers to Bamean in the course of a few days, when we shall cross ridges of 12,000 to 13,000 feet high.

"I can only find three kinds of fish in this neighbourhood. I have been making some drawings, and collecting a few plants which continue to be entirely European."

Peshawur : November 17th, 1839.

"I hope some day or other to turn out a real traveller. I am now in hopes of becoming a decent surveyor, and before many years have passed a decent meteorologist. I leave the Army here, and shall part with it, particularly Thomson and Durand of the Engineers, with regret. I start in a short time to travel up the Indus with little before me but difficulties, however *à la renommée*. If I can do something unparalleled in the travelling way I shall be content for a year or two at least.

"I have obtained some few specimens of fossil shells from the shingly beds of the Khyber Pass. They seem to be a Spirifer with a very square base, quite different from the common species of the Bolan Pass, which is like a large cockle, and of which I have one beautiful specimen. How I regret not seeing Bukkur, for with a few days' leisure, a number of fossils might be obtained. The older I grow the less content am I scientifically: would that I had received a mathematical education. I was much interested with some quotations from Lyell's Elements in a late *Calcutta Courier*, especially about the Marine Saurian from the Gallepagos. What further proof can be wanted of the maritime and insular nature of the world during the reigns of the Saurian reptiles ? What more conclusive can be expected about the appearance of new species ? This point would at once be settled if the formation of these islands can be proved not to have been contemporaneous with the Continents. Then the animal nature of chalk !

"I am doing nothing in botany, but learning Persian, and the use of the theodolite, with nothing but difficulties to look at all around. I begin to feel of such importance, (do not think me conceited in relation to my collections and information on geographical botany,) that I am not overpleased with the idea of facing dangers alone : however I suppose every thing is as usual exaggerated."

Bamean : August 3rd, 1840.

"Yesterday I crossed the Hindoo-koosh by my former route, and this morning while out, i. e. trout fishing, was most agreeably interrupted by the post. The fishing was ended forthwith. Indeed the sun in this country even at elevations of 12,000 feet is very hot, and has excoriated my hands, beautifully white as they were after my sickness, but not before I had caught 3 barbels, evidently different from those of the other side of the range. I caught some trout yesterday evening, it is a most beautiful fish, I was particularly struck with the size of the eye, its prominence, and expressive pupil, in opposition to the sluggishness of the eyes of carps.

"It is strange that Botany has always been the most favoured of the natural sciences, it is strange that in spite of what all do say it is the least advanced of any. How can I reconcile my own splendid opportunities with those of more deserving naturalists in other branches? and I would willingly share them on the principle of common fairness with others, who I know would turn them to a better account. Oreinus takes the worm greedily; in the Helmund, 11,000 feet above the sea, it is abundant. It is the same species I think as that in the Cabul river; but in the Cabul river, Barbus is the predominant fish: in the Helmund it is the reverse. How can one account for the small elevation at which fish are found in the Himalayan? I cannot imagine it is owing as some think to the relative impetuosity of the rivers, which after all is only an assumption.

"This Bamean valley is the strangest place imaginable, its barrenness and the variegated colours of the rocks convey the idea of its volcanic origin, and give it a look as if it had come out of the furnace. I cannot make out where the stones so universally found all over the slopes of the mountains, came from, for very generally they seem water-worn. I find no great peculiarity in the flora of this side of the range, except an abundance of odd-looking Chenopodiaceous plants, probably resulting from the saline saturation of the soil. There is a very singular spring on the other side of the range, about 11,000 feet above the sea: the water very clear, with no remarkable taste, but every thing around is covered with a deposit of a highly ferruginous powder. I shall write next from the fossil locality, which is said to be about forty miles from this. I am as stout as ever, but by no means so strong."

Bamean: August 21*st*, 1840.

"I am now out of the region of trees, excepting a poplar, of which I will send you a bit, as the same tree grows in much lower places. The want of rings in wood is by no means unusual in tropical vegetation. For the production of rings, some annual check to vegetation is required: their absence is particularly frequent in climbers. The walnut will not be a good instance, because even if you can get it from Java, it is a tree that requires cold, and must consequently be found at considerable altitudes. Your instances must be taken from subjects that can bear a great range of climate: you have some in the apricot, vine, etc. I will not fail in sending you what you want from Cabul, and also from Peshawur, in which almost the extremes of temperature can be contrasted. I will also get the woods of apricots, cherries, etc., at the highest elevations on my road back, as I hope to pass through the grand fruit country of Affghanistan. No Jungermannias are obtainable in this part, nor anywhere indeed, except towards the true Himalayas. I do not remember having seen the pomegranate growing at Cabul: the place is too cold for it. I think however, I can get some from Khujjah, where snow lies in winter. I leave for the Provinces early in October, and shall travel 30 miles a day. I want to get to Seharunpore, 15 or 20 days in advance of my time, as I must run up to Mussoorie and fish in the Dhoon. I shall be in Calcutta in all February."

Cabul: September 26th, 1840.

"I despatch to-morrow the first of the bits of wood, the duplicates will be sent on the 28th or 29th: on this latter day I leave for Peshawur, and right glad am I that the time has come at last. I will send you the same woods from Peshawur, but shall scarcely be able to send you pomegranate from any thing like a cold place.

"On receiving your specimens of vine, the following question occurred to me. If wood is a deposit from the leaves or fibres sent down from the leaves, how is the presence of wood to be accounted for in tendrils, which have no leaves, but yet which are evidently branches? The theory of the formation of wood, which considers it as above, is deemed ingenious, but it will not I think be found to be true. The bark evidently has a great deal to say to the matter.

"I shall be most rejoiced at a remote prospect of again setting to work. I take no interest now in the vegetation of this country. I hope to be at Loodianah *early* in November; my present intention is to run up to Simla, thence to Mussoorie, and descend on Seharunpore. If I do this, I shall only leave one point unfinished, and that is the Hindoo-koosh Proper, where however I shall have the advantage of Major Sanders of the Engineers, who will pick up a few plants for me. I wish much to take notes of the vegetation about Simla and

Mussoorie, this I can do at a bad season. I shall afterwards be able to compare the Himalayan chain at very distant points."

Serampore, — 1841.

"I will send you to-morrow dissections of Santalum if I can get a small bottle for them: under $\frac{1}{2}$ inch lens you can easily open the pistillum of Santalum having previously removed the perianth: it is a concial body; you must take care to get it out entire, especially at the base, then place it in water, and dissect off the ovula of which there are three or four, as per sketch. I shall not say what I see, as I want to have your original opinion unbiassed, etc.; but whenever you see the tubes with filaments adhering to their apices, pray mark attentively what takes place, both at the point and at the place where the tube leaves the ovulum; your matchless $\frac{1}{1500}$ would do the thing. Try iodine with all such, after having examined them in water.

"Should you find any difficulty in dissecting away the ovula, light pressure under glass will relieve you. I shall be very anxious to know what your opinion is, particularly with regard to the tubes and all adhering filaments; the question now occupying botanists being this, is the embryo derived directly from the boyau or is it derived from some parts of the ovulum?

"I hope you can understand these sketches."

Peshawur: 13th December, 1839.

"What a shame it is that botanists should know nothing whatever of the formation and structure of wood! They look at a section of a piece of oak, and imagine they have discovered the secret, and write volumes on this imagination, yet they have been told over and over again, that nothing is to be learnt on such subjects without beginning at the commencement, which they are too idle to do. To name an abominable Aster, is among them of much higher importance than to discover the cause of the growth of wood. Medullary rays are most difficult, because they are very often deficient particularly in climbers. I am horridly idle, and yet what can I do without books; yet with regard to books, the more originality we possess, the less we require them? There is nothing to be got here except a few marsh plants coming into flower. One beautiful Chara, which might disclose the secret, had I good glasses, it is a most graceful pellucid form: an undescribed duckweed, a floating Marchantiaceæ. Would that I were settled with a Ross on one hand, and a

Strongstein on the other, around my collections with good health and good spirits. Tell —— I have in view the division of the vegetable kingdom analagous to radiata, they include all the Marchantiaceæ, and are, to all intents and purposes, Vegetable Radiata."

Pushut, 1st march beyond Kooner: January 29th, 1840.

"This will be a letter of odds and ends, you know I was to return to Jallalabad; well I reached that place, but left the encampment and crossed the river, where an advance road making partly for the Kooner expedition were employed, and having originally determined on going to Kooner, I accompanied them two marches, when they were overtaken by the army, to avoid which, I halted one day, and on the next proceeded onwards by the north bank of the river, thus saving all the fords of this horrid river. I should call it beautiful at any other season. The road was bad, and the last one and a half mile into camp most difficult, the path winding round and over spurs of sharp limestone rocks which must have had abundance of silex in them they were so very hard. At the very worst part, my headman being in front, all of a sudden I heard three shots in quick succession with the usual hallooing, and then I was called on in advance, meeting my headman wounded: he has lost the two fore-fingers of his right hand. All I saw was three men scrambling up the face of the hill, on whom I opened a fire as soon as my guns came up, and had the pleasure of hitting one on the shield.

"Such a scene ensued! for when there are three or four on such occasions we may reasonably expect thirty or forty, and my object was to get out of the bad road, and so be close to camp. Some of, or rather all, my people became dismayed, I had therefore to cheer, to point my double barrels, and in fact to enact a whole legion. One fellow tried to shoot me but his powder proved faithful, the others were wounded: however they kept in sight, and to make matters worse, in one place within twenty yards, six or seven of my loads were thrown; evening drawing on, and prospects disgusting, when at last having passed over one bad part and got down into a ravine, a number of people were seen closing down on us, but my man had run off to camp, and by shouts succeeded in calling five or six *sepahis,* part of the rear-guard, to our relief, and so we escaped bag and baggage, the rascals making off when the red coats appeared. I was sick at heart at the loss of poor Abdool Rozak's fingers: he is an Arab with an English heart, bearing his loss most manfully, and when his fingers were removed expressed anxiety alone about me and my *Sundoogs* (collections). Well then, where should I have been had I been assailed as Abdool Rozak was, I should have been unprepared, and if riding, my mare would certainly have jumped into the river beneath. Thomson* said when he left me, G—. you are rash and Abdool Rozak is rash, take care or you will get into trouble. My moving about without a guard was imprudent, and I now return to Jallalabad to get one, or if not successful to wait there until the spring and its floral excitements call me out: what I dislike is danger without any recompense, not a flower is to be had; with excitement it is nothing. I have now had two escapes, one from the buffalo in Assam, and this, which is a greater one, because had not the army been delayed by accident at the ford, it would have been eight or ten miles in advance, and consequently there would have been no rear-guard at hand.

"The country is disturbed, and one can only stir out in the valley itself close to camp, which is the more tantalizing as the mountains are accessible, and covered with forest. Our halt here should put us in possession of much information respecting these forests. As it is, I shall leave probably as wise as I came, except in having ascertained that the change from the well-wooded Himalaya mountains to those of the Hindoo-koosh, without even a shrub five feet high, takes place to the east of this. My employment is surveying and collecting data for ascertaining the heights of the hills around. But wherever I turn, the question suggests itself, what business have I here collecting plants, with so many in Calcutta demanding attention? How I am living! alone, without a table, chair, wine, or spirits, with a miserable beard, and in native clothes! but one thus saves much time; how unfortunate that mine now is not worth saving!

"I have been reading Swainson's volumes in Lardner's Cyclopædia, in which there is a little to which severe critics may object, but a vast deal more that is beautifully sound. I am quite certain I never appreciated them before. How wonderful that no one before Macleay and Swainson thought that living beings were created on one plan.

* Major Thomson, C. B., Engineers, from whom as well as all the officers of the same corps, Mr. Griffith experienced much kindness in Affghanistan.

I have imbibed all the important parts with the hope of bringing them to bear on Botany, which is in a shameful state. One talks of the typical nature of polypetalous or monopetalous plants; another ridicules the idea, because as he wisely says, some polypetalous plants are monopetalous, and vice versâ!! he objects, in fact to what constitutes the great value of a character, *its mode of variation.* All Swainson's propositions appear to me philosophical and highly probable, but none of the present generation have eyes young enough to bear such a flood of light as he has thrown upon them. There are faults I acknowledge, but a man who writes for money does not always write for fame; rapid writing and much more rapid publishing is a vast evil, but one which is too often unavoidable. I have four or five drawings of fish, one of the spotted carnivorous carp, the most carnivorous type of all except Opsarion, and perhaps a new subgenus;* one of the Sir-i-Chushme and Khyber *Oreinus*, and a Perilamp with two long cirrhi on the upper lip. I intend in my travels now I am alone, to stop at every fertile place. I am ascertaining the limit of the inferior snow in these latitudes, which I fancy will be 3,500 feet. Is it not curious that here 1,000 feet above Jallalabad we have had no snow, while at Jallalabad there has been abundance. I attribute it to the narrowness of the valley at this place, and to the forest. When I glance at the subject of botanical geography, how astounding appears our ignorance! we have no data, except to determine the mere temperature and amount of rain: yet men well persist in the rage for imperfect description of undescribed species, and pay no attention to what is one of the most important agents in preserving things as they are in our planet,—i. e. vegetation. On this point Swainson is less happy than on others when he ascribes such importance to temperature, and points out the fact that countries in the same latitudes, and having the same temperatures, produce different animals."

Cabul, September 25th, 1839.

"I am just on the eve of re-entering Cabul from a visit to Bamean, a singular place on the other side of the Hindoo-koosh, celebrated for its idols and caves. It has amply repaid a march of 106 miles

* *Racoma nobilis*, Calcutta Journ. Nat. Hist. Vol. ii, p. 577. t. xv fig. 4. Subfam. SCHIZOTHORACINÆ.

and back again. I never saw a more singular place, and never enjoyed myself more: we crossed several high ridges between 11 and 13,000 feet, but so poor is the flora that I have only added 200 species to my catalogue, now amounting to 1200 species instead of 2,400 as I fully expected. But I must say I was as much pleased at the acquisition of a genuine *Salmo* in the Bamean river (which is a tributary of the Oxus,) as at any thing.

"Unfortunately we were so hurried, that I had only one afternoon and that an unfavourable one, for indulging in my fishing propensities: the chief fish seems to come very near the English trout, and so far as I can judge, is not found on this side the Himalaya. The other fish of these rivers are a fine Schizothorax or Oreinus, allied to the *Adoee*, a flat-headed Siluroid, a loach, and a small Cyprinus. This is a singular country, quite unlike any thing I have seen, and as distinct from the Himalaya in its vegetation, etc. as can well be imagined. Generally it is very barren, and after travelling over so much of the country I have yet seen only three parts of it decently cultivated. It is reported to be rich in minerals.

"But it will never bear comparison with Hindoostan. It is however capable of much improvement. It consists of a succession of barren valleys, divided from each other by barren ridges, and is generally deficient in the great fertilizer of all things—water. There is scarcely an indigenous tree in the whole country, and generally very few cultivated ones, except about Cabul, although they have poplars and willows well suited to the climate. It has been subjected to so much misrule that the natives have become indifferent to its improvement, (if they ever felt alive to any such interest.) The Zoology is very poor, quite at zero. There is a species of Ibex, an *Ovis*, and a *Capra*, which from the frequency of their heads and horns about sacred places and gateways of towns, must be common; but I have never seen more than a portion of one fresh specimen of the sheep. Furs are brought from the Hindoo-koosh, but are all too mutilated to be of any use, except to a Zoologist with antiquarian eyes: one Jerboa. Hares are rather common in some parts, and about here there is a Lagomys. Of birds there are but few, but as the vegetation is chiefly vernal, these creatures may perhaps be abundant. The game birds are quail, three species of partridge, a huge Ptarmigan? Pterocles of Loodianah. The fauna is richest in Saurian reptiles, and of these one might make a very good collection. I have only seen two snakes, and both are I believe lost."

Mirzapore: April 26th, 1841.

"Request —— to refrain from abusing compound microscopes. Why should not compound and simple microscopes each have their merits? Valentine, who is a great authority, and an unrivalled dissector, says, the simple lens must be suspended. I only wish I could dissect with a compound microscope: what things might not one get access to. The simple lens is quite useless with opaque objects; it only does for transmitted light. Now dissections of opaque objects have been too much neglected. How odd it is that all improvements are ridiculed at first.

"I enclose a bit of Sphagnam, a curious moss, with curious incomplete spiral cells in the leaves. I dare say it will bear preservation in Canada balsam. I have received a new microscope, a queer-looking thing, very portable; one object glass of a quarter inch focus, by Ross; two eye-pieces magnifying linearly 200 to 300 times. I have put it up, but I am not well enough to decide on its merits. Now that I have arranged all my things, I am literally frightened at the work I have to do.

"I am quite annoyed at the idea that German artists make better microscopes than English. I was aware that the lenses were better, but otherwise I imagined that any comparison would be vastly in our favour. I am curious to know the price, and where to apply for one, as your account makes me quite ashamed of mine. Who knows what a fine penetrating power of 1100 may not disclose. I am very much pleased with your idea of anointing cuts with nitrate of silver; this hint I will bear in mind.

"I enclose the first list of fish, No. 2, not that it is of much use.—What nonsense it is to collect without knowledge.

No.	Native Name.	Family.	REMARKS.
1.	Kuggur, ..	Siluridæ.	
2.	Soonnee, ..	Cyprinidæ, ..	Back greenish, otherwise pearly-white.
3.	Dhurra, ..	Cyprinidæ, ..	Fins reddish, red spot on opercule, back greenish-brown.
4.	Moogullee, ..	" Perilampoid,	Diaphanous, silvery, head reddish.
5.	Peedur, ..	" " ..	Like the preceding.
6.	Moorr, ..	" " ..	Ditto ditto.
7.	Bhanghun, ..	" " ..	Ditto ditto.
8.	Kundura, ..	" Perilampus,	Back greenish, otherwise quite silvery.
9.	Pullee, ..	" " ..	Same as 4, 5, 6, 7.

No.	Native Name.	Family.	REMARKS.
10.	Goolla. ..	Ciprinidæ.	
11.	Khunnuree, ..	*Percidæ,* Chanda of Buchanan, ..	Diaphanous.
12.	Sur-ri-rha, ..	Cyprinidæ Perilamp,	Silvery-green on back.
13.	Gundhan, ..	,, Perilampoid,	Same colours.
14.	Mhukk, ..	,, ,, ..	Ditto ditto.
15.	Ghurr, ..	,, ,, ..	Ditto ditto.
16.	Dhoalee, ..	Ophiocephalus, ..	Colour brown, with usual marks and bars.
17.	Ahaiha, ..	Siluridæ, ..	Diaphanous, 3-5 irregular longish stripes.
18.	Mhullee, ..	Silurus, ..	Silvery-blueish.
19.	Mhoarree, ..	Cyprinidæ, ..	Yellowish-green, fins reddish, 5 seers.
20.	Dhumpurra, ..	,,	Brownish-green, 6 seers.
21.	Pho-eikee, ..	,, Perilampoid.	
22.	Putollee, ..	Cyprinidæ, ..	Back and sides light-green.
23.	Poapree, ..	,, ..	Back greenish-brown, sides greenish.
24.	Shingra, ..	Siluridæ, ..	No stripes, lightly tinged with brown.
25.	Dhimmurr, ..	Silurus.	
26.	Ghoa-gha, ..	,, ..	Back greenish, punctulate, head reddish.
27.	Mokkhurr, ..	Opiocephalus.	
28.	Dhujjha. ..	,,	
29.	Thailla, ..	Cyprinidæ, ..	5 to 6 seers.
30.	Mhorakkee, ..	,, ..	Much like 19.
31.	Singarhee, ..	,, ..	Much like 4, 5, 6. 7.
32.	Logurr, ..	Siluridæ, ..	3 to 4 faint punctulate longish lines.
33.	Ghoje, ..	Not noted.	
34.	Tupree, ..	,,	
37.	Ghunghutt, ..	Perilampus.	
38.	Soourr, ..	Siluridæ, ..	Diaphanous. Faint punctulate lines.
39.	Soonaree, ..	Cyprinidæ.	
40.	Phunnee, ..	,, Perilampoid.	
41.	Kutchoo, ..	,, ..	Much like the preceding.
42.	Saisurr, ..	,, ..	Ditto ditto.
43.	Coommee, ..	,, ..	Much like no 4.
44.	Saluree, ..	,, ..	Ditto ditto.
45.	Shumsheer, ..	,, ..	So called because of its voracity; (Shumsheer a sabre.)
46.	Ghora, ..	,, ..	Same as Soonee.
47.	Saboan, ..	,, ..	Same as the preceding.
48.	Bhambhun, ..	Cyprinidæ, ..	Same as Dhurra.

All the above from the Indus, at Shikarpore.

No.	Family.	River.	REMARKS.
49.	Cyprinidæ, ..	River Nari, ..	Small size, colour-silvery, except upper back, which is bluish-green.
50.	Siluridæ, ..	Mysore river.	
51.	Ophiocephalus,	,,	
52.	,,	,,	
53.	Cyprinidæ, ..	,, ..	Same as 49.
54.	,, Systomus,	,, ..	A beautiful fish, bright green back, otherwise bright orange-red, fins stained with black colours; fugacious.

No.	Family.	River.	REMARKS.
55.	Cyprinidæ, ..	Mysore river.	
56.	„ Systomus,	„ ..	Back greenish, opercle orange spotted, one black spot near tail.
57.	Percida Chamda,	„	
58.	Perilampoid, ..	„	

Water of both these rivers, quiescent: bunded up.

No.	Family.	River.	REMARKS.
59.	Cyprinoid, ..	Dadur river.	
60.	„	„ ..	Same as 54.
61.	„ Systomus,	„ ..	Same as 56.
63.	Cyprinoid, ..	„	
64.	„	„	
65.	„ ..	„	
66.	„ ..	„ ..	Same as 59.
67.	Cobites, ..	„	
68.	Cyprinoid, ..	Bolan river, ..	Bluish-green, blue bars and dots. Takes the fly.
69.	Barbus? ..	„ ..	Intestines very long, much like Naipoora.
70.	Gonorhynchus?	„	
71.	„ ..	„ ..	Probably a small specimen of 69.
72.	Cyprinoid, ..	„	
73.	„ Gonorhynchus,	Gurmab, ..	Same as 70?
74.	„ ..	„	
75.	Cyprinoid, ..	„ ..	Closely allied to the Mahaseer.
76.	Ditto Mahaseer	„ ..	Beautiful fish with yellow-brown back, golden sides. Takes fly greedily.
77.	„ Gonorhynchoid,	„	
78.	„	„	
79.	Silurida, ..	„ ..	In Bolan river, deep still water.
80.	Cyprinoid, ..	„ ..	In small streams.
81.	Macrognathus.	„ ..	Tenacious of life, belly puffy, common throughout; a good deal like a Gudgeon.
82.	Loach, ..	Quettah river.	
83.	Cyprinoides, ..	„ ..	A beautiful silvery-leaden backed fish, with a streak of bright-red along the side. Common, very like the preceding: of these Quettah fish No. 83 is the most common, 82 the least so.
84.	Cyprinus, curious, not being a mountainous form,	„	
86.	„ ..	„	
87.	Cyprinoides, ..	Lora river, ..	Same mountain form, Gonorhynchoid.
88.	„ ..	„	
89.	Loach, ..	„ ..	Ditto ditto ditto.
90.	„ ..	„ ..	Perhaps same as the preceding.
91.	Cyprinoides, ..	„	
92.	„ ..	„ ..	Like the Adoee.
93.	„ ..	„ ..	Mountain form.
94.	„ ..	„ ..	Large size for the genus.
95.	„ ..	„ ..	*Note.*—Probable number of species 47, deducting those supposed not different.
96.	Cyprinoid, ..	Urghundab.	
97.	Loach, ..	„	
98.	Siluridæ, ..	„	

"I subjoin a list given me by a fisherman at Shikarpore, with his divisions into large and small :—

Large.	*Small.*
Dhumpurra,	Ghunghut,
Buree Phookee,	Pedir,
Buree Thaillee,	Soonnee,
Mhoarrhee,	Phokee,
Mookkur,	Mogullee,
Gundhan,	Dhimmur,
Singaree,	Ghoagar,
* Pulla,	Khuggur,
	Seenra,
	Mhorr,
	Bhangun,
	Ghurr,
	Soourr,
	Morakee,
	Tupree,
	Ghogee,
	Phopree,
	Thaillee,
	* Pulla,
	Punnotee,
	Dhaiee,
	Ghogura,

These lists may be of some small use compared with Burnes's collection. To a certain extent they may be useful as showing the preponderance, etc. of certain forms. You may rely on my distinctions between Cyprinidæ, Siluridæ, and Percidæ.

I send this list as all the specimens are not lost, and some are among the plants. Most of the species are, I think, distinct, and when they have appeared to me not to be so, I have generally noted it on the spot.

The mountain forms are very distinct, the mouth being under the snout, or head, the intestines long, peritoneum covered with a black pigment. These forms commence at Dadur, 800 feet above the sea: this stream abounds in rapids.

Gurmab is 1,100 feet.

Quettah, 5,600 feet.

Lora river, 3,6'0 feet.

Urghundab, 3,600 feet.

"To-morrow I will send the other list of specimens No. 3, which will I hope reach you ; of all the fish in these parts, the Sir-i-Chushme and Cabul river *Oreinus* travels farthest up. I have caught it at nearly 11,000 feet in the Helmund river. Then come loaches, and the beautiful trout-like Opsarion; other Cyprinidæ ascend 2,000 or 3,000 feet, the Mahaseer scarcely more. Above that, come the genuine mountain forms.

No.	Family.	Locality.	Remarks.
1.	Cyprinidæ, Oreinus?	Streams from Sofaid-koh,	A brown fish, with irregular black spots.
2.	Cyprinidæ, ..	"	
3.	" ..	" ..	A sombre looking Gudgeon-like fish, back blackish, sides yellowish, punctulate with groups of blackish spots.
4.	Loach, ..	" ..	Colours and patches obscure.
5.	Perilamp, ..	Jallalabad river, ..	Usual silvery-bluish hues.
6.	Cyprinidæ, mountain form, Schizothorax.	"	
7.	Cyprinidæ, *Pooteoides*,	" ..	Colours obscure, scales minute, dorsal spine very strong.
8.	Cyprinidæ, ..	" ..	A stout fish, of obscure colours, each scale with a transverse more or less wavy red line (like the Nepoora of Assam), mouth nepooroid, intestines very long, very thin, very frangible, packed in longish folds, Peritoneum covered with a black pigment. Herbiv.

No.	Family.	Locality.	Remarks.
9.	Cyprinidæ. Perilampoid,	Jallalabad river, ..	Back metallic bluish-brown, otherwise silvery.
10.	Cyprinoid, ..	,,	
11.	,, Schizothorax, ..	,,	
12.	,, ,, ..	,, ..	Back greenish, fins reddish, snout elongated.
13.	,, ,, ..	,, ..	Colours brownish, tinged with yellow; perhaps it is the same as the Helmund and Cabul species: intestines packed in a few folds, moderately long, 4½ inches longer than body: diameter of body 2 inches. Peritoneum with the black pigment. *Carneo-herbivorous.*
14.	Cyprinoid, ..	,,	
15.	Ophiocephalus,	Jheels, etc., Bussoollah,	Colour rather a rich brown, pectoral fins barred with chesnut.
16.	Cyprinoid like a Bleak, Schizothorax.	,, ..	Back brownish: this colour limited to a narrowish line, otherwise entirely pearly. Peritoneum covered with black pigment. Intestines rather large, in 3 or 4 folds.
17.	Cyprinoid. A narrow deep fish. Perilamp. An Opsarion?	,, ..	A very pretty species, brownish back, marked faintly both longitudinally and transversely with iridescent patches, abdominal fins reddish.
18.	Cyprinoid, ..	Jheels, etc., Bussoollah, very common,	A handsome species allied to the Mahaseer; back black, otherwise yellowish, fins tinged with red, scales as it were bordered with dusky-black. Intestines short.
19.	,, ..	,, ..	An oval, rather thick fish, of obscure colours.
20.	,, Schizothorax,	,, ..	An elegant species, back obscurely brown, otherwise pearly. Peritoneum black, covered with pigment. Intestines very long and narrow.
21.	Racoma nobilis.*	Lalpoor, Cabul river,	A stout fish, with a large head, not unlike a trout at first sight. Sides bluish silvery grey, back obscurely brown, remarkable for frequent irregular well-defined black spots, faintest in small specimens, fins tinged with reddish. Head flat at top, with some spots. Peritoneum with black pigment. Intestines of large size, loaded with fat, short, not twice the length of the abdomen, cavity loaded with fat. As usual no cæca. A remarkable type: aspectu omnino carnivoris.
22.	Loach, ..	Khyber range stream, from Sir-i-Chushme spring, temper. 75°, from limestone rocks,	A very small and slender species, light brown, speckled and barred with brown, attracted immediately by scraping up the bed of the outlet of the spring.

* Calcutta Journal Natural History, Vol. II. p. 577, t. xv. f. 4.

No.	Family.	Locality.	Remarks.
23.	Cyprinid, Oreinoides,	Same place, but occurs down to Khyber ghat stream,	Back brown, with some iridescent hues, sides yellowish-brown, dark spots confined to back and sides, small but distinct; fins tinged with reddish. Peritoneum loaded with black pigment. Intestines in short loops across abdomen of intermediate size, as to length and diameter. Air bladder small; very common. Swarm in deepish pools under limestone rocks, takes bait, *i. e.* offal and worms with great avidity. Like many other species, it is asserted to be the English trout: it rises to the surface.
24.	Loach, ..	Same place common,	Shape subcylindrical, pale greenish-brown, with very broad bars of brown, fins spotted with black, otherwise fuscescent; at root of tail a deep black bar. Head depressed, in old specimens broad, closely spotted with black, snout attenuated, apex with cirrhi; upper jaw in the centre with a bony process not unlike an incisor tooth.
25.	Cyprinid, Opsarion, ..	,, ..	A beautiful trout-like fish, back bluish-black, triangular bars of azure blackish, ending in a point towards glandular line, fins tinged with orange, tail tipped with black. Peritoneum spotted slightly with black.
26.	,, Opsarion,	,, ..	Possibly young specimens of preceding, colours same but fainter."

Memorandum on return from Affghanistan.

"As I considered on my arrival at Peshawur in December 1839, that a great deal remained to be done, I obtained permission to remain another season in Affghanistan. I immediately mentioned my wishes of travelling to General Avitabili, who strongly advised me not to attempt leaving Peshawur in any novel direction, as the whole of his district was much disaffected. Soon afterwards I heard of an expedition being on the point of leaving Jallalabad for Kooner, and I determined on joining it. I re-traversed the Khybur Pass alone, and arrived at Jallalabad just in time to go in the advance. I was present at Pushut, 18th January 1840; and on the return of the force I remained behind with Captain Macgregor. In February 1840 I accompanied Captain Macgregor to Chugur-Serai, and thence to Otipore or Chugur-Serai-Balu on the immediate frontier of Kaffiristan, and through his influence I was enabled to remain there, and to increase my materials in an extremely interesting direction. I remained about Otipore for some weeks, making arrangements for penetrating into Kaffiristan and little Cashgur, and in daily expectation of being joined by the late Capt. E. Connolly; all my plans, which first seemed to promise success, were completely frustrated by the disturbances which broke out in Bajore, consequent on Meer Alum Khan's absence at Jallalabad. Capt. Connolly barely escaped with his life from the hands of the Momauds. Meer Alum Khan found on his return towards his government that he could not leave Chugur-Serai, and at last, circumstances threatened so much around Otipore and Chugur-Serai, that Meer Alum Khan insisted on my leaving Otipore and on returning with him to Jallalabad. I did not leave a moment too soon, for shortly after, Syud Hoshin turned Otipore by crossing the hills to the north of Deogul, and very soon possessed himself of Otipore. Meer Alum and I reached Jallalabad in safety, having been attacked once on the road.

"I remained at Jallalabad a few days, and was driven thence to Khaggah by the necessity of obtaining medical aid. I reached Khaggah in a high fever, and was confined to my bed for six weeks: during my severe illness, I experienced the greatest kindness and attention from Dr. Thomson and Dr. Andrew Paton, of the H. C. European Regt.

"Early in July I proceeded to Cabul for change of air, and as soon as I recovered a little strength, started to join Lieut. Sturly, who was surveying on the Toorkistan frontier. I met that Officer at Syghan the day he left to prosecute his surveys, which had been interrupted by the Kamard disturbances: he was recalled to Syghan, in consequence of heavier and more serious disturbance.

"I returned to Cabul, as I found it impossible to proceed beyond Syghan, and then waited with impatience for a season that would enable me to cross the Punjab without great risk to my still debilitated constitution.

"My establishment of collectors consisted of unintelligent Affghans, who were particularly prone to abrupt abscondings, and my supplies of materials and carriage very limited.

"The botanical collection is as extensive as could be expected from the nature of the country and the climate. It is in excellent order, consisting of about 1500 species, and a great number of duplicates. This collection has been formed on the principles which have guided me on former travels. Those principles I conceive to require the collection of every form in numbers, and in various localities, so that the geographical limits of each may be estimated, and the examination be open. They also require information as to habitat, locality, climate, whether the plants are gregarious or not, and whether they contribute to giving peculiar features to the country. I do not hesitate to say that this collection contains almost all the plants that existed in flower or fruit along the line of march of the army between Cabul and Syghan, about Chugur-Serai, Otipore, and Pushut, and in the neighbourhood of Khaggah.

"The extent over which it was formed is about 1,600 miles, and on the variety of geographical position a considerable part of its value depends. If the plants between Cabul and Peshawur are less rich, as my journeys between those cities always occurred at unfavourable seasons, the deficiency has been lessened by my friend Dr. Ritchie.

"The Ornithological portion of the collection, consists of about 350 specimens, is in good order, and contains many objects of interest, valuable for throwing some light on the geographical distribution of birds.

"To the fish of the various tracts I paid considerable attention, but owing to the difficulties of travelling and of climate, the collection has suffered severely. At Shikarpore I made an extensive collection of the fish of the Indus. I had collected most of the fish of the river, of the Bolan Pass, of the streams of Quettah, and of the Urghundab, near Candahar, unfortunately I relied too much on the preservative powers of alcohol. Subsequently I took the additional precaution of preserving skins separately; and it is to these which amount to about 150 specimens, that the collections are chiefly limited. The collections contain the fish of the Cabul river, between its source near Sir-i-Chushme, and Peshawur, of the Helmund at an altitude of 11,500 feet, of the Bamean river, and of the Chenab, Ravee, and Sutledge.

"This collection is particularly interesting, as showing that while the plants, quadrupeds, and birds of the southern and northern declivities of the Kohi-Baba, the continuation of the Hindoo-koosh, are much alike, yet that a total difference exists in their fish.

"Lord Keane, and Sir Willoughby Cotton, left me in complete possession of my own time, a great kindness due no doubt to the considerate instructions of Lord Auckland, but for which I was not the less grateful.

"I always found Sir Alexander Burnes very considerate and very willing to forward my views, and put me in possession of information.

The late Dr. Lord also showed himself anxious to assist me in my duties, and very kindly asked me to join the Mission to Toorkistan, so suddenly put an end to by a suspected outbreak in Kohistan.

"To Captain Macgregor I was under great obligations during the whole time I continued in his district. Through his influence I was enabled to remain at the outer borders of Kaffiristan; and that deservedly warm respect which he was held in by all the chiefs, would, I am confident, have gained me access into Kaffiristan, and towards Cashgur, at any less unsettled period. I have seen Captain Macgregor in the closet and in the field, and I cannot sufficiently express the respect with which I have had cause to regard him in both situations.

"Captain Sanders, of the Bengal Engineers, was always eager to swell my stock of materials, and during periods of occasional indisposition, I relied almost entirely on him. Captain Sanders had also made for me a collection of plants between Candahar and Herat, which, I regret to say, was nearly entirely destroyed in crossing one of the rivers on that route.

"It is to Dr. Ritchie, of the Bombay Medical Service, the companion of the justly celebrated Major Pottinger, during his return from Herat via Jhomunna, that the Botanical collections are mostly indebted. Dr. Ritchie not only placed unreservedly at my disposal a very interesting collection made on that journey, but also a larger one made between Peshbolak and Peshawur. Both these are of considerable value, the one shows that the Affghan forms prevail as far as Herat on both sides of the Paropamisus, the other shows that Affghanistan, even in its hottest parts, has a majority of European forms. To the contents of these collections, notes of the localities are also added, enhancing their value very considerably. I may be excused for adding, that Dr. Ritchie is acquainted with route surveying; in this and his knowledge of Botany, he possesses two valuable requisitions of a traveller.

"Dr. Grant, of the Bombay Medical Service, formerly in Medical charge of Dr. Lord's Mission, liberally presented me with an excellent series of specimens from the valley of Syghan.

"While I am beyond measure indebted for Zoological collections, to Captain Hay, of the European Regiment."

"The following notes addressed to Emanuel Fernandez, plant collector at Malacca, may perhaps be useful as containing instructions for the collection and transmission of plants and seeds. They are perhaps worthy of insertion on other grounds, as an example of the pains taking, and patient manner in which Mr. Griffith made his wishes known to the persons employed by him in his pursuits."

To Emanuel Fernandez.

"I have received the open box of seeds, and the large case of plants, per '*Tenasserim.*' The Ebool seeds were coming up, the dried plants are in good order, and are of very good kinds.

"Before you put in the palms and fruits with other collections, you should see that they are quite dry, as otherwise they rot and injure the dried plants. When you send up more fruits, etc. put them into open rattan baskets, so that they may be aired.

"I send a list of palms and *rotans* wanted very much, and two more glazed cases for seeds: water the earth inside a day before closing the boxes and sending them off to Singapore. Whenever you get any good seeds, dry them, and put them in a letter, directed to me. Seeds spoil by being kept, particularly if kept among wet fruits and dried plants.

"If you can get flower-pots in Malacca buy two or three dozen, and whenever you get seeds sow them in a pot, and keep them, until you have enough pots filled to occupy one of the cases, then put mould between the pots, and sow more seeds in this mould, fasten the lid down and send off the box to Singapore."

May 30th, 1843.

"The cases of plants, etc. have arrived: the fresh plants were nearly all dead.

"You planted them very well, and cleverly, but some how or other the lids of the boxes were nailed down, and so the plants died, because plants will not live without light.

"Some of the Ebool seeds have sprouted, one Lanjoot arrived alive, and also the Pakoo Galowe.

"I will send soon two glazed cases, in which you may put plants as before, and seeds of palms, or any good plants: sow them in the same manner, and three or four days before the cases are despatched water the earth and plants moderately; then screw down the lid, when the plants, if they have rooted in the earth, will not die, because the glass admits light to them. But to be sure of the plants having rooted, you must keep the cases with you for three weeks, and if any plants are sickly, take them out and put in others.

"I send a list: when your next despatch arrives, I will increase your pay. If you send plenty of seeds, etc. often, that is once a month or six weeks, I will keep you in my service even if I do not come back to Malacca.

"I also send a box with a large bottle in it of spirits of wine, this is for monkey cups (Nepenthes). Take the finest ones you can get of all sorts, and put them in the bottle, leaves and all, do not squeeze them into the bottle, then send it to me."

"I send two empty glazed cases for plants: when these reach you, fill them with moist earth and plant in them ripe fresh seeds of the following palms * * * You need not wait until you have obtained all, but such only as you can get at once; but remember when you have got ripe seeds of any kind to sow them in the case. Take care the earth is not too wet. The seeds you sent, sown in an open box, came up, and we have now six or seven live Ebools, &c.

"Send me up some ripe fruits and seeds of the Epoo, those you sent were not ripe. If you can get any ripe ones, also sow some with the palm seeds."

Calcutta: March 26th, 1844.

"When you prepare Rotangs do not cut off the stalk of the leaf close to the stem, but six inches from it, and do not cut off the thorns, but tie all up in mats or gunny bags: at the same time send the leaves of each dried in paper like other plants and flowers, all with names written plainly in English and Malay.

"Send live plants according as you receive boxes for them."

"Whenever you find ripe fruits or seeds, dry them in the sun, and then send them to the Post Office for despatch in paper bags. Sow palm seeds in open boxes as you did before, the Ebool having come up."

January 14*th*, 1844.

"The plants dried and living have been received, and do you great credit. The live plants particularly are in excellent order. I have sent two more cases, when they reach you, fill them as you have done before, and despatch them to me. I send some cards on which you can write the names plainly, and tie them on the specimens. I will also send you a pocket English Dictionary, and make you a present of the English and Portuguese one."

PRIVATE JOURNALS

OF

Wm. GRIFFITH, F.L.S.

CHAPTER I.

When proceeding with the Assam Deputation for the Examination of the Tea Plant.

September, 1835.—We arrived at Pubna on the 9th of September, and left it on the following morning, pursuing the course of the Pubna "Karee," which is exceedingly tortuous and of about an average width of 100 yards. On the evening of the 10th, we halted in the same river near its termination. This morning we reached the "Beera," into which the Pubna Karee enters, and which at the mouth presents a vast expanse of water. Among the jheels which occur on every side, we noticed in abundance the *Tamarix dioica.* About noon we entered a narrow river, and in the evening a very narrow creek in which in two places we experienced a great difficulty in getting the boats along. We noticed *Alpinia allughas, Nymphæa pubescens, Oxystelma esculentum, Apluda aristata,* in abundance. Up to this period the two most conspicuous grasses continue to be *Saccharum spontaneum,* and *Andropogon muricatus.*

Sunday, 13*th.*—Arrived at Shiraz-gunge, about half-past 8 A.M., from which place the people say Jumalpore is a three days' journey. The country through which we proceeded after leaving Shiraz-gunge is nothing but a net-work of rivers, several of vast size, and low islands, occupied almost exclusively by *Saccharum spontaneum,* and in some places abounding in *Typha elephantina,* in fruit. We halted at a small village in the evening, where we procured *Centrostachys aquatica.*

September 14th.—Came in sight of distant very elevated land, which we suppose to be the Kassiya Hills. This morning (15th) the Hills are very plain, and bear nearly due north. The country through which we passed yesterday presented no change whatever. *Andropogon muricatus* has now nearly left us; but the *Saccharum* reaches to a large size, and is incredibly abundant. The natives use it for thatching their huts. We were visited by a heavy squall in the evening.

16th.—Strong winds from an easterly direction. About noon we succeeded in reaching a creek, in which we are completely sheltered. During our route here, we were employed in examining a new species of *Crotalaria*, and one of *Mitrasacme!* In pools close to us are *Damasonium indicum, Nymphæa cærulea, Myriophyllum tetrandrum, Polygonum rivulare*, and a species of *Villarsia, V. cristata.*

19th.—Left the creek, and arrived at Jumalpore about 2 P.M.; the cantonment of which occupies the right-hand side of the Burrampooter, along the bank of which the officers' houses are situated; indeed this is the only dry line about the place, as immediately inland there are nothing but jheels and rice fields. Jumalpore is about $\frac{3}{4}$ of a mile from the junction of the Jenai with the Burrampooter or rather from the point of exit of the former river.

24th.—We left the cantonment about 11 A.M., and proceeded down the Burrampooter, which is a very uninteresting river, and appears more like a net-work of water and sand banks; opposite Jumalpore, the banks are about a mile apart, but the distance between the extreme banks, leaving the island opposite the cantonment out of the question, is much more. During the dry weather *this* part of the river is passable, and indeed is in some places nothing but a dry bed of sand, so that people walk across it. During our stay at the above place we met with many interesting and new plants, among which a new species of *Villarsia* occupied the most prominent place. *Cyperaceæ, Gramineæ*, and aquatic *Scrophularineæ* abound. *Solanum spirale* occurs in abundance, and the trees commence to be clothed with ferns. I observed only one *Epiphytica Orchidea*, probably an *Aerides.*

The banks consist hitherto of nothing but sand, covered with *Saccharum spontaneum. Andropogon muricatus* is scarcely to be met with.

26th.—We left Mymensing this morning, and proceeded down the Burrampooter, the banks of which still present for the most part nothing but a succession of sandy banks covered with *Saccharum spon-*

taneum. The stream is not very rapid, and the river, owing to the numerous islands and banks, does not present so imposing an appearance as the Ganges. For the last week strong easterly winds have prevailed.

27th.—We entered the mouth of the Soormah, or, as the natives seem to call it, the Barak. The water of this river or portion of the Megna? is remarkably clear, compared with that of the Ganges; as indeed is that of the Burrampooter.

30th.—Some time after we entered the Soormah we apparently left its channel, and up to this morning we have passed through a tract of jheels with a few clear and very deep channels. The villages are built on small eminences, and are entirely surrounded with water; they have the usual form, and those houses adjoining the water have fences of an *Arundo,* which they tell us are intended to keep out the grass. We have since entering these jheels passed through and between immense beds of vegetation, formed principally of *Oplismenus* (Panicum) *stagninus, Leersia? aristata,* which by-the-bye is a distinct genus. *Villarsia cristata, Nymphæalotus,* Palomogeton, *Azolla Salvinii,* etc. etc. The only novel things we have met with are *Ischæmum cuspidatum,* Roxb. (sui generis,) and a small grass intermediate between Panicum and Chamæraphis. The wild form of *Aryza sativa, Panicum interruptum* and Leersia? *ciliaris,* Roxb. also occur; the two former in abundance. On the more dry tracts, that occasionally though very rarely occur, *Andropogon muricatus* appears. No Saccharum presented itself since the 28th. High ground was visible yesterday evening, apparently at a great distance.

October 1st.—We have continued to pass through immense jheels: about 6 A.M. we arrived at Hubbe-gunge, a large native town, situated on the Barak, which does not deserve the name of a river. The actual distance from this place to Chattuc is about 42 miles, and the high land in that direction was faintly visible for about 2 hours in the morning. The ground to the Eastward is losing the "Jheel" character, and appears densely wooded, and to the S.E. rather high hills are visible. Altogether this land of jheels is very remarkable, particularly on account of the great depth of the water, which except in one point has hitherto always exceeded 6 feet, and yet the water has fallen in all probability two or three more. As the head quarters of tropical aquatic plants, it is well worthy of attention; the profusion of *Leersia aristata,* Roxb. is immense, but this is almost exceeded by *Oplismenus stagninus.*

On the 3rd October, we left the tract of jheels, and proceeded by small rivers, overhung with jungle and fine bamboos; on the 5th we re-entered the Soorma and proceeded down it to Chattuc, which is situated on the left bank of the river, and which we reached in the afternoon. During our passage down the river we had beautiful views of the mountains, which do not however strike one with an idea of great height. We could plainly distinguish two or three waterfalls shooting over scarped precipices.

Churra Punjee, October 30th.—After a residence of 20 days here, I wrote to Mr. Solly, stating nothing particular, except that Bucklandia has coniferous tissue, and that Podostemon will probably prove Monocotyledonous and allied to Pistiaceæ. Our stay here has proved a source of great delight, and accumulation of botanical and geological treasures. The cantonments of Churra are at an elevation of 4200 feet above the sea, the native village being situated half way up the ascent which closes in the table-land on which the cantonment is situated towards the N. and W., and it is hence about 300 feet higher. The country immediately adjoining the cantonment is flat, with here and there a rounded hillock, destitute of any covering but grasses and a few low, half shrubby plants. To the Eastward there is a very deep and beautiful valley, the west side of which in particular is densely covered with jungle, but this does not contain any large trees. The opposite side, fronting our bungalow, runs nearly N. and S., presents a succession of ravines, and a most picturesque and varied surface. This valley, along the bottom of which as is usual a torrent runs, opens into the low country at Terrya Ghat, which is situated at the foot of the ascent to Churra. Directly to the south, and at a distance of about two miles from the cantonments, there is another valley likewise occupied below by a torrent fed by the Moosmai falls. The commencement of all these vallies, that I have at least seen, is a sheer precipice, which often, and particularly at Moosmai, assumes the form of a vast amphitheatre, over the brink of which cascades, especially at Moosmai, fall in tolerable plenty. It is in these places that the immense depth of the sandstone is best seen; the depth of the valley of Moosmai is, I am told, 1500 feet, the country above these precipices is generally level, and is in fact table-land. The most beautiful valley is at Maamloo, a village to the Westward of Churra, and about five miles distant. The approach to Churra is pretty enough, and gives the best view of the cantonment. The coal mines are to the Westward, and close to

Churra. These I have not yet seen; the coal is of the very best description, it does not splinter, gives remarkably few ashes, affords an admirable fire and the best coke. Water-courses are plenty about Churra, but the body of water is at this season small, although it becomes considerable after a few hours rain; it is then that the great fall at Moosmai becomes really beautiful, the water shooting over the precipice and falling into a bason about 150 feet below. By a succession of these falls, although of more limited height, it at length reaches the bottom of the valley. It is only on the precipices about the fall that the Chamærops appears to grow; at the foot of a precipice a little to the right (going from Churra,) a tree fern grows, which I have Wallich's authority for stating to be Polypod giganteum, a fern which occurred at Mahadeb, and which I have seen in somewhat similar situations at Mergui. All my excursions have been confined to this valley and to the water-courses immediately around Churra; once only have I quitted the table-land and proceeded to Maamloo, and yet in this very limited space the profusion of objects has been such as to enable me only to embrace a very limited proportion. The above excursion proved very rich. About half way to Maamloo I discovered a solitary tree fern *(Alsophila Brunoniana,)* and to the left, and up the broken sides of the calcareous cliffs that occur here and between Maamloo and Moosmai, a group of several magnificent specimens, of which on the succeeding day we brought home three. We saw none above 30 feet, although the specimen in the British Museum from these hills measures 45. Their axis is of small diameter, and is nearly cylindrical, the vascular fascicles being disposed in covered bundles, often assuming the form of a Ш near the circumference of the very dense cellular tissue of which the axis is chiefly composed. Towards the base it is enveloped in an oblique dense mass of intermottled rigid fibres (roots) which, as they are developed in the greatest extent, the nearer they approach the base, give the trunk a conical form. Their growth is essentially endogenous, and will probably be found when examined aborigine to approximate to that of Cycadeæ, although these last are of a more exogenous than endogenous nature. Nothing however is known of the growth of Palms, Cycadeæ, or tree ferns. I have above alluded to the calcareous rocks or cliffs; these are of the same formation with those that occur so abundantly on the Tenasserim coast, although they are much more rich in vegetation. These I first saw at Terrya Ghat; like those of Burmah they abound in caves, and assume the most varied and picturesque forms; they appear to be the head quarters of Cyrthandraceæ, of which we found a noble species with the flower of a Martynia growing among the tree-ferns. They are very rich in ferns and mosses, of which last near the tree-ferns I gathered four species of four genera without moving a foot. The cliffs in which, or at the foot of which the coal is found, bound the Churra cantonments to the Westward. These are chiefly calcareous. The entrance to Churra lies between this and the precipice at Moosmai. Very few animals of any description are to be seen about Churra. I have seen one small species of deer, about half as large again as the mouse-deer of Mergui, and one young flying squirrel of a greyish black colour, with a very bushy tail. Leopards are, they say, not uncommon. Tigers do not generally come so high. Of birds, I mean about Churra, there are several species of hawks, and their old companions crows and swallows; but I have seen no sparrows, which is singular enough. There is one beautiful species of jay, with crimson orange beak and legs, and a pretty king-fisher; but, except perhaps in the valleys, birds, I should say, are very scarce. With respect to shooting, scarcely any is to be had; wood-cocks are found in the dells about Churra, but sparingly. I have seen only one snipe and one quail.

Regarding the natives, I have little to say. They are a stout-built, squat, big-legged hill tribe: the women in regard to shape being exactly like their mates; and as these are decidedly ugly—somewhat tartarish-looking people, very dirty, and chew pawn to profusion—they can scarcely be said to form a worthy portion of the gentler sex. They appear to be honest; but that is a quality which, from the example of their European lords, they are said to be losing fast. They have no written character; every thing being transmitted by tradition, and performed by the interchange of tokens. They drink like fish, and manufacture a bad kind of arrack, the pernicious effects of which were experienced by the European invalids when the Sanatarium was in existence. They pay respect to their dead by the erection of a sort of kairns and large erect slabs of sandstone rounded off at the upper end: of these, I believe, they put up three or five to each friend, according to their means and, probably, rank. The Churra people cultivate nothing but a little cotton, and perhaps a species of Eleasine. They depend upon the plains for their support and supplies, and this is good management since rice at Terrya Ghat is sold at 70 or 80 seers a rupee. Their hire is, considering the cheapness of their food, very expensive; a man being rated at four annas a day, a woman at three, and a boy at two. I should add, that they have no caste.

The climate is certainly very cool and cold, the thermometer ranging from about 56° to 66° in-doors at this time of the year. The rains are said to be the coldest part of the year; they are excessive, commencing in April and ceasing in October. It occasionally rains for fifteen or sixteen days in succession, and without intermission; and nine or ten inches have been known to fall in twenty-four hours. Since we have been here, inclusive of this, we have had four days of wet weather, of which three were continued rain. Both were ushered in by the sudden irruption of heavy mists from below, which soon spread over the country, obscuring every thing. These sudden irruptions occur during the partial breaking up of the rain, during which time the valleys are completely choked up with dense mists, the summits of the hills on the opposite side to that on which one stands being alone visible. After the rains were over, in the first instance, the plains, or rather the mass of haze hanging over them, presented a most curious spectacle.

The coldest weather we have yet experienced was at Maamloo, on the 27th, the thermometer at 8 P.M. being at 52°. This is remarkable, as Maamloo is rather below Churra. There is however a good deal of wood round the place.*

With regard to Botany, the chief vegetation about Churra, as indeed is at once indicated by the appearance of the country, consists of grasses. Along the water-courses, which intersect this portion of the country, *Bucklandia populnea*, a species of Ternstræmia, Pandanus, Eugenia, Camellia, are found; while Compositæ, Eriocaulon, and ferns abound in the same places. The vegetation of the valleys is very rich and very varied; and, an affinity is indicated with the botany of China by the existence of a species of Illicum, I. khascanam, and several Terustræmiaceæ. The great orders are grasses, ferns, compositæ. During a trip to Maamloo, a beautifully situated village on the brink of the table-land, we discovered abundance of the tree-fern *Alsophila Brunoniana*, the highest of which measured 25 feet. The appearance of the tree is that of a palm. The flora surrounding these tree-ferns we found to be exceedingly rich. Among Nepal ferns, I may mention *Anisadenia, Saxifraga ligulata.*

Interior of the Khasyah Mountains.—On the 2nd, we left for Surureem; at which place we halted a day. Bucklandia here occurs,

* It is also on a northern declivity.

of a very large size, perhaps 50 or 60 feet. It is a rugged-looking tree, many of the branches being decayed. There we observed the first *Rhododendrum arboreum.* Our next stage was to Moflong; during our march thither, or rather mine, I had a fine view of the Himalayas, but not upon the regular road to Moflong. The European forms certainly increased in number between Surureem and the above place. Two great acquisitions occurred on the road; a new Crawfordia, and a Podostemon which W. has named after me. This I found in the clear stream adjoining the Bogapanee growing upon stones, and adhering to them very firmly. It is on the hills about the Bogapanee that the firs first make their appearance, but do not attain to any great size. The valley of the Bogapanee is exceedingly deep, and both the descent and ascent are very difficult.

Moflong is a bleak exposed village, and the bungalow or residence for travellers very bad. The number of European forms we found to increase considerably about this place. The only woods that occur are of fir, but the trees are of no great size; their frequent occurrence, however, stamps a peculiar feature on the scenery. We here experienced nearly three days of continued rain, and, as the place is bleak, we were miserable enough. We left for Myrung on the 9th, and the greater and all the first part of the long march was very uninteresting. At Mumbree, however, there is a decided improvement, and the scenery is very good. One here notices the occurrence of woods —of oaks, etc., and their form reminded me somewhat of the woods of Buckinghamshire. No woods of fir occur; all the trees occurring isolatedly. I should mention that the country between Molee and Moflong is quite peculiar in geological structure, abounding in Cyanite, the masses of which are of very considerable size. I imagine that the vegetation farther on in this direction would be more rich in European forms than elsewhere, at least between Churra and Mingklow.

Myrung is certainly far superior in every point to any place that we have yet seen; and, as the climate is peculiarly fine and the bungalow good, the degree of enjoyment is as great as can be expected. The features of the country are similar to those of Mumbree. The groves or woods are composed chiefly of oaks, intermixed with Magnolias, which attain a very large size. These forests seem all to have a northern aspect. Orchideæ abound in these woods, and so far as herbaceous forms go, European vegetation is on the decrease. From the bungalow one has occasionally a remarkably fine view of the Hima-

From a Sketch made on the Spot by W. Griffith. M & N Hanhart lith. Printers

VIEW FROM NUNKLOW.

layas, mountains intercepted by large tracts of very high land, probably Bootan. The coldest weather we have experienced here was when the thermometer sank to 46°; even in the middle of the day the sun is not oppressive. It is singular enough, that the first attempts, so to speak, at a Fauna occur here. The woods abound with small birds. I shot one squirrel, with a very short tail and rounded head. Red deer (the Gyee of the Burmese) occur, though rarely. Two or three solitary snipes may be found during a day's excursion, and perhaps a brace of quail, which are nearly as large as English partridges. Pheasants are reported to occur in the woods. I should add, that both here and at Nunklow snipe of a very large description, and of the habits of the solitary snipe, are found in small numbers. They are very brown, as large as a wood-cock, and their cry is that of a common snipe. Lieutenant Townsend informs me, that these birds are a totally distinct species. Lieutenant Vetch tells me, that the Khasiyas declare that they are the females of the wood-cock, in other words, wood-hens, and that in March wood-cocks abound in the places with these wood-hens. He likewise informs me, that the only difference he could ascertain to exist between these birds and wood-cocks, consists in their having very short and thick legs.

I have seen two of this particular description, but have never shot any.

After Myrung one can speak much less in favour of these hills. Nunklow is a pretty spot, and commands a really magnificent view of the Himalayas, of the Bootan mountains, and of the plains of Assam. Altogether this view is the finest which, in my limited experience, I have ever seen : I did not however like Nunklow, nor do my wishes recur to it.* The route thither is pretty enough, and not fatiguing. I may mention Nunklow as the station of some fine trees, among which is a Betula, two Æsculi, oaks, etc. in abundance. The pine is in fine order, but not large. Much more cultivation is carried on in this portion of the hills than elsewhere, and paddy is cultivated apparently to some extent. The temperature is much warmer, and the air by no means so bracing as that of Myrung. Perhaps at this place the flora resembles that of lower Himalaya more than other place we have yet seen. The march from Nunklow to Nowgong is very long, and, as we started late, owing partly to mismanagement and partly to the want of

* On a hill near the Bungalow are the tombs of Lieuts. Burlton and Beddingfield, two distinguished officers murdered by the natives in 1829.

coolies, we were most agreeably benighted in the jungle. The descent is very sudden and commences at Nunklow; the valley, on the brink of which it is situated, being perhaps 2000 feet deep. It is in this valley or on its walls that the finest pines we have seen occur, but even here they do not attain a greater height than 60 feet, and perhaps a diameter of a foot or a foot and a half. As Mr. Brown of the Sillet Light Infantry informed me most correctly, many would make fine spars; but Mr. Cracroft's language in one of the Journals of the Asiatic Society when describing these firs, seems rather overwrought. During our march I picked up a pretty species of Sonerila. A small stream runs at the foot of the descent, by what name it goes I know not. Near the Busta-panee, flowing along a valley about two hours' walk from the last mentioned water. Wallich discovered abundance of his favourite and really splendid Polypodium Wallichianum, which I may accuse with justice of being an additional reason for our benightment. The stream is really the only respectable river we have seen, or rather the second one that can be called a torrent, the other being the Bogapanee. It boils along, and the body of water is great, even at the season of the year at which we passed it. It has forced enormous holes, frequently round, in the large masses of rock that form its bed, and then in and a few yards beyond the bridge of bamboos by which we crossed, it falls, they say, 70 feet into a fine bason, which however is only partly visible from above. They who have been on the edges of this bason say that the fall is really fine; it certainly has not much of this when viewed from above, neither can it, I think, even in the rains come up to Mr. Cracroft's description. Moosmai is, *après tout* I will venture to say, the king of the falls between Terrya Ghat and Ranee Godown. On the farther side of this water, small trees of Cycas first make their appearance, but we had no time now or rather then to examine any thing. As the shades of evening lengthened we quickened our paces, and at last when it became dark, came up with the coolies in a most rugged road, and when it was dark, after stumbling about a good deal, I made my way to the foot of the descent, and reached a small stream, where we made preparations for a halt, and where we passed the night, during which we were treated with a slight shower of rain. As the season was far advanced we all escaped, scot-free, from fever, and reached the Bungalow called Nowgong about 10 o'clock next morning, where we spent the day.

From this time we were, I believe, all anxious to leave the hills, which had lost all their charms, although the vegetation was still

From a Sketch made on the spot by W. Griffith

THE VILLAGE OF NUNKLOW

more gigantic and interesting. But we were now confined to the road, which is very good, all digressions being prevented by the thickness of the jungles, and then in some places swarms of wild elephants. These animals appear most numerous about Onswye, near which there is a marshy place literally trodden up by them, and their tracks were so fresh that no traces of Wallich or his coolies could be identified, although they had preceded us only about half an hour. It was in this particular place that I gathered a solitary specimen of *Butomus pygmæus*. Beyond Nowgong, saul first comes into view, and many trees attain a considerable size. Some fine ferns and two beautiful Acanthaceæ, I may mention, as collected about that place. We reached Jyrung by an easy march the next day; every step adding only to a greater renewal of acquaintance with old faces, or at least old plain plants. Between Jyrung and the foot of the hills, we fell in with *Henslowia glabra* in fine flower: Wallich took many fine specimens, all of which were males. This species is, as well as the former, liable to deceive one as to the sex of the plant; but all the seeming ovaries beginning to enlarge are due to insect bites or punctures. To conclude: at the foot of the hills we were embraced with *Marlea Byonifolia, Bauhinia purpurea*, etc. almost exactly as at Terrya Ghat. Between the foot of these really delightful hills and Ranee Godown, I fell in with one plant only, deserving of mention. *Dischedia Rafflesiana;* this is worthy of notice, as our Indian Asclipiferous species have not hitherto been found, I believe north of Moulmain, nor otherwhere than that peninsula and the archipelago. From Ranee Godown we had the pleasure of walking nineteen miles to Gowahatty, which place we reached on the 23rd November.

All I can say in its favour is, that it is very cold in the mornings, always at this season cool; that it is very pretty, being situated on the Burrampooter, and surrounded with hills; that the women are good-looking, and the whole body of officers among the best. Of its botanical riches I can only say, that in a short afternoon's excursion we found *Cardiopterus harnulosa*, or rather saw it, and a species of Apocynea in fruit, probably the same with one I have from Tenasserim, and which is remarkable for the very many fleshy alæ of its fruit. Gowahatty is particularly known as the station for *Cycas circinatis*, one fine specimen of which Captain Jenkins shewed us, and the height of which is perhaps 20 or 25 feet.

It was dichotomous, but only once. The rings formed by the scars of the foot stalks, as well as those of the fruit stalks, were most distinct on the two branches only, and gave them a very rich and less elated appearance. The examination of this specimen only strengthens me in my opinion derived chiefly from examination of those in the Botanic Gardens, that these rings which certainly afford the age of each branch, one being added of either sort every year, are not to be distinguished in the stem below its division. So that after all, *Brongniart* is only half-wrong, although he is ignorant of the saving clause.

I may add, that we were on the hills about thirty-eight days, of which seven and a half were rainy, a proportion of 1 in $5\frac{1}{2}$.

On the 2nd December, our party left Gowahatty for Suddiya, on the morning of the 4th I proceeded in advance in Captain Matthie's express canoe for Tezpoor, which place I reached on the evening of the 6th, and at which I met with a most kind reception from Captain Matthie, Principal Assistant to the Agent to the Governor General, and in Civil charge of the district of Durrung. Tezpoor possesses many advantages over Gowahatty, from which place it is about 120 miles distant, that is, following the river. It is situated on the banks of what was once a portion of the Burrampooter, but which is now nothing but a nullah, nearly dry at the present season. It is a completely new place,* Captain Matthie having arrived here about a year since, at which time it was a complete jungle. Some small hills run along the side of the nullah, on one of which Captain Matthie's house is situated. The clearings have already reached to a considerable extent, and there are two good roads for buggies. The great advantage it has over Gowahatty consists in its freedom from fogs, which evidently hug the Meekur hills on the opposite side of the Burrampooter, bearing about E. S. E. from Tezpoor. It is perhaps owing to the proximity of these hills that Nowgong until 10 A. M. appears completely enveloped in fog, while all round Tezpoor it is completely clear.

From this place the view of the Himalayas and of the intervening Bootan hills is very fine. The chain is of considerable extent, and presents three grand peaks, of which the most westerly one is the largest. They do not appear very distant, and are distinctly seen at this season at all times of the day. They are more soft and picturesque towards evening, at which time the different shades are better

* Although in former times it must have been of some note, the vicinity is strewed with sculptured stones and columns, of which the modern buildings constructed. These remains present the form and proportions of European Architecture, and exhibit considerable taste.

From a Sketch on the spot by W. Griffith. M & N. Hanhart, lith. Printers

VIEW of CAPT^N MATTHIE'S CUTCHERRY, THE BOOT HILLS & HIMALAYAH, FROM TEZPORE

developed. The degrees of ascent of the Bootan hills are well shewn; the hills forming the lowest range being of no considerable height. It is at once obvious, that the ascent into Bootan from this place would occupy several days.

The view to the S. and S. S. W. is barren enough, and is completely flat; the country presenting nothing whatever but high grass, with an occasional peep of the river. That to the north is, owing to the Himalayas, very striking and picturesque.

Cultivation is carried on to a great extent about Tezpoor, and the district is populous, although few villages are to be seen, as they are all concealed among trees. Paddy is the principal grain cultivated, and this is carried on in low places, which appear on a casual examination to have been originally beds of rivers. Captain Matthie however tells me, that many of these have abrupt terminations and commencements, such may have been old jheels. Sursoo, opium, and sugar-cane are likewise cultivated, especially the former.

The whole land indeed, with the exception of the rice-places and the evidently old beds of the Burrampooter, are much more elevated than the land round Gowahatty. Both Tezpoor and Durrung are consequently less damp, and more healthy than the above-mentioned place. In fact, as a residence I would infinitely prefer Tezpoor to Gowahatty. With regard to the *shikar*, (shooting) both large and small game abound. Tigers are frequent as well as bears. Buffaloes are to be seen on the *churs* (islands) in large herds. Pea-fowl and jungle-fowl abound, as well as water-fowl; floricans and partridges, both black and red, are by no means unfrequent.

Upper Assam, *Jan.* 15*th*.—We arrived at Kujoo, a rather large village of Singfos, and within half a day's journey of which the tea is found in its native state. This is the first Singfo village I have as yet seen, and is situated on the skirts of a plain of small extent, and covered to all appearance by extensive grass jungles, among which trees are interspersed. The houses are not numerous, but they are of large size, and are raised in the Burman fashion on piles from the ground. Within one, many families are accommodated. The people themselves are fair, much like the Burmese, but still quite distinct. The male dress resembles the Burmese much; the females is more distinct, consisting chiefly of a sort of *gown;* and whilst tattooing is confined to the males in Burma, it here appears to be indulged in chiefly by the ladies; all the legs I saw during the day, being ornamented with rings of tattoo. The men are a stout, rather fine race; free, easy, and independent, and great admirers of *grog* in every form.

During our journey hither, and indeed en route from Kujoo Ghat, we passed over a clay soil and through a dense jungle, comparable to which I have seen but little. Our direction has been nearly south from the above place. The jungle consisted chiefly of trees, here and there large patches of bamboo or tobacco occurring: there was but little underwood. Among the trees the most gigantic was a species of Dipterocarpus, probably the same with that I have gathered on Pator hill, Mergui. We picked up likewise very large acorns with a depressed lamellated cap, and two fruits of Castanea, one probably the same with that from Myrung. But of all the vegetation, that of ferns is the most luxuriant and most varied.

Jan. 16th.—This day we gave up to the examination of the tea in its native place. It occurs in a deep jungle to the south of the village, and at a distance of about three miles from it. Our route thither lay through first a rather extensive grass jungle, then through a deep jungle. We crossed the Deboru once on our route; it is a mean and insignificant stream.

Nothing particular presents itself in the jungle until you approach the tea, on which you come very suddenly. This plant is limited to a small extent, perhaps to 300 yards square, the principal direction being N. and S. It grows in a part of the jungle where the soil is light and dryish, and throughout which, *ravinules* are frequent, due, Mac. tells me, to the effect of rain dropping from the heavy over-shadowing foliage on a light soil. In addition to this, small mounds occur about the roots of the large trees; but chiefly around bamboos, which are by no means unfrequent. This, however, is of common occurrence in all bamboo jungles. The underwood consists chiefly of Rubeaceæ, a small Leea, Cyrthandraceæ and Filices, *Polypodium arboreum*, *Angiopteris orassipes*, and a large Asplenium are common. Among the arbuscles are a large leaved Tetranthera a Myristica, Anonaceæ, *Pæderioidea fœtidissima*, foliis ternatis; stipulis apicee subulata, 3-fidis, etc. And among the forest trees are a vast Dipterocarpus, the same we met with en route to Kujoo, *Dillenia speciosa*, etc. Piper and Chloranthus are likewise not uncommon. There is no peculiar feature connected with the existence of the tea in such a place, and in such a limited extent. We were fortunate enough to find it both in flower and fruit, owing to its site; its growth is tall and slender, and its crown at least that of the smaller, very small and ill developed. Large trees are rare; in fact, they have been all cut down by the Singfos, who are like all other natives excessively improvident. The largest we saw, and which Wallich felled, was, including the crown, 43 feet in length. Small plants are very common, although Bruce had already removed 30,000. Mac. thinks they grow chiefly on the margins of the ravinules or hollows. Their leaves were all large, of a very dark green, and varying from four to eight inches in length. The pith of the tree felled was excentric, the greater development taking place as usual on the southern side; it was two and a half inches N., three and a half S.; but about 10 feet above the base this excentricity was nearly doubled. The wood is very compact, and the tree apparently one of slow growth. The largest that Bruce has seen, and which he felled last year, was 29 cubits in length. The jungle was so thick that all general views as to its real extent, and the circumstances limiting it, must be very superficial. To the East the cessation of the lightness of the soil and of the hollows is very abrupt, and strongly influences the tea, only a few small straggles being visible in that direction. The jungle here was choked with grasses, and the large viscous Acanthaceæ of which we have elsewhere en route seen such abundance. The tree evidently, even in its large state, owes little gratitude to the sun, at least for direct rays, none of which I should think ever reach it. The Singfos however say, that it will only thrive in the shade. We halted after gathering a crop of leaves under a fine Dillenia, which was loaded with its fruit. Here the Singfos demonstrated the mode in which the tea is prepared among them. I must premise, however, that they use none but young leaves. They roasted or rather semi-roasted the leaves in a large iron vessel, which must be quite clean, stirring them up and rolling them in the hands during the roasting. When duly roasted, they expose them to the sun for three days; some to the dew alternately with the sun. It is then finally packed into bamboo chungas, into which it is tightly rammed. The ground on which it occurs is somewhat raised above the plain adjoining the village, as we passed over two hillocks on our route to the tea, and the descent did not evidently counterbalance the ascent.

Jan. 17th.—We arrived at Kujoo-doo this afternoon, having passed through a great extent of jungle, which I am sorry to say presented the usual features. We crossed the Deboro once during our march, and several tributary streams which, as may be supposed, from the size of the *larger* recipient river, are excessively insignificant. The soil throughout, a good part seemed to be of clay. The only plants of interest we found were two Bambusæ in flower, and two species of Meniscium, and a *Polypodium venulis* tertiariis simplicibus. A *Sarcopyramis Sonerilæ* was also found, but rather passed flowering, and an Acrostichum? or Lomaria? We did not observe any ravinules or hollows, although mounds were by no means uncommon.

Jan. 18*th.*—We proceeded in a Southerly direction, and after marching for nearly seven hours arrived at, and encamped on, a largish plain, on which paddy had been extensively cultivated. The whole route lay through a vast and deep jungle, the road running partly on the side of an old bund: part of our road was through very wet ground, part through rather dry elevated woods, bamboos of two species occurred abundantly. We saw several vast specimensof Dipterocarpus, one which had been cut down measured from the base to first branch 110 feet. Ferns still continue in excess. I gathered another species of *Sarcopyramis;* a *Goodyera, Chrysobaphus Roxburghii* in flower, but rare; and an Apostasia not in flower.

Jan. 19*th.*—We reached Negrigam early in the forenoon although we did not leave our ground before 10 A. M. the road to the village was pretty good. Negrigam is a largish village on the north bank of the Booree Dihing, which is here a considerable though not deep stream. This bank is at the site of the village very high. The population seemed to be considerable. To the south, large ranges of hills were visible, the first of which were close enough to admit of one's distinguishing them to be wooded to the top. The inner ranges were lofty. We had some difficulty in ascertaining where the tea was located, the accounts being rather contradictory. At length we proceeded up the bed of a small river, Maumoo, which runs into the Booree Dihing close to the village: after wading along in the waters for two hours we arrived at a khet where we encamped. The direction being from Negrigam N. W. along the banks of this stream. The Pavia I first observed at Silam Mookh, was abundant, and some of the specimens were very fine, the largest was a handsome, very shady tree, of perhaps thirty feet high. The only plant of interest was *Gnetum scandens.* On a high land bank I gathered a species of Polytrichum, and one of Bartramia.

January 20*th.*—This morning we crossed the small streamlet Maumoo, ascended its rather high bank, and within a few yards from it came upon the tea: which as we advanced farther into the jungle increased in abundance; in fact within a very few yards, several plants might be observed. The plant was both in flower and ripe fruit, in one instance the seeds had germinated while attached to the parent shrub. No large trees were found, the generality being six or seven feet high; all above this height being straggling, slender, unhandsome shrubs: the leaves upon the whole were, I think, smaller than those of the Kujoo plants. With respect to the plants with which it is here associated, I may observe that they were nearly the same with those of the Kujoo jungle, but here there was nevertheless one striking difference, that the jungle was by no means so dark in consequence of the smaller size of the jungle trees. The underwood consisted chiefly of ferns, among which *Polipodium unitum* was very common, and a Lycopodium. Bamboos occurred here and there, although by no means so extensively as at Kujoo.

Chyrsobaphus Roxburghii, and a new *Dicksonia*, *D. Griffithiana*, Wall. were the plants of the greatest interest. With regard to the limits of the tea, it is by all accounts of no very great extent; but this is a point upon which it is difficult to say any thing decisive, in consequence of the thickness of the jungle. The space on which we found it may be said to be an elbow of the land, nearly surrounded by the Manmoo river, on the opposite side of which, where we were encamped, it is reported not to grow. Within this space the greater part consists of a gentle elevation or rather large mound. On this it is very abundant, as likewise along its sides, where the soil is looser, less sandy, and yellow (McClell.); along the base of this I think it is less common, and the soil is here more sandy, and much darker (McClell.) We partly ascertained that it was limited to the west, in which direction we soon lost sight of it. To the south and eastward of the elbow of land it is most common, but here it is, as I have said above, stopped by the river.

The greatest diameter of the stem of any plant that I saw in this place, might be two or three inches, certainly not more.

Nadowar, Feb. 17th.—Our route from this village, at which we were encamped, to the tea locality in the neighbouring forest, lay for the first time partly over paddy fields, the remainder over high ground covered with the usual grasses, with here and there a low strip; all was excessively wet. We next traversed a considerable tract of tree jungle, perhaps for nearly a mile; this was a drier and higher soil than the rice ground. On the northern flank of this, and close to the edge of the jungle we came to the tea, situated on a low strip of ground.

This plant here occupies an extremely limited space, and its greatest, and indeed almost only extent, is from south to north. It is in one spot excessively thick, and many of the plants had attained a considerable size, but the largest had been cut down, when it was visited by people from Suddiya in search of tea some short time ago. It had just passed flowering; all the plants looked well, better I think than those of Kujoo. The soil was very much like that of the Kujoo and Negrigam jungles, and was remarkable for its great dryness and looseness, in spite of the long continued and heavy rains. That near the surface was dark brown, below yellow brown, and the deeper it was examined the more yellow it seemed to become. We satisfied ourselves that its depth extended lower than two feet from the surface. The space the plant occupies in any numbers certainly does not exceed forty yards in length, by twenty-five in breadth. About fifty yards to the north several plants occurred, but the soil here was of a much darker tint, although it appeared to be nearly as dry as the other. The accompanying diagram may give some idea of its situation.

February 17*th*.—We arrived at Rangagurrah, the capital of the Muttack country, and the residence of the Burra-seena Puttee, [or Bengmara. Our route thither occupied us, inclusive of the day spent in examining the tea at Noadwar, five days. During the three first, we passed through a low country admirably, and almost exclusively, adapted for rice cultivation, and consequently abounding in wild wading birds and water-fowl.

As we approached Rangagurrah the ground became higher, in addition to which it is better drained. We crossed about two miles from Rangagurrah a small rivulet, a tributary of the Deboroo; no plants but one of much interest was detected *en route*. That one was a fine forest tree affecting damp low places, apparently very limited in extent. It is a new genus, belonging to Hamemelideæ, and we have called it *Sedgwickia cerasifolia*. On our arrival at Rangagurrah we were met by the Burra-seena Puttee, 'Big warrior,' who escorted us to the houses he had caused to be erected for us, and which were at a little distance from the village itself. During our association with him or with his country, he was remarkably attentive and civil, and as he is an independent man he pleased me much. On the — Feb. we reached Tingrei, a poor village about ten miles to the S. E. of Rangagurrah, situated on the west bank of the rivulet of the same name, another tributary of the Deboroo. On the same morning as the march was very short, we proceeded to examine the tea, and the following day was likewise given up to another examination. The tea here

From a Sketch made on the spot by W Griffith.

M & N Hanhart, lith Printers

THE HIMALAYAH FROM RANGAGURRAH MUTTACK

may be characterised as dwarf, no stems that I saw exceeding fifteen feet in height; it had just past flowering. It occurs in great abundance, and to much greater extent than in any of the places at which we had previously examined it. But here it is neither limited by peculiarity of soil or such slight elevation as the place affords; it grows indiscriminately on the higher ground where the soil is of a brownish yellow, and on which it attains a larger size than elsewhere, or on clump occurring in low raviny ground and associated with fine bamboos. This ground was intersected by a very tortuous dry nullah bed, on the banks of which tea was very abundant. On either side of the jungle in which it is found, extensive clearings occur, so that it is impossible to say what its original extent may have been; I am inclined to think, however that its limit was with the commencement of a small clearing running to the N. W. of a village situated on the west bank of the Tingrei, and that not much has been cut down.

The extent may be roughly estimated as follows, reckoning from the entrance into the jungle in a south easterly direction: the one in fact of our route from the village to the tea.

S. E. 180 yards, after which it disappears, but shews itself again sparingly about 100 yards further on, and in the same direction.

To the S. of this I found none, its direction being totally changed; its general direction being now,

N. W. or N. N. W. in which, and in about 200 yards from the place at which it ceased towards the south, it becomes very abundant, and continues so in a

W. N. W. course for about 220 yards.

Thence it appears to be interrupted for the space of 80 or 100 yards.

It then recommences a course

N. by W. for about 100 yards, when it is terminated by cultivated ground to the east, and low raviny ground to the west.

200 yards to the north, and close to a small village, it is very abundant, and at least its stumps with numerous shoots, occupy almost the whole of a small clearing bounded on the N. E. by the rivulet Tingrei. It may be supposed to extend for a little distance into the contiguous jungle to the N. W.

On the whole, it may be said to occupy a narrow strip of jungle, extending from the village Tingrei in a S. E. direction about a $\frac{1}{4}$ of a mile. I consider the plants here as finer than in any of the other tea jungles, the crown being much better developed owing at least in some parts to the less denseness of the jungle. The fact of the shoots appearing from the bases of the stems which had been cut down in the small clearing above mentioned, gave us good opportunities of seeing the effects of exposure to the sun. This they seemed to bear well, but the shoots were rather too much elongated, and the leaves had too much of a yellow tint to indicate that such was their natural situation. No part of the soil on which tea was found was like the soil of Nadowar or Manmoo; still, although stiffer than the others, it was characterised by a certain lightness.

The superstratum was very light, and brownish black, the remainder yellowish brown, the yellow tints as well as the stiffness increasing downwards. The soil was here deeper than in any of the other sites.

Many parts of the ground were excessively low, and very probably inundated during the rains.

From the fact of its occurring in such abundance in the small clearing to the N. W. of the village, I am induced to suppose that it had at some period extended down the large clearing which runs 200 yards to the south of the above village.

The associated vegetation presented no peculiarities; several plants, with which we had not previously met, occurred. One, a Stauntonia, was found, which may be supposed from analogy to indicate a certain coldness of climate. But on the other hand, it was associated with so many tropical forms that not much reliance can be placed on this isolated fact.

On the 25th we returned to Rangagurrah, where the elephants and dowaniers (*drivers*) were dismissed. On the 26th we commenced returning by the Deboroo, the descent of which occupied two days and a half.

Here let me express my opinion that in cases like ours, where a set of men are deputed to examine countries, time spent on rivers is absolutely thrown away. Of course in many instances such must be the case, but where it is avoidable, marching, and especially returning by a different route, should be adopted. Rangagurrah, be it known, is only two days' march from Suddiyah in a direct line, yet we have been a month proceeding by the circuitous line of rivers between these places.

CHAPTER II.

Journal of a trip to the Mishmee Mountains, from the Debouching of the Lohit to about ten miles East of the Ghalooms. Lat. 27° 50′ *to* 28° 10′ *N.; Long.* 95° 20′ *to* 96° 40′ *E.*

I left Suddiya on the morning of the 15th October 1836, and halted at Noa Dihing Mookh, (river mouth) a place abounding in fish, and promising excellent sport both in fly and live-bait fishing. The temperature of the Noa Dihing, an indolent stream flowing over a flat, sandy plain, was 79°; that of the B. pooter, which falls in large volume rapidly from the mountains, was 67°. Fish congregate in vast numbers at the junction of rivers of different temperatures, and are there more easily captured than in other situations, a fact that ought to be borne in mind, whether for the mere object of sport or the more practical purpose of fisheries in India.

The following day (16th) we passed Choonpoora, where the rapids commence, and where stones first appear; one rapid, a little above Choonpoora, is severe. There is a severe one also at Toranee Mookh, on which the Copper temple is situated; and one at Tingalee Mookh, on which Lattow is situated. The river now commences to be more subdivided; there is but little sand deposited alone, but vast beds of sand and stones occur together. The banks are clothed with jungle, and are occasionally skirted with tall grasses, but the *churs* or islands disappear it may be said with the sands, and are only formed in lower and more distant parts from the mountains, where the velocity of the current is less. Temperature at 6 A.M. 66°, 4 P.M. 76°, (water of B. pooter 64.65,) 7 P.M. 72°.

Buffaloes abundant, but I only saw a few.

The most interesting plants were a Cyclocodon, Lyriodendron, Sanicula: 32 species were collected.

Oct. 17th.—Reached Karam Mookh, about noon. Rapids much increased, some very severe, especially that opposite Karam Mookh, which we crossed without accident, although as we crossed a confluence of two rapids, the water in the middle being much agitated; it was a wonder that no canoes were upset. The bed of the river is still more divided, the spots between the streams being for the most part entirely composed of stones. The lowest temperature of the B. pooter was 63°. A severe but short rapid occurs at Karam Mookh itself, the fall being very great, but the body of water small. The water of this river is beautifully clear. Its temperature at the Mookh 72°. The jungle extends down to both edges of the water, and the stream is not divided into branches. My guide in the evening disgusted me by asking how many days I intended to stop at the Koond before my return to Suddiya, when I had engaged him expressly to go into the Mishmee hills, and not merely to Brama Koond, as the above question implied. But such is the way in which our best designs depending on native agency are often tampered with. Thermometer at 8 P.M. 64°. Species of Conaria grow abundantly on the banks!

Oct. 18*th.*—We are still in the Karam river. Reached about noon the Kamptee village, Palampan, or rather its Ghat. This Karam river is tortuous, generally shallow, with a more or less stony bed; it is nothing more in fact than a succession of rapids, between each of which the slope is very gentle, so that one makes good progress. Temperature at 6 A.M. 66° in the canoe; but in the hut in which I slept, it is as low as 60°. The dews are very heavy, and the jungle, as before, comes down to the edges of the water, but scarcely affords any marked feature. *Kydia calycina* is common, as is likewise a large Mimoseous tree. There is apparently very little diminution in the volume of water, though several minor streams were passed between this and the Mookh. Liriodendron is becoming more frequent. The views of the mountains are very varied, and that of the Koond defile or Chasm, very beautiful; water-falls seem to be distinctly visible down one hill or mountain, in particular. The finest view however is on the Lohit, opposite Dyaroo Mookh, at which place the three huge, ever snowy peaks, characteristic of the Mishmee portion of the mountains, are distinctly seen.

Left the Ghat for the village which is situate on the Dea-soon or Simaree, which flows into the Tenga-panee, and which is said now to carry off so much water from the Karam that this river ceases a short distance above this place to become navigable for boats like mine. The path we pursued ran in a S. E. or S. S. E. direction for about a mile; it is good, and leads through a thick jungle: the village contains probably fifteen houses. The Gohain, or *chief*, is a most respectable-looking man, and of very fair complexion. His people are for the most part stout. The women also of very fair complexion, with their hair tied in a large knot on the top of the head, in a peculiar way, putting one in mind of fat Norman damsels. Temperature in the boat to-day 76°, the sky beautifully clear. The B. pooter seems still the only river, the temperature of which is always below that of the air. One interesting Elæocarpus occurred—Petal. viridibus apice dentatis; calice griseo viridi, *vix valvato*. I may remark, that the æstivation of Kydia is scarcely valvate. I saw a, to me, new kingfisher and wood-pecker. The black and white kingfisher, *Dalcedo rudus*, is not found on the B. pooter beyond the termination of the sand banks.

Oct. 18*th*—Temperature in my hut at $5\frac{1}{2}$ A. M. is 56°, outside it is $52\frac{1}{2}$°, that of the river water 63°. We left about 8, and proceeded up the Karam, which presented nothing singular. The volume of water is now less, and rapids are more frequent: heavy snow is visible from a little above Palampan Ghat, where the river bends to the northward; and a little further on a fine view of the Koond occurs. The Chasm is bounded in the rear by the fine rugged peak so distinctly seen from Suddiya due east. About 11, we reached the Ghat, beyond which boats, except of the smallest description, cannot pass; and about 1, started for the Mishmee village Jing-sha, situated on the Karam. Our course was along the bed of the river, and nearly due east. Formerly boats were able to reach the Ghat of the village, but the water has become shallower, owing, they say, to a larger portion being carried off by the Dea-soon, which runs into the Tenga-panee. We reached the village Ghat about four in the afternoon, but our people arrived very little before six o'clock. The march was tedious and difficult, owing to the numerous stones which are strewed in the way: and the necessity for crossing the river was so frequent, that all idea of shoes was quite out of the question. To increase the difficulty, the stones in the bed of river are very slippery, and as we crossed rapids, it frequently required some care to prevent our falling.

We were met by the Gam, or chief, before any signs of the village there were visible. The population is small; the people fair, but begrimed with dirt: the dress consists of a loose jacket without sleeves. The primary article of clothing is indeed so scanty, that the less one says about it the better. The women are decently clothed, and have generally enormous calves, certainly bigger than those of the men: their favourite ornament seems to be a band of silver, broadest across their forehead, which encircles their head. This village is close to the hills, and within a day's journey of the Koond, at least for a Mishmee. One Assamese slave is among the inhabitants, who was sold when a boy. A few of the men have Singfo dhaos or swords, others miserable knives, and some the usual spear so general with the tribes on this frontier. But in general the weapons of these people are most insignificant. The view of the hills is not fine from this place; it is too close to see any of great height, and they soon disappear to the westward. In the evening that of the Koond, which bears E. N. E. by N. is fine, particularly one mountain, which is known at once by its numerous cascades or appearances of water-falls, which, although they appear like streaks of white to the eye, are distinctly visible through a telescope. The bed of the Karam is almost entirely stony, and the immediate banks are clothed with grass. The jungle is of the usual thick description. The Gam, whose name is Jingsha, is a respectable looking man, fair in his dealings, and willing to oblige. They all have tobacco pipes.

Oct. 19*th.*—Halted to enable the people to bring up the baggage, and we shall in all probability have to halt to-morrow. I paid a visit to the Gam's house, Jingshi; it is to the S. E. of the Ghat, and about a mile and a half distant from it. The houses are all detached, and almost buried in jungle. Jingsha's house is a good one, very long, and well built; he has only about five skulls.* *Mont* was handed round to the Mishmees in large bamboo cups. From our encampment, abundance of clearances for cultivation are visible on the hills. Those to N., S., S. E. are of some extent, and belong to a Mishmee Gam, Tāpā. Some fine timber trees exist on the road to the village, and a very large Ficus: no particular plants occur except a Chloranthus, fructibus albis, which is also common towards Palampan. Thermometer at noon, in imperfect shade, 83°.

Oct. 20*th.*—The temperature of the air at $5\frac{1}{2}$ A. M. was $57\frac{1}{2}$°. That of water, 60°. I was obliged to halt again to enable the rice to be brought up. To-day we gathered on the banks of the Karam, a tree in fruit, Fol. alterna, impari-pinnata, stipulis caducis. Cymi compositi dichotomi; calyce minuto, 4 dentato, reflexo; corolla coriacea, viridi, rotata; stamina 4, hypogyna, gynobasi, maxima; carpulis 4, aggregatis, 1, 3, fecundalis, globosis, atro-cyaneis, baccatis; stylis lateralibus; semen 1, exalbumosum arbuscula mediocris; one Chrysobalanea? one Ochnacea?

Yesterday they brought me a beautiful snake, Collo gracillimo,

* The rank of the chiefs of various nations on the frontiers of Assam depends on the number of skulls of vanquished enemies, which decorate their houses. The Mishmee trophies, as appears from the author's account in the Journ. As. Soc. May 1837, consist of the skulls of cattle only.

colore pulchre fusco, maculis aterrimis, capite magno ;* has all the appearance of being venomous. To-day we passed another place for catching fish : the water is prevented from escaping, (except at the place where the current is naturally most violent,) by a dam composed of bamboos, supported by triangles, from the centre of which hang heavy stones: the fish are prevented passing down except at the above spot, and here they are received on a platform of bamboo : the stream is so strong through this point, that when once the fish have passed down they are unable to return. One of these fish-traps on a larger scale exists below Palampan.

The Karam debuts from the hills a little to the S. of east of Jingsha Ghat : the chasm is very distinct. Temperature at 2 P.M. 87°, at sunset 76°, 8 P.M. 68°.

Oct. 21*st.*—Left the Ghat about 9, and proceeded over the same difficult ground down the Karam until we arrived at Laee Mookh. This occupied about an hour ; our course thence lay up the Laee, which runs nearly due east. The bed of the river throughout the lower part of its course is 60 or 70 yards across : the journey was as difficult as that on the Karam. Towards 2 P.M. we were close to the hills, and the river became contracted, not exceeding 30 or 40 yards across. It is here only that large rock masses are to be found, but the boulders are in no case immense. We arrived at the place of our encampment about 4 P.M., the porters coming up much later. The march was in every respect most fatiguing. Temperature about 6 A.M. 58°, outside 57°. Water 60°. Temperature of Laee at sunset 66°. Of the air 71°.

Oct. 22*nd.*—Cloudy : during the night we were much annoyed by heavy gusts of wind sweeping down the river. Left our encampment at 7½, and struck into the jungle, the porters still continuing along the course of the river ; after crossing some rising ground we reached a path, which is tolerably good. Our course lay about N.E. ; we crossed over some low hills, and after marching for about an hour and a quarter, came upon the Koond Chasm, or great defile ; of which, however, from the thickness of the jungle, we had no view. We then descended a very steep, but not very high hill, and came upon the Koond ; of which nothing is at first seen but large masess of rock strewed in every direction. We were accompanied by a number of Jingsha Gam's people, and in the evening we were visited by Tāpān

* *Trigonocephalus mucrosquamatus*, afterwards described in Proc. Zool. Soc. 1839, *Vid. Cal. Journ. Nat. Hist. vol.* 1, *p.* 77.

Gam himself, with a train of followers. This man assumes the sovereignty of the Koond. We encamped immediately under the Faqueer's Rock, which is known to the Mishmees by the name "Taihloo Maplampoo." The south bank is wooded to its brink, but not very densely: it is excessively steep, and in many places almost perpendicular. The strata composing it is partly limestone, lying at an angle of 45°, and in many places at a greater one. The scenery is picturesque and bold: on either side of the river are hills rising abruptly to the height of a few hundred feet, but the hills are continued longer on the north side. From the Rock the river seems to run W.N.W. for a quarter of a mile, and then bends to the S.W. The breadth of the bed is a good hundred yards, but the stream at this season is confined to the fifty yards near the south bank, the remainder being occupied by rocks in sitû, or boulders and sand: the edge of the N. bank is occupied by stunted *Saccharum*. The appearance of the water is characteristic, of a greyish green tinge, giving the impression of great depth. It is only here and there that it is white with foam, its general course being rather gentle. It is in various places encroached upon more or less by the rocks forming its bed, some of which are quite perpendicular. A little to the west of the Faqueer's Rock there is an immense mass of rock in the bed of the river, between which and the south bank there is now very little water and no current. The rocks are generally naked; here and there they are partially clothed with Gramineæ, and a Cyperaceous-looking plant, something like an Eriophorum. The river, a short distance beyond the Deo-panee, takes a bend to the north; at the point where it bends there is a considerable rapid.

The Faqueer's Rock itself is a loose mass of rugged outline, about 50 feet high: access to its summit is difficult to any body but a Mishmee; it is, however, by no means impracticable. The path by which it may be gained, leads from the eastward. At the summit is an insulated, rounded, rugged mass of rock, on which the faqueers sit. It is however the descent by the path to the east which is difficult, and people generally choose another path to the west. This rock is clothed with ferns epiphytical Orchideæ, an Arundo, and a few stunted trees are very common at its summit. Between it and the hill is another much smaller mass, and the intervening spaces are occupied by angular masses of rock. These spaces both lead westward to that corner of the river into which the Deo-panee falls. Eastward they lead to the margin of the bank.

From a Sketch made on the spot by W Griffith

M & N. Hanhart, lith Printers

[illegible] GROUND AND FAQUEERS ROCK

From a Sketch made on the spot by W Griffith

M & N Hanhart, lith Printers

THE MURI-PANE [illegible] THE KHOOND

The north face of the Faqueer's Rock is excavated into a hollow of the Deo Dowar. It has no resemblance to a Gothic ruin, which form is, I believe, peculiar to calcareous rocks. It is this rock which, by its eastern extremity projecting into the water, forms the reservoirs into which the Deo-panee falls, or rather at this season runs; the place resembles merely a sort of bay. The water-mark of floods visible on some of the rocks, is probably eight feet above that of this time of the year. The reservoir is completed by a projection from the rocks forming the south bank, but it is almost entirely abstracted from the stream. The south bank immediately beyond this is extremely precipitous, and very high. The Faqueer's Rock is three-peaked; two peaks can only be seen from the Deo-panee, the third is the low one to the west, the middle is the highest, and is perforated: the eastern represents a sugar-loaf appearance. Two distinct streams run into the reservoirs, the bed of one forms the second defile before alluded to: this is very insignificant. The other occupies the corner of the bay, and can only be seen from a low station on the sand beneath: it is an attempt at a small water-fall.

Oct. 23*rd.*—To-day I have been employed in collecting plants. Nearly due east of the Koond, and at a distance of about 40 yards, the face of the hill is perpendicular, and in some places overhanging; its extremity juts out into the stream, which here flows with great violence; the banks are occupied by masses of rock strewed in every direction, resulting from a landslip of great size: some of these masses are enormous. The greater portion of the slip is clothed with herbage and trees, so that it is of some age, or standing; but in one place over the river it is clean, as if fresh formed, and white-looking much like chalk. This cliff in many parts is a dripping well, particularly in one extremity where a good deal of water falls. It is clothed with the Eriophorum, which hangs down in long tufts; the moist parts with an Adiantum much like A. C. Veneris, a beautiful Pteris, a Pothos or Arum foliis pulchre nigro tinctis, and some mosses; B. speciosa out of flower, and some Hepaticæ, Ruta albiflora, etc. Between this and the Deo-panee a small stream enters the Lohit: following this up to some height, one arrives at a pretty water-fall; here it is inaccessible in this direction, but by following a branch of the stream to the west, one may arrive at the summit of the hill, from which however no view is to be obtained. The summit is ridge-like, and excessively sharp; the descent on either side almost precipitous. I found several fine ferns up this hill; at its base an Acer and fine Equisetum.

The Koond is apparently formed by the Deo-panee and Mori-panee. In the rains it must be a rather striking object, now however it is at this season, lost amidst the fine surrounding scenery. How the Faqueer's Rock and the rock between it and the Mori-panee were detached, is difficult to say. It is evident, however, that formerly the two rivers were not united to form the Koond as at present, but that they had each their own channels when the Faqueer's Rock must have stood between them. In fact both channels, in which water has flowed, still remain. My broken Thermometer pointed out the low temperature of the Lohit water, and 208° was the point at which water boiled in two experiments. All attempts at passing along the river on this side would be vain, owing to a cliff which is totally impracticable. The Mishmees know of no rivulet called the Mtee; probably this has been mistaken for the Mishmee name for water, *Mchee*. The way Wilcox went I am at a loss to ascertain; as he could not have passed the Koond, he must have gone above it; although the hills are said to be impracticable for loaded coolies.

Oct. 25*th*.—The Koond is obviously little frequented. I left sometime after the coolies, pursuing the path leading to Ghaloom's, which extends to the eastward. An hour and a quarter brought me again to the Laee-panee, and three hours and a half to Laee Mookh : from this place to Jingsha Ghat is scarcely an hour's walk. The day's journey occupied about five hours inclusive of stoppages : the distance is probably about twelve miles. I came to the determination of returning, owing to the known difficulty of the route pursued by Wilcox, and the impossibility of making a collection of grain. The Tapan Gam, or Lord of the Koond, particularly insisted on the impossibility of ordinary coolies going this way, and as he offered men to bring up grain from the plains, I at once acceded to his proposal of making a granary in his village. This man had no delicacy in asking for presents : he at once said, "You must give gold, silver, and every thing in the calendar of presents to the Deo," meaning himself. As I found it impracticable to satisfy him, I sent him off with a small present, promising more when he should have amassed the grain. His brother, a tall, stout, and much more useful man, (as he does not refuse to carry loads,) on seeing me rub salt on a bird's skin, remarked, "What poor devils we are! Bird's skins with salt supply the Sahibs with food, while we can't get a morsel." They promised to take me all over the country, and to be my slaves, if I would point out to them where salt is to be found.

From a Sketch made on the spot by W. Griffith.

M & N. Hanhart, lith. Printers

THE DEO PANEE AS IT ENTERS THE KHOOND

I saw nothing particular in the woods. I picked up the fruit of a Magnolea and Castanea, and observed an arborescent Leea. Some of the timber is fine. A large Acrotirchea abounds between Laee and the Koond, as well as Chloranthus. Near the Laee a climber, the base of whose stem is elephantopoid and enormous considering the slender stem, is abundant. I could not get any of the leaves. At the Koond, Buddleia Neemda, a Prunus, etc. occur. Cælogyne polleniis 4 obovatis, faciebus incumbentibus complanates materie pulverea, mediocri. Dundoons are rather troublesome; they are flies, and nearly as large as an ordinary house fly: their proboscis is large, and leaves spot of extravasated blood where they bite, nearly of the size of an ordinary pin's head.

Oct. 27th.—My people brought me in a beautiful snake, *Coluber porphyraceus,* ventre albo, cæterum pulchre coccineo-badio, capite lineis nigris tribus quarum centralis brevior, dorso lineis nigris duabus postea gradatim evanescentibus, lineis circularibus minus conspicuis, iridibus carneis.*

Oct. 28th.—Yesterday evening two elephants arrived with grain, so that I have every prospect of being fairly on my way in a day or two. Nothing worth seeing has occurred, except a man who by some accident had the lobe of his ear torn, and had the fragments stitched together with silver wire.

Oct. 31st.—Halted at the Laee-panee, and gathered an Oberonea, and specimens of fish.†

Nov. 1st.—Dirty weather; rain looking much as if it were going to continue for several days. There is a small drupaceous fruit found here and at Beesa, the Singfo name of which is Let-tan-shee; it is the produce of a large tree probably the fruit of a Chrysobalanus, testibus stylo *laterali,* stam, perigynis: cotyledonibus crispatis. The flavour is acid, rather pleasant, and somewhat terebinthinaceous.

Nov. 2nd.—I thought it best to set off, although it was raining heavily. Our course lay in an E. direction up the Karam for about two hours, when it diverged: it thence after passing through some heavy jungle continued up the steep bed of the now dry Dailoom; it next diverged again about 2 P.M., when we ascended a small hill; it continued

* Subsequently described from this specimen in the Proceedings of the Zoological Society, March 12, 1839. *Cal. Journ. Nat. Hist. vol* 1, *p.* 82.

† *Gonorhynchus bimacalutus, G. brachypterus, Perilompus æquipinnatus,* and *Cobitis phoxocheila,* which have been all since described from these specimens in the 19th vol. As. Res. Beng.

thence through heavy jungle chiefly bamboo, until we descended in an oblique manner on the Laee-panee, about a mile up which we found our halting place. The whole march occupied, including a few halts, seven hours; and as the pace was pretty good for six full hours, I compute the distance to be about fifteen miles. Hill Flora recommenced in the bamboo jungle; two fine species of Impatiens and several Urticeæ making their appearance; *Camellia axillaris* and some fine Acanthacea: the best plant was a species of Aristolochea. The latter part of the day was fine, and the elephants with grain from Suddiyah arrived.

Nov. 3rd.—Passed the forenoon in ascending the hill opposite our encampment: it is of no great height, but like all the others very steep. To the N. W. of this has occurred a large slip, but long previous to this time; on it two or three Phæniceous palms may be found. Pandanus still occurs. The hill was barren of Botany, excepting a few ferns towards base.

Nov. 4th.—Left Laee-panee at 9½ A.M., and reached the encampment at 3½ P.M. Our course diverged almost immediately from the last encampment, and we ascended for some time up the bed of a torrent. The first hill we ascended occupied an hour, and the remainder of the day's journey consisted of ascents and descents along the most difficult path imaginable. All the hills are very steep, and the paths when they wind round these, are very difficult; a slip would cause a dangerous fall. About 1 P.M. we reached; two or three houses constituting a village.

From this, one has a fine view of the plains, and of the B. pooter near its exit from the hills: it is much intersected by islets covered with jungle. Leeches are not very numerous. Dundoons or sand flies very annoying. I have gathered plenty of plants, especially ferns. Wallichia continues; *Wulfenia obliqua*, and a Companula were the best. At our halting place I found the fruits of *Sedgwickia* in abundance. Passed two or three streams. Found the flowers of a large Loranthus, or rather its very large flowers on the ground. They are eaten by the natives, but the acidity is unpleasant, owing to its being mixed with a bitter; the flowers are two inches long: tubo 4 angulato, basi-coccinescenti, laminis viridibus interstibus carneis, coccineo lineatis præsenti transverse, antheris syngenesis. *Sarcocordalis*, common.

Nov. 5th.—Left at half-past 8, and reached extensive *kheties* (cultivated fields) with dispersed houses at about 1 P.M. This place is called Dilling. Our route consisted of the same fatiguing marching: we passed over some hills, from which we had fine views. The first gave us a fine sight of the Patkaye mountains,* S. E. of Upper Assam, which reach apparently a great height. The second, of the plains of Assam. The exact summits of all the hills are covered with a coarse Bspicate Saccharum. On one we met with a Melampyracea. The Botany is improving greatly; two species of Viola, two fine Cyrthandraceæ occurring. I also noticed Sedgwickia again, and got abundance of ferns, a Buddleia, and a fine Amaranthacea. Halted on a cleared ground immediately under the Red mountain so plainly seen from Jingsha. There is now no appearance of water-falls on it, but there are several white spots owing to slips: the brink or brim of this hill is woody, but there is a considerable space covered only with short grass. The strata are inclined at an angle of 45°. I here got two or three fine mosses. All the Mishmees have the idea, that on some hills at least rain is caused by striking trees of a certain size with large stones, some hills are again free from this charm; it was ridiculous to hear them call out not to throw stones whenever we approached one of these rainy hills. The people appear to get dirtier the farther we advance. I saw plenty of snow on two high peaks, and had a peep of the Lohit beyond Brahma Koond. Wallichia continues, as well as Bambusa, Saccharum Megala. The kheties are either of rice or Cynosurus or Ireia. Tobacco is not cultivated, but left to take care of itself. Buddleia Neemda and wild plantain continue, the latter is probably a distinct species; leaves subtis glauco niveis. Pandanus continues. The name of the Red mountain before alluded to, is Thu-ma-thaya, the rivulet at its base is Tus-soo-muchee. Tus-soo Dee-ling is the name of the place; a large mountain bearing N.N.E., is Sun-jong-thaya. It is obvious that Dee-ling must be of some extent, as my site does not agree with that of Wilcox. The view to the E. is entirely limited to Thu-ma-thaya, and to the N. N. E., by Sun-jong-thaya; no B. pooter is visible, nor is Ghaloom's house. The snow collects on the Thu-ma-thaya this month: the clearings for cultivation on the declivities of Thu-ma-thaya are called Chim-bra: the houses, although at great distances from the village, are called *Yeu*.

Nov. 6th.—We arrived at our halting place after a march of seven hours, over a most difficult and fatiguing road: we skirted throughout the whole time the base of the huge Thu-ma-thaya; I never saw a worse road, if road it may be called—part of it lay over places where

* Afterwards crossed by the author in his journey into Burma.

a false step or slip would be very dangerous, if not fatal. We came suddenly on the B. pooter; but as the place was not a good one for crossing, we prepared to go a little higher up the stream, and though the distance we had to go was not above 100 yards, yet as the river side was impracticable, it became necessary to ascend and descend by a most difficult path where a slip would have precipitated one into the river sixty or seventy feet below. What rendered this passage most difficult and dangerous, was the jungle which, while it caused you to stoop, at the same time concealed your footing. It is one of the characteristics of Mishmees, that they sooner risk their necks than take the trouble of cutting down underwood.

We have scarcely passed Thu-ma-thaya, so that the distance we have travelled in a direct line from Deeling must be very small. The stream of the Lohit is not forty yards broad, but the bed is about sixty. It has the appearance of great depth, and roars along amidst rocks in some places in fine style. I here picked up some small branches of an elm, very like U. virgata; the tree was too late to reach fruit. I also gathered a fine Acanthacea, and some good ferns. The north bank of the Lohit here has the same structure as the south at the Koond, and is perpendicular. The water of the Lohit is certainly much cooler than any of the mountain streams. Vast blocks of rock, of many sorts, lie strewed on the south side; one in particular is quartzose, remarkable for the indentations on its surface. I here gathered some mosses, and a good Marchantiacea, very nearly allied to Octoskepos, but culiculate. Pandanus still continues, as also Marlea, Wallichia, Caryota, and Pentaptera. Passed several streams, and a pretty fall, the water falling down a cliff almost perpendicular, about 100 feet high. The Mishmees use the fibres and *reti* of Caryota as an ornament to their baskets, from which it likewise keeps the rain. Wild plantain continues. Our encampment is on a fine bed of sand.

Nov. 7th.—Rain throughout the night at intervals, and sharp cold in the morning; we left at 9 A.M. and arrived at our encampment about 1½ P.M. The first part of our march was very difficult, it in fact consisted of crossing a precipice overhanging the Lohit; the difficulty was increased by the slipperiness occasioned by the rain; no one could pass some of the places unless aided by ratans fixed to trees, etc. We came to the Sung river about 12 noon, but were delayed some time in building a bridge. This river appears to me to be in some places fordable, but the Mishmees say that it is not; the water is beautifully clear. The first cane suspended bridge occurs here; I did not fancy it, although I observed the Mishmees cross, the passage taking barely half a minute. *Throughout the whole time* the Mishmees use their legs and arms, to accelerate or determine their progress; the inclination caused by the weight is slight. I preferred one of our own erection, about 100 yards distant from it. The height is not great over the river, and the width is perhaps thirty yards. The Bourra crossed after some delay; we were then obliged to make two halts: we followed the Sung down to its mouth, which is barely 200 yards: its bed is rocky; at its junction there is a large bay formed, on the N. side of which is a fine sand bank. The Lohit there runs nearly N. and S., and is excessively violent in its course, certainly ten miles an hour. The scenery is pretty, but no hills of great height are seen to any extent. This is the most romantic spot I have seen in my course of travels as yet. We forded the bay about its centre, and encamped on the sand: the path we are to follow is said to be above, and very difficult. We here gathered some fine ferns and a Bleteoid Orchidea. A Gentianacea likewise occurred. The Tapan Gam, on my inquiring, said, that Wilcox passed by the upper path, the Lohit at that time running under the cliff which forms one side of the bay.* The course of the river, he says, has since changed by the occurrence of a large slip, principally of mica slate.

Nov. 8th.—The commencement of our march to-day was up a hill, the ascent, as in all the other cases, being very steep. From its summit we could see Dilling in a horizontal distance extremely near. We then proceeded skirting the hill, and descended subsequently to the *O.* rivulet, which is of no size. We then ascended another considerable height, and found ourselves on the site of Ghaloom's old dwelling. The situation was delightful; to the N. E., a high range was visible, which is covered with snow, the pines on the lower parts of the ridge standing out, in fine relief. To the N. was a noble peak bare at its summit, on which snow rests during some months, its centre being prettily marked out with numerous patches of cultivation. To the N. again the Tid-ding might be seen foaming along the vallies; the hills are evidently improving in height and magnificence of scenery. We reached this at 12 o'clock, our march having lasted five hours. We thence descended crossing a small

* For a narrative of Lieut. Wilcox's visit to the Mishmee mountains, see As. Res. vol. xvii. p. 314.

stream at the base of the hill, on which Ghaloom's former house stood, called the Dhaloom Basee.

I thence proceeded over some nasty swampy ground with a few low elevations until we reached Ghaloom's, which we did about 2 P.M. A small spot was allotted to us some distance from the village, on which we erected our huts. Ghaloom changed his residence to this place, owing to the death of two of his people, which was attributed to the unhealthiness of the former site; but as might be expected from the nature of the place he has chosen, he has suffered very severely from fever since his removal. As soon as our huts were built, Ghaloom and his brother Khosha visited us, preceded by the hind quarter of a pig. Their appearance is somewhat better than the ordinary run of Mishmees, but they are just as dirty. Khosha is a little man, with a mahogany-coloured wrinkled face. Great attention was paid by their attendants to all they said, and Khosha himself is evidently the Demosthenes of the Mishmees. When interrupted, he commanded silence in an authoritative way. Krisong was not present. Khosha declares that Rooling, the Mezhoo chief, is nobody, and that Wilcox gave him his present unknown to them. The acquisitions in Botany consisted of some fine Cyrtandraceæ, a Cymbidium, and some ferns. One of these Cyrtandraceæ is very singular: the runners are long, producing one stem with a very small terminal leaf, and a very large flower. Afterwards this leaf enlarges, becomes a large cordate Begonioid one, bearing from its bosom apparently one or two Siliquæ; Pandanus Bambusa continue. The fine Quercus is common, *Megala, Podomolia,* Triumfetta, Siegesbeckia, Cynoglossum, Callicarpa, Urena, Rottlera and several other low tropical forms continue. The Cymbidioid has pollena 4, incumbentia postice aliquoties minore, glandula nulla?

Nov. 9th.—Halted. Went to the suspension bridge over the Lohit, which is about 60 yards across, or double the length of the one we crossed on the 7th. The passage by Mishmees takes two, or two minutes and a half, requiring continued exertion the whole time, both by hands and feet, as above described. Both banks are very steep, yet the natives are so confident of safety, that of this bridge only one cane is trustworthy. Bathed in the river, which is very cold and deep, but comparatively quiet.

Nov. 10th.—Went to the Lohit, gathered Cymbidium giganteum, two or three ferns, and a Rafflesia in its several stages. I have not however yet seen the perfectly expanded flower, the natives do not know it, although it must be a sufficiently striking object, the alabastri before expansion are about the size of an orange. Went to Ghaloom's house, which is of great length, built of bamboos, raised high from the ground, divided into about twelve compartments, and containing 100 men, women, and children.

Nov. 11*th.*—Left for Khosha Gams; crossed the Lohit on a raft, and left its banks at noon. Followed the river for some distance, and then diverged towards the N. W. and reached Khosha at 3 P.M., the march owing to the heat was very fatiguing. Found very few plants; noticed a flower of a Ternstrœmiacea nearly allied to the genus Camellia, cor. rotat. lacin. reflexis, albis fauce carnea. stam. 00, epipet. anther. erectis-apice dehiscent, and of a large Hibiscus; the Cælogyne of the Koond was also found. Two species of Castaneæ occur in these woods, one with very stout thorns to its cupula, and not eatable fruit; the other has long slender prickles, and its fruit about the size of an acorn, is eatable, and not at all disagreeable. On all the hills of any height with grassy tops Compositæ are among the most striking forms. Areca parva continues, Pentaptera, and Fici continue. Saccharum Megala very abundant and fine. Cupuliferæ are becoming more abundant. The roofs of the houses which are built of bamboo, are covered with the leaves of the Marantaceous genus—capitulis densis lateralibus *culmis* 1-foliosis. Buddlea Neemda and Callicarpa continue.

Want of means forms the only limit to the number of wives of a Mishmee. A rich man who has at his disposal numerous cattle, etc. will give 20 *mithuns*;* but the wife appears to bring with her slaves, etc. as a return. A poor man will get a wife for a pig. Whatever the number of wives may be, each will have a separate khetee, (field) and each khetee has a separate granary. All the wives live in the same house; in fact, one house forms the village. Theft is punished by a fine inflicted by a meeting of all the Gams; if the fine is not paid, or the offender refuses to pay, he is slain in a general attack. Murder is punished in the same way, but by a heavier fine: adultery against the consent of the husband, or at least elopement, is punished by death; if with the consent of the husband, the delinquent is fined. There appears to be no regular law of succession: the favourite son succeeding without reference to age.

Nov. 12*th.*—I went out for plants, and descended to the Paeen rivulet, which is of small size: followed up its course some way, and

* Mithun is, according to the author, a peculiar species of Ox.

then returned over a low hill to Khosha's. The guide who was some distance behind, came up with a Rafflesia bud. I returned with him, and saw it to perfection; he likewise succeeded in tracing the roots to a gigantic Cissus, the fruit of which I have before observed is eatable, and not unlike a greengage. I returned home loaded with this undescribed genus: I found likewise a fine Buddlea, and Menispermum, with some rare Compositæ, among which was an arborescent Eupolanisia and a gigantic thistle, a Prunus in flower and fruit, and a neat Liparis, Calamus, Tree-fern, Tupistra, Pandanus, were likewise observed, and a beautiful Viburnum, Corol sterilibus, 4 phyllis, foliis niveis carneo venosis: petal fertil calyptratis, deciduis, intus cæruleo tinctis: staminibus cyaneis, ovariis pallide cæruleis, stigmatib. carnosis.

Nov. 13th.—Opposite Khosha's, or rather his granaries to the E. is a high mountain excessively steep, only partially clothed with trees, and with stunted ones at its summit, which in December and the colder months is covered with snow: this they call Thayathro.

Khosha positively refuses to take me any farther into the interior, and Krisong begs that I won't come and see him. It is obvious that they are under great fear of other tribes. Khosha says, he should be attacked by all the Mishoos or Mizhoos, were he to conduct me any farther now, and that very probably the Lamas would attack him likewise. He says the only chance of success in penetrating to Lama, is to send previously a present of salt, (about a seer) to all the chiefs, and request their leave, without which preparatory donation, they would cut up any messengers he might send. He offers to do this at any time, and to let me know the result. He declined taking me to the Chibong Gam, a few days' journey up the Diree, although the man is a relation of his own, and a Deboro Mishmee. It is obvious that there is no chance of getting further at present, nor would it be fair even if one could bribe them. He says no reliance whatever is to be placed on Rooling, the Mizhoo who deceived Wilcox, and whom he represents to be an underhand person. I tried to overcome his scruples by assuring him that I only wanted to go as far as Rooling, but he declines taking me. He says I may go any where to the west of this, but to the north he dare not conduct me. I shall therefore go to Premsong to-morrow, and if that is not a favourable place, return forthwith to Ghaloom's, and thence to Deeling to botanise on Thuma-thaya.

Nov. 14th.—Proceeded to Premsong's, which we reached in less than two hours. Our march was in a westerly direction across a hill of some elevation: the remainder of it was over kheties and level ground. The plants evidently increase in interest as we advance in the interior, Compositæ and Labiatæ being most numerous. A large tree occurs not uncommonly, which is either a Birch or a Prunus, most probably from the venation of its leaves, the latter; the bark is exactly like that of a Birch. Close to Premsong's I gathered a Clematis, Valerian and a fine Botrychium, a Carex and a Cuscuta. The mountain on the base of which Premsong's house is situated, is a very high one; it is the one that is so striking from Ghaloom's old site: it is named Laimplan-thaya; its summit, which is a high peak, is very rugged, partially clothed with vegetation, in which, as in all the others of the same height autumnal tints are very distinct. Thai-ka-thaya is a smaller peak to the S. S. W. of Premsong's house. One of my Mishmee Dowaneirs tells me that the Mishmee (Coptis) teeta Khosha gave me last evening, is cultivated near his native place; its flower buds are just forming and are enclosed in ovate concave squamæ. The leaves are of a lively green, not unlike those of some ferns, but at once to be distinguished by the venation; it is very evident that the Mishmees know nothing about the period of its flowering, as they told me it flowered in the rains, at the same time as the *dhak* flowers in Assam; the radicles are numerous, tawny yellowish, the rhizomata are rugged tortuous, the bark and pith are of yellow orange colour, the woody system gamboge: this is the same in the petioles: it tinges the saliva yellow. It is a pure intense bitter of some permanence, but without aroma: it is dried over the fire, the drying being repeated three times. Judging from it in its fresh state, the test of its being recently and well dried is the permanence of the colors. The *Bee*, flowers during the rains: its flower, (*on dit*) is white and small; they pretend that it is very dangerous to touch, causing great irritation; both Coptis teeta, and Bee, are found on high hills on which there is now snow; one of them, the Ummpanee or Mŏochee, is accessible from hence in three days.

The Mishmee name for the Teeta, is *Yoatzhee;* of Bee, *Th'wee; Ghe-on* is the Mishmee name for the smelling root, which the Assamese call Gertheon. The smell of this is a compound of Valeriana and Pastinaca; it is decidedly aromatic, and not at all disagreeable, it is white inside and abounds in pith, but has scarcely any taste.

Yesterday evening I visited Khosha's house, which is of immense length, and considerably longer, though not so high from the ground as Ghaloom's: it is divided into upwards of twenty apartments, on the right hand side of the passage are ranged the skulls of the cattle Khosha has killed, including deer and pigs; on the other side are the domestic utensils, the centre of the floor is occupied by a square earthen space for fire-place: the bamboos, of which the floor is composed being cut away. From the centre of each room over the fire-place, hangs a square ratan sort of tray, from which they hang their meat or any thing requiring smoke; their cooking utensils are, I believe, confined to one square stone vessel, which appears to answer its purpose remarkably well. The women appear to have no shame; they expose their breasts openly, which from their dirty habits by no means correspond with the exalted character of the sex. On hills to the N. E. of Khosha's first residence, forests are very visible, descending far down the sides.

On an open spot a little distance from Premsong's, there is a fine view of the course of the Lohit, and of the more remote (now) snowy ranges. The hills beyond this exactly answer to Wilcox's description, being very high, and all descending as it were unbroken to the Lohit.

Went out for about two hours over a tolerably level portion of the hill, covered with Artemesia; found abundance of interesting plants, Crawfurdia campanulacea, a Clematis, Acer, Prunus, Camellia axillaris, Cyathea, Myrica, Rhus, Sedgwickia, Polygala, Galium; and a beautiful very fragrant climbing Composita.

Great part of the side of the hill is covered with a small hard bamboo, which forms excellent walking sticks. An Urticea foliis peltatis, was among the novelties. The Paeen Panee forms the nearest ravine. The Polygonum, paniculis densissimis, is a certain indication of some elevation. I observed Calamus, and Torenia asiatica. There is likewise a large Mimoseous plant, which we found in fruit.

Nov. 15th.—Spent the greater part of the day attempting to reach the summit of Laim-planj-thaya, but my guide did not know the way. We ascended for upwards of four hours, slowly of course, but were still a long way from its summit. The face of the mountain is entirely occupied by woods, with but little underwood. Found abundance of plants, chiefly ferns, only saw 4 Orchideæ, of which 2 were in flower. The novelties were a Polygonatum, Camellia, and Quercus lamellata.

I observed no less than 5 Araliaceæ, of which I succeeded in getting 4: an Acer, probably that from Brahma Koond: and several *incertæ.* Near Premsong's the varnish tree was shewn to me, it is obviously a species of Rhus. The Assamese name of the varnish plant is *Ahametta Gas.* I took specimens of it in fruit.

They obtain the juice by ringing, and the only two specimens I observed were evidently well drained: no preparation is required for the varnish; and it is applied one day, the next day is hard; it has a fine polish, and is of an intense black. It is the same probably with two small trees I had previously seen in Capt. Charlton's garden at Suddyah. Kydia continues; a fine Palm, caudex 8-10-pedali; it probably belongs to the genus Wallichia? Camellia is only found towards the top; the Polygonatum also does not descend far. I saw also species of an undescribed Bucklandia, likewise one specimen which had been damaged: the capituli pluriflori. Towards the middle a small bamboo becomes plentiful; the lower joints, from which no branches proceed, are armed with a verticillus of spines. I did not observe Pandanus, but it is used for constructing large mats: Megala continues, but not up the hill.

Nov. 16th.—Attempted to ascend Laim-planj-thaya by the Paeen rivulet which proceeds from the centre, but after proceeding about half an hour we found our progress effectually stopped by a water-fall, the sides of the stream being so precipitous as to render all idea of clambering over, or proceeding round ridiculous. Gathered two or three rare ferns, and a pretty Lobelia. On our return through the open grassy parts near Premsong's, we found a fine Choripetalum and Crawfurdia campanulacea, beautifully in flower; the flower is rose-coloured. Anthistiria arundinacea, the same Sambucus found at Suddya, Solanum 10 dentatum, a Kydia and Torenia continue.

Nov. 17th.—Left and returned to Khosha's, as we were all out of rice, and it was impossible to get anything in Premsong's absence. The march on return occupied us about two hours, but the path was so excessively slippery, owing to the grass not being cut away on either side and to the dry weather and heat, that our progress was very slow. Noticed Lactuca exalata and a Rottlera on the road; more snow has fallen on the hills E. N. E. The descent on returning, owing to the slippery state of the roads, was more fatiguing than the ascent. Hedychium angustifolium I also observed on the road.

I have as yet observed the following grains used by the Mishmees. 1st, Oriza, rice; variety of this called *Ahoo Da*; 2nd, a species of Eleusine, *Bobosa;* 3rd, Zea Mays, *Gorm* dan; 4th, Panicum Panicula nutanti, densa clavata. 5th *Konee,* Chenapodium sp. panicula simili.

The Mishmee names are as follow: *Dan-khai* rice; *khai hoo, bobosa, Mdo.-zea, or Maize, Ma-bon-konee-yo* Chenopodium; *Thenna,* a kind of Polygonum; *Hubra-Aloo, Ghee-kuchoo-shoom,* Sweet potatoe; *Gaihwan,* Plantain; *Puhee Dhoonhwa,* Tobacco. They likewise cultivate Sesamum.

Nov. 18th.—Found more of the Rafflesiacea on low hills along the Paeen; it was attached to the roots of the same species of Cissus, on which it was found before.* I also gathered a Euonymus and a fine Engelhardtia. The hairs of the fruits of Engelhardtia create a disagreeable itching. All the Mishmees decline shewing me the road a foot in advance of this place. I tried every way I could think of, to overcome their objections, but to no purpose. They have so little regard for truth, that one cannot rely much on what they say: I begin to think that it is all owing to the Tapan Gam, who I suspected was insincere in his professions.

Nov. 19th.—Yesterday evening Premsong arrived, he is a man about 35, the best looking of all the Gams: but has rather a cunning Jewish face. The brandy I gave him made him at first wonderfully obliging, for he seemed disposed to enter into my views. This morning however he came with Khosha and Tapan, by whom it was at once obvious that he has been overruled; not only will he not take me to the Lama *Dais* (plains,) but he won't even shew me the road to Truesong's, a Digaroo, whose village is only distant about five days' journey. Premsong I know wishes to go, induced by the promise of 200 Rs. but he is afraid of incurring the displeasure of Khosha, etc. I shall therefore return towards Deeling, and devote a few days to botanising on Thuma-thaya.

Nov. 20th.—Returned to Ghaloom's: gathered the Martynia, finely in flower, and observed the Rafflesiacea along the banks of the Lohit.

Nov. 21st.—Halted at Ghaloom's, the Rafflesiacea is found all about, anth. bilocular, apice poro-gemino dehiscent, pollen simplex, materie viscosa cohærenti, ovula antitropa, tegumento unico. Made every arrangement with Premsong. According to this Gam we are to go up the Diree, and then cross over high mountains, leaving the Lohit entirely. He says the Lamas wear trowsers, socks and shoes, and

* Subsequently described by the author in an important communication to the Linnæan Society.

that they dress their hair *a la mode Chinoise ;* their houses are built on posts, and raised from the ground : they erect forts like the Chinese, and have plenty of fire-locks. They have also abundance of cattle, consisting of about seven kinds, but no *Mithuns ;* and three sorts of Horses, which alone they use as beasts of burden. Their staple food is Ahoodan. The *Mithun* of the Mishmees appears to me intermediate to a certain degree between the Bison and the wild Bull ; their head is very fine, and as well as the horns that of a Bull, but their neck and body have, so to say, the same awkward conformation as those of the buffalo. I have not seen a large living one ; the largest head I saw was three feet from tip to tip of the horns, the diameter of the forehead being probably about one-third of the above.

Nov. 22nd.—Returned to Loong Mockh. I cannot reconcile Wilcox's description of Ghaloom's old site with the reality, because the scenery is decidedly fine, embracing the Tidding, and the (in comparison with the near surrounding hills) gigantic Laim-planj-thaya, which from this presents the appearance of a vast cone with a peaked summit. Premsong's village is obviously at a considerable elevation. Found another Acrostichum, a Bolbophyllum, a rare Aristolochia foliis palmatis, 7 lobis, subtus glaucis ; sapor peracerbus, floribus *siphonicis.* The Huttaya I have not seen : it occurs at a greater distance in the mountains than I have been. In addition to the plants I have gathered, Asplenium nidus is very common. Tradescantia and Camelina both occur ; Ricinus also occurs, the Mishmees do not however put it to any use ; Melica latifolia is common on some of the hills. Anthistiria arundinacea occurs in abundance. Likewise a small Areca and Chloranthus.

It is at Ghaloom's old site that these hills commence putting on an interesting appearance, those previously seen, excepting however Thuma-thaya, being entirely covered with tree jungle ; but beyond this site, the lower spaces unoccupied by jungle become much more numerous. The Mishmee word for bitter, is *Khar.* Query—why should not the name of the plant Coptis teeta, be changed to Coptis amara, although the species of the genus Coptis are probably all bitter ? Sauraussa and Bombax both occur at Ghaloom's, as well as Pentaptera ; Sesamum is used for oil.

I should have mentioned the top of the hill, surmounted in going immediately from Loong Panee towards Ghaloom's, is occupied almost entirely by a species of Fraxinus.

On my arrival at Ghaloom's on the 20th, I found that the coolies had played me the same trick as they had done previously, though not to such an extent. Instead of each man having 20 days' provisions, scarcely one had more than 5 or 6 : as they had 20 days' given them in addition to that they would require on the road, it is obvious they must have thrown much away. Were all the Gams disposed to take one to Lama, it could not be done with Assamese coolies: and, above all, Seerings or Ahooms are the very worst; and although often good sized men, they are very deficient in strength. Nagas and Mishmees are the best, then Kamptees.

I gave before leaving a packet of salt to Premsong, according I suppose to their own custom of proceeding. Yesterday he went to Roomling, Krisong's eldest son, and gained his consent. I mention this to shew how active he is. He is a friend of the Dupha's,* and to my surprise, told me he saw Capt. Hannay at Hookhoom, who gave him a jacket, and tried to induce him to shew him the road to Suddiya. He is certainly the best of all the Gams, and appears to be very liberal.

Nov. 23rd.—Arrived at Deeling after a tedious march of 8 hours : we did not traverse the two cliffs near the Lohit, but pursued a longer, but more commodious cattle path: our Mishmees, however, preferred the shorter one. Gathered Sabia, Martynioidea, Alsophila, Menispermum at Paeen in fine flower. At Ghaloom's old site a large Euphorbia fol obovatis, ramis 4 angulato-alatis occurs, and Cymbydium giganteum in fine flower. *En route* hither I noticed the following: Bauhinia, Hoya, Urtica gigas, Mucnna, Curculigo, Panax, foliis supradecompositis, Dalbergia, Laurus, Abroma, Lactuca exaltata, Uncaria. Liegesbeckia, Megala, *Podo-Molee*, and a species subscandent of bamboo, internodiis vix cylindricis, gracilibus; this is of great use where it occurs, in assisting one's ascent and descent.

Nov. 24th.—Left about 11 for Thuma-thaya: we first descended the Dissoo ravine, then up a very steep hill, the top of which was cultivated, then descended and crossed another stream, the remainder of our march consisting almost entirely of an uninterrupted steep ascent: during our progress we gained partial views of the Plains and the Naga Hills, but on crossing a high ridge on which I observed Betula Populus ? Rhododendrum arboreum. The view to the East and West was very fine. That to the W. embracing the greater

* One of the most influential of the Singpho chiefs, whose influence at this period kept Upper Assam unsettled.

part of the plains about Suddiya and the Abor Hills, stretching along to S. W. the more distant Naga Hills. The Lohit could be traced for an immense way, the Dihong, Dibong, Digaroo, Dihing were all partially visible. To the N. E. Thegri-thaya was finely seen, then some rugged peaks among which Laim-planj was conspicuous. It embraced the course of the Lohit, at least its right bank, ridge surmounting ridge: the loftier ones tipped with snow; and lastly it was closed by a huge wall, all covered with snow, especially its peaks, stretching away to the N. From this we descended to Yen, where, as usual, I took up my quarters in a granary. During the latter portion of the journey, I gathered a Passiflora ? Lobelia two species, a Scitaminea, Spiræa, and a curious aromatic plant, pedunculis bracteæ adnatis, bracteis, coloratis, petal videis.

Codonopsis, etc. Dicksonia, stipitibus atris 3 canaliculatis, frondibus amplis, 10 pedalibus; in fine fructification; this is the same with the Manmoo plant. I observed likewise an arborescent Sambucus, a Bonnaya, a huge Begonia: Coix was seen cultivated.

Nov. 25th.—Spent the day in botanising. Gathered Adamia, some fine ferns, a bamboo, spiculis dense congestis, bracteis scariosis interspersis, and Schizosfachyum, Nees ab E. etc.

Another and much finer species of the Fumariaceous genus, I found on Laim-planj, Deutzia, a rare Quercus, a fine species of Antonia, (Br.) in fruit, a Bartramia, Trematodon, Neckera, etc., noticed a fruit something similar to that of Combretum, allis 2 maximis, 2 minimis: cotyledonibus hæmisphæricis.

Saurauja, Prunus: 3 species of Aralia, Castanea, Quercus, etc. A species of Panicum is here cultivated; the Assamese know it by the name Cheena, 3 species of Polygonatum, including that from Laim-planj, one foliis carnosis oppositis. 2 species of Begonia, making altogether six. The Amaranthacea of Deeling is here found extensively, it often assumes the form of a climber of considerable size. Musa farinosa grows to a great size, 20 to 25 feet. Bambusa in flower has stems about two inches in diameter. Sterculia flowers were observed on the ground. In the afternoon it rained slightly. This is the coldest place I have visited on these hills: in the evening and earlier parts of the night there is a very cold draught down Thuma-thaya.

The Anthistiria found on the more elevated portions of these hills, is probably different from that of the plains. Urticea are here found in abundance.

Nov. 26th.—This morning the atmosphere being beautifully transparent, very high land plentifully sprinkled with snow was visible to the N. W. by W., and to the N. W. a slight peep of the Himalayas was gained. Started at 9, and commenced the ascent; we arrived at our halting place at 11½. The greater part of the march was a steep ascent through dry woods, the ground being very slippery owing to the leaves. Bucklandia occurs in abundance and of a large size, and attains a much greater height than Sedgwickia : found many interesting plants and a small Conifera, probably an Araucaria or a Taxus.

I continued the ascent until about 12, but the scene had totally changed; the whole face of the mountain on the S. side being entirely destitute of trees, and in many places quite naked. The ascent was not very difficult, and occupied a little more than an hour. This acclivity is chiefly occupied by Graminea, all past flowering, all adhering very firmly to the rock, which is quartzose and greyish blue outside, excessively angular: Gentianeæ 2: a beautiful Campanula, Hypericum, Viburnum, Spiræa, Bryum Neckera, Pteris, Scabiosa, some Compositæ, one or two Vaccinioidea, and a curious shrubby Rubiacea evidently a Serissa, were observed. The top, which represents a ridge, is partially wooded, the trees being the continuation or rather termination of the jungle that covers the whole northern face of the mountain. Here I saw Bucklandia, a Pomacea, Crawfurdia, Deutzia, Cynaroidea, Viburna 2, some ferns. Brachymeum, Neckera, Lichens several : a Caryophyllea and a Berberis.

All these were somewhat stunted. The various views were beautiful, embracing a complete panorama, but unfortunately obscured towards Lama by trees. The Lohit was seen extensively from the Koond to Ghaloom's, and to the plains to an immense distance. The whole range of Abor Hills and a great portion of the Naga, some of which appeared very high, were likewise seen: to the S. E. high ridges not far distant and covered with snow, limited the view; slight snow was visible on the peak seen from Suddiya. The descent was very tedious owing to the excessive slipperiness of the grass: it was dangerous, because a slip would have frequently dashed you to pieces, and in all cases would have hurt one severely.

Nov. 27th.—Descended to Yen : near our halting place we gathered a fine Pomacea arborea in fruit: a Symplocos, and observed Wallichioideæ and Calamus. The plants of the greatest interest gathered were an Acer, and Epilobium, a Hoya grandiflora, Eurya,

Hypericum, a fine Arundo, Bucklandia: Cotoneaster microphylla, a Sabia, Coriaria, Abelia ? a rare Dipodous Orchidea of the same genus as a dwarf plant of the Cossiya Hills. Rhododendron, scandesent Eleodendron.

The ascent for the greater part is a steep wooded ridge; the first change indicated or induced by elevation is the diminution of the size in the trees, and the frequent occurrence of a Betulus ? out of flower. Proceeding onward one comes to a ridge, the S. E. declivity of which is nearly naked, the opposite being wooded with shrubs, Viburnum, Conaria, Mespilus, Pomacea, Rhododendron, Rubiacea Serissa, Cupulifera and some Compositæ occur. Then Arbutus Vaccinium; Nardus: Filix cano-tomentosa, Lycopodium; Dicranum atratum; one or two Hypna, a Bryum, and Neckera fusca. Descending slightly from thence the ridge is observed to be wooded on both sides; it is at the termination of this that we halted. The ascent is continued up a rock, and the whole of the mountain is, excepting the ravines, covered with Graminea, Cyperacea, Filix cano-tomentosa, etc. but the Ericoidea are not so fine. The grasses of the summit are two Andropogons: an Arundo Festucoidea, Panicum, Isachne, Nardus ceasing below, it is towards this that Crepis ? and Campanula are common.

The Ceratostemmata are found towards the summit, none descend any distance, except one of Roxburgh's; they are all generally epiphytes. Orchidea become more common towards the halting place; beyond this I observed only two past flowering, one Habenaria, and a Malaxidea; the others are two Cælogyne, a Dipodious Orchidea, labelli ungue sigmoideo very common, a Bolbophyllum, and a few ditto epiphytes out of flower, one terrestrial Bletioidea is common in some places. At our halting place, I observed an arborescent Araliacea, a Cissus, an Acanthacea and a Laurinea. A little below, Pandanus occurs here and there, and attains a large size, the largest in fact I have ever seen. Castanea occurs about half way up, it is that species with rigid compound spines to the cupula. I gathered also a fine Geastrum, but the specimens are lost. Bucklandia occurs extensively; it is a distinct species owing to its many flowered capitula; Sedgwickia comes into play towards Yen, where Bucklandia appears to become scarce: a large Vitex floribus roseo-purpureis is the most conspicuous tree of all, it ceases towards the summit; Cyathea I observed only above half way. Camellia axillaris occurs below, but I missed the Laim-planj plant. I may here observe that almost all plants with red flowers, at least in this quarter, are acid: the Assamese always appear to expect this, the proofs are Loranthus, Ceratostemma, and Begonia, in which red is generally a predominant colour.

Antrophyllum I noticed about Yen; towards Yen, I diverged from the path to visit the place whence the stones are procured, which the Mishmees use as flints for striking lights: this stone is found on the S. Western face of the mountain: the stones or noduli are frequently sub-crystalline, and are imbedded in a sort of micaceous frangible rock: they are very common, of very different sizes, with glassy fracture; the best are hard; the bad easily frangible, their weight is great. The inclination of this bed is considerable; overlying it at an inclination of 45°, is the grey quartzose rock which forms the chief part, and perhaps nearly the whole, of the mountain. The Mishmee name for the noduli is *Mpladung*.

In the jungle at Yen occurs a huge Palm evidently Caryota, foliis maximis supra decompositis; the diameter of the trunk is $1\frac{1}{2}$ to 2 feet. It is said to die after flowering: the natives use the central lax structures as food. The Yen Gam promises to send me specimens to-morrow. The Palms I have hitherto seen are Wallichia, one or two Calami: Wallichioidia trunco 5-10 pedali, and a Phænicoidea, but this I only saw at the foot of the mountains near Laee Panee, and the small Areca common about Negrogam. The name of the large Palm in Assamese is *Bura Sawar*. All the plants common to these and the Cossiya mountains, with one or two exceptions; flower much earlier here, those being all past flowering which I gathered in flower on the Cossiya hills in November last. This is owing to the greater cold, and the consequent necessity for the plants flowering at an earlier and warmer period.

A species of ruminant, or, according to the native account, a species of Pachydermata called the *Gan Pohoo*, occurs on Thumathaya. At the summit of the mountain the ground was in one place rooted up, the Mishmees said, by this animal, which they describe as a large Hog, but which I should rather take to be a kind of Deer.

Nov. 28*th.*—Returned to Deeling. At the commencement of the principal descent we gathered Betula and another Cupulifera, both moderately sized trees. Anthestina arundinacea, is about this place very common, and an Andropogon, Culmis ramosis which I had previously brought from the Abor hills. About half way down by a present of *kanee* (opium), I succeeded in getting the arborescent vitex, which is the most striking tree of all when in flower. Lost sight altogether of Bucklandia, nor did I observe Sedgwickia. Gathered at the foot of Thuma-thaya a Cælogyne in flower, allied to C. Gardneriana; Alsophila is common towards the base.

In the evening the Yen Gam came up according to his promise with the gigantic Palm, with male inflorescence, it is a Caryota; he likewise brought Sarcocordalis, Rafflesiacea, and a curious pubescent Piper. He also added the female flowers of another Palm, which, according to him, is another species of *Sawar*, or Caryota: the inflorescence is of an orange yellow. A tree with the habit of Pterospermum occurs on Thuma-thaya, low down Habenaria uniflora on rocks in the Dirsoo Panee, or river; Kydia occurs about Yen, but not higher.

Nov. 29th.—Reached Laee Panee after a march of five hours; and without Assamese coolies, it might be done in three. I noticed below Deeling, but still at a considerable elevation, Crawfurdia campanu lacea, Adamea, Engelhardtia, Vitex speciosa, and Magnolia in the order in which they are thus given, Quercus, cupulis echinatis occurs comparatively low down, Castanea ferox still lower, Dracæna comes into view towards the base. At the village first reached in the ascent there is a Meliaceous Azedarach looking tree.

At our old halting place, and which is near Deeling, another *Ahum-metta Ghas* was shewn me. This attains, I am told, a large size: it is not very unlike in habit a Melanorrhæa, and its young leaves are tinged with red, the mature ones are coriaceous, I have not seen it in flower; the juice, at least from small branches, is not very abundant, and at first is of a whitish colour; it is, *on dit*, after drying that it assumes the black tint; at any rate it is excessively acrid, for one of my servants who cut it incautiously, had his face spoilt for a time: the swelling even after four days had elapsed was considerable. With this as well as the Rhus they dye the strings of the simple fibres of *Sawar*, which they all wear below the knee: if not properly dried these strings cause some inflammation: the strings are ornamental, light, and when worn in small numbers graceful, but when dozens are employed, and all the upper ones loose, they deform the figure much; some of the women, perhaps anxious to restrain the protuberance of their calves, tie two or three lightly across the calf.

At Nohun, near Deeling, Cocoloba aculeata *baccis* cyaneis occurs here the same as at Mumbree in the Cossiya hills, and at Suddiya.

Nov. 30*th.*—Halted. Put all the grain into the Tapan Gam's hands, amounting to 60 maunds. In the evening received as a present a long sword from Premsong. Found a fine Impatiens and a shrub coming into flower, Calyce æstiv. valvato? Stamen 4, connectivo ultra antheras longe producto, ovarium adnatum, foliis oppositis, exstipulatis. Meyenia coccinea, finely in flower. An arborescent Urticea (Bæhmeria?) foliis subtus candidis is common.

Dec. 1*st.*—Reached the Tapan Gam's after a sharp march of four hours. We are not yet quite at the foot of the hills. Gathered *en route* 4 new Acanthaceæ, not previously met with on this trip, among which is a beautiful Eranthemum. At Laee Panee one of my people brought me a fine Aristolochia, very nearly allied to that from Ghaloom's, but at once distinct by its ferruginous pubescence, Antrophyum, and a Polypodium not before met with were among the acquisitions. The Tapan Gam has behaved very handsomely for a Mishmee, having killed a hog, and given five kuchoos of beautiful rice, and feasted my people. Found two snakes, which inhabit the inside of bamboos. Color superne brunneo-cinereus, margines squamarum nigri, gula nigra, fascicula subtus antea alba, postice lutescens.

Noticed Jenkinsia near Laee Panee, and some gigantic specimens of Pentaptera, the Hool-look of the Assamese, the timber of which is used for large canoes; and Lagerstræmia grandiflora occurs on the banks of the Kussin Panee.

CHAPTER III.

Revisits the Tea Localities in the Singphoo and Muttack Districts, Upper Assam.

Dec. 2nd.—Returned to Jingsha viâ Kussin Panee, or river, and Karam Panee, the march being a tolerably easy one. Found along the steep banks of the former a fine Meniscium, frondibus 6-8 pedalibus, and an arborescent Polypodium, caudice 12-15 pedali, partibus novellis densissime ferrugineo-tomentosis; frondibus subtus glauco-albidis. The caudex is altogether similar in structure to that of Alsophyla, equally furnished with strong black bristly radicles towards its base.

Dec. 3rd.—Left for Husa Gam's about 9; and arrived at the village which is on the Kampai of the Singfos, Tup-pai of the Mishmees about 4½ P.M. The first part of our march was to the E. up the Karam, we then traversed for a long way heavy jungle in a S. direction, and then came on the dry bed of the Kampai, up which we ascended to the village. Found a Ruellioidea, *Cyananthus, mihi. Oom* of the Assamese, with which the Kamptees dye their black blue cloths. Noticed an arborescent Araliacea inermis, foliis supra decomposita; panicule patentissima. The Husa Gam treated us very handsomely forming a striking contrast with the Mishmees; he declares positively that no tea exists in this direction; I shall therefore proceed direct from Luttora to Beesa. Roxburghia occurred on the route. The village is on the left bank of the river: the direction from Jingsha's being about N. W.

Dec. 4th.—Reached Luttora after an easy march of three hours and a half, for the most part along an excellent path. We passed the following villages *en route* Chibong, Wakon, Mtarm, and Mcyompsan: three of which are of some size; none however so large as Nsas. This is the largest Singfo village I have seen, and probably contains 400 people. This village and all the others are situated on high ground, the ascent from the Kampai being probably 70 feet. The country consists of level, apparently good soil, with here and there broadish ravines in which bamboos are abundant. Cultivation is common, and of considerable extent. On a similar eminence is situate Luttora, and it has been well chosen, for on both sides that I approached it, the ascent is steep and capable of being easily defended; the south side is bounded by the Ponlong Panee, which runs into the Tenga Panee. If any ascent it is an easy one, and must be to the westward; to the north, there is a small stream, but neither this, Ponlong or Tenga are any thing but mere rills, which may be easily leaped over in the dry seasons. Our route from Nsas was to the W. of south. No stockades appear to exist in this quarter.

Luttora is not so large as Nsas; formerly the Luttora Gam was the chief of all this soil, but he has been partly deserted by two bodies of men who have respectively chosen Nsas and Htan-tsantan.

The Gam visited me in the evening at our halting place on the Ponlong; he is a large, coarse, heavy looking man, nearly blind, and excessively dirty. He proposed of himself to me, to become the Company's ryott in accordance with the wish, he said, of the Dupha Gam; but when I told him he ought to send or go to the Suddiya Sahib, or Political Agent, he said he wanted to see the Dupha first: he was accompanied by a very loquacious oldish man, who had just returned from Hook-hoom, to which place he had gone with the Dupha. They left apparently not much pleased at my being empty handed.

Dec. 5th.—Left at 6½, reached the Muttack Panee about 8½, having come through much heavy bamboo jungle; we then ascended the dry bed of the Muttack, and ascended after some time the Minaboom. This was most tedious, as we continued along the ridge for two hours; we then commenced our descent, but did not reach the Meera Panee much before 1 P.M. Down this we came here, and then along some curious chasms in the sandstone, and encamped about 3. The difference of soil between the Minaboom and the Mishmee hills is most obvious; on the N. E. declivity there is much soil; but on the opposite side little but rounded stones which supply the place of soil, and in places we saw nothing but sandstone conglomerate? or indurated soil with many boulders imbedded in it, and a blackish greasy clay slate; while on the Mishmees, on the contrary, all is rock, hard and harsh to the touch; or where loose stones do occur on the face of the hills, they are all angular. The vegetation of sandstone is likewise far more varied; and that of the Meera Panee district, abounds in ferns, among which is Polypodium Wallichianum. The Tree-fern of Kujing I observed in the Muttack, Sedgwickia in Minaboom, two Magnoliaceæ, one bracteis persistent, induratis, and a Dipterocarpus. The chief vegetation of the ridge consists of grasses, among which bamboo holds a conspicuous place. A Begonia was common along the Muttack. The Meera Panee would well repay a halt of two or three days.

At our halting place we met four Burmese, despatched by the Maum,* who has arrived at Beesa on a visit to the Luttora Gam.

Dec. 6th.—Reached Beesa after a sharp march of six hours. Our course lay at first down the Meera Panee; here I observed more of the Polypodium Wallichianum, which is common throughout the Singfo hill country, and appears to be used as grog, at least the juice of the petioles. We then diverged to the westward through heavy jungle, and the remainder of our march consisted of uninteresting dense jungle, water-courses, and excessively low places. Observed Sabia in some of the jungles; the only interesting plants gathered were an Impatiens and two or three Acanthaceæ. About 2½ P.M. we came on the Noa Dihing, which is now nearly dry, the water having flowed into the Kamroop. No boat, not even a dâk boat, can come near Beesa. It is obvious that this river here never presented any depth, both banks being very low; the bed consists of small hard boulders.

Dec. 7th, 8th.—Halted at Beesa.

Dec. 9th.—Started for the Naga village, at some distance, and

Dec. 10th.—Left for Kujoo or Khoonlong, which we reached about 1, after a march of five hours. At 10, we arrived at Dhoompsan or Thoompsa, a large village with extensive cultivation. The remainder of our march was through heavy jungle, many parts of which were very low, and crowded with a fierce Calamus. The higher parts abound in a Dipterocarpus, and two Castaneæ. I found many fine ferns, all of which however we collected last year. Chrysobaphus, not uncommon. Apostasia rare.

Dec. 11th.—Visited the tea in the old locality at Nigroo. No steps have been taken towards clearing the jungles, except perhaps of tea. The Gam tells me, that the order for clearing was given to Shroo, Dompshan, and Kumongyon, Gams of three villages near the spot. Noticed Dicksonia *en route*, so that we must have passed it last year. Æsculus also occurs here.

Dec. 12th.—Arrived at Kugoodoo after an easy march of two hours and a half. At 12, went to see the tea which lies to the S. S. W. of the village, and about ten minutes' walk to the W. of the path leading to Negrogam, and which for the most part runs along an old

* A Burmese authority.

bund road. After diverging from this road we passed through some low jungle, which is always characterised by Calamus Zalaccoideus; and then after traversing for a short time some rather higher ground, came on the tea. This patch is never under water; there is no peculiarity of vegetation connected with it. It runs about N. and S. for perhaps 150 yards by 40 to 50 in breadth. The Gam had cleared the jungle of all, except the larger trees and the low *herbaceous underwood*, so that a *coup d'œil* was at once obtained, and gave sufficient evidence of the abundance of the plants, many of which were of considerable size, and all bore evidence of having been mutilated. They were for the most part loaded with flowers, and are the finest I have seen in the Singfo country. Young buds were very common, nor can I reconcile this with the statement made by the Gam, that no young leaves will be obtainable for four months. From the clearing, the plants are exposed to moderate sun; it is perhaps to this that the great abundance of flowers is to be attributed. The soil, now quite dry at the surface, is of a cinereous grey; about a foot below it is brown, which passes, as you proceed, into deeper yellow; about four feet deep, it passes into sand. No ravines exist, and mounds only do about a few of the larger trees. The soil as usual is light, friable, easily reduced to powder, and has a very slight tendency to stiffness.

Dec. 13*th*.—Left for the Muttack: our course lay through dense jungle, principally of bamboo, and along the paths of wild elephants; these beasts are here very common. We halted after a march of seven hours on a small bank of the Deboro; the only plant of interest was my Cyananthus in flower.

Dec. 14*th*.—Continued through similar jungle along the Deboro; bamboo more frequent. About 2 P.M. we left the undulating hillocks, and the jungle became more open. At 4, we reached Muttack, but had still to traverse a considerable distance before we halted at Kolea Panee. We crossed the Deboro *en route;* no particular plant was met with. I shot two large serpents, *Pythons;* one 8, and the other 10 feet long. The Kolea Panee is of some width, but is fordable.

Dec. 15*th*.—After marching for about seven hours, halted at a small village. The country passed over was, like most of this part of Muttack, open, consisting of a rather high plain covered with grasses, T. sperata, Saccharum, and Erianthus, with here and there very swampy ravines; the soil is almost entirely sandy, light at the surface; the yellow tint increasing with the depth, which is considerable.

Crossed the Deboro by a rude wooden bridge. I found no particular plants *en route*.

Dec. 16th.—Reached Rangagurrah, after a march of about an hour : and halted for the day.

Dec. 18th.—Started to visit Sedgwickia at the wood, where we found it in February last. Reached the spot, which is at least ten miles from Rangagurrah, in two hours and a half. The trees had evidently not flowered last year; many of the buds were of some size, and such contained flower buds, each capitula being in addition enveloped in three bracteæ densely beset with brown hair. The natives assured me, it will flower about April, or at the sowing of *halee*. When we before found it, the buds were all leaf buds, which at once accounts for the non-appearance of flowers. Gathered Sabia in the Sedgwickia wood. The Major* arrived before I got back.

Dec. 20th.—Revisited the tea locality of Tingrei, which we reached after a five hours' march. The portion of it formerly cleared is now quite clean : all the plants, and they are very abundant, have a shrubby shady appearance; the branches being numerous, so that the first aspect is favourable. But one soon detects an evident coarseness in the leaves, the tint of which is likewise much too yellow; altogether their appearance is totally unlike that of teas growing in their natural shade. That part, and the more extensive one which we first visited in February last, is now clearing; almost all the large trees have been felled, and all the underwood removed. The branches, &c. are piled in heaps and set fire to, much to the detriment of the plants: all the tea trees likewise have been felled. My conviction is, that the tea will not flourish in open sunshine; at any rate, subjection to this should be gradual. Further, that cutting the main stem is detrimental, not only inducing long shoots, but most probably weakening the flavour of the leaves. It appears to me to be highly desirable, that an intelligent superintendent should reside on the spot, and that he should at least be a good practical gardener, with some knowledge of the science also.

Dec. 24th.—Reached Suddiya. The country passed through was, for the first two days, of the same description as before; *i. e.* rather high grassy plains with belts of jungle, and intervening low very swampy ravines. The soil precisely the same as that of the tea localities. The last march was, with the exception of Chykwar, through low damp dense jungle.

* Probably Major R. Bruce of the Rajah's service, one of the Superintendents of Tea Cultivation.

*Extract from the Author's letter to Captain F. Jenkins, Commissioner of Assam, regarding the Mishmees. December, 1836.**

"I had thus become acquainted with all the influential chiefs near our frontier, and by all I was received in a friendly and hospitable manner. In accordance with my original intentions, my attention was in the first place directed towards ascertaining whether the tea exists in this direction or not, and, as I have already informed you, I have every reason to think that the plant is unknown on these hills. From what I have seen of the tea on the plains, I am disposed to believe that the comparative want of soil, due to the great inclination of all the eminences, is an insuperable objection to its existence.

"As I before observed to you, during my stay at *Jingsha*, my curiosity had been excited by reports of an incursion of a considerable force of Lamas into the Mishmee country. It hence became, having once established a footing in the country, a matter of paramount importance to proceed farther into the interior, and, if possible, to effect a junction with these highly interesting people; but all my attempts to gain this point proved completely futile; no bribes, no promises would induce any of the chiefs to give me guides, even to the first Mishmee village belonging to the Mezhoo tribe. I was hence compelled to content myself for the present, with obtaining as much information as possible relative to the above report, and I at length succeeded in gaining the following certainly rather meagre account.

"The quarrel, as usual, originated about a marriage settlement between two chiefs of the Mezhoo and Taeen tribes: it soon ended in both parties coming to blows. The Mezhoo chief, ROOLING, to enable him at once to overpower his enemies, and to strike at once at the root of their power, called in the assistance of the Lamas. From this country a force of seventy men armed with matchlocks made an invasion, and, as was to be expected, the Taeen Mishmees were beaten at every point and lost about twenty men. The affair seems to have come to a close about September last, when the Lamas returned to their own country. Where it occurred I could gain no precise information, but it must have been several days' journey in advance of the villages I visited.

* For the whole of this able communication, detailing the object and results of his visit to the Mishmee mountains, See Journ. As. Soc. Beng. May 1837.

"It was owing to the unsettled state of the country, resulting from this feud, that I could gain no guides from the Digaroos, without whose assistance in this most difficult country, I need scarcely say, that all attempts to advance would have been made in vain. These people very plausibly said, if we give you guides, who is to protect us from the vengeance of the Mezhoos when you are gone, and who is to insure us from a second invasion of the Lamas? Another thing to be considered is, the influence even then exercised over the Mishmees near our boundaries by the Singphos connected with the Dupha Gam; but from the renewal of the intercourse with our frontier station, there is every reason for believing that this influence is ere this nearly destroyed."

"The natives of this portion of the range are divided into two tribes, Taeen or Digaroo and Mezhoo, these last tracing their descent from the *Dibong* Mishmees, who are always known by the term crop-haired. The Mezhoo, however, like the Taeens, preserve their hair, wearing it generally tied in a knot on the crown of their head. The appearance of both tribes is the same, but the language of the Mezhoos is very distinct. They are perhaps the more powerful of the two; but their most influential chiefs reside at a considerable distance from the lower ranges. The only Mezhoos I met with are those at *Deeling-Yen*, a small village opposite *Deeling*, but at a much higher elevation, and *Tapan*. I need scarcely add that it was owing to the opposition of this tribe that Captain Wilcox failed in reaching *Lama*. The Digaroos are ruled by three influential chiefs, who are brothers Drisong, Khosha, and Ghaloom: of these, Drisong is the eldest and the most powerful, but he resides far in the interior. Primsong is from a distant stock, and as the three brothers mentioned above are all passed the prime of life, there is but little doubt that he will soon become by far the most influential chief of his tribe. Both tribes appear to intermarry. The Mishmees are a small, active, hardy race, with the Tartar cast of features; they are excessively dirty, and have not the reputation of being honest, although, so far as I know, they are belied in this respect. Like other hill people, they are famous for the muscular development of their legs:—in this last point the women have generally the inferiority. They have no written language. Their clothing is inferior; it is, however, made of cotton, and is of their own manufacture;—that of the men consists of a mere jacket and an apology for a *dhoti*,—that of the women is more copious, and at any rate quite decent: they are very fond of ornaments, especially beads, the quantities of which they wear is very often quite astonishing. They appear to me certainly superior to the Abors, of whom, however, I have seen but few. Both sexes drink liquor, but they did not seem to me to be so addicted to it as is generally the case with hill tribes:—their usual drink is a fermented liquor made from rice called *mont'h:* this, however, is far inferior to that of the Singphos, which is really a pleasant drink.

" *Religion.* Of their religion I could get no satisfactory information: —every thing is ascribed to supernatural agency. Their invocations to their deity are frequent, and seem generally to be made with the view of filling their own stomachs with animal food. They live in a very promiscuous manner, one hundred being occasionally accommodated in a single house. Their laws appear to be simple,—all grave crimes being judged by an assembly of Gams, who are on such occasions summoned from considerable distances. All crimes, including murder, are punished by fines: but if the amount is not forthcoming, the offender is cut up by the company assembled. But the crime of adultery, provided it be committed against the consent of the husband, is punished by death; and this severity may perhaps be necessary if we take into account the way in which they live.

" The men always go armed with knives, Lama swords, or Singpho *dhaos* and lances; and most of them carry cross-bows—the arrows for these are short, made of bamboo, and on all serious occasions are invariably poisoned with *bee.* When on fighting expeditions, they use shields, made of leather, which are covered towards the centre with the quills of the porcupine. Their lances are made use of only for thrusting: the shafts are made either from the wood of the lawn *(Caryota urens)* or that of another species of palm *juice*—they are tipped with an iron spike, and are of great use in the ascent of hills. The lance heads are of their own manufacture, and of very soft iron. They have latterly become acquainted with fire-arms, and the chiefs have mostly each a firelock of *Lama* construction.

" With *Lama* they carry on an annual trade, which apparently takes place on the borders of either country. In this case *mishmee-teeta,* is the staple article of the Mishmees, and for it they obtain *dhaos* or straight long swords of excellent metal and often of great length; copper pots of strong, but rough make, flints and steel, or rather steel alone, which are really very neat and good; warm woollen caps, coarse loose parti-colored woollen cloths, huge glass beads, generally white or blue, various kinds of cattle, in which *Lama* is represented as abounding, and salts. I cannot say whether the Lamas furnish flints with the steel implements for striking light; the stone generally used for this purpose by the Mishmees is the nodular production from *Thumathaya*,—and this, although rather frangible, answers its purpose very well; with the Singphos they barter elephants' teeth, (these animals being found in the lower ranges,) for slaves, dhaws, and buffaloes.

" With the Khamtees they appear to have little trade, although there is a route to the proper country of this people along the *Ghaloom pânee*, or *Ghaloom Thee* of Wilcox's chart; this route is from the great height of the hills to be crossed, only available during the hot months.

" With the inhabitants of the plains they carry on an annual trade, which is now renewed after an interruption of two years, exchanging cloths, Lama swords, spears, *mishmee-teeta*, *bee*, which is in very great request, and *gertheana*, much esteemed by the natives for its peculiar and rather pleasant smell, for money, (to which they begin to attach great value), cloths, salt and beads: when a sufficient sum of money is procured, they lay it out in buffaloes and the country cattle."

The following is a list of collections of Plants from the Mishmee Hills to the extreme East, Upper Assam.

Dicotyledones.		*Dicotyledones.*	
Compositæ, { Ligulatæ, 9; Cynaraceæ, 4; Corymbiferæ, 76 }	80	Ericineæ,	7
		Verbenaceæ,	8
		Boragineæ,	2
		Labiatæ,	50
Valerianeæ,	1	Gesneriaceæ,	22
Dipsaceæ,	1	Acanthaceæ,	38
Caprifoliaceæ,	6	Scrophularineæ,	19
Rubiaceæ,	42	Solaneæ,	6
Apocyneæ, } Asclepiadeæ, }	5	Convolvulaceæ,	8
		Primulaceæ,	1
Gentianeæ,	7	Myrsineæ,	19
Oleinæ,	2	Escalloniaceæ ?	3
Jasmineæ,	6	Malvaceæ,	6
Campanulaceæ,	7	Cruciferæ,	3
Lobeliaceæ,	7	Polygaleæ,	1
Vacciniaceæ,	2	Violaceæ,	5

Dicotyledones.	
Passifloreæ, ...	1
Modeceoideæ, ...	1
Samydeæ, ...	1
Ampelideæ, Leea, ...	6
Balsamineæ, ...	15
Sileneæ, ...	6
Aurantiaceæ, ...	5
Meliaceæ, ...	5
Sapindaceæ, ...	3
Acerineæ, ...	4
Malpighiaceæ, ...	3
Hypericineæ, ...	2
Ternstrœmiaceæ, ...	11
Symplocineæ, ...	3
Ebenaceæ, ...	1
Terebinthaceæ, { Rhus, 5; Buchanania, 1; Phlebochiton, 1; Sabia, 2 }	9
Zanthoxyteæ, ...	5
Conareæ, ...	1
Trygophylleæ, ...	1
Rutaceæ, ...	2
Ranunculaceæ, ...	4
Fumariaceæ, ...	2
Myristiceæ, ...	2
Anonaceæ, ...	4
Magnoliaceæ, ...	1
Berberideæ, ...	1
Lardizabaleæ, ...	1
Menispermeæ, ...	5
Rosaceæ, ...	16
Leguminosæ, ...	31
Philadelpheæ, ...	2
Saxifrageæ, ...	3
Melastomaceæ, ...	9
Onagrariæ, ...	3
Myrtaceæ, ...	2
Cucurbitaceæ, ...	6

Dicotyledones.	
Begoneaceæ, ...	6
Umbelliferæ, ...	4
Araleaceæ, ...	12
Rhamneæ, ...	1
Celastrineæ, ...	9
Amaranthaceæ, ...	8
Polygoneæ, ...	12
Chenopodeæ, ...	1
Plantagineæ, ...	1
Urticeæ, ...	14
Ulmaceæ, ...	1
Euphorbiaceæ, ...	21
Scepaceæ, ...	1
Stilagineæ, ...	5
Myriceæ, ...	1
Juglandeæ, ...	1
Cupuliferæ, ...	4
Betulaceæ, ...	5
Salicineæ, ...	1
Laurineæ, ...	8
Hamamelideæ, ...	2
Thymeleæ, ...	1
Santalaceæ, ...	1
Loranthaceæ, ...	2
Proteaceæ, ...	1
Elæagneæ, ...	1
Aristolochiæ, ...	3
Combretaceæ, ...	2
Chloranthеæ, ...	1
Piperaceæ, ...	14
Coniferæ, ...	1
Incertæ, ...	17
Unarranged, ...	8
Ditto, ...	14
	725

Monocotyledones.	
Smilacineæ, ...	14

Monocotyledones.		*Acotyledones.*	
Dioscoreæ, ...	1	Pteris, ...	21
Peliosantheæ, ...	5	Blechnum, ...	1
Tupistraceæ, ...	2	Dicksonia, ...	1
Commelineæ, ...	10	Davallia, ...	12
Tacceæ, ...	1	Lindsæa, .. .	2
Aroideæ, ...	6	Asplenium	27
Scitamineæ, ...	6	Allantodioides, ...	6
Orichedeæ, ...	43	Aspidium, ...	22
Apostaceæ, ...	1	Nephrodium, ...	16
Palmæ, ...	3	Cyatheæ, ...	7
Cyperaceæ, ...	22	Trichomanes, ...	4
Gramineæ, ...	73	Hymenophyllum, ...	2
	——	Gleichenia, ...	1
	187	Angiopteris, ...	1
	——	Botrychium, ...	1
Acotyledones.		Lygodium, ...	2
		Lycopodium	6
Acrostichum, ...	12	Tinesipteris	1
Ceterach, ...	2	Equisetum, ...	1
Grammitis, ...	3		——
Polypodium, ...	56		224
Pleopeltis, ...	8	Monocotyledones, ..	187
Niphobolus, ...	1	Dicotyledones, ..	725
Cheilanthes, ...	3	Mosses unarranged, about	50
Adiantum, ...	3		——
Vittaria, ...	1	Total,	1186
Lomaria, ...	1		——

N. B.—The plants enumerated above, were transmitted to the India House in 1838, together with former collections made *in the Tenasserim* Provinces.

CHAPTER IV.

Journey from Upper Assam towards Hookhoom, Ava, and Rangoon, Lat. 27° 25′ to 16° 45′ N., Long. 96° to 96° 20′ E.

We left Suddiya on the 7th of February 1837, and reached Kedding on the 10th; stayed there one day, and reached Kamroop Putar, where I found Major White and Lieut. Bigge on the 12th. The jungle to this place was similar to the usual jungle of the Singpho country, very generally low, and intersected by ravines. We crossed *en route* the Karam river, the Noa Dihing, or Dihing branch of the Booree Dihing, on which the Beesa's old village was situated; and lastly the Kamroop. Kamroop Putar is close to the Naga hills; it is a cultivated rice tract, on the river Kamroop. This river is fordable, with frequent rapids. The only curious things about it are the petroleum wells, which are confined to three situations. The wells are most numerous towards the summits of the range; and the place where they occur is free from shrubs. The petroleum is of all colours, from green to bluish white; this last is the strongest, partaking of the character of Naptha, it looks like bluish or greyish clay and water. The vegetation of the open places in which the wells are found, consists of grass, Stellaria, Hypericum, Polygonum, Cyperaceæ, Mazus rugosus, Plantago media, etc., all of which are found on the plains. One of the wells is found on the Putar, or cultivated ground; the petroleum in this is grey. The Kamroop river above this Putar, strikes off to the eastward, and the Kamteechick, a tributary, falls into it from the south; this last is a good deal the smaller; the banks of the Kamroop are in many places precipitous. About two miles from the Putar, a fine seam of excellent coal has been exposed by a slip:* the beds are at an inclination of 45°, and their direction is, I think, nearly the same with that of the left bank of the river in which they occur; immediately over the seam there is a small ravine, where three of the veins are still farther exposed. Coricea, a new Dicranum, Alsophila ferruginea, Polytrichum aloides, Bartramea subulosa, and Jungermanniæ are common near this spot.

* See Reports of the Coal Committee, 1841, p. 3.

Left Kamroop on the 19th, and proceeded in a S. W. direction for twelve miles, when we halted on the Darap Kha, at the foot of the Naga hills, opposite nearly to Beesala. Nothing of interest occurred.

Feb. 21*st.*—Commenced the ascent, and after marching about ten miles, halted in a valley near a stream. Temperature 66°. Water boiled at 210½°, giving an altitude of about 77°, or 383 feet above Suddiya. The road was very winding, the path good, except towards the base of the hills: the soil sandy, in places indurated, and resting on sandstone; but there is not yet sufficient elevation to ensure much change in vegetation. Found Kaulfussia* below in abundance, observed Castanea and a Quercus; three species of Begonia, and three or four species of Acanthacea. In other respects the jungle resembles that of the Singpho territory. Dicksonia is abundant. Dipterocarpus of large size occurs. Caught two innocuous snakes at the halting place.†

Feb. 22*nd.*—The distance of the march is about 12 miles, and we halted after crossing the Darap Panee; some parts of the route were difficult, at least for elephants. No particular features of vegetation yet appears. The summit of the higher hills looks pretty. Tree jungle considerable, open places with low grass, is the surrounding feature of vegetation. The hill first surmounted from the halting place is covered with a Camellia or *Bunfullup*, (*i. e.* bitter tea) of the Assamese. The fruit has loculicidal dehiscence. In habit it is like that of the tea, but the buds are covered with imbricate scales. At the summit of the hill, it attained a height of 30 or 40 feet. Begoniacea, Urticaçeæ, Acanthaceæ, Filices, are the most common.

Feb. 23*rd.*—Halted to enable the elephants to come up; they arrived about 10 A.M. Temperature of the air 75°, water boiled at 210°, altitude 1029 feet. The Darap is a considerable stream, but is fordable at the heads of the rapids. Fish abound, especially *Bookhar*, a kind of Barbel,‡ which reaches a good size. Clay slate appears to be here the most common rock, and forms in many places the very precipitous banks of the river. Alsophila ferruginea, Areca,

* See Description by the Author, As. Res. Bengal, Vol. xix.

† Since described from these specimens as *Calamaria monticola*, and *Dipsas monticola*. Vide Proc. Zool. Soc. March 12th 1839, and Cal. Journ. Nat. Hist. Vol. i. pp. 80-85.

‡ As. Res. Vol. xix. p. 336.

Calami, Fici., Pentaptera, Laurineæ, Myristiceæ continue. Kaulfussia assamica, is common along the lower base of the hills.

Feb. 23*rd.*—Started at 7, and after a march of five hours, reached the halting place on the Kamtee-chick, some distance above the place at which we descended to its bed. Distance 12 miles, direction S. S. E.; crossed one hill of considerable elevation, certainly 1000 feet above the halting place, which we find by the temperature of boiling water to be 1413 feet above the sea. The tops of these hills continue comparatively open, and have a very pretty appearance. The trees, however, have not assumed a northern character; their trunks are covered with epiptytes. The Kamtee-chick is a small stream fordable at the rapids, the extreme banks are not more than 30 or 40 yards. No peculiarity of vegetation as yet occurs; the fruit of a Quercus continues common, as well as that of Castanea ferox. I met with that of a Magnolia; Tree ferns, Calami, Musa, Areca, and the usual sub-tropical trees continue; Acanthaceæ are most common, Gordonea plentiful on the open places on the hills, Sauraufa two species, Byttneria, etc. etc. Altogether, I am disappointed in the vegetation, which, although rich, is not varied. Wallichia continues common. A Begonia with pointed leaves, and a Smilacineous plant are the most interesting, and a large Quercoid Polypodium, the laceneæ of which are deciduous; and these I found in abundance on the Mishmee hills, although I did not succeed in getting an entire frond.

Feb. 24*th.*—Marched about ten miles all the way up the bed of the Kamtee-chick, now a complete mountain stream, the general direction being S. S. E. Traversed in places heavy jungle, but for the most part we ascended the bed of the river. The only very interesting plant was Podostemon, apparently Griffithianum, which covers the rocks on the bed of the river. The usual plants continue, viz. Scitamineæ, Phrynium capitatum, Tradescantia, Pæderia and Isophylla, Pothos 2 or 3 species, Ixora 2, Leea, which occasionally becomes arborescent. Cissus 3 or 4, Panax ditto, Pierardia sapida, Elæocarpus, Smilax, Areca, Calami 2 or 3, Asplenium nidus, Fici several, Pentaptera, Cupuliferæ, the latter rare; Bauheniæ 2, Acanthaceæ, one of which attains the size of a large shrub, Guttiferæ 2, Phlebochiton, Rottlera, Millingtonia simplicifolia, Inga, Wallichia, Pentaptera, Malvacea, and Acanthacea convallariæ flore. I observed Pandanus to be common, (one Sterculia was yesterday observed). Equisetæ 2, the larger being the plant of the plains. Erythrina,

Lagerstræmia grandiflora. Chondospermum, Polypodium, Acrostichoides ferrugineum, and the fruit of Cedrela Toona, Megala. Choranthus was not seen.

Feb. 25th.—Proceeded about 100 yards up the Kamchick, then crossed the Tukkaka, and commenced the ascent of a high hill, certainly 1000 feet above the elevation of our last halting place on the Kamchick: the lower portion is covered with tree jungle, the upper portion of the mountain is open, covered with a tall Saccharum and an Andropogon, among which are mixed several Compositæ, and an Ajuga. Among the grass, occur trees scattered here and there, chiefly of a Gordonia. From the summit we had a pretty view of the Kamchick valley, closed in to the S. W. by a high and distant wall, being part of the Patkaye range. All the hills have the same features, but it is odd that their highest points are thickly clothed with tree jungle. Observed Kydia, Alstonia, ***Eurya***, Triumfetta, Celtis, Engelhardtia, Rhus, Rottlera, Loranthus, Callicarpe and Dicksonia all at a high elevation, but this latter is scarce. No pines visible. ***Dhak***, Fici, Musa farinacea, Bambusæ continue. Compositæ are common on the clearings. A Mimosa occurs on the summit, and Andrachne, 3-foliata. Thence we descended for a short distance, and halted at the foot of the Patkaye near the stream.

Direction S. S. E. Distance four miles.

Elevation 3026 feet. Temperature 66°. Boiling point, $206\frac{1}{2}$°.

All the trees have a stunted appearance.

Feb. 26th.—Halted.

Feb. 27th.—To-day ascended a hill to the W. of our camp, certainly 500 feet above it; its features are the same, Porana alata. Bignonia, a Leguminous tree, a ditto Mimosa. Panax, Lobelia zeylanica, Artemisia, Cordia. Panicum curvatum, Anthistina arundinacea.

Panicum *plicatoides*, Smithea, Hypericum of the plains, and Potentilla, Sida, and Plantago all plain plants, are found at the summit. To the S. W. of our camp are the remains of a stockade, which was destroyed by fire, it is said, last year. The only interesting plants gathered were a Cyrtandracea, Æschynanthus confertus mihi, a Dendrobium, and a fine Hedychium, beautifully scented, occurring as an epiphyte. Of Ficus several species are common. On the large mountain to the N. E., either birch or larches are visible, their elevation being probably 1000 feet above that of our camp.

The party halted until the 3rd March; I had one day's capital fishing in the Kamtee-chick with a running line.

March 2nd.—A Havildar arrived, bearing a letter from Dr. Bayfield,* stating that he would be with the Major in two or three days.

March 3rd.—Capt. Hannay and I started in advance; we crossed a low hill, then a torrent, after which we commenced a very steep ascent. This ascent, with one or two exceptions, continued the whole way to the top of the Patkaye range, which must be 1500 feet above our halting place. The features continued the same. The Patkaye are covered with dry tree jungle on the northern side. The place, whence the descent begins, is not well defined: at first winding through damp tree jungle. After a march of four hours we descended to a small stream, the Ramyoom, which forms the British boundary; this we followed for some distance through the wettest, rankest jungle I ever saw: thence we ascended a low hill, and the remainder of our march was for the most part a continued descent through dry open tree jungle, until we again descended into the damp zone. We reached water as night was setting in, and bivouaced in the bed of the stream.

The former vegetation continued until we reached the dry forest covering the upper parts of the Patkaye, and here the forms indicating elevation increased. Polygonatum, Ceratostemma, Bryum Sollyanum, and a Ternstrœmiacea occurred, Epiphytical orchideæ are common, but were almost all out of flower. Owing to the thickness of the jungle, and the height of the trees, we could not ascertain what the trees were; but from the absence of fruit, etc. on the ground, I am inclined to think that they are not Cupuliferæ. *Betee bans,* (of the natives) a kind of bamboo, perhaps the same as the genus Schizostachyum, N. ab. E. is common all over the summit, and descends to a considerable distance, especially on the southern side. On this side the prevalence of interesting forms was much more evident. Along the Kamyoom I gathered an Acer, an Arbutus, a Daphne. Polypodium arboreum ferrugineum was likewise here very common. Succulent Urticeæ, Acanthaceæ swarmed: a huge Calamus was likewise conspicuous. On this side there is plenty of the bamboo called *Deo bans,* articulis spinarum verticillis armatis, habitu B. bacciferæ. Among the trees on the descent, Magnoliaceæ occur; the petals of one I picked up were light yellow, tinged with brown in the centre. A species of Viola occurred low down. I believe it is V. serpens. On both sides, but especially the south Ceratostemma,

* Dr. Bayfield was deputed by the Resident at Ava to meet the party from Assam on the Burmese Frontier.

variegatum occurs; this is common still lower down the Kamyoom. The trees along this portion of the boundary nullah, are covered with masses of pendulous Neckera and Hypna. On the summit I observed two species of Panax, a fruitescent or arbusculous Composita, Asplenum nidus, Laurineæ, etc.

The direction of the day's journey was about S. S. E. The distance 15 miles.

March 4th.—We reached almost immediately the real Kamyoom, down which our route laid; we halted in its bed at 3, after a march most fatiguing from crossing and recrossing the stream, of about ten miles: general direction E. S. E. The features of this torrent are precisely the same as those of the Kamteechick, but Sedgewickia is common. I gathered a Stauntonia, Ceratostemma variegatum, and some fine ferns, and two or three Begoniaceæ, Magnoliaceæ three species occur, among which is Liriodendron; Cupiliferæ are common, especially Quercus cupulis lamellatis, nuce depressa; a Viburnum likewise occurred. The stream is small; the banks in many places precipitous. In one place great portion of the base of a hill had been laid waste by a torrent coming apparently from the naked rocks; trees and soil were strewed in every direction. Clay-slate is common.

I should have mentioned that Dicksonia occurs at 4000 feet, as well as (Camellia) *Bunfullup*, after that the former ceases. The two Saurauja of Suddiya continue up to 4000 feet of elevation; on the first ascent I observed a large Thistle, but out of flower. No cultivation was passed after surmounting the first ascent; we passed the remains of a stockade on the 4th, in which some Singphos had on a previous inroad stockaded themselves. The hills are generally covered with tree jungle, except occasionally on the north side where they have probably at some early period, been cleared for cultivation. To this may be added the curious appearance of the trees indicating having been lopped.

Equisetum continues in the bed of the river. Nothing like a pine was observed.

March 5th.—Proceeded in an E. S. E. direction towards Kamyoom for a distance of four miles, where we met Dr. Bayfield. As we found from him that it was impossible to go on, as there were no rice coolies, etc. to be obtained, we returned to our halting place; where I remained chiefly from supposing that the Meewoon will start less objections when he sees that I am in his territory without coolies, etc.

Fished in the afternoon. The Bookhar, or large Barbel already mentioned, still continues; but there is another species still more common, of a longer form, ventral fins reddish, mouth small, nose gibbous rough;* it takes a fly greedily, and is perhaps a more game fish than the other. All the birds inhabiting the water-courses of the north side of the Patkye continue. Barking Deer are heard occasionally.

Gathered one fine Bleteoidia Orchidea, racemis erectis oblongis, sepalis petalisque fusco-luteis, arcte reflexis, labello albido, odore forti mellis. Engelhardtia occurs here, Pentaptera, Wallichia, Calamus, Saccharum, etc.

March 7th.—To-day the Meewoon arrived, accompanied by perhaps 200 people chiefly armed with spears; he was preceded by two gilt chattas. He made no objections to my remaining, and really appeared very good-natured. The first thing he did, however, was to seize a shillalah, and thwack most heartily some of his coolies who remained to see our conference. He did not stay ten minutes.

March 8th.—To-day I examined superficially the ovary and young fruit of Ceratostemma variegatum, Roxb. The placenta which is very green, is 5-rayed. The substance of the walls of the ovary which is thick and white, projects towards the axis not only between the lobes, but also opposite to each; so that the fruit is really 10-celled, but 5 of the cells are spurious. The production opposite the placentæ necessarily divides the ovula of one placenta into two parcels, and these are they that have no adhesion with the axis. At present I can say nothing about the relative site of the lobes of the placentæ, otherwise there is nothing remarkable, beyond the production of the ovary opposite the lobes of the placentæ.

March 12th.—Yesterday evening Bayfield returned alone, leaving Hannay on the Patkaye, unable to come on or retreat, owing to his having no coolies. It was decided, that there was no other step left me to follow than going on to Ava, and I thus am enabled to obey the letter of Government, relative to my going to Ava, which reached me on the 10th by the Havildar. The Meewoon can give me no assistance towards returning, although he will spare me a few men to carry me on to Mogam. For the last three days I have been indisposed. Altitude 2138 by the Therm. Temp. 208°, at which water boils.

* This is one of the Mountain Barbels, *Oreinus*, probably *O. guttatus*, As. Res. vol. xix. p. 273.

March 13*th.*—Left and proceeded down the Kamyoom, or properly Kam-mai-roan, according to Bayfield, in an E. S. E. direction for about seven miles, when we reached the previous halting place of Dr. Bayfield. We passed before arriving at this a small Putar on which were some remains of old habitations; on it limes abound, and these are a sure test of inhabitation at some previous period.

The vegetation continues precisely the same as that of the Namtucheek, even to Podostemon Griffithianum, which I to-day observed for the first time.

March 14*th.*—Proceeded on, still keeping for the chief part of our march along the Kammiroan. We left this very soon, and crossed some low hills on which the jungles presented the same features. We left the village Kammiroan to our right. We did not see it, but I believe it consists of only two houses. Passed through one khet, the first cultivated ground we saw after leaving that on the Kamchick; then we came on to a few more Putars, in which limes continue abundant. On these I find no less than three species of Rubus; in those parts on which rice has been cultivated a pretty fringed Hypericum likewise occurs, and these are the most interesting plants that have presented themselves. Our course improved much yesterday; it extended E. by S., and was rather less than seven miles. Halted at Kha-thung-kyoun, where the Meewoon had halted, and where the Dupha Gam had remained some time previous. The same vegetation occurs, Engelhardtia, Gleichenia *major* longe scandens, Equisetum both species, Euphorbiacea nereifolia, Dicksonia rare, Scleria vaginis alatis, Plantago media, Zizania ciliaris, Melastoma malabathrica, Lycium arenarum, Duchesnia indica, Mazus rugosus, the Suddiya Viburnum, Millingtonia pinnata, Pentaptera, Erythrina; an arboreous Eugenia fol. magnis, abovatis, is however new, and Polypodium Wallichianum which occurred to-day growing on clay-slate. But considering the elevation at which we still remain to be tolerably high, the products both of the vegetable and animal kingdom are comparatively uninteresting. There are more epiphytical Orchideæ on the south sides of these hills, than the north. Musci and Hepaticæ are common, but do not embrace a great amount of species. Machantia asamica is common. Another new tree I found is probably a Careya or Barringtonia; the young inflorescence is nearly globular, and clothed with imbricated scales. Sedgewickia has disappeared. No tea was seen. There is but little doubt that on hills, the ranges of which rise gradually, the acclimatization of low plants may take place to such a degree, that such plants may be found at high elevations; can they however so far become acclimated, as to preponderate? I expected of course to find the same plants on both sides of the hills, but I did not expect to find Rottleræ, Fici, tree-ferns, etc., at an elevation of 4000 feet and upwards.

The fish of the streams continue the same, as well as the birds. The Ouzel, white and black, long-tailed Jay, white-headed Redstart, red-rumped ditto, all continue. Water Wagtails were seen to-day. This bird is uncommon in hill water-courses; one snipe was seen yesterday. Ooloocks (Hylobates agilis), continue as in Assam. With regard to fish, both species of Barbel occur*; the most killing bait for the large one, or Bookhar of the Assamese, is the green fucus, which is common, adhering to all the stones in these hill-streams: it is difficult to fix it on the hook. The line should be a running one, and not leaded, and the bait may be thrown as a fly. To it the largest fish rise most greedily; plenty of time must be allowed them to swallow before one strikes, otherwise no fish will be caught. All the same Palms continue except Calami, Areca, and Wallichiana.

Balsamineæ are uncommon. There is one however, although rare, probably the same as the bright crimson-flowered one of the Meerep Panee. Urticeæ have diminished; the Suddiya Viola occurred yesterday, the Asplenium, fronde lanceolat. continues common.

March 14th.—Halted. Water boiled 209°. Temp. 59 and 60°. Elevation 1622 feet.

March 15th.—Left the Meewoon about 8, and proceeded about 100 yards up the Khathing. Thence we struck off, and commenced the ascent, which continued without intermission for some hours, the whole way lying through heavy tree jungle. Ascent in some places very steep. On reaching the summit, or nearly so, the jungle became more open, and the route continued along the ridge. We then descended for 50 feet, and halted on an open grassy spot where we ascertained the altitude to be 5516 feet. Boiling point 202°. Temperature of the air 63°. The vegetation increased in interest; I noticed near the Khathing, Buddlea neemda, Pladera Justicioidea, which continues however all along even to 5000 feet. Thunbergia coccinea, Chondrospermum, Dicksonia; near and on the summit Magnoliæ and two or three Cupuliferæ, Daphne Strutheoloides, nobis,

* A Barbel, and an Oreinus, or Mountain Barbel.

Gymnostomum involutum, Berberis pinnata, the same as the Khasiya one, but scarce. Laurinea arborea, Bambusa monogynia, Rubus moluccanus: Frutex Ruscordeus, Loranthus, Anthistiria arundinacea, Melastoma, Cyathea, Compositæ, Conyzoideæ two or three, Correas one, Hedychium, Eurya, Gleichenia, Hermannia, Lycopodium ceranium, Hoya teretifolia, Acanthaceæ two or three, Bucklandia.

We thence descended, and after a longish march reached the Natkaw Kyown, and finally halted on the Khusse Kyown. During this portion I gathered some very interesting plants, a new Ceratostemma, Adamia, two or three Orchideæ, a beautiful large flowered Cyrtandracea, the same Daphne, an Umbellifera. Vaccineaceæ, four species of Begoniæ, a Viburnum. Crawfurdia and Polypodium Wallichianum, which roofed in our shed; Musci increased as well as Succulent Urticeæ in shady places. Smilacinæ were common, especially one at elevations of from 3 to 5000 feet inflorescentia cernua. The features are the same, the drier woods crowning the ridges. On the trees of these, Orchideæ and Filices are common, as well as in low parts in which Acanthaceæ abound. I saw no *Betee-bhans* nor Deo-bhans, (peculiar bamboos). Of the above, Ceratostemma, Daphane, Smilacinæ, Cyathea, some of the Begoniæ, the large flowered Cyrtandraceæ, Umbelliferæ are sure indications of considerable elevation. The course was nearly south. Distance about 13 miles. Thermometer in boiling water 206.° Temperature of the air 50½°. Halting place, 3516.

March 16th.—Started before breakfast, and reached the Khusee Kyoung without any material descent. Thence we continued descending on the whole considerably until we reached Namthuga, at 10 A.M. Thence the descent increased. Halted on Kullack Boom. General direction S.; distance 13 miles. Noticed Areca up to 3800 feet, as well as Cheilosandra obovata, Bletea melleodora, and Begonia palmata as high as 3000 feet.

At Namthuga a Sambucus, probably S. Ebulus, a Mimosa, Pothos decursiva, Hedychium, Urtica urens, Gleichenia major, Tradescanthia panicularis. Between this and Kullack Boom Acanthaceæ are the most common; Pæderia triphylla appears near the Boom, together with Arum viviparum. Black Pheasants were likewise heard on our route. On the open halting place, grasses preponderate. Anthestiria arundinacea, arbusculous Gordonia, and Saurauja, a Laurinea, Styrax, etc. Æsculus asamicus is common, and profusely in flower, and Pteris as on Thuma-thaya; Musa glauca made its appearance. From this open space an extensive view is obtained of Hookhoom valley, bounding which occurs a range of hills stretching E. S. E. and W. N. W. These in the centre present a gap in which a river is seen running S. The view to the E. is impeded by the trees on that face of the hill. The valley is as usual one mass of jungle, with here and there clear patches occurring, especially to the W. of S., but whether from cultivation or not, I am unable to say. The Namlunai river is visible; winding excessively, especially to the E. S. E., it appears a considerable stream with much sand: it passes out towards the gap above alluded to, winding round the corner of the hills.

During the 16th, my attention was particularly directed towards Tea, which was said positively to exist. I obtained some of the bitter sort, or *Bunfullup*, but the plant which was pointed out to me as tea certainly was not, although resembling it a good deal. There is no reason for supposing, that it exists on these hills, and if *tea* is brought hence, it is I should think a spurious preparation. The soil is in many places yellow, in many brick-dust coloured. If the Tea existed in abundance, I must have seen it.

The hills which confine the valley, at least those which are obvious outliers of the Patkaye range, are characterised by conical peaks, and there is a bluff rock of good elevation to the W. S. W. ½ S.

March 17th.—Boiled water at 206°. Fahr. Thermometer in the air 61°. Elevation 3270. Commenced the descent, which continued without interruption to the Loon-karankha, where we breakfasted. The bed of this, which is a mere mountain torrent, is of sandstone. Here Ceratostemma variegatum is very common, and has larger, broader and more obovate leaves, than before observed; Polypodium Wallichianum, a Begonia and Orchideæ are common on its boulders. Continued our course at first up a considerable ascent, thence it was nearly an uniform descent. Crossed the Namtuwa, along which our course lay for a short time. The latter part was through low wet jungle, along small water-courses, till we reached the Panglai Kha, along which we continued for some time. Reached our halting place on the Namtuseek about 2 P.M. General direction E. S. E.; distance about ten miles. Noticed Podostemon Griffithianum, on rocks on the Namtuwa. My collector gathered one Daphne, Acanthus Solanacea occurred very abundantly, corinfundib. lab super postico, infer reflexo, laciniis bifidis. Low down observed the usual Dipterocarpus, Uncaria and Kaulfussia asamica, Dracæna. Mesua ferrea occurred during the first part of the march. Noticed the

From a Sketch made on the spot by W Griffith.

M & N Hanhart Lith Printer

VALLEY OF HOOKHOOM

tracks of a Rhinoceros. At 5 P.M. water boiled at 210°. Temperature 69°. Elevation 1099 feet.

The most interesting plants were an Arum, an undescribed Ceratostemma, and a Celastrinea.

The collection formed between this place and Suddiya now amount to about 500 species. The vegetation of the lower portions is the same, or nearly so, on either side of the hills; but I did not observe near this the Polypodium ferrugineum arboreum, although there is a small arborescent species of this genus. On either side, the lower ranges are clothed with heavy wet tree jungle, the undershrubs consisting of Acanthaceæ, Rubiaceæ, Filices, Aroideæ, and Urticeæ; Kaulfussia does not ascend so high on this side. Acanthacea solanacea appears peculiar to this side, although there is a species of the genus on the Kammiroan.

The plants indicating the greatest elevation are Acer, Ceratostemma miniatum, and angulatum, Vacciniaceæ; Daphne, particularly the Patkaye one, and D. struthioloides, most of the Smilacineæ, Berberis, etc. etc. Bucklandia Crawfurdii, Begoniæ, some Viburnia, Cyathea, etc. of Ceratostemma (Gay Lussacium?) several, perhaps not less than seven species occur; all have the same habit, and the same depot of nourishment in the thick portion near the *collet*. No Coniferæ exist, although the elevation is more than sufficient to determine their appearance. In Orchideæ the flora is certainly very rich, but few species are in flower.

[*Memo*. To compare these elevational plants with those from the Mishmee hills, on which, speaking from memory, they are more abundant.]

March 18th.—Left at half-past 6, and arrived (after halting about one hour and a half) at 3 P.M. The road was very circuitous, for the first part E. by S., subsequently for some time N. N. E., and even N. E.; the general direction is perhaps E.; the distance certainly 18 miles. The greater part of the route lay through heavy but dryish tree jungle; but during the latter half, and especially towards Nempean, Putars or cultivated fields increased in number, and extent. We crossed one stream only. The soil is yellow and deep, occasionally inclining to brick-red; it is apparently much the same as that of Muttack. The low spots were uncommon. We saw only two paths diverging from ours; one of these led to Bone, which is about two miles from our path, in a south direction, and at no great distance from the Namtuseek.

The features of the country and its productions are much the same as those of Upper Assam, indeed strikingly so. During the earlier part of our march we observed a fine Shorea in abundance; it had a noble straight stem, but the leaves were too small for Saul. The only new plants I found were Styrax floribus odoris, ligno albo close grained, arbor mediocris a Bæobotrys, two Goodyeræ, a Laurinea, Sparganium! Tabernæmontana fructibus magnis, edulibus, fol. obovatis, and a species of Shorea.

I noticed the following plants in the following order from Namtuseek: Dicksonia, Areca, Calamus, Bambusa, spiculis pubescentibus, deformatis, a species of Phrynium, Pladera justicioides, Chrysobaphus Roxburghii, Phyllanthus, Embilica, a species of Wendlandia common in places that appeared to have been formerly cleared; Gnetum lepidotum, Celastrinea *foliis Leguminosarum*, Bombax (inerme) Saccharum Megala, Imperata cylindica, Anthistiria arundinacea, Ingæ sp., Saurajæ sp. Entada, Gleichenia, Hermannia, Blechnum orientale, Bæobotrys, Meniscium 3-phyllum, Sonerila, Acanthus leucostachys, Diplazium of Kujoo, Podomolee, Saccharum foliis apice spiraliter tortis, Osbeckia, Rottlera, Lygodium, Rubus moluccanus, Centotheca, Zizania ciliaris, Viola asamica, Potamogeton nutans, foliis linearibus, Limnophila, Pontederia dilatata, Lobelia Zeylanica, Hypericum venustum. Panax foliis supra decompositis spinosis, Callicarpæ 2 spec, Duchesnea indica, Combretum, Melica latifolia, Magus rugosus, Vandellia peduncularis, Villarsia pumila, Artocarpus integrifolius, Piper, Lagerstræmia grandiflora, Roxb. Dillenia speciosa, Spathodea. All these exist in Assam.

The birds are the same. As for instance, common Maina, Doves, the Picus of low swampy places, and the *Lark* of the plains of Assam. Squirrel, ventre ferrugineo. Black Pheasant, *Phasianus leucomelanus*, Laurineæ, Acanthaceæ, Rubiaceæ and Filices, are common in the jungles.

The Putars are clothed with the same grasses as in Assam. Imperata cylindrica, Anthistiria arundinacea, Megala in low places with Alpinea Allughas, in those lately under cultivation, the Campanula of the B. pooter occurs, together with Hypericum, Gnaphalium, Poa and Carex.

From the frequent occurrence of these Putars, I should say that the capabilities of the country, at least the latter half of our march, improves as far as regards *halee* cultivation.

Throughout the march nothing occurred to shew that this part of the valley is inhabited. We passed, however, an old and extensive burying ground of the Singphos. Of the Putars only small portions were cultivated, and the crops did not appear to be very good.

Nempean, which is a stockaded village, is about a quarter of a mile from the encampment of the Mewoon, and about S. E., and within 200 yards to the N. N. E. is a similar stockaded village called Tubone. Both these villages are on the right bank of the Namturoon, which is a large stream, as big nearly as the Noa Dihing at Beesa. B. measured it, and finds its extreme bed to be 270 yards broad. The volume of water is considerable, the rapids are moderate; it is navigable for largish canoes. On this bank, *i. e.* right, there is an extensive plain running nearly N. and S.; no part of it seems to be cultivated. The scenery is precisely the same as that of Upper Assam, viz. open, flat, intersected by belts of jungle. With the exception of the W. and the points between this and south, hills are visible, some of considerable height. To the S. E. there is a fine peak, which reminds one much of the Mishmee peak, so remarkable at Suddiya. It is in this direction that the hills are highest.

No tea is reported to exist here. B. met with it on his road hither, and shewed me the specimen; there is no difference between this and the Assam specimens in appearance, neither are the leaves at all smaller. As a new route has been cut out I cannot visit it, but shall wait until I arrive at Meinkhoom.

The Chykwar Mulberry occurs, and to a larger size than I have seen it in Assam. The Singphos, however, as they have no silkworms, do not make use of it; I have seen some little cultivation on the Tooroon belonging to Bon: Kanee or Opium formed portion of it.

Thermometer in shade at 2 P.M. 85°.

March 21*st*.—7 A.M. Thermometer 60°. Yesterday at 2 P.M. 86°! under a decently covered shed.

Boiled water at 209½ Fahr. Thermometer 70°, which gives 1399 feet of elevation.

Started at 9, and arrived at Kidding on the Saxsai, a small stream which *now* falls into the Tooroon. Distance about four miles and a half from Nempean: general direction about S. S. E. The road runs along the Tooroon S., and a little to the W. of S.; it then diverges up the Saxsai, which runs nearly W. and E. Near the mouth of the Saxsai, and about 400 yards above, there is another small stream, the Jinnip Kha. Both these are on the left bank of the river. On the opposite side, and about a quarter of a mile, is a village, which like all the rest is stockaded. Kidding is larger than either Tubone or Nempean; it is on the left bank of the Saxsai. Rapids are common in the Tooroon, but are not of any severity.

The vegetation remains in a remarkable degree similar to that of Assam. The Lohit Campanula is very common in the stony beds of either river.

Brahminy Ducks seen at Nempean, and the ravenous Geese of Kamroop Putar. Fished in the Tooroon, and had excellent sport, killing in the afternoon twenty fishes, average weight half pound; some weighing nearly two pounds. Three species occurred, and all were taken with flies; the smallest are a good deal like the *Boal* of Assam. The large-mouthed, trout-like Cyprinida* occurs, and to a larger size than in the Noa Dihing. The third is the *Chikrum* of the Singphos; it is a thick, very powerful fish, a good deal resembling the Roach: one of two pounds, measures about a foot in length. Outline ovate lanceolate, head small, mouth with four filaments; eyes very large, fins reddish, first ray of the dorsal large spinous. It affects deep water, particularly at the edges of the streams running into such places†. It takes a fly greedily even in quite still water; but as it has a small mouth, the smaller the flies the better. Black hackle is better for it than small grey midges. On being hooked it rushes off with violence, frequently leaping out of the water. It is a much more game fish than the Bookhar: the largest I took with flies; with worms I took only one small one. With regard to the Bookhar, it is strange if it is not found in the streams running through this valley, as in the Kammaroan it occurs in abundance.

Black and white Kingfisher, *Alcedo rudis*, Snippets, Curlews of the B. pooter, with chesnutish back occur in the valley, together with Toucans: and Ravens occur as in Assam.

At the village of Kidding there are silkworms fed.

March 22*nd*.—Started at 6 P.M., reached Shelling khet on the Prong Prongkha in about two hours; it is distant about seven miles. The village is now deserted. The nullah is small, with a very slow stream; direction from Kidding nearly S. E. It was at this place that Bayfield got his specimen of tea, but on enquiry we found

* *Opsarius gracilus*, As. Res. vol. xix. p. 419.

† A species of Barbel; probably *B. deliciosus*, As. Res xix. p. 352.

that it was brought from some distance; it is said to grow on a low range of hills. We started after breakfast, and reached Culleyang, on the same nullah, about 12 o'clock. Total distance thirteen miles; direction S. S. E. Path very winding. The country traversed is much less open than that of Nempean, but few Putars occurred; and the whole tract is covered either with tree or Megala jungle. Water boiled at Shelling khet at 209½ Fahr. Temp. of the air 68½°. Elevation 1340 feet. Noticed but very little clearing for cultivation, neither did the Putars appear to have been lately under cultivation.

Culleyang is a village containing about eight houses; it is not stockaded, and has the usual slovenly appearance of Singpho villages. The natives keep silkworms, which they feed on the Chykwar or Assam morus, which they cultivate. I noticed likewise Kanee, or Opium, and Urtica nivea, which they use for nets; Acanthaceæ, Indigofera, and Peach trees.

Close to the village are the burying places of two Singphos. These have the usual structure of the cemeteries of the tribe, the graves being covered by a high conical thatched roof. I find from Bayfield, that they first dry their dead, preserving them in odd shaped coffins, until the drying process is completed. They then burn the body, afterwards collecting the ashes, which are finally deposited in the mounds over which the conical sheds are erected. Between the village and the graves I saw one of these coffins which, if it contained a full-grown man, must have admitted the remains in a mutilated shape; and close to this were the bones of a corpse lately burnt.

To-day I shot the beautiful yellow and black crested Bird we first saw on the Cossiya hills, *Parus Sultaneus*, and two handsome Birds, *Orioles*, or *Pastor Traillii*, quite new to me, blackish and bright crimson, probably allied to the Shrikes.

Of fishes, Cyprinus fálcata, or *Nepoora* of the Assamese, together with the Sentooree* of the Assamese, both occur. Of plants, we noticed Stauntonia, Vitis, Cissampelos, Butomus pygmæus, Dicksonia, Hedychia 2, Croton Malvæfolium of Suddiya, Xanthium indicum; Cheilosandra ferruginea, Pothos scandens decursiva, etc., Liriodendrum, Kydia. Ficus elastica? Asplenium nidus, Conyza graveolens, south of the old clearings. Lemna, Valisneria, Azolla, Æsculus asamicus in abundance. Limes in profusion near Culleyang;

* Since described as *Cyprinus semiplotus*, As. Res. vol. xix. p. 346.

Pæderia fætida and the other species, Naravelia, Hiræa, Phrynium dichotomum, Gærtnera, and Carallia lucida. New plants, Ophioglossum, Carex, Gnetum sp. nov. Choripetalum, and two *incerta.* Noticed Pladera justicioides during the first part of the march, and the small Squirrel of Kujoodoo.

Six A.M. Temperature 58½. Water boiled at 210° Fahr. 8 P.M. Temperature of the air 66. Altitude 1064 feet.

March 23rd.—Started at 6 A.M. and reached Lamoom about 8, where we breakfasted. Reached Tsilone, the Dupha's village, at noon. General direction S. W. Distance about ten miles. Lamoom is a small *un*stockaded village on the Moneekha. Tsilone is a moderate sized Singpho village on the right bank of the Nam Tunail. The river is of considerable size, with scarcely any rapids: stream slow. The village is situated on a rather high bank.

The country continues the same, perhaps a little more open, at least Putars are of frequent occurrence, although they are all narrow. Observed Cryptolepis, Celastrus *leguminoideus* Cuscuta Uncaria racemis pendulis. Of birds the smaller Maina, common house Sparrow, blue Jay, and the larger grey Tern occur. We halted on a sandbank about one mile and a half higher up to the south of Tsilone. New plants, the Campanula of Chykwar, ditto Lysimachia, Dopatrium, Jasminum, Rhamnea, Pothos, Lasia, Riccia, etc.

March 24th.—Thermometer 58°. Boiling point 210. Altitude 1064 feet. After a long and hot march of seven hours we reached Meinkhoon; general direction — distance 17 miles. During the first two hours we marched along the bed and banks of the Nam Tenai, subsequently over grassy plains intersected by belts of jungle. Country much more open than that we saw yesterday. To the W. low ranges of hills, about one-third of a mile distant, occurred throughout the day. We passed two or three small nullahs, in one of which I observed lumps of lignite.

The Nam Tenai continued a large river, extreme breadth varying from 250 to 350 yards. We crossed at once, about half a mile from our encampment, deepest part of the ford four feet; its banks are either thickly wooded or covered with Kagara jungle. The day's march was very uninteresting. I observed a few Mango trees, a Mucuna, Laurineæ are common, as well as a Wendlandia in open grassy places. Sagittariæ sp. was the only novelty. Noticed the Hoopoe bird, *Upapa Capensis.*

From a Sketch made on the spot by W. Griffith.

M & N Hanhart Lith Printers

MEINKHOOM.

March 25*th*.—Meinkhoon is situated on a very small nullah, the Eedeekha. The village which is large and well stockaded, is divided into two by this nullah. The population of both cannot, including children, be less than 200. They belong to the Meerep tribe. The women wear the *putsoe* somewhat like those of Burma, which seems to me quite new in Singpho women ; and is not the fashion with those in Assam. To the S. W. there is a group of somewhat decayed Shan Pagodas, and a Poonghie house, around which are planted mango trees and a beautiful arboreous Bauhinia, B. rhododendriflora mihi, ovariis binis ! Around the village is an extensive plain, and to the S. E. one or two more Pagodas. This Bauhinia has flowers 1½ inches across, calyx spathaceus, petalis, sub-conformibus, obovatis, repandis læte purpureis, vexillo coccineo-purpureo, colore saturate venoso, carinæ petalis distantibus, odor Copaivæ ! Stam. 5 declinata, cum petalis, alternantia. Ovaria 2 ! anticum posticumque, longe stipetata, difformia superiore minore, aborticate, ambobus vexillo oppositis ! Stylus ruber pallide ; stigma capitatum. One B. variegata, W. Roxb. Fl. Indic. vol. ii. p. 319, quamvis auctor de ovario antico silet.

Two snakes were captured, approaching in shape to the green snake of the Coromandel Coast. Under surface throughout bright gamboge colour ; upper surface throughout, excepting about a span or less of the back of the neck, bright ochraceous brown. The space above alluded to is in one faintly, in the other strongly variegated with black and white. Irides, gamboge-coloured.

March 26*th*.—Visited the amber mines, which are situated on a range of low hills, perhaps 150 feet above the plain of Meinkhoon, from which they bear S. W. The distance of the pits now worked is about six miles, of which three are passed in traversing the plain, and three in the low hills which it is requisite to cross. These are thickly covered with tree jungle. The first pits, which are old, occur about one mile within the hills. Those now worked occupy the brow of a low hill, and on this spot they are very numerous ; the pits are square, about four feet in diameter, and of very variable depth ; steps, or rather holes, are cut in two of the faces of the square by which the workmen ascend and descend. The instruments used are wooden-lipped with iron crowbars, by which the soil is displaced ; this answers but very imperfectly for a pickaxe : small wooden shovels, baskets for carrying up the soil, &c., buckets of bark to draw up the water, bamboos, the base of the rhizoma forming a hook for drawing up the baskets, and the Madras lever for drawing up heavy loads.

The soil throughout the upper portion, and indeed for a depth of 15 to 20 feet, is red and clayish, and appears to inclose but small pieces of lignite; the remainder consists of greyish slate clay increasing in density as the pits do in depth: in this occur strata of lignite very imperfectly formed, which gives the grey mineral a slaty fracture, and among this the amber is found.* The deepest pit was about 40 feet, and the workmen had then come to water. All the amber I saw, except a few pieces, occurred as very small irregular deposits, and in no great abundance. The searching occupies but little time, as they look only among the lignite, which is at once obvious. No precautions are taken to prevent accidents from the falling in of the sides of the pits, which are in many places very close to each other (within two feet): but the soil is very tenacious.

We could not obtain any fine specimens, indeed at first the workmen denied having any at all, and told Mr. B. that they had been working for six years without success. They appear to have no index to favourable spots, but having once found a good pit they of course dig as many as possible as near and close together as they can. The most numerous occur at the highest part of the hill now worked. The article is much prized for ornaments by the Chinese and Singphos, but is never of much value; five rupees being a good price for a first-rate pair of earrings. Meinkhoon is visited by parties of Chinese for the purpose of procuring this article. There are at present here a Lupai Sooba and a few men, from a place three or four days' journey beyond the Irrawaddi, waiting for amber. These men are much like the Chinese, whose dress they almost wear: they squat like them, and wear their hair like them; shoes, stockings, pantaloons, jackets, tunic. They are armed chiefly with firelocks, in the use of which at 50 yards two of the men were expert enough. They talk the Singpho language.

The vegetation of the plains, proceeding to the mines, is unchanged. Noticed Apluda, a Phyllanthus, Cacalia, Poa, etc. That of the hills is the same as that of the low ranges before traversed. The only new plants were a Celtis? a Krameria (the Celtis is the Boolla

* This would seem to be Coal formation, in which amber is frequently found. It occurs, for instance, in the spurious coal of Kurribori, E. of Rungpore.

of Upper Assam,) Ventilago, Quercus or Castanea, Compositæ, etc. In the damp places a largish Loxotis, two or three Begoniæ, ditto Urticeæ occur. I noticed among and around the pits a species of Bambusa, Celtis, Kydia calycina, Clerodendrum infortunatum, Calamus, Areca, Dicksonia, Ficus, Pentaptera, and Rottlera. Pladera has ceased to appear.

Last night a sort of alarm occurred, and in consequence, this evening, the head cooly gave his orders to his men in the following terms: "Watch to-night well." Nobody answering him, he continued, "Do you hear what I say?" Then addressed himself to them in the most obscene terms, which habit and uncivilized life seem to have adapted to common conversation amongst these people without any breach of modesty or decorum; and amongst the Assamese such expressions likewise form not an uncommon mode of familiar salutation.

March 27*th.*—Left about 7, and proceeded over the Meinkhoon plain in an easterly direction, in which the highest hills visible from the village lay. We continued east for some time, our course subsequently becoming more and more south. On reaching the Nempyokha, we proceeded up its bed for about two miles, the course occasionally becoming west. We reached Wollaboom at 12½. General direction S. E.; distance thirteen miles. The greater part of the country traversed consisted of low plains, splendidly adapted for *halee* cultivation. No villages were passed. Saw two paths, one leading to the N., one to the S. not far from Meinkhoon; of these the N. one leads to the hills, the S. to a Singpho village. And we passed burial places of some antiquity, and considerable extent. New plants; a Loranthus floribus viridibus, petalis 6 reflexis. Zizyphoidea, and an arborescent Bignonia foliis cordatis oppositis, integris, basi bi-glandulosis, paniculis racemiformibus, solitariis et axillaribus vel terminalibus et aggregatis. Marlea Sporobolus, Castanea edulis, Pteris dimediata, etc., occurred. Noticed the tracks of a Tiger, of Elks, and the Peewit or Curlew.

Woollaboom is rather a large village on the Nempyokha, which is here scarcely 40 yards broad; it is of no depth, and has not much stream. The villagers are Meereps, but seem to bear a small proportion to their Assamese slaves. It is not stockaded, but was so formerly. The Souba, like a Hero and a General, has erected a small stockade for himself near his house, out of which he might be with ease forced by a long spear, or a spear-head fastened to a bamboo.

He is an enemy of the Duphas, indeed almost all appear to be so. Whatever events the return of this Gam to Assam may cause, it appears obvious to me, that the feuds in Hookhoom will not cease but with his death. So much is he hated, that B. informs me that his destruction is meditated directly the Meewoon retires to Mogam.

Water boiled at 210° Fahr. Elevat. 1064 feet.

List of Plants observed in Hookhoom, which occur likewise in Assam.

Eclipta floribus albis,
Pogonatherum crinitum,
Verbena chamædrys ?
Phlebochiton extensum,
Ehretia arenarum,
Erythrinæ, sp.
Trematodon sabulosum,
Marchantia asamica,
Euphorbiacea nerifolia,
Adelia nereifolia, Roxb.
Spilanthus,
Convolvulus flore albo,
Mimosa sudiyensis-stipulis amplis foliaceis,
Vandellia pedunculata,
Bonnayæ sp. fol. spathulatis floribus saturate cæruleis,
Cordia of Suddiya,
Ricinus communis, (See Journal, p. 174.)
Buddlea Neemda,
Urtica gigas,
Plantago media,
Cotula, 2 species,
Coladium nympheæfolium,
Millingtonia pinnata,
Uricariæ sp.
Saccharum spontaneum,
Eleusine indica,
Cynoglossum canescens,
Æsculus asamicus,
Cynodon,
Dactylon.
Cardamine.
Sisymbrium.
Gærtnera.
Phrynium capitatum.
——— dichotomum.
Hiræa.
Naravalia.
Liriodendrum.
Pæderia fœtida, and another.
Azolla.
Lemna.
Conyza graveolens, on clearings.
Asplenium nidus.
Ficus elastica.
Kydia calycina.
Pothos scandens.
Croton malvæfolium.
Hedychium.
Hedychim, bracteis obtusis, apice reflexis, concavis.
Dicksonia.
Phlogacanthus, *major*.
Vitis.
Butomus pygmæus.
Cissampelos.
Stauntonia.
Apludæ sp.
Clerodendrum infortunatum.
Vandellia pedunculata.
Mangifera indica.

Ardisia fol. obovatis, umbellis nutanti-pendulis, on the hills.
Cheilosandra.
Loxotis major.
Bauhinia variegata.
Cacalia rosea.
Briedelia.
Marlea.
Pteris dimidiata.
Centotheca.
Castanea edulis.
Sporobolus.

CHAPTER V.

Continues the Journey from Hookhoom Valley, Lat. 26° 20′ N., 96° 40′ E. Long., towards Ava.

March 28*th.*—Started at 5½ A.M., and arrived at a halting place at 3½ P.M. General direction nearly south. Distance 22 miles. Throughout the first part we followed the Kampyet, on the left bank of which Wulloboom is situated. We thence diverged into jungle. The remainder of the time was occupied in crossing low hills, with here and there a small plain. We halted on a nullah, which discharges itself into the Mogam river.

In the Kampyet I saw abundance of Bookhar fish : these indeed actually swarm. The country throughout was uninteresting, although in the tree jungle clothing the small hills we crossed there are noble timber trees. I saw one of the finest Fici, I ever saw. The Botany of these hills was very interesting; for instance, a Conifera taxoidea occurred, a new Cyrtandracea, ditto Acanthaceæ 2, Begoniæ 2, Tankervillia speciosa, a species of Bletea, etc. etc.

I also observed Lindsæa, and Pteris in abundance. Hymenophyllum, Davallia atrata, Diplazium, Begonia Malabarica? Bambusa spiculis hispidis, Hypni sp. spinioenio prop. Dicranum glaucum, etc. etc. A fine Alpinia occurred near Wulloboom.

We observed no other signs of population than an old burial ground, near where you strike off into the hills.

March 29*th.*—Marched in a southerly direction from 5½ to 1½ P.M., inclusive of a halt of two hours nearly: distance fifteen miles. Country, etc. continue the same. Crossed same nullahs *en route*, before we reached the Mogam river at 11 A.M. Our course continued down it for 300 yards; we then crossed into the jungle, and traversed a low rising ground: subsequently we descended on the bed of the river. The jungle was for the most part dry.

Fish abound in the Mogam river; in one place I never saw such swarms of Bookhar, thousands must have been congregated. The river is of no great size, the extreme banks being at our halting place about 30 yards distant. No rapids occur here, and the stream is in general gentle.

Noticed the Shorea, which is the *Foung bein* of the Burmese. Some occurred of gigantic size. It is strange, but a considerable change has occurred in the Flora since we left Hookhoom. Thus, Jonesia and Peronema, Jack? or at least one of the involucrate Vitices occurred, as well as a large Byttneria? fructibus echinatissimis. A climbing species of Strychnos, a Diospyros, a Sapindacea, were the principal new plants. Dicksonia and Polypodium Wallichianum continue.

Slackia of Cuttackboom has white infundibuliform bilabiate flowers, tubo brevi, deorsum leniter curvato, lobo medio labii inferioris reliquis minore, lab. super. intus biplicato, plicis sursum convergentibus, stam. quinto valde rudimentario, antheris apice cohærentibus. The new Cyrthandracea of yesterday is suigeneris, Ramondiæ affinis. Of this there are three species, two of which I have not seen in flower. Calycis laciniæ lineari-subulatæ. Cor. rotata, subregularis Stam. 4, subsessilia connectivis amplis, quinto minimo dentiformi. Stylus declinatus, Stigma subsimplex, Capsula (per junior) siliquosa. Herbæ vel suffrutices, hispidæ, habitu peculiari. Folia alterna! vel summa sparsa vel ob approximationem sub-opposita: intervenia areolata, areolis piliferis, pilis basi bulbosis. Inflorescentia axillaris, cymosa, dichotoma.

The Tankervellia (or Pharus?) has sepala pet. conformia extus alba, intus fusco-brunnea, labellum cucullatum, breve, calcaratum; intus inconspicue bilamellatum; extus albidum margines versus exceptis qua uti intus fusco-sanguineum, fauce saturatiore. Columnæ albæ clavale sursum subulata. Anthera fere immersa, Rostellum integrum ut in omnibus glandula orbotis Pollinia 8. 5 A.M.—Temperature 62.210.

March 30*th*.—Marched for about thirteen miles along the bed of the river, and a more uninteresting march I never had. We breakfasted about four miles from our halting place at the granary of the Meewoon. The bed of the river continues wider, and more sandy: the water being in general shallow. The only acquisitions met with to-day are Grislea, an arborescent Capparidea, and a pretty Grewia. Of birds, I noticed the Avocet, or curved-billed Plover, the grey Kingfisher, the green Pigeon, and the snake-bird, Plutus Levalliantia. The plants occupying the banks and the bed of the river are the same, viz. Ehretia, Saccharum spontaneum, spirale; *Kagara*, Erythrina, Ficus, Gnaphalia, Podomolee, Bombax. Of fish, Cyprinus falcata, and *Nepoora mas*, occur in this river.

Temperature at $5\frac{1}{4}$ A.M. 61. Water boils at 210.

March 31*st*.—Continued our march down the Mogaung river, passing through a most uninteresting, inhospitable-looking tract. General direction S. E., distance fourteen miles. The river is not much enlarged: it is still shallow, and much spread out, and impeded by fallen trees and stumps; it is navigable for small boats up to the Mywoon's granary. Noticed Æsculus in flower. Of birds, saw the grey and black-bellied Tern.

The Botanical novelties are an arborescent Salix, a ditto Cordia floribus suave odoratis, Phyllanthus Embelica.

Saw some cultivation on low hills to the S. E. and E. inhabited by Kukheens. 1*st April*. Temperature 63. Water $210\frac{1}{4}$ altitude.

April 1*st*.—Started at $5\frac{1}{4}$. Leaving almost directly the Mogaung river we traversed extensive open plains, halting for breakfast on the Wampama Kioung. This we crossed, continuing through open plains until we came to patches of jungle consisting of trees, and quite dry. We subsequently traversed more open plains until we reached the Mogaung river, on the opposite (right) bank of which Camein is situated. These plains were in many places quite free from trees; they are, except towards the south, quite surrounded with low hills, the highest of which are to the E., and among these, Shewe Down Gyee, from which the Nam Tenai rises, is pre-eminent, looking as if it were 3000 feet high, and upwards. The hills although generally wooded are in many places quite naked; and as the natives say, this is not owing to previous cultivations, I suppose that they are spots naturally occupied entirely by Gramineæ. The plains slope towards the hills on either side. They are covered with Gramineæ; among which Imperata, occasionally Podomolee and Saccharum, Anthistiria arundinacea, a tall Rottboelia, and Andropogon occur; and in the more open spaces a curious Rottboellioidea, glumis ciliatis, is common. In addition a Polygala, a Crucifera with bracteæ and white flowers, an Acanthacea, Prenanthes? Centranthera tetrastachys are met with. The trees are quite different from those of Hookhoom; the principal one is a Nauclea; Bombax, Wendlandiæ sp., a Rhamnea, Phyllanthus, and Bignonia cordifolia occur; the Nauclea giving a character to the scenery. The Botany of the patches of jungle is varied. Strychnos Nux-vomica is common; Congea tomentosa, Engelhardtia, etc. Bauhinia arborea, and Costus also occur.

Teak occurred to-day for the first time, but not in abundance, neither were the specimens fine: it was past flowering, it occurred only between the patches of jungle among grass. I should have mentioned, that throughout the first portion of the plains traversed, a dioceous dwarf Phœnix was not rare, as well as an Herpestes. A beautiful Rose occurs on the banks of nullahs, and at Camein, on the Mogaung river: it has large white flowers, involucrate; smell sweet like that of a Jonquil.

The general direction of the march was S. S. E. Distance fourteen miles.

Camein consists of two stockaded villages: the smaller one being situated on a small hill on the Endaw Kioung, which comes from near the serpentine mines, and falls into the Mogaung river here; this has about twelve houses: the one below about twenty, the inhabitants are Shans chiefly, and appear numerous and healthy. Assamese slaves are not uncommon.

Observed the large blue Kingfisher of the Tenasserim coast, *Alcedo sinensis*.

The day's Botany was very interesting, more so than that of any other days, excepting two on the higher ranges of the Naga hills. The Crucifera is highly interesting. In the woods Alstonia and Elephantopus; Salvinia is common in marshes.

April 2nd.—Left at 10 A.M., proceeding over the low hill to the W. of lower Camein; our course continued traversing low ranges and small intermediate plains, which we skirted. At noon we reached the Tsee Een nullah, where we found a large party of Shan Chinese, returning from the mines; they had but few Ponies, and still fewer Mules. Their dress, appearance, habits, etc. are those of the lower orders of Chinese. After leaving this our course continued over similar country, until we reached the Endaw Kioung at 3 P.M., which we crossed, halting on its left bank; it is a stream of much strength and a broad bed, but shallow. We saw some cultivation on low hills to the W. N. W., and could distinguish two or three houses; it is a small village inhabited by Meereps.

The vegetation of the valleys or plains continues the same, but in addition to the Rottboelleoidea minor, is a curious Andropogon, and on the skirts of the hills a large Anthistiria; some of the finest specimens of teak also occurred. Bamboo in abundance; otherwise the trees are, with a few exceptions, completely changed. A fine arborescent Wendlandia, Bignonia indica? fructibus siliquo-formibus spiraliter tortis, arborea, Kydia, Eurya arborea, and many other fine trees occurred, but these I leave until my return. On one plain I noticed a Cycas, caudice simplici vel dichotomo, and the Phœnix of yesterday. In the Endaw Kioung two species of Potamogeton, Azolla, and Pistia, Villarsia and Ceratophyllum occur.

April 3rd.—5¼ A.M. Therm. 55. Water boiled at 210. Elevation 1064 feet.

Continued our journey over similar country, marching from half-past 5 to 1 P.M., including an hour's halt. Distance fifteen miles: general direction S. S. W. Passed many streamlets, and continued for some time close to the Endaw, which is still a largish river, apparently deep, with a sluggish stream. The plains continue, but of much narrower diameter. Met many Shan Chinese and two parties of Mogaung people returning from the mines.

The most interesting plants of to-day are a Santalacea, a climbing species, racemis subpendulis, of Citrus—Citrus scandens, Cardiopteris of which I found old fruit alone, a new Roydsia, R. parviflora mihi.

The vegetation of the plains continues unchanged, a Dillenia with small yellow flowers is common on their skirts, Bignonia cordata occurs as a large tree; no one has seen teak. There is something peculiar in the appearance of the trees of the plains, especially of the Nauclea; they look scraggy. I picked up the flowers of an arborescent Hibiscus, and the fruit of Lagertræmia grandiflora.

Halted on an old rice khet, near a pool of tolerably clear water.

Bignonia cordata has sweet smelling flowers, lab. medio labii inferioris bicristato. Is it not rather a Viticea, owing to the absence of the 5th stamen? Phlebochiton, Sambucus, Butomus pygmæus. Many portions of the hills are covered with plantains in immense numbers, (not Musa glauca). On hills bounding to the south, one or two spots of cultivation belonging to a village in the interior occur. The Shans wear curious sandals made of a sort of hemp, at least those who do not wear the usual Chinese shoes. *4th.*—5¼ A.M. Temperature 55½. Water boiled at 210. Elevation as before.

April 4th.—Continued our course through exactly the same kind of country, the plains becoming much narrower. Reached the path leading to Keouk Seik after five hours' marching, and up to this our course was nearly the same with that of yesterday, between W. S. W. and S. W. We did not see the village; several (seven or eight) houses are visible on the hill, which here extends north and south, and along which runs a nullah, the Kam Theem.

From this place our course continued almost entirely over low hills not exceeding 800 feet above us, until we halted on the margin of a plain bounded to the W. by the Boom, which runs N. and S., the direction being W. N. W. Distance seventeen miles. On our march we met several parties of Shans, Burmese, and Singphos. The path from the village to this is much better, and much more frequented than any of the other parts. Most of the parties were loaded with Serpentine. Noticed *en route*, both on the plains and on the hills, Teak; in the latter situations many of the specimens were very fine. Another noble Dipterocarpea arborea was observed. I observed Drymaria, Vallaris solanacea, and a Spathodia, which is common on the plains. Teak is remarkable for the smoothness and peculiar appearance of its bark, so that it seems to have had it stripped off.

Gathered on the hills Ulmus and Hyalostemma, the petals of which are united into a tri-partite corolla, a Cyrtandracea in fruit, and an Olacinea, floribus tri-sepalis, appendicibus 6 apice fimbriatis, stam. 3, sepalis oppositis, racemis erectis.

April 5th.—Reached the mines after a march of about four hours; our course was winding, continuing through jungle and small patches of plain, until we reached the base of that part of the Kuwa Boom which we were to cross, and which bore N. W. from the place at which we slept. The ascent was steep in some places, it bore in a N. N. W. direction, principally through a bamboo jungle. From a clear space half way up, we had a fine and pretty view of the hills and plains, especially to the S. and S. E. In the former direction, and distant about fifteen miles, we saw on our return, the Endaw Gyee, but we could not estimate its size or figure; it is evidently however a large sheet of water; the natives say, several miles across. From the summit, we likewise had a fine view of the country to the E.; very few plains were visible in this direction. Nearly due east, and about thirty miles off, was visible Shewe Down Gyee, and this will make Camein nearly due east also, or E. by S. The descent passed through similar jungle, that at the foot being damp. The course continued in a direction varying from S. to W., or rather between these points, through damp jungle. We then ascended another steep hill, but not exceeding 5 or 600 feet in height; descending from this, and passing through low tree and then bamboo jungle, we reached the mines.

The road was, up to the base of Kuwa Boom on the W. side, very good, thence it was in general bad; wet, slippery, much impeded by blocks of serpentine, and foliated limestone (Bayfield) crossing several streams, mountain torrents, the principal one being Sapya Khioung. This takes its name from a spring of water of alkaline properties, which bubbles up sparingly from under its rocky bed, and which must be covered during the rains. The water is clear, of a pure alkaline taste, and is used by the natives as soap.

The mines occupy a valley of a somewhat semi-circular form, bounded on all sides by hills clothed with trees, none being of very great height. The valley passes off to the N. into a ravine, down which the small stream that percolates the valley escapes, and in this at about a coss distant other pits occur. The surface of the valley apparently at one time consisted of low rounded hillocks; it is now much broken, and choked up with the earth and stones that have been thrown up by excavating. The stone is found in the form of more or less rounded boulders imbedded with others, such as quartz, etc. in brickish-yellow or nearly orange clay. The boulders vary much in size. There is no regularity in the pits, which are dug indiscriminately; some have the form of ditches, none exceed 20 feet in depth. They are dug all over the valley, as well as on the base of the hill bounding it to the W. and N. W. We could not obtain any good specimens, nor is there any thing in the spot that repays the visit. No machinery is used, the larger blocks are broken by fire. But that they are of importance in the light of increasing the revenue, is evident, from the fact that B. counted, since we left Camein, 1,100 people on their return, of whom about 700 were Shan Chinese. The loads carried away are in some cases very heavy; the larger pieces are carried on bamboo frames by from two to five men, the *lesser* on a stout piece of bamboo lashed to and supported on two cross or forked bamboos, the stouter joint resting on the bearer's neck, the handles of the forks being carried in his hands. The most obvious advantage of this is the ease with which the load may be taken off, when the bearer is fatigued. The revenue yielded last year, B. tells me, was 320 viss of silver, or about 40,000 rupees. The length of the valley from E. to W. is about three-quarters of a mile; its breadth varies from 460 to 800 yards.

On our return we boiled water at the Soap spring, which is about 50 feet above the mines, Temp. of the air 80½. 2½ P.M. of boiling water 209. Elevation 1600 feet. And on the top of Kuwa Boom, which is crossed at a comparatively low place, at 4½ P.M. Temp. of the air 76, of boiling water 207. Elevation 2678 feet.

I can say nothing as to the peculiar features of the vegetation, in the woods towards Kuwa Boom. I gathered three Aurantiaceæ; the Olacinea of yesterday is common, a large arborescent Artocarpus fructibus oblongis sub-informibus, sub-acidulis, $\frac{3}{4}$ uncialibus; Teak rarely; Tonabea, noble specimens occur; on the Kuwa Boom, a large Gordonia arborea, two arborescent Myrtacea, large Mangoes, Bamboo, a Morinda; Magnoliæcea occurs on its western face, as well as the Conifera toxoidea before gathered. Dicksonia and Pladera justicioidea both occur. Dianella nemorosa, etc. The Serpentine is carried from Keoukseik in boats down the Endaw Kioung, thence to Camein, and from whence it goes to Mogam, which is probably the principal mart. Calamus spioris petiolorum uncialibus verticillatis occurs in abundance in all the damp jungle.

We returned in the afternoon to our halting place of yesterday, from which the mines are distant ten miles, four of which occur from the side of Kuwa Boom to the West. The Endaw Gyee is situated on a plain, but it is enclosed by hills on every side except the S. E. Those to the south are very high.

April 6th.—Returned, diverging from the path to the village Keoukseik. Noticed Leriodendron, Æsculus, Achyranthis aspera, Vallaris solanacea, etc.

The village is situated to the S. of the road to the mines; it is close to the Nam Theen, and on a small elevation; it is stockaded. The number of houses is about sixteen; of inhabitants, including children, 120: all the houses, except two, being small. The merchants, etc. empoyed about the mines, halt on the Nam Theen, which is up to this point navigable for small boats.

Thermometer 66. $6\frac{1}{2}$ A.M. Temp. of boiling water 210.

April 8th.—Reached Camein at noon: halted on the 7th at our former hut on the Endaw Kioung. The additional plants noticed are Duchesnia indica, common in wet places; a Bamboo, paniculis (culmis) nutantibus aphyllis, amplus. Pandanus; Curculigo pumila, floribus sub-solitarius ante folia, 6 vel. 4 partitis; a Careya, Dillenia, arborea floribus numerosis parvis luteis.

Æschynomena, Anthistiria arundinacea, Composita arborea, 40-50 pedalis. Another species of Anthistiria, common on the margins of hills during the march. Fir trees are reported to exist on *Lioe Peik,* which bears South from Kioukseik. Volcanic hills reported to exist near the Endaw Gyee, but no salt rock occurs. This mineral is said to be found three days' march from Kioukseik on the Nam Theen. The revenue said to accrue from the Serpentine mines, is probably highly exaggerated; and the supply of the stone is said to be diminishing yearly. Casually found on the Nam Toroon, a Sterculia arborea, florib-masculis clavato, infundibul. coccineis, pubescentibus: a Sophora, floribus albidis pallidissima ceruleo tinctis, of which the flowers alone were seen; Prenanthis flosentis citrinis, a Polygala and Hypericum were likewise found.

April 9th.—Left Camein at 6, and reached Mogoung at 6 P.M. after a march of at least twenty-five miles. The course at first was nearly due east, until we reached the Nam Pong, but subsequently it became more southerly. Camein bears from this about S. S. E. The country traversed was the same, generally comparatively open, that is to say, grassy plains with Rhamnea, Nauclea, Bombax, etc. For some distance the path extended through shady woods. No villages, nor any signs of such were observed *en route.* We passed many streamlets particularly during the latter half of the march. Our original intention was to have come to Mogoung by water, and with this view Bayfield told the man sent by the Myoowook to procure two or three canoes. At 6 A.M. the Havildar came up to our hut, and said that the headman of the village was disputing violently about our taking the boats. Bayfield proceeded down to the river side, where the Yua Thugee was very insolent, and he and his followers drew their *dhaos* (swords) on Bayfield, who slightly pushed the Thugee. It ended in our going by land. We had previously heard of the rebellion at Ava: the Thugee's behaviour evidently arose partly from this. I did not observe the dispute, as I remained near the stockade.

Noticed a Lonicera in low places, and the Viola of Suddiya on the plains, a Cardiopteris, Kempferia, Curcuma, a Bambusa vaginis collo barbatis, a scandent Strychnos, an Aerides, Ardisiæ 2, some Acanthaceæ, Loxotis major, Urticeæ 2 or 3, Santalacea as before, Tetrantheræ, Davallia atrata, Asplenium fronde simplici, etc. etc.

April 10th.—We halt, and hear a report of the death of Mr. Kincaid, and that a Burmese army is *en route* here. The whole country is most unsettled, all the Singphos and Khukeens being in open rebellion. It appears that Thurrawaddi is meeting with success in his summons for men. No resistance shewn to his authority hitherto except by one Myoowoon. Our Myoowoon has absented himself, and the Myoowook determined on surrender. Bayfield under all circumstances, and failing authentic intelligence of Mr. Kincaid, resolves on remaining here.

Mogam is a rather pretty town, situated on the right bank of the Mogoung river, at the confluence of a river 100 yards broad, the water of which spreads out, in some places, to a considerable breadth and depth. The country is however low, flooded in the rains, and surrounded by hills, except in the direction of Shewe Down Gyee. In many places it is only covered with grass. The town is large, and was formerly stockaded, the remains of the timber stockade being still visible. It contains about 300 houses, about 2,500 inhabitants, mostly Shans. The houses are generally raised, in many cases like those of the Kampties, the chopper coming low down, shaped like a turtle's back. There is a very distinct opening or chasm in the hills between S. D. Gyee and a low range to the North, but no river makes its exit there. Sunday, 16th.

April 18th.—Halted up to this date, waiting for information especially regarding the army at Tsenbo.

In this place two fragrant Dipterocarpeæ are found; as also Bixa, Tamarindus, and Carthamus, which last is cultivated and used both for food and dyeing. About the Poongie houses some remarkable Fici occur, the trunk being divided so low down as to give the idea of a group of several trees. The roots in addition are made to spread over the conical mounds, thrown up at their bases.

A race of wild-looking short men, called Lupai Khakoos, inhabit this vicinity, wearing a jacket, and dark-blue cloth with an ornamented border, worn with the ends overlapping in front. They wear garters of the Suwa. Their hair is worn either long or cropped, and a beard is also occasionally worn by the elders.

In this place very few regular Chinese are to be found, and the few that are here seen, are ultra-provincials; none are acquainted with the manufacture of tea. This article is procurable here, but at a high rate; it is sold in flat cakes of some diameter; it is black, coarse, with scarcely any smell, and in taste not much superior to the Assamese article; 20 tickals weight sells for 1¼. All the blue cloths of the Shans are dyed, Bayfield informs me, with Ruellia, or jungle indigo.

It is with these people that the only trade seems to be carried on, and this is limited to amber and serpentine. They are very dirty, and excessively penurious, but industrious. Owing to their habits and extreme penury, there is no outlet for our manufactures in this direction; so that I fully agree with Hannay's statement, that 500 rupees worth of British goods would be unabsorbed for some years. Rosa is common, also a Rumex; a Sisymbroid plant also occurs. Among the trees, all which are stunted, Gmelina arborea occurs. There are some Assamese slaves here among the people, one of them is said to be a relation of Chundra Kant, the Suddiya chief: slaves are held in very small estimation with the Burmese. Thus Bayfield asked his writer, who such a one standing near him was, whether a Shan or Singpho? The man answered, "My lord, it is not a man; it is a Waidalee."

Altogether, Mogoung is an uninteresting place; the surrounding plains are barren-looking, and inhospitable, and clothed with grass. Here and there a ragged Nauclea, Careya, etc. is visible with Gmelina arborea. The under shrubs are chiefly a Rhamnoidea, and a Phyllanthus. Rosa is common; Rumex and Nasturtium are both met with.

News arrived yesterday evening to the effect, that the King is drowned, the heir-apparent in the palace: and that Colonel Burney is with Thurrawadi!!!

My collections up to this place amount to 900 species.

April 19th.—Left at 12, and halted after having gone about four miles. The river continues the same as above; it is a good deal impeded by trees, and much more so by sandbanks.

April 20th.—Reached Tapaw in the afternoon; our progress is, however, very slow the stream being slight, but the river is much improved; being less spread out, owing to its greater proximity to the low hills: often very deep, generally clothed with jungle to the water's edge. On the hills near Tapaw are some Khukeens of the Thampraw tribe, and on these hills bitter tea is reported to be found. This the Khukeens bring down for sale.

April 21st.—Continued our course, performing about twelve miles between 7 and 5, inclusive of one hour's halt. At some distance from Tapaw and thence throughout the day, here and there occur rapids, which are much worse, from the stream being impeded by large rocks. In some places it is divided, in others, compressed between hills, and here it is very deep.

April 23rd.—Arrived at the Irrawaddi. The Mogoung river is very uninteresting; the stream being generally slow, sandbanks very abundant, as well as stumps of sunken trees. At its mouth it is deep, and about seventy yards across. The banks are either overgrown with trees or else grassy; the grasses being Arundo and Saccharum. On the steep banks of the hills where these descend into the river, ferns are common together with an Amaryllidea out of flower. Cadaba is common, as well as a large Mimosea. Rosa continues; as also Æsculus. On the road by which the Chinese branch off from Tapaw to the Irrawaddi, I gathered an arborescent Apocynea foliis suboppositis, and a Homalineous tree, floribus tetrameris; Salix is common all down the river. Teak only occurs occasionally. In one place I gathered Lonicera heterophylla, a fragrant Valeriana? and Jonesia in abundance; this last being here apparently quite wild. Adelia nereifolia, a Ficus, Ehretia arenarum, and the usual sandy plants occur on the banks. Pistia, Salvinia and Azolla are common.

The Irrawaddi opposite the entrance of the Mogoung river, is 600 yards across. It is a noble stream; has risen a good deal, and presents one unbroken sheet of water. The banks are by no means high, and are grassed to the brink. The water is cold and clouded; its temperature is 66½°, that of air in a boat 88½. We reached Tsenbo about 1 o'clock, having passed five or six villages, mostly small, and inhabited by Shans. Tsenbo numbers about 30 houses, but these as throughout Burma, as far as we have seen, are small; it is situated on a low hill on the left bank. Both banks are hilly, especially the right. The river has risen enormously during a halt here—many feet. In one hour we found it to rise about 16 inches. At this place I gathered a fine blue Vanda, and a curious tree habitu Thespiæ: stigmatibus 4. Between this and the entrance to the narrow defile Kioukdweng, which is about 1½ miles distant, three villages occur. This entrance is well marked, the river becoming suddenly contracted from 300 to less than 100 yards. We halted about 6½ P.M. at Lemar. Noticed four or five villages between Lemar and the village at the entrance of the defile. All these villages are inhabited by Poans, a distinct hill tribe. Passed through two fearful places, one in particular where the whole body of water rushes through a *gate*, formed by huge rocks not 50 yards wide.

April 24th.—Continued our course, and arrived at Bamoo about 5½ P.M.; the greater part of the journey extended through the Kioukdweng, or defile, in which some terrific places occur, one in particular known by two rocks which are called the Elephant and Cow. Passed several small villages before we made our exit from the K. dweng: all inhabited by Poans. Between this and Bamoo the country along the river is truly magnificent, and is well inhabited.

The largest village contains about 70 houses; at least seven or eight occur, between the points above noted.

The Kioukdweng is a remarkable and an awful object. The greatest breadth of the river while confined within this defile does not exceed 250 yards, and in all the bad places it is contracted to within 100, occasionally 50. From the enormous rise of the river, which, last night alone amounted to an increase of ten feet, the passage is one continued scene of anxiety. In the places above referred to the river rushes by with great velocity, while the return waters caused on either side by the surrounding rocks, occasion violent eddies and whirlpools, so as to render the boat unmanageable, and if upset the best swimmer could not live in these places. The rocks are serpentine and grey limestone, presenting angular masses which project into the stream; the former in all places within high-water mark is of a dark-brown colour. Micaceous slate? likewise occurs, although rarely. The depth is of course enormous, in the low state of the river, when Bayfield passed up, in many places no bottom was found, at 25 or even 40 fathoms, and at this season the water had no doubt risen 40 feet higher. Some idea of the rise that has taken place may be formed from the fact, that in places where, when Bayfield passed up, the stream did not exceed 70 yards in width, it was now 200; and of course a rise of 20 feet in the open river, would determine one of at least 40 within the K. dweng. After passing the Elephant and Cow, which have the usual resemblance implied by their fanciful names, the river widens and becomes tranquil. The whole of this Kioukdweng is truly remarkable, and in many places very picturesque.

The vegetation is, I imagine, similar to that of the low hills about Mogoung; but so dangerous was the passage, that I had but few opportunities of going ashore. The hills are thinly wooded, and all bear many impressions of former clearings; but the spots now under cultivation are certainly few. Besides, we must bear in mind, that the spots cultivated generally throughout thinly populated parts of India are deserted after the first crop, so that a very limited population may clear a great extent of ground. Bayfield tells me, and I consider his authority as excellent, that the population is almost entirely limited to the villages seen during the passage. These do not exceed twelve, and they are all small. None of the hills exceed 500 feet in height (apparently,) they do not present any very peculiar features.

Below the maximum high-water mark the vegetation is all stunted, at least that of the rocks ; a tufted Graminea is the most common. Adelia nereifolia (Roxb.), a Celastrinea, a curious Rubiacea, which I also have from Moulmain, two Myrtaceæ, a Rungia, are the most common. I did not observe Podocarpus. In the occasionally sandy spots Campanula, the usual Compositæ, Panica three. Eleusine, Clenopodium, and Atriplex are common, a Stemodia, and Asclepiadea likewise occur. One Clematis carpellis imberbibus, and the Lonicera are met with. No mosses appear to occur. One remarkable tree, *Belhoe* of Assam, 70 feet high, cortice albido, foliis orbato, panculis (fructus) pendulis, occurs : it has the appearance of an Amentaceous tree.

April 27th.—We have remained at Bamoo; nothing appears to have been settled below, and the river is reported to be unsafe. It has fallen at least three feet since our arrival. Bayfield measured the left channel yesterday; it is nearly 750 yards wide.

Bamoo is situated on the left bank, along which its principal street runs. The town is a very narrow one, the breadth averaging about 200 yards; its extent is considerable, but it scarcely contains 600 houses, and of these 105 are Chinese, and only has one good street, *i. e.* as to length. Neither are the houses at all good or large, so that the population cannot be established at more than 3000. I allude only to those within the stockade; out of this, and close to Bamoo are two or three small villages. The stockade is of timber, *pangaed,* or fenced outside for about 30 yards; it has just been completely repaired, as an attack is expected from the Khukeens.

The Chinamen live all together, in a street of low houses built of unbaked bricks; these are not comparable to the houses at Moulmain. There is but little trade now going on. Within the stockade and without, low swampy ravines occur, that cannot be but injurious to the healthiness of the town. The Myoowoon spends all his money in pagodas, none of which are worth seeing: all the roads and bridges he leaves to take care of themselves.

The *inferior caked tea,* sugarcandy, silk dresses, straw hats, and caps are procurable, but at a high price. Pork is plentiful, and the bazar is well supplied with fish. It is a much more busy place than Mogoung, as well as considerably larger. The chief export trade with the Chinese is cotton; the revenue however by no means equals that of the Mogoung district.

The country around is nearly flat; on one side of the stockade there is an extensive marsh well adapted for paddy. Otherwise the ground is dry, and tolerably well drained; it appears to have been formerly wooded; at present the environs are occupied by undershrubs. I have observed no peculiar botanical feature. Among the undershrubs are Phyllanthæ 2, Apocynea arborescens, Gelonium, Combretum, Strychnos, Vitex, Melastoma. When I say undershrubs, I mean that such is their present appearance. The only new plant is an elegant Capparis, subscandens, floribus albis, odoratis demum filamentisque purpureo-roseis. About old Pagodas, Pladera of Moulmain, a Labiata, Stemodia, and Andropogon occur.

The cultivated plants are those of the coast, Hyperanthera Moringa, Bixa Orellana, Calotropis gigantea, Artocarpus integrifolia, a Phyllanthus, Cordia Myxa, Carica Papaya, Citrus medica, Plantains, a large and coarse Custard Apple, Mango, Zyziphus, Cocos, Taliera, Agati.

The climate is dry and sultry, the diurnal range of the Thermometer being from 28 to 32°. At this season, viz. at 6½ A.M. from 66 to 68; 4 P.M from 94 to 96. North winds are common, daily commencing from that quarter, or terminating there. They are not accompanied by much rain, although the weather is unsettled.

May 2nd.—A Khukeen whom Bayfield sent for tea returned, bringing with him many specimens out of flower. The striking difference between this and the tea I have hitherto seen, consists in the smallness and finer texture of the leaves. For although a few of the specimens had leaves measuring six by three inches, yet the generality, and these were mature, measured from four to three, by two to three. As both entire and serrated leaves occur, the finer texture was more remarkable. The bitterness, as well as the peculiar flavour were most evident. Young leaves were abundant.

The Khukeens make no use of the tea. The Chinese here talk of this as the jungle tea, and affirm that it cannot be manufactured into a good article. They talk of the valuable sorts as being very numerous, and all as having small leaves. Neither here nor at Mogoung are there any real Chinamen, nor is there any body who understands the process of manufacturing tea. The caked tea is not made to adhere by the serum of sheep's blood, it adheres owing to being thus packed before it is dry. The plain around Bamoo is intersected by ravines, which afford good paddy cultivation; no large trees occur within 1½ mile of the town. At this distance a large Dipterocarpea is common. In the underwood around the town, a Dipterocarpus, arbuscula, foliis maximis, oblongo-cordatis, Gordonia, Lagerstræmia parviflora, Elodea, Nauclea; Leguminosæ 3, Gelonia, Combretum, Jasminum occur. In the marshes Ammannia rotundifolia, Cyrilla, Azolla, Marsilea, and Salvinia, Serpicula, Ceratophyllum; a Campanula *arenosa* reaches thus far.

Every day indecent sights occur in the river, owing to the women bathing without clothes, and either with or near the men. They appear to be indifferent to the concealment of their person, breasts, and hoc genus omne, being freely exposed. They swim very well, and in a curious way. They make their escape by squatting down in the water, unfolding their cloth, and springing up behind it. As for the men, they appear to take a pride in exposing every part of their bodies. No gazers-on occur among these people, such not being the fashion.

The Shan Tarooks who trade with this place use oxen in addition to other beasts of burden; the breed appears good, resembling the smaller kind of India.

The Irrawaddi here is between the extreme banks a little less than 1½ miles broad; the channel on which Bamo is situated is the largest, and is 800 yards across. Two other channels exist, of which the west is the smallest, and carries off least water. The river is a good deal subdivided by sandbanks, but is, compared with the Burrumpooter a confined river. Since our arrival here it has sunk several (say five or six) feet, and no longer looks the noble river it did on our arrival.

The sandbanks when they do exist are either naked, or clothed with partial and not gigantic grassy vegetation. I have not seen any thing comparable to the churs of the B. pooter in this respect. The temperature of the river is not particularly low, and is much higher now than during the rise. From Bamoo the opening of the Kioukdweng is not conspicuous, nobody unacquainted with the course of the river would imagine that it passes through the range of hills to the N. and NNE. The highest hills visible are to the east. They are within a day's journey, and are clothed to their summits. Some appear 3000 feet high.

Low hills inhabited by wild Khukeens, are visible nearly all around, except perhaps due west. The wild fierce nature of these people is attended with a great extent of mischief, quite unchecked, without eliciting even precautionary measures on the part of the Burmese Government.

There are a few angles in the Bamoo stockade, and these exist because a straight line cannot be preserved; and large torches are placed out on levers for illuminating the enemy, and loop-holes are cut through the timbers; watch-houses are likewise placed at certain points. There are two rows of *pangahs* or fences outside, but not the Singpho pangahs. Notwithstanding all this the river face is quite defenceless.

The soil is dry and sandy, and cultivation is carried on principally on the churs. Pumpkins and Gourds are abundant; Yams, (Dioscorea,) not very good. Rice is sold at the usual price, a basket full for a rupee. The town is dirty, and not kept in any order.

May 6th.—We left Bamoo, and in three hours reached Kounglaun, a rather large village on the left bank, containing 100 houses, many of which are respectable, better indeed than any in Bamoo. It contains many small ruined pagodas. A gigantic tree grows within the stockade, which is a very poor one. Punica Granatum, and Beloe, were the only plants of interest observed in the neighbourhood.

We passed several (six or seven) villages, none except one with more than thirty houses; the one alluded to had sixty. All the houses continue small. The river is here much subdivided, and in many places shallow; sandbanks are common. Vegetation of banks is almost entirely Gramineæ, and coarse strong-smelling Compositæ. The grasses are different from those previously met with, except the Arundo. Rosa continues; Salix is common. Between Koungloung and Tsenkan, which is on the same bank, and close to the entrance to the Kioukdweng, three villages are met with; but none of any size. Tsenkan is prettily situated on a high bank, or rather low hill. The houses are about 100 in number, all poor and small. The stockade is a miserable affair. There are some good Poonghie houses, and a very pretty group of pagodas on a small rock. The country is jungly; just above the town a nullah enters the Irrawaddi: it is down this that large quantities of teak is brought, from hills two days' journey to the eastward; some large rafts were seen, but although some of the timbers were stout, none were of any great size. I gathered a pretty Hippocrateaceous plant in the jungles, as well as a Combretum; a Vitex, an Amyridea, etc. Phrynium dichotomum occurs here; Rosa continues; Jatropha is cultivated.

May 7th.—Started at 5 A.M., and entered the Kioukdweng almost immediately. We halted about 7, at Tsenbo. Noticed Æsculus, Sisymbrium, Campanula, Adelia neriefolia, Dillenia speciosa, the usual Compositæ, and largish Dipterocarpeæ. The river is a good deal narrowed, but never less than 130 yards across, and as there are no rocks in any direction to impede the stream, the water flows but slowly and very placidly. Almost all the rocks forming the hills are grey carbonate of lime. These hills are covered to high-water mark, with scanty somewhat stunted trees, the most of which have no foliage. The scenery is by no means so bold as in the upper K. dweng, although just above Tsenbo, there is a noble cliff, 300 feet high, and almost perpendicular; under its ledges we observed great numbers of bees' nests. The rock when exposed is rather greyish black, and in many places reddish. Serpentine occurs, but is not common. A good deal of lime is prepared in this Kioukdweng, and some portions of it in the rugged serrated appearance, remind one of the limestone cliffs on the coast. Above Tsenbo and nearly opposite the cliff, is a small village of eight houses. Tsenbo numbers fifteen; it is on the left bank, and is a miserable place. Here we were left by our escort which accompanied us from Tsenkan, and the Thogee refused positively to give us two or three men to row. Although master of a miserable hole, he had made preparations for defence, and had set on foot a custom house. We saw a good many boats passing up, all evidently containing families moving away from their villages.

In this Kioukdweng a fine Palm exists, which I have never seen before. Caudex 10-15 pedalis, crassa, petiolorum basibus processubus vestitis, frondibus pinnatis, 10 pedalibus, pinnis ensifornibus 2-2½ pedalibus, subtus glaucis, diametro 1½ uncialibus, basi valde obliquis, bilobis! lobo inferiore maximo, decurrenti, uninervi: floribus in spadicibus nutanti-curvatis, amplis, basi spathaceis spicato-paniculatis. Florib. masculis polyandris.

Petiol. bases cretosæ, intus processubus atris, subulatis, longissimis robustis quasi panicillatis.

Habitus quodammodo Wallichiæ. Hab. in Umbrosissimis.

An arbuscula Anonacea, floribus dioicis, Mas. corollæ petalis apice valvatim cohærentibus, basi apertis, potius distantibus, Ovariis (fæm) pedicellatis, also occurred.

Fructus elliptico-oblongus, subuncialis, hinc a basi ad styli punctum linea tenui exsculptus, unilocularis, unisporus. Endocarp, ac testa viscoso-gelatinosa. Testa ac tegumen intera membr. chartacea. Albumen copiosum hinc et suturæ fructus oppositæ, profundius exarat. sectione transversa-reniformi. Carnoso albumeni germen secus sulcum affixium. Embryo in axi albuminis, radicul super. Cotyledones foliaceæ, albæ, amplæ, curvat seminis sequentes: suturæ placental, oppositæ. Ejusdem generis cum Menispermea: in sylvis Singfoensibus cum Wallichia: vide Icones.

Arrived at Kioukgyee at 5 P.M. Waited on and dined with the Meewoon, who is a gentlemanly, spare, lively man with grey hair. Dinner was good, and clean. Preserved dried jujubes from China, as well as some preserved by himself were very good. Kioukgyee is on the right bank of the river, which is here undivided by islands, and about 1200 yards broad. Just above the town there are some rocks. The number of houses is about eighty-five, most of them arranged in a broad street running along the river, and the best that I have seen for some time.

The village is surrounded by a new and wretched stockade, the outskirts being fenced or *pangaed;* the people are on the qui vive, and the whole village seems to be in a constant state of alarm. All the jungle immediately adjoining the town is cut down; many of the houses are unroofed, and all the gates are guarded. Visited this morning the lines occupied by the attacking force; these were not 300 yards from the village, and occupied the skirts of the jungle: trees had been felled and earth thrown up, but not in such a manner as to obstruct in any way tolerably brave men. We saw none of the slain, we may therefore doubt if there were any, but it was evident from platters, etc. strewed about, that the flight of the robbers had been very precipitate. We passed some little distance above this, a holy island, the numberless small pagodas on which, had a very pretty effect. Close to these there was a small village, Sheweygyoo, which had been just burnt down by the Kioukgyee people, for giving assistance to the robbers; this as well as two other contiguous villages before occupied a good extent of the left bank, and numbered probably 150 houses. Most of the inhabitants have retreated up the river.

May 8th.—Reached Katha at 6 P.M. Throughout the day saw little of interest. What we did see, gave evident tokens of disturbances: villages deserted; dogs starved, howling piteously; canoes without owners. At one village a few miles below Kioukgit, our arrival caused much excitement, and a gun was fired off as a signal of alarm on our approach.

May 9th.—Katha is on the right bank of the Irrawaddi; it is situated on an eminence, and commands a fine view of a fine reach of the river; the situation indeed is excellent. It contains nearly 200 houses, but these are not of the better description. To the west is a fine chain of hills, the lowest ranges of which are distant about one mile and a half; the highest peaks are perhaps 1500 feet. No signs of alarm or disturbances are here visible, although part of the force that invested Kioukgit came from this village. We here learn the agreeable news that the country below is quiet, and that no robbers now infested the road. The Thogee is a fine looking young man; very polite. This village boasts of some pretty pagodas, well grouped, and a very fine *Kiown*, the workmanship of which astonished me, particularly the carving; it is built of teak, the posts being very stout, and very numerous. Several merchant boats left before us, apparently anxious for our escort.

Behind the town is a large plain used for the cultivation of paddy. Otherwise the jungle comes close to the houses, although the larger trees have been felled for firewood, etc.: the woods are dry, and tolerably open. In the morning I went out towards the hills; the chief timber trees are a fine Dipterocarpus, and a Hopea; Pentapetes likewise occurs; Terminalia Chebula. Gathered a fine Arum, somewhat like A. campanulatum. An arboreous Gardenia, as at Mergui; Myrtacea, Vitex, Bauhinia of yesterday; Randia, Andropogon aciculare; some stunted bamboos were likewise observed. Altogether Katha is the prettiest place I have yet seen. The river opposite it is confined to one bed, about 500 yards broad.

May 9th.—Left at 7 A.M., and reached the mouth of the Shwe Lee at 1 P.M.; the distance according to B. being sixteen miles. Passed a few villages, but none of any size; the houses of all continue of the same description. The river presents the same features. Salix continues. Sandbanks occupied by annual Compositæ occur, two Polygona, Campanula, a Ranunculus, much like that of Suddiya, a Labiata, Paronychia, two Spermacoces; Bombax occurs just below Katha; Salix and Rosa continue. Shwe Lee is a considerable river, at the mouth between 4 and 500 yards broad; but one-third of this is unoccupied by water, and the stream is not deep, although of the ordinary strength. Above, it narrows considerably.

7½ P.M. Temperature of the air 76°. Of Irrawaddi 74°.

May 9th.—Tsa-gaiya. This is a mean village on the left bank, about eighteen miles from Katha; it is close to a low range of hills, and occupies part of a plain, which is adapted for paddy cultivation. Near the village to the North, is a small *jeel*, covered to a great extent with a large Scirpus, Jussiæa, Azolla, Salvinia, etc. Water-fruits are abundant; round this paddy is cultivated, and they appear to cut it at this time. Lowground near the jeel is covered with a low, handsome Stravadium or Barringtonia, as well as a Xanthophyllum, resembling exceedingly in appearance a Leguminosa: the wood is hard. Calamus is also common. A handsome Nauclea occurs, and on the grassy margins of the plain a small Euphrasia is common.

During our stage I observed large quantities of Bombax, and a tree apparently the Beloe of Assam; the banks were either grassy or wooded, especially on the right bank, which is skirted entirely by hills of the same barren looking description. The grasses are all small compared with those of Assam.

May 10*th.*—Reached Tagoung late in the evening at 7½: distance thirty-two miles. The river continues the same; the hills on the left bank are much broken into ravines: all continue clothed with the same stunted vegetation.

May 11*th.*—Tagoung is a miserable village on the left bank; it occupies a rocky eminence, and contains less than 100 houses. It is the most inferior village I have yet seen, the streets being dreadfully dirty and the houses very mean. We visited an old pagoda, about a mile from the town, which is surrounded by an antique wall, much obscured by jungle, and more resembling a bund. On our route hither we landed at Thigan, a village containing about forty houses, and prettily situated at the foot of a hill of micaceous sandstone, on the right bank. At this place are the remains of a fort built by the Chinese, of slabs of the rock forming the hill. Similar remains exist at Myadoung, on the opposite bank, as I learn from Mr. Bayfield. I gathered a Sida, Capparis, Prionitis, Gnaphalium, and a Xanthoxylia petiolis alatis armata; an Adiantum grows between the slabs composing the wall. At Tsenkan I observed an Agave, a different Cactus, a fleshy Euphorbia; and an Ananassa is common all about.

About Tagoung the botany is varied, and interesting. I gathered about fifteen plants that had not occurred before, two Poæ, two Andropogons, a Zanthoxylum, and an Olax. The most interesting is an Apocynea, floribus infundibulifor. lamina reflexa, fauce squamis dentatis 10, serie duplici dispositis, interioribus petalis oppositis et majoribus, antheris, in conum stigma omnino coadunatis. Cotton cultivated here; plants taller than usual. The villages around are all forsaken owing to one of them having been attacked by Khukeens, and two men carried off. Hence the population at Tagoung, although usually scanty, is now much increased from adjoining places. A small river falls into the Irrawaddi immediately above Tagoung.

May 12*th.*—Reached Malé about 6 P.M. Passed *en route* a few villages, none of any size or importance. The river varies in width, *i. e.* the channel, from 400 to 600 yards. The banks are either alluvial or rocky, and there are hills on the right bank skirting the river; those on the left, are more distant and higher. Borassus commences to be common; it is a taller, and more slender tree than that of Coromandel, and the trunk is not covered with the persistent bases of the petioles.

The village of Tsebainago is opposite to Malé, and appears nearly of the same size. Both are situated close to the mouth of the third Kioukdweng. Malé contains 150 houses, all small; it is a place of no trade. To the north is a hill forming the river bank, and covered with pagodas; it is the prettiest place we observed after Katha. The soil has now put on the dry sterile appearance of the Coromandel coast, all the trees of which, except the figs, are common; and often render the banks very pretty. Tectona of Hamilton is very common; it is a tree not exceeding in height 40 feet, much resembling in habit the more valuable species; the flowers are blueish, particularly the villi; the leaves have the same excessive rough feel. Two other Verbenaceæ, a curious Capparidea, caule laxo, foliis lineari-oblongis, basi hastato-cordatis, and a Ximenia are common. On the banks Stravadium, and an arboreous Butea, a Combretum, are common. Low stunted bamboos likewise prevail; and all the bushes are prickly. Nyctanthes is cultivated. The rocks as well as those forming the Kioukdweng, are of coarse sandstone, here and there affording nourishment to abortive Compositæ, stunted grasses, Mollugo, etc.

Left Malé, and entered immediately the last Kioukdweng on descending, or the first defile on ascending against the stream. This is a pretty passage, and moreover has no dangerous places; the hills are low, lower than those of the two former passes, consisting of sandstone partially clothed with the same scanty vegetation, presenting the same barren appearance. Olax, Fici, Leguminosa, stunted bamboos, Hippocrateacea, Mimosa, and Stravadium, occur. Celsia on sandy spots, together with Campanula, but this last is becoming rare. Adelia nereifolia continues. An arundo occurs on the naked rocks; Cassia fistula, Tectona Hamiltoniana are also present.

We are much impeded by south-west winds; and owing to this and the slowness of the stream, we were compelled to remain some time at Thee-ha-dau. We there had excellent opportunities of seeing the fish, which are so very tame as to come up to the sides of the boat, and even to allow themselves to be handled. The faqueers of the place call them together; but I think they are not much disposed to come from mere calling, for they seem to require more substantial proofs of being wanted, in the shape of food: they are found in still water in a small bay, which is closed up still more from the influence of the stream by a round island, constructed superficially on a rocky base, and on which pagodas are built. They resemble a good deal the Gooroa Mas of Assam, but have no large teeth as this has. They are very greedy, of a blueish grey colour, occasionally inclining to red; the feelers are in some forked: they have no scales.

We continued our course when the wind lulled; halted to dine on a sandbank, and proceeded on afterwards, until we reached Kabuct about 8½ P.M. On the sandbank where we dined I gathered a Crotalaria, Campanula, Cleome, a Graminea, Polygonum, Cyperaceæ, and a Dentelloidea. The villages seen were all small.

May 13th.—Left Kabuct before 6. Halted to breakfast on a steep bank, finding it impossible to proceed against the south-west winds, which have now become prevalent.

At this place, which is hilly, I gathered Gmelina villosa, an Anonacea, calyce 6 sepalis, cor. tripetala, pet. patentissimis, margine revolutis, luteis. A Carissa, Grewia, Malpighiacea samaris, 3-alatis, alis dorsalibus abbreviatis, a curious Graminea, a green Orchidea, terrestris, bulbosa, flore ante folia evoluta, a Diospyros, Polygala, Plectranthus, Rungia, Pladera, etc.

Halted at Movo, owing to the wind. This is a very pretty village; of no great size, and of no importance. A delightful tope formed by Mango, Fig, and Garcinia, or Xanthochymus, the dense shade of which is most agreeable; Averrhoa, Ægle Marmelos is cultivated here; Borassus is common, trunks of which are often of very irregular diameter. Low grassy places occur running along the back of the village, with abundance of a Combretum fruticosum; and a nullah at either end of the village presents many trees on its banks, particularly a very large and handsome Myrtacea, Hemarthria compressa. Stravadium racemis longe pendulis.

We were compelled to put into Malá on the right bank, about a mile above Tsengoo, by a severe storm from the north-west. This village consists of about forty houses, many pagodas, and has a good many potteries, and some fine trees. It is at the entrance of the Kioukdweng. Observed Jatropha Curcas, and Vitex negrendo. In the evening we proceeded to Tsenbou.

May 14*th*.—Left Tsenbou, and breakfasted at Nbat Kiown-wa. Just above this are several villages, two of which number nearly seventy houses each. This is the most populous part I have seen. To the east of this are the Ruby mines in the Shan hills; and to the south-east low hills from which the marble is procured, from which they make the idols. The river features continue the same; namely, low hills close to the right bank, and more distant as well as higher ones on the left. On the Shan hills to the east, teak forests occur; on those to the west, tea also grows. In Polong tea districts also occur; but the tea is very coarse, and said not to be drinkable. Hemarthria, and Hoya viridiflora were found.

Here I found Solanum, Tribulus, a Mimosa, lime trees, Carissa, Mimusops, Stemodia ruderalis now appear. The most interesting is a small diffuse Caryoplylleous-looking plant, with white Campanulate flowers; it is probably a Frankeniacea. On the pagodas an Aristella grows. Certain features prevail in the vegetation similar to those of the Coromandel coast. Fig trees often surrounded at base with brick-work; this never lasts long, the roots tearing up the masonry in every direction.

The exit from this 3rd Kioukdweng is very pretty. Tsengru with its numerous white pagodas; the noble river expanded into a broad bay; the Eastern hills are very beautiful, and the Marble hills which form a back ground to Tsenbou are no less so. The banks towards the exit from the defile are sloping, often covered with grass. The Palmyra trees and Fig trees have a very pleasing effect. At Kiougyoung there is a large brick fort, built by Alompras. The village contains about 150 houses: no large village is passed between this and Kubuct.

Halted above Sheemnaga to look at Gaudama's foot, a piece of workmanship contained in a pagoda; it is a very large foot, with a central circular impression. This is about a mile below Endawka.

Sheemnaga never contained more than 400 houses. I counted upwards of 180, and although extensive traces of fire, and of new houses existed, I should reckon it to have contained only about 300. At the Pagoda I gathered a curious Rutaceous-looking decandrous thorny tree, with foliis bijugis.

Reached Mengoon about 7 P. M. Landed at the commencement of the sandstone hills, which in some places assume the form of cliffs: texture very loose. They are full of holes, and abound with blue rock Pigeons. Gathered a Murraya. Trichodesma indicus and Compositæ, Asclepiadea, Calotropis gigantea, and a curious Arenariod-looking plant.

May 15*th*.—Mengoon boasts of a huge unfinished Pagoda, consisting as it now stands of an immense square brick mass, surrounded by four fine broad raised terraces; it would have been, had it been finished, upwards of 700 feet high. The dome was to have been with angular sides. Height 170 feet; the basement, as may be supposed, is immense. The plan or model of it was first built in a small adjoining grove to the south, by the grandfather of the present king. The whole kingdom must have been occupied in its erection. The entrance to it is guarded by two huge Griffins. Several large bells lie close to it. The country around is hilly; the hills low, raviny, and clothed with stunted vegetation. Beautiful topes exist along the river bank, between this and the cliffs before alluded to, consisting chiefly of fine mango trees, noble Fici likewise occur. About Mengoon, Jatropha Curcas is common. Gymnemea, Calotropis gigantea, and Argemone abound. We found a Pergularia, Lippia, Zyzyphus, and one or two small Euphorbiaceæ. The soil is dry, sandy, and barren.

We reached Ava about 1 o'clock.

May 21*st*.—Went to Tsegai on an excursion: the hills in this vicinity are low, none exceeding 300 or 400 feet, dry and barren, chiefly composed of grey carbonate of lime, and in some places Kancha occurs. Pagodas are very numerous, but none are very large, or bearing the stamp of great age. A fine view of country is however afforded: large plains are seen to the east of the city, and between the hills and the river two large jheels are visible from the hills.

The vegetation almost entirely consists of low stunted, very ramous shrubs, and these are generally thorny. Not a tree visible except Bombax and Tamarindus, but this last is planted. A large subarboreous Cactus, spinosus, ramis 4 angulis, is common. Noticed four species of Capparis, and the following plants, Barleria, Prionitis, Tamarindus, Ægle, Zizyphus, Cocos; Borassus, Bixa, Cordia, Punica, Ricinus, Melia Azederak ; Citrus Cassia, near houses and on the hills ; Euphorbia 2, Ximenia, Cleome, Boerhaevia, Adhatode, Cassia sennoidea, Sidæ, Andropogon, a lax Linaria common on old pagodas ; Calanchoe, Sedum, Pommereulla, Vinca rosea, Tectona Hamiltoniana, but not of such size as at Malé. Bambusa stunted and rare, Blepharacanthus, Polygala, Labiatæ 2, Æruæ, sp. Fici one or two, an Alstonia, Celosia mollugo, Solani sp. Stemodia, Combretum, Heliotropium indicum, and the Euphorbiacea of Mengwong. It will at once be seen that the vegetation has some similarity with that of the Carnatic, for in addition I found Asplenium radiatum, and Lemonea Monophylla, a Carissa, Ximenia, Flacourtia, etc. etc.

Ava is a fine town, surrounded with an excellent brick wall : the streets are wide, and kept clean ; the houses are regular, and as trees are interspersed, a pleasing effect is produced. The appearance is much improved by a lattice before each house. The houses also are of a superior description, a few only are of brick. The fort is surrounded by an additional wall, and a broad but shallow ditch. The palace is a handsome, irregular, gilt edifice ; but its precincts are not kept so clean as they might be. The Shwottoo is a handsome hall. The town altogether conveys an idea of importance. The river is about 800 yards broad opposite the Residency ; but above, it is encroached on by a sandbank. Boats are numerous, and opposite Tsegain there is a busy ferry, especially now the king is at Tsegain. This is a much preferable place, and rendered much more pleasing by its superb Tamarind trees, with their most elegant foliage and sculptured trunks. The plants cultivated about Ava are Palmyra, Cocoa (rare). Tamarinds abound ; Carica Papaya, Punica Granatum ; Mangoes, which are of good description ; Cordia, Plantains, Ægle Marmelos.

The country is flat, and destitute of trees to the south and south-west. The whole of this is cultivated during the rains, chiefly for Gram, Tobacco, Capsicum, and a Melitotus. At present the plains are barren, the low places being almost exclusively occupied by a Combretum ; the rest give a new Polygonum, Lippia, 2 or 3 Compositæ, and a curious dwarf grass. On the walls Linaria is common. Noticed near one of the gates, Cryptostegia grandiflora ; the waste places and banks are occupied by Argemone, Mollugineæ three, Xanthium, Dentella, and low annual Compositæ.

May 26th.—Visited Tsegain in the evening, and returned to Ava on the following morning.

May 27th.—Noticed Phœnix sylvestris. The Euphorbia is common; it is not a Cactus, but a species of this genus, ramis complanatis, is found though not common; as well as an Agave or Aloe, but this is a doubtful native. Poinciana pulcherrimea, both red and yellow, Rhus ? sp. arbuscula, Vallaris solanacea. A small Lycopodium, Gmelina asiatica ? The additional Madras plants are, Cissus quadrangularis. There is likewise another fleshy species fol. 3 phyllis, Sarcostemma viminale, Indigofera, Kalanchœ laciniata is common; so is the white Cyperacea on barren spots! I met with Sarcostemma ciliatum; Wall. ? petalis extus viridescent, intus ciliisque purpuro sanguinies, but it is rare. Cardiospermum pubescens is certainly distinct, the flowers are twice as large as those of C. Halicacabum, fructibus inflatis vix alatis, ovalibus, dehiscentia septicida, septis axi adnatis, persistentibus. Semin. solitarii centro loculi affixis, pisiparvi magnitudine, atris.

NOTE.—Where any discrepancy occurs with regard to the native names in the preceding Journal, it is requested that such may be corrected from the Report to Govt. Chapter VII. p. 115.

From a Sketch made on the spot by W. Griffith.

M & N Hanhart, Lith. Printers

VIEW FROM BEESA

CHAPTER VI.

Botanical notes connected with the foregoing Journal.

[*February* 19*th.*—The finest view of the hills from Upper Assam is obtained on a reach or turn of the river just above Palankar, the river bending to the NNE. Snow is plentifully seen on one back range from the Sugar-loaf peak. Another reach shortly after presents a fine view of the Burrampooter chasm, terminated by the rugged peak so distinctly seen from Suddiyah, due east. This view might be chosen, as a general characteristic of the Scenery of Upper Assam.

It embraces the Mishmee mountains to the left, the higher peaks of which are covered with perpetual snow. These lie to the NNE. of Beesa. To the east, is the continuation of the Himalaya, to the South-east and South, the Patkaye, and Naga ranges; the whole forming a panorama, rarely if any where surpassed in beauty. Temperature of the river at 6 A.M. 67°

Musa. Many flowers from the axil of a bract; no bractioles interspersed, hence we may expect racemose or spicate partial inflorescences. The perianth is unilateral, 5 cleft, the two smaller segments, which are intermediate, being internal, or belonging to a different series. Within this petaloid perianth is a membranous one, together with a boat-shaped bracteolate body, entire. The stamens are five, evidently opposite to the segments of the petaloid perianth, staminibus adnatis, the sixth is not developed, but is rudimentary, and exceedly minute, opposite to the bracteoid body. The carpella three, alternate as they ought to be with the last series of stamina, and hence they are opposed to the larger and outer segments of the petaloid perianth, but this last point deserves further examination.

The base of the bracteoid sepal is filled with a gelatinous, sweet, transparent, unicoloured ½ fluid.

I am unaware whether this explanation has occurred to any body else.

It is curious as compared with Scitamineæ, in which the posticous stamen is alone fully developed. Pl. 1. Fig. 3. *a.* bracteoid body, *b.* sterile stamen, *c. c. c.* outer series, *d. d.* inner ditto.

The fact of the outer smaller laciniæ belonging to a second series is not very apparent, but is corroborated by the evidently internal situation of the bracteoid scale, and by the evidently elevated lines visible in the inner.

(*April 3rd*, 1837.—On march towards the Serpentine mines) the face of the perianth, corresponds to these smaller laciniæ.

April 7th.—Thunbergia grandiflora has the pedicels of its flowers twisted, or not twisted, according to the situation of the flowers. Thus if the flower be so situated that the raceme has the direction of the axis, or in other words is erect, the pedicel is straight, but if the raceme, as generally happens, be pendulous, the twisting of the pedicel is resorted to, to secure the flower that situation which it would have, were the raceme erect.

The above is obvious in flowers which from elongation of the axis of inflorescence, have fasciculate or aggregate flowers. An obvious inference is, that the twisting of the pedicel is not of generic, nor of specific importance; and that it is capable of being produced artificially.

This resupination is not uncommon in the order; it is most evident in Thunbergia coccinea, in which the racemes are always pendulous. There is nothing, at least in this species, in the situation of the genitalia to account for the resupination.

Pedicelli demum apicem infra articulati, the inflorescence of this order is always centrifugal, the partial axis being invariably as well indeed as the general, disposed to dichotomy. Hence the very common presence of three bracteæ to each flower, the central one presenting the leaf from whose axil the partial branch springs.

Stipulæ—if the analogy of these be difficult to ascertain, the structure and functions would appear to be as of leaves, in addition to the function of protection. In most cases they are certainly not double organs; in Naucleaceæ they are apparently so. Can this be explained by supposing them to form a bud with four scales, the scales instead of being imbricate, being on one plane. Stipellæ of Leguminosæ are certainly single; these being all probably stipulate plants, are to be considered as having terminal buds, the buds being either totally, or partially protected by the stipulæ. The difficult nature of ochreæ of Polygoneæ is certainly to be acknowledged, but they are similar to those of Costus, and hence not stipulæ, but an extension of the margin of the vaginate petiole, from which veins are prolonged into it; the functions of these are not stomatose, since they are membranous, the veins being the only green parts.

I see no reason why the stipulæ of Rosæ are not to be considered as belonging to, or dilatations of the petiole. They have no distinct vascular fascicles to indicate a distinct origin. And further, in Lowea no stipulæ exist.

Jonesia: pedicellis apice articulatis, basi bracteolatis, ideoque infloresc. magis composita esse debet; laciniis anticis ? corollæ ? perianth compositum, binatum præbentibus, emarginatio et situs stam 5ti rudiment. Staminis laciniis alternatis ? basi in annulum, seriem 2 indicantem coalit.* The situation of the stamens is somewhat obscure, the two lowermost however alternate with the segments, the two intermediate being sometimes sub-opposite.

Of course if they be opposed, the perianth will be referrible to a calyx if not to a corolla.

Lepidostachys or Scepa. Fruit dicarpillary, stigmata four, hence they are placentary not costoid. bilocular, loculis dispermis, ovula 2 pend; 1 abortiv. semiunceum, testa vix arillus obsacuit clause lutescens carnosa et ab nuclei inter adhæren. Rad. sup. embryo junior viridis.

Stipulæ cad. Gemmam oblegent.

Homalineæ, Calycis; laciniæ 4, petal 4, Glandulæ 4 totidem sepalis oppositæ. Connat; stamin 4, petal opposita; styli 4. Ovar non ext.

Arbor magna. foliis alternis stipulatis, paniculæ racemoso-axillares, Flores minut. viridescent. Pet. et sep. fimbriat. æstiv. imbricat.

Clematis has semina pendula.

The stipulæ of Ficus obviously belong not to the leaves, their insertion taking place $\frac{1}{2}$ a line above that of the petiole. Hence they belong as obviously to the elongation of the axis above the leaf; their coloration is curious, especially as they are green when young. Their vernation is conduplicate and plicate.

Combretum presents several points in common with Rhamneæ; valvate calyx, and tendency to want of petals; to Elæagneæ in calyx and furfuraceous scales; a decandrous Rhamneæ would differ but little in flowers from Combretum.

My idea of the origin of stigmata is proved to be correct by a Phyllanthus, the carpella of which are ovuliferous below, the upper part being fleshy, the stigmata are two to each, obviously corresponding to the placentary inflexions, while the sinus terminating the dorsal suture is totally naked; it is this which should bear the stigma if Lindley's view were correct.

* The reading of this passage is obscure, the MS. being very faintly written in pencil.

*

The true place of Moringa seems to be near Xanthophyllum with which genus it has some remarkable points of resemblance, witness the papilionaceous corolla ; unilocular stamina, their situation, ovary, placentation, and lastly glandulation.

To this Lindley has made an approximation by placing the order near Violarieæ. Its chief difference from Polygaleæ, is habit, foliation, and the perigynous insertion of corolla and stamina, and consequent union of the sepals. As in Xanthophyllum there is no albumen.

(An additional Xanthop. which until to-day I have always taken for a Leguminosa.)

Tamarindus cal 4 partitus, sepals 2, superiorib. connatis. Pet. 3, vexillo, sepalo postico composit ; opposit ; stamen tria ; sepalis 3, inferior opposita. Stylus æstivation deflexus. Pl. 3—Fig. 4.

Pedicelli apice articulat. Folii petiol. basi articulat. Stipulæ minimæ stipellæ.

In Jonesia, there are no petals. Humboldtia comes near Tamarindus, through H. Brunonis, which agrees in calyx and petals.

Thorns of Prionites, what are they ? They are axillary, and yet buds are produced between them and the axis. They have no connection with the leaves. Were it not for the buds above alluded to, I should say that they were abortive branches (bearing one pair of leaves) reduced to spines.

Olacineæ. Certainly in habit, corolla, etc. Olacineæ are allied to Aurantiaceæ, but they are nearer akin to Santalaceæ. The processes are indubitably modified stamina, with a great tendency to irregularity ; in one species from Tagoung only three fertile, and five sterile stamina were observed : the three fertile generally, but not invariably, alternate with the petals.

To Santalaceæ they approach in processes, valvate corolla, and placentation, also to Loranthaceæ.

Eight stamina thus accounted for ; when two opposed to petals, belong to outer series—also single one.

In Punica, the structure of the ovaria is highly curious. We find the bottom of the tube is occupied by two cells, partially filled with ovula, which are attached both to the axis and to the base, as well as to the lower part of the outer paries of each cell ; so far, it does not depart from the order, for in Aplexus the placentation is tolerably similar.

Above these two, are 4-5 cells, filled with ovula, which are attached entirely to the outer wall of each cell, but the placentæ however would seem to have an obvious connexion with the axis, although this is very doubtful.

The formation of the stigma decidedly indicates a binary formation of carpella.

If these 4 upper cells are 4 constantly, and the base of the ovary is as constantly two celled, then the explanation is sufficiently obvious, though different from that given by Lindley.*

First, we have in the bottom from which the mere structure of an ovary is deduced, the normal dicarpellary structure, and there is in addition a tendency in excess toward a parietal placentation.

The anomalous formation arises first from parietal placentæ being produced to the axis, and from spurious growth from the sides of the ovary also meeting in the axis, by which the ovula are divided into four bundles.

Lindley's view seems to be questionable, because as in all cases the styles and stigmata are more permanent than ovaries, there should be as many styles, etc. as ovaries. 2nd, because according to this view the placental suture of the carpella would be turned from the axis, (look at Pomaceæ,) although his view of Pomaceæ being right would indicate an additional affinity with Mespilus, etc. which it does in habit and abbreviated lateral branches.

Are all Myrtaceæ dicarpellar ?

The true nature of the case is pointed out in the instance cited by Lindley of a permanent variety of apple, which has 14 cells and 14 styles ! With regard to Nicotiana and Nolana; have these one or two rows of carpella ?

TECTONA.

Arbores, trunco crasso, cito ramoso, cortice albido, lævi, tenui.

Folia siliceo-aspera, inflorescent dichotoma.

Calyx æstiv. valvat. cor infundibul, subregularis laciniis, 5 rotundatis, demum reflexis æstivat. laciniis super 2, omnino exterior, facies barbato-villosa.

Antheræ longit dehiscent, stylus stigma simplex.

Pubescentia stellata.

Modo Asclepiadeæ, corolla rotata.

GMELINA VILLOSA.

Lab. super. æstivat. omnino exterior fl. axi fere paralleli, pedicell apice bibracteolat.

Cal. minim. 5 dentat.

* Introd. Nat. Syst. p. 44.

Cor. infundibul campanul. bilab; 4 partit. stigma bilabiat-lab infer longiore.

AROIDEUM.

Radix maxime napiformis, undique radiculas exserens, et superne e centro spadicem. Spadix pedunculum 3-uncial terminans. basi squamis magnis membranaceis, lineari-oblongis stipatus sursum in corpus fungoiden, capitatum, maximum, purpureo-sanguineum, superficie rugose dilatata.

Ovar bilocul, diovulat.

Medio antheras bipoross confertissimas, sessiles, numerosas, basi ovaria distantiora gerens.

Ovaria fusco-purp, stylus elongatus clavatus, stigma clavato, capitat.

Odor-floris præserti marcescentis pessimus.

Katha in sylvis aridis.

The fruit of Lagerstramia grandiflora can, I think, be explained by assuming it to consist of several carpella, which by not becoming united near the axis, leave an irregular shaped space in the centre; the placentæ are fleshy, the ovule inserted all around. This view does not take into consideration the situation of the stigmata. The deeper sulci visible externally correspond to the inflexions of the carpellary leaves; in addition to this, the centre of the dorsum of each of these is marked with a line. Pl. 1. Fig. 4.*]

* The preceding eight pages within brackets are written faintly in pencil.

CHAPTER VII.

Report to the Government of India, 12th July, 1837.

In the following report, I have divided the marches into series, corresponding with the countries through which they were made, reserving a table of the whole for a subsequent part. These series will be as follows—

1. From Sadiya to Beesa Lacoom.
2. From Beesa Lacoom to Namtusseek.
3. From Namtuseek to Wullabhoom.
4. From Wullabhoom to Mogoung.
5. From Monoung to Ava.

I. From Sadiya to Beesa Lacoom.

Country traversed belonging to the British Government, and forming part of the south-east extremity of the valley of Assam.

1. From Sadiya to the Noa Dihing river mouth or Mookh. Direction east. Distance 6 miles performed in boat, the course lying up the Burrumpootur.

2. From Noa Dihing Mookh to Rangagurrah on the Noa Dihing. Direction SSE. Distance 12 miles, course lying along the dry bed of the Noa Dihing.

3. From Rangagurrah to Moodoa Mookh, on the same river. Direction south-east, the distance being 12 miles.*

4. From Moodoa Mookh to Kidding. Direction south, the distance 9 miles, course south-east, along the bed of the Noa Dihing as far as Wakhet, thence diverging to SSW. through heavy jungle.

5. From Kidding to Namroop Puthar. Direction, nearly south, the distance being 12 miles, course lying through very heavy jungle, crosses the Karam Panee,† which here is not fordable, and another considerable feeder of the Booree Dihing, and lastly up the Namroop.

* The usual route is to Kujoo Ghat, about five miles below Moodoa Mookh, thence through Sooroo, Kujoo, etc. to the Booree Dihing.

† By the Karam and this other branch, on which old Beesa was situated, all the water which formerly supplied the Noa Dihing now passes into the Booree Dihing.

6. From Namroop Puthar to Beesa Lacoom. Direction south-west, the distance 12 miles, the course extending at first over low hills and difficult ground, thence through heavy jungle intersected by narrow plains, lastly chiefly along the banks of the Darap Panee.

Nature of the country.—It will be seen that with the exception of the three first marches, and part of the fourth, the country is occupied by the heavy jungle so prevalent in these parts. The chief difficulties our party experienced arose from the limited manner in which the jungle had been cut for their passage.

Rivers.—The only one not fordable in the above route, is the Karam Panee, but this does not hold good either above or below the place I crossed. They all discharge much water during the rains, and even in the dry season are navigable for small canoes.

Villages.—These are as follows :—

1. *Digalo Gohain Goung.*—On the right bank of the Noa Dihing it is inhabited by Kamptees lately settled in our territory, and is a respectable village. The Noa Dihing here ceases to be navigable even for small canoes.

2. *Wakhet.*—This is a new but wretched village, inhabited by Singphos. Wakhet Gam was an adherent of the Duphas, and is by all account one of the worst-disposed Singpho chiefs. He is said even at this period still to traffic occasionally in slaves.

3. *Kidding.*—A temporary village, containing about 10 houses, inhabited by Nagas, now naturalised to the plains.

4. *Namroop Puthar.*—So called from a plain on the left bank of the Namroop. The village, which is a mean and despicable one, is on the opposite bank.

5. *Beesa Lacoom.*—Is situated on the right bank of the Darap Panee, which is fordable at the heads of the rapids. It contains 12 small houses. The Gam is, I believe, an uncle of the Beesa Gam, and exercises exclusive controul over the tribe of Beesa Nagas. This influence he appeared to exercise to our disadvantage. He is a discontented man, and his behaviour to our party was very unsatisfactory.

*Population.**—This is scanty enough, particularly when we consider that the houses in the above villages are much smaller than in the better sort of Singpho villages. With the exception of the

* Most of the Singphos subject to our controul are located between Kujoo Ghat and the Booree Dihing, as well as on the banks of this river and in the valley of the Tenga Panee.

Kamptee village the average number of people to each house cannot exceed five. Another small Singpho village exists on the Namroop, about 3 miles from Namroop Puthar, and not far from the site of the coal mine.

Capabilities of the Country.—These are of the usual description. The soil is productive enough, but the labour of clearing the drier spóts is excessive. Excellent rice grounds exist in abundance between Beesa Lacoom and Namroop Puthar, but the cultivation of this, as well as of all the other necessaries, is limited to the quantity absolutely required. Scarcities of grain are of frequent, indeed almost of annual, occurrence; and this is chiefly owing to the pernicious influence of opium or Kanee, to which all our Singphos are immoderately attached. Of the *Mineral Productions*, coal and petroleum were the only ones we met with.

The coal occupies the greater portion of a precipitous part of the sandstone composing the left bank of the river Namroop. Three large veins have been completely exposed by the cutting away of the bank. The coal is I believe of good quality. The river immediately under the veins is very deep, and were it not for the rapids which intervene between the site of the mineral and the Booree Dihing, it would be difficult to conceive a spot affording similar facilities for the transmission of the mineral. I must however, observe, that even in the dry season the river is navigable for small canoes as far as the site alluded to. During the rains no difficulty whatever would be experienced in the carriage, as rafts might be made on the spot. No use is made of the coal by the natives, nor did they seem to be aware of its nature.

Of *the Petroleum** no use whatever is made, although we have ample experience from its universal use by the Burmese, that it is a valuable product both as affording light, and preserving in a very great degree all wooden structures from rot and insects. The springs occur in four different places, all close to the Puthar: of these three occur on the low hill which bounds the Puthar to the southern side, and one on the Puthar itself, at the foot of the range alluded to. The springs are either solitary, as in that of the Puthar, or grouped, a number together; the discharge varies extremely from a thin greenish aqueous fluid to a bluish grey opaque one, of rather a thick consistence: the quantity poured out by these latter springs is very

* The existence of Petroleum is of value as connected with the solution of Caoutchouc.

considerable. On the surface of all, but especially on these last, an oleaginous, highly inflammable fluid collects in the form of a thin film. The jungle surrounding the springs ceases abruptly, the ground around, and among them, being covered with stunted grass and a few small herbaceous plants. Elephants and large deer are frequent visitors to the springs; of the former, the tracts are frequent, and they are sometimes shot here by the natives.

Vegetable Products.—The jungles afford several kinds of bamboo, some of which are of value; generally speaking the trees are not large, with the exception of a gigantic Dipterocarpus, wood-oil or dammar tree; of this particular tree I have seen specimens measuring 100 feet from the base to the first branch. The wood is of no value, nor have I seen any use made in Assam of the resinous secretion, which is in great vogue on the Tenasserim Coast for the construction of torches, etc.

II. From Beesa Lacoom to Namtusseek.

COUNTRY TRAVERSED FORMING PARTS OF THE NAGA RANGE OF HILLS, AND OF THE SOUTHERN BOUNDARY OF THE VALLEY OF ASSAM: THE NORTHERN SIDE IS SUBJECT TO BRITISH, THE SOUTHERN TO BURMESE CONTROUL.

1*st.* STAGE.—*Halting place* in the jungle, at an elevation of 770 feet above the sea. Direction SSE. Distance 12 miles, course over low hills covered with dense jungle.

2nd. Darap Panee.—Altitude 1029 feet. Direction SSE. Distance 12 miles, passed over some difficult places; crossed the Darap twice before we reached the halting place, course through very heavy jungle, except on the summits of the higher hills, which are tolerably open.

*3rd. Namtusseek,** or Tusseek Panee, altitude 1413 feet. Direction SSE. Distance 12 miles, country more open: summit of the hills covered with grass and scattered trees. The highest hill surmounted was certainly 1000 feet above our halting place.

4th. Namtusseek, or Tusseek Panee, altitude (not observed). Direction SSE. Distance 10 miles, course almost entirely up the bed of the river over boulders, occasionally skirting the stream through heavy and wet jungle.

* The affix *Nam*, signifies in the Shan language a river or stream.

5*th. Yoomsan nullah,* near the foot of the Patkaye. Alt. 3026 feet; direction SSE. distance 4 miles. Course for a short time along the bed of the Namtusseek, until we crossed a small stream, the Tukka-kha: then ascended a mountain, about 3500 feet high; on reaching the summit we descended until we reached the halting place.

6*th. Nam-maroan,* or Maroan-kha.* Alt. 2500 feet. Direction ESE. Distance 15 miles. Ascended until we reached the summit of the Patkaye; the ascent was in some places very steep, and owing to the unsettled state of the weather, very difficult. Reached the boundary nullah, along which we proceeded for some time; we then commenced the descent, which was steep, and continued so, until we reached the Nam-maroan. The extreme elevation we reached was rather more than 5000 feet.†

7*th. Nam-maroan.*—Altitude estimated 2000 feet. Direction ESE. Distance 10 miles, course along the bed of the stream; ground difficult, and much impeded by boulders.

8*th. Nam-maroan.*—Altitude not taken. Direction ESE. Distance 7 miles. Course the same, but of a less difficult nature.

9*th. Khathung khioung.*‡—Altitude 1622 feet. Direction E. by S. Distance 7 miles, course continues along the Nam-maroan, the whole way: ground much less difficult. Passed close to a Singpho village of two houses; some Puthars which bore traces of having once been cultivated and inhabited occurred on this march.

10*th. Khussee-khioung.*—Altitude 3516. Direction E. by S. Distance 13 miles, left almost immediately the Khathung Kioung, and commenced ascending. Ascent in some places very steep and difficult, and continued until we had reached an elevation of 5600 feet. The descent then commenced, and continued until we reached the Khussee-khioung, passing along for some distance the Natkaw-khioung. The descent was occasionally difficult, owing to broken ground; tree jungle occurred almost throughout the whole distance.

11*th Kuttack Bhoom.*§—Altitude 3270. General direction S. Distance 13 miles. Left the Khussee-khioung, but reached it again before long. Continued to descend considerably, until we reached the Nam-thuga, thence the descent increased considerably. Halted on an open grassy spot, from which an extensive view of the valley of Hookhoom is obtained.

* The word *Kha* is Singfo, and signifies a river.

† Here Capt. Hannay and myself were met by Mr. Bayfield.

‡ Khioung, or Kioung, signifies a small river in the Burmese language.

§ Bhoom is the Singfo word for mountain.

12th. Namtusseek.—Altitude 1099 feet. General direction ESE. Distance 10 miles. Descended from Kuttack Bhoom, until we reached the Loonkharankha, then ascended considerably. The descent then recommenced, until we reached the Namtusseek. Heavy jungle occurred throughout. Path occasionally difficult, becoming as we approached the base of the range very wet. We crossed several small mountain streams.

General features of the hills.—The prevailing formation appears to be sandstone, and connected with this we have rounded summits, not attaining a great elevation, and a considerable depth of soil. The lower ranges are throughout covered with heavy tree jungle. This becomes excessively thick and wet along the water courses, which are of frequent occurrence towards the base of the range, both on the northern and southern sides. But from an elevation of 1000 feet to that of Yoomsan, a great change for the better takes place on the northern face, the hills being covered with clay, and generally not very high grass jungle, among which trees are scattered. This character is particularly evident along both sides of the valley drained by the Namtusseek of the northern side. The Patkaye is wooded to its summit; the jungle on the south side being much more humid than that on the northern. Indeed on this face of the range, with the exception of the Puthars on the Nam-maroan, scarcely more than two open spots exist, and both of these are of small extent. Of these one exists at an elevation of 5500 feet, and one at Kuttack Bhoom.

The paths although very often steep, are easy enough for coolies, except during wet weather, when they become very slippery. With some degree of preparation the worst places might be made passable for lightly loaded elephants, and this would be facilitated by the soft nature of most of the rocks. The most difficult marches are those which lie along the beds of the streams, and these, it has been seen, are far the most numerous; they are particularly difficult for elephants, the boulders affording a very precarious footing to these weighty animals. The difficulty is much increased by rain, when even coolies find considerable difficulty in making any progress. Several elephants accompanied Major White as far as the Darap Panee, and a small suwaree elephant, loaded with a light tent, succeeded in reaching Yoomsan. The southern side of the range is decidedly of a more difficult nature than the northern, and it is in addition of greater extent: the highest point traversed is 5600 feet above the level of the sea. The range might be traversed by a lightly loaded active native in six days.

Streams.—These all partake of the usual nature of mountain torrents; they are all fordable during the cold weather, the principal ones being crossed at the heads of the rapids. The boundary nullah is a mere streamlet: it runs between two ridges of the Patkaye: its course being about ESE. and WNW. Owing to the frequency of the streams and their mountainous nature, I should imagine that this route is impracticable during the rains.

Villages.—Not a single village or house exists directly on the route. One small Naga village is visible from the Namtusseek below Yoomsan, and a detached hut is visible here and there on a high mountain close to, and NE. of Yoomsan. On the Burmese side there is, as I have mentioned before, a village consisting of two houses close to the route. This village has lately been established by some Singphos from Nimbrung, several marches to the eastward.

Population.—I certainly did not see 100 Nagas throughout the time passed in traversing these hills, although I am satisfied that every man within a reasonable distance came into Camp in the hopes of sharing in the extensive distribution of presents. From the appearance of the country about Yoomsan, and the valley of the Namtusseek, I am inclined to think that the population was at one time considerable. The openness of the country, which is as I have previously said chiefly clothed with grass, and the peculiar and generally imperfect aspect of the trees, can only be accounted for, by supposing the country to have been extensively cleared, particularly when it is remembered that the highest portions of the range are thickly wooded. But allowing this supposition to be correct, it is no proof, that the total population has been on the decline, for we must take into account, the wandering nature of all hill tribes. In forming an opinion of a hill population, which in all times and places has, in this country at least, been found scanty; we must take care not to confound the temporary huts, erected in khets, for the purpose of protecting the cultivation, with actually inhabited houses; to the former description I think the detached houses mentioned as being visible from Yoomsan are to be referred.

The Nagas, at least the men, for I saw no women, are a small, active, large-legged race, with Tartar faces. They are divided into very many tribes, each of which has some peculiarity of costume. Those I saw were decidedly inferior to any of the other hill tribes, with which I am acquainted. Their clothing is miserable, the chief protection consisting of a number of rings, made of rattan, which encircle the abdomen. They are as usual excessively dirty, and much attached to the use of tobacco and ardent spirits. Their wants are few, but even these are miserably supplied. They entertain an unbounded fear of the Singphos, who appear to make any use of them they think proper. Their only weapons are spears, Singpho dhas and battle axes.

The Singphos cannot be considered otherwise than as encroachers. Invasions of these restless, marauders appear not to have been uncommon up to a late date. The remains of two stockades, in which they had entrenched themselves were extant, one close to Yoomsan, the other on the S. face of the Patkaye. I have before said that the puthars on the Nam-maroan bore evidence of having been inhabited, and apparently to some extent. But even during the stay of Major White on these hills, an irruption of Singphos from Nimbrung had taken place, and had totally unsettled the peace of the native inhabitants. Such things must be expected to occur, particularly when it is well known that the Burmese, the only power to which they are subjects, can exercise no authority over the Singphos in any one direction, except when they have a large armed force in the valley of Hookhoom.

Of the Capabilities of the country it would be vain to attempt giving an opinion. Scarcely any cultivation was passed on the route. The soil is generally deep, more or less yellow, and somewhat clayey; the hollows having a thin superstratum of black mould. Taking the deserted state of the country into account, this part of the Naga range is of little importance, except as forming portion of a most natural and well defined boundary, compared with other portions of the same range to the westward.

Products.—The principal mineral product is salt, an article which is procured abundantly in some other more available points of the range. We saw one small spring on the Namtusseek, from which supplies had been lately taken.

Vegetable Products.—Fine timber trees occur here and there. Oaks, Magnolias and Chesnuts occur not uncommonly, the Magnolias being of these in this range the most characteristic of elevation. The horse chesnut of Assam, (Osculus Asamicus mihi) occurs on both sides of the range, but does not ascend further than 3,000 feet. No Fir trees exist on the route, nor is it probable that they exist on the range in this direction. One of the most interesting plants is a new species of tea, which I believe to be a genuine Thea; it is called Bun Fullup, or jungle tea, by the Assamese, in contra-distinction to the true tea plant, which is called Fullup. This species makes its appearance at an elevation of about 1,000 feet, and is met with as high up as 4,000 feet. It attains the size of a tree of 30 feet in height; it is used only as a medicine. No real tea exists on this route; several plants were pointed out to me as tea, but all were spurious instances. The higher portions of the ranges have a flora approaching in many instances to that of northern latitudes. As examples of this, it will be sufficient to allude, in addition to the trees mentioned above, to the existence of two species of Daphne, one of Barberry, several species of a genus nearly allied to the Whortle Berries, a Violet, and several species of Smilacineæ, to which order the Lily of the Valley belongs.

In concluding this part of my report, I may perhaps be permitted to advert to the question of the possibility of transporting a body of armed men into the Burmese dominions by this route. Although there is nothing in the nature of this portion of the boundary which would render this operation very difficult, yet considering the state of the adjoining parts of Upper Assam, and that of Hookhoom, it becomes almost impracticable. I allude to the extreme difficulty of procuring grain in Upper Assam, in which, at least around Sadiya, annual scarcities are by no means uncommon, and to the utter impossibility of drawing any supplies from Hookhoom in its present miserable state. All the necessary supplies would require to be drawn from Lower Assam, and for the transport of these the scanty population of this extremity of the valley would by no means be sufficient. Bearing on this point it must be remembered, that from the 1st of April to the 1st November, these hills cannot be traversed except by their native inhabitants, without incurring great risk from the usual severe form of jungle fever.

III. From Namtusseek to Wullaboom.

Country traversed subject to Burmese authority, forming greater portion of the Valley of Hookhoong, or the Paeendweng.

March 1. *From Namtusseek to Nhempean.*—Direction E. Distance 18 miles, crossed the Namtusseek, then passed through heavy tree jungle, and subsequently over extensive grassy plains.

2. *From Nhempean to Nidding.*—Direction SSE. Distance 4½ miles, course along the Namtoroan, thence up the Saxsaikha.

3. *From Nidding to Kulieyang.*—Direction SSE. Distance 13 miles, country covered either with tree or high grass jungle. Passed a deserted village, Thilling Khet.

4. *From Kulleyang to Isilone.*—Direction SW. Distance 10 miles, country rather more open. Puthars are of common occurrence; passed a small village, Damoon.

5. *From Tsilone to Meinkhoong.*—Distance 17 miles, course at first along the Namtunai,* country open, consisting of grassy plains; several nullahs occur.

6. *From Meinkhoon to Wullabhoom.*—Direction SE. Distance 13 miles. Course over plains intersected by tree jungle, subsequently up the bed of the Nempyo-kha.

Nature of the Country.—The valley of Hookhoong, or as the Burmese call it, in allusion to its amber mines, Paeendweng, is of small extent. Its greatest diameter is in the direction of E. to W.† its southern termination being within a few miles from Wullabhoom. It is surrounded on all sides by hills, the highest of which are towards the NE. and E. none however would appear to exceed 6000 feet in height; and from their appearance, I imagine they are wooded to their summits. The lowest hills are those which form the southern boundary, and these scarcely deserve the name. From Kuttack-bhoom a fine view of the valley is obtained; it is here very narrow, and does not I should think exceed 25 miles in breadth. The features of the country are in a striking degree similar to those of Upper Assam, that is, it presents a plain surface intersected frequently by belts of jungle, the parts at the base of the boundary hills being exclusively occupied by heavy jungle. The general elevation of the plain above the sea may be estimated at about 1000 feet, so that it is several hundred feet above the level of Sadiya, But although this is the case, the valley of Hookhoom undergoes the same changes during the rainy season as Assam, the greater part being during that period under water.

Of the Climate it is perhaps presumptuous to give any opinion: it is however by no means so cold as that of Upper Assam. In April the daily range of the thermometer was very considerable, from 60°

* Which we forded a few miles below Isilone; depth of the ford from two to four feet.

† In this direction the valley is nearly 65 miles in length.

to 88°. The rains set in later than on the northern side of the Patkaye, and they are said to be much less severe.

The rivers are numerous, the principal one is the Namtunai,* which subsequently assumes the name of Kyeendweng. This is in the places I saw it a large, generally deep and sluggish stream, varying in breadth from 270 to 350 yards. The next in size is the Namtoroan, which has more of the character of a mountain stream; it is of considerable breadth (opposite Nhempean it is 270 yards across,) and presents numerous rapids. Both of these rivers are navigable for boats of some size. The other rivers are small and insignificant; all fall into the Namtoroan or Namtunai.

Villages.—Of these the following were passed on the route:—

1. *Nhempean*, on the right bank of the Namtoroan, is situated on an extensive open grassy plain, it is stockaded: it contains about 12 houses, the river is here navigable for middling sized canoes.

2. *Tubone*, on the same bank, but lower down, and within quarter of a mile of Nhempean, it is of about the same size, and similarly stockaded.

3. *Nidding*, on the left bank of the Saxsar-kha, about three-quarters of a mile above its junction with the Namtoroan: it is a stockaded village, and about the same size.

4. *Calleyang*, on the Prong-kha contains about 8 houses: it is not stockaded.

5. *Lamoon*, on the Moneekha, is a very small village, containing four or five houses: it is not stockaded.

6. *Tsilone*, on the left bank of the Namtunai. This is the Dupha Gam's village: it is of the ordinary size, and is stockaded in the usual manner.

7. *Meinkhoon*, on the Cadeekha, by which it is intersected; it consists of two stockades, separated by the above stream; and contains about 25 houses, none of which are however large. It is here that the first Pagodas (Poongye houses) occur. The village is situated on an open grassy plain of considerable extent.

8. *Wullabhoom*, on the right bank of the Nemokapy, an insignificant steam. This village is not stockaded; it contains about 10 houses, of which several are of the Singpho structure.

The Gam of this village was in expectation of an attack from the Dupha people, and had in consequence erected a small square

* This river rises in a conspicuous range, well known by the name of Shewe Down-gyee, or great golden mountain.

stockade for his own use; he had however built it so small that he might easily be dislodged by means of a long spear.

In addition to these, there is a village called *Bone*, on the Namtoroan; the path leading to this is crossed soon after leaving Namtusseek, and another stockaded village, on the right bank of the Namtoroan, a little below the mouth of the Saxsaikha.

None of the above villages are situated on strong positions. The stockades are as usual of bamboo, and are but weak defences; the space between the stockade and the outer palisades is covered with short pointed bamboos, placed obliquely in the ground: these are called Panjahs by the Assamese; they inflict very troublesome wounds, and are universally employed by the Singphos. The interiors of the stockades are dirty, the houses are built without order, and generally fill the stockade completely, so that the people inside might be burnt out with the greatest ease. The average number of houses in each of the above villages, may be estimated at about 12, of these the largest occur at Wullaboom. They are built on muchowns, and resemble in all respects those of our Assam Singphos. They are generally thatched with grass (Imperata cylindrica.*) The larger kinds have invariably one end unenclosed; under this *portico*, which is usually of some size, all the domestic operations are carried on. The Dupha Gam's is not distinguished above the rest in any one way.

Population.—No country inhabited by sets of petty chieftains belonging to different tribes, which are generally at enmity with each other, can be populous; it is therefore with considerable surprise that I find it stated that the number of houses in the north and eastern sides of the valley is estimated at not less than 3000, which at the rate of 7 men to one house, which is, considering the great size of very many Singpho houses, rather underrated, would make the population of these portions of the valley amount to 21,000 souls. The part of the valley which I have traversed, and during which route 75 miles of ground were passed over, does not present a single sign which, in the absence of direct evidence, would lead one to suppose that it contained a considerable population. During the before mentioned marches, I saw only four paths, crossing or diverging from that which we followed. Of these, one *leads*, as I have mentioned, to Bone, one to the hills on the NE., one to a Singpho village, some miles to the south of our track, and the fourth diverged from the

* This is certainly not the Ulukhor of Buch. Hamilton's statistics of Dinajpoor.

path leading to the Amber mines through the village of a chief called Tharapown Hhoung. The population on the above route of 75 miles, would at the rate of 7 men to one house, and 12 houses, to each village, amount only to 840, but I think that 1,100 or 1,200 would be a fairer estimate. From Kuttack-bhoom, as I have mentioned, a great portion of the valley is distinctly seen, and nothing meets the eye but jungle, broken here and there by the waters of the Namtunai: not a clearing is even visible; instead of a population of 30,000, as has been stated I should imagine that the whole valley of Hookhoom does not contain more than 12,000.

The above population consists almost entirely of Singphos and their Assamese slaves, and these last form a considerable portion. This was particularly evident at Wulla-khoon, where they certainly out-numbered their masters.

The Singphos of Hookhoong resemble exactly those located in Assam: they are however less given to opium eating. They are of the same indolent habits, and content themselves with cultivating sufficient grain to keep themselves from starving. The women wear the Thumein, or Burmese dress, a costume which is entirely unknown among the Singphos of Assam. The most superior men I saw belonged to the Luppai tribe, from the east of the Irrawaddi; they had come to Meinkhoon for the purpose of procuring amber. In manners and dress they resembled the Shan-Chinese, they were provided with firelocks, in the use of which they were certainly adroit. The usual weapons of the Hookhoong Singphos are dhas and spears. I saw very few muskets.

The behaviour of these people was throughout civil, and perhaps friendly. Their hatred of the Burmese is excessive, the visits of the armed forces of this nation being most harassing and oppressive. They are sub-divided into tribes, among whom there is but little unanimity. The Dupha Gam is much disliked, as he is considered the cause of the visit of the Burmese. His power has been much exaggerated; he is not capable of bringing 500 men into the field. So unpopular was he, that it was reported to Mr. Bayfield, that he was to be cut off immediately the Burmese force had left the valley.

In giving the foregoing low estimate of the population of the valley, I believe I have taken into consideration every circumstance of importance. The occurrence of several old burial places on the route, some of which are of considerable extent, might be considered by some as a proof, that the population has undergone a decrease; but

I conceive that it is sufficiently accounted for by the wandering habits of the people.

Capabilities.—The greater part of the valley is well adapted for the cultivation of rice, and as the soil is generally rich, approaching in external characters to that of some parts of Upper Assam, particularly Muttack, it is capable of supporting a large population.

Products.—Of the mineral productions, the most remarkable is Amber, for which the valley of Hookhoong has been long famous, and from the existence of which it derives its Burmese name. The mines are situated in low, wooded hills, from which they are distant between five and six miles; of this distance the first three miles traverse the plain on which Meinkhoong is situated. The pits now worked give occupation to about a dozen people; they occur on the brow of a hill: they are square, and of various depth, the deepest being about 40 feet, the diameter not exceeding three feet; the workmen ascending and descending by placing their feet in holes made in two faces of the square. No props are used to prevent the sides of the pits from falling in, the tenacity of the soil rendering this precaution unnecessary. The instruments used, are small wooden shovels, a wooden crow-bar tipped with iron for displacing the soil or breaking the rocks, baskets for removing the substances so displaced, buckets made of the bark of trees* for removing the water which is met with in the deepest pits, and rude leavers similar to those used in Madras for the purposes of irrigation, for carrying the soil, etc. from the pits to the surface; these however are only used in the deeper pits, a hooked bamboo answering the purpose in the shallower ones.

The soil throughout the upper portion, and indeed for a depth of from 15 to 20 feet, is clayey and red: the remainder consists of a greyish-black carbonaceous earth, increasing in density with the depth, and being very hard at a depth of 40 feet. The amber occurs in both these, the clue to its existence being the presence of small masses of lignite. The searching occupies but very little time, as the presence of the lignite is readily ascertained; all I saw dug out occurred as small irregular deposits; it did not appear to be abundant. The people appear to have no guide for the selections of favourable spots on which to commence their operations; but having once met with a good pit, they dig other pits all around, and often within a distance of two feet from the first one sunk.

I could not succeed in procuring a single fine specimen; indeed

* Probably from a species of Sterculia.

the workmen denied having found any of value during the last six years! It is an article in great request among the Chinese and Singphos; at the pits, however, it is not high priced, and a first rate pair of ear-rings are procurable at Meinkhoong for 5 tickals; in Assam 10 rupees are occasionally given. Meinkhoong is annually visited by parties of Shan-Chinese, for the purpose of procuring this mineral; the caravan at the time I passed this village had returned, and I believe was met by Mr. Bayfield. There was a small party of Lupai Singphos from the East of the Irrawaddi, consisting of a Tsonba and six or seven followers still waiting for a supply.

The spot occupied by pits is considerable, but three-fourths of these are no longer worked. Compared with the Serpentine mines, they are but of small value.

Both *Coal and Salt* exist in the valley; the only indication of the existence of the former I saw, was a mass of lignite in the bed of a nullah between Tsilone and Meinkhoong.

Vegetable products.—Fine timber trees,* which belong to the same genus as the Saul, occur between Nhempean and Namtusseek, and elsewhere towards the foot of the hills surrounding the valley.

The Mulberry of Upper Assam occurs likewise, and the leaves supply with food a species of silkworm. From the silk a coarse species of cloth is manufactured, but the use of this appears to be very limited.

Tea appears to be of uncommon occurrence. The only specimens I saw were given me by Mr. Bayfield, they were procured from low hills some distance from Shellingket. On this subject Mr. Bayfield made very frequent and minute enquiries, and the result appears to be that the plant is of rare occurrence; none exists towards or about the amber mines.

The Room of Upper Assam (Ruellia Indigofera Mihi) is in use for dyeing cloths, but not so much so as in Assam.

The cultivated plants are of the ordinary kind; and the produce is just sufficient to meet the wants of the inhabitants. Owing to the presence of the Myoowoon's force, rice was scarce during my visit; the price was seven tickals a basket, each of which contains about 30 days' supply for one man.

The domestic animals are of the ordinary description: fowls forming the only poultry. But on this subject it is unnecessary to enlarge, as the habits and manners of the people are precisely the same as those of the Assamese Singphos.

* The Toung-bein of the Burmese.

IV. From Wullabhoon to Mogoung.

Country traversed forming considerable portion of the Mogoung Valley, throughout subject to Burmese authority.

March 1. *Halted* on a small stream, a tributary of the Mogoung river.—Direction nearly S. distance 22 miles, course at first along the Namphyet, thence over low hills, forming part of the S. boundary of the valley of Hookhoong.

2. *Halted* on the Mogoung river.—Direction S. distance 22 miles, over similar low hills until we reached the Mogoung river after a a march of four hours, soon descending into its bed, which we followed.

3. *Mogoung* river.—Direction S. distance 13 miles, course along the bed of the river.

4. *Mogoung* river.—Direction SE. distance 14 miles, course continued along the bed of the river.

5. *Kamein.*—Direction SSE. distance 14 miles: on starting left the Mogoung river: course throughout over fine open high plains intersected by belts of jungle.

6. *From Camein to Mogoung.*—Direction SSE. Distance 25 miles, course over high open plains and dry woods. Many nullahs occurred on the route: crossed the Mogoung river opposite to Kamein.

Nature of the Country.—The low hills which are passed before reaching the Mogoung river, are covered with tree jungle, but they afford scarcely any thing of interest; they are here and there intersected by small plains, covered with the usual grasses*. The country traversed while following the Mogoung river, is most uninteresting, the road following almost entirely the sandy bed of the river, the banks of which are either covered with grass or tree jungle. On leaving this most tortuous river, the face of the country improved and became very picturesque, presenting almost exclusively fine high, and rather extensive plains covered with grass, and partially with trees, while here and there they are intersected by strips of dry tree jungle. Low hills are visible frequently, especially to the eastward.

* Many of these hills are inhabited by Kukkeens, who do a great deal of mischief, and whose annual depredations remain unchecked and unpunished.

Villages and Towns.

1. *Camein*, on the right bank of the Mogoung river, at the junction of the Endaw-khioung, consists of two stockades, one on a small hill the other at the foot. Both together contain about 32 houses. The inhabitants are Shans. It is a place of some consequence, as it is on the route from Mogoung to the Serpentine mines. From Kamein Shewe Down Gyee, a conspicuous mountain, so called, bears east.

2. *Mogoung*, on the right bank of the river of the same name, just below the junction to the Namyeen Khioung, contains rather fewer than 300 houses. Although it contains so few houses it is a place of considerable extent. It is surrounded by the remains of a timber stockade, similar in construction to those of Burmah proper. The houses are mostly small, and I speak within bounds when I say, that there is not a single one that bears the stamp of respectability. There is a bazaar, but nothing good is procurable in it. Tea and sugar-candy are rare and high priced. Pork is plentiful. Mogoung is situated in a plain of some extent, this plain is surrounded in almost every direction by hills, all of which, with the exception of Shewe Down Gyee, are low: the nearest of these are about three miles off.

The inhabitants are mostly Shans, there are some Assamese, the chief of whom is a relation of Chundra Kant, the ex-Rajah of Assam. The best street in the town, though one of small extent, is that occupied by the resident Chinese, none of whom however are natives of China proper. Of this people I should say there are barely 60 in Mogoung, and, judging from their houses, none of which are of brick, I should say they are very inferior to their fellow-countrymen residing in Bamo.

During our stay in Mogoung, which was protracted owing to the disturbed state of the country, the population was much increased by Shan-Chinese returning from the Serpentine mines; and as there was a considerable number of boats engaged by them for the transportation of the Serpentine, the town looked busier than it otherwise would have done.

The Mogoung river is here about 100 yards broad, but it is much subdivided by sand banks: it is navigable for moderate sized boats a considerable distance above the town. In the upper part of the course this river abounds with fish to an unprecedented degree; of these the most numerous is the Bokhar of Assam, and of this I have seen shoals of immense extent.

The Namyeen is a small and shallow stream. Although from the extent of the stockade Mogoung has evidently in former periods (during the Shan dynasty) been of extent and consequence, it is at present a mean and paltry town. It derives any little consequence it possesses from being the rendezvous of the Shan-Chinese, who flock here annually for procuring Serpentine.

The most valuable products of the Mogoung district is the Serpentine; the mines producing which, we visited from Kameim. The marches are as follows,

1. *From Kamein to Endawkhioung.*—Direction SSW. Distance 10 miles, course over low hills covered with jungle, with intervening grassy valleys of small extent; crossed the Isee Een nullah.

2. *Halted on a plain,* on a patch of ground lately under cultivation. Direction SSW. Distance 14 miles. Course over a similar tract of country; continued for some time close to the Endawkhioung; crossed several nullahs.

3. *Halted in the jungle.*—Direction WNW. Distance 17 miles. Country the same: we changed our course on reaching the path which leads to Kionkseik, a Singpho village, diverging to the N.; halted within a short distance of Kuwa Bhoom.

4. *Reached the mines.*—Direction WNW. Distance 10 miles, course over small plains and through jungle until we reached Kuwa Bhoom, which we ascended in a WNW. direction, extreme altitude attained 2,799 feet. The descent was steep, varied by one or two steep ascents of some hundred feet in height. On nearing the base of the range we continued through heavy and wet jungle, until we arrived at the mines.

These celebrated Serpentine* mines occupy a valley of somewhat semi-circular form, and bounded on all sides by thickly wooded hills of no great height. To the north the valley passes off into a ravine, down which a small streamlet that drains the valley escapes, and along this, at a distance of two or three miles, another spot of ground affording Serpentine is said to occur. The valley is small: its greatest diameter, which is from E. to W. being about three-quarters of a mile, and its smallest breadth varying from 460 to 600 or 700 yards.

The whole of the valley, which appears formerly to have been occupied by rounded hillocks, presents a confused appearance, being dug up in every direction, and in the most indiscriminate way; no steps being taken to remove the earth, etc. that have been thrown up

* Serpentine is occasionally found in the bed of the Nam-marsan.

in various places during the excavations. Nothing in fact like a pit or a shaft exists, nor is there any thing to repay one for the tediousness of the march from Kamein.

The stone is found in the form of more or less rounded boulders mixed with other boulders of various rocks and sizes imbedded in brick-coloured yellow or nearly orange-coloured clay, which forms the soil of the valley, and which is of considerable depth. The excavations vary much in form, some resembling trenches; none exceed 20 feet in depth. The workmen have no mark by which to distinguish at sight the Serpentine from the other boulders; to effect this, fracture is resorted to, and this they accomplish, I believe, by means of fire. I did not see the manner in which they work, or the tools they employ, all the Shans having left for Kamein, as the season had already been over for some days. No good specimens were procurable. The workmen reside in the valley, drawing their supplies from Kioukseik.

On our road to the mines we met daily, and especially on the last march, parties of Shan-Chinese, Burmese, and a few Singphos on their return. Of these in all Mr. Bayfield counted about 1,100, of whom about 700 were Shan-Chinese: these were accompanied by ponies, which they ordinarily use as beasts of burden. The larger blocks of stone were carried by four or five men, on bamboo frames; the smaller, but which still are of considerable size, on ingenious frames which rest on the nape of the coolies' neck; the frame has two long arms which the bearer grasps in his hand, and which enables him to relieve himself of his burden, and re-assume it without much sacrifice of labour, as he props his load against a tree, which is then raised by the legs of the frame some height from the ground. The valley we visited affords I believe the greatest quantity of the stone, which is said to be annually diminishing, neither are pieces of the finest sort so often procurable as they were formerly wont to be.

The path to the mines is on the whole good; it is choked up here and there by jungle, and the occurrence of one or two marshy places contribute to render it more difficult. It bears ample evidences of being a great thoroughfare.

The greater part of the stone procured is removed in the large masses, to Kioukseik, and thence by water by the aid of the Endawkhioung to Mogoung. At this place duties are levied upon it. Hence almost the whole is taken to Topo by water. From this place the Shan-Chinese carry it to their own country on ponies.

From the stone various ornaments are made; from the inferior kind, bangles, cups, etc. and from the superior, which is found in small portions generally within the larger masses, rings, etc. The stone is, I am informed by Mr. Bayfield, cut by means of twisted copper wire. The price of the inferior kind is high.

It is from these mines that the province of Mogoung derives its importance; so much so, that its revenue is said to exceed that of any other Burman Province. The sum derived from the Serpentine alone is stated to be occasionally as high as 40,000 Rs. per annum.

Owing to the avidity with which this product is sought after by the Chinese, it is highly desirable to ascertain whether it exists in Assam, which indeed is probably the case. I believe it is reported to exist near Beesa; at any rate, blood-stone is found in this extremity of the valley of Assam, and this, in Chinese eyes, is of considerable value. If the Serpentine is found, specimens should be sent to Mogoung. As the Shan-Chinese are reported to be a most penurious race, a small reduction in the price below that of the Burmese, would suffice to divert the current of the trade into Assam. Another interesting product, although of no value, exists in the shape of an Alkaline spring on the Sapiya Khioung, which hence derives its name. The water of this spring bubbles up sparingly and quietly from under the rocky bed of the above mountain torrent, it is quite clear, of a decided and pure alkaline taste: it is used by the natives for the purpose of washing, and it answers this remarkably well. Of this interesting spring Mr. Bayfield took specimens for analysis.

Salt is procurable within a distance of three or four days from Kioukseik.

Vegetable products.—Teak, and some of it is of a fine description, occurs both on the route between the Mogoung river and Kamein, as well as between Kamein and the Serpentine mines. The natives do not however appear to cut it, probably owing to the want of water carriage. Fine timber trees, nearly allied to the Saul, likewise occur on the road to the mines.

I met with the tea but once. This occurred among the low hills dividing the Mogoung district from the valley of Hookhoong, close to the Dupai-beng-kheoung, or Tea tree Nullah. There was no difference in the specimens brought to me from the plant of Assam, with the exception that the leaves were even larger than in the plant alluded to; it did not occur in abundance. It exists I believe in another place on this route, and among the same hills, but I did not succeed in procuring specimens. Throughout both routes scarcely any cultivation was seen. Between the Mogoung river and Mogoung town considerable portions of some low hills to the East, presented the appearance of clearings. It must however be observed, that the appearance of clearings is a most fallacious ground on which to form an estimate of the population; 1st, owing to the habits of a nomadic population; 2ndly, because a spot once cleared, keeps up the appearance of a clearing for a long time; and 3rdly, because some particular spots are, from some local cause or other, exclusively inhabited by grasses, the prevalence of which will at a little distance always give one the idea of cultivation.

Population.—This in the somewhat extensive tract of the Mogoung district traversed, is very scanty. That of Mogoung and suburbs may be estimated at about 1,600, and that of Kamein at 250. In addition to these places, I have to mention a small Singpho village of three or four houses, seen on a range of hills during our first march towards the mines, and bearing about WNW., and Kioukseik. This latter place we visited on our return from the mines, it is a stockaded village, containing 16 houses, and about 120 souls. It is situated about 100 yards from a small stream, the Nam Teen: it is inhabited by Singphos: it is about a mile from the divergence of the road to the mines, and bears from this spot nearly due south. During the season of operations at the mines it is a place of some consequence, as all the necessary supplies of grain are procured from it. At the time of our visit, there was a good sized bazaar along the Nam Teen, which was likewise a good deal crowded by boats.

The neighbouring hills are inhabited here and there by Kukkeens, the most troublesome perhaps of all mountainous tribes; but there are some other villages about the lake, called the Endawgyee. We had an opportunity of viewing from a distance the above lake on our return from the mines. From an open spot on the eastern face of Kuwa Bhoom, it bore nearly due south, and was estimated as being 15 miles distant. We could not distinguish its outline, but we saw enough to satisfy us that it was a large body of water. It is situated in an extensive plain near a range of hills, part of which form portion of its banks. From the same spot we could see Shewe Down Gyee, the large range from which the Namtunai takes its course, bearing nearly due east, and at an estimated distance of 35 miles; the situation of the mines is therefore nearly due east from Kamein.

V. From Mogoung to Ava.

The whole of the distance between the two above places was performed by water.

The time occupied in descending the Mogoung river was three days. This river is exceedingly tortuous, generally a good deal subdivided, and its channels are in many places shallow. The chief obstacle it presents to navigation consists in rapids, which commence below Tapan, and continue for some distance; these rapids are not severe, but are rendered difficult by the presence of rocks, many of large size. These rapids commence immediately the river in its course approaches some low ranges of hills. Boats of considerable size however manage to reach Mogoung; they ascend the severer rapids in channels made along the sides of the river, by removing and piling up on either side the boulders which form great part of the bed of the river in these places. The descent is managed in the same way, the speed of the boat being retarded by the crew exerting their united force in an opposite direction. On leaving the proximity of the hills, the river resumes its natural and rather slow character, and towards its mouth there is scarcely any stream at all. The channels are much impeded by stumps of trees. The country through which the Mogoung river passes is very uninteresting, and almost exclusively jungle, either tree or high grass.

Only one village, Tapan, is met with; this is small, and is situated on the right bank; with the exception of its river face it is stockaded. At this place the Shan-Chinese leave the river, striking off in an E. direction towards the Irrawaddi, which they reach in one day. We observed a small Kukkeen village on some hills near Tapan; with these exceptions no sign of inhabitants occurred until we reached the Irrawaddi. On the hills above alluded to, the bitter Tea is reported to exist. The Mogoung river at its mouth is about 70 yards across. The Irrawaddi even at the mouth of the Mogoung river, and at a distance of nearly 800 miles from the sea, keeps up its magnificent character. At this point it is 900 or 1,000 yards across; when we reached it, it had risen considerably, and the appearance of this vast sheet of water was really grand. Its characters are very different from the Ganges and Burrumpooter, its waters being much more confined to one bed, and comparatively speaking becoming seldom spread out. Generally speaking it is deep and the stream is not violent. It appears to me to afford every facility for navigation; in one or two places troublesome shallows are met with, and in several places the channel near the banks is impeded by rocks. It is only in the upper defile, or Kioukdweng, that the navigation is during the rises of the river dangerous, and at times impracticable. On our reaching Tsenbo, which is about 12 miles below the junction of the Mogoung river with the Irrawaddi, the river continued to rise in a most rapid degree, Mr. Bayfield ascertaining by measurement that it rose 16 inches an hour. We were consequently compelled to push on, as we were informed that the next day the defile would be impassable. The Kioukdweng alluded to commences about two miles below Tsenbo, the river becoming constricted from 1000 to 150 yards. The rush of water was great, and was rendered fierce by rocks which exist in the midst of the river. Still further within the defile the difficulties were increased; at one place the whole of the enormous body of water rushes through a passage, and it is the only one, certainly not exceeding 50 yards in width. The passage of this was really fearful, for on clearing it we were encountered by strong eddies, backwaters and whirlpools, which rendered the boat nearly unmanagable. These scenes continued, varied every now and then by an expanded and consequently more tranquil stream, until a gorge is passed, well known by the name of the "Elephant and Cow," two rocks which are fancifully supposed to resemble the above named animals; the defile then becomes much wider, and the waters flow in a tranquil and rather sluggish manner. The depth of the river in this defile is, as may be supposed, immense; Mr. Bayfield ascertained during his passage up, at a season when the waters were low, that in many places no bottom was to be found at a depth of 45 fathoms. The necessity of this enormous depth is at once evident, and is pointed out by the configuration of the banks, which are in many places sheer precipices. Two other defiles exist between Bamo and Ava, of these the middle or second is the shortest, in both the steam flows sluggishly, and there is no impediment whatever to navigation. In these the depth is great, but owing to their greater width, much less so than in the upper.

The temperature of the waters of the Irrawaddi is as usually obtains, except during the rises of the river caused by the melting of snow, when it is higher than usual.

Tributaries of the Irrawaddi between Mogoung river and Ava.

The number of tributaries even to Rangoon is unprecedently small: this tends to increase the astonishment with which one regards this magnificent river.

The rivers that fall into the Irrawaddi within the above distance are,

1st. The Mogoung river.

2nd. Tapien Khioung, above Bamo.

3rd. Shewe Lee Khioung.

These are about the same size, and only discharge a considerable quantity of water during the rainy season. The Shewe Lee at its mouth, is between 5 and 600 yards wide, but only an inconsiderable portion of this is occupied by water, and this to no depth.

The great branch from which the Irrawaddi derives its vast supply of water still remains to be discovered, and will probably be found to be the Shoomaee Kha. It is evident, at any rate, that the great body of water comes from the eastward, for between the Mogoung river and Borkhamtee, in which country Captain Wilcox visited the Irrawaddi, and where it was found to be of no great size, no considerable branch finds its way from the Westward: neither are the hills which intervene between these points, of such height as to afford large supplies of water.

On the whole it is, I think, probable, that the Irrawaddi is an outlet for some great river, which drains an extensive tract of country; for it appears to me that if all its waters are poured in by mountain streams, a tract of country extensive beyond all analogy, will be required for the supply of such a vast body of water.

In addition to the above three rivers, few nullahs exist, but these are scarcely worthy of consideration.

Nature of the country.—From the mouth of the Mogoung river nearly to Tsenboo the country is flat, and the banks wooded or covered with grass to the brink. The range of hills which form the upper Kioukdweng there commence, and continue for a distance of 16 or 20 miles, during the whole of which they from the banks of the river. These hills are scantily covered with trees, most of which are in addition stunted. The vegetation within the maximum high water mark consists of a few scraggy shrubs. The rocks composing these hills are principally serpentine, which within the influence of the water is of a dark sombre brown colour. Limestone occurs occasionally.

From this Kioukdweng to the second, the entrance of which (coming from above) is at Tsenkan, the features of the country are of the ordinary alluvial description, and the river is a good deal spread out and subdivided by islands, covered with moderate sized grasses. On leaving the second Kioukdweng the same scenery occurs, the banks are generally tolerably high, often gravelly or clayey. About Tsagaiya, a few miles below the mouth of the Shewee Lee, low hills approach the river, and they continue along one or both banks* at variable distance until one reaches Ava. These hills are all covered with a partial and stunted vegetation, chiefly of thorny shrubs, and present uniformly a rugged raviny and barren appearance. The scenery of the river is in many places highly picturesque, and in the upper Kioukdweng and portion of the second, where there is a remarkable cliff of about 3,000 feet in height, bold and even grand.

Villages and Towns.—These although numerous compared with the almost deserted tracts hitherto passed, are by no means so much so as to give an idea of even a moderate population. From the mouth of the Mogoung river to the Kioukdweng there are several villages, but all are small, mean, and insignificant. Strange to say, they are defenceless, although the neighbouring Kukkeens are dangerous and cruel neighbours. Nothing can be more calculated to shew the weakness of the Burmese government than the fact, that the most mischievous and frequent aggressions of these hill tribes always go unpunished, although a short time after an attack the very band by whom it has been made will enter even large towns to make purchases, perhaps with money the produce of their robberies.

The upper Kioukdweng has a very scanty population, consisting of a distinct race of people called Phoons: who are sub-divided into two tribes, the greater and lesser Phoons. About 12 villages occur in this defile, and Mr. Bayfield says that the population is almost entirely confined to the banks of the river: all these villages are small.

Between the defile and Bamo a good number of villages occur, the largest of which does not contain more than 100 houses, the generality are small and mean. Bamo, which is a place of celebrity, and is perhaps the third town in Burmah, is situated on the left bank of the river, which is here, including the two islands which subdivide it into three channels, about a mile and a quarter in width; the channel on which Bamo is situated is the principal one. The town occupies

* Especially on the right bank.

rather a high bank of yellow clay, along which it extends for rather more than a mile, its extreme breadth being perhaps 350 yards. It is surrounded by a timber stockade, the outer palisades being well pangoed; the defences had just undergone repair owing to an expected attack from the Kukkeens. It contains within the stockade rather less than 600 houses, (the precise number was ascertained personally by Mr. Bayfield,) and including the suburbs, which consist of two small villages, at the northern end, one at the southern, and one occupied by Assamese at the eastern, it contains about 750 houses. These are generally of the usual poor and mean description; indeed, not even excepting the Governor's house, there is not a good Burman or Shan house in the place. One street which occupies a portion of the river bank, is inhabited by Chinese, and contains about 100 houses; these are built of unburnt brick, and have a peculiar blueish appearance; none are of any size. The best building in Bamo is the Chinese place of worship. Those occupied by the Burmese have the usual form. The country adjoining Bamo is flat, dry, and I should think unproductive; it is intersected by low swampy ravines, one or two of which extend into the town. To the south there is an extensive marsh, partially used for rice-cultivation.

The population of Bamo including the suburbs, may be estimated at about 4500, of whom 4 or 500 are Chinese. The governor is a bigoted Burman, of disagreeable manners; he expends much money in the erection of Pagodas, while he leaves the streets, roads and bridges by which the ravines are passed, in a ruinous and disgraceful state.

The Bazaar of Bamo is generally well supplied: British piece goods and woollen cloths are procurable, but at a high price: the show of Chinese manufactures is much better, particularly on the arrival of a caravan; considerable quantities of Tea are likewise brought in the shape of flat cakes, of the size of a dessert plate, and about two inches thick. This tea is of the black sort, and although very inferior to the Chinese case teas, is a far better article than that of Pollong. In addition to this, warm jackets lined with fur, straw hats, silk robes, skull-caps, and sugar-candy are procurable; pork of course is plentiful, and is excessively fat; grain, vegetables and fish are plentiful. On the whole Bamo is a busy and rather flourishing place: it derives its consequence entirely from its being a great emporium of trade with the Chinese, who come here annually in large numbers; for the accommodation of these people and their caravans, two or three squares, fenced in with bamboos, are allotted.

The principal article of Burmese export is cotton, and this I believe is produced for the most part lower down the Irrawaddi.

The climate of Bamo is in April dry and sultry: the range of the thermometer being from 66° or 68° to 94° or 96°. North-westers are of common occurrence in this month, and are frequently of extreme severity. I saw very little cultivation about Bamo, some of the ravines alluded to had lately been under rice-culture; the chief part of the cultivation for vegetables, &c. is confined to the sandy islands, which occur here and there.

Of the numerous villages passed between Bamo and Ava not one deserves especial notice, nor is there one, with the exception of Umeerapoora, the former capital, which contains 500 houses. Shewegyoo, which formerly occupied a considerable extent of the left bank near the south opening of the second Kioukdweng had been burnt by the orders of the Monein Myoowoon, on account of their having supplied troops to the emissaries of the Tharawaddi. Kioukgyee, the residence of the above governor, had a short time before our arrival been invested by a force in the interest of the Tharawaddi, but had been repulsed. The governor was to proceed with the whole population, amounting to several hundred souls, to Bamo, to join his forces with those of the Bamo governor. This part of the country was most unsettled and almost deserted. On reaching Catha the state of the country was more tranquil, all the people below this point having espoused the cause of the Tharawaddi. Katha contains 200 houses, and has a rather respectable bazaar; it is well situated, and has the most eligible site in my opinion, of all the towns hitherto seen. The most remarkable object is a noble Kioung, or Mosque, built by the head-man of the place; this is one of the finest now existing in Burma.

The only other large place is Sheenmaga, about a day's journey from Ava. This is said to contain 1,000 houses. An extensive fire had lately occurred here. I counted 200 houses, and judging from the extent of the ruins, I should say it might probably have numbered between 4 and 500. There are several villages contiguous to this, and I think that the district immediately contiguous is more populous than any part hitherto seen.

During the above portion of the journey our halts were as follows:—

1. Tapaw.
2. Mogoung river.
3. Mogoung river.

4. Lemar, in the upper Kioukdweng.
5. Bamo.
6. Tsenkan.
7. Kioukgyee.
8. Katha.
9. Tsagaya.
10. Tagoung.
11. Malé, at the entrance of the lower Kioukdweng.
12. Kabuet, in the lower Kioukdweng.
13. Malé.
14. Menghoon.
15. Ava.

This distance down the Irrawaddi may, in a fast boat, be performed in ten days, but owing to the disturbed state of the country we were compelled to avail ourselves of the first opportunity that offered to enable us to reach Ava; in addition the proper number of boatmen was not procurable, every body being afraid of approaching the capital even a few miles.

The chief product I saw was Teak, of this there were large rafts at Tsenkan and elsewhere. This tree seems to abound in the hills forming the NE. boundaries of Burmah. I did not, however, see any of large size.

Tea is found on hills to the east of Bamo, and at a distance of one day's journey from that place. Through the kindness of Mr. Bayfield, I was enabled to procure specimens; the leaves were decidedly less coarse, as well as smaller, than those of the Assamese plants, and they occurred both serrated and entire. No use is made of the wild plants in this direction, and the Chinese at Bamo, asserted that it was good for nothing. It must be remembered, however, that none of them had seen the plant cultivated in China. Indeed the only real Chinaman we saw, was one at Kioukgyee, serving the Myoowoon as a carpenter: this man had been to England twice, and talked a little English.

Cotton is, I was informed, extensively cultivated.

But the most valuable product is the Ruby, which is procured from hills to the eastward of Tsenboo, and which are, I believe, visible from the opposite town, Mala. From the same place and to the SE., low hills are visible, from which all the marble in extensive use for the carving of images, is obtained; this marble has been pronounced by competent authority to be of first-rate quality.

Population.—This must be considered as scanty. From a list of towns and villages, observed by Captain Hannay, between Ava and Mogoung inclusive, I estimated the population at 1,00,000 souls, but from this one-third at least must be deducted. In this estimate of the number of houses, Captain Hannay was probably guided, either by the Burmese census, or by the statement of the writer who accompanied him. From the numbers given by this officer, in almost every case one-third, and occasionally one-half, or even more, must be deducted: as instances, I may cite his statement of the number of houses in Bamo and Katha.

In almost every case Mr. Bayfield counted all the houses, and in all doubtful cases, I counted them also at his request, so that I am enabled to speak with great confidence on this point.

As a collateral proof of the scanty population of this extensive portion of the Burmese territory, I may allude to the fact that Bamo, the third place in Burmah, and the emporium of great part of an extensive Chinese trade, contains only even at the rate of seven souls to each house, which is two too many, 4,250 inhabitants. The capital may be adduced as an additional instance; for including the extensive suburbs, no one estimated it as having a larger population than 1,00,000. It must be remembered also, that there is no doubt, but that the banks of the Irrawaddi are more populous than any other portion of the kingdom.

Throughout the above rather long journey, we were treated, with one exception, tolerably well; indeed our delays arose from the unwillingness, real or pretended, of the authorities to forward us on while the country remained so unsettled. The headman of Kamein on our first arrival was extremely civil, but on our return after he had received news of the revolt of the Tharawaddi, he behaved with great insolence, and actually drew his dha on Mr. Bayfield. It must be remembered however that he had been brought to task by the Mogoung authorities for having, as it was said, accepted of a douceur for allowing us to proceed to the serpentine mines.

The general idea entertained by the people through whose countries we passed, was, that we had been sent to report upon the country prior to its being taken under British protection. Of the existence of this idea, Mr. Bayfield met with some striking proofs.

On reaching Katha our troubles ceased, and these, excepting at Kamein and Mogoung, only arose from the evident wish of the natives to keep at a distance from us, and not to interfere in one way or the other. At Mogoung I consider it probable that we should have been detained had it not been for the firm conduct of Mr. Bayfield, and his great knowledge of the Burmese character. At this place the authority of the Myoowoon, who was absent in Hookhoong, was totally disregarded, and his brother the Myoowoah, was in confinement, the Shan Matgyee having espoused the cause of the prince Tharawaddi.

Conclusion.—For the brief and rapid manner in which I have run through this last section of my report, as well as for having forsaken the arrangement adopted in the previous sections, I trust I shall be excused. In the first place, this portion of the route had been previously travelled over by Captain Hannay and by Mr. Bayfield, by whom much additional information will be laid before Government; and in the second place, I would advert to the hurried nature of this part of our journey, and to the disturbed state of the country. For similar reasons I have only drawn up this account to the period of my reaching Ava. It will be at once seen that the information might have been much more extensive, especially as regards the revenues of the districts, but I abstained from interfering with subjects which were in every respect within the province of Mr. Bayfield; and the minute and accurate manner in which this officer performed the duties consigned to him, reconciled me at once to the secondary nature of the objects which were left for my examination.

I subjoin a tabular view of the marches, this will not agree entirely with those given in the body of the report, as one or two of those were unavoidably short. I give the table to shew the shortest period in which the journey could be accomplished by an European without constantly overfatiguing himself. If the total distance be compared with an estimate made from charts, all of which however are imperfect so far as the country between Meinkhoong and Beesa is concerned, the tortuousness of our course will be at once evident.

Marches,	1.	From Sadya to Noa Dehing Mookh,	Miles	6
,,	2.	To Rangagurreh, ...	,,	12
,,	3.	To Moodoa Mookh, ...	,,	12
,,	4.	To Kidding, ...	,,	9
,,	5.	To Namroop Puthar, ...	,,	12
,,	6.	To Beesa Lacoom, ...	,,	12
,,	7.	To Halting place in the hills, ..	,,	12
,,	8.	To Darap Panee, ...	,,	12
,,	9.	To the Namtuseek, ...	,,	12

Marches,	10. Namtuseek,	Miles	10
,,	11. To the Boundary Nullah,	,,	12
,,	12. To the Namaroan,	,,	15
,,	13. Namaroan,	,,	13
,,	14. To Khathung Khioung,	,,	15
,,	15. To Khussee Khioung,	,,	13
,,	16. To Kuttack Bhoom,	,,	13
,,	17. To Namtuseek,	,,	10
,,	18. To Nhempean,	,,	18
,,	19. To Kulleyang,	,,	17
,,	20. To Tsilone,	,,	10
,,	21. To Meinkhoong,	,,	17
,,	22. To Wullabhoom,	,,	13
,,	23. To Halting place towards the Mogoung river,	,,	22
,,	24. Mogoung river,	,,	15
,,	25. Ditto ditto,	,,	13
,,	26. Ditto ditto,	,,	14
,,	27. Kamein,*	,,	14
,,	28. Mogoung,	,,	25
	Total number of miles,		378

The remaining distance performed in boats may be thus estimated down the Mogoung river to the Irrawaddi,	,,	45
From the confluence of the Mogoung river down the Irrawaddi to Ava,	,,	240
		663

Allowing twelve days for the performance of this last portion, which however is too short a time, the entire distance may be performed in forty days.

* It must be observed that Kamein is several miles out of the route from the Mogoung river to Mogoung itself, we visited it en route to the Serpentine mines.

CHAPTER VIII.

Notes made on descending the Irrawaddi from Ava to Rangoon.

[28*th May.*—I left Ava and halted about two miles above Menboo.

29*th May.*—Continuing the journey, the country appears flat with occasionally low hills as about Kioukloloing, no large villages occur; the river is sub-divided by churs; no large grasses to be seen, and the vegetation is arid. Bombax is the chief tree: Mudar and Zizyphus occur: Guilandina, Crotolaria a large Acanthacea, and a Jasminioides shrub are the most common plants: Borassus is abundant: Fici occur about villages. The banks are generally sandy, not high.

Yandebo. This is a wretched village; barren plains bounded to the east by barren rather elevated hills; base jungly. Observed the tree under which the treaty was signed with the Burmese at the close of the late war. It is an ordinary mango, near a pagoda on a plain with two large fig trees. I counted to-day 28 boats sailing up between this and our halting place of yesterday, mostly large praows. The banks present few trees, are flat, barren, and from being occasionally overflowed, adapted to paddy.

Halted at Meengian, which is a middling sized village on the left bank, about a mile below Tarof myoo.

30*th May.*—I made an excursion into the country which is dry, barren, and sandy, with a descent towards the banks of the river. Zizyphus, Acacia, Euphorbia 20 feet high, Calotropis, Capparis 2, etc., occur all the same as before, only one Ehretiacea appears to be new. Hares are very common. Likewise red and painted Partridges, and Quail. Carthamus and Tobacco are cultivated, specially the latter at Meengian. The most common tree here, is Urticea procera? which has always a peculiar appearance. The country towards Pukoko becomes prettier, the left bank wooded, and the ground sloped very gradually up to Kionksouk, which is barren, and 2,000 feet high at least, with the slopes covered with jungle.

31*st May.*—Passed Pagam, a straggling town of some size, famous for its numerous old pagodas of all sorts. The surface of the country is raviny, and the vegetation continues precisely the same. Below Pagam, the range of low hills becomes very barren: altogether the country is very uninteresting.

The low range of hills on the right bank is nearly destitute of vegetation. The hills present a curious appearance of ridges, sometimes looking like walls. The country continues the same.

Halted opposite Yowa.

June 1st.—A low range of hillocks here occurs on the left bank, and as in other places, consisting of sandstone with stunted and scanty vegetation.

Tselow is a large place on the left bank, the river is here much spread out, with large sand banks. The hills on the right bank present the same features; passed Pukangnai, a large village on the left bank. Passed Pukkoko, Pagam, Tselow, etc., the hills about this last place abound with Prionites. Strong wind prevails.

June 2nd.—Yeanangeown 10 A. M. The country continues exactly similar to that already observed—hillocks intersected by ravines, loose sandstone, very barren in appearance. Vegetation is the same, but more stunted; fossil wood is common, especially in the bottom of ravines.* Of fossils very few were seen, but more are to be procured by digging. The most common trees are Zizyphus, Acacia, and a Capparis: the most common grass Aristida. Arrived at Yeanangeown, a busy place judging from the number of boats.

Wind less strong. At 2 P. M. stopped at Wengma-thoat, where Zizyphus is extremely common. Euphorbia seems rather disappearing.

The plants met with at the halting place six miles above Yeanang, were Euphorbia, Olax, Zizyphus, Mimosa, Carissa, Ximenia, Prionites, Calotropis, Gymnema, Capparis pandurata et altera species arborea, Murraya rare, Gossypium frutex 6-8-petal, Xanthophyllum blue, petiolis alatis of Tagoung, Sidæ sp. On the right bank flat churs continue covered with a small Saccharum. Vegetation more abundant and greener than before. Ficus again occurs and Stravadium occasionally.

Passed 5 P. M. Memboo at a large village on right bank, containing perhaps 200 houses. The river below this runs between two ranges of low hills, similar in every respects to those already passed. A Kukkeem woman was observed, who appeared to have a blue face, looking perfectly frightful.

June 3rd.—Maguay. Reached this place at 8 P. M. It is on the left bank. It is a place of some importance. Many boats lying in the stream. The country, is of the same dry, arid description: the banks of the river are however lower than previously observed.

* This is the site of the fossil bones discovered by Mr. Crawfurd.

Passed Esthaiya, a small village on the right bank, at 6 A. M. Adelia neriefolia continues common in some places.

Dhebalar, Meemgoon, two villages nearly opposite, neither of these villages large. Ficus and Bombax are common ; no Euphorbia was observed.

We are now evidently getting within the influence of the Monsoon, as the vegetation is more green.

Passed Mellun, a village on the right bank. The hills on either side of the river are higher and better wooded than before observed, and the river itself is not more than 350 yards broad.

Observed gold washers below Meegyoung-yea, where they find gold, silver, and rubies by washing the sands. Here Bombax is very common on the right bank.

Passed Thembounwa, a village on the left bank. The country presents the same ridges of singular hills formed of veins of slaty, tabular, brown rock, this is very conspicuous at Thembounwa. The hills on the left bank above Meeaday are very barren ; the banks rocky.

Halted at Khayoo, just above Meeaday, at 7 P. M.

June 4th.—Passed Teiyet myoo, a village on the right bank, which seems to have some cotton trade; the houses along the bank are wretched in appearance. Meeaday was passed during a squall, I was thus prevented from making any observation on it. Teiyet is the largest place I have seen. The country we are now passing is very slightly undulated, soil light and sandy. Fine tamarind trees occur, also Terminalia. In addition to the usual plants a Lagerstræmia occurs, which attains the size of a middling tree, and a frutescent Hypericum, Aristolochia, and Hedyotis occur. Strong south wind prevails so that we can make no progress whatever, I therefore went into the jungle and found Stravadium, a fine Bignonia foliis pinnatis, floribus maximis, fere spitham. infundibulif. subbilabiat. lacinus crispatis : one or two Acanthaceæ, two Gramineæ, two Vandelliæ, Bonnaya, Herpestes, Monniera, Rumex, Dentella, three or four Cyperaceæ, Ammannia, Crotalaria on sand banks, Triga in woods and Bauhinia, Dioscoria, a pretty herbaceous perennial Ardisia, etc. We have not made two miles since breakfasting at Teiyet, about four hours ago. Convolvulus pileatus and dwarf bamboo are common on the low hills. The Lagerstræmia has petals none, or minute squamiform.

Reached Caman Myoo, a village on the right bank, at 7 P. M.

June 5th.—Many boats are here, owing to there being an excellent place of anchorage in still water, protected by an Island, but there are not many houses in the village.

Below, the river again becomes confined between hills, but above this it expands. These hills are rather bare: no Euphorbia exists, and the whole vegetation is changed.

Now passing hills, chiefly covered with bamboos. Bignonia crispa occurs, and a Scilloid plant out of flower is common. Aroideum, similar to that of Catha, is common, a new species is likewise found, but it is a Roxburghia, and rare.

Stravadium has very minute stipules, the habit and gemmation is that of Ternstræmiaceæ, and it perhaps connects this order with Myrtaceæ; Punica from this is certainly distinct, owing præter alia to its valvate calyx. Soneratia belongs I suspect to Lythrarieæ, connecting it with Myrtaceæ.

The Roxburghia above alluded to, is a distinct genus.

Planta quam juniorem tantum vidi vix spithamæa. Radices plurimæ filiformes, cortice crassa, tenacissima obfibras foliiformas ad vaginam redacta, superiora petiolique purpureo-brunnei, vernatione involutiva, flores solitarii in axillis foliorum et vaginarum, albi carneo tincti. Pedicellis subtereti apice, articulatis, monoicis.

Perianth sub-companulat, 4-sepalum, sepalis lanceolato-oblongis a medio reflexis, estivat imbricat.

Stam. 4. sepalis alterna, filam subanth. magna, subsagittat, connectivo magno supra in apiculum longum product, et inter loculos in carinam (carneam) purpuream, loculi angustissimi, viridis, alabastrus lutescens. Pollen viridescens. Fæmin flos, infimus, unum tantum vidi sepala longiora herbacea, stam. 0.

Ovarium compressum, fol. carpell ⊃, stylus conicus, ovar viridis, stigma sub-simplex.

Char. gen. Flores monoici Per. 4, sepalum, stam. 4.

Arrived at Prome on the left bank, the stockade seemed to be out of repair: the water front of the stockade is about 800 yards in length: it extends about 200 yards back from the river, and beyond the hill on which are pagodas: opposite the pagodas it is of brick, and beyond this a long line of houses or huts extends; there is no appearance of improvement going on. The hills on the opposite side present the same features, trees just commencing to leaf; every thing indicates a temporary sterility caused by the long hot season. Above this place we passed a village extending 500 yards along the river. Cocoa trees thrive well here, and are not uncommon. Borassus continues.

Shwe Doung, 6 miles from Prome, is as large as Prome itself: the country beyond this expands; no hills were seen near this part of the river; some way below Palmyras are common; Bombax, Ficus, and Tamarind are the chief trees.

Passed Reedan, a straggling place on the left bank. A range of hills occur, extending close along the right bank, and which, as well as the distant ones, are wooded to the summit, as the hills are on the Malay Coast.

Passed Thengyee, a village on the right bank. Hills at this place approach close to the river for a short way, but soon cease. They are covered with Teak, scarped, and many images are carved in the recesses of the rock, apparently sandstone. Thengyee, just below this, seems to be a great place for boat-building.

Halted at Talownmo at 7½ P. M.

June 6th.—At this place there are no hills near the river, which is sub-divided by islands. Painted partridge continues. Kioungee; palmyra trees continue in plenty. Talipat never seen dead, but with its inflorescence. Passed Meāvion and Runaown. Palmyras here occur: great numbers of boats passing up and down. Traffic considerable.

Moneu, a village on the left bank, at which many boats were observed.

The river banks throughout are to day flat and alluvial, and those of the Islands are covered with moderate sized grasses; extreme banks jungly. Palmyras continue.

Halted at Thendan, on left bank.

June 7th.—The country here has the usual alluvial features; few villages are seen, but as the river is sub-divided, one must not judge from this and the consequent barren appearance, that the country is less populated than above.

Stravadium is common in the woods: on the banks, noticed Acrostichum difforme; Epiphytical Orchideæ are common. Urticea fructibus late obcordatis.

Passed Tharawa, a village on the left bank, and Theenmaga myoo on the right bank, which seems a large place; here Pandanus commences. Palmyras were seen, together with a few Areca. At 4 P. M. I saw at Zulone myoo, for the first time during the descent, a Crocodile, which is an indication of our approach to the coast. A Bombax is now common on some of the islands, the banks are now generally grassy.

This Bombax is apparently the same as that of Assam; the river here resembles the B. pootur about Chykwar.

Halted at a small village about six miles above Donai-byoo near Dollong.

June 8th.—Donai-byoo, 7 A. M. This is a large place, on the right bank, having a good many boats.

Niown Sheedouk on the left bank, three miles below Donai-byoo, is likewise a large place.

Tides exist here, and their influence extends upwards as far as Zulone, that is to say, the stream is much diminished during the flood. Entered Rangoon river at 1 P. M.: it is here not more than 200 yards broad. Nioungdoa is a middling sized village, situated about a mile from the mouth or entrance, at which were observed plenty of boats. The banks of the river are here grassy; tall Saccharum and Arundo occur, but not so large as those of Assam. The river a small way below the mouth is not more than 100 yards wide. Bombax and Ficus are the most common trees: Lagerstræmea grandiflora forms a little tree jungle: Butea likewise occurs.

Passed Tsamaloukde, a small village on the right bank.

June 9th.—Halted at 6 this morning at a small village on the left bank. The features of the country now become paludosal. Acanthus ilicifolius, Cynometra acacisides, Cyperaceæ, Soneralia acida, Avicennia, Stravadium, Croton malvæfolium are very common, Creni sp. Cæsalpinia, and a leguminous tree, fructibus 1-spermis, drupaceis, Webera, Premna, Cissi sp. potius *Vitis,* Clerodendri sp. Heritiera fomes, Flagellaria indica, Hibisci species populneæ affinis, Arundo, Ambrosinia 2 species.

Country open, low, and quite flat, admirable for rice cultivation.

Crinoid giganteum, Excæcaria, Agallocha, no Rhizophores, Ipomæa floribus maximis, hypocrateriform, albis, foliis cordatis. Soneratia apetala less common, but becomes more so as we approach Rangoon, it is an elegant tree with pendulous branchlets. Heritiera is very common and conspicuous when in flower, it is then of a yellow brown tint: Acrostichum aureum, Calamus, and Lomaria scandens occur.]

CHAPTER IX.

Journal towards Assam and to Bootan—contains notes on distribution of Plants.

Left Calcutta a second time on the 31st August 1837, arrived at Serampore on the 1st September, and spent the day with the Voights.

September 3rd.—Continue on the Hooghly: paddy cultivation prevails and Crotalaria juncea: this last is sown broad cast in low places, but not quite so low as paddy. Bengallees are but slovenly husbandmen; grass, etc. collected by them in small cocks, and covered with a small thatch, which answers its purpose as well as a narrow brimmed hat would answer that of an umbrella. Broken earthenware not unfrequently visible in the banks, in some places at the depth of 3-4 feet. Unsettled weather, with gusts of strong wind from the S. and SSE. Thermometer 78° 82′. The usual Calcutta birds continue, jackdaw-like crow, Falco pondicherainus, two common mainas, Ardea indica, and the white one.

Came on the Ganges about noon; on passing Chŏbda had the horror of seeing the bodies of burning Hindoos, the friends who are present at these funeral rites turning them about with sticks, so as to give each side its share of fire. The women bathe in their ordinary dresses: these though ample are of fine cotton fabric, so that when wet more of the shape is disclosed than is deemed desirable in Europe, but exposure of person has no repugnant effect on Asiatics.

The Matabangah is a small, very tortuous, stream, not exceeding 70 yards in breadth: the banks are low, either wooded to the edge or covered with grass, such as Cynodon. Excellent pasturage prevails, as indicated by the number of cows.

Monday 4th.—Wind SE. There are not many villages in the vicinity of the river; passed yesterday Kranighat, where there is a toll, from which officers on duty are exempt; but as no precautions seem to be taken to keep the river clear, no toll whatever should be taken: although the latter is high, the receipts must be very small. Passed Arskally about noon, the banks are composed occasionally of pure sand, and the country becomes more open, with very little jungle, much indigo cultivation occurs. Thermometer 78° 85′.

Tuesday, 5th.—Wind SW. The country continues the same as before. At 2 P. M., we reached Krishnapoor.

Wednesday, 6th.—8 A. M. We left the Matabangah river and entered a less tortuous nullah. The country continues the same. Much indigo cultivation still occurs. We saw yesterday evening a large herd of cows swim across the Matabangah; they were led by a bull, who kept turning round every now and then to see whether his convoy was near him. To-day I saw a rustic returning from his labours, with his plough thrown easily across his shoulders; to a strong Englishman the feat of walking home with such a plough, cattle, and all would not be very difficult. Indigo is cut about a foot from the ground, then tied in bundles. Water for steeping it in is raised from the rivers by something like chair-buckets, only the buckets are represented by flat pieces of wood, the whole is turned on an axle by the tread of men; the water is carried upon an inclined narrow plane; the machine answers its purpose very well, and the natives work it with great dexterity. At 5 P. M., we came on a stream 100 yards wide, down which we proceeded.

Thursday, 7th.—The country continues much the same. Of birds the black and white peewit is not uncommon;—cormorants, etc. also occur. P. M. Thermometer 90°.

Friday, 8th.—The country is more low and more sub-divided by rivers than before. Abundance of indigo. Pumps also used, as before observed, for raising water. Passed Moodoo Kully at 5 P. M., and left its river for a small nullah. Indigo abundant on all sides throughout the day's journey.

Saturday, 9th.—Continue in this nullah. Country wooded. Phænix sylvestris very abundant: Areca and Catechu also becoming abundant. A good deal of cultivation occurs, mottled chiefly with sugar-cane and vegetables. The habits of the black and white kingfisher, Alcedo rudis, are different from those of the other Indian species: it never perches, choosing rather the ground to rest upon: it builds in banks: takes its prey by striking it from a height of 20 feet or thereabouts, previously fluttering or hovering over it. The size and figure of this bird when resting on the ground, resembles the two common Indian Terns.

Palms, contrary to what might be supposed from the nature of these plants, can put forth additional buds;—this is exemplified in phænix sylvestris, the stems of which are deeply and alternately notched by the natives for procuring toddy. When this is carried to a great extent, the tree either dies or a new apex is formed laterally. The old notches, as might be expected, at length, become much obliterated. It is from the study of such palms that much light will be thrown on the growth of monocotyledonous stems. The vegetation of jheels is now obviously commencing. Pistia stratioles, Nymphæa, Potamogeton, Potamochloa, Oplismenus stagninus, and Villarsia occur. Reached Furreedpore at 7 P. M.

Sunday, 10th.—Came on the Paddo, an immense stream 1½ miles wide, with a very strong current, about a mile to the East of Furreedpore. Lagerstræmia Regina here occurs.

Monday, 11th.—The country is become much lower since leaving Fureedpore, and is inundated during the height of the rains. The peculiar vegetation of jheels predominant; that of the jungle continues much the same. Plhugoor continues plentiful. No palmyras. Mangoes plentiful, but small. Passed a deserted Roman Catholic Chapel, and Priest's house. White-winged long-nailed water-hens becoming plentiful.

Tuesday, 12th.—The country abounds more in jheels: in many places nothing is visible but water, in which huge plains of floating grasses occur. The villages are very numerous, and occupy in fact almost every spot of ground not subject ordinarily to inundation. Damasonium Indicum, Nymphæa pubescens occur in profusion. The grass which exists in such vast quantities is, I believe, Oplismenus stagninus. The water of these jheels is clear, black when deep, which it often is to a great extent.

Wednesday, 13th.—Reached Dacca about 2 P. M.: it is a large and populous place. The numerous grass of the jheels is sown there: it is the red bearded *dhan* or paddy grass: of this vast quantities are cut for fodder, for, the whole face of the country being overflowed, it follows that the cattle are throughout the rains kept in stalls.

Thursday, 14th.—Left about noon, and proceeded down the Dacca river about 5 miles, then diverged into a narrow creek running nearly south. Along this were observed fine specimens of tamarind trees. Stravadium in abundance. Sonninia scandens, and Mango, both in abundance. Passed at 5 P. M. Neerangunge, a large native town, and below it Luckepoor. A vast expanse of water appeared near this, viz., the Megna. A good deal of native shipping occurs, consisting of brigs: great quantities of rice being exported from both places. Pelicans I observed here to roost in trees.

From a Sketch made on the spot by W. Griffith. M. & N. Hanhart Lith. Printers

VIEW IN THE JHEELS

Friday, 15*th*.—In the midst of jheels: the whole face of the country is covered with water several feet deep. Vast quantities of Oplismenus stagninus still occur.

Saturday, 16*th*.—Still in jheels. The same features continue. The country is still very populous, all the more elevated spots having villages. Oplismenus stagninus still prevails in vast quantities.

Sunday, 17*th*.—Jheels in every direction:—nothing indeed seen but water, with occasional grassy or reedy, and elevated spots occupied by villages:—here and there a round-headed tree springing apparently out of the water. Hills visible to the east. Cormorants, Ciconia nudiceps, paddy-birds, the common white ones with black feet, are abundant, and associate in flocks: there is one very nearly allied to this, which is solitary, having black feet with yellow toes. The boats of this district are very simple, something like a Bengal *dingy* reversed, but they are sharp in the bows and ought to be fast; their only mode of progression is to be pushed along by means of poles. There appears to be a great number of Mussulmans, who would here seem to form the majority of the population. Strong winds from the south interrupt our progress.

Monday, 18*th*.—Delayed by bad weather.

Tuesday, 19*th*.—Continued to pass through same kind of country, but less jheelly. The Cook boat was left behind on the 17th in a squall, and has not come up yet, so that I dine with the boatmen.

The black and white long-toed water-hen continues plentiful: when alarmed by kites, etc. it pursues them uttering a low mournful scream, until it has succeeded in getting its enemy off to some distance; it then returns, I suppose to its young; otherwise its cry is something like the mewing of a cat, or rather a low hollow moan. The hills are plainly visible to-day, lying towards the north.

The males of the white and black water-hen have tails something like those of a pheasant. There are two other species: one that is found on the Tenasserim coast; the other is much larger,—the size, of a large domestic fowl: one of the sexes, has red wattles on its head. The white and black one is far the most common; it feeds apparently, in flocks: the Maulmain one is the least common. These with Ardea Indica, the white, black-toed, yellow-beaked Ardea, Ciconia nudiceps a small brown *chat?*, Pica vagabunda, are the birds of the jheels or rather the dry spots in them. I saw yesterday a flock of the black Ibis, flying *in a triangle* (∧) *without a base*, the party was headed by one of the white paddy-birds! Villages have become very numerous, and the population abundant and flourishing. The cattle are, as I have said, stalled and fed with paddy grass, quantities of boats being employed for its conveyance. Oplismenus stagninus appears less common about here.

Thursday, 21*st*.—Still among jheels; our progress is necessarily very slow; we are indeed scarcely moving, there being no tracking ground: jheels occur in every direction, although the hills are not 15 miles distant. Pelicans with white and black marked wings occur, together with the slate-colored eagle with white tail, barred at tip with black; it is common in the low wooded places surrounded by jheels. Black-bellied Tern occurs, but not that of Assam.

Friday, 22*nd*.—Arundo and two species of Saccharum occur, among which S. spontaneum, is very common and of large size. We reached the Soorma river about 12 o'clock, 3 or 4 miles above Mr. Inglis's house.

I arrived at Chattuc on the 21st, which place I left for Pundoa the following day. There are no mountains of this name as would seem from the habitat of some plants given in Roxburgh's Flora Indica. The mountains therein called Pundoa are the Khasya or Cossiah range; Pundoa, is the name of a village called by the natives Puddoa. The jheels are for a great part under cultivation. The paddy cultivation is of two kinds; it is either sown in the jheels just at the commencement of the inundation, or it is sown on higher portions, and then transplanted into the jheels. Jarool, Lagerstræmia Regina is the chief timber, it comes from Kachar; it is a dear and not a durable wood.

Dalbergia bracteata, first appears, on low hills about Chattuc; there is also a Grimmia here on the river banks.

Porpoises are often seen in the Soorma; alligators or crocodiles, very rarely.

Jheels continue nearly to the foot of the mountains; these last are not wooded more than half way up; the remaining wood being confined to ravines, the ridges appearing as if covered with grass. Here and there, scarped amphitheatres are visible, down which many fine cascades may be seen to fall.

Arrived at Mr. Inglis's Bungalow at Pundoa about 3 P. M., and here regulated my thermometers; temperature of boiling water taken with the large thermometer 210½°, by means of the one in wooden case 210½°, temperature of the air 92½°, red case thermometer indicated the boiling point at 206°!! nor would the mercury rise higher.

Saturday, 23rd.—Commenced the ascent, from Terya Ghat. Up to which point the country is perfectly flat low and wet, covered for a great part with gigantic Sacchara; among which partridges are common. Osbeckia nepalensis, Marlea begonifolia, Gouania, Bignonia Indica, a Panax, Byttneria, Hedysarum gyrans, Pueraia, Mimosa stipulacea, a very large Rottboellia, Bauheniæ 2, Bombax, Tetranthera arborea, Grewia sepiaria may all be observed. On the Terya river among stones, and where it is a pure mountain stream Eugenia salicifolia, as in the Upper Kioukdweng, between Terya and the foot of the hills occurs; Alstonia, Ophioxylon, Trophis aspera, Urtica naucleiflora, Varecæ sp. Impatiens in abundance, oranges in groves occur; at the foot Cryptophragmium venustum; rather higher, Argostemma, and Neckera are common; Æschynanthus fulgens, jack and sooparee commonly cultivated. Then Oxalis sensitiva, a small tender Lycopodium; pine-apples, Pogonatherum crinitum; Gordonia soon commences, probably at 400 feet. Polytrichum aloides appears on banks with Gordonia; Eurya commences above the first cascade. Choripetalum, Modecca, Sonerila about two-thirds up to Mahadeb, and Commelina, C. bengalensis, and Anatherum muricatum continue to Mahadeb, as also Andropogon acicularis, the Impatiens, etc. No change takes place, in fact the vegetation being all tropical. Up to this place thick tree jungle continues; the ridges sometimes are covered with grass, either Saccharum, Anthistiria arundinacea or Manisuris; scarcely any oaks occur. Euonymus occurs at Mahadeb. Beyond Mahadeb the scene becomes changed especially after surmounting the first ridge, the face of the hills is covered with grasses, interspersed with rocks; the clumps of wooded vegetation being small, irregular, and composed of barren looking stunted trees.

Above this ridge the country puts on the appearance of a table land. At Mahadeb, Staurogyne, Ruellia Neesiana, and Cryptophragmium are common, a little above these is a species of Zalacca; Impatiens bracteata is very common from near the foot to beyond Mahadeb; but it becomes small and disappears before Moosmai is reached. Cymbidium bambusifolium commences 600 feet above Mahadeb. Linum trigynum commences at Mahadeb; Scutellaria a little above, but I have found this at the foot.

Dianella is found 1,000 feet above Mahadeb, as also Camellia caudata; Plantago, and Eriocaulon 2 sp. appear about 500 feet above Mahadeb; and continue to Churra. Randia, the common one, is found up to 4,000 feet. Cinchona gratissima appears at Moosmai. The first Viburnum, also occurs here. Impatiens graminifolia a little lower. Salomonia, which appears half way to Mahadeb, continues to Moosmai and Churra, but is stunted.

Vaccinium, Ceratostema, Crotalaria Hoveoides, Gnaphalia appear towards Moosmai. Wendlandia at Moosmai. Ruellia persicæfolia straggles a little lower than these. Smithia commences at Moosmai; Pandanus also; this is excessively common on hills to the left, towards the caves. Dipsacus commences above Moosmai.

Monday, 25th.—Churra is situated in a plain surrounded in every direction by low rounded hills, except to the E. and SE., on which side there is a deep ravine, the whole plateau rising considerably towards the north, in the direction of Churra itself. Ravines exist here and there; it is along these, and the water-courses, that the only woody vegetation is to be found. The rest of the surface is clothed with grasses, of which a number of species exist, they are chiefly Andropogoneæ. Two or three Osbeckias exist; a Tradescantia (T. septem clavata) covers certain patches with its bright blue flowers. Three species of Impatiens, two with bright pink flowers are common. Spathoglottis, and Anthogonum occur on the flat rocks, which frequently prevail; Arundinaria is seen every where as well as a Smithia? with lotus-like blossoms. With regard to birds, the Motacilla or water-wagtails are seen at Churra and at Pundoa, are generally of yellow colour in place of white.

The woody vegetation consists of Berberis, Viburnum, Bucklandia, Cleyera floribus fragrantis, petalis sepalis oppositis, Myrsine and many others, too numerous indeed to mention.

The woods, towards Churra, assume that rounded and very determinate form, which is seen so commonly in some parts of England, Bucks for instance. None of the trees arrive to any great size. The generality are low, rounded, and stunted. It is in these, that Quercus, Viburnum, and Pandanus may be seen growing side by side.

October 4th.—Took the height of the station, which I make to be 3,921 feet; temperature 74°; water boiled at 205°; in the small metal thermometer 198°! centigrade 97°; large metal 205¼°; wooden scale 204°.

October 5th.—Left for Surureem. On the first height on which the village is situated, a Potentilla is to be found, and this becomes more abundant as we continue to ascend. The next European form that appears, is Fragaria, the height of which may be estimated at 4,200 feet, this too becomes more common as we ascend; Caryota may be seen, or at least, a palm tree, in ravines as high as 4,000 feet; Daucus appears at 4,300 feet in grassy plains; Prunella at about the same, Gerardia at 4,500 feet; Gaultheria and an Impatiens with very small yellow flowers at 4,800 feet, as well as Othonna.

With the exception of these, the vegetation is much the same as that about Churra: but the Balsams of that place disappear almost towards Surureem, as well as the Tradescantia 7-clavata. Plants which are not in flower about Churra, are found towards Surureem in perfection.

After the first considerable ascent is surmounted, and which is probably 4,750 feet, the country becomes more barren, the grass more scanty and less luxuriant. Spathoglottis, and Anthogonium disappear; Xyris continues in abundance, likewise Eriocaulons, especially the middling-sized one; Bucklandia becomes more common and more developed; a frutescent Salix commences at 4,800 feet, as well as a Gramen Avenaceum vel Bromoideum.

Surureem is a small village, 100 feet above the rude bungalow, provided for the few travellers who pass this way; close to it is to be found Zanthoxylum and Hemiphragma, which last commences at Moosmai. The simple leaved Rubus of Churra, petalis minutis carneis, has ceased; a trifoliate one foliis cordato-rotundatis, existing instead. Most of the grasses continue, but all are comparatively of small stature. Two new Andropogonoids make their appearance; of Compositæ, a Tussilaginoid and a stout Senecionidea, the former not uncommon about Churra, but out of flower. Salomonia ceased.

The height of Surureem I calculate at 4,978 feet; temperature 65° Fahr.; of centigrade 19°; water boiled at 95½° of centigrade; 203° Fahr., wooden scale; 203½° large metal; small ditto 195½°!; Temperature of the air at 6 P. M., 63°.

October 6th.—Temperature 6 A. M., 63½°. Left for Moflong. There is a considerable rise at first, then the country is tolerably level until one reaches the Kala Panee, the descent to this is about 7 or 800 feet, thence the rise is great, with a corresponding descent to the Boga Panee, which I estimate at 4,457 feet, and which is certainly 1,000 feet below the highest ground passed on this side of the Kala Panee. After crossing this torrent, by means of a miserably unsteady wooden bridge, the ascent is very steep for about 1,200 feet, thence there is a small descent to Moflong, which I find to be 5,485 feet. Most of the plants continue. Tradescantia and Commelina become much less common towards the Kala Panee, as well as the Impatiens of Churra, but their place is supplied by others. Along 100 yards of the

Kala Panee, upwards of four species may be met with. Polygonum (Bistorta,) becomes more common on the higher ground between Surureem and Kala Panee, thence diminishing in size and frequency. Polygonum Rheoides becomes abundant towards a height of 5,200 feet, when Pyrus, an apple-like species, and Spiræas make their appearance at 5,300 feet. On the Kala Panee, Bucklandia re-appears, but thence would seem to cease: on the brow of the ascent from this, Pedicularis appears in abundance among grasses, with it *Sphacele?* At the same height, which cannot be less than 5,400 feet, Carduus or Cnicus, appears. Solidago commences in the valley of the Kala Panee, but becomes more abundant at higher elevations. Sanguisorba appears at 5,400 feet, but in small quantities, and at this height Anisadenia recommences. Epilobium appears at 5,300 feet, continues at the same elevation to Moflong, where it is common. On the descent to the Boga Panee, an European form of Euphorbia appears at 5,000 feet with Viola Patrinia and a Galium asperum. Hieracium appears at about the same height. Cuscuta is very common from 5 to 5,500 feet, continuing even to Moflong; the scales of this genus are, it appears to me, mere appendages of the filaments, and not due to non-development or suppression of parts. Erythrina, which is found about Churra, is seen on the road to Kala Panee, apparently quite wild; altitude 5,200 feet: it recommences at Moflong, where it is common about villages, but never exceeds the size of a small tree. Commelina bengalensis? continues throughout here and there, and may be found even about Moflong.

The most striking change occurs, however, in the Pines, which, although of small stature, exist in abundance on the north side of the Boga Panee; so far as may be judged of by the naked eye, they disappear on this side, about a mile to the westward, very few cross the torrent, and few indeed are found 100 feet above its bed on the south side. I took the height of the bed of this torrent. Temperature of the air 72°; water boiled at 204°; which gives the height about 4,400 feet. Between Surureem and the Boga Panee, many new plants occur; grasses continue, as also at Moflong, the prevailing feature. The principal new ones occur on the descent, consisting of two large Andropogons, one closely allied to A. schæranthus and a tall Anthistiria habitu A. arundinacea; a beautiful Saccharum occurs here and there, especially before reaching the Kala Panee and the Gramina Bromoidea, which is the only really European form. On the Kala Panee, scarcely any Podostemon griffithia; except a few small ones, very few signs or appearance of fresh plants. Along the Boga Panee, among the wet rocks which form its banks, a fine Parnassia; a trailing Arbutoidea; a very European looking Quercus; Anesadenia pubescens, a Circæa, Campanulæ 2, Æschynomene, Crotalaria, a Serissa?; this last continuing to Moflong, a fine Osbeckia, and Gnaphalium aereonitus may likewise be found. On the ascent, few new plants occur; Rhinanthoidea, Osbeckia nepalensis, and capitata, Conyzoidea, Dipsacus, Gnaphalium foliis linearibus, Crotolaria hoveoides, Colutoidea, Pteris (Aquilina.) Scutellaria, Potentilla, Smilax occur at 5,000 feet with Plantago, Fragaria and Artemisia, as well as lower down. The most striking plant is a Delphinum, which, at about 5,000 feet, occurs stunted; this is common about Moflong.

Agrimonia range from 3,500 to 5,500 feet, where they are very common, Hypericum three sorts occur, H. myrtifolim commences, about Churra, re-occurs here and there on the road to Moflong, about which it is very common. H. ovalifolium, is more elevational, scarcely descending below 5,000 feet; H. japonicum is found from towards Mahadeb to Moflong; H. fimbriatum foliis decussatis, scarcely below 5,000 feet; Leucas galea brunneo villosa on grassy hills is common towards Boga Panee, and continues as high as Moflong.

Quercus commences about Mahadeb: a new species occurs on the edge of woods towards the Kala Panee; altitude 5,000 feet; it nearly commences with two Rhododendra, which, at least the arborescent one, arrives at perfection on the Kala Panee.

Viburna continue; Salix (fruticose) commences about 5,000 feet, continues here and there to Moflong. Buddlea Neemda is found about Churra, but not commonly; and soon disappears. B. 4-alata commences beyond the Churra Punjee, and continues as far as Moflong.

Thibaudia buxifolia becomes less common beyond 5,000 feet; other forms of Ericineæ appear in places about 5,000 feet, Gaultheria continuing as far as Moflong. Eurya species alterum, commences about the same elevation, continuing to Moflong.

Three species of Spiræa are found between Surureem and Moflong, none perhaps below 5,000 feet; Prunella occurs about the same height, continuing as far as Moflong.

On crossing the Boga Panee, the country becomes perhaps more undulated and much more barren, scarcely any arborescent vegetation is to be seen, the little woody vegetation consisting of stunted shrubs. Immediately around Moflong, the country is excessively bare, not a tree is to be seen, even the sides of ravines being clothed

y

with stunted shrubs. Berberis asiatica, Viburna, Spiræa *bella?* Eurya *camellifolia*, Betula *corylifolia*.

To the north, fine woods are seen, and to the east, fir woods, the nearest being about 4 miles off. The village is small and wretchedly dirty, the paths being the worst of all I have seen on these hills. The houses and the adjoining fields are surrounded with hedges of Colquhounia, Erythrina, Buddlæa.

In waste places Colquhounia *micrantha*, Cysticapnos, Verbesina, Pteris, Davallia, etc. are to be found, as well as Codonopsis viridiflora. The hills are covered with low grass, almost a sward. On this, Potentilla, Agrimonia, Geranium as well as in fields, Pisoideum floribus cyaneis, Campanula, Aster disco azureo may be found; on low spots a very small Parnassia, and a still smaller Ischæmum.

Ranunculus, one species, but this is uncommon; Delphinum is common in thickets, etc.

The only cultivation is potatoes, a few years since introduced, and which answers admirably, some turnips and Glycine tuberosa. Cattle, goats and pigs abundant.

On the whole this is to be considered as the place where the peculiar vegetation of Churra, arrives at its boundary, for although many of the plants of the plains are to be found, they are all in a dwarf state.

Noticed a Hoopoo, but birds in general are not frequent.

CHAPTER X.

Continues the Journey towards Assam and Bootan.

The annexed table of the distributions of plants in relation to altitudes of the Khasyah mountains may render the subject of the preceding observations more clear and distinct. The dotted line along the left hand margin represents the elevation of the mountains, the greater height of which is something better than 6,000 feet.

Surureem alt. 4,900 feet.

o .—Dauci species Tussilaginoid, Zanthoxylum, Swertia, Micrantha.
.—Rhododendron arboreum, species, altera fruticosa.
.—Quercus foliis subtus glaucis, Rosa, Salix.
.—Myrica, Photinia.
.—Clematis, Cuscuta,
.—Gramen, Bromoideum.
.—Swertiæ species duæ, Gerardia delphinifolia.
.—Arbutoid.
.—Gaultheria.
.—Pyrus.
.—Eurya, Hypericum ovalifol. myrtifolium.

{ Potentilla Fragaria. Clematis. }

Kala Panee.

Xyris discontinues.
Ditto, large Eriocaulon.
Tradescantea Commelina uncommon.

.—Bucklandia.
.—Solidago, Lactucoidea floribus cyaneis.
.—Rhododendron arboreum, Impatiens 4, Camellia, Begonia, Pomacea.
.—Quercus.
.—Crawfurdia speciosa, Utricularia in Moses.
.—Anisadenia.
.—Sphacelia.
.—Pedicularis, Solidago, Rhus.
.—Hypericum fimbriatum, Tofieldioideæ.
.—Cinicus, Parnassia pygmæa.
.—Galium asperum.
.—Colquhounia micrantha.
.—Epilobium, Clitoria, Asteroid, Hieracium.
.—Euphorbia, Viola Patrinii.
.—Potentilla altera species.
.—Podostemon Griffithii, Anthistiria, Desmodium.

Boga Panee altitude 4,400.

Temp. 9½ P. M. in doors. 64
6 P. M. 60°

.—Circæa, Campanula? Æschynomene, Crotalaria, Parnassia.
.—Pinus Khaseyanus, Arbutoid, Serissa, Andropogon, Quercus, Anisadenia.
.—Delphinium, Viburna, Salix, Quercus fruticos.
.—Colquhounia micrantha.

.—Agrimonia, Potentilla, Urtica petrophylla, Cuscutæ sp.
.—Colquhounia? Pisoideum, Cysticapnos, Macrocapnos.
.—
.—Ranunculus, Hypericum, Campanula, Cobonopis Geranium.
o.—Spiræa bella, Asteroid, Desmodium, Quercus.

Moflong alt. 5,500 feet.

October 8th.—Visited the fir wood, which is about three miles to the eastward; the road runs over the same *downey* ground. The first plant that appears is a Boreal Euphorbia, allied to that previously mentioned. A Sanguisorba of large stature occurs in low wet places. Epilobum not uncommon. The Pines appear first straggling, and they only form a wood in one place, and even there not of much extent; none are of any size. Musci Lichens and fungi abound in the wood, as also Circæa and Herminium?

Osbeckia Nipalensis, Hedychia 2, a small Goodyera, Tricyrtis Hedera, Polygonum, Polypodium, Gaultheria, Viburnum, Thibaudiacea fructibus gratis, subacidis. Eurya. Valeriana, Quercus, may likewise be found. Salix occurs on the skirts in low places. The hills around are clothed with grasses, among which is a large Airoidea; in the low vallies between these, intersected with small water-courses, three species of Juncus, a curious Umbellifera fistulosa, and Mentha verticillata, occur. Another Hypericum is likewise found in lately cleared places.

Some cultivation occurs about the place on the slopes of hills, chiefly of a Digitaria, sown broad-cast, and tied up in bundles when nearly ripe; together with Glycine tuberosa, and Coix Lacryme.

To the eastward the hills become more rocky, affording little vegetation, the chief plant is an Othonnoidea; another Herminioidea, and a Habenariod, both out of flower, may be found, the former on hills, the latter in low places; a tall Campanula was among the new plants, and an Umbellifera with curious foliage.

The height of this ridge is 5,768 feet, the temperature being 74°, and water boiling at 201$\frac{3}{4}$°.

Took the elevation of Moflong bungalow. Temperature of the air 65°; water boiled at 202$\frac{1}{4}$°; this gives 5,410 feet.

There are several high rounded hills about this place, (one to the south of the Boga Panee,) the generality of which are more elevated than those on the northern side; the most conspicuous is the hill near Moleem, the north face of which is wooded, and which is at least 1,000 feet above Moflong.

8 P. M. Temperature 58$\frac{1}{2}$°. 5 P. M. 65°.

October 9th.—Rain as usual in the morning. Thermometer at 7 A. M., 58$\frac{1}{2}$°.

October 10th.—A fine bracing cold morning, with the thermometer at 53$\frac{1}{2}$°. 7 A. M. left for Myrung. The march to Syung is uninteresting, passing over precisely the same country as that about Moflong, with vegetation much the same. A tall Carduaceous tree with pink flowers was found in the swampy bottoms of the valleys. About Syung, a seneciois tree foliis angustissimus. It is about this place that the sides of the ravines become clothed with forest, and from this northward, Pines increase in abundance. Anthistiria speculis villosissimis continues here and there; a good deal of cultivation passed on the road, especially under Syung to the south, where there is a large valley. The chief cultivation appears to be Coix, Glycine, and some rice, but the produce seemed very small. At the foot of Syung on the north side, large tufts of Juncus occur, and on the first ascent another species of Valeriana foliis radicalibus reniformi cordatus occurs. Urena lobale was noticed as high as 5,300 feet. Between Syung and Myrung, especially about Nungbree, Parnassia recurs, with another species of Epilobium, Xyris, Juncus, the Senecioneæ, etc.; a new Impatiens occurs towards Myrung. Generally speaking, the plants are much the same as those about Moflong; but several new Compositæ occur.

The road leaves Nungbree to the right, leaving the most interesting parts of the march behind. Altogether not more than 20 additional plants occurred in a journey of 6 hours. Many parts are wet and marshy, and there is an absence of all tree vegetation, until one reaches Syung. This makes the first part of the way somewhat tedious. At Syung an Elæagnus occurs; Colquhounia as usual in hedges; Styrax occurs at foot of the hill the altitude of which is 5,000 feet.

An anemone is common on road sides, especially on this side of Syung; a new Potentilla occurs; and the only Boragineous plant hitherto seen by me on these hills, a Cynoglossum closely allied to C. cunescens. The altitude of Syung is 5,594 feet. The temperature being 70°, and water boiling at 202°. Myrung 6 P. M. Thermometer 65°.

October 11*th*.—Myrung 7 A. M. temp. 63° Fahr.; noon 67°; 6 P. M. temp. 65°; 9 temp. P. M. 62½°. Weather unsettled, showery, and very cloudy, a very fine view is had of Bootan and the Himalayas from this place, particularly about 7 A. M. when the atmosphere is clear, the Durrung peaks being most magnificent. The vegetation of the hills about here is much the same as about Moflong. The woods are fine, composed chiefly of oaks; a Magnolia, which is a very large tree, likewise occurs together with Gordonia, an occasional Pinus, Myrica integrifolia. The most curious tree is one which with the true appearance of an Elæagnus, seems to be a Loranthus, the first arborescent species yet found, although, as one or two other exceptions occur to parasitism, there is no reason why there should not be a terrestrial arborescent species, as well as a fruticose one. The wood to the east of the bungalow, which clothes a deep and steep ravine, has a very rich flora; a dryish ridge on the other side of its torrent abounds with Orchideæ, and presents an arborescent Gaultheria. The ridge in question may be recognised by its large rocks which are covered with Epiphytes Mosses, etc. In this wood Pothos flammea is very common, climbing up the trees as well as hanging in festoons. The marshes which are frequented by a few snipe, present grasses, the usual Cyperaceæ, Xyris, occurs but is not common; Panicum stagninum? Eriocaulon spe. fluitans! Burmannia Rungioidea floribus carneis magnis, Senecionides, Ammannia rotundifolia, Sphagnum, Carduacea floribus roseis, Limnophilæ sp. Mentha verticillata, and the others previously found in similar situations. *Goldfussia* so common about Churra, recurs here, but rarely.

The wood abounds with several species of birds, among which a green *Bulbul* is the most common, then the fan-tailed Parus, with its coquettish airs; judging from the voice there is a species of Bucco. Both species of Phænicornis, yellow and crimson, described in Gould's Century as male and female, and the black Edolius are found. The only animals are two species of squirrel, and a genet, of which I shot one, but although it fell from a height of 70 feet or so, I could not succeed in securing it; it is a lengthy animal, black and grey, with a long tail, climbing trees with great facility. The ring-dove of Churra continues.

The weather during the four days I stayed at Myrung was unsettled; fine usually in the morning, but cloudy and showery in the evening; the range of the thermometer from 53°, at 6½ A. M. to 68° in the afternoon in an open verandah. The place, however, is not a cheerful one, for the aspect on every side except to the E. and NE. is dreary, marshes and the usual bleak grassy hills being alone visible. My favourite spot in this direction would be the Nungbree hill, the altitude of which, at least of that part over which the road to the village runs, is 5,439, (or probably 5,700,) temperature of the air being **, and water boiling at 202½°. There is a beautiful and very extensive wood at Nungbree, the largest I have yet seen; it consists, at least at the skirts, principally of oaks; a large Pyrus is also not uncommon. Eurya, and an arborescent Buddlea likewise occur.

From a sketch made on the spot by W. Griffith.

M. & N. Hanhart lith. Printers

OK-KLONG ROCK

At this place Plectranthus azureus makes its appearance, otherwise the vegetation is that of Myrung; the most remarkable plant is a huge Sarcocordalis, parasitic on the roots of a large climbing Cissus cortice suberosa, foliis quinatis, on the wet parts of the wood, especially towards the mountain foot, mosses abound, chiefly the pendent Hypna and Neckeræ.

On the 13th, I went to a celebrated rock called Kullung, (Pl. 10,) bearing about NW. from Myrung, from the heights surrounding which it is visible; the road runs off from the Nunklow nearly opposite Monei, near to which village one passes; the village is of no great size, and as well as others in this direction is inhabited chiefly by blacksmiths, the iron being procured from the sand washed down the mountain torrents; the sound of their anvils when beaten is very soft and musical, not unlike that of a sheep bell. The road to the rock is very circuitous; it finally ceases, and for an hour one traverses ridges on which no path exists, having the usual vegetation. The rock is certainly a vast mass, forming a precipice of 700 feet to the westward, on which side it is nearly bare of vegetation, gradually shelving to the east, and covered with tree-jungle, among which huge mosses are to be found. At its foot some fine fir trees occur, one at its very base measured nine feet in circumference, but had no great height. The forest consists of Oaks, Pines, Panax, Erythrina Eurya, Gordonia.

The base of the rock is covered with mosses, Hepaticæ, a Didymocarpus, Cælogyne and some other epiphylical orchideæ, among others Bolbophyllum cylindraceum.

All these continue to its apex, except the mosses and Hepaticæ, which are gained by clambering, and proceeding up fissures clothed with grasses. The apex is rounded, presenting here and there patches of grass, Aira, and Nardus, together with a few stunted shrubs—Viburnum, another Rhododendron, and Didymocarpus common, Cælogyne in profusion, Bolbophyllum cylindraceum in abundance, mosses, Lichens, an Allium also in abundance on the slopes, Stellaria in the woods towards the middle.

The view to the westward in particular was pretty, embracing a fine well-wooded undulated valley, with several villages and a stream of sòme size. The plains of Assam and the huge Brahmapoutra were likewise seen, but not very clearly. The distance from Myrung to the Kullung rock is certainly not less than eight miles, the time it took was 4 hours. The altitude of the rock is 5,392 feet, temperature 76°, water boiling at 202½. Wild hog are found round its base.*

October 14*th.*—I left for Moleem, the march is long and fatiguing; the road leaves the Moflong road at about four miles from the village of that name, continuing over similar barren hills, clothed with scanty grass. On reaching Morung firs become common, but they are small. The view of Moleem, from this direction is remarkably pretty; the country being better wooded, especially with young firs, and the effect being much increased by the quantities of large boulders that occur strewn in every direction. The Boga Panee is here a contemptible stream, not knee deep. Moleem is a place of some size on the left bank of the river, occupying the side of a hill of considerable height. Thermometer 7 P. M. 58°.

October 15*th.*—Temp. 7 A. M. 53°, at 3 P. M. 70½°, water boiled at 204°, altitude 4,473 feet, or perhaps rather more. Walked towards Nogandree; between this and a stream resembling the Boga Panee there is a pretty valley, the eminences generally well-wooded with young firs. Pretty and eligible sheltered sites might here be chosen for a Sanatarium. The vegetation is the same as that of Moflong—Delphinium, Ranunculus, Anemone, Potentilla, Tricyrtis, Codonopsis, Lilium giganteum, Spiræaceæ, Viola, Pyrus, Galium, Carduus, Viburna.

The woods are not very frequent, they consist, when not exclusively of Pines, chiefly of Oaks and Chesnuts. Underwood almost entirely of Acanthaceæ. Rhus Bucki-Amelam is common here, an Oxalis occurs in very shady places with fleshy leaves, it is so large that it is scarcely referrible to O. corniculata. Berberis asiatica is very common. 6 P. M. thermometer 58°, 9 P. M. 60½°.

October 16*th.*—7 A. M. 842½°. Ascended the Chillong hill, which is among the highest portion of this range, it is said that from this both the plains of Bengal and of Assam may be seen, not because it overtops all the intermediate ground, but because that happens in some places to be rather low; the termination of the 1st elevation above Churra, is seen to be very abrupt, but nothing can be seen beyond the elevated plateau of this part towards the south. To

* The Kullung rock is a most striking object from its artificial dome-like appearance. It is composed of granite resting on an elevated plateau of soft friable gneiss. This last in mouldering away, leaves numerous rounded boulder-like masses of granite on the surface, which from their hardness, resist the action of the atmosphere amidst the surrounding decay of the softer rock.

the east and west the view has the usual appearance—grassy vallies and hills—with a great disproportion of jungle.

The summit is gained after an easy march of two hours; the ascent is gradual. The highest ridge is naked of trees, but to the north the slope is in one portion covered with heavy tree-jungle, in which the underwood is as thick as I have ever seen it: it consists of an Acanthaceous plant; the forest itself of oaks, chesnuts and Rhododendron arboreum, which last is common on the highest margin. A few Pines occur, but scarcely above the middle of the hill. To the north very high ground is visible, as likewise from Myrung, and between this and Chillung is an elevated plateau which appears to me likewise very eligible for the sites of European residences.

But many places about Moleem are so, especially towards Nonkreem; and it is much to be regretted that some situation in this part of the range had not been selected for the site of a sanatarium instead of Churra. The Rhododendra were covered with mosses and other epiphytes, among which Otochilus occurred. Bambusæ, 2 Fici sp. Andropogon, Gaylussacia, etc. occur about the wood. The vegetation of the grassy hills was precisely the same, Aroidea, Erianthus, Tofieldioidea, Parnassia nana *potius collina*, Sphacelioidea, Osbeckia, Arbutoideæ, etc. I got scarcely a single new plant; the best was a fine large Neckera, sect. Dendroidea. The temperature being 70°: water boiled at 201°, making the altitude 6,167 feet. No view of any particular beauty was obtained, nor did any thing occur to repay me for the trouble and fatigue of the journey.

About Moleem an Osmundoid is common enough, but not in *flower*: the northern forms are Ranunculus, Anemone, Parnassia, Pyrus, Pinus, Viola, Galium, Campanula, Clematis, of which an additional species occurs, Bromoideæ, etc. etc., as at Moflong. I took the height of this place again; the mean of the three thermometers gave 4,502 feet, the temperature being at 60°: water boiling at 95°, 203¾°, 204°. It must, however, be remembered that my residence is not 100 feet above the bed of the Boga Panee, so that it would be easy to attain an elevation of 5,000 feet in the village itself.

October 17th.—I returned to Churra to send away my collections and to consult with Major Lister as to the routes proposed for me by Capt. Jenkins, viz. through the Garrows, or through the Cacharees. Nothing particular occurred en route. I met with Hydrangea exaltata along a torrent flowing into the main-feeder of the Boga Panee, and two other Araliaceæ. The highest ground crossed is towards the ravine of the Boga Panee, and from this a good view of Moflong is obtained, and also of the Himalayas in clear weather. Cœlogyne Wallichiana was commencing to flower; this plant occurs in profusion in some rocky spots about Moflong. The only additional thing I remarked was, that Luculia scarcely reaches the Kala Panee.

On my return to Churra, a change was observed in the character of the vegetation, all the Tradescanteas had ceased, as well as most of the Impatientes, and Eriocaulons. The grasses had become more withered, and the general tint was brown. No kites (Falco milvus) are to be observed out of Churra.

The plants which were particularly conspicuous about Churra, were past flowering in the interior; thus Osbeckia Nepalensis? was not to be met with in flower in the interior, while it is in profusion about the station. The same may be said of other instances.

After all Churra presents the richest flora of any other place in the Khasyah hills, because there is a greater extent of wood near it, than is found in any other locality, much greater *altitudes* and deeper descents in its ravines, and it is as it were the transit point between a tropical or sub-tropical, and a temperate vegetation. I have no doubt, that within a circle of three miles of Churra, 3,000 species might be found in one year.

The principal plants pointing out the tropical nature of the vegetation are Pandanus, which is almost limited to the limestone formation, on which it is excessively abundant, Chamærops Martiana? which from its affecting particularly the walls of the amphitheatres so conspicuous about Moosmai, Mamloo and Surureem, and the depths of whose sides is probably at Mamloo 1,000 feet, might have been better named. I have never seen it on any other places. The Alsophila Brunoniana is likewise apparently confined to the limestone hills, while the tree fern, Polypodium, is found on sandstone, as well as Impatiens, Tradescantia, Commelineæ, Eriocauloneæ, Xyres, almost all the grasses, Melastomaceæ, almost all the Leguminosæ and the preponderance of tropical Rubiaceæ, which are, however, few, Scitamineæ, Epiphytical Orchideæ, Urena Labiata, etc. etc.

On the 23*rd* I went to Mamloo, which is about four miles to the west of Churra. To this place the limestone ridge, extending from Churra, nearly approaches: its vegetation is not rich but always stunted: rocky amphitheatres are very remarkable at Mamloo, they are of excessive depth; their walls being generally perpendicular, often somewhat overhanging. The manner of their formation is now to be seen in the amphitheatre immediately contiguous to the village, although it appears to be very slow. It is thus, bodies of water falling from the edge of the table land, seem to undermine the sandstone below, producing land slips, which occur in this manner year after year. Since 1835, the edge of the Moosmai fall has receded at least 10 feet, and ample evidence remains of the recession to take place next rains. This simple undermining will suffice for the formation of ravines, which *are* formed by their sides merely slipping down without being carried away, this last only occurring in the immediate vicinity of the strength of the torrent. All the different stages may be easily seen. The edge of the table land I take to have been originally at Mahadeb. The time that has elapsed between the falling of the first cataract over its edge, and the formation of the edge over which the waters at present fall, must be immense, since that edge has now receded several miles. Allowing the annual recess to be 5 feet, and the distance 5 miles; the time occupied would be 5,700 years: that the time has been great, is proved by the sides of these places being clothed with large tree-jungle to the base of the scarp.

October 25th.—I went in search of the fossil marine beach, (found during our first visit in 1835,) but passed it, and my journey ended at the site of the Jasper beds: this occupies a ridge where roads strike off leading to the Orange villages, so called from the groves of orange trees by which they are surrounded, and from which they derive their name. From this spot, 3 villages are seen occupying sheltered situations, none much above 2,000 feet in elevation. Luckily I was accompanied, (although going down I was unconscious of it,) by a boy who had been with McClelland when he originally discovered the fossil remains, so I recommenced the ascent, after digging in many places without any success. The site is scarcely 1,000 feet below Mamloo, which is 3,153 feet; it is below the ridge along which the road is visible from the village, and is about 100 yards farther from it than the second square stone erection. One would imagine that one was passing through rocks presenting nothing interesting: the rocks are in many places very hard, particularly when they have been long exposed to the atmosphere, in which case they are less red than when sheltered by vegetation, when they are soft and of a reddish colour: the fossils are by no means frequent, the cylindric *tubes* appear to occupy the outer or rather upper surface of the sandstone, in the interior of which Medusæ or Cyrtomæ are most frequent, accompanied by shells, some of large size, the largest bivalves resembling *scolloped oysters;* the next in size looking like oblong cockles: for only in one position did I see a conglomeration of minute shells; this occurred above the others and nearer the jungle. I brought away with me, two boxes full. Owing to my presuming that I should meet with water near, I omitted the precaution of taking some with me, so I could not ascertain exactly the height of the place. All the fossils are easily friable.*

From the Jasper, which is scarce 1,800 feet, in elevation, the following plants occurred nearly in succession—Holmskioldia, this is scarcely found above 2,000 feet; Porana in abundance, gradually diminishing above; Callicarpa arborea abundant, continuing to about 2,200; Triumfetta, Urena lobata, Arundo the same as above, Melica latifolia, Panicum plicatum, and one or two other species; a Polygonum, Andropogon, small Commeline, Leea, Erythrina are very close to the spot, and the only Churra plant, except the Arundo and Wendlandia is a Labiata, Geniosporum? so is Composita arborea; indeed the vegetation is almost decidedly tropical. The following plants are then seen —Tetranthera, Flemingia as at Mahadeb, Vitis, Drymaria, Panicum eleusinoides, Eurya, Panax foliis decompositis inermis, Pogonatherum crenitum, Wallichia, which occur before one has gained an ascent of 2,000 feet: Osbeckia nepalensis descends to this but in small quantities; then I remarked Bidens, Ætheilema, Caricineæ, Rottlera, Didymocarpus, Begonia, Cheilanthes dealbata, Stemodia ruderalis? Scutellaria, Impatiens bracteata, Rungiæ sp. Sida, Elephantopus sp. and Bambusa, Gordonii occurring there at an elevation of about 2,100 feet. Then Centotheca lappacea, Deeringia, Panicum *centrum*, Gouania, Caryophyllus, which last occurs on all the chain of Himalayas, and which I have seen as high as 6,000 feet in the Mishmee Mountains, latitude 28°. Panax foliis palmatim partitis, Clerodendrum nutans, Ficus feruginea and F. hispida, foliis cordatis, serrato-dentatis: then Saurauja micrantha; before 2,300 feet were reached. There Oxyspora sp. paniculis cernius ramis ascendentibus, frutex, Croton of old, Ruellia persicæfolia appeared, and about 2,400 feet, the 1st Quercus appeared. Here, as at Mahadeb, Ruellia Neesiana became common, and Linúm trigynum, Uncinia, etc. Grasses commence to preponderate at about 2,800 feet, but not the grasses of Churra. Holcus, Airoides, etc. not being found, but Panica varia, and Rottboellia which ceases above this.

At the raised Marine Fossil Beach, a queer Cephalanthus? Legumenosa arbuscula fol. pinnatis impari (Pongamiæ) Legumenibus secus suturam quamque alatis, Mangifera indici, Anthistiria arundinacea are found, and an arbusculous Mimosa, but unarmed. Shortly above this,

* For original notice of the discovery of this raised beach, see Journal of the Asiatic Society, September 1835, p. 523; and an account of the difference of level in Indian coal fields, vol. vii, 1838, p. 65 of the same work; also description of Cyrtoma a new genus of Fossil Echinida, Calcutta Journal of Nat. Hist. vol. i, p. 155.

Holcus, Andropogons, etc., begin to preponderate, and thence the vegetation is nearly that of Churra. The woods of Mamloo consist of Bucklandia, oaks, chesnuts, Panax, Hyalostemma, Eurya, and Oleineœ; Epiphytes are very common. The most remarkable tree is one foliis alternis bistipulat; corymbis denis, Calycibus hinc fissis, petalis 5-albis, Antheræ sinuosæ columna terminans, et ovarium et stigma occultantes ? fructibus pendulis stipilatis ovato oblongis, carpellis 5-latere marginatus.

This has some affinities apparently with Sterculiaceæ; the flowers are perhaps polygamous.

Here Cypripedium insigne, Venustum, and various other fine Orchideæ may be found.

The only bird I saw was a Bucco, which in voice resembled the green one of the plains.

The elevation of Mamloo is 3,153, the temperature being at 7 A. M. 63°. The large metal thermometer rose at the boiling point to $206\frac{1}{4}$°: wooden one to $206\frac{1}{2}$°: centigrade $96\frac{7}{10}$°: small metal 200°.

One of the most curious places about Churra is situated over the ridge in which the coal is found; on surmounting this, which is steep and perhaps 400 feet high, one soon commences to descend gradually until you come to a water-course; on proceeding along this a short way you come to a precipice. The water falling over this, has cut a deep well in the limestone: the road to the bottom is precipitous and dangerous. On reaching the water-course again no signs of the well are observable, access to this is gained by subterranean passages, of which two, now dry, exist. The scene inside is very striking; you stand on the rugged bottom of the well which is 70 or 80 feet deep, the part above corresponding to the fall, being of about the same depth; the water now escapes through a chasm below the bed of the well, the other fissures or passages being above, and probably now rarely letting off the water. After a severe fall of rain the scene must be grand.

November 4th.—Nonkreem $6\frac{1}{2}$ A. M., thermometer 31°: hoarfrost. Marched hither from Surureem. Vegetation the same until you reach the Boga Panee, when Delphinum, Anemone, and Ranunculus make their appearance. On the high ridges before reaching Boga Panee, found an Astragalus; at Nonkreem, a Scrophularia. Nonkreem, is a curious place, the village of no great size in a valley: the sides of the valley are covered with boulders; those at the entrance from Churra of huge size, and thrown together with great confusion. Pines at this place occur of some size, but they are distinctly limited in this direction to the granitic formation. The downs have now assumed a withered wintry appearance. Nonkreem is a great place for iron; this is found in coarse red sandstone, or it may be fine granite, forming precipices; this is scraped or pushed down by iron rods, it is then washed by a stream turned off on to it: the stream is dammed up, and the irony particles by their weight fall to the bottom: they are very heavy, of a dull blackish appearance. All the streams are of a whitish colour, and the rocks are covered with Cælogyne Wallichiana.

The elevation of Nonkreem is 4,578 feet, the temperature of the air being 52°. The large thermometer indicated boiling water 203°: centigrade 96½°: wooden 204°: small 197°. In the Nonkreem jheel, Alisma, Villarsia! and Potamogeton occur.

November 5th.—The march to Suneassa continues over high downs, the vegetation being precisely as before, viz. Cnicus, Carduus, Prunella Pedicularis, Gaultheria, Gnaphalia, Bromoid acroideum, Tussilaginoid Andropogon, Sphacelia Daucas, Hypericum, Hedychium, Polygonum rheoides, Smithia but rare, Tradescantia clavigera, Parnassia collina, Pteris aquilina, Euphorbia, Dipsacus, Salix, Osbeckia capitata, Æthionnia, Eriocaulon, Knoxia cordata, and Campanula. In short, the higher ridges have the vegetation of those between the Kala and Boga Panee, the less elevated, that of Surureem. Along the watercourses Pyrus, Betula, Corylifoliæ, and Eurya.

As one approaches Suneassa the ravines become wooded, and the aspect of country more diversified. The woods consist of a Castanea, 2 oaks, Rhododendron arboreum and R. punctatum, Panax, Eurya, Thebaudiaceæ variæ, no less than 4 or 5, of these, one is a Gaylussacia; Saccharum megala makes its appearance at Suneassa.

This is a small straggling village, on the brow of the ravine of the same name; it is like Moflong, each house being hidden by hedges composed as usual of Buddlea, Colquhounii, Solanum spirale? Erythrina, Ficus, and Rhus. Sugarcane, but of poor quality, is here cultivated, as well as capsicum, but this is also of inferior quality; the houses are worse than usual. Near this place several Nunklow plants appear, as Plectranthus cæruleus, Labiata foliis verticillatis of Suddya. Its elevation is 4,362 feet, the temperature being in the air, 59°. Big thermometer boiling point ditto 204°: wooden ditto 204°: small 298°: centigrade ditto 96°. Pines occur here and there towards Suneassa, but of no size and no abundance.

November 6th.—Left Suneassa and proceeded down the ravine which is probably 1,200 to 1,500 feet deep. The scenery is very pretty, the sides being much wooded; the woods open, consisting chiefly of pines, which are of moderate size, Gordonia, Castanea, and Quercus: Mimosea occurs, also Saurauja. The grasses are as before, except that the Anthisteria of Nunklow appears, with Volkameria, Verbena Primulacæ, and Osbeckia capitate, foliis lineari oblongis, floribus carneis. Towards the foot, the scenery still improves.

The woods consist of pines and a Quercus foliis castaneæ cupulis echinatis, Arbor mediocris; the slopes as well as the valley are cultivated chiefly for rice, this last often assuming the terrace fashion. The river is of considerable width, 50 to 60 yards, but of no depth: two here flow together, and at the end of the valley a still larger stream not fordable in the rains, at least where I crossed, meets it. On the streams at the base of the Suneassa acclivity, Salix, Ligustrum, Ficus frutex humelis, and a fine Indigofera occur. Moving thence along the valley the vegetation becomes tropical, although pines descend nearly to its level. Pontederia the small one of Bengal, ditto Sagittaria Vandelliæ, Poæ 3, Apluda, Cyperaceæ, Saccharum megala, and spontaneum, Elytrophorus, Ammannia, Erianthus, Cnicus! Artemisia as before, Arundo exalum, Cirsium, Carduus! Scitamineæ 2, Panicum curvatum, Setaria glauca, Swertia angustifolia! Volkameriæ sp., Ranunculus hirsutoideus! Zizania ciliaris.

Those marked with, [!,] have probably straggled down. The cultivation is chiefly of rice, Eleusine, Coix, and the edible seeded Labiata. Grasses abound; in addition to those above several new ones occur, Rottboellia exallata, Anthisteria of Nunklow, Arundinaceæ, Andropogones several, Saccharum fusco-rubum, 25 species might certainly be collected.

Fine pines occur on the other ascent from its base to apex. Here also occurs Phœnix pumile, which as well as the Rottboellia, which I think I have seen in the Magoung valley (during the journey to Ava), and Buddlea neemda.

The ascent gained, the country appears level, covered with the usual grasses. The ravines are well wooded, but few pines occur, although they may be seen here and there. The woods appear the same as those of Churra. Pandanus sp. altera? occurs. In one ravine gathered a new Thebaudiaceæ allied to T. variegata, differing in its short greenish flowers and its smoothness.

o.—Pinus, Pyrus, Quercus. Delphinium, Anemone.

Nonkreem. 4,578 feet.
.—Alisma, Vellarsioid, Potamogeton, Scirpus, Cyperaceæ, Ammannia rotundifolia.

.—Grassy tracts without wood. Delphinium ceases. Vegetation as about the downs of Surureem; Erucus, Carduus, Holcus.

.—Andropogon, Bromus, Gnaphalia, Osbeckia capitata, Æthionnia.

.—Pinus to the northward and east.

.—Pyrus, Betula corylifolia.

.—Quercus 2. Thibaudiaceæ, Rhododendrum arboreum punctatum.

.—Senecio.

Suneassa 4,362 feet.
o.—Luculia, Buddlea, Colquhounia, Ficus, Rhus, Rubus, Fragaria, sugarcane, capsicum, rice, Digitaria, Eleusine.

.—Quercus, Castanea.

.—Gordonia, Anthistiria, Verbena primulacea, Pinus, Saurauja, Volkameria, Eria, Sarcanthus, Cirsium.

.—Quercus castaneoides, Pinus.

.—Rice cultivation, Eleusine, Coix, Labiata, Andropogones, Rottboellia, Sacchara 3, Elytrophorus Vandellia, Pontedenia, Sagittaria, Ligustrum, Indigofera Salix, Anthistina arundinacea, Ranunculus Zizania, Carduus, Cnicus Verbena primulacea Artemisia, Scitamineæ, Swertia, Exacum.

.—Pinus, Gordonia Phœnix.

.—Panax, Thibandia, Polyagonum, Pothos.

.—Grassy level, table land, ravines and sides of hills with rounded woods. Elephants. Vegetation much as at Churra, Pinus ceases. Woods of oak, chesnuts, Symplocos, Bucklandia occur.

Amwee. 3,500 feet.
.—Quercus castanea Symplocos, Pandanus, Bucklandia, Garciniæ Nepenthes, Chrysobaphus, Gnetum, Elæocarpus. o

Amwee is situated on an undulated plain or table land; the undulations are gentle, separated by marshy tracts: no steep ravines occur, the face of the undulations is covered with grasses, among which are seen most of the Churra plants, the sides are covered with fine woods with defined edges, consisting chiefly of oaks, chesnuts and Bucklandia. The aspect of the country is pretty, resembling some woodland scenery in the south of England; close to Amwee is a fine stream 40 yards wide, this winds through the valley, and on its upper part fine cascades occur. No fish are to be found besides those of Churra. The river is crossed by a stone bridge consisting of pillars of single slabs of large size, one measuring 20 feet in length by from 4 to 5 in breadth. The temperature varies from 50 to 68 during the day in an open verandah. Fogs are not so common, nor is the rain so heavy as at Churra. The space being much greater, and the country more level, it would be better as a sanatarium than Churra, besides which, its access is as easy, it being reached in one day from Jynteapore. There is, however, a Toorai about Jynteapore, which is unhealthy. Its altitude is 3,500 feet, or nearly 500 below Churra.

The vegetation is nearly the same as about Churra, some new Castaneæ and an Elæocarpus occur, and Pandanus of large size in the woods. Epiphytical Orchideæ abound; Nepenthes occurs here. Altitude from three observations 3,530 feet: 1st observation 3,439: 2nd 3,597: 3rd 3,624.

November 10*th.*—Joowye: this is north from Amwee, and about 8 miles distant. Two vallies have to be descended, one rather steep. The country alters immediately after the 1st ascent, the woods nearly disappearing except in the more favoured spots. Pines soon commence. In the second valley, the stream of which is large, and of which pretty views are to be obtained, the pines reach on the south side to the bank of the stream, on the north scarcely any are to be seen. In the woods about Amwee, Eugenia is very common: noticed on the route Lonicera.

Joowye is the largest village I have seen, it is of great extent but straggling; near its entrance is a breast-work now nearly complete. The houses are of a better description than those generally met with. They are surrounded by wood, especially fine bamboos, in habit not unlike B. baccifera. They are also surrounded by excellent timber palings. The people are different from Khasyas Proper —perhaps they are not so fine a race. Their features approach more to those of Bengallees, particularly the women, who dress their hair like those of Assam, indeed the dress generally of both sexes assimilates to that of Assamese, although their language seems to be Bengallee. In the wood surrounding this place curious features of vegetation occur, and beautiful lanes and pathways. One may see a beech now naked of leaves, standing out in graceful relief close to the elegant foliage of a bamboo. Bamboos surround all the houses —sugarcane, kuchoos, mustard, hemp, Musa, Ricinus were observed.

The plants are beech, which is common and of large size. Pyrus of Moleem, Pinus rare, Marlea begonifolia! Betula corylifolia common. Verbena chamædrys, Rubi 3 or 4, Tetrantheræ? Rubia cordifolia, Morus, Cerasus, Panax 3 species, Gleicheniæ 2, Eurya, Juncus, Ranunculus, Viola, Verbesina of Moflong, Sida, Clematis *pubescens*, Caricineæ, Myrica, Gordonia, Polygonum 3, among them Rheoides Engeldhaardtii common, Viburna 2, Wendlandia, Osbeckia capitata and nepalensis. The grasses chiefly Andropogons; Mussænda, Bucklandia, Saurauja, Hiræa, Dipsacus rare, Camellia oleifolia, and C. axillaris, Begonia laciniata, Ficus, Vitis, Sonerila, Plectranthus azureus, Randia, Mephitidia, Psychotria, Galium, Clerodendrum infortunatum, Pyrus or crab, Fragaria, Potentilla, Urena lobata. The diversified nature of the vegetation, both tropical and temperate, is at once evident.

The altitude is 3,553 feet—temperature of the air 62°; large thermometer boiling point 205½°: wooden ditto 206¾°: centigrade ditto 96°: small ditto 199½°.

The higher ground about the place is about 4,000 feet: Joowye being situated in a hollow. Viola and Peristrophe occur.

November 11*th.*—The march to Nurtung occupies about 6 hours. The country is level, or merely undulated, with no considerable descent, the steepest being that to the river on which Nurtung is situated. The vegetation continues the same, the trees except in the ravines almost exclusively pines, those on the ravines consisting of oaks, Rhododendra, Betula corylifolia, Betula moroides, Solidago, Verbena, Primulaceæ, Othonna, occur; Anthistiriæ, *both* those of Nunklow are common, Rottboellia Manisuris in low vallies: here and there Phœnix pumila is common. The country just before Nurtung is unintéresting, scarcely any thing but grass being visible in some directions. Indeed it falls off on leaving Joowye.

Rhinanthus, Corolla infundibulif. subbilabiat. lobis 2, superioribus minoribus, stam. ascendent. stigmati inclusi decurvo.

November 12*th.*—Nurtung is a large place for these hills, perhaps next in extent to Joowye, it occupies principally both sides of a sufficiently sheltered hill. The lanes adjacent to the place are narrow, often very wet, and always very dirty. The gardens are enclosed with wooden palings and are screened still further by bamboos. The houses, at least the better order, are still better than even those of Joowye. The exterior is of the same construction as all Khasya houses, but the lawns and the comparative cleanliness of the front makes them look much better. The market, which took place to-day, is outside the village and close to our bungalow : it is well attended, but the amount of persons could not exceed 100 to 200, and these form a considerable amount of all the persons capable of bearing burdens from the neighbouring villages. The luxuries exhibited are all Khasyan, consisting of stinking fish, some other things of dubious appearance and still more dubious odour, millet and the inferior grains, and the fashionable articles of Khasya clothing and the adjuncts to that abominable habit pawn eating. There was plenty of noise, but still order prevailed : no other rupees than the *rajah's* were taken, and even pice were refused. Iron implements of husbandry of native manufacture were vended, in short all the various luxuries or necessaries of a Khasya are obtainable.

This place bears evidence of having been ruled over by some chief pretending to Hindooism. This is observable in the large fig trees in some of the buildings, in most of the houses in the presence of some brahmins, in the tanks, and in a sacred lake. At any rate it is attended with bad effects, and to see a Khasya attempting the formalities of a rigid Hindoo is ridiculously absurd.

It must be a wealthy place, many of the natives are well off; and I saw a *lady* of a decidedly superior nature to the Khasya women, clad in snow white, reclining in oriental fashion on a platform. The *vegetation* of this place forms a curious melange around our huts : Rhus bucki ameli, two Artimiseæ, Anthistiria arundinacia, Pteris aquilina, Callicarpa *lilacina,* Eurya, Bombax, Osbeckia nepalensis and linearis, Marlea begonifolia, Pyrus, Pinus, Urticia fructibus aurantiaceus capitulatis, Polygonum rheoides, Rubi 3, Swertia angustifolia, Polygonum globuliferum, Valerianæ, Cacalia, Randia, Gnaphalia nervosa, and G. revoluta, Smilax, Plectranthus azureus, Trichosanthes, Leea, Tradescantia clavigera, Geniosporum, *Butea,* Hypericum, Knoxia cordata, Rice cultivation.

Along the path to the village are to be found, Carduus, Myrica crotalaria, *Hacyoides,* Cariceneæ, Panicum curvatum, Arundo, Mentha verticillata, Cyperaecæ usual, Zizania ciliaris, Panax, Wendlandia

Salvinia, Isachne bigeniculata, Betula corylifolia common, Pontedera, Tetranthera, Erythrina, Celtis, Salix, Buddlea, Gordonia, Calamus abundant, Juncus, Arum macrophyllum, Cordiaceæ, Urena lobata, Cynoglossum canescens, Bambusa, Verbesinea, *Lavinia*, Magnolia of Myrung, Camellia oleifolia, Gualtheria.

About the village, Porana, Musa, Verbena, Xanthophyllum, Xyris, Urtica herophylla, Sambucus, &c.

The cultivation consists of rice, millet, Soflong? pumpkins and tobacco; guavas and oranges, are also to be seen.

Daphne cannabina occurs here, as well as Loxotis obliqua, the Cardaminum, Plantago, and Martynia.

From a fresh observation and taking the mean, I find the elevation of Nurtung to be 3,302 feet.

On enquiry I find that Rulung is one march off, that the country is similar, and that pines grow there to a large size. From this place to Koppilee river it is said to be nine marches. A fuqueer from Cutch said several, six to ten—and as the distance is nearly fifty miles and the ground difficult, he was probably right.

You then come to the Meekir country. To get into Tooly Ram's country would require at least nine days, but with loaded people probably twelve or fifteen. The station between Rulung and the Koppilee is Hush Koorah. Thermometer varies here from 45 to 85 in the sun, in shade from 52 to 74.

November 13th.—Left for the Borpanee.

The country traversed is easy, consisting chiefly of undulations covered with grassy vegetation. There are no steep ascents nor descents; and the only obstacle is the Borpanee. The march is of about six hours' duration.

Butea suffruticosa is very common about Nurtung, but ceases soon after leaving its environs. All the valleys near this place are cultivated: the ground being now inundated in proportion. Dipsacus valeriana continued, and a short distance from Nurtung pines become very common. Thence the country became more undulated and scarcely a tree was met with: Hedysarum gyrans commenced shortly after leaving Nurtung: a sure sign of decreasing elevation. The country subsequently improved, being more diversified with wood: firs became abundant, Callicarpa arborea commenced. About Nonkreen, a small village to the east, close to our path the trees became mostly different. Kydia appeared, a tree like the mango, and some others unknown to me. Bauhinia, Randia, Phyllanthus Embelica, and a stunted arboreous Symplocos, Anthistiria arundinacea common, with chesnuts (Castaneæ).

Close to this, Gordonia, pines of some size, Anthistiria arundinacea and Cassioides. The grasses continued the same, but two new Andropogons and a small Rottboellia appear ; Holcus, Airoides, etc. of Churra have ceased : the other are Sacchara and various Andropogons. On approaching a considerable descent the woods became open, consisting at first entirely of pines, Betula of Joowye, etc. then of pines, Quercus castaneoides which attains a large size. It was here that the pines became large, one felled measured sixty-nine feet to the first branch, most are straight, the greatest diameter not two feet. Gordonia occurred here of large size, the woods are really delightful, reminding one much of England. Here Myrica occurs but rarely, Lematula, Flemingia, Elephantopus, Vanda, Quercus callicarpifolius commences, Biophytum appears a short distance hence. Also, Liriodendron, Dipterocarpus, Bambusa, Pinus but of smaller size, Engelhaardtia, Dioscorea, Castanea, Quercus callicarpa, which is very common.

Here Bombax appears somewhat lower, with it Castanea, Kydia, Gordonia. No pines now occur except on the neighbouring heights.

The descent to the Borpanee is not great, say 400 feet; on its banks Thunbergia grandiflora commences, but the Castanea castaneoides of large size, Camellia oleifolia, Daphne cannabina, Rhododendron punctatum variety. Engenia Wallichii (which commences), Quercus castaneoides, etc. may be found along its banks.

This is a large stream, not fordable at any time, nor passable in the rains; both banks are high, rocks of course break the stream, which is gentle at the points crossed. Breadth is 50 to 60 yards, the elevation of its bed is 2,508 feet, water boiling at 207½° : temperature 74°.

The ascent of the north bank is great, on surmounting it one returns to grassy undulations, the vegetation of which is the same as before, Rottboellia of Suniassa as well as Manisuroides here occur. The village Madan is very small, the people, of course, as they have scarcely ever seen a white face, very polite and obliging : it is situated on a hill, but is still below the north bank of the river. Its altitude is 2,753 feet—temperature of the air 67° : boiling water 207°.

Nurtung, 3,302 feet. O.—Butea suffrutex.

.—Andropogon (novum), Holcoides.

.—Pinus very common.

.—Grassy hills with no vegetation.

.—Nonkreem Bauhinia, Kydia commences.

.—Gerardia, Andropogons.

.—Rottboellia humilis, Andropog. sursum.
.—A. deorsum.

.—Pines very common, of large size.
.—Quercus castaneoides, Q. callicarp. commences.
.—Castaneæ, Gordonia, Dioscorea, Kydia.

.—Quercus callicarpifolius, abundant.

.—Liriodendron: Kydia.

.—Castanea, Kydia, Camellia oleifol., Rhodod. punctat.
.—Cuscuta.

Borpanee, 2,508 feet.

.—Grassy naked hills.

Madan, 2,753 feet.

The birds, as well as those of the Nurtung river, are the water-ouzel, the greyish-blue water-chat, the red and black ditto with a white head-top, and the black bird, *durn-durns* or bird producing that cry occurs, but not in great numbers. Pea-fowl at Madan. Elephants are abundant, especially towards the descent to the Borpanee. *Fly wheel (?)* insect is here common at Kokreen, a small village close to Nonkreen. Equisetum occurs along the Boga Panee as well as a new species of Podostemon, P. fronde profunde lobato, lobis liniaribus simplicibus vel lobatis saxis arcti adpressis, floribus marginalibus distiches. Polygala occurs at 3,000 feet and continues higher.

November 14*th.*—The march to Mengtung occupies about six hours, it is by no means difficult, and the only ascent of any length is that before descending on Nungtung. Throughout the 1st part, all the bottoms of the valleys are cultivated, thence all is jungle, either of high grass or of trees.

Near Madan, Arundinaria bambusifolia may be found, although at an elevation of 2,800 feet, Volkameria is common. The same grasses continue. In the rice field Butomus lanceolatus, Herpestes, Jussæia, Juncus, Eriocanlon, Zizana ciliaris.

We then came after traversing such low swampy ground for sometime to a wood composed of Quercus castaneoidea, of large size; its bark is thick and somewhat corky, its diameter three feet. Quercus callicarpifolius appeared soon after, with Polygala linearis, Scitamineæ are common in the valley. In similar low places, Impatiens graminifolia of Churra was seen, and Hedysarum gyrans.

Oolooks* and parrots are both found: Cnicus floribus roseis, Gerardia, Apluda, Senecio pubescens, were found in similar spots.

After traversing a low valley with gentle undulations presenting the usual grasses, we came to a wood presenting many tropical features. Oaks and chesnuts still continuing to be the usual trees. Much underwood, consisting of Acanthaceæ, Laurineæ, Anonaceæ, Rubiaceæ, among which Pœderia triphylla and Mephitidia were common. Centothca sp., Sarcopyramis, Garcinia, Triumfetta were observed.

Thence we came to pines. Then a low valley, the altitude of the stream of which was 1,979 feet, the thermometer being in the air 82°, boiling point $208\frac{1}{2}$°. Then a wood.

In it Castanea ferruginea continued common, Quercus dalbergioides, Daphne cannabina, Acanthus leucostachyus (1st appearance), Oxys-

* *Simia Hylobates agilis.*

pora and Polypodium Wallichii were found; ascending a few feet, say 60, Randia microphyllum, Aneilema aspera, and pines appeared in the woods, with straight trunks and high branches, occasioned by the abortion of the lower branches, sometimes dichotomously forked, bark grey, and scaley, branches horizontal, approximated; cones inclining towards the axis. The descent occasioned a loss of pines, oaks and chesnuts continuing, Orthopogon, Pederia triphyllum.

This wood was of great extent, the path running along the precipitous or steep edge of a very wet water-course. Castanea ferruginea very common, Cyrtandracea.

Begonia malabarica, Achyranthes, Tradescantia flagellifera, Phlogacanthus, Acanthaceæ, Sarcopyramis, Magnolia, Eupatorium arboreum, Laurineæ, Gleichenia minor.

Pinus subsequently appears but is rare, Eurya.

Daphne involucrata, Gaultheria arborescens, Knoxia cordata, Polypodium arborescens, Thibaudia, Viburni sp., Vareca, Leucas galea brunacea.

Then still gradually ascending, open woods occurred.

Pines, Q. castaneoides.

Thence the ascent is still through open woods of pines. Castanea, Quercus castaneoides and callicarpifolia, Polygala here appears, Knoxia linearis, Flemingia, Æschynomene.

On the top no Pines. Oaks, chesnuts, and Gordoniæ appear.

Thence a second but small ascent, pines re-appear with birch, Scutellaria, Erythrina, Melica latifolia, Epiphytes common, especially on Gordoniæ. The altitude of the summit before descending on Nungtung was 3,359 feet: thermometer 75°. boiling point 206°.

The altitude of Nungtung is 2,862 feet, Temp. 64°. Big Therm. in boiling water 206½°, ditto wooden 207°, small ditto 201°, centigrade 97¾°.

Madan ○.
2,753 feet. —Arundenaria.

—Andropogon castratus.
—Jussiœa, Herpestes, Butomus lanceolatus, Zizania ciliaris, Xyris.

—Quercus Castaneoides and Q. callicarpifolius.

—Hedysarum gyrans, Impatiens graminifol. Cnicus, Apluda, Senecio, Dysophylla.

—Tropical wood, underwood of Scitamineæ, Laurineæ, Myrsineæ, Anonaceæ Rubiaceæ, Castanea common, Calamus, Polypodium arboreum.
—Pines.

—Pines.

—Grassy hills.

1,979 feet. —Quercus, Hedysaroid, Daphne cannabina, Acanthus leucostachyus, Castanea, Polypodium Wallichii.
—Pinus of large size.

—Oaks, Chesnuts, Orthopogon, Celastraceæ, Garcineæ, Acanthaceæ Bamboo and other tropical features.
—Then open woods, oaks, chesnuts.

—Open woods, pines, oaks, chesnuts.
—Polygala, Leguminosa.

Nungtung. ○
2,862 feet.

Nungtung is a small village not containing more then 12 houses; these are on michaowns,* and are built entirely of bamboos. The doors of curious construction, consisting of bamboos strung longitudinally over a transverse one, so that they can be only opened by pushing on one side. The pigs have similar doors to their houses and appear well acquainted with the mode of ingress and egress.

Tobacco flourishes here. Here also I saw Sesamum and Ricinus, sure signs of increasing temperature, Labiata edulis. The first part of the march lay through an oak and chesnut wood; then through the valley which is under rice cultivation; then through part of an oak and fir wood; I then turned off to NNE. traversing undulated hills entirely covered with grass; here and there an oak and chesnut wood occurred; this continued until 1 P. M., when the path joined the great road as it is called, but which is nearly as bad as the Nungtung one. The marching was very disagreeable, owing to the path being choked up with grass, particularly in the swampy valley just before Onkreem. In this valley wild elephants were first seen.

After leaving the halting or resting place under a large oak (Q. castaneoides) at Onkreem, the path improved and is only rendered bad by the swarms of elephants, by which animals we were disturbed twice; it continued until 6 P. M., over undulated ground becoming lower and lower until we arrived at the large valley of Onswye, which is even now at this advanced period of the season, the middle of November, considerably swampy.

Oaks and chesnuts continued, but pines ceased about half way between Onkreem and Onswye.

* Raised on posts.

Nungtung 2,862 feet. O .—Labiata edulis, Sesamum, Nicotiana.
.—Bryum argenteum, Gnaphalioid, Globba.
Eleusine, Urena lobata. .—Didymocarpea, Chirita, Composita, Panicum echinatum, Ajuga azurea, oaks and chesnuts, Q. castaneoides, pines.

Few kairns such as indicate Khasyah habitation; any that occur are used by the elephants as rubbing stones or scratch-sides.
.—Oaks, etc. ditto.
.—Chloranthus inconspicuous.

.—Rice.
.—Q. castaneoides.
.—Pinus of large size.
.—Camellia oleifolia.
Ravine-wooded, oaks, chesnuts, Pinus, Buddlea Neemda, Crocus roseus, Gordonia.
.—Rice.
.—Viola Patrinii, Lactuca.
.—Grassy undulated hills, with scarcely any trees. old clearings covered with rank grass, with Hibiscus.
.—Labiata edulis, Lab. uncifera, Tagetes, Cannabis, Citrinus.
.—Large Sacchara, Imperata cylendrica.
.—Arundo, Digitaria.
Elephants ravines, all forming marshy bottoms.
.—Same continue.

.—Hedyotes, Tradescantia.
.—Pueraria.
.—Pogonatherum cornitum, Apluda.
.—Cnicus roseus. Trichosanthes cucumerina.
.—Arundinacea bambusifolia.
.—Swertia angustifolia.

.—Kydia, Bambusa, Bombax.

.—(View of Himalayas from this place.)

.—Valeriana Hardwickii, Kydia, Bauhinia, tropical trees.
.—The same grasses continue.
.—Anisomeles, Phyllanthus, Emblica, Linum pentagynia.
.—Briedleia, Rottboellia exaltata, Sacchara, Andropogones.
.—Anthistiria minor, Pteris aquilina.
.—Gordonia.
.—Quercus callicarpifol, Lobelia baccifera, Commelina.
.—Bambusa, Castania, Eurya, Rubus, Gleichenia minor, Serratula.
.—Begonia Malabarica, Ajuga, Plectranthus albus.
Elephants seen. .—Curculigo, Rottlera arborea.
.—Oaks, Hedysarum gyrans.
.—Blechnum, Knoxia cordata.
.—Cirsioides, Pteris aquilina.
O .—Coarse grasses as before.

O .—Low marshy valley, coarse grasses, Saccharum, Rottboellia, etc. as before.
.—Firs.
.—Quercus.
.—Ficus.
Pica vagabunda. .—Q. callicarpifolius, Melica latifolia.
.—Gordonia.
.—Malvacea arborea.
.—Composita arborea.
.—Low grassy valley, Rubus.
.—Castanea.
.—Quercus Castaneoides, Vareca.
Onkreem 2,400 ft. .—Æsculus, Betula.
.—Valeriana, Costus, Mimosa arborea.
.—† Sterculia fol. palmatis, Strobilanthes.
.—Bambusa, Leea, with the same grasses as before.
.—Osbeckia nepalensis, Labiata of Suddya, Elephantopus.†
Elephants swarm. .—Eupatorium arboreum, Melica latifolia.
.—Anonaceæ, Schænanthus.
.—Rubus moluccanoide. Heavy grass—Arundo, Melica latifolia.
.—Tetranthera, Panicum eleusinoides, Rottboellia *cernuosa*.*
.—Pteris aquilina, Arborescent Leguminosæ, Laurineæ and Euphorbiacæ.
.—Betula. Q. callicarpifol.
.—Wendlandia, Eupatorium arboreus : Bombax.
.—Symplocos scraggy ! Quercus callicarpifol.
.—Hastingsia.
.—Gordonia, Arbusculi incerta, fruct pyrifom pendulis. Sterculia—Betula, Viscum *loranthophillum*,* Castanea homda, ferruginea.
.—Myrtacea.
.—Phyllanthus, Emblica, Betula.
.—Mimosa scandens.
.—Bignonia indica ! Celtis !
.—Grassy Hills. Wood.
.—Careya ! Q. callicarpif !
.—Ficus. Dianella, Verbenaceæ ! Semicarpus.
.—Verbena Primulacea, Castanea Betula.
.—Phœnix,† Briedelia—Pteris aquilina—Anthistiria minor.
.—Ficus,
.—Pines a little to the right.
.—Betula.
.—Sterculia, Careya.
.—Level grassy ridge, the grasses much as before.
.—Simool, Pinus one specimen, Betula, Careya Arboreous, Leguminosa.
O .

* Would seem to be MS. names.

O .—Bambusa, Uvularia ! Sida corylifolia.
Phlogacanthus ! .—Scleria inflata !
.—Eurya, Castanea.
Grasses continue throughout. .
.
.
.—Bambusa.
.—Leea, Careya.
.—Quercus vestita, beech.
.—Inga, Magnolia, Castanea, Chloranthus.
—Pinus, Quercus, Chesnuts.
.
.
.—Polypodium arborescens.
.—Pinus.
.
.
.—Semicarpus.
.—Bambusa, Linum pentagynum.
.
.
.
.—Plectranthus albus.
.
.
.—Symplocos scraggy.
Blechum, .—Q. castaneoides, Melica latifolia, Osbeckia nepalensis.
.
.
.—Senecio hirsutus, Isachne, etc.
.—Semicarpus, Symplocas scraggy.
Here a miniature Kollong village occurs. .—Anthistiria of Nungklow. Andropogon species binatis deflexis.
.
.
.
.—Bambusa, Castanea.
.—Rottlera.
.—Quercus vestita—Castanea ferruginea.
Same grasses continue. .—Dimeria.
.—Pteris aquilina.
.—Rottlera arborea: Castanea ferruginea.
.
.
.
.—Symplocos memecylifolia.
.—Quercus, Castanea.
Country much undulated, ravines marshy. .—Phœnix.
.
.
.
.—Pteris aquilina, Semicarpus.
.—Quercus Castaneoides.
.
.
.
.—Castanea, Quercus vestita.
.—Eugenia. Semicarpus.
.
.
.
Valley of Onswye 1,632 feet. .—Hygrophila, Arundinaria, Zizania ciliaris. Menthoid verticellat. Senecio pubescens, Andropogons, Rottboellia, Oryzæ nov. sp., Cacalia, Aneilema paniculata. Impatiens graminifolia, Andropog. castrat. Burmania aphylla. O .

Ammania rotundifolia. O .—Verbena primulacea, Alisma, Damasonium.
.—Phœnix pumile.
.—Kydia.
.—Bambusa, Sterculia.
.—Semicarpus.
Altitude 2,232 feet. .—Elephantopus.
.—Rhus, Castanea, Symplocos, Quercus.

.—Undulated hills covered with the usual grasses, barely wooded, forming North side of the valley.

Water boiled 207¾°. .—Altitude 2,550 feet.
.—Anthistiria of Nungklow, Acroides of Mahadeb.
Temperature 85°: .—Arundo, Rottboellia, Hedychium, Erianthus.
altitude 2,002 ft.† .—Sacchara, Scleria, Rottboellia Verbena.
.—Primulaceæ, Solanum glaucum, Andropogoni binatus, both species.
.—Bambusa.
.—Eupatorium arboreum, Erythrina.
.—Wendlandia, Bombax.
Altitude 1850. .—Saccharum—fuscum, Coarse large grasses as before.
.—Dicerma !
.—Anthistiria, Andropog. binatus 2 as before.
.—Chesnuts.

.—Dimeria.

Same grassy undulated country.
.—Bamboos, Rottlera arborea, Linum pentagynum.
.—Knoxia cærulea.
.—Tree jungle, Cedrela Toona ! Elephantopus.
.—Vanda cærulea.
.—All tropical trees and usually with pinnated leaves.
.—Sterculia, Emblica, Leea crispa.
.—Leguminosæ arboreæ.
.—Strobilanthus, Orchideæ epiphytic subulifolia.
Grasses continue. .—Cirsioid, Hedera terebinthacea, Costus ! Bignonia indica.
.—Hastingsia, Spathodea, Kydia, Careya.
.—Pendulous grey lichens.
.—Semicarpus, Labiata of Suddya.
.—Bridelia, Crotalaria juncea, Mimosa, Kydia.
.—Spathodea, Cedrela, Emblica.
.—Bambusa.
.—Hastingsia, Serratuloid.
.—Acanth. leucostractyus, Centotheca lappacea, Ruellia Neesiana, Bombax.
.—Æsculus, Phlogacanthus, Begonia malabarica, Hastingsia, Elephantopus.
.—Airoid, Schænanthis, Semicarpus, Sterculia, Labiata, of Suddya, Andropogons, Eria.
.—Anthestiria minor.
1,500 feet. O .—Grassy ridge with trees.

O .—Terebinthacea? fructicosa racemis pendulis.
.—Dillenia! Hastingsia.
.—Saurauja, Panax, Begonia malabarica.
1,500 feet. .—Ruellia Neesiana.
Heavy Bamboos .—Acanthus leneostachyus.
down descents. .
.
.
.
.
.—Tradescantia flagelliformis.
.—Succulent urticeæ.
.—Ruellia Neesiana.
Heavy jungle. .—Andropogon tenerum.
.—Uvularia.
.—Zingiber, Pothos pertusus.
.—Succulent urticeæ.
.—Bamboos Hastingsia.
.
.
.
.
.—Bauhinia arborea.
.—Angiopterus, Aneilema paniculata.
.—Acanthus leucostachyus, Pladera justicioides.
.—Dillenia.
.
.
.
.
.
.—Sabia* Lasia.
.—Anonaceæ, Rubiaceæ, Myrsineæ, Lycopodium.
.—Scitamenæ, Acanthus leucostachyus.
.—Ophiorhiza paniculata, Acrostichum, Guaicanæ.
.—Sabia, Acrostichum flagelliferum.
.—Hastingsia, Centotheca lappacea.
.
.
.
.
.—Elephantopus, Bauhinia, Trichosanthes.
.
.
.
Tree jungle.
Pheasants.
.—Sambucus!
.—Alpinia Allughas, Bambusa.
.—Careya, Dillenia, Cinchona, Semicarpus!
.—Elephantopus, Panax fol. supra decomposita, inermis, black.
.—Hoya! Sterculia, Bambusa, Phlogacanthus thyrsiflorus.
.
.
.
.—Cymbidium alæfolium, Hastingsia, Bauhinia, Carallia.
.—Aerideæ, Pæderia sapida, Millingtonia simplicifolia, Myrioneurum.
.
Dullagong.
.—Urtica gigas, Tetranthera macrophylla, Bæhmeria, Calamus.
.—Convolvulus, Convol. lupulifolius. Naravelia, Deeringia.
.—Adhatoda, Trophis aspera, Cæsalpinia, Tall Sacchara.
.—Mangifera, Gomphostemma, Erythrina Ætheilema.
.—Elephantopus, Pæderia fætida, Eleodendrum infortunatum.
.—Tabernæmontanæ, Nauclea pendula, Boerhaavia.
O .—Cryptolepis, Urtica pendula.

Onswye is a small village, seated on a low hill, and entirely hidden by trees: the access to it is pretty. Its elevation is 1,632 feet, temperature 63°. Water boils at $98\frac{3}{4}$° of centigrade, small ther. $202\frac{1}{2}$°, big ditto $208\frac{3}{4}$°, wooden ditto 210°: taking 209° as the mean.

It is a Lalung village. These people have distinct habits and language from their neighbours: their dress is like that of the Khasyahs. They approach to Hindoos in not eating cows. They inhabit the lower northern ranges of these hills, but do not extend further east, nor into the plains at the foot, and are far less civilized than the Khasyahs.

They have religious houses or places of worship, deo-ghurs, in one of which I slept, having it first cleansed, and the deity appeased by some most villanous music, and a procession of men with knives.

At this village Carica, Ficus elastica, Ficus cordifolius, Ricinus, Artocarpus intigrifol, Tamarind, Guava, Musa, Solanum Melongena, tobacco, etc., are cultivated.

Caryophyllea scandens, Desmochæta, Plumbago, Plectranthus azureus, Phlebochiton, Cassia tora, Orthopogon, Adhatoda, Mangifera, Croton malvæfol, Hastingsia, Torenia asiatica, Caricinea, Leea, Prunus! Congea! Antidesma, Rottleria, Clerodendron nutans, Calamus, Xanthochymus. Mesua ferrea, Garcinia Cowa, Leea arbuscula, Dalhousia, Roxburghia, are found on the ascent which is moderate and pretty.

The heavy tree or bamboo jungle does not begin until you attain 12 or 1,500 feet, up to that, the ridges present the former grasses. Rottboellia, Andropogons, Erianthus, Saccharum, Anthistiria, and the trees are scattered consisting of Arborescent Leguminosæ, Sterculia, Cedrela, Semicarpus continues to the tree jungle, but rarely.

The road to the village runs through heavy woods, the plants forming which I have already mentioned, it is in good order. The village is a Lalung one.

At Dullagong, which is situated in the plains of Assam, at the foot of the range the temperature being 66°, $8\frac{1}{2}$ A. M., water boiled at $211\frac{1}{10}$° in the large thermometer. 100 centigrade, and above the boiling point in the wooden. $205\frac{1}{2}$° in the small metal thermometer.

Between this and Goba, the path is generally through grass or tree jungle. I noticed Exacum, Careya, Butea arborea, Ficus, Cinchona, Kydia, Saccharum Megala fuscum masus, Spathodea, Alstonia, Bombax, Semicarpus! Ægle Marmelos, Emblica, Panax, Elephantopus, and Lagerstræmia Reginæ succeeds about Goba: and between this and Dhumria, the country being low and highly cultivated, presents generally the appearance of one sheet of rice. In this march I observed one or two instances of the absolute enclosure of Dicotyledonous trunks by Fici. This enclosure arises entirely from the excessive tendency to cohesion between the roots and radicles of some of the species of this genus. With these, an expert gardener might produce any form he likes; the tendency exists in all to throwing out additional roots; in few only to excess. In the generality it is limited to the trunk and often to its base. Nobody can understand this genus who cannot study it from living specimens.

Cardiopterus is very common along the foot of these hills: it abounds with milky juice, and in habit and some other points approaches nearer to Chenopodiaceæ than Sapindaceæ.

December 7th.—Returned from Jeypore, whither I had been to report on the Caoutchouc trees.*

These trees appear to be limited to the belt of jungle or toorai which commences towards the foot of the Aka and Duphla hills, and which in the part in which I examined them is about 8 miles wide. They are said to be found likewise among the neighbouring villages, but I saw no instance of this. They occur solitarily, or at most in groups of two or three. They appear to be more frequent towards the immediate base of the hills, and to prefer the drier parts of those humid and dense forests called toorai. They are frequently of vast size, and by this as well as their dense head, may be at once recognised even at a distance of a few miles. Some idea of their size may be formed from the following measurements of a large one:

Circumference of main trunk,............	74 feet.
Ditto, including the supports,...........	120 ,,
Ditto, of space covered by crown branches,..	620 ,,
Height, ditto ditto,......................	80 to 100 ,,

The roots spread out in every direction on reaching the ground; the larger running along the surface, their upper portion being uncovered: occasionally they assume the form of buttresses, but never to such a marked degree as occurs in some other trees, such as the Simool, Herietiera, etc. The supports are only thrown out towards the base of the principal branches, not as in the banian at indefinite distances. The trunk is a compound one, formed entirely by the mutual cohesion of roots; not as in almost all other trees by

* See Journal Asiatic Society of Bengal, vol.—Feb. 1838.

the growth of parts in an ascending direction. Its aspect is picturesque and varied, occasionally putting on the appearance of sculpture. It is, I think, doubtful whether this as well as some other species of the genus are not to be considered as genuine parasites, at any rate they generally cause the destruction of the tree on which they originally grew. If this be the case the parasitism is the reverse of that which occurs in Cuscuta, in which the plantule draws its first nourishment from the earth, relinquishing this when sufficiently developed to enable it to draw its supply from other plants. I may here observe, that parasites are common on the peepul, contrary to the statement of M. DeCandolle.

The destruction of the foster-mother takes place by the mutual interlacement of the roots, which descending irregularly, form at first a strong net-work, subsequently becoming a cylindric binding, in the strongest possible way to the trunk, and preventing all lateral distinction. The hollow occupied by the trunk when dead may become filled up, when this has passed away, by other roots. The adhesion of the roots commences by abrasion of the bark, the union subsequently becomes of the most intimate kind. The supports are perfectly cylindrical; they become conical only towards the earth, on approaching which they divide into roots: they are strictly descending growths, and as such, under ordinary circumstances, they never produce leaves, etc. Roots likewise issue from every section of the bark of sufficient depth to reach the outer layer of wood, with the outer fibres of which they are obviously continuous. To such an extent is this carried, that transverse sections of young supports assume the appearance of coarse paint-brushes or tails. The lenticells, which are very numerous, have nothing whatever to do with their production; if the bark remains entire, no roots are thrown out except by division of the apex. The branches ascend obliquely, the outermost running nearly horizontally.

The juice is obtained from the larger; that from young parts is less thick: an exposed semi-denuded root, is selected for transverse incisions through the bark, from which alone the juice flows, a small hole is made in the ground immediately beneath the incised parts into which a leaf, generally of Phrynium capitatum is placed: it is collected in this simple manner in a very clean state, far more so than that which can be collected from the tree in any other situation. On issuing, it is of a very rich pure white; if good, of the consistence of cream: its excellence is known by the degree of consistence, and by the quantity of caoutchouc it contains. This is ascertained by rubbing a few drops up in the palm of the hand, which causes the watery juice to separate (probably by evaporation) from the caoutchouc which remains in the form of small, oblong, or round portions; and by kneading this in the hand, and striking it sharply once or twice with the fist it acquires elasticity, so that an additional test of excellence is at once pointed out. Many incisions are made in one tree, the juice flows rapidly at first, at the rate of sixty drops a minute from an ordinary incision, but this soon becomes so much diminished that it dwindles to eight. The bleeding is continued for two or three days, when it ceases spontaneously by the formation of a layer of caoutchouc over the wound; and it is to the commencement of this that the rapid diminution in the number of drops is perhaps to be attributed. The quantity obtained from one tree has not exactly been ascertained; by some it is stated to be as much as four or five maunds, while others say that a moderate tree will only yield one gurrah full, or about ten seers. From the slowness with which it flows, I should consider half a maund to be a fair average for each bleeding. The juice is, however, said to flow faster at night, but this demands verification.

The operation is repeated at the end of eighteen or twenty days. In seven miles of jungle we observed eighty trees, by far the greater portion of which were of large size. Lieutenant Vetch has made a calculation, (on the assumption that they are equally plentiful throughout Chardowar,) that the number in this district alone is — trees.

I calculate the number to be about 20,000. There is no reason for supposing that they are not equally abundant throughout Noadwar, nor in fact on any line where toorai prevails between Goalpara and Bishnath; beyond this, however, the increase in latitude may occasion their decrease both in number and size. On the southern side of the valley there is every reason to believe it to be equally common. The general geographic range may hence be said to be in latitude 24°, to 26½° in longitude. It has been stated by Mr. Royle that it does not extend beyond Pundua, Jynteapoor, and Churra Punjee, but on no other authority than that it had not been found elsewhere.

Taking the number of trees at 20,000, and the produce of each from four bleedings at two maunds, the annual supply that may be obtained from Durrung may be estimated at 13,000 maunds of the caoutchouc itself, assuming Dr. Roxburgh's proportion of one to three to be nearly correct. Some idea may be formed of the extent to which it is procurable, when from the mere outskirts of the forest, 300 maunds of juice may be collected in one month.

On the excellence of the Assam product as compared with that of America, it does not become me to pronounce. If strength, elasticity, clearness, and perfect freedom from viscidity, be tests of excellence, then this product may be considered as equal to any other. It has been pronounced by persons in Calcutta to be excellent, but no details have been entered into except by Mr. Bell, who objects to its snapping: if by this we are to understand snapping on being pulled too much, in contradistinction to breaking, it only proves its excellence. It is declared to be inferior to the American by Mr. McCosh, evidently on examination of the worst possible specimens.

The size of the trees as they generally occur in the limits above alluded to, entirely precludes all idea of any great liability to be destroyed by the extraction of juice, the amount of which must be so minute, compared to that of the whole tree. Still it may be considered desirable for the security of the tree to limit the bleedings to the cold months, and this is rendered more necessary by the inferiority of the juice during the season of active vegetation. And if it be possible to limit the number of bleedings of each tree to four or five during the above period, I consider that the present 3,000 stock cannot fail to be kept up. But to venture on still larger supplies, to meet the demand for this most useful article, a demand to which limits can scarcely be assigned, the formation of plantations should be encouraged, the sites chosen to be near the villages bordering on the line of the natural distribution of the tree. Propagation by cuttings or layers cannot fail to be of easy and rapid application; and if we consider that the tree is the most valuable receptacle of the lac insect, there is every reason to suppose that the natives will readily enter into such views.

The jungle in which the tree occurs is of the usual heavy description, presenting in fact no one feature in particular. The trees are all of a tropical nature, except towards the foot of the hills, when two species of chesnut and one of alder begin to shew themselves.

CHAPTER XI.

Journey from Assam towards Bootan.

Left Gowahatti on the 21*st* and halted at Ameengong ghat.

December 22*nd*, 1837.—Left at twelve and proceeded to Hazoo, which is nearly due west of Ameengong, and distant thirteen miles. Road, through grassy plains; much cultivation throughout the greater part. Passed several villages, and forded one stream. Hazoo is at the foot of some low hills, on one of which is a temple of great sanctity with the Booteahs. The hills above this, as well as between this and Ameengong, abound with Cycas, many of which were once dichotomous; on these hills a fleshy Euphorbia likewise occurs, a sure indication of barren soil. Pea-fowl abound. The light-blue Jay figured in Hardwickii, Sterna, Haliætus pondicerianus, Chat, Butcher-bird, Edolius, Plovers, Hoopoe, and Ardea indica, were met with.

December 23*rd*.—Hazoo, a large village, extending nearly north and south, all the houses surrounded by trees. Areca bamboos, Ficus elastica, F. indicoides, F. religiosa, Sapotea (Mimusops) Arborea, Erythrina. Country to the east very jheely, and one huge expanse of paddy cultivation. Fine Loranthus, Hingtstha repens.

December 24*th*.—Nolbaree, seventeen miles nearly, N. by W., throughout the latter half of the way, the country consisted of highly cultivated plains, intersected by bamboo jungles, etc. Villages very abundant, surrounded by trees, especially bamboos. The hedges are made of a dwarf Pandanus. Crossed four streams, two not fordable. Grallatores and water-birds innumerable throughout, but especially after passing the Borolia, Bec ouvert or Anastomus coromandelianus, Pelicans, Water-hens, Divers, Ibis bengala, Cigoines (Ardea Pavonia) Syras, Mangoe-bird, large King-fisher, Hawks abundant, of which we observed five species; this is, generally speaking, one of the richest parts of Assam I have hitherto seen.

December 25*th*.—Dum Dummia, distance ten miles, direction north, country very open, in parts less cultivated than before, scarcely any jungle towards Dum; this is a straggling place on the banks of a small stream called Noa Nuddee.

The bamboo continues common, as well as Pandanus, Pterocarpus marsupium, Bombax, Diospyros ebenum, which are the most common trees. Villages are very numerous, but as usual, entirely concealed from view by jungle.

December 31st.—Up to this morning we remained at Dum Dummia, and had the Booteas alone been consulted, we should have remained there till to-morrow. It is a very uninteresting place, the country consisting of one extensive plain, diversified only by trees wherever there are villages. There is a good deal of cultivation, chiefly however, of rice; some sugarcane is visible, but it is of inferior quality, and evidently not sufficiently watered. Sursoo is considerably cultivated. The river Noa Nuddee is about seventy yards wide, with a stream of three miles an hour; it is full of sand-banks and of quicksands, and is crossed with great difficulty on elephants; by men it is easily fordable. The only shooting about the place is Floriken, which are very abundant, ten or twelve being seen in one day.

We left for Hazareegoung, a Bootea-Assam village to the north. We passed through a similar open country not much cultivated, but overrun with grassy vegetation. The path was of the ordinary description, and not kept at all cleared: crossed a small stream twice, with a pebbly bed and sub-rapids, a sure indication of approaching the hills. These, in their lower portion, have a very barren appearance, but this may arise from the cultivated patches: land-slips are of very frequent occurrence.

The grasses of the enormous plains, so prevalent every where in this direction, are Kagaia, Megala, Vollookher, Saccharum spontaneum, this is soft grass, and affords an excellent cover for game, Cymbopogon hirsutum, which is more common than the C. arundinaceum, Erianthus, Airoides, Rottboellia exaltata, Arundo, (?) Anatherum muricatum, Apluda, Trizania cilearis, is common in the old rice khets.

Among these occur a tall Knoxia, Plectranthus sudyensis, and P. uncinatus.

I observed Vareca, Grislea, about Dum Dummia. Elytrophorus is common in rice khets.

Towards Hazareegoung we came on a high plain, covered principally with S. spontaneum. Among this occurred Lactuioides, Premna herbacea, Grewia, with here and there Pterygodium. I observe here Bootea bamboo baskets made water-proof by caoutchouc; this is a practice much adopted by the Booteas: and the trees are here. The large coloured stipulæ are peculiar to the young shoots cultivated, they are often a span long. The young fruit is enveloped by three large coloured scales, which originate from the annuliform base; this is hence a peduncle, not a bracte, as I before supposed.

January 1st, 1838.—Halted.

January 2nd.—Marched to Ghoorgoung, a small village, eight miles from Hazareegoung and nearly due north. We crossed similar grassy tracts: the country gradually rising as we approached the hills.

Very little cultivation occurred. Crossed the Mutunga, now dry, but the breadth testifies to its being a large stream in the rains, as the boulders do to its being a violent one. The same plants continue; small jungle or wood composed of Simool. Trophis aspera, Cassia fistula, Bauhinia, Butea scandens, Byttneria, underwood of Eranthemum, and another Acanthacea.

About this place Cnicus and Arundinaria occur, and a small Santalaceous or Olacineous plant, with the habit of a Polygala. Merops apiaster is very common.

January 3rd.—To Dewangeri, distance eight miles.

Our route hither lay for the greater portion up the bed of the Durunga, the stream of which makes its exit about one mile to the west of Ghoorgoung. After ascending its bed for some time, the ascent becomes steep, for perhaps 800 or 1,000 feet, when we reached a portion of Dewangeri, but two or three hundred feet below the ridge on which the village is situated. The hills bounding the watercourse are very steep, many quite perpendicular, owing to having been cut away; generally they are of decomposed granite as at Dacanara, in some parts of conglomerate.

The torrent contains but little water, and very few fish, the banks are wooded tolerably well, as soon as the lower barren ranges are past.

At the base Cassia fistula, Leguminous trees, Artemisia, Simool, Spathodea, Bignonia indica, Sterculia, Cæsalpinea, Phlogacanthus thyrsiflorus, Pæderia fætida, Eugenia, Rhamnea, Croton malvæfoliis are found among the usual grasses, which form the chief vegetation.

These continue along the sandy bed for some time, but afterwards the usual small Andropogons usurp their place. Anthistiria arundinacea continue longest; with some of the large Saccharum, Rubus moluccanus soon appears, with Melica latifolia, and a species of Rhus.

Leptospartion is very common up to 1,000 feet, Pandanus 3-500 feet, but soon ceases; the higher precipices abound with an elegant palm tree, habitu Cocos.

Fleshy urticeæ and Aroideum become common at 300 feet, along the shaded watery banks, and continue so long as shade and humidity are found. Equisetum commences at 300 feet, Arundo, Saurauja, Pentaptera, which last ascends to 1,000 feet, as does Dillenia speciosa, Castaneæ feorox commences at 500 feet. Between this and the Choky, Polypodium, Wallichianum arboreum, Davallia grandis, Oxyspora, Musci, Goodyera, and Composita arborea are found.

At the Choky, the elevation of which is 965 feet, Œsculus begins. Wallichia,* Œschynanthus, Urtica gigas,* Derngia,* Govania,* Anthistira arundinacea, Alstonea, Angiopteris, are found. Grislea is found as high as 1,000 feet. Ficus obliquissima is found at 300 feet, and Ficus altera species as high as 700 feet.

At 1,200 feet Rubi sp., Panax, Cordia, are found, and on the steep ascent, Hastingsia,* Gordonia, Eurya, Corisanthera, Griffithia.

At one place the jack fruits, Ficus elastica, Compositi arborea, Panax altera species.

Dewangeri occupies a ridge 200 feet above our halting place, the elevation of which is 2,031 feet. The view to the north is confined to a ravine of 1,500 feet deep, at the bottom of which runs a considerable mountain torrent: to the SW. plains are visible, to the east and west the view is hilly.

The village itself is a poor one, containing perhaps sixty houses, but these are divided into three or four groups; the houses, with the exception of three or four stone and lime ones, are of the usual build, viz. of bamboo, and raised on muchauns. Filth and dirt abound every where, and the places immediately contiguous to the huts are furnished plentifully with various ordures.

Along the ridge three or four temples occur, these are of the Boodhistical form: they are composed entirely of slate, are white-washed; none are of any size, and the workmanship is rude in the extreme; on each face of the square basement, slabs of slate with inscriptions are visible, and in one instance many of these are ranged along a longish wall. The Pagodas are surrounded with long banners, with inscriptions fastened longitudinally to bamboos. On the west side of this the view is remarkably pretty, embracing all the temples, part of the village, and the Rajah's house. The hills adjoining being considerably diversified and remarkable, and for India over picturesquely wooded.

The pucka houses are ungainly structures, the height being out of all proportion to the width, the walls are very thick, and composed of slate slabs, the roof is choppered with projecting eaves, the windows are very narrow. Each has three stories, the middle one being occupied by the owner, this is divided into several rude compartments, each of which has one or two balconies.

The steps are rude and awkward, consisting of notches cut into large blocks. The cooking is carried on, on the ground floor, much to the edification of the residents above. Dirt abounds in every direction. The doors are rudely constructed of wood.

January 4th.—To-day was occupied by moving up into the village, in which we occupy a pucka house.

January 5th.—Visited the Sooba or Rajah, his house is very picturesque, reminding me much of the pictures of Swiss cottages: it is white-washed, with a red belt. The interior is capacious; the state room has hangings, which are decorated with native pictures on cloth. At the east end is a recess in which are some well-executed Chinese statues, the chief figure is of large dimensions, and is intended to represent the Durmah Rajah, whose statue is supposed to give infallibility. Two bells were suspended, one from the centre, the other from the balcony, the tongues of which were long, of ivory, and moved by a string. The Rajah received us in state, amidst discordant sounds of horns, pipes, and drums; his followers for the most part were badly clothed, the few decent looking persons being only decent externally. He was seated on a raised *dais* and was well dressed. He is a stout Chinese looking man, about 50 years old, and his deportment was certainly easy and dignified. The meeting was very friendly, but it is evident that we shall be delayed here at least seven days.

The central room in the Rajah's house is used as a guard house! arms were fixed round the walls, but they seemed to consist chiefly of spears, swords, and bucklers.

January 6th.—I walked this morning to a village, a mile to the west, in which there is a picturesque pucka house of religion. What pleased me especially was a specimen of a juniper, of extreme elegance, with drooping branches. The house itself was of the usual form, and one end was occupied as usual by an ornamental window and balcony. I noticed in addition Ulmus and Quercus.

The vegetation hitherto seen about this, consists of mango trees, several species of fig, among which were Ficus indica, elastica, terminalioides, Papyrifera, etc. two with cordate leaves occur. Ulmus,

Quercus, Bombax, Juniperus and Pinus, both cultivated. Aralia or Panax, four or five species, Croton malvæfolium, Justicia, Adhatoda, Peristrophe, Amaranthaceæ, Artemisia, Urtica urens? and heterophylla, Pogostemon, Triumfetta, (these occupy the old cleared spots,) Castaneæ sp.? Artocarpus integrifolium, Erythrina, Sambucus ebulus, Rubi, three species, Solanum farinaceum, Engeldhaardtia, Pandanus, Leptospartion, Calamus, Nauclea, Euphorbia carnosa, foliis ligulatis, Artocarpus chaplasha, the fruit of which is eaten, Phlebochiton extensus, Sedgwickia cerasifolia, Callicarpa arborea, Porana, Randia, sugarcane, citrons, tobacco.

The fauna contains two or three squirrels, one of which is the small one of Upper Assam, Trocheloideus, the lesser Edolius or Drongo minor. Mainas, two kinds, carrion crows, Bucco, Muscipeta flammea, and one or two other species, Parus, two or three species, kites, large tailor-birds, sparrows. The black-bird of the torrents, and the usual water-birds, black pheasants; bulbuls very common, Bucco barbatus, parroquets, barking deer.

The temperature being 58° 61′, water boiled at 208°. The meanof two observations accordingly gives the altitude as 2,165 feet above the sea.

The number of houses is about 130, but these form two or three detached villages. The population is considerable, and there is no want of children. The people are stout and very fair, with ruddy cheeks, but abominably dirty. Some of the men are six feet in stature. We had one opportunity of witnessing their practice with the bow, but only two or three of the dozen candidates were decent shots. The mark was a very small one, and the distance 120 steps, but none hit it during the time we looked on, nor even the circular patch of branches, on which the slab of wood of this form was placed. The practice was accompanied with the usual proportion of noise and gesticulations.

There is very little cultivation on the hills around, so that this people are, at least about here, evidently dependent on the plains for their supplies. The cattle are a good breed, and totally different from those of the plains. Ponies and mules are by no means uncommon; there are likewise pigs and fowls, both of which are abundant, and of fine description.

January 16th.—Every thing leads me to conclude that the Booteas are the dirtiest race in existence, and if accounts be true, they are equally deficient in delicacy. Although much beyond other mountain tribes inhabiting either side of the Assam valley, in the structure of their houses, in their clothing, in their language, and probably in their religion, they are inferior to them in other points. Thus their looms are perhaps really primitive, and of the most simple construction; neither in their weapons of defence are they at all superior.

On the 14th I ascended a peak to the eastward, and certainly 1,000 feet above the village: on the summit of this, where there were the remains of an old clearing, I observed Pyrus, Acer, Rhus, Tetrantheræ, three or four species, Bigonia species picta, Carex, Composita arborea, Pteris aquilina, Kydia zyziphifolia, Saurauja, Eurya, Mæsa Panax, Artemisia, Hedyotis scandens, Callicarpa arborea, Camellia, Cælogyne, Oberonia, Otochilus fuscescens, Ficus, Cinnamomum, Æschynanthus, Pholidota, Cyrtandra, Piper, Citrus, Corysanthera, Hypoxis, Tupistra, Bambusa.

Sanicula appeared at 2,500 feet with Bartramea spectabilis, and a small Ophiorhiza, Acer at 2,800 feet, as likewise Rhopala; at 2,000 feet, Costus and Abroma, Thunbergia grandiflora.

January 19th.—I find that large quantities of Mungista or madder are sent to the plains from this, where the plant is very common; it is exchanged for ill preserved salt-fish, one bundle of madder for one fish. This fish is of an abominable odour, and probably tends to increase the natural savour of the Booteas, which, considering their total unacquaintance with soap, is sufficiently strong.

P. tells me that the Kampo country is situated north of this, and that it may be reached by a Kampo, in twenty-six days.

The language of the people we are now among, is distinct from that of Assam, as will be observed from the names given to the common grains cultivated in both countries, their principal grain is barley, which is of a fine description; very little cultivation being carried on here, the people drawing all their supplies from the plains. The following is a list of grains cultivated those marked* are Cerealea :—

	Assam.	*Bootea.*	
1*	Lalkonee dhan,	Yungra,	Panici sp.
2*	Legaid ditto,	Ditto,	
3	*Boot*, Tel,	Hnam,	A Sesamum.
4	*Cultivation* in Upper Assam,	Braime,	Polygonum Fagopyrum, grains very large.
5*	Bhobosa,	Khongpo,	Eleusine sp.
6*	Goomdam,	Peihnam,	Zea Mays.
7	Gellei-ma,	Linjee,	Phaseoli sp.

Ghoorgoung in Assam. ○ .—Santalacea, Gramineæ, Cnicus, Arundinaria, Cersium.

.—Cæsalpinia, Cassia fistula, Croton malvæfolia terminalia.

.—Palma sp. Phœnicis ? trunco altiusculo.

.—Polytrichum aloides.

.—Rubus Moluccanus.

.—Polypodium Wallichianum, Angiopteris, Polypod. arboreum.

Chokey, alt. 965 feet. □ —Plectranthus cæruleus, Leptospartion, Œsculus.

.—Cordia.

.—Pogostemon. Rubus. Jasminum.

.—Bamboo, Jack, Ficus pyrifera, indica, elastica, etc.

.—Artemisia. Urtica urens, U. heterophylla, Justicia, Adhatoda, Phlogacanthus.

.—Sedgwickia, Quercus, Castanea 2, Bombax, Spondias.

Dewangeri, alt. 2,165 feet. ○ — Rhus, Cordia, Cyrtandria, Æschynanthus, Artemisia, Croton malvæfol. Cupressus.* Pinus longifolia, Ulmus, Citrus 2. Saccharum, Rubia cordifolia, and munjista, Erythrina, Mangifera.

.—Clematis, Panax 4-5. Saccharum megala, Bolbophyllum, Costus, Abroma.

.—Thunbergia grandiflora.

.—Clematis, Exacum, Andropogon, Dicranum.

2,500 feet. .—Sanicula.

.—Acer, Rhopala, Eleocarpus.

.—Thibaudia.

.—Hypoxis, Orthodon.

.—Begonia picta, Pteris, Aspidum, Tupistra.

.—Acer, Pyrus, Kydia, Mæsa, Oberonia.

.—Cælogyne, Otochilus, Ericinea, Loranthus.

3,000 feet. .—Tetranthera, Artemisia, Citrus.†

The palm from the cliffs on the road hither is evidently a species of Phænix, pinnulis inferioribus spiniformibus reticula copiosa, pinnulis liniaribus acuminatissimus, apicem versus canaliculatis reticulo copioso, the height must be about that of a moderate Areca. No specimens of the trunk, none of flowers and seeds have been brought to me.

The temples here have a good deal of the Burmese shape, but the dome is more like that of a Mussulman mosque.

January 22*nd*.—Yesterday evening Mr. Blake's Khidmutgar died rather suddenly, he had been ailing for some days, but apparently not serious; his indisposition was owing to over-loading the stomach with radishes, &c. in which all partook too freely during the protracted halt, thus causing a good deal of sickness.

This place is so straggling that it is difficult to make a guess at the number of the houses, the greater number of the people are temporary residents and mostly are natives of Kampo,* they are more dirty than the Booteas, and seem to have an especial predilection for begging. When wishing to be very gracious they bow and gesticulate awkwardly, shewing their tongue at the same time. Their principal dress is coarse woollen clothes, and in lieu of turbans they wear caps or hats. Their beasts of burden are principally asses, which are perhaps, from bad treatment, undersized: they likewise use goats, and largish animals between goats and sheep in appearance; of these we saw one male only, it had *once spiral* horns. Even a little black kid was not exempt from carrying its share, this was ornamented by woollen tassels of a red colour, fastened through a hole in the ear.

Pemberton tells me, that most of these people come hither with the view of going to Hazoo, a place of pilgrimage in Assam; some remain here as a security for the return of their brethren in three months, the period during which leave is granted by our friend the Rajah of this place. Their language is totally different from that of the Booteas. The day before yesterday an edict against catching fish, being taken off as I supposed it would be on shewing the Rajah some flies, Blake and I went down, and repeated our visit yesterday; the bed of the river at the debouchment of the path leading towards Tongsa, is elevated 1,431 feet, ($70.209\frac{4}{5}$), it is of no great size, and is generally fordable; the fish are almost exclusively Bookhar.† I saw one or two Sentooreahs,‡

* Eastern Thibet.

† *Barbus hexagonolepis,* Asiatic Res. xix.—Pl. f. 3, pp. 170, 313, 336.

‡ Cyprinus Semiplotus As. Res. xix.—Pl. 37, f. 2, pp. 274, 346.

and caught a long thin Bola,* beautifully banded with purplish-blue. The Bookhars as usual take a fly well, especially red hackles ; the largest was caught by Blake, and must have weighed nearly three pounds.

Very little worth noticing occurred in the vegetation. Sedgweckia is common and of very large size, 2,400 feet above the river, as well as tree ferns.

Equisetum occurs in the bed of the river; in some places at the same level a species of Ranunculus, Aroidea, Succulent Urticeæ were common; along the edges or in the small churs, that have established themselves here and there, and which are covered with the usual Sacchara, but of smaller size; Erythrina, Leptospartion, Sambucus, Bœhmeria tomentosa, Kydia calycina, Grislea, Tupistra, Leea occurred, Ficus elastica is not uncommon, one specimen presented itself, which had sprung up on another tree, fifty feet from the ground; this it had destroyed, and the appearance was singular enough.

The juice is used for water-proofing bamboo vessels. The general rocks are slate, and this was the only one we saw *in sitû;* the vegetation is rather barren.

Near the bed of this river, which is called the Deo Panee, I found a curious Menispermous genus, Columnea, Clypeæ perianthia uncialata, ore integeriuscula, a Myrtacea, Uncaria, Abroma augusta, etc.

On ascending, Murraya exotica, Magnoliaceæ, Pæderia fætida, and Bignonia, occurred at low elevations, Lobelia baccata, Wulfenia obliqua, Costus, Chloranthus, Justicea orchidiflora below 600 feet, Eurya occurred scarcely below 1,800 feet with Millingtonia simplicifolia.

The cattle here are really noble, particularly the bulls; they are much like the Mishmee Methuns, but are distinct,† they are very quiet.

January 23rd.—Left at twelve, and arrived late at Rydang on a nullah, distant eight miles. Passed no villages, but passed a bridge erecting over the Deo Nuddee, at which place a Lam Gooroo or high Priest was employed: vegetation continued the same, and only two new plants occurred, a Stemodia with large yellow flowers, and a Begonia, with branched stems. Rydang is, 2,404 feet, above the sea (55.208½.)

January 24th.—Started early in the morning, (at 8 A. M.) the coolies mostly leaving at daylight. Yet although the distance was

* Opsarius gracilus, As. Res. vol. xix.

† See p. 35.

only eleven miles, we did not reach till 5 P. M. and many of the coolies did not arrive till late at night. The fact is the ascent was nearly uninterrupted during the day, the highest point traversed being about 6,000 feet. We then descended slightly to Khegumpe, our halting place, the altitude of which is 5,395 feet (46. 202,) at the highest point Fahr. thermometer stood at 42° at 1 P. M.

The first part of the road lay over grassy sparingly-forested hills, until we reached 4,000 feet. Here or a little below this the change in the vegetation commenced, the first elevational plants being Serissoid; Gaultheria, and Rhododendron commenced at about 3,600 feet on dry rocky eminences, which it always prefers.

On the 1st eminence, 600 feet above Rydang or 3,000 feet above the sea, Quercus, Castanea, Sedgwickia, Polypodium Wallichii, Lobelia, Pyramidalis, Composita arborea, Gordonia, Pteris aquilina, Anthistiria, Gramen airoides, Callicarpa arborea, Artemisia, Tephrosia, Flemingia, Govania, and these continued up to 4,000 feet. We here met with Kampo Tartars with their laden sheep, the children being generally placed cradle-fashion on the top of the loads, each in its own basket. Itea macrophylla, occurred at 3,200 feet, with Clematis, Hastingsia, Bignonia, Euphorbiacea, Briedleia.

At 3,300 feet Kydia zyziphifolia, Rhopala, Composita arborea, Hypericum,* Triumfetta, Smilax, Indigofera.*

At 3,600 feet, the same with Panax, Wendlandia, Myrtacea arborea, 1. Melica latifolia.

At 3,800 feet, Hedychium, Gaultheria, Habenaria, Serissoides, Gnaphalium, Gordonia, here very abundant, covered with Lichens and epiphytical Orchidea, Phyllanthus, Emblica.

At 4,000 feet, Rhododendron arborea, Eugenia, 1. Gaultheria arborea, Echinanthus, Bambusa, microphylla.* The same trees continue.

At 4,200 feet, Hedychium, Briedleia, Pyrus, Ficus,* and Rhododendron in flower, Gordonia, Itea macrophylla, Pteris aquilina, Osbeckia nepalensis, Artemisia major, Airoides, Flemingia.

At 4,500 feet, Myrica, Callicarpa arborea, Verbenaceæ, Buddlæoid,* Ardisia, Mæsa, Panax, Piper, Styrax, Camellia,* Polygonum rhæoides, Cyrthandra common, Mimosa arborea, Betula,* Ficus, foliis cordatis hispidis, Kydia calycina, Inga, Rubus moluccanus. Anisadenia, Begonia, Otochilus latifolius, Tussilaginoides, Neckeræ, Urtica, Gaylussacia, Lobelia, Panax, Æschynanthus venosus of Churra,* Lycopodium of Surureem,* Smilax ruscoideus,* Liparis, Rhododendron arboreum verum, Bucklandia of vastsize. Hoya fusca, Ophiopogno,

Viola, Hymenophyllum, Croton heterophyllum, Convallaria oppositifolia, Plectranthus Roylii, Begonia picta, Isachne, Cerastium, Spiræa, Hedera, Hypericum, Peliosanthes, Carex gracilis rupium, which commenced at 5,500 feet, Bambusa microphylla.

The forests here were damp and tropical so far as herbaceous underwoods were concerned, the trees were loaded with mosses chiefly pendulous Neckeræ and Hypnea, as well as the rocks, Epiphytes were common.

We then continued along ridges about the same elevation, Ranunculus, Hemiphragma, Thibaudia buxifolia, Polygonum rheoides, Pyrus indica. Gnaphalium common, Pteris aquilina, Airoides, Artemisia on sunny spots, Gaultheria, Galium of Churra, Arundo. The trees were about this all scraggy, but of picturesque appearance. Choripetalum, Panax, Laurineæ,* Piper, Cissus, Photinia and Gleichenia major, Thibaudia myrtifolia,* Potentilla, Calophyllum,* Hydrangea arbuscula,* Thalictrum majus,* Crawfurdia speciosa,* Macrocapnos,* Daphne papyrifera.*

Our march now wound round a huge hill with rocky head, lowering several hundred feet above us, the road being narrow, rocky, overhanging vast precipices. All the trees were scraggy, stunted with tufted grasses. Here about Dipsacus of Churra occurred, Buddleia, Phlomoides, Lonicera, Rosa, *Jubrung*, Cheilanthes dealbata of Brahmakund, Asparagus, Urticea arborea floribus fæm. capitulatis aurantiaces, Spiræa bella, Hymenopogon, Saxifraga ligularis,* on the rocks Primula,* in the crevices, with Hydrocotyla, Thalictrum renatum, Umbelliferæ,* Scirpus, Stemodia, Compositæ, Hypericum, Didymocarpus contortus of Oklong, Erianthus, Gymnostomum, all these on the bare rocks. Along the path, Codonopsis, Cnicus, Valeriana, Hardwickia, Lobelia.

Hence we passed along nearly at the same elevation through romantic paths, the vegetation being European, and comparatively open: the trees covered with moss, with grassy swards here and there: the scenery was beautiful, the descent hence to Khegumpa was gradual and easy, along similar paths.

Noticed the following trees, &c. in the following order: Tetranthera, Gaultheria arborea, Tradescantia cordifolia,* Acer, Polygala, Deutzia, Tradescantia, Jasminum triphyllum, Plectranthus azureus, Macrocapnos, Rubia cordifolia,* Cucurbitacæ Cissampeloid, then forests of Rhododendron, on the paths Swertia, Potentilla, Fragaria, Alnus Acer folius palmatum lobatis oppositis, Porana.

This day I gathered about 130 species, the march was really delightful. The plants marked thus* indicate elevation.

Madder is furnished by both Rubia munjista and R. cordifolia, these species are quite distinct, the latter affecting greater elevations than the former, scarcely descending below 4,000 feet.

Scarcely any water occurred on the route; from just above Khegumpa, a beautiful valley is seen to the left, with a good deal of cultivation. No large villages were seen.

Rydang O.
altitude
about
2,000 ft.
* See section of route.—Sedgwickia &c.

—Quercus, Callicarpa arborea, Euphorbraceous trees.

—Gordonia covered with Epiphytes.
—Hypericum, Lobelia pyramidalis.
—Seressoides, Gaultheria, Gnaphalia, Habenaria.

—Rhododendron, Thibaudia myrtifolia.
—Bucklandia, Garcinia? Eugenia.
—Quercus lamellata.

—Gaylussacia, Masdevallia, Otochilus major.

7,000 feet. —Bucklandia, Lomaria, Otochilus major, Quercus lamellata.

—Artemisia major, Gnaphalia, Arundo, Composita arborea.

—Acer sterculiaceum, Rhododendron.
—Scirpus, Umbelliferæ, Hypericum, Primula, Stemodia, Compositæ, Thalictrum.

—Rhododendron.
—Dipsacus Macrocapnos, Thalictrum majus, Cissus, Rubus potentilla folius, Treefern, Polypodium.
—Woods with pretty glades and swards, Oaks, chiefly Bucklandia, Swertiæ.
—Phlomoides, Viburnum. Spireaceæ, mosses abound.

Khegumpa. —Abies, Pyrus, Rhododendron, Lobelia, Viburnum, Potentilla.
O

January 25*th*.—Khegumpa. This is a pretty place; but the whole country has a wintery appearance from the trees having mostly deciduous leaves; it is a small village, not containing twelve houses. Pagodas with the inscription-bearing walls occur as usual; on a small hill rising from just below the village, a large house with out-houses belonging to a Lam Gooroo, is the prettiest bit of architecture I have yet seen. We put up in a small house, of the usual poor construction, capable of containing four or six people, the roofs are of wood, the planks being kept down by stones. The evening was very cold, but the thermometer did not fall below 44°. Here a solitary specimen of Pinus was seen.

A beautiful tree, with pendulous leaves and cones, which resemble those of Abies, occurred. Rhododendron is common here. Around the hut I observed Lobelia, Rumex, Quercus, Ranunculus, Plantago, Leucas ciliata, Gnaphalia, Rubus, Urtica urentior, Rubi 2, Pteris aquilina, Geranium, Galium, Artemisia major, Fragariæ, Betula? ramis pendulis, foliis lineari lanceolatis, *Jubrung*, Phlomoides, in flower, Spiræa bella, Tetranthera, Daucus, Gleichenia major, Oxalis corniculata, Dipsacus. The trees were covered with Lichens; the only cultivated plants I saw, and of these only straggling individuals, were tobacco and Bhobosa.

In a wood at the base of the hill on which the Lam Gooroo's house is situated, Saurauja hispida, and S. arborea,* Woodwardia,* Rubia cordifolia, Oaks, Spiræa bella, decomposita, Stemodia, Cerasus, Curculigo, Pogonatherum,* Carduus, Polygonum rheoides, Panax, Bucklandia, Berberis asiatica and Porana, occurred.

Our march, after passing this hill, commenced by a descent through a damp wood of Oaks, Eurya. Here Swertiæ 2 occurred on banks. Clematis verbesina, Gordonia, Erythrina, Myrica. Thence we passed along a ridge, the forests being stunted and wintery, abounding with Rhododendron and oaks. Myrica, and pendulous lichens occurred in abundance, but grasses predominate, chiefly Airoid and Andropogons.

From this to the right was seen a beautiful valley with a moderate-sized village and picturesque houses, with considerable and very clever cultivation.

Thence we crossed to the other side of the ridge, descending a little and then continuing through forests of oak, consisting of a species found on the Khasyah hills, and approaching Q. Robur: as all the leaves had fallen, the whole appearance was that of winter. Here I shot the Jay figured in Royle's work: continuing to descend very gradually, I observed Epilobium,* Neckera, Fissidens, Brachymenium, Nerioideum in fruit and half buried in the fallen leaves; a pretty Gentiana, Ruta albiflora, Potentilla. After passing along this for some way we commenced a sharp descent. At about 4,800 ft. Vitex simplex, occurred. Indigofera re-appeared, with Saccharum rubro nitens of Churra, the other grasses being Andropogons, 2-3, and Orthopogon, Hedychium, Gordonia soon re-appeared: to the east, cultivation was visible, and to the north, Pines were visible in every direction stretching away far below us to a considerable torrent. About one-third of the way down this steep ravine, at the bottom of which a torrent was heard roaring, Wendlandia, Spiræa bella, Hedychium, Gaultheria arborea, Aspera Rhododendron, Pteris aquilina, Artemisia, Saurauja hispida, Indigofera, Eurya, Mimosa arborea, Mæsa angustifolia of yesterday, Osbeckia nepalensis, Viburnum, Tetranthera, Ficus, Gleichenia minor, Crawfurdia speciosa, Polygonum rheoides, were found. Hitherto the woods had been dry, or rather so, but on turning to the east, we came into damp woods presenting many tropical features, along which we continued descending gradually for some time: at the commencement in this, Callicarpa arborea, a weeping Beech, Dipsacus verbesina, and the Alnus, of Thumathaya occurred, Arbutoideus, Hydrangea, Urtica heterophylla, Neuropeltoid aromatica. Then below we came on Piper, Deeringia, Cerasus, Sanicula, Cyrtandracea, Cheilosandra gracilis, and fleshy Urticeæ. Underwood, herbaceous forms of Acanthaceæ, Ferns, as Davallia, Asplenium, all more or less succulent. Darea, Glycine, Buchanania, Saurauja ferruginea, Thalictrum majus, Pothos, etc. Hypericum, Begonia, Panax terebinthaceus, Magnoliacæ, Garciniæ, Valeriana cordifolia.* Passing on at the same elevation, we suddenly rounded a ridge, and in one moment came on dry, sunny, rocky, grassy ground, the trees being exclusively Rhododendron, oaks and a few Gordonias with Airoid, Andropogons, Pteris aquilina: we then came on the brink of the ridge up to which Pinus longifolia ascends; the elevation of this was 4,132 feet (60-204½.*) From this all around Pinus is visible in profusion; we then dipped to the south, this face being occupied by thick forest, having Rhododendrons on the skirts. From the above spot Saleeka was visible, with a fine grove of Pines, it is 1,500 feet, at least above this.

* Such figures; may be thus read. Temp. of the air 60° Fah., that of boiling water 204½°.

The descent was steep, we soon came on Callicarpa arborea, Celtis megala, Pogostemon, Stemodia grandiflora; this was about 4,300 feet, where a clearing had been commenced: close to this I observed Martynia, Pteris, Composita arborea, Desmodium vestilum, Flemingia, and gathered at 4,000 feet a Verbenaceous shrub, looking like a Plumbago, and a Bœhmeria; continuing, without descending much, I came on Pinus, Rhododendron, Gaultheria.

Loranthus was here a common parasite on Pinus, oaks occurred but the species was changed; this had small leaves, white underneath; and descending we continued through pine woods, Artemisia minor, together with the usual grasses and Aspideium macrosomum.

Here we travelled along a hill just above a ravine. Either side of this was covered with grasses and pines, the ravine being crowded with oaks, etc. Panax, and Composita arborea occurred.

A little below this, Hastingsia, common, Desmodium hispidisum, Artemisia minor, Briedelia, Mimosa, and several Compositæ: we continued descending very steeply, and observed Holcus elegans, Melica latifolia, Erianthus Apludoid Circium.

At 2,600 feet, came on Scutellaria; Pines had ceased, but on the opposite side of the nullah, they descended lower. Knoxia scandens, Kydia calycina, Hastingsia, Hedyotis linearis, Ficus pedunculis radiciformibus pendulis, Leguminous trees as Dalbergia, Truimfetta; Bœhmeria, Asparagus, Buchanania again, Solanum, 10-dentat., Urtica urens,—1. (66-208½.*)

The altitude of the bed of the Cameon nullah is here, 1,937 feet, its banks are formed by hills cut away and hence precipitous, those to the east are covered with Pines, Oaks descend to this. Here Arundo Karka, Leptospartion, Erythrina, Artemisia major, Solanum farinaceum, black pheasants of which I shot a male. Ficus Dumooriya, Grislea, Rhamnoid scandens, Pandanus, Bœhmeria torrentum, Urtica pendula, Barleria Prionites of Dgin, Sida cuneifolia, Dalbergioid.

Thence we ascended 100 feet or thereabouts, and descended to another and larger torrent. Anonaceæ, Phlogacanthus thyrsifloris here occurred.

The bed of this stream is 70 to 80 yards wide, but the volume of water is inconsiderable. The hills forming the opposite bank are lofty, not under 4 to 5,000 feet; their bases and the nullah above alluded to have the vegetation of Dgin, otherwise they are clothed with the

* See note p. 212.

usual grasses and noble Pines. The brown bird with crooked bill was heard here.

At 500 feet above the torrent Menispermum, Bidens albiflora, Megala, Leptospartion, Verbenacea, Plumbaginea, Mucuna, Desmodium hispidum and Ficus were seen as before: Phyllanthus, Emblica, and Grislea occurred at 800 feet: Grewia at 1,000 feet: and Osbeckia linearis occurred at 1,200 feet in rocky places; with Poa, Cynosuroides of Churra, and Bassia at 1,300 feet, with Emblica, Labiata sudyensis, Osbeckia nepalensis, Ficus.

On rounding the ridge to the east, which is 200 feet above this place *Sassee*, we came on a forest of oak, Rhododendron, Viburnum, Pothos pinnatus.

January 26th.—Sassee. Our coolies left us here, they are not very good ones, not equal to Khasyah, they are however merry, and whistle or sing when tired, their feet are generally naked, but occasionally they wear leathern sandals. Thermometer 60°: water boiled at $204\frac{1}{2}$°: altitude 4,109 feet.

About this place I first met with Thlaspi bursa pastoris, Malva rotundifolia also occurs, Ligustrum, Adhatoda! Euphorbia ramis 4-gonis, foliis? in spinis abeuntibus! Bambusa, Urtica urentior, Geranium, Rumex of Khegumpa, Pancratium or Crinum! Peristropha triflora, Holcus elegans, Pteris aquilina both Artemisias, Panicum cynosuroides! Stemodium ruderalis! Callicarpa arborea! Cerasus, Pyrus indica and malus, Barleria prionitis! Ervum, Hedychium coronarioides! in wet places, Buchanania, Peperomia, Moschosma! Dendrobium! Thibaudia myrtifolia, Gordonia, Dioscoreæ! Tetrantheroid arbor magna, Pinus longifolia, Quercus, 2-sp. Rhus, Citrus also is found. Thus the mixture of forms is nearly excessive, those marked ! thus indicate usually low elevations. Rubia cordifolum.

The whole four leaves of this plant are petiolate, but one pair is perhaps always unequal, one occasionally abortive, I look upon this as a proof that the so-called stipulæ of Stellatæ are real leaves. There is this difference then between Rubiaceæ and Stellatæ, the one has covered buds, the other not. The development of the lamine before the petiole is particularly conspicuous in this plant.

Buck-wheat with trisulcate seeds, and Cannabis sativa are found here; barley is cultivated.

January 27th.—Sassee: temperature 58°, big metal thermometer. Tomato found here; Leptospartion ascends woody ravines as far as this; of birds, the larger dove is abundant; Verbena officinalis.

January 28th.—On walls about this a Lobelia, and Stemodia ruderalis occurred. Sassee is a ruined village, said once to have been large, now containing not more than five or six houses, an equal number being in ruins.

January 29th.—Commenced to descend almost immediately, until we reached the Giri Nuddee, we then ascended again 5,600 feet, and continued over excessively precipitous rocky ground, until we reached the nullah again.

The same vegetation continued until we had descended some hundred feet. Pinus, Quercus, Rhododendron, Viburnum, Indigofera, Osbeckia nepalensis, Desmodium, Gaultheria arborea, Rubus, deltoidifolius, Conyza, Saurauja ferruginea, Crawfurdia speciosa,. Labiata sudyensis, Dipsacus occurs but is rare, Gordonia, Rubus idæus, Gleichenia minor, Pendulous lichens, Galium asparajus, Engeldhaardtia, Smilax.

The descent was steep. Thibaudia myrtifolia, Peperomia, Stemodia grandis, Airoid, Otochilus linearis.

At 300 feet Composita arborea, and penduliflora, Polygonum rheoides, Flemingia, and a cleared spot with Zea Mays. 400 feet Pteris aquilina, Rubus moluccanus, Aspidium Polypodioides, Lygodium, Aspidium macrosorum, Moschosma, Mimosa arborea, Millet, Cerasus, Hedyotis, Plectranthus, Roylia, Knoxia Scandens, Ruta albiflora, Rottlera, commenced at 500 feet. Stemodia, Hovenia, Cerastium, 4-ovulatum, Carex.

Khegumpa, 6,900 feet. O .—Abies, Tetranthera, Salix, Jabrung, Geranium, 6,900 feet Artemisia.

.—Tobacco, Dipsacus, Rumex,* Gnaphalium, Bhobosa.

Saurauja hispida. .—Thalictrum, Epilobium, Rhododendron, Panax, Berberis asiatica, Ruta albiflora.

.—Damp wood of Oak, Eurya, Laurineæ Swertiæ 2, Spiræa, Compositæ, Gillemoides.

.—Dry open ridges, rocky ground covered with Andropogonous grasses, Ichanthus.

.—Airoides, Conyzoid, Quercus, Rhododendron, Myrica, Cirrhopetalum.

.—Dry open wood composed almost entirely of Quercus, Roburiordes, Gentiana, Nerioides.

.—Rubi, Saurauja, Artemisia major, Saccharum aristatum.

.—Betula, Alnus, Arbutoides, Neuropeltis, Ficus.

.—Humid woods, *herbaceous underwood*, Acanthaceæ, Ferns. abundant.

.—Cheilosandra, Buchanania, Pothos, Urtica heterophylla, Cerasus.

.—Urticeæ abundant.

.—Dry open woods, rocky ground as before. Rhododendron abundant.

.—Pinus longifolia ascends on the western face thus far.

4,200 feet. .—Rhododendron, Quercus.

.—Humid wood, Celtis, Callicarpa arborea, Quercus, Eurya, Composita arborea, Verbenacea Buddleoid, Martynia.

.—Gaultheria.

Chilluree Nuddee, 1,937 feet. .—Pinus longifolia, Rhododendrons.

.—Mimosa, Pinus, Mæsa, Compositæ, Artemisia minor.

.—Buchanania.

.—Arundo, Leptospartion, Bœhmeria torrentum.

.—Anonacea, Phlogacanthus thyrsiflorus.

.—Callicarpa arborea.

.—Pinus longifolia, with grasses as before.

.—Verbena plumbaginea.

Ficus.

.—Berberoides, Emblica.

.—Round ridge, then again Pinus longifolia.

Sassee, 2,400 feet. O .—Rhododendrons, Oaks.

Carex, Kydia, Jujubifolia, Randia, Hovenia, occurred at 600 feet, with Rhopala, Panax, Ficus obliqua.

Then shady jungle commenced, underwood of Ferns, Acanthaceæ, Urticeæ, Andropogons, Stemodia secunda occurred at 700* feet. Hastingsia, Pogostemon, Kydia calycina, Glypea, Curculigo, 750 feet, with Clematis Cana, Cerasus, Quercus Robur, this came down a ridge. Rhus acidissima.

Scleria, Lycopodia, Mæsa, Sterculia Balanghas, and Kydia Jujubifolia, at 900* feet. Phlomoides, Acanthacea specicosa, Pothos pinnatus, Choulmoogrum, Malpighiacea, at 1,000* feet. Buchanania, Magnolia, Achyranthes, Murraya exotica, Sedgwickia, Urtica Gigas, Chloranthus inconspicuus, Peliosanthes, Phænix pygmæa, Hedysarum acenaciferum, at 1,200* feet.

The altitude of the bed here is 3,112 feet (64, 206 $\frac{1}{5}$: of Woollaston, 6.4.3)† and along its banks Cissus, Woodwardia, Megala, Polygonum Rheoides, Mimosa arborea, Curculigo, Woodwardia, Andropogon fuscum, Conaria, Potentilla, Rumex, Rubia cordifolia, Drymaria, and Begonia occurred.

The ascent was steep, leading over several land slips, the same vegetation continuing. Oaks, Pines, Rhododendrons occupying the more exposed faces, and the usual humid jungle characterising aspects not so much exposed. Pinus longifolia strays down to within 100 feet of the nullah. We passed a pretty cascade discharging a considerable body of water : here at 200* feet above the nullah, I observed Crotalaria juncea, the Betula of Thumathaya, Quercus lanatus, Leea crispa, Panax terebinthaceus, Indigofera, Scutellaria, Clematis, Cana, Panax altera, Mimosa, Porana, Arundo karka, Flemingia, Conyza, Aspidium macrosomum.

At 400* feet, Itea macrophylla, Ficus, Composita arborea. The woods are dry, but little occurring underneath the trees, except the usual grasses, Andropogons and Airoides. At 500* feet, Thibaudia myrtifolia, Triumfetta mollis, Composita penduliflora, Lysimachia, Pinus, Rhododendron. The ground now became excessively rocky, the road winding along at the same elevation, not more than a foot wide.

At 600* feet, Desmodium vestilum, Artemisia, Acanthacea lurida, Gentiana, as before. Gordonia, Bambusa, Microphylla, Arum viviparum, Tussilaginoid, Wendlandia, Thibaudia, *variegatoides*, and a myrtifolia; Sedum, rocks strewn in every direction covered with Sedum and epiphylical orchideæ.

* Relative heights.

† These figures refer to Woollaston's thermetrical barometer.

On rounding a ridge with a north-east aspect we came without altering our elevation, on a humid jungle. Pothos pinnatus and red, Ferns, Acanthaceæ, Choripetalum, Calamus, Acrostichea, Blakea, Grammitis decurrens, Moschosma. We descended through similar jungle with Pandanus also occurring until we again changed our aspect, when the oak woods, etc. reverted with Rhododendron and Thibaudia myrtifolia; again changing, we returned to an intermediate jungle, gradually assuming all the humid characters of those places passed before. Here I observed Tupistra, Asplenium nidus, at 200 feet above the bed of a nullah. Rottleria, Mimosa arborea, Crawfurdia, Speciosa, Zanthoxzlon triphyllum.

Along the bed of this nullah, Crawfurdia speciosa, Potentilla, Choripetalum, Eurya, Ranunculus, Cardamina, Juncus! Oxyspora, Saurauja hispida, occurred; some in a sort of marsh, with Thibaudia variegatoides. The places along which torrents formerly flowed were occupied by Typha elephantina, Kujara, Megala, Arunda, the Alnus of Bhailseeree, Artemisia major, Rubus deltoidifolia, (Corysanthera hispida with Juncus;) here Anthistiria arundinacea, Artemisia minor, Bucco grandis (Bird), Polygonum rheoides, Bæhmeria torrentum, Gaultheria deflexa, Indigofera, Oaks, Gordonia, Holcus elegans, Conaria nepalensis in flower, and Erythrina occurred along the bed, up which we proceeded about a mile.

We then ascended among Pines and Oaks, Callicarpa arborea, and others, ascending up the humid ravines, which in the rains give exit to torrents—at 300 feet noticed a different Pinus, which is observed in abundance on a mountain on the opposite side, up which it ascends 2 or 3,000 feet.

Callicarpa azurea, Buddlea Neemda, Eugenia, Serissoides, and the Saccharum of Churra, occurred here.

The ascent was continual but gradual, rounding the almost precipitous face of the hill, the path was stony, often loose and frequently not above a foot wide, with a precipice lowering above and yawning beneath. The vegetation had, with the exception of the Pines, Oaks, and Rhododendrons, all been burnt, so that the ascent was uninteresting. As we neared the summit it became bitterly cold, a strong biting wind nearly cutting us in two: we reached Bailfa, which is on the summit but sheltered, at 6 P. M.

Conaria occurs at the top! being more advanced in flower than below; in one instance with young capsules. I noticed Pogonatherum, Didymocarpus contortus, Serissoides, Gaultheria fruticosa, Polytrichum fuscum, gathered at 7,000 feet, previously: at 1,200—1,500 feet above the nullah, Indigofera reaches the top. In a sheltered place here I found a beautiful Gaultheria; a small Campanula occurs on the rocks at from 1,000 feet upwards.

Bailfa or *Bulphai.*—This place is 6,808 feet above the level of the sea, yet on the east and south are mountains towering far above it. Snow is said to fall in February, but sparingly—the hills around are bleak, thinly vegetated, except those on the south of the Geerea, which are more wooded. There are only a few houses. Turnips and barley are cultivated here, and in these fields may be found a Cruciferous annual, and probably a small species of Lamium. The chief cultivation is visible in the valleys below. Buckwheat is among the number.

January 29th.—To-day I sallied out a few hundred yards to the west, on turning over the ridge, the south side of which is so bleak, thinly covered with Q. lanata and Rhododendrons, I found myself in a thick shady jungle, the chief tree being a species of oak, widely different from Q. lanata. The trees and shrubs are loaded with mosses, especially pendulous Neckeræ, Daltoniæ, Hypne; Hookeria, Fissidens, etc. occurred on the ground. I imagine, I gathered twenty-five species of mosses here. Ferns were likewise abundant; I noticed Daphne papyracea, Berberis asiatica, Conyza nivea, Smilax ruscoides, Œschynanthus venosus, Hedera, Ophiopogon linearis, O. latifolius, Cymbidium veridiflorum, Ardisia crenata, Carex, Piper? Clematis, Gordonia, Spiræa decomposita, Composita volkamerifolia, Cissus, Smilax, Bambusa microphylla, Viburna, as before. Gaylussacia serrata and microphylla, the former in fruit. Thibaudia lanceolata, buxifolia, Gaultheria of yesterday.

On the exposed face Santalacea, Gentiana, Hypericum decussatum of Moflong, Leucas ciliata, Ischæmum pygmæum, on Rhododendron, Loranthus obovatus. The mosses of this side were Brachymenium, Tortula, Famaria, Trichostomum, Neckeræ, Polytrichum fuscum, Zygodon? Dendrobium and Otochilus, occur here. A stray and small Abies occurs on the ridge itself.

About the village of Bailfa occur Urtica urens, Artemisia major, Saccharum aristatum, Rubus triphyllus, Senecio scandens, Rumex, Chickweed, Stemodia ruderailis, Lactucoidea murorum, Carduus, Phlomoides, Rubus deltoidifolies, Achyranthoid, densa.

January 30th.—Thermometer at 7 A. M. 40°. The houses here are roofed with split bamboos, and they are tied on by rattans, a precaution rendered necessary by the boisterous winds which prevail.

The place is very cold; the thermometer varying from 40° to 52°: mean temperature of the day 46°.

In the barley fields I noticed Fumariæ sp., Potentilla and Cynoglossum, Erythrina ascends to this! Pyrus Malus and Spiræa bella occur.

January 31*st*.—Our march this day commenced with an ascent of a ridge lying to the north-east of our halting place, this occupied us some time, and at last we reached a pagoda, visible from Bailfa, and which is nearly 1,000 feet above that place. Thence we descended about a hundred feet, through a well-wooded situation. Emerging thence at about the same elevation, we crossed barren bleak downs, the ravines being alone wooded, and hence the woods had that rounded, defined appearance, so remarkable in some parts of the Khasya hills.

Thence the descent was continued to Roongdong, the march is an easy one, about seven miles.

The first new plant that occurred was an Allium on rocks, but it had been dried up by the fires which had bared the surface of the hill of every thing, except the trees and stouter shrubs, capable of resisting its action.

Toward the pagoda, on the summit of the ridge, Pendulous lichens were abundant, Epiphytes were common, consisting chiefly of Orchideæ, with the 2 Gay Lussacias, Rhododendron punctata, Hymenopogon parasiticus, Orthodon, Tussilaginoid, Alnus occurred at 7,300 feet. The other vegetation continued.

At 7,400 feet, a new Quercus appeared, this, which has in its young state, leaves much like those of the Holly, and may therefore be called *Q. elicifolia!* Andropogon, Viburnum cærulium, Neckera, Bambusa microphylla, Fragaria, Potentilla, Conyza nivea, Scabiosa Spiræa decomposita, Gillenioides, Smilax ruscordeus, Hyperica of Moflong, Campanula, Swertia, Dipsacus.

At 7,500 feet, Epilobium, Rosa, Vaccinum cyaneum! Rhododendron coccineum, Tetranthera.

At 7,800 feet, Abies pendulifolia, Hemiphragma.

At the pagoda, and about it, Grimmia was found on rocks, with the usual pendulous Neckeræ, Q. elicifolia, Vibura, Hipericum.

Abies Brunoniana, a large solitary tree, with pendulous branches, Tetranthera, Laurineæ, Smilax gaultherifolia, Ilex, on the wooded side of the ridge. Ferns and mosses were abundant, Ilex! Daphne papyracea.

Eurya, Panax rhododendrifolia, Rhododendron arborea, minus et majus. The tree of Thumathaya* foliis ad apicem ramorum aggregatis,

* Page 32.

petiolis colorat., Celastrinea Euryifolia, Tetranthera another species without leaves. In the more moist places a small Urticeæ, Lonicera as before, on the exposed side stunted Q. elicifolia, Dipsacus, Gnaphalia, Vaccinium cyaneum, and Gramineæ, Hemiphragma, Potentilla, Campanula, Tussilaginoides. Long-tailed grey monkeys.

The ridge we crossed, runs up into a bleak ridge on which are houses, and which cannot be under 9,500 feet high, about the descent through the wood, which did not extend many hundred yards. I noticed Galium, Valeriana, Crawfurdia fasciculata, Sphæropteris Betula corylifolia, Hypericum, Spiræa gillenioides, Rubus cordifolius, Senecio scandens, Juncus effusoideus, in wet places, Rhododendron majus, coming into flower, (flower white) Cerastium bacciferum, arborea, canescens, Cissus, Rubus moluccanus, Elæagnus, Rubus potentillifolia, Plantago, Ligustrum, Berberis pinnata and asiatica, which last is generally covered with lichens.

Xanthoxylum, Lilium giganteum ! Polytrichium fuscescens, Trichostomum anielangioides, Pohlia, on walls and rocks, Adoxa ! in wet places under banks, with a fleshy Urticea : about this was observed the brick-red and black bird.*

Along the naked ridge and on the downs, which had a most wintery appearance, and where it was bitterly cold, the Lycopodium of Surureem was found, also Vaccinum cyaneum, Gnaphalium, Pteris aquelina stunted, Hypericum of Moflong, Swertia stunted, Hemiphragma.

The defined woods are formed of oaks and stray Abies pendulifolia, Panax rhododendrifolia, Berberis asiatica, and B. pinnata.

Mespilus microphyllus, Rhododendron minus, and R. arborea, (Euphorbia, and Juncus on the swards.) Eurya, Gaultheria arborea, Stauntonia. From this ridge a village near Benka is visible, as well as a large stream, the Goomrea, and several villages. The one we now inhabit, being the best looking and occupying a deep valley, is surrounded with much terrace cultivation.

Descending still farther we left the downs, first coming into the scraggy woods of Oaks, Rhododendron, Quercus, chiefly Q. robur.

About here we met abundance of people going to Hazoo from Kampo; they were accompanied with asses chiefly carrying burdens of one maund weight; few goats; one yak was seen of a black colour; a low compact animal, much resembling, except in the absence of a hump, the bison : it was not a handsome specimen. We

* Centropus nigrorufus.

also passed a village to the left, containing about twenty houses, here a Nai gooroo, or person of rank, resides, and here I also got fruit bearing specimens of Abies pendula.

Noticed, as I descended, Pyrus, Cerasus, Magnoliacea, Gaultheria arborea and frutex, Pteris aquelina, Quercus sclerophylla of Bulphai, Viburnum cærulescens and angustifola.! Rhododendron minus, Ilex! Aspid. nidus, Gordonia, Q. lanata, Woodwardia, Rubia albiflora, Gleichenia major, Pyrus indica. Then we came to a pretty temple built like a house, with a fine specimen of Cypress pendula, altitude of the place 7,000 feet. From this a fine view of Roondong is obtained.

Still descending a short distance came to another temple, with a dome of the ordinary form, and a large square terraced basement, and inscribed slabs in the recesses. Hence the ascent was very steep. Erythrinum, Buddlea! Indigofera! Spiræa bella, Artemisia major! Polygonum rheoides! Rubus deltoidens! Curculigo, Conaria nepalensis, Thalictrum majus! Asparagus, Jubrung! Oxalis corniculata, Clematis cana, Eurya ferruginea! Santalacea australas, Pyrus malus! Elæocarpus! Mæsa salicifolia. We then crossed a small torrent, and ascended about 100 feet to Roongdong; noticed Stemodia grandiflora! Spiræa bella, Conaria, Erythrium, Elæagnus spinosus, Salix? buds with velvet or woolly hairs, Martynia! Hedera! Citrus! Woodwardia.

The transitions of the flora were this day well shewn. The plants which indicated the greatest elevation are, Vaccinium, Abies Brunoniana, Saxifraga, or Adoxa, Q. ilecifolia, Rhododendron formosum, R. arboreum majus, Sphæropteris, Ilex, Eurya acuminata? Panax rhododendrofol., Berb. pinnata and B. asiatica, Mespilus, Microphylla, Juncus.

The occurrence of the Urticea at such elevation is curious, the proofs of the wonderful effects of humidity, and non-exposure were particularly shewn, between the exposed south face of the Bulphai mountain, and the north-east face which was wooded.

From scarcity of grass, horses were here seen to feed on boughs so high as to be obliged to stand on stones, to get at their food. They are likewise fed on maize and tares; the poultry is of a large brood. The cocks are atrociously noisy, two in particular had such lengthened, cracked or quavering voices, that they were quite a nuisance. We put up in the house of the Dumpa or head man. It is situated on the top of a stony, and a bitter cold place, exposed to the four winds of heaven. House very large, and our host a little man with great airs, and a red coat or wrapper of coarse English cloth, drinks intensely.

During our stay at this place he invited Pemberton and Blake to shoot pigeons; the poor man thought that they would not be able to hit them, on finding out his mistake, he put an end to the sport.

Atriplex is cultivated here, Mooreesa of Assam, Hempstee of the Booteas, though seeds are used as well as the leaves.

The loads of salt brought down by the Tibetans on asses are packed up neatly in coarse cloths, and weigh upwards of forty seers each.

Bulphai, 6,808 ft. o .—Erythrina, Cnicus, Crucifera.
[Q. lanata Sclerophylla. .
Rhodod. minus, Daphne, .
Piper. .
.—Hypericum, Swertia.
.—Gymnostomum.
.—Q. ilicifol.
.—Allium.
.—Vaccinum, Scabiosa, Campanula.
.—Andropogon, Polytrichum.
.—Spiræa.
About 8,000 ft. .— | Trichosanthes on rocks.
. } Ilex, Abies Br. Daphne.
Gaultheria nov. .— | Ferns, Urticea. Smilax geal.
Long-tailed ape. .—Sphæropteris, Crawfurdia.
.—Rhododendron 2.
.—Saxifraga.
Barren grassy downs. Stunted .—Polytrichum Trichost., Pohlia.
Pteris aquilina. .—Marchantiacea.

Woods occupying ravines with .—Vaccinium cyaneum.
rounded distinct outlines, .
Quercus, Abies pendul., Mes- .
pilus, Microphyllum Berbe- .
ris 2, Panax, Rhododendif., .—Abies.
Daphne papyra, Vaccinia, .— |
Rhododend. minus. . }
. — |

Villages occur here with a .—Ilex, Magnolia, Cerasus.
good deal of cultivation. .
.—+-Cypressus pendula.
.—— |
. }
.—— |
.—Magnolia.
.—Woodwardia, Ruta albiflora.
.— |
. }
.— |
.—Buddleæ, Erythrina.
.—Conaria nepalensis, P. rheoides, Pyrus Malus, Artemisia major.

Roongdong, .
6,000 ft. o .—Citrus, Pol. rheoides, Mæsa, salicifolia, Hedera.]

February 1*st.*—Our march commenced by descending gradually at first, then very rapidly to the Dimree nuddee: crossing this at the junction of two streams, we ascended a little and then kept along the side of the ridge forming the right bank of the nuddee, until we came over the Monass: thence proceeding about one and a half mile, we reached Tassgong or Benka which is situated on this river, and about 1,000 feet above it. This we crossed by a suspension bridge.

But little interesting botany occurred to-day: Chenopodium sp. occurs in fields at Roongdong. The terrace cultivation here had just yielded a crop of rice, and was now planted with wheat. Agriculture would appear to be at a low ebb, and if the country is populous, the people must be half-starved.

Water was abundant throughout the route: the Monass is a large stream, but not generally very deep, although from its rapidity it must discharge even at this season a great body of water. Composita penduliflora descends to the Dimree, the altitude of which is about 3,000 feet, so in fact did most of the plants found about Roongdong. Pyrus continues half-way, Rhododendron to the bottom. Hovenia at an altitude of 5,000 feet, Randia—as also Tetranthera oleosa, and a new Flemingia.

At 4,900 feet, *Jubrung* occurs.—Clematis, Cana, Luculiæ sp., Conyzoidea nivea, Kydia calycina, Mimosa arborea, began at 4,800 feet: Gaultheria, arborea, Gordonia, descend to the bottom: Crawfurdia speciosa, Oxyspora, Aspidium, Macrostomium, and Polypodioides, Saurauja hispida, Hypericum, Spiræa bella, Gillenioinis, Quercus, Rubus, and Viburnum cærulescens. A tree yielding lac, which had lately been cut, and Meliaceæ, Rhus triphyllum. Hence some snow was visible on a lofty ridge above our heads, at least 9,500 feet, the snow descending a considerable way down ravines. Of birds, Bulbuls and Bucco, were here observed.

At —— feet, Leguminosa arborea, Loranthus Scurrula, Kydia Wendlandia, Celtis, Osbeckia nepalensis, a Vitex, Grislea, Pteris aquilina, Indigofera! Acanthacea cærulea.

At —— feet, Triumfetta mollis, Composita arborea, Pterospermum, fructibus 10-valvibus, valvis lobatibus, Sem. alatis. Santalacea australasica, here a large shrub.

At the nullah, Fici sp., Saccharum Megala, Verbenacia? foliis apice craso lobatis. On the opposite side, Pinus longifolia, to within 200 feet of the nullah, Phlibochiton extensus! Solanum farinaceum! Achyranthes densa! a Plumbaginacea ,which is a Pæderioid Rubiacea, and another Ficus, Hastingsia, Bassia, Labiata Sudyensis, Grislea, very common, Emblica, Ficus obliquus were found along the road, after crossing the nullah. The ridge of the mountain was rocky, barren, covered chiefly with grasses, the Butea of Nurtung, Artemisia minor, Umbelliferæ, Desmodium vestilum, Kalanchœ, also occurred. At the few houses below our path, we saw plantains! and bamboos as well as mangoes! The terraces here are fronted with stones: Lemna occurred in water; Linaria on rocks; Conaria and a fleshy Euphorbia, this last, about villages.

The occurrence of plantains and mangoes here is curious, and a sure sign of mild climate, as Kalanchoe is of dryness; nothing could well exceed the barrenness of the road, from crossing Dumria to Benka.

Benka is a straggling place, built on a ridge overhanging the Monass, and on exceedingly rugged ground, the north face of the ridge being nearly equally steep; the southern face, contains about fifty houses, all of which are small and a few in ruins. The only large house is the Rajah's, which is said to be of Chinese construction.

This day the Rajah paid us a visit; a tent was pitched for his reception on the open ground before our house, consisting of a small silken pall, with two high silken parti-coloured kunnauts. He arrived about eleven, preceded and succeeded by followers amounting to less than a hundred. On reaching the ground, he was carried or shuffled off his horse and deposited in the tent amid most terrific screechings. He took an immense time to arrange for our admission. We found him seated on a shabby throne, with a head priest, a coarse looking man, on his right, on a less elevated seat. Brass cups, etc. were arranged before him. Our chairs occupied the left; a present of fruits, onions, etc., the floor. The meeting was friendly, and he promised us coolies in two days. He is a youngish man with a square face, and was well dressed.

After we had taken leave, he feasted his attendants and the spectators with salt-fish and rice. He departed about 2 P. M. The procession was as follows, both going and returning—

A large, black, shaggy dog led by a chain.

A drum and drummer; a gong with a melodious sound; a clarionet played by an old and accomplished musician, rivalling in its strains that beautiful instrument the bagpipe; a man bearing a wooden painted slab on a pole, on this was an inscription; a banner looking like a composition of rags; a white flaglet; fifteen matchlockmen; fifteen bowmen; the Dompa of Roongdong; five horses and one mule led.

The household; Natchees; guitar; sundries. Personal attendants, looking like yeomen of the guard in red cloth dresses, variegated with yellow; the Rajah wearing a chinese copper hat.

Lastly, the priests, of whom there were about six.

These were the best clothed and best mounted, and evinced satisfactory tokens of being corporeally well off. Their dress consisted of a sombre jacket with no sleeves, with either a yellow or red silk back, over this is a sombre scarf. They are great beggars, and the headman was well pleased with a present of four rupees. In return, he gave P. two, B. and myself each one paper of salt, similar to those given to the lookers-on.

The ponies were all poor, excepting two or three of the Rajah's own, which were handsomely equipped; these had their tails raised on end, exactly like hobby-horses. In addition to this, each was supplied with supernumerary yâk tails, one on either side.

The whole people collected did not amount to more than 300. The arms, at least were wretched, consisted of culverins, which went off with an enormous report, and matchlocks with short rests, like the end of a pitchfork. The bows were long and good. The helmets were worn on the head when going and coming, but were allowed to sling on the back while resting here; they are rude iron things, like bowls, but covered for some way up the sides with cloth in a most unbecoming way. Dirt and noise were predominant; the dancing women, evidently not what they should be, had clean faces, but horridly dirty feet, and were very plain. The dancing was poor, consisting chiefly of ungraceful motions of the hands and fore-arms; the singing pleasing, harmonious but monotonous.

A peculiar kind of spirit called *Chonghoons* is in great requisition: this liquor is pleasant, perfectly clear like whiskey and water, with a small matter of malt in it.

Fumaria is found here much more advanced than that at Bulphai, Drymaria ovata. They cultivate one sort of Legume, perhaps more; mangoes, jacks and pomegranates; all these trees bear fruit towards the end of the hot weather. A young mango tree was observed with opposite leaves, uppermost pair one abortive nearly: thus the Mariam of Burma, may probably present the normal form of foliation. *Adoce* fish* found in the Monass.

Bheirs, papia, tobacco, banyan, of these last, poor specimens may be seen here. The place is miserably poor, and as it is reckoned one of

* *Oreinus progastus*, As. Res. vol. xix. pl. 40, fig. 4.

some importance, its condition shows the barrenness of the country. The Rajah's house is a large one, apparently consisting of a quadrangle with an elevated story. News arrived yesterday to the effect that tumults still prevailed: the Deb it was said had been deposed by treachery: that a new one had been permanently appointed: but that the usurper did not wish us to come on. Tongsa, however, said that after we have come so far, we should advance, and that we may settle our plans at his place.

February 5th.—Left: descended immediately from the town to the bridge over the Monass. The descent is steep but winding, the face of the hill being nearly precipitous. Close to the river we passed a small field of Cajanus, used for feeding the lac insect. The bridge is a suspension one, the chains, one on either side, being of iron in square links the curve is considerable, in the form of the letter V, the sides being of mat. Hence it is difficult to cross, and this is increased by the bridge swinging about considerably: it is seventy yards in span, and about thirty above the Monass.

The Monass is 1,300 feet below Benka, it is a large river, the banks being about eighty yards apart, but this space is not generally filled with water. Its violence is extreme.

We continued along this river some time, gradually rising from its bed until we ascended nearly 1,000 feet. We continued at this elevation until we reached Nulka, to which place we descended a little. The whole march was through a barren, rocky, burnt up country. The Monass was in sight nearly the whole distance. Passed two villages, both small, one on the right and one on the left bank of the river. No change in vegetation occurred except that we came upon pines, P. longifolia about a mile and a half from Nulka, coming into flower. I am almost inclined to think this is different from the Khasya species, Kurrimia, Indigofera pulchra, Desmodium, Buddleia sp., were the only plants of a novel nature that occurred. The hills are chiefly clothed with Andropogoneous grasses, very little cultivation was observed, but there seemed to be more on high hills to the east.

Bheir, jack, pomegranate, mango, banyan, Santalaceæ, Jasminum.
Ficus, tobacco, papia, Euphorbia, Solanum farinaceum.
Stemodia secunda, Hastingsia, Pæderia fœtida, and P. cyaneceum.
} Tassgong 3,182 feet.

Rhus pendula, Grislea, Kalanchoe.
Artemisia minor, Andropogonous grasses, Deeringia.
Vitex negundo.

Cajanus, mango.

Monass river, or Goongree 1,400 feet above the sea.

Emblica, Pterospermum. —Bauhinia, Mimosa, Arundo, Rottlera.

—Kurrimia, Ficus oblique.

Andropogoneous grasses, Arioides, all burnt up, Kalanchoe. —Indigofera, Cassia fistula.

—Pinus longifolia.

—Lactuca hastata.

—Buddlæa.
—B. neemda.

—Vitex negundo.

Pomegranate, plantain, China rose, sugarcane. Rice cultivation along the Monass, which is 800 feet below this place. —Nulka 2,200 feet.

CHAPTER XII.

Continuation of the journey in Bootan.

The following table affords the result of observations made with the view to determine the relation between temperature and altitude, in these parts.

	Difference of Temperature.	Difference of Elevation.	Value in height of 1° of Temperature.
Benka and Monass,....	13° Fahr.	1,222 feet.	94 feet.
,, and Nulka,.......	4 =	406 =	$101\frac{5}{10}$
,, and Khumna,...	13 =	1,110 =	85-5
Khumna and Nulka,.. ...	16 =	1,516 =	89-3
Monass and Nulka,.....	9 =	816 =	90-6
Monass and Khumna,...	26 =	2,332 =	89-9
			6)550-8

Mean value of 1° of Fahr. as indicated on the barometer. 91-8

Second series of observation.

Benka and Monass,....	13° Fahr.	1,193-4 feet	91-8 feet
,, Nulka,.....	4 =	367-2 =	91-8
,, Khumna,...	13 =	1,178-1 =	90-6
Khumna and Nulka,....	17 =	1,557-0 =	91-10
Monass and Nulka,....	9 =	826-2 =	91-8
,, and Khumna,..	26 =	2,386-8 =	91-8
			6)549-8
			91-6

The Monass is called Goongree by the Booteas; its bed is very much inclined, and tranquil pools are of rare occurrence: it is not fordable in any place, although many of the rapids are not very deep. The singular bridge is said to be of Chinese construction, and that it serves the purpose of a chief thoroughfare, is a proof of the extremely small population of the country.

Onions grow at Nulka, plantains, sugarcane, tobacco.

Bheirs are common. Weeping cypress occurs, but stunted.

The entrance to this village on the north-side, is through a square building, the ceiling of which is painted, and the walls decorated with figures of deities, white and red.

From a Sketch made on the spot by W. Griffith.

M & N Hanhart, lith Printers

KOLLONG BRIDGE

February 6th.—We descended immediately to the Monass, keeping along its banks throughout the greater part of the march; rising however, over one or two spurs that dip into it.

This river varies a good deal in width, its bed, however, is generally confined, and the stream fierce; occasionally, however it spreads out and becomes here and there more placid. We continued along its banks, crossing one or two small streams until 12 o'clock, when we reached a large torrent, the Koollong, up which we proceeded three or four hundred yards, but at some height above its bed. We crossed this by a wooden bridge of similar construction with that over the Deo Panee, and the idea of which is ingenious. It is nearly fifty yards wide, and about twenty above the torrent. It is in a bad state, and unprovided with railings throughout the central level part. The houses into which the inclined supporting beams are fixed are strong, and built on rock. The fastenings are altogether of cane, and the whole presenting the appearance given in the annexed drawing.

Hence we ascended a black, rocky, burnt up mountain until we reached Khumna, the ascent amounted to nearly 2,000 feet, and occupied more than an hour.

But little of interest occurred, in fact I never saw a more barren country. We passed a small village of two or three houses, and two good patches of rice cultivation, one just below Nulka, one at Ghoomkhume, the small village just alluded to.

Pinus longifolia descends nearly to the bed of the Monass, which below Nulka is about 2,200 feet above the level of the sea. Along this I noticed Hiræa, Eugenia, Vitis, Jasminum, Pæderia fœtida, Ficus, Loranthus, Scurrula, Desmodium, Aerides, Vanda, Flacourtia, Kalanchoe, Leguminosa, *Vanillidora* of *Solani mookh*, Ceanothus, Bergera, Dischidia bengalensis, Leguminous trees, Euphorbia, Bassia, Cheilanthes of Brahmakoond common, Coccoloba cyanea. In rice khets at Ghoomkurrah, I found Lemna, Cardamine, Rumex of Khejumpa, Cirsium decurrens, Gnaphalia, Datura, Simool in flowers; Spathoidea, Oxalis coriculata, Cannabis, Verbesina.

I observed water-ouzels, bucco, water-wagtails, bulbuls, ordinary and yellow-rumped.

Nulka 2,200 feet. —Sugarcane, Bheir, tobacco, onions.

—Bhobosa, maize, rice Buddlæa.

—Indigofera, Santalacea, Desmodium.

—Flacourtia, Pinus.

—Bauhinia, Dischidia bengalensis, Ficus, Pterosperma.

—Leguminous trees, Hiræa, Saccolabium.

—Simool, Flemingia secunda, Gnaphalium, Rumex.

—Cirsium decurrens.

All the features tropical. Pines not within 300 feet; grasses, etc. as before, about Benka.

Koollong bridge. Monass and Koollong rivers join at this point.

—Ixora, Euphorbia.

Bleak, rocky, burnt up hills, without a blade of grass.

Khumna 4,292 feet. —Pinus longifola.

Passed cotton cultivation in two places, one close to the Monass, and one to the Koollong, both equally bad, and observed Begonia edule, which they call Sheemptsee, and which they eat.

The road to-day was generally good, overhanging in one place the Monass at a height of forty yards above, and below scarped precipices. The road here was constructed or supported artificially. Distance six miles.

February 7th.—To Phoollong. Left at 9½ A. M., and immediately commenced ascending. The ascent was at first steep, then gradually wound round the Khumna mountain, which was most barren throughout. The ascent continued but very gradually until we came near Phoollong, to which we descended, and then ascended about 100 feet. About half-way, and when we had ascended perhaps 1,000 feet, we came on new vegetation, oaks, Rhododendra, etc. as before, and this continued improving in denseness until we reached the village. The distance is five miles, ascent about 1,500 feet, but so gradual, that one would not imagine it more than 800 feet. At Khumna, I noticed Pinus longifolia, Pyrus malus, Achyranthes dense, Citrus, Urtiça urens, tobacco, Musa, Datura, Artemisia major. Hogs are fed here in large circular platters made of stone scooped out

Commencing the ascent, I observed Ficus cordata of Bhamru, Rhus pendula, Indigofera *elatior*, Conaria, Pteris aquilina, Cerasus commenced at 5,000 feet. Then Desmodium vestilum, Artemisia minor, Conyza laculia, Rubus deltifolius, Labiata Sudyensis, Acanth. cærulescens.

Quercus robur commenced at about 5,200 feet, but stunted. Flemingia secunda, then Gaultheria arborea, Gnaphalium nivea.

Here there was a high ridge to the right, crowned with a wood of Q. robur, all the leaves of which had fallen. Myrica, Rhododendron, Jubrung, Didymocarpus contortus on rocks, Cnicus, Clematus cana, Polygonum rheoides. At a village here, which contained ten houses, observed Cupressus pendula, Citrus, wheat, Bambusa, then Juncus. Primula of the Khasya hills. Q. robur abundant, Composita penduliflora, Saurauja hispida, Equisetum, Rubus cæsius, Alnus of Thumathaya, Elæagnus spinosus, E. macrophyllus 5,300 feet: Plantago, Coriaria, Erythrina, Rhus acidum, Cerastium cœnum, Dipsacus, Viburnum microphyllum, Rubia cordifolia, Barleria, Tetranthera oleosa, Hedera, Gentiana, Myrsine, Blasia, Fleshy urticea, Q. robur, Gordonia, Adamia, Neckera jungermannoides and læta, Primula in abundance, Acorus, Calamus, Scirpus kysoor of Churra, Gram. latifolia, Andropogonoides of Suniassa.

Coming on a well-wooded ravine close to Phoollong, the first I have seen since leaving Balphai, found Quercus 2, Castanea, Gordonia, Spiræa decomposita, and S. Bella, Hydrangia, Rhododendron, Thalictrum, Quercus, Curculigo, Viburnum cærulescens, Indigofera elatior, Gnaphalium niveum, Sempervivum on rocks, Panicum eleusinoides, Thibaudia myrtifolia, Swertia major, Alnus as before, Rubus moluccanus, Salix lanata, Primula Simsii, Phlomoides, Orthodon.

Throughout the march we observed many detached houses on the mountains forming the right bank of the Koollong, and much cultivation, all of the terrace sort. Passed one village beneath us about 700 feet, containing, twelve houses, and the one mentioned above; as usual, ruined houses occur.

Cattle furnished with litters of leaves; a curious low was heard, like that of an elephant.

Booteas work their own cotton, much of which is cultivated along the rivers at low elevations.

Higher land, certainly 11 to 12,000 feet high, was visible to the north side: on this a good deal of snow was visible.

Khumna, 4,292 feet. — Citrus, Pinus longifolia. Sugarcane, Urtica urens.

Barren, rocky, bleak, burnt up hill. —Andropogonous grasses, Artemisia minor. —Conyza, Rhus pendula, Ficus.

At this point the vegetation commences to change. —Quercus robur. —Rhododendron, stunted Pines,

Chalee, 5,200 feet. — Citrus, Bambusa, Cupressus pendula.

—Primula.

Viburnum microphyllum. —Quercus robur, Gordonia. —Primula, Neckera jungermannoides. —Acorus, Juncus.

Hills all more or less wooded, ridges covered with woods of Q. robur. *Jay* as before.

—Quercus, Castaneæ, Spiræa. —Hydrangea, Thalictrum. —Primula.

—Sempervivum. —Fleshy urticeæ, Primula.

Lofty range overtopping this, 8,500 feet, on which there is snow.

— Phoollong about 6,000 feet.

February 8th.—Towards the morning it commenced to rain; snow has fallen on both sides the Koollong: it has fallen on the road we came by yesterday, and on the hills above to within 200 feet of us, or in some places to the level of this. Exemption in favour of this place is to be attributed to local causes. The trees in the neighbourhood are completely covered with it, and it is said to have fallen here twice during the night.

The Bootea houses are ill calculated for rain, they leak all around as indeed might be expected from the nature of the roofs, which consist of boards, kept *in situ* by stones. It would be curious to ascertain the temperature under which snow does not fall, and if possible the temperature here and among the snow. In the morning, sleet with a few flakes of snow fell also, but only occasionally.

Snow continued to fall throughout the day, and steadily too: it commenced slightly: as the cold increased it ceased to melt on reaching the ground, and at length all around was a sheet of white. The variations of the thermometer were considerable and frequent, the wind blowing pretty steadily from the south-east.

At	10	A. M.	37	degrees	Snow commencing.
,,	$10\frac{1}{2}$	,,	36	,,	South-east wind.
,,	$10\frac{3}{4}$	,,	40	,,	Wind from the north, snow rather heavy.
,,	$11\frac{3}{4}$	,,	37	,,	South-east.
,,	12	,,	35	,,	ditto.
,,	$12\frac{1}{2}$	,,	36	,,	ditto.
,,	$2\frac{1}{2}$	,,	37	,,	ditto.
,,	4	,,	39	,,	ditto.
,,	6	,,	37	,,	ditto.
,,	9	,,	38	,,	ditto.

Fine moonlight night. View to the north beautiful; every thing silvered with snow; the deep and black ravine of the Koollong is particularly conspicuous, and on some cultivated spots the pendulous cypress with its sombre head and branches covered with snow, was also remarkable, altogether a beautiful scene. Larch-like firs were visible 500 feet over the road leading to this from Khumna.

February 9th.—Fine sunny morning: thermometer at 7 A. M. 35°: at 8 A. M. 42°. Hills around covered with snow. High ridge to south plainly visible, a good deal of snow visible. Went out at noon over to the south-east, in which direction a pine wood was visible; this I ascertained to consist of Pinus or Abies pendula, which has much the habit of a Larch. The altitude of this above Phoollong is certainly 1,000 feet; snow covered the ground in all sheltered spots. The woods here are formed chiefly of Q. robur, Q. elecifolia also occurs here and there, Gordonia, Cerasus, Rhododendron minus.

Mosses and Jungermanniæ abound, and were in high perfection owing to being saturated with moisture. Polytrichum, Neckera, Brachymenium, Dicranum, Weissiæ, Fissidens, Hypnum, Didymodon, Diastoma, Orthodon, were found in perfection. The only new plant were a Campanula and a Chimaphila, which last was found at 7,000 feet. Berberis asiatica scarcely occurs below 6,000 feet, Hedera. The birds seen were the jay, barbet, red-and-black-headed, variegated short-wing, large ditto of Khegumpa, orange-breasted Trochilus, brown Fringilla, green woodpecker, black pheasant, and small squirrel of Assam was also found.

From the fir wood, Tassyassee was distinctly visible, bearing nearly due south, distance 10 or 12 miles. Koollong was also seen: all the high ground between that and Bulphai was covered with snow. The high range to the south is, I think, the same as that which runs up behind from the pagoda above Bulphai.

A few plants of the Assam Indigo, Ruellia indigofera, are kept here, and preserved with care, but stunted and obviously unsuited to the climate. Montario, our taxidermist, says that it is the fourth plant he knows from which indigo is procured. First, Indigofera —Second, the custard-apple, *shereefa*—Third, a climbing plant used in Java, etc. probably Marsdenia tinctoria—Fourth,— ?

February 10th.—Fine weather: thermometer at 7 A. M. 40°. Started at 9 A. M., and reached Tassyassee at 3 P. M.; the distance being nine miles. We continued throughout nearly at the same elevation, rounding the hill on which Koollong is placed. About three miles from this we descended about 500 feet to a nullah, which we crossed over by means of planks, thence we ascended about the same height, and continued at nearly our former level until we descended to the Koollong, which we crossed by the usual form of wooden bridge. Thence we ascended 400 feet to the village, which is chiefly constituted by the Rajah's house, a very large edifice. The Koollong is still a considerable stream, but appears to be fordable, at least in the present season.

The vegetation continued the same almost throughout. In ascending from the nullah above mentioned, we came on plenty of Pinus longifolia, and on getting still nearer Tassyassee the Abies pendula became more and more common, until it forms on the opposite bank of the Koollong opposite this, a large wood; Pinus longifolia disappearing. The hills continue openly wooded, the woods consisting of oaks, chiefly Q. robur and Rhododendrons. In the ravines which are thickly wooded, oaks, chesnuts, Cerasus, Rhododendron arborea, mosses; Panax two or three species, among which is a new one, *P. æsculifolia*, arbor parva armati, foliis 7 digittatis, paniculis nutantibus. Hydrangea, Viburnum cærulescens, and Microphyllum, Galium, Ferns abundant, Bucklundia likewise occurred here and there! Tetranthera, Valeriana, Scabiosa, Conaria, Holcus elegans.

In the broken ground before reaching this, Gaultheria nummularifolia, Primula minor, in crevices of rocks. In some places Erythrina was very common, Gentiana, Dipsacus, Sedum and Didymocarpus contortus on rocks, Saccharum aristatum, Salix lanata, Woodwardia, Primula minor, which grows in shade on the Khasya hills, is found here in sunny wet places. The scenery in some places is very romantic, and occasionally grand; the valley of the Koollong being closed far to the north by a high ridge and beautiful peaks, all heavily snowed. The Rajah's house is visible from a considerable distance. As we approached, some parts were rugged and bold. Water abundant throughout.

Phoollong 5,929 feet. Wheat, Bhobosa, Cupressus pendula, Room.	Solanum melongena, Thlaspi arista.
	Ervum, Crucifera, Ajuga.
Oak woods; chiefly Q. robur.	
Oak woods with Rhododendrons. Usual Andropogoneous grasses.	
	Conaria.
Tetranthera, Viburn. cærulescens and microphyllum.	Valeriana, Scabiosa, Galium.
	Hydrangea, Castanea, Quercus.
	Holcus elegans, Galium.
	Erythrina, Artemisia major.
Hooked-tailed Finch, large, short-wing. Orange-breasted Trochilus.	Alnus.
Didymocarpus contortus.	Bucklandia, Rhodod. arbor. maj.
Sedum, Sempervivum.	Panax æsculifolium.
	Orthodon, Orthotrichum, Grimmia.
Thalictrum majus.	Primula minor, Spiræa decomposita, Gilleneoides.
	Fleshy urticæ, Woodwardia, Begonia !
	Panax palmata.
	Primula Stuartii, Pinus longifolia.
	Alnus.
Lycopodium pendulum.	Pinus longifolia, with Abies pendula.
	Saccharum aristatum, Salix lanata.
Green Pigeon.	Gaultheria nummularifolia.
	Primula Stuartii.
Hypna, Funaria.	Abies pendula in woods, Composita pendulifora.
Koollong river.	
	Tassangsee 5,387 feet.

February 11*th.*—Went out at 1 P. M.; descending to, and crossed the Koollong, then ascending along its banks for about a mile.

The bridge over this is about thirty yards wide, abutting from two houses of ordinary structure, built on solid rocks: the river is underneath the bridge apparently of great depth; above it is a succession of rapids, it is even at this, the dryest season, a considerable river. The path leads in a winding direction either over rice cultivation or on precipitous banks. I noticed Berberis asiatica, pinnata, a Pomacea spinosa, foliis spathulatis, Stauntonia latifolia, Hedera, Gaultheria two or three, Thebandiaceæ, Artemisia major, Erythrina, Primula Stuartii in abundance, Juncus, Alnus, Myrsina, Prunella in grassy spots, Rumex of Khegumpa, Daphne papyracæ, Peperomia quadrifolium, Spiræa bella, Viola, Ophiopogon linearifol., Hypericum, Smilax, Elæagnus, Conaria, Lonicera villosa, Epilobium sericeum, a common plant in all watery places, Cardamina Swertia, Viburnum microphyllum. Rhododendrum arborea and minor, Leucas ciliata, Thistles, Pteris aquilina, Neckeræ, Osbeckia capitata of Churra, Oaks, Catharinea, Xyris, Gordonia, Fragaria, Potentilla two, Festucoidea, Cupressus pendula.

The greatest acquisitions were a beautiful pink farinaceous ascapous Primula, and a new genus of Hamamelideæ. This plant I have long known, and called *Betula corylifolia*, as I had only seen it in fruit, and not examined it; it is found on the Khassya hills at elevations of between 4,000 and 6,000 feet. It will be worth dedicating it to some distinguished geologist, thereby associating his name with that of Bucklandia and Sedgwickii.

No fly-fishing is to be had in this stream, nor indeed in any at such elevations. The Adoee is found, but always keeps at the bottom, the structure of its mouth pointing out its grovelling habits. The Bookhar does not, I think, ascend more than 2,500 feet. Water-ouzels, white-fronted Sylvia occur. Observed for the first time the religious vertical revolving cylinders, these revolve by the action of water, which runs on the cogs of the wheel by means of hollowed out trunks of trees. Flour mills are common here, the grindstone revolves on another by means of vertical spokes, which are set in motion by a horizontal wheel, and moved by a stream let on it in the same way.

Funaria heygrometrina abounds in the larch wood here.

This is a very cold place, although 550 feet below Phoollong: it is much colder than that place: thermometer at 7 A. M. 34°.

Snow still remains on the height around; heavy snow on the lofty ridge to the north: strong south-east winds prevail here.

From a sketch made on the spot by W. Griffith.

M & N Hanhart Lith Printers

TASS-GOUNG FROM THE KOLLONG

February 12th.—Tassyassy, which is also called Tassangsee, is a small place apparently consisting of one large house, belonging to the Soobah, and some religious edifices, the other houses belonging to it are scattered about among the adjoining cultivation. The Soobah we have just learnt is absent at Tongsa, so we have no opportunity of comparing his rank with that of the Tassgong man. His house is however, much larger; it is situated on a promontory formed by the debouching of a considerable sized torrent into the Koollong. The bridge is at the foot of this hill, which is about 400 feet high: the house is accessible to the north and west only. Half-way up a high hill to the north-west is a fort! and between the foot of this hill and the Rajah's house there is a wall with a tower at the north-west end, and a house at the south-east. In the afternoon the weather threatened snow, but it ended in very slight rain.

February 13th.—Thermometer at 7 A. M. 33°: at 9 P. M. 31°: cloudy. Observed Conyza nivea, Composita penduliflora, Agrimonia, Stemodia grandiflora, a species of Alopecurus in inundated rice fields, Fragaria, in the wood, Arenaria, Gymnostomum on the terraces. An Arabis in cornfields with a Viola, probably V. patrinia, Gaultheria deflexa and Gerardia of Churra. The fir woods are comparatively bare of mosses and lichens. Shot an Alauda, a Fringilla, and a curious climber with the tail of a woodpecker, at least so far as regards the pointing of the feathers, plumage of Yunx, and beak of Certhia.

Fine cypresses were seen opposite Tassangsee.

February 14th.—Left Tassangsee, diverging from the Koollong at that place, and following the nullah, which falls into that river below the Soobah's house. The march was a generally, continued, gradual ascent; we crossed two considerable streams by means of rude wooden bridges, and the whole march was a wet splashy one, owing to the abundance of water. Snow became plentiful towards the latter end. The direction was west, the distance about seven miles. We passed two or three deserted villages.

We commenced ascending through woods of stunted oaks, Rhododendrons, Gaultheria arborea. The chief under-shrubs being Daphne papyracæ, Gaultheria fruticosa, Primula Stuartii, Lycopodium of Surureem, Thibaudia myrtifolia continue, the Alnus of Beesa occurred plentifully along the bed of the nullah. Spiræa decomposita, Valeriana simplicifolia, Conaria, Scabiosa, Fragaria, Potentilla, Geranium, Artemisia major, Spiræa bella, Hedera, Viburnum cærulescens, Q. robur, Crawfurdia speciosa also occurred.

Ascending, the oaks and Rhododendrons became more developed the latter being the smaller species, Bambusa microphylla, Gordonia, Sphœropteris, Antrophyum trichomanes, Oxalis major ! commenced. Larches on the opposite side, Saccharum aristatum, Gillenioides, Gleichenia major, Hemiphragma, Abies Brunonis commence.

At 6,500 feet Smilax ruscoides, Senecio scandens, Lilium giganteum. The Rhododendrons here are large, forming with oaks, open woods, mosses and lichens, very abundant. Here we came on snow, with it commenced Eurya acuminata, Rhododendron formosa, majus, Rhododendron fruticosa on ruins, Pyrus malus, Dipsacus.

At 6,800 feet, Q. ilecifolia, Q. glauca, Dalibarda, Bambusa very common, Sphagnum abundant, Rhododendron formosa, majus, Quercus ilecifolia larger and more common at 7,000 feet, Gaultheria nummulariodes very abundant, Daltonia, Lomaria of Khegumpa, Gaultheria flexuosa, Thibaudia acida, Tetranthera nuda, Lycopodium of Sureem, Primula Stuartii, Hyperici sp., also *H. moflongensis*, are found up to 7,400 feet. with Hemiphragma, Elæagnus spinosus, microphyllum, Juncus, Alnus of Beesa, Saccharum aristatum.

The village is a ruined one apparently, and never contained more than four or five houses, situated on an open spot, surrounded by woods. This spot is covered with sward, a fine Q. ilecifolia occurs about the centre of the village. Its altitude is 7,983 feet.

The vegetation is the same, Abies pendula, Oaks, Rhododendron formosa, majus, the other has disappeared, Bambusa microphylla, Thibaudia acida, Primula Stuartii, Juncus.

Tassangsee 5,387 feet. Gneiss and mica slate. .—Cupressus, the pendula, larger. Trogon with small wing.

.—Spiræa decomp. Primula Stuartii, Hamamelis.

.—Alnus.

.—Scabiosa, Valeriana, Rhododron. Daphne papyracæ, Conaria, Geranium, Potentilla.

.—Fragaria, Spiræa bella, Crawfurdia speciosa.

.—Villarsia fragilis.

At 6,000 feet, Bamb. microphyllus, Oxalis, Antrophyrum. .—Gleichenia major, Gordonia.

.—Sphæropteris, Rhododendron, oaks.

At 6,500 feet, Hedera. .—Abies pendula, Brunonis, Gillenia.

.—Smilax ruscoideus, Lilium giganteum.

.—Pyrus.

At 6,800 feet, Bambusa microphyllus. Tetranthera nuda. .—Rhod. formosa, majus, Q. ilecifolia.

.—Sphagnum, Dalibarda, Daltonia.

Lycopodium of Surureem. .—Lomaria of Khegumpa.

Hypericum, H. moflongensis, Elæagnus. Saccharum aristatum, Alnus. .—Q. glauca, ilecifolia, Gaultheria flexuosa.

Juncus. .—Primula Stuartii.

Sanah 7,983 feet. Mica slate.

February 15*th.*—We started very early; the coolies were all off by 6½ A. M. Our march was first over undulating ground, either sward or through green lanes. We then commenced ascending a steep hill visible from Sanah, the face of which was covered with sward; at the top of this, snow lay rather thick, especially in the woods. The ascent continued, soon becoming very steep, snow laying heavily on the path, until we reached the summit of the second ridge; thence we descended a little, soon ascending again very steeply until we surmounted the highest ridge. The descent from this was at first most steep, the path running in zig-zags, and being in many places very difficult. About 1,000 feet below, we came on sward, with wood on the right, along which we descended, diverging subsequently through a thick wood, until we reached sward again. Here the coolies who had come up had halted, refusing to go on, as it was already dusk. Learning that Pemberton and B. had gone on, I hurried on likewise, expecting that the coolies would follow, and continued along the swardy ridge, the path running occasionally between patches of wood, the descent being gradual; the path then struck off into wood, and the descent became rapid. I continued onward, until it was quite dark, and finding it impossible to proceed, and meeting with no signs of B. and P., I determined on returning. I reached the coolies about eight, covered with mud, the path in the wood being very difficult and excessively slippery. I had nothing but broken crusts to eat; I procured some sherry however, and my bedding being up, I was glad to take shelter for the night under the trees. Next morning on overtaking P. and B., I found that they had remained all night in the wood without any thing to eat, and without bedding, and that no habitation was near. We reached the village about 9½ on the 16th, fatigued and dispirited. Nothing was at hand, and we had no meal until 5 P. M. except some tea, and an egg or two.

Many of the coolies came up late on the 16th, and some have not yet arrived (17th.) The distance was fifteen miles, to the halting place about twelve. The amount of ascent about 4,500 feet, and descent 6,100 feet, the road being difficult and very slippery: snow was heavy throughout, and the elevations between 9 and 12,400 feet; icicles were frequent. The trees were all covered with frost, and the aspect was wintry in the extreme; luckily there was no wind, and no snow fell. The summit of the ridge was 12,477 feet high. No views were obtained throughout the 15th and 16th; the weather being cloudy and very disagreeable. No bad effects were experienced from the rarefaction of the air; we all suffered of course from colds owing to exposure at night, at an elevation of nearly 9,500 feet; the servants bore it tolerably well.

At Sanah, the altitude of which is 7,983 feet, (Pemb.) I observed Quercus ilecifolia, on it Neckeræ, Antymenium, Senecio scandens, Rhododendron arboreum, majus, Juncus effusus, Swertia, Pendulous lichens, Dipsacus, Artemisia major, Primula Stuartii, Berberis asiatica, Bambusa microphylla, Lycopodium of Surureem, Orthotrichum!

At 8,000 feet, Smilax ruscoideus, Senecio scandens, woods of oak and Rhododendrons, the ground and the trees covered with mosses. Gnaphalium, Daphne papyrif., Mespilus microphyllus! Gaultheria nummularioides, Spiræa gillenioides, and S. bella, Hypericum, Gnaphalium lanceolatum, trivenum, Sambucus! but withered, Tetranthera nuda of Bulphai, Abies Brunonis which is probably a Podocarpus.

At 8,300 feet, Tussilaginoides of Churra, Primula Stuartii common on swards with Swertiæ, etc. as before, Funaria and Weissia Templetonia common, Sphæropterus! Quercus ilecifolia, Abies pendula, Rhododendron arboreum, majus! Dalibarda, Rubus, Ilex dipyrena! Rhododendron undulatum!

At 8,400 feet, the road running along, and above a ravine, rocky ground to the right, Eurya acuminata! Composita penduliflora. Thibaudia rotundifolia, and in a swampy sward a small dwarfed very narrow leaved bamboo, Primula Stuartii, Gnaphalium densiflorum, Swertia monocotyledonea, Prunella in the woods, Salix lanata, and Panax rhododendrifolia.

Just above this, 8,500 feet, the first Abies cedroides appeared, soon becoming very common, and extending up to 9,500 feet, its habit is like that of a cedar, and it is a tall handsome tree, Rubia* cordifolia! Geranium scandens, Baptisioides.

Crossing a nullah, we commenced a steep ascent, Thibaudacæ rotundifolia, Abies cedroides, Lomaria of Khegumpa, Crawfurdia speciosa, Andropogon, Gaultheria nummulacifol. Ilex, Epibolium Vaccinum cyaneum! Here a sward commenced with vegetation as before, the summit of this ascent was 9,050 feet. Here Ilex, Daphne papyracæ, Rhododendron, Scleria, Lomaria of Khegumpa! Primula pulcherrima! Spiræa bella, Gnaphalium trivenium, Rubus moluccanus, Thibaudia, Ericinea orbiculens, Spiræa decomposita, Gaultheria, nummulariod., Scutellaria prunella, Gaultheria flexuosa, Scandent composita, Cerastium bacciferum. The trees covered with mosses,

Neckeræ, Dicranum, Daltoniæ, Abies pendula ceased, its limits visible below. Hence the ascent was gradual at first: snow became heavy at 9,100 feet. Hemiphragma, Rhododendron abundant.

At 9,500 feet, much the same vegetation, Abies densa commenced, cedroides ceased. Woods entirely of A. densa, with a small baccate-like deciduous leaved tree. Hydrangea! Spiræacea! Urticeæ?! Pedicularis elatior.

At 10,000 feet, some trees all covered with frost; snow very heavy, quite crisp. Juncus niveus, Cerastium inflatum! bamboos, other plants of 9,500 feet, continue. Old Cretins!

At 11,270 feet, thermometer 39°, the same trees, scarcely any thing but Abies, Arenoid, Dicranum macrocarpus, Orthotrichum, Lichen pendulum atratum.

Thence we descended a little, soon to re-ascend.

At the same elevation Parnassia, Epilobium monus, Gnaphalium densiflor., Vaccinum pumilum, Gentiana, Polygonum (?)

At 11,000 feet, icicles were common, and snow very heavy. Woods of some Abies, a species of rose very abundant, a shrub of four feet high; other plants continue as before.

From this to the summit the ascent was very steep; Abies continues. Rhododendron (?) very common, with rose, Parnassia, Saxifraga, Composita arenoid, Gentiana, Polygonum (?), Pedicularis dwarfed, Triticoides, Aroides. Many pines dead as if blasted. Summit nearly bare of trees, which appear confined to slopes, Rhododendron very common, Umbellifera crassa, figured in Royle, Lilium unifloria.

At 12,000 feet, after descent, commenced Hymenophyllum, Xyris on rocks, Pyrus at 11,500 feet, Rhododendron ellipticum common, summit strewed with rocks, Rhododendron pumilum.

At 10,000 feet, the Spilus microphyllus, Polygonum, as well as on ascent Gaultheria nummularioid., swards abounding with Gramen nardoides (?), Dipsacus minor, Epilobium parnassia, Swertia, Umbelliferæ, Primula scapigerc. floribus in globum densum, pedalis, Habenariæ herminioid.

At the halting place 9,700 feet, Berberis ilecifolia, Daphne papyracæ, Thibaudia myrtifolia, Baptisia, Dipsacus, major, Swertiæ pedicularis, Andropogones, Ilex dipyrena, Rumex of Khegumpa, Betula, Euonymus cornutus, Abies cedroides, and Brunonis, Geranium scandens, Pyrus, Hypericum moflongensis, Hemiphragma, Mespilus microphyllus, Panax rhododendrifol., Rhododendron obovatum.

At 9,500 feet, Rhododendron arborea, majus, Abies cupressoides, Gaultheria nummularioides flexuosa, Thibaudiacea rotundifolia, Primula Stuartii, stunted juncus.

At 9,000 feet, Q. ilecifolia, Rhododendron undulatum, Primula pulcherrima, Tetranthera nuda, Chimaphiliæ! Andropogons, Rhododendron arbor, majus, common, which varies much in size of leaves, Dalibarda, Smilax ruscoideus.

At 8,500 feet, Berberis pinnata, asiatica, Buddlæa purpurea, Eurya acuminata.

At 8,000 feet, Gnaphalium trivenium, Baptisia, Spiræa, (Gillenioid) bella, Artemisia major. 7,500 feet, Rhododend. minus arborea, Leucas ciliata, and woods of Q. robur, as usual deciduous.

Sanah 7,983 feet.—Q ilecifolia, Anhymenium, Rhodod. majus, Swertia, Juncus.
Mica slate and gneiss. .—Primula Stuartii.

.—Abies, Brunonis, Rhodod. undulatum.

.—Baptisia, Primula Stuartii.

.—Abies cedroides, Thibaudia rotundifolia.

First ascent. .—Primula pulcherrima, Abies cedroides.
.—Daphne papyracæ, Berberis, mosses abundant

.—Abies densa, Pedicularis, Spiræa.
.—Urticoidea, Betuloidea, Polygonum.
.—Rheum.

.—Abies densa, Rhododendron.
.—Betuloidea, Rhododendron.

Ridge composed of gneiss. .—Labiata, Xyris, Rosa.
Doonglala Peak 12,478 feet. .—Parnassia saxifraga, Pedicularis.
.—Abies densa.
.—Rosa.
.—Triticoides Polygonum,
.—Umbelliferæ.

.—Rhododendron pygmeum.
.—Xyris.

Sward. .—Primula globosa, Umbellifera.
.—Dipsacus minor, Swertiæ.
.—Nardoides.

Halted for the night. .—— } Berberis ilecifolia, Tetranthera nuda, Rhodod. ferrugin. Betula, Abies.

Mica and talcose slate resting on gneiss. .—Brunonis cedroides, Rumex of Khegumpa.
.—Sphieropteris.
.—Chimaphila, Rhodod. majus, Q. ilecifolia.
Linge, 9,602 feet. .—Rhodod. minus, Artemisia major.

All the plants above 10,500 feet, had perished, not a single one being found in flower. The descent was so hurried, that it was impossible to note down more plants; and the same applies to the descent to this from the halting place. Starvation being to be added to discomfort.

Of Rhododendrons, the species observed, may be characterized as follows:—

Floribus in racemis umbelliformibus.

1. R. *arboreum*, arboreum, foliis oblongo obovatis, subtus argenteis.

2. R. *ferrugineum*, arboreum, foliis obovatis, supra rugosis, subtus ferrugineis.—No. 654.

3. R.———fruticosum, foliis oblongis, subtus ferruginea lepidotis.—No. 652.

4. R. *ellipticum*, fruticosum, foliis ellipticis.—No. 653.

5. R.———fruticosum, foliis ellipticis basi cordatis subtus glaucus reticulatis.—No. 659.

6. R.———fruticosum, foliis lanceolato oblongis, sub-obovatis, subtus punctatis.—No. 655.

7. R. *undulatum*, fruticosum, foliis elongati lanceolatis, undulatis subtus reticulatis.—No. 656.

Floribus solitariis.

8. R. *microphyllum*, fruticosum, lotum ferrugineo lepidotum, foliis lanceolatis parvis.

February 17th.—Snow has fallen during the night all around, but not within 1,000 feet of us: this will make the snow line here about 7,300 feet, the village being 6,335 *supra marem*. Mildness of climate would appear to be indicated by the abundance of rice cultivation round this place, chiefly, however, about 1,000 feet below. In every direction ranges of 9 to 12,000 feet are visible: villages are very common, especially so in a hollow on the western side of the ravine of the Kooree, in which I counted sixteen or eighteen; one containing between thirty and forty houses. The space alluded to is one sheet of cultivation, chiefly rice and wheat. Lingè itself is an ordinarily sized village, containing about twelve houses. The wooded tracts cease for the most part, about 1,000 feet above this. The face of the country, where uncultivated, being clothed with harsh Andropogoneous grasses, Salix pendula, Thuja pendula, Pyrus malus, Erythrina, Quercus, Juncus effusus, Porana of Churra, Plantago, Barleria, Polygonium rheoides, Stellaria media, Rubus deltifoliis, Cnicus, Rhodod. arboreum minus, but rare, Smithea occurs also.

February 18*th*.—Our march commenced by a steep descent on the south face of the hill, the coolies proceeding by a more direct one to the north, but which was said to be difficult. We continued descending in a westerly direction, until we came in sight of the Kooree river which flows along the ravine, and which is a large stream, one-third less than the Monass. We then turned to the north following the river, the path running up, about 800 feet above it. We then came to another ravine, and descended to the torrent, which we crossed by a rude wooden bridge: then followed again the Kooree, to the bed of which we descended, and along which we continued for some time. We then ascended where the banks were of such a nature as not to allow a path, descending again here and there. Then we came on the Khoomun, a large torrent, which we crossed by a wooden bridge about 100 yards above its bed; re-descended to the Kooree, reached its bridge; and thence descending rather steeply, and for about one and a half mile to Ling-Ling, or Lengloon, which is plainly visible from the bridge over the Kooree.

After turning to the north along the Kooree, and indeed after passing the cultivation below Lingè, which chiefly occupies a sort of plateau, we passed through a most miserable country, the hills being rocky, nearly destitute of trees, and chiefly clothed with the usual coarse Andropogoneous grasses, especially lemon-grass, occurred between Lingè and Lengloon.

At 5,000 feet, observed Desmodium, Santalacea australasia, Gaultheria arborea, Indigofera, as before, Clematis cana, Acanthacea cærulescens, Pteris aquilina, Viburnum cærulescens, Oxyspora, Panicum eleusinoides, Anthestiria, Conyza, Ficus cordifoliis of Bhamree, Labiata Suddiensis, Corearia, Rhus pendula, Airoides major, Flemingia secunda and major.

At 4,800 feet, Desmodium vestilum, stunted, Q. robur, Dipsacus, Epilobium, Elæagnus microphyllus, spinosus.

At 4,600 feet, Sedum, Campanula, Osbeckia capitata, Citrus in villages, Emblica, Artemisia minor.

At 4,000 feet, Pæderia cyanea, lemon-grass, Panax, Terebinthaceus, Pinus longifolia, here and there, Ficus obliqua, Grislea, Cirsium.

At the bed of the torrent 4,000 feet, Bassia.

Over the Kooree, Euphorbia antiqorum, a sure sign of aridity. Didymocarpea contorta, D. canescens, which differs from the other in being hirsute, Menispermum, Holcus elegans.

Along its bed, Sedum of Phoollong, Eugenia, Achyranthis, Ingoides arborea, Aspidium polypodioides, Briedleia obovata; Desmodium of Nulka! Arundo, Buddlæa neemdoides, Jasminum of Benka, Composita, involucri squamis ciliatis. Rice fields, in these Gnaphalium aureum, Phleoides of Tassangsee, but in full flower, Lysimachia majus, rugosus, Oxalis comiculata, Hieracioid, Composita, Lactucoid purpureseus, Ammannia, Bidens alba, Drymaria.

Then along the wooded banks, Wendlandia, *Pomacea?* Mimosa arborea, Camunium, Butea suffruticosa, Pterospermum of Bhamree, Luculia, Ulmus, as before, Pinus longifolia, Rottlera, Melica latifolia, young plants of Q. robur on rocks, along with it Goodyera articulata, Urticoid rhombifolia, carnosa; on rocks up Khoomun, Orthotrichum corcalypta. At the bridge over this, a Myrtaceous tree and the Simool occur. The plants occur during the ascent, as in the descent. Water-wagtails, blackbirds, tomtits, were observed, as also white-pated and white-rumped water-chats.

February 19*th.*—Ling-Ling or Lengloon.

February 20*th.*—To-day we visited the Soobah, who is a young man, certainly not more than twenty years old, with a good humoured countenance. The meeting was cordial but unattended with any state, and judging from appearances only, this Soobah is inferior to the others we have seen, and especially to him of Tassgong. No armed men were present, and the whole bystanders scarcely amounted to 100. It was agreed that we remain here until the baggage, now in the rear, arrives. Tonsa is, we hear, only four or five days journey from this.

The meeting took place in an open plot of ground below the Soobah's house and on the skirts of the village, the ground was matted and a space enclosed with mats: we sat in the open air; the Soobah under a silken canopy. Altogether he seemed a person of no pretensions, crowds, speaking comparatively, of priests attended as usual, they were the slickest looking of the whole, and the greatest beggars. A hideous party of *nachnees* were in attendance, and ready to perform any more pleasing duties they might be required; they were however so ugly, that not much self-denial was required in declining their offers. They were dressed in red, with abundance of cumbrous silver ornaments, and dirty leggings; one was additionally ornamented with incepient goitre.

Sugarcane (but stunted), almonds, or peach, oranges, castor-oil, datura, pear, simool, may be found here. Oranges are poor enough, the pear no better. Pinus longifolia, Cupressus pendula, are almost the only trees: the hills being barren, covered with coarse grasses.

February 23rd.—Marched to Tumashoo: our march commenced with a steep ascent, but which may be avoided by going through the village, it commenced and continued throughout in the direction of Lingè, opposite to which place we found ourselves on our arrival, but on the right bank of the river. The highest part reached, before we descended to this village, was 6,350 feet, or about the height of Lingè. The march was nearly six miles, it was easy, the road being throughout excellent and apparently more frequented than any we had hitherto seen. Generally we moved along through open Rhododendron woods, frequently very much stunted, at 6,000 feet. These were intermixed with Quercus tomentosa. The only spot well wooded, occurred in the ravines, giving exit to small streams.

The first ascent from Leng-Leng, gave the same vegetation, scarcely any trees being visible. Tradescantia clavijera of Churra on rocks, Galium of Churra, Santalacea, Desmodium vestilum, Indigofera canescens, Artemisia major and minor, Oxyspora, Luculia, Conaria, Sambucus in wet places, Lobelia pyramidalis, Spiræa bella and decomposita, Thalictrum majus, Gaultheria fruticosa, Woodwardia, Saurauja hispida, Rhododendron minus, and lemon-grass, occurred in the order of ascent.

Turning hence along the ridge at the same elevation, Gaultheria arborea, Quercus tomentosa, Rhododendron minus, Hedychium, Holcus elegans, Leucas ciliata. In wet wooded spots Gaultheria duplexa, Bucklandia, Viburnum cærulescens, Polyg. rheoides, Erythrina, Gordonia, Porana, Neuropeltis aromatica, Catharinea, Thibaudia myrtifolia, in open massy woods of Rhododendron minus and Quercus tomentosa, Rosa, Cnicus, Pyrus, Gleichenia major, Agrimonia occurred at the same elevations.

From one spot seven villages were visible, on opposite bank of Kooree and between Lingè and the Khoomun. A few stunted P. longifolia: one or two of Abies pendula, occurred 100 feet above the highest point of the former: at 6,350 feet, woods of the deciduous Q. robur, were observable.

On the descent at 6,000 feet, Mimosa spinosa, Primula Stuartii, Rhus, Juncus, and others, as before.

We passed several villages, some containing twenty or thirty houses, and on halting found ourselves towards the edge of the cultivated tract alluded to, as seen from Lingè.

Cattle are here kept in farm yards which are well littered with straw; as in other places they are noosed round the horns: they are fed, while tied up, on straw of a coarse and unnutritious description, which they do not seem to fancy much. Pigeons abound, but they are of no use as they cannot be caught; they may help to feed the sparrowhawks, which are generally found about the villages, and which are very bold.

February 24*th.*—Left at 8 A. M. after the usual trouble about coolies and ponies. We ascended at first about 1,000 feet, passing over sward with woods of P. longifolia on either side, crossing the ridge through a hollow, we then commenced a steep descent to the west, until we reached a water-course, the elevation of which is about 200 feet below that of Tumashoo. We then struck off, again to ascend, and continued to do so until we attained 7,800 feet, from which point we descended gradually at first, then abruptly to our *mokan.* The direction was nearly west, the distance 11 miles, the march pretty easy, as the road was good, and the ascent gradual.

Up to the ravine and indeed throughout, nothing new occurred in the vegetation. The hill up which we ascended to again descend, was bare, covered with the usual coarse grasses, Campanula linearis and C. cana, foliis undulatis, Desmodium vestilum, Santalacea.

In the ravine Gordonia, Photinia, Pothos flammea and another species, Mæsa, Polygonum rheoides, Ficus of Bhamree, and in the *khets* Hieraceoid, Gnaphalium aureum, Ajuga, and Veronica occurred.

Up the first ascent and at about 5,500 feet, there was a field of peas, in very luxuriant condition. Our road lay through open dry woods of oaks, either Q. robur or Q. tomentosa, principally the latter, Rhododendron minus, and Pinus longifolia preponderated in some places, but few trees of Abies pendula occurred.

The march was so far interesting as establishing nearly the limits of Q. robur, Q. tomentosa and Q. ilecifolia, which last only commenced, and then in a small state, at 7,300 feet, I should say that Q. tomentosa was to it the next indication, as well as Q. glauca. But it must be understood that only full grown trees are now considered. Mosses were common in the woods on reaching 6 to 7,000 feet, principally Dicrana, Hypna, Orthotricha, Pendulous lichens frequent; about 7,000 feet, Primula Stuartii in its old situations between 6 to 7,00 feet, Hypericum of Moflong, 7,000 feet.

We crossed several small water-courses, along these, the dry woods ceased, and the usual humid jungle made its appearance: mosses very numerous.

Lengloon 4,523 feet, mica slate.

.—Primula Stuartii.

Buddlæa purpurescens. .—Composita penduliflora.

At 7,300 feet, Quercus tomentosa, Ilecifolia glauca in wet places, Neckeræ. .—Shlotheimia, Chimaphilia, Daphne papyracum.

Scabiosa, Thibaudia myrtifolia. .—Didymocarpus canescens.

Bambusa microphylla. .—Gordonia, Berberis pinnata.

.—Smilax auriculata, Thalictrum majus.

Pinus longifolia. .—Spiræa decomposita, S. bella, Woodwardia.

Hills covered with Andropogoneous gramineæ: woods of Q. tomentosa, Q. robur, with Gaultheria arborea, fruticosa. .—Anthestiria.

Abies pendula, Viburnum *canum*, Pisum, Conarea. .—Indigofera canescens, Rubus delboideus.

.—Pothos, Q. Photinia, Gordonia.

In *khets* here Veronica, Hieraceoid Gnaphal. aureum, Ajuga. .—Mæsa.

Andropogons, Santalacea, Ficus cordifolia of Bhamree, Campanula linearis, canescens and undulata. .—Barren steep declivity. .—Rhus pendula.

Traces of primary limestone. (Pemb.) .—Pinus longifolia.

Cultivation.

Tumashoo 5,000 feet, mica slate.

The above plants continued throughout, after reaching an altitude of 6,000 feet, the woods consisting of oaks and Rhododendrons.

The route for the most part wound along the course of the Kooree, but considerably above, we left this track about 3 P. M. on the river turning to the southward. Lingè was in sight nearly the whole day; we have been six days (including a halt) performing what might with ease be done in one, for there probably is a road in a direct line between this part and the opposite bank of Kooree. The small-crested finch, and red-beaked and red-legged fare occurred, the former is a noisy bird, inhabiting chiefly woods of Q. robur, the flock were loth to leave one particular spot, so that we obtained five specimens: the finch occurred at 7,800 feet.

Various temples and walls were passed en route, and a few villages, with one exception of average small size, were visible in various directions.

February 25*th*.—Our route hence continued for some time at about the same level, when we descended rather rapidly, until we reached a considerable stream, the Oongar, which is crossed by the ordinary wooden bridge; about 200 yards further, it is again crossed by means of a rude bridge, and the remainder of the march is a steep, long, and unmitigated ascent. I reached the tent about 5 P. M.; we passed one village situated near the larger bridge, with this exception the country seemed uninhabited: very little cultivation was visible in any direction.

The vegetation was the same, for the most part, the drier faces of the hills being covered, i. e. at about the level of Oongar, with oaks and Rhododendrons, the wet ravines being more densely, and more variously wooded. On sward about Oongar, I noticed a Pedicularis, Artemisia major, Stellaria angustifolia, Berberis pinnata in woods at the same elevation, Plantago, Crawfurdia speciosa, Rubus deltoideus, Alnus of Beesa, Otochilus, Gordonia, Lilium giganteum, Bucklandia.

In one spot near this place mosses were very abundant. On one rock I gathered, Weissiodes, Orthodon, Pohlia, Brachymenium bryoides, Weissia, Bartramioides, Didymodon, Daphne papyrifera, and Eurya acuminata, this being about the lowest elevation at which I have seen this plant. In cultivated spots Crucifera, Ervum, and at a temple about a mile from Oongar, Cupressus pendula, and a juniper, Arbor parva, of aspect scraggy, trunco lævi, Cannabis, Cerastium canum in cultivated places. The most common oak was Q. robur. The Jay, larger Brachypodium, which always goes in large flocks, orange-breasted Trochilus and blackbird, were likewise seen, as well as the brown finch, which was seen feeding on Rhododendron minus. On rocky ground I procured a really fine Acanthus, leaves all flesh-coloured, subscandens, spic. maximis lanato-ciliatis, tetrastich. on this the black cattle appear to be fed, as large bundles were brought in at Oongar. In the woody ravines Panax curcasifolia was common, in these I noticed Cerastium scandens, Elæagnus, Clematis, Tetrantheroidea habitu, Sedgewickiæ ! Orthotrichum pumulum ! Phlomoides, and in wet spots are Epilobium. The descent shewed nothing remarkable: towards the nullah I noticed Engelhaardtia, tree fern, and Gaultheria deflexa. Obtained a beautiful woodpecker at 5,000 feet, with the chesnut-pated lesser tomtit, Yunx, and speckled Brachypodium in woods here; this last has the habit and manners of the crooked bill of Dgin.

The wood between the two bridges was very pretty and open; the trees covered with mosses. The ascent shewed nothing remarkable until 2,000 feet had been surmounted, the plants forming the vegetation below this were Q. robur, Rhododendron minus in abundance, Thibaudia myrtifolia, Gaultheria arborea, Saurauja hispida uncommon, Viburnum cærulescens, Conyza nivea, Oxyspora towards the base with paper plant, and Bambusa microphylla. About 5,000 feet, a Daltonia, D. hypnoides, was found in abundance both on rocks and trees.

The change takes place about the situation of a spacious open sward; here the jungle is thick, the trees consisting principally of Q. glauca, which is a noble tree, with immense lamellated acorns, Pendulous lichens are here common, Hymenopogon parasiticus, Lomaria of Khegumpa ! Berberis asiatica ! Hemiphragma, Gaultheria nummulareoides, Panax Rhododendrifol.

At 7,500 feet, Rhododendron majus appears, the wood preserving the umbrageous humid aspect, Eurya acuminata, Hydrangea, and about this snow commenced sparingly, but soon became thick. At 8,000 feet, Rhododendron undulata, Tetrantheroides baccis nigris. At 9,000 feet, Rhododendron ferrugineum. The evening now became so misty that it was impossible to discern any thing; in addition, it was snowing: these circumstances added to fatigue made me press on for the halting place, before coming to which I passed through heavy snow.

Pémee, where we put up, is a miserable hut, is upwards of 9,000 feet above the sea, situated on an open sward, now densely covered with snow, the accommodations being of course very miserable. Icicles of large size were seen here; and we had nothing but snow for water.

February 26*th*.—Leaving this, we commenced a long and at last very steep ascent, the snow increasing in thickness as we increased our elevation, the march commenced with undulations, but soon passed off into an excessively steep ascent, in some parts indeed precipitous. We crossed at twelve and a half P. M. the Pass of Rodoola, on which are some slabs, with mystic characters, but even here the ascent did not terminate, but continued, although very gradually for perhaps two miles more. Before coming to the summit, a small hut is passed. The descent was at first very rapid, then we proceeded along the side of the mountain for a long way, at nearly the same level through woods of Abies densa. On recommencing the descent, swardy patches commenced, surrounded by fir woods, these increased in frequency. At length we reached extensive fir woods, from whence a valley was visible, percolated by a large stream to which we descended over open country with beautiful patches of firs, and at length over extensive swards. I reached the village at 5 P. M., after a march of nearly nine hours, the direction was west, the distance eighteen miles. The road was very bad; in one place our ponies escaped with difficulty, the road having apparently fallen in, and the only footing being afforded by the thickness of the snow: one poney was saved by placing branches under him. The highest portion of the Pass near the peak was good enough. Snow was heavy on the road, until we descended into the open fir-wooded country, it became scanty at 9,500 feet. The day was gloomy and misty, for a moment, the sun appeared while I stood on the summit, disclosing deep ravines, one formed by the valley in which we now are, surrounded in every direction by equally high land, as that on which I stood, and certainly not under 12,000 feet. Nothing visible but dense forests of firs. The highest point crossed was 12,035 feet, estimating the summit to be 300 feet above the Pass itself, which is so narrow as scarcely to admit of the passage of a loaded mule.

In the open spot around the hut, Tofieldioid, which continues as high as 10,500 feet, Cerastium inflatum, Labiata species, Conecis, which, as on Dhonglaila, continues up to 12,000 feet, Dipsacus, Prunella, Gaultheria nummularioides, Pteris aquilina, stunted, Juncus niveus, Gnaphalium. No firs were visible, but the trees were so covered with snow, that I was not able to distinguish them.

At 9,800 feet, along an open ridge, Spiræa belloïdes, Buddlæa, B. purpurasæ, Khasyanæ affinis, Andropogones, Mespilus microphyllus, Hydrangea, Taxus, Swertia, Gnaphalium, Thibaudia orbicularis, commences, continuing up to 10,500 feet, Brachymenium bryoides, Bambusa very common, forming frequently the chief bulk of the forest, even up to 10,500 feet, Acer arbuscula foliis palmatum lobatis!! Pyrus arbor magna fol. obovat. serratis subtus albus, fructibus cerasi magnitudinum.

At 10,000 feet, Composita penduliflora! Hemiphragma, Lobelioides, Brachymenium bryoides, Rhododendron minus ferrugineum, arboreum vel arbuscula, Rhododendron obovatum, foliis subtus albus, Rhododendron hispidum, Rosa microphylla, Bambusa, Spiræa of former ascent.

At 10,200 feet, Polygonum, Rheum, Hydrangea! Spiræa belloides, Hydrangea, Betuloides.

At 10,500 feet, Abies densa, but sparingly, Rhododendron ellipticum, foliis basi cordatis, Hypericum, Rhododendron microphyllum.

At 11,000 feet, no firs: nothing almost but Rhododendrons, R. ellipticum, and R. ellipticum foliis basi cordatis.

At 11,500 feet, Vaccinium, foliis ovatis spinuloso-dentatis, atratus fructex pygmæus repens.

Towards the Pass, the face of the mountain became more and more rugged, the vegetation more scanty, consisting of nothing but Rhododendrons.

At 12,000 feet, Eriogonum minus, Polygonum, Rheum, Rhodod. microphyllum and ellipticum foliis basi cordatis.

About the Pass, Trichostomum, *Xyris*, Abies densa, one small plant, Rosa, Eriogonum minus, Rhododendron microphyllum and ellipticum foliis basi cordatis.

On the more level ridge between this Pass and the summit, Rhododendrons still were most frequent, Triticoides umbellifera of Royle, Eriogonum majus, woods of Abies densa occurred a little below the path, Gentiana maxima, 4-pedalis folliculis bipollicaribus, Lilium uniflorum, Potentilla common between this and 9,000 feet, Rosa microphyllum, Juniperus, Epilobium minus of Dhonglaila, Rheum. Large black crow, Pedicularis, Saxifraga, Umbellifera alia, Compositæ, Spiræa.

At the summit, no woody vegetation was visible, except Rhododendrons; the firs being confined below.

The descent at first through Rhododendron, then for a long time entirely through vast woods of Abies densa, most of the larger trees of this are apparently blasted, it has a tabular form, and very sombre appearance, and can be recognized even at great distances by its black columnar palm-like appearance.

At 11,000 feet, Acer sterculiacea, Rosa microphylla, Ribes, which ceases below 10,000 feet, it is confined to the A. densa woods.

At 10,500 feet, Saxifraga, two species on moist banks, A. densa woods, small Umbellifera.

The sward commences at about 10,000 feet, and is common at 9,500 feet. It is clothed principally with the small bamboo noticed in similar places above Sanah. Berberis spathulata commences. It is with this sward that a new fir, with a larch-like look, which I call temporarily Abies spinulosa, commences, and continues down to the nullah, becoming more abundant as A. densa becomes less abundant, and finally usurping its place entirely. Rhododendron microphyllum continues to 9,600 feet, at which point Baptisoidea commences.

The vegetation hence to Bhoomlungtung consists entirely of Abies spinulosa, intermixed with a species very like Abies pendula, this appears at about 9,500 feet. The sward consists of small grasses, Juncus niveus, Gnaphalium, Hypericum of Moflong, suffrutex incertus, Juncus effusus at 9,000 feet, with Prinsepia utilis.

The marked indicators of great elevation are A. densa, Polygonum, Rheum! Eriogona! Rhododendron microphyllum, ellipticum, and ellipticum foliis basi cordatis, Epilobium, Triticoides, Holcoides, Umbellifera of Royle, Saxifragæ, Ribes, Juniperus.

The most marked peculiarity is the comparative absence of A. densa on the east side of the mountain, and its excessive abundance on the west. This valley may be justly called the valley of pines, for in no direction is any forest to be seen but those composed of pines. The change indeed is extraordinary, in other respects as indicated by the presence of a new Rosa and Prinsepia utilis. Another peculiarity is the appearance for the first time of A. spinulosa. The range of which is between 8 to 10,000 feet; this is a beautiful tree, and disposed in beautiful groups. The valley altogether is a beautiful one, and actually repays one for the trouble endured in getting access to it.

The temperature in crossing the ridge was below that on Dhonglaila, and below the freezing point at times. No inconvenience was felt by us from the elevation, but many of our servants suffered probably as much from fright as cold.

February 27th.—Halted.

February 28th.—This valley is certainly the prettiest place we have yet seen, the left bank is particularly level, but neither are of much breadth, the hills adjacent present rounded grassy patches, interspersed with beautiful groves of pines. The level space, as well as the more favourable sites on the slopes of the hills, are occupied by wheat cultivation, which is carried on in a more workman-like manner, than any of the previous cultivation I have hitherto seen. The fields are occasionally surrounded with stone walls, but generally only protected from the inroads of cattle by branches of thorny shrubs strewed on their edges. They are kept clean, and above all, manure is used: it is however dry and of a poor quality, apparently formed of animal and vegetable moulds. In some of the fields the surface is kept very fine, all stones and clods being carefully removed and piled up in various parts of the field, but whether these masses are again strewed over the ground. The plough is used, and penetrates to about four inches. Hoes and rakes are also used, but the angle of the handle is much too acute. Radishes are grown with the wheat: no rice is cultivated here.

The village Bhoomlungtung, at which we are stationed is, on the left bank of a branch of the Bhoomla nullah, a river of some size, but fordable in most places, its bed being subdivided. It is 8,668 feet above the sea. The houses are ordinary, but they are surrounded with stone walls. Our's, which is a portion of the Dhumpas or headman's, has a court-yard, surrounded by a stone wall, and the entrance is defended by a stout and large door. The natives invariably wear dark clothing, the colour being only rivalled by that of their skins, for I never saw dirtier people. The Bhooteas hitherto visited, were quite paragons of cleanliness compared to those we are now among. Half ruined villages are visible here and there, although otherwise the appearance of the valley is prosperous enough. The valley is surrounded on all sides by hills of great altitude, the lowest being 10,500 feet high. Snow is plentiful on the ridges, but it does not remain long below, although falls are frequent. No fish are to be seen in the river, which is otherwise as regards appearance as beautiful a trout stream as one could wish to have. The birds are the common sparrow, fieldfare, red-legged crow, magpie, skylark, a finch which flies about in large flocks, with a sub-forked tail, raven, red-tailed stonechat, larger tomtit, syras, long-tailed duck, and quail, which is much larger than that found in Assam. The woods are composed entirely of Abies pendula, a few A. spinulosa occur, intermixed, but the woods of the latter species are scarcely found below 9,500 feet. The ridges are clothed with the columnar Abies densa. In thickets a smaller Rosa, Rhododendron ellipticum, foliis basi cordatis, Rhododendron elliptica, foliis subtus argenteis, Rhodod. gemmis viscosis. Berberis asiatica, Hamamelidea? Bambusa microphyllum, Philadelphus, Thibaudia orbicularis, Mespilus microphyllus, Taxus or Abies Brunonis, Ilex dipyrena, occur. The sward shews small grasses, all past flower, Hemiphragma, Thymus, Dipsacus, Juncus niveus, Gnaphalia 2, 3, Potentilla.

The fields have Crucifera Lamium and Verbascum, a late biennial species, Caule simplici, Hemiphragma.

The marshy spots abound with Juncus effusus, and shew also a Primula out of flower, and a Xyris past flowering.

Along the bed of the river, Hippophae is the most common plant. Lastly, a few trees occur of Q. ilecifolia, which assumes a very handsome character, looking much like a Conifera at some distance, one group occurs near the village, and a solitary tree or two elsewhere. The other woody vegetables are Rosa fructibus hispidis, Cycnium, Pomacea arbuscula, and one or two other deciduous shrubs. The willow tree is also common.

March 1st.—Marched to Byagur, we were told that the march was a short one, and that we should continue throughout along the Bhoomlungtung river, which is called Tung-chiew. We did keep along this for about two miles, when we struck off into the hills: passing through a village, we continued rising for perhaps 1,000 feet, when we descended to a small nullah. Leaving this we commenced an ascent, and a very long one too, and continued to ascend until we surmounted the ridge overlooking the river, on which Byagur or Iugur is situated. To the place we descended, the march was fourteen miles, direction westerly. Highest ground traversed about 9,500 feet high. Road throughout winding round and up hills, through woods of Abies pendula: nothing of interest occurred. Magpies, crows, chatterer feeding on pine cones, common in woods at 9,000 feet. Passed two or three villages, all containing ruined houses. Direction we pursued was that of the Tung-chiew river, until we reached the ridge guiding the Byagur river to it: their junction takes place two or three miles below this place, Cycnium occurred on the road in plenty, also Sarcococea.

Horseshoe curlew, the same as we shot at Daimara, common in the Tung-chiew, along which the chief shrubs are Hippophae and Elæagnus, particularly in the islets which are not uncommon in its bed. The common water wagtail also occurs.

I find that the root of the common Potentilla is used here, as about Nunklow, as a substitute for *sooparee*, it is unpleasantly astringent.

Observed Rhododendron microphylla on the loftier ground; very high land, 18,000 feet visible to the south along the course of Tung-chiew, covered with heavy snow: Abies pendula is occasionally a beautiful tree, 100 feet high, and in appearance something like a cedar, the finest occurs at a monastery under a bluff rock, about one and a half mile from Bhoomlungtung on the Tung-chiew; Daphne papyriferæ occurred at 9,000 feet. The heaps of earth piled up in the fields before sowing, consist of burnt rubbish, the ashes are subsequently spread out. The manure consists entirely of vegetables: here I find that the pine leaves are piled up, and formed into manure by fermentation.

March 2nd.—Byagur, the Soobah's house is about 500 feet above us, and is a huge rambling edifice. We are in a village situated in a rather capacious valley, percolated by a large river, twice the size of the Tung-chiew, which is crossed by an ordinary bridge, the river runs close to the hills, which form the left bank, the right is a sort of plain, occupied by wheat cultivation, and which has apparently at a former period, been the bed of the river. In this valley other villages are visible, but they are small, and nothing indicates either fertility or prosperity. The valley is surrounded on all sides by high mountains, those towards Bhoomlungtung being lowest. To the north-east very high land is visible. The ridge which separates us from Tongse is, in the highest parts, certainly 12,000 feet, and covered with snow. The people are dirty to an excess.

Crow, sparrow, Alauda, are the birds here. Saw a fox, an animal of some size, with a beautiful brush. The botany is poor, the hills are clothed with the usual grasses, abundance of Abies pendula. The khets or fields present the old Lamium and Crucifera. The only trees are one of Q. ilecifolia, and one or two of Salix lanata.

March 3rd.—Cycnium is found here, but is put to no use. The crops which are now springing up are very poor, the soil being extremely bad, they are irrigated by means of canals, but terraces are not in use, the ground being too level, the embankments are much smaller than those used in rice cultivation.

The place is bleak in the extreme, and here, as often on the western face of the Himalaya, at this season a fierce diurnal wind rises directly the sun gets power, which always blows up the ravines or against the streams; draining these, it dies away towards evening, generally. It is cold in the extreme, and must check vegetation extremely. Syras, common here, as at Bhoomlungtung.

The ridge above this which is crossed coming from Bhoomlungtung, is 9,947 feet high, yet no snow was on the ground. The contrast between it and Pèmee in regard to snow and vegetation is remarkable; there the woods were thick, luxuriant, and varied, here nothing is to be seen but Abies pendula. I consider this a proof that A. pendula is a native of places below much snow, and that where snow abounds, it will not be found to extend above 8,000 feet. The dwarf bamboo of Sanah is common here, covering large patches of ground, Lamium of Bulphai in the vicinity of temples, and enclosing pagodas. The people here evince great skill in figures, but none in architecture.

The Soobah's house a castillated heterogeneous mansion, spread over much ground, the defences on one side reaching nearly to the level of the valley. The Kumpa dogs are fierce and handsome, with the bark of a mastiff, they are not apparently deterred by threats, but rather the contrary. A woman with dropsy, wrapped in filthy clothes, presented herself and evinced great anxiety to have her pulse felt, but the dirt of her clothes was such, that I made excuses.

Manure for the land consists of pine leaves, etc. mixed with cow-dung. The cattle are well littered; and grass is here of rather better description: all cattle are however in wretched condition notwithstanding, and the cows give very little milk. The houses of the poorer orders, are unornamented, but those of the better classes are always ornamented with a belt of red ochre outside. There are no large boulders in the river here, although it runs with violence. This is owing to the softness or tenacity of the rocks.

March 4th.—Our march commenced with a steep ascent up the ridge, forming the west boundary of the valley, surmounting this we proceeded on for some distance at about the same level, and thence descended rapidly to a nullah. We then ascended slightly, and subsequently descended to the valley, in which the village Jaisa is situated. The distance was nine miles; the march was pretty, almost entirely through fir woods, three villages were visible in a valley to the left, which is in fact the termination of the Jaisa one, but beyond the valleys no cultivation whatever was visible.

The first part was up a barren grassy slope, after which we entered fir woods, these at first were almost entirely constituted of Abies pendula.

At 9,000 feet Chimaphila, Berberis spathulata, Abies pendula, Bambusa microphylla of Sanah, Mespilus microphyllus, Rhododendron elliptica, foliis basi cordatis subtus argenteis, Philadelphus Lycopod. of Surureem, Gaultheria nummularifolia, Rhododendron viscosum.

At 9,300 feet, Abies spinulosa becomes more common, Rosa hispida and microphylla! Pinus cedroides commences, Dalibarda, Daphne papyracea, Thymus, Gnaphalia, Mespilus and Berberis, as before, Potentilla.

At 9,500 feet, snow lying on the path in sheltered places, Euphorbia, Gaultheria arboreoides, Hypnum rubescens, scolopendrioids, Pteris aquilina, Melianthus, Rosa, frutex erectus ramis hispidissimis, ramulis subglabratis, fructibus pendulis glabris, tubo-ovato, sepalis lanceolatis. Salix arbuscula, gemmis rubur glabris, foliis lanceolatis subtus glaucis, amentis fæminies pendulis, Bupleurum, Hydrangea, Spiræa densa belloides! Prunella, Pinus cedroides common at Potentilla.

At 9,700, 9,800, to 10,000 feet, Abies densa, a few trees, as usual many blasted, from lightning confined entirely towards the summit, Acer stercuilacea, Aruncus, Thibaudia orbicularis, A. spinulosa very common, A. pendula ceases, or at most only stunted plants occur, Mespilus microphyllus, Berberis spathulata, Baptisia, these were very common on west face, which is level enough and open.

Here also Pedicularis, Bupleurum, stunted Pteris aquilina, Polygonum, Rheum! Avena! Pendulous lichens luxuriant. Along the level tracts, the woods consisted entirely of Abies spinulosa, a minute Gentiana common on the sward.

The descent was steep to the ravine; half-way down A. pendula commenced to flourish, and towards the ravine it was more common than A. spinulosa, Rhododendron microphyllum was seen on this face at 9,500 feet, Verbascum at 9,200 feet, but most of the plants seen on the east face were not found on this. Acer sterculiacea, however occurred at 9,800 feet, otherwise pines were the most prominent feature.

At the nullah, Dipsacus, Elæagnus, Salix lanata, Artemisia major, Daphne papyracea, Rhododendron viscosum, Mespilus microphyllus, Rosa hispida, spinus acutissimis, Bambusa of Sanah, Plectranthus a large suffruticose annual species, common in all the same altitudes, were observed. The subsequent descent was through woods of A. pendula, with a few of A. spinulosa intermixed.

The limits of A. densa, A. spinulosa and A. pendula, Melianthus, Acer sterculiacea, Thibaudia orbicularis, A. cedroides, Rosa microphylla, Pedicularis, Hydrangea, Baptisia, Berberis spathulata were well determined. They may be expressed as follows: A. densa, 10 to 13,000 feet, A. spinulosa, 9 to 10,500 feet, A. pendula, 6 to 9,000 feet, Melanthus, 9,500 feet, Acer sterculiaceum, 9,800 to 10,000 feet, Thibaudia orbicularis, 10,000 feet, A. cedroides, 9,000 to 9,800 feet, Rosa microphylla, 9,800 to 13,000 feet, Pedicularis, 10 to 12,500 feet, Hydrangea, 4 to 10,000 feet unless two species are confounded, Baptisia, 9 to 9,800 feet, Berberis spathulata, 9 to 10,000 feet.

Jaisa is a good sized village for Bootan, and the houses are rather large. We were lodged in the castle, a large building, with a capacious flagged court-yard, surrounded by galleries: we were housed in the grand floor of the higher portion fronting the gate. A good deal of wheat cultivation occurs around. The village is situated in a small nullah, surrounded on all sides by pine-clad hills. The vegetation is precisely the same as at Juggur, with the exception of a Ligustrum, which is common along the nullah. Larks, red-legged crows and ravens, abound here.

March 5th.—Our march consisted of a progress along levelish ground up the river, occasionally rounding small eminences: we then commenced the ascent of a ridge, the summit of which we reached about half past-twelve. Snow is common above 9,000 feet. The descent was steep and uninterrupted from about 2,000 feet, when we reached a small river. Thence we ascended a little to descend again, we continued over a ravine at nearly the same level, for sometime proceeding over undulated ground: on reaching the debouchure of the ravine into a larger one running north and south, we commenced to descend rapidly until we came to an elevation situated above Tongsa, to this place the descent was excessively steep. The march was thirteen miles long, the direction west.

At a temple near Jaisa found the Juniper of Oongar in flower, and arboreous, attaining a height of about 40 feet. The whole march up, nearly to the summit, was through pine woods, A. pendula and spinulosa being intermixed for sometime. I noticed Primula globifera, Eucalypta, Thibaudia orbicularis, Aruncus, Rosa ramis hispidis, Dipsacus, Prunella, Potentilla, Gnaphalium, Sphagnum, Daphne papyracea, Tofieldia, Gaultheria nummularoides, as we approached the base of the ridge or rather the spot at which the ascent commenced. At this place Abies cedroides commenced, and Abies pendula became uncommon.

On a bank here, I gathered abundance of mosses, Bartramia, Dicrana, etc. and some Jungermanniæ.

The ascent was through precisely similar vegetation, in one place it was exceedingly pretty, consisting of sward with pines. Here snow was lying on the ground in sheltered places to the depth of several inches. The ground hence was levelish, but between this place and the summit a rise of a hundred feet took place. Between these places Abies densa, cedroides and spinulosa, occurred, but this was uncommon, Rosa ramis hispidis, Salix of yesterday, Bambusa of Sanah, stunted Pteris aquilina, Betuloidea, Hydrangea, Hypnum rufescens, scolopendrioid as well as below: Spiræa belloides, Rhododendron obovatum, which varies on the same plant with ferruginous and white leaves, Sphagnum, Thibaudia orbicularis. On sward Gentiana minima.

As the snow increased, Abies cedroides became less, Abies densa more common. At the very summit Parnassia, Polygonum rheum, Composita penduliflora, Rhododendron hispidum, Berberis spathulata, which had occurred previously, Vaccinium pumilium, ciliatum, Gentiana minima, Swertia, Cnicus, Compositæ frequent, Labiata spicata of Dhonglaila.

The descent was at first open, through swardy places: here Acer sterculiaceum, Geranium scandens, Avena, Abies densa, Juniperus fruticosa, raro arbuscula.

At 9,800 feet, Rhododendron foliis lanceolato-oblongis subtus ferruginea tomentosis, arborea, became very common, forming large woods, Abies densa interspersed, Juniperus, Betuloidea which has six or seven layers of bark, the *boj-putah* of Hindoostan according to Blake, Rosa microphylla, Hemiphragma, Daphne papyracea, Dicranum atratum, etc.

At 9,500 feet, Clematis, Berberis asiatica, commences, Betula, common Andropogoneous grasses.

At 9,300 feet, Primula pulcherrima, Abies cedroides very common, Abies densa ceasing, Buddlæa purpurescens, Aruncus, Bupleurum.

At 9,200 feet, Lonicera villosa, Vaccinium cyaneum, Bambusa alia, Abies densa ceasing.

At 9,000 feet, the jungle now became humid, Gaultheria flexuosa, Mespilus microphyllus, Quercus ilecifolia, Tetrantheroides baccis nigris, Gaultherium nummularifolia common, Rubia cordifolia! Hydrangea.

At 8,900 feet, Junipers ceases, woods of Q. ilecifolia and Pinus cedroides, Rosa microphylla, shrubby Rhododendrons, that which was arboreous previously now becoming shrubby, Berberis asiatica,

Taxus or Abies brunonis! Lomaria of Khegumpa, Rhododendron foliis oblongis subtus punctatis ferrugineis, Rubus, Primula Stuartii! Quercus folliis, Castaneæ, Ilex, Betuloid, continues.

At 8,500 feet, Panax rhododendrifolia, Thibaudia obovata, Taxus ophiopogon angustissimus, Rhododendron formosum majus! Smilax ruscoideus vel gaultherifolia! Primula pulcherrima, very common.

At 8,200 feet, Spiræa decomposita, Thibaudia obovata very common. No firs, woods of oaks and Rhododendron majus, Panax rhododendrifolia and another species; Bambusa.

At the nullah, same vegetation, Tetranthera nuda, Primula pulcherrima, Valeriana violifola, Eurya acuminata, Daphne papyrifolia, Fragaria, Potentilla supina, Rumex of Khegumpa, Poa annua, Stellaria media and angustifolia, Rhodoracea deflexa!

At 8,000 feet, the woods at this elevation have the same characters, Rhododendron argenteum becomes common, Q. ilecifolia and Castaneæ facies, both very handsome and large trees, covered with pendulous mosses, Sphæropteris, Saxifragea viridis, fleshy Urticea, Oxalis major on sward at the same elevation, Vaccinium cyaneum, Mespilus microphyllus, Artemisia major, Gnaphalium, Dipsacus, Elæagnus in woods, Tetranthera nuda, Taxus, Gaultheria flexuosa nummularifolia, Vaccinium cyaneum, Lomaria, Lonicera villosa, paper plant, Thibaudia orbicularis, Hedera.

At 7,800 feet, towards open barren hills, Indigofera canescens, Q. robur, Spiræa decomposita, Anthistiria minor, Composita penduliflora, Alnus of Beesa, Juncus effusus, Viburnum cærulescens, Xyris, Scripus fuscescens of Tassangsee, Gaultheria arborea and fruticosa, Polygonum rheoides, Smilax auriculata, Saccharum aristata, Lobelia pyramidalis, Stauntonia latifolia, Salix lanata, Deutzia.

At 7,500 feet, Quercus tomentosa commences, between this and Tongsa, Berberis asiatica is very common, Rosa sp., quarta, Cyaneum dycopod. of Surureem, Ilex dipyrena, Tuipus, Kysoor of Churra, Apple, Gleichenia major, Rubus deltoideus. In wheat fields, 7,500 feet, Crucifera, Thlaspa, Lamium, Ervum, are found, Vaccinium cyaneum continues to 7,000 feet, this Mespilus microphylla, Berberis asiatica, Cycnium, Lycopod. of Surureem, Ilex, Daphne papyriferæ, are the only elevational plants found between 8 and 9,000 feet, and which continue low down. All the others ceased with the jungles.

March 13th.—Tongsa: this, although the second place in the kingdom, is a poor wretched village, the houses, always excepting the palace, are poorer than ordinary, abounding in rats, fleas, and other detestable vermin. Our reception would seem to be uncordial: we are miserably housed in the heart of the village, which is a beggarly one. On descending the hill some people in the Pillo's house behaved very insolently, roaring out, and making most insolent signs for me to dismount, of which of course I took no notice: sparrow-hawk was seen at 8,000 feet. There is but little cultivation, indeed the adjoining hills are barren in the extreme. The little cultivation there is of barley, which is now in the ear, and decent enough; the crops being much better than any we have yet seen, although in many fields it is difficult to see any crop at all. The village, including the houses on the surrounding adjoining heights does not contain thirty houses. There is one flock of sheep, which are in good condition, some small shawl-goats, and a few cattle, but of a lighter breed than the Mithans, from which they are very distinct, and which we have scarcely seen since crossing Dhonglaila, the first high ridge. There is some rice cultivation along the nullah or torrent, on which the village is situated. Pears, peaches likewise occur, and are now both in flower. The hills around are bare, nothing but shrubby vegetation being visible, the tree-jungle not descending below 7,500 feet, except on one spur to the south-west, on which it reaches nearly to our present level.

The shrubby vegetation consists of Hamamelidæ, Salix, Gaultheria fruticosa, Rosa, Rubus, Pomacea, Elæagnus, Berberis asiatica, among which Artemisia major occurs on sward. Primula Stuartii, Potentilla and P. supina, Oxalis acetoseltoides, Juncus, Bartramia, Polytrichum glaucum, Fragaria vesca. In the fields Lamium, Crucifera, Thlaspi, Gnaphalium aureum, Prenanthoid, Fragaria indica, Viola, Ranunculus, Oxalis acetosella, Poa annua.

Urtica urens, and urentior occur about the houses, Cupressus pendula and a Magnoliaceous tree, with exquisitely fragrant blossoms.

The palace is a huge, long, straggling piece of patch-work, of ordinary construction, and less imposing than that of Byagur, which the Pillo makes his summer residence on the Bhoomlungtung; it is however ornamented with three gilt umbrellas. It is situated on the bank of the nullah, and defended by some outworks, 6 to 700 feet above it; to the east, these might, from their situation, be easily demolished by stones. The palace itself is commanded in every direction, particularly by the hill, along which we came from Jaisa; indeed a person might jump from the summit of this on to the outpost, and thence on to the palace; so precipitous is the descent.

The people, above all those hitherto seen, are dirty in their persons, uniting curiosity with no small share of obstinacy and impertinence in their manners. The birds are the blackbird, a black mina, the house-sparrow, sparrow-hawk, larger crow, domestic pigeons, kites, and hoopoo. The red-legged crows I have heard once, but far above, nor do I think that they ever visit this. The productions being essentially different from those of the elevated valleys we have lately quitted. Can those valleys be the *steps* to the table-land of Thibet to which they must be near, and which is reached sooner in that direction than any other? The idea of the high vallies in question being steps to table-land is perhaps corroborated by the fact, that the table-land is said to be within two days' journey from Byagur.

Our interview with the Pillo took place on the 15th, it was conducted with some state, and with some impertinence. The latter was indicated by delaying us at the door of the audience room, the former by the attendance of more numerous and better dressed attendants than usual. Two Pillos were present. The incense as usual was burning, and the Pillos, both old and new, were seated [illegible]ore some large Chinese-looking figures. The only novel ceremo[illegible]s the praying over a mess of something which I imagine was meant for tea; in the prayer all joined, when finished the beverage was handed to the Pillos, who, however, were contented with merely tasting it. Before this some was strewn on the floor in front, and some to the right of the chieftains. The castle was in places crowded with people, no less than 5 to 600, but all were as dirty as usual. None but the immediate attendants appeared armed. The new Pillo is a dark low-looking man, with an incipient goitre, the old one a more decent aristocratic looking person, good-looking and very fair. The presents were of course beggarly, consisting of indifferent oranges, wretched plantains, sugarcane of still worse quality, and ghee of an abominable odour.

March 17*th*.—We still remain here, and do not expect to leave for two or three days. The weather is unsettled, and the sun increasing in power daily. The new Soobahs left to-day for their appointments, with the exception of the Dewangur one. Pigs are here fed on boiled nettle leaves: old ladies may be seen occasionally busily employed in picking the leaves for this purpose, and which they do by means of bamboo pincers or tweezers. A few plantains may be met with here, but in a wretched state. Rice may be seen 500 feet above this, on the north of the castle, the slope of a hill being appropriated to its cultivation; the terraces above, owing to the inclination, are very narrow, and from the paucity of straw, the crops must, I should infer, be very poor.

March 22*nd*.—To-day we took our leave of the Pillo, who received us in a room to the south of the castle. He was friendly enough, but begged for presents unconscionably. He was surrounded by a considerable number of more mean looking persons than ordinary. On the previous meeting he talked openly of being at enmity with the present Deb Rajah, but on this occasion he said little on the subject.

The castle is an ill-built, and worse arranged building, the windows and loopholes being so placed as to afford every facility for shooting into the air. In a court-yard, several tiger skins brought from the plains, are suspended.

It now appears that this Pillo, who said previously that the new Deb was never installed, is himself an usurper, previously handing the old Deb from the throne. This latter personage appears to be by far the more popular of the two. The Pillo must now have great influence, as all the posts in his division, are either held by his own sons, or by his more influential servants. The sons by the bye are, so long as they remain in the presence, treated like ordinary servants. Joongar is held by one of his sons, a lad of about eighteen, of plain but pleasing appearance and of good manners. He visited us yesterday, and his newly acquired rank sat easily on him. The old Pillo no doubt owes his rank to his having been the father of the lad chosen to be Dhurma Rajah, he is himself very evidently low-born and low-bred, and compared with the former one, so poor a specimen, that the greater popularity of the former is not to be wondered at. From all we have heard, they are contemptible rulers, as they appear to do nothing but intrigue for power among themselves. Changes are hence excessively frequent, and were they attended with much bloodshed, the country would be depopulated.

This evening we had ample proof that the Bhootea houses are not water-proof. Heavy showers occurred with thunder and dense clouds from the south-west.

March 23*rd*.—We left Tongsa, proceeding through the castle, and thence struck down to the river Mateesun. The descent was very steep, and amounted to about 1,200 feet. The river is crossed by an ordinary bridge, it is a large and violent stream and contains fish, some of which, seen by Blake, were of large size. Crossing this, we continued throughout the remainder of the march, gradually rising along the ridges bounding the Tongsa river. We continued rising until we reached our halting place, Taseeling. In one or two places, the road was completely built up; ascending by zig-zags up, in some degree, perpendicular cliffs. The distance was seven miles.

Proceeding to the bridge, observed Rubus deltoideus, Pomacea, Quercus tomentosa, Artemisia major, Cycnium, Gaultheria arborea and fruticosa, Buddlæa, Quercus altera, Indigofera cana, Gaylussacia serratoides, Hedera, Thibaudia myrtifolia, Pomacea sauraugifolia, Viburnum cærulescens, Quercus robur budding, Pterogonium, Fragaria, Duchesnia.

The remaining hills were much similar, generally very bare, clothed with partial woods of Q. tomentosa, Rhododendron minus; the oak changing to Q. robur, as we increased our elevation. Near the bridge noticed Bucklandia, Erythrina, which is likewise found at Tongsa, Maesa salicifolia, Urena lobata, Cnicus, Mimosea! Arbuscula inermis, Senecio scandens in flower, Araliacea subscandens, Didymocarp. contort., a Solenia, Betuloideus, Panax curcifolia, Alnus, Arundo, Anthistiria arundinacea, Cerasus, Tricerta unisexualis, at 6,000 feet.

At about the same elevation Rhododendron minus becomes common, Primula Stuartii, Dipsacus, Verbenacea exostemma, Scleria, Valeriana, Tradescantia on rocks, with Saxifraga ligularia in full flower at 6,500 feet.

About this, 6,500 to 6,800 feet, Spiræa decomposita, Hamamelidea here a tree, occasionally but small, Erythroxyloides, Conyza nivea and communis, Gleichenia major, Parochetus communis on wet dripping rocks, Woodwardia, Clematis ternata.

At 7,000 feet, Berberis asiatica, Q. tomentosa ceased, its place being supplied by Q. robur, Verbascum, Juncus, Gaultheria nummularioid, Mespilus microphyllus, Scirpus fuscus of Tassangsee, Thibaudia gaultherifolia, Rubia cordifolia, Azalea, and Daphne capitulis pendulis, Ranunculus uniflorus, Hydroctyle.

Taseeling is situated about 2,000 feet above the Mateesun, on a nakedish hill; about it there is some cultivation, and one or two villages, one towards Tongsa and above Taseeling of some size. The place itself consists of a large house, with some fine specimens of Cypressus pendula, the east face of the house has the red stripe, indicative of rank. Its elevation is about 7,300 feet, close to the house I observed the Lamium of Bulphai, Bursa pastoris, Oxalis corniculata, Cnicus out of flower, Artemisia major, Fragaria vesca, Daphne pendula and papyracea, Hemiphragma, Composita pendulifolia, Lycopod. of Surureem, Hypericum, Berberis asiatica, Juniperus; Barley cultivation, and a Pomaceous arbuscula, armat. ovar. 5-discretis. The red-legged crow occurs here, and a thrush much resembling our English one. The raven of course occurs. A curious opening occurs in the hills at Taseeling, affording a prospect of the Bag Dooar plains, seven days' journey distant, but the road is bad.

March 24th.—Leaving Taseeling we commenced to ascend until we rounded a ridge, when we turned to the west, we then commenced to descend, but slightly, winding over undulated surfaces of barrenish hills. After sometime we reached heavy tree jungle, the road proceeding in the same undulating manner, so that it was impossible to say whether we had risen or descended. About one we came on the river, up the ravine of which we had been advancing ever since turning to the west. This stream is of some size, very violent and rapid, but fordable. Near this is a large pagoda, built after the old Boodhistical style, and the only respectable one we have yet seen, its site is pretty, and it is ornamented above with eyes and a fiery-red nose. Leaving this we ascended along one bank of the river, until we reached Chindupjee, our halting place; this was distant from the pagoda three miles, and from Taseeling twelve. This latter part reminded me of Bhoomlungtung; firs being the prevailing trees, and the valley having more pretensions to the name than usually happens.

We encamped in a beautiful spot, the house being situated on fine sloping sward, surrounded by picturesque trees of Q. ilecifolia, a few tall Cypressus standing up in the centre. The village is a few feet above, and of average size, although it looks from a little distance to be of considerable size. The march throughout was beautiful, especially after entering the wooded tract; this reminded me of the march near Khegumpa, the woods were here and there very picturesque, glades and swards abounding, water was very abundant here, and this no doubt causes the development of so much vegetation.

At 7,800 feet, Thibaudiaceæ very common, Rhododendron two species, Gaultheria flexuosoides, Thibaudia obovata, Caudata myrtifolia, Hydrangea, which I find to be a climber, Rhododendron majus, commencing, pine wood; chatterers heard here. Hills naked or covered here and there with stunted wood; marshy places common.

At 7,600 feet, Lomaria of Khegumpa, Tetranthera nuda, Sphæropteris, pear and apple, Q. tomentosa, Magnolia grandiflora begins, Polygonum rheoides, Daphne pendula, which is used, as well as the other, both here and in Nipal in the manufacture of paper: brick-red black-pate.

At this same elevation farther on, Rosa hispida! Gillenia, Juncus, Rhododendron deflexa, Smilax gaultherifolia, Spiræa bella, Dipsacus, Spiræa decomposita, Ilex, Vaccinium cyaneum, Magnolia grandiflora very common. The country now becomes more wooded, the woods being confined to moist ravines, and in other situations where water is very plentiful, the woods throughout become continuous, and forming the large forests before mentioned :, having the open spaces between the woods covered with sward, on which Gentiana pygmæa, and Fragaria are very common.

As we approached the wood or forest, Pinus cedroides commenced, and towards the valley of Chindupjee this species became very common, Rumex occurred throughout in wet places, also at Taseeling. Geranium is common also in wet places, Stauntonia latifolia, Potentilla, Duchesnoides, Tussilago of Churra, on the confines of wood and on it. Here the orange-breasted trochilus occurred. The mass of the wood is formed of a fine Quercus, resembling Q. glauca, it is a beautiful and a shady tree. Next to it in abundance is Rhododendron majus, now in full flower, and forming a beautiful object, Rhododendron minus ceases with the barrener tracts. Magnolia is very conspicuous, Pinus cedroides common towards the pagoda; Eurya not rare, Gaultheria nummulifolia continues throughout, Valeriana violifolia, Oxalis acetoselloides, Bryum, Butia purpurea, Sambucus, Saxifraga of Bulphai, and another species, Bambusa microphylla, Swertia, Luzula, Thibaudia orbicularis, Primula Stuartii, occurred between the commencement of the ascent and the pagoda; at between 7,300 to 7,600 feet, Magnolia odoratis.

At the pagoda and village, Pinus cedroides, P. pendula, Bambusa of Sanah, Mespilus microphyllus, Magnolia grandiflora, Berberis asiatica, Q. anthoxylia, Coriaria, Rosa altera of Bhoomlungtung, Elæagnus, Salix and Allium of Bulphai, occur.

Chindupjee is situated on a rivulet close to the confluence, with a larger stream. Around it, or at least between the village and the larger stream, picturesque patches of sward bordered with a very picturesque oak. Q. ilecifolia occur; this tree predominates all about the village, it is certainly the prettiest place we have yet seen.

Some cultivation occurs around, chiefly of barley, with a little portion of radishes. The valley is surrounded by comparatively low mountains, most of which are rather bare, many are transversely furrowed on the surface, this may arise from their having been at some former period under cultivation.—The prevailing trees on the surrounding heights are firs, Pinus pendula and cedroides. No fish are to be seen in the river. The birds are the raven, white-necked starling, *bull-finch*, crimson and yellow shrikelets, blue tomtits, lesser ditto with two stripes on the head, white-rumped waterchat, red-tailed chesnuty sparrow.

The plants are Q. ilecifolia, Magnolia grandiflora, Laurinea, Hamamelidioides, Castanea aromatica, Pinus cedroides and pendula, Bambusa microphylla, and B. of Sanah which may be a variety depending on its marshy sites, Rhododendron minus, Salix, Mespilus microphyllus, Gaultheria nummularoides, Elæagnus, Marchantia, Swertia, Rumex, Daphne papyracea, Dipsacus, Artemisia major, Berberis asiatica, Rosa hispida, Rubus cæsius, Stauntonia latifolia, Tofieldioid of Sanah and Pemee, Taxus, Mespilus microphyllus, Ilex dipyrena, Oxalis acetoselloid, Thymus, Lycopodium of Surureem, Juniperus.

Bamboos split and inverted, and then placed in the ground, are used to scare away beasts from the cornfields.

March 26th.—Left at seven and a half and proceeded along the river which runs by Chindupjee, the path running over the spurs of the hills, forming its right bank. After proceeding about four miles, we crossed the nullah, changing our direction, and proceeding up a tributary, until we reached a prettily situated, and rather large village, thence we commenced to ascend over naked slopes with intervening woods, until we reached the base of the chief ascent, which is not very steep, although of good length, chiefly over naked hills. On reaching the summit, which is about 10,000 feet high, we commenced to descend, and the descent continued uninterruptedly and steeply until we reached Rydang, where we halted.

We passed only one village, which is about five miles from Chindupjee, and of similar size, but we passed in the more elevated places two temporary ones, apparently intended for the residence of the herdsmen of yâks or chowry-tailed cows, as a herd of these animals was seen feeding near each place.

The march throughout was beautiful, in the more elevated and drier portions, winding over swardy slopes or through woods of fir trees: on the descent from 9,000 feet downwards, passing through beautiful forests, chiefly of oak, and diversified in every possible way. The long-tailed pie was met with in the first portion, about 7,800 feet, the speckled chatterers at 8,500 feet, red shrikelet at 7,800 feet, and a new hawk at 8,300 feet. I observed the water-ouzel again as high as 8,000 feet. The new plants were a Carex, 6,500 feet, a sileneous plant past flowering, from the *same* limestone formation.

At 7,800 feet, and not far from Chindupjee, Pinus spinulosa again re-appears, it becomes common towards the village alluded to, and continues throughout the ascent, up to 9,300 feet, P. cedroides was uncommon during the first part of the march, its place being occupied by P. spinulosa, afterwards it re-appeared, and continued abundant up to 9,300 feet, it re-appeared on the descent about the same elevation, and continued to about 8,000 feet. Abies densa commences at the base of the chief ascent: at 10,000 feet, it is the only fir to be seen, it descends but a short way on the Rydang side. In the higher portions it occurred mixed with a Juniper, which in proper places becomes a small but elegant tree.

At the village on 7,000 feet, observed Rosa hispida, Ligustrum of Jaisa, Philadelphus, Pinus spinulosa common, as also Pinus cedroides, Bambusa of Sanah very common. Near this, larks were heard soaring high above us.

At 8,500 feet, Pendulous lichens becoming plentiful, Lonicera villosa.

At 9,000 feet, Abies densa appears, Acer sterculium, Betula, Bogh Pata, Rhododendron fruticosa, foliis ellipticis basi cordatis.

At 9,300 feet, Abies densa common, P. cedroides rare, spinulosa 0, pendùla 0, Rosa hispida, Gaultheria nummularioid, which as usual continued throughout, Hypnum scolopendroid, Sphagnum, Bogh Pata very common, Rhododendron foliis ellipticis basi cordatis subtus argenteis, which I found on the descent as low as 8,000 feet.

At 9,500 feet, Bogh Pata very common, trees covered with Pendulous lichens, Bambusa of Sanah, Abies densa everywhere.

At 10,000 feet, Abies densa, Juniperus, Rhododendron obovata, foliis subtus argenteis; I am not sure whether this, is a variety or not, but it indicates greater elevation than the ferruginous one, Rhododendron gemmis, viscosis, foliis lanceolatis, supra venosis, subtus subargenteis very common, Gnaphalium, Mespilus microphyllus, Rosa hispida, Swertia, Berberis spathulata, Orthotuck, Cerastum inflatum, Hemiphragma, Bogh Pata, Primula globifera, Pedicularis, Dicranum nigrescens, etc. Limonia, Laureah.

Daphne papyraceæ occurs at the same elevation, chiefly on the side of the descent. From this place an opening is visible to the north-west, occupied by low hills. Juniperus very fine occurs. Compositæ abundant. Snow lies in the hollows and sheltered woods.

At 9,600 feet, Lonicera villosa, Rosa microphylla, Buddlæa purpurescens! Berberis spathulata, Spiræa belloides, Hydrangea! Rhododendron foliis lanceolatis, etc. as above, forming thick woods, Abies densa, Bogh Pata, Bambusa, Limonia lanceolata.

At 9,400 feet, Prunella, Cerastium inflatum, Labiata spicata, Baptisia! High ground 14 to 15,000 feet, is seen forming a lofty heavily snowed ridge to the north.

At 9,000 feet, Pinus cedroides re-appears, Bogh Pata, Rhododendron as before, Daphne papyraceæ, Thibaudia orbicularis, Limonia lanceolata, Dalibarda, Polygonum rheum!

At 8,800 feet, Rhododendron hispida, Abies densa ceased, Limonia lanceolata common, Lonicera villosa, Rubus triphyllus, Acer! Taxus! Primula Stuartii! Rubia cordifolia!!

At 8,500 feet, Chimaphila, Rhododendron obovata-ferrugina! Pinus cedroides, here and there, of immense size, diameter of one-six feet, Lycopodium of Surureem, Bogh Pata, Gaultheria flexuosa, Q. ilecifolia, also a very large and tall tree.

At 8,400 feet, Taxus very common, Smilax gaultherifolia, Olea, Sarcococea very common, Thibaudia orbicularis, Laurinea, Hamamaloides. Beautiful glades here occurred, trees covered with mosses: another fine oak, Q. castaneoides commences, Daphne papyraceæ very common, Composita penduliflora, Hemiphragma, Rhododendron elliptica, foliis basi cordatis subtus punctatis, Ilex! Berberis intermedia, Laurinea uniflora, large Umbellifera of Rodoole descent.

At 8,000 feet, Acer, Primula Stuartii, Rhododendron majus! R. argentea commences.

At 7,500 feet, Cedar ceased, Rhododendron majus very common, Taxus diminishing, Sphæropteris, Ericinia solorææfolia, Lomaria of Khegumpa, Thibaudia orbicularis ceases.

At 7,300 feet, Berberis pinnata, Spiræa bella, Cycnium, apple tree. Here we emerged on open space in front of a hill, on which several detached houses stood, around which Pinus pendula was very common. Barley cultivation. Several small villages visible around, and to the north, in front of the snowy ridge, a curious truncated mountain was seen, its apex covered with snow.

Magnolia! Conaria! Cycnium, Viburnum canescens! Gaultheria arborea, Berberis intermedia very common, Fragaria.

At 7,200 feet, Q. tomentosa! the others have ceased, Gaultheria fruticosa, Rhododendron arborea, minus and argentea, in fine flower, Eurya æcuminata, Smilax, Gaultherifolia, Thibaudia caudata, Q. robur, Gleichenia major, Salix as before, Artemisia major, Rumex, Valeriana violifola, Rosa, Berberis asiatica, Ervicia crucifera, Thlaspi, Callitriche, Calamus.

The curious features are, the absence of Thibaudia obovata on the descent, and of Mespilus microphyllus, the substitution of Thibaudia orbicularis, and its low descent, the abundance of Taxus, size of the cedar and Q. ilecifolia, the re-appearance at same elevation of Magnolia grandiflora, occurrence of Rubia cordifolia, at such an elevation, etc.

Rydang is prettily situated towards the bottom of a rather narrow valley. There is a good deal of barley cultivation about it. I also noticed Cycnium, Celopecurus, Acorus Calamus, Corydalis! Fragaria, Cardamina, Rosa, Berberis, Ilex, Plantago, Rumex, Viola, Artemisia major, Daphne papyraceæ, Gentiana pygmæa of Khegumpa, Houttuynia! Pomacea, Callitriche, Dipsacus, Berberis pinnata, Elæagnus, Q. robur, ilecifolia. Of birds the long-tailed pie! is common. Berberis asiatica, Viburnum, Caneun, apple, Quercus microcarpus, Orthodon, Pteris aquilina, Ophiopogon, Angustis, Valeriana violifolia, Urtica urentium, Stellaria media, Eurya acuminata, Betula.

March 27th.—Our march commenced with a steep descent to the Gnee, a river of average size. We then continued descending along it for sometime, crossing it once on our way: we then diverged up a small nullah, and then commenced a very steep ascent, of about 2,000 feet. After attaining this, we proceeded through woods, or over sward at about the same elevation, still continuing along the Gnee. We subsequently commenced to descend at first through fine oak woods, then over barren naked hills. We reached Santagoung, about three and a half miles distance in a direct line, but fourteen miles by the road, highest point traversed 8,000 feet; lowest reached 6,000.

During first part of descent, noticed one or two straggling cedars and Taxus, Primula Stuartii, the woods were formed by Quercus robur, tomentosa, Gaultheria arborea, Rhododendron minus, Scabiosa re-appears, Clematis nova species, Sambucus, Rubus cresius, Composita pendulifolia, etc. as at Rydang.

Along the Gnee, the beech became plentiful, as also two Viburnums, both trees, together with the Cupulifera of Tongsa was here common and in fine foliage. Juglans, Incerta of Boodoo, Gaultheria, Mimosa arborea, Cupressus pendula, Conaria, Berberis racemosa and pinnata, Quercus microcarpus, Woodwardia, Thibaudia myrtifolia, Marlea! Cucurbitaceæ menispermoides, Alnus of Beesa, Polygonium rheoides, Mespilus microphyllus! Gentiana pygmæa, Salix, Pyrus. The birds were the usual water birds, viz. ouzel, slaty-white rump, slaty-red tail, white-pated chat.

On the smaller nullah Bucklandia, Viburnum microphyllum, Bucklandia!

The ascent was at first through dry woods of Rhododendron minus, Q. tomentosa, Gaultheria arborea, a Taxus or two occurred at 7,000 feet, Indigofera cana, Rosa, Gaultheria fruticosa of Sanah aristatum.

At 7,000 feet, the same vegetation continued, Rhododendron minus very common, Pendulous lichens commencing.

At this elevation, in more moist spots, woods thick, differently constituted, Quercus glauescense, Castaneoides ilecifolia, here and there Rhododendron majus, Magnolia grandiflora.

Gaultheria fluxuosa, Pinus cedroides rare, Vaccinium cyaneum, Rosa hispida! Saxifraga! Thibaudia orbicularis and caudata, Mespilus microphyllus, Azalea, Ilex, Symplocos, Tussalago of Churra, Acer, Thibaudia obovata, Pendulous mosses abundant.

The remainder of the vegetation afforded little of interest; consisted of stunted oaks, Q. tomentosa, Gaultheria arborea, Rhododendron minus: Serissoides reappears near Santagoung, Pinus longifolia, plantains.

The valley to the left towards Santagoung is on the left side well populated and cultivated.

March 28th.—Santagoung, a small village 6,300 feet above the sea, situated on bare hills, between two loftier ridges. Country around well inhabited and well cultivated in the terrace style: villages numerous. Pinus longifolia, Rosa, Azalea, etc. occur here as before. A lake or jheel was observed 500 feet, below the village of some extent, formed in a natural hollow, abounding with Scirpus trigueter of Churra, and Hydropeltis. Water-fowl, snipe, and red pie-like peewit or plover.

The march commenced with a steep descent, which continued until we reached the river.

Crossing this we ascended 1,000 feet, and then proceeded in an undulating manner over naked hills until we reached Thain, distance six miles; the greatest descent was about 1,800 feet, ascent 1,000 feet; the country naked; no forest. The hills for some extent towards Thain appeared from some cause very red.

But little interesting vegetation occurred: noticed a huge Cupressus pendula, half-way to the Gnee. Vegetation otherwise much the same as towards Tassgong, Valeriana violæfolia, Azalea, Campanula linearis, Rubus deltoides, Aspidium macroser., Artemisia major, Pinus longifolia straggling, only plentiful near Thain, Anthistiria minor! Primula Stuartii, Mimulus, Gentiana pumila, Alnus, Flemingia secunda, Morus rubescoides, Salix, Quercus, Viburnum microphyllum.

At the river Cæsalpinia! Ficus obliqua! Desmodium, Salix, Indigofera cana, Arundo, Luculia.

On the ascent Holcus, Elæagnus, Santalacea, Clematis cana, Senecionoides, Conyza vulgaris, Emblica, Schænanthus, Phyllanthus ruber, Q. tomentosa, Desmodium vestilum, Briedleia obovata! Nerium canum, Euphorbia antiquorum, Jasminum of Benka, Ligustrum conaria, Mesp. microphyllus (are these two species confounded by me, as the larger-leaved one never descends so low?), Lerissoides, Osbeckia linearis, Euphorbia, Gordonia, Gymnobotrys. Red-legged crow; in descent altitude 5,800 feet, the most common plant is a species of Berberis very nearly allied to B. asiatica. Rain in the afternoon.

March 29th.—Mimulus, Acorus Calamus, Quercus robur, Rhododendron minus, P. longifolia, Gymnobotrys, Campanula linearifolia, Rosa tetrapetala, Gordonia, Salix, Verbena officinalis, majus, rugus, Lemna, Gentiana, Hypericum japonica, Indigofera cana, Schænanthus, Senecio, Buddlea of Nulka, Pyrus, wheat, Ervum, Vicia, Potentilla, Q. tomentosa, Cypressus, Ficus, Berberis, Phyllanthus ruber.

Blackbird, sparrow-hawk, and Hoopoe about houses; it has a curious hoop, varied with a grating chirp.

The blackbird frequents houses here; its voice is very discordant and singular, sparrow-hawks were seen to pursue wounded pigeons. Houses few, built of unbaked and large bricks or rather cakes of mud. The village of Wandipore is visible to the south-west, about one and a half mile. Snow on ridges to west, all which are lofty. The country around Wandipore is tolerably populous, though not so much so as about Santagoung.

We were compelled to halt at Phain or Thain, until the 1st instant, owing to the admirable management of the Bhooteas. It appeared at first as if the Zoompoor or Governor of Wandipore was determined that we should not be gainers in time by not going through his castle, but subsequently it turned out that the Deb had, with infinite consideration, wished us to remain in order to rest ourselves after our long journey. This may have been merely said to shelter the Wandipore man, who had the impudence to send one evening to us saying, that the Deb and Durmah were coming to Wandipore next morning, and that we were to meet them there, and return the same evening to Punukha. This turned out untrue. Pemberton was at last compelled to write to the Deb, and the consequence was the arrangement for our advance next morning.

April 1st.—The march to Punukha extended over a most barren dried up country, the features presented were the same as those about Phain. We proceeded at first in the direction of Wandipore, then diverged, proceeding downwards in the direction of the villages. The remainder of our journey extended either just above the base of the hills, or along the valley: the distance was nine miles. The march was an uninteresting one; the only pretty part being the river that drains the valley, and it is one of considerable size, fordable in but few places; the rapids are frequent, but the intermediate parts flow gently. We were all dreadfully disappointed in the capital, the castle even is by no means so imposing as that of Tongsa or Byagur; the *city* miserable, consisting of a few mean houses, and about as many ruined ones.

The surrounding cultivation is chiefly poor wheat; the hills the most barren conceivable. On arriving near the palace we made a detour, to avoid exposure to the usual regal insolence: our plan was effectual. From some distance I had espied our quarters, and although our mission, is one sent by the most powerful eastern government, yet we had allotted to us a residence fit only for hogs.

It consisted of a court-yard, surrounded by walls, and what had evidently been stabling; the apartments were numerous, but excessively small, the roof of single mats. The place swarmed with vermin. In this we determined not to stay, and so proceeded to the city, (for sure there cannot be a capital without a city,) and there, after some delay, procured two houses, in one of which the present Tongso Pillo had lodged before his present exaltation. But imagine not that it was a palace. The two houses together furnished three habitable rooms.

I imagine not that the houses were procured for us by the local government. We only obtained them by Pemberton's liberality was well known. The Sepoys' lines were transported hither not by Bhooteas but by our own people. In addition the people are in many cases insolent, and it was only after a peremptory message to the Deb, stating what the consequences would be of such a system of annoyance, that we got any assistance.

April 3rd.—We have heard nothing of the Mutaguat. It appears that the country is unsettled now. The old Deb having possession of Tassisudon, and the people here declaring they will stop all supplies if the Deb does not, according to custom, repair at the usual period to Tassisudon. A Deewan here, who has held office under four Rajahs, says, that the present truce is owing to the hot weather; Bhooteas only admire fighting in the cold season, in conformation of which, he says that in the cold season the contest will be renewed. There will then be an additional bone of contention for the present. Nor should I much wonder if the Paro Pillo then comes forward and takes the Debship and all away. The Deewan's account of the past fighting, places the Bhooteas in a most contemptible light: it appears that when they fire a gun, they take no aim, their only aim being to place their bodies as far as possible from the weapon; the deadly discharge is followed up by the deadlier discharge of a stone. At plunder they are more adroit.

The following plants may be found about this place; Ligustrum, Salex pendula, Valeriana orolifolia, Campanula linearis, senecionideæ, Viola, Jasminum, Rosea, Conaria, mangoe one tree in the gardens, Citrus two or three species in ditto, Jubrung, Diospyros, Acorus, Veronica, Ranunculus, Sclerossophalos, Alopecercus, Agrostides, Bombax, stunted weeping cypress, Pinus longifolia, Punica, Dipsacus, Potentilla, Potamogeton 2, Hyperia japonica, Lysimachia, Chenopod. Ajuga, Anisomales.

Birds—great kingfisher, diver snappet, white-pated rumped chats, no ouzels. Part of the gardens extend from the palace up the river to the village; the breadth is fifty to seventy yards, the length 200. They are surrounded by a dilapidated stone fence. Although an Assam malee or gardner resides in them, they are kept in miserable order: the soil seems good, the trees flourishing, mangoe, Diospyros, Jubrung, oranges, citrons, pomegranates, are the principal trees. The south side has a streamlet running along it outside the fence, for the supply of water. This streamlet abounds with Acorus Calamus.

April 9th.—Our interview with the Deb took place. We dismounted at the boards over the streamlets above mentioned, and then

2 o

proceeded over the wooden bridge across the Patcheen, which is here a wide and deep stream: the bridge was partially lined with guards, in different dresses, few in uniform; it was besides armed with shoulder wall-pieces, capital things for demolishing friends. We then crossed a sort of court-yard and then ascended a steep and extraordinarily bad flight of steps to the door of the palace. Here we found the household troops all dressed in scarlet with two door-keepers, one seated on either side of the door: this led us into a quadrangle. The citadel being in front, the side walls were rather low, although viewed externally they appear of good height, but the ground of the interior is much raised. We crossed this diagonally, passed into the opposite quadrangle on the west side, and thence ascended into a gallery, hung with arms, and filled with followers, from this we passed after a little delay into the Rajah's room.

This was handsomely decorated with scarfs, the pillars were variously ornamented. The Rajah was seated on an elevated place in the corner, and appeared a good-looking well-bred man. He received the Governor General's letter from P. with much respect, getting up from his chair: the visit was a short one, and entirely of ceremony. The presents were deposited on a raised bench in his front. Communications were kept up by the Deewan and the Zimpay, formerly Joongar Zoompoor or Governor. On retiring we were presented with fruits, oranges, walnuts, horrid plantains, ghee, eggs and rice.

The whole business went off very well, no attempt at insolence. The concourse of people was greater than I expected. Swarms of Gylongs, the more curious of whom received whacks from leathern straps, wielded by some magisterial brother.

April 10th.—Yesterday we saw the Dhurma, to whom we had to ascend by several flight of steps, which are most break-neck things, the steps overlapping in front, and being often lined with iron on the part most subject to be worn. We found him in the south room of the upper story of the citadel. We waived our right to sitting in his presence as the question was put to us with respect and delicacy. The Rajah is a good looking boy, of eight or ten years old: he was seated in the centre, but in an obscure part of the room, and was not surrounded by many immediate attendants. The balcony was filled with scribes with handsome black, gilt, lettered books before them. Two other scribes were likewise engaged on our right, noting down what passed, but they seemed to be very bad writers. The visit went off well. The room was tastily, but not so profusely ornamented with scarfs as was the Deb's.

On returning we found the household guard drawn up in front to prevent our passing out without paying a fee. This matter was soon settled forcibly, and the durwan, or door-keeper, lost by his impudence the present he would otherwise have had from P., besides being in a great fright lest the affair should be reported to the Rajah.

April 11th.—The rains appear to have set in: the sky is constantly over-cast, and showers are by no means unfrequent. One of our dawks arrived opened: this no doubt took place in the palace, although the Deb strenuously denies it. Messengers are to be sent to Tassgoung, where the accident is said to have happened. The cause of its having been opened, is no doubt the report that there was a letter in it from the old Deb.

April 14th.—A violent squall unaccompanied by rain, came on yesterday from the west: roofs were flying about in every direction, and many accidents occurred from the falling of the stones by which they were secured. Part of the palace was unroofed. The storm has stopped all our amusements, particularly as the Gylongs attribute it to our firing. The Kacharies, our servants, were likewise requested not to play any more on the esplanade. This is just as it has been in every other place in Bootan, nothing is said against amusement until the presents have been received, and then we are requested to do nothing, and the authorities become disobliging!

The potters fashion their earthernware entirely with their hands, the upper half is finished on a flat board; the lower being added afterwards; the finishing is done chiefly by a wet rag, the operator revolving around the pot. The vessels chiefly used for carrying water are oval, these are covered with black glaze.

Some Didymocarpi very fragrant, one near Chindupjee most grateful, resembling quince and sandal wood; the odour is permanent, and appears to reside in the young leaves before their expansion: Iris, Hypericum, Viola, Ligust., Ranunculus, Verbasena, Gymnostomum, Serratula arenaria, Veronica.

CHAPTER XIII.

Return of the Mission from Bootan.

May 9th, 1838.—We left Punukha at twelve, having been delayed throughout the morning, on account of coolies. We crossed the palace precints, and the two bridges unmolested. Our road lay in the direction of our entering Punukha for sometime, but on the opposite bank of the river. We gradually descended throughout this portion. Then at about eight miles turning round a ridge, we followed a ravine to the west, some distance above its base, gradually descending to the watercourse draining it. Thence we ascended in a very circuitous route to Telagoung, the castle of which is in a ruinous state: it is visible from the place whence one turns to the westward.

Up to this point, which was certainly 1,200 feet above Punukha, no change occurred in the vegetation. The country remained barren, the ravines in favourable places being clothed with underwood, and as we increased our elevation, with trees. Noticed a Bupleurum, Viburnium sp., Ficus obliqua.

At 3,500 feet, Sambucus, Bupleurum sp., Potentilla as before, Gentiana pinnata, Serissoides, Campanula.

At 3,800 to 4,000 feet, Pinus longifolia more common though still a stunted tree, Emblica, Pæderia cyaneum, Q. tomentosa, Primula Stuartii, Parochetus, Pogonantherum, this is a most common grass about here, it becomes more stunted as we proceed lower, and its extreme elevation does not exceed 6,000 feet, Acorus very common, Adhatoda!

At 4,000 feet, Simool, Dipsacus as before, Aspidium, Macrodon, Rhododendron minus re-appears.

On rounding the ridge, although we did not increase our elevation, the country became more wooded. In some places Q. robur, Gordonia, Pyrus were common, others and the greater portion were composed of Pinus longifolia, Bucklandia re-appears at 4,500 feet, Azalea, Saccharum aristatum, Hedera, Didymocarpus contortus, on rocks.

Towards the nullah we passed a village with some wheat and buckwheat cultivation; Plantago, Ranunculus, Thymus, were interspersed. Along the watercourse Symplocos styracifolius, which becomes a middling-sized tree, was seen, and Stellaria cana, petalis albis profunda partitus, as well as S. media.

Our section was as follows :—

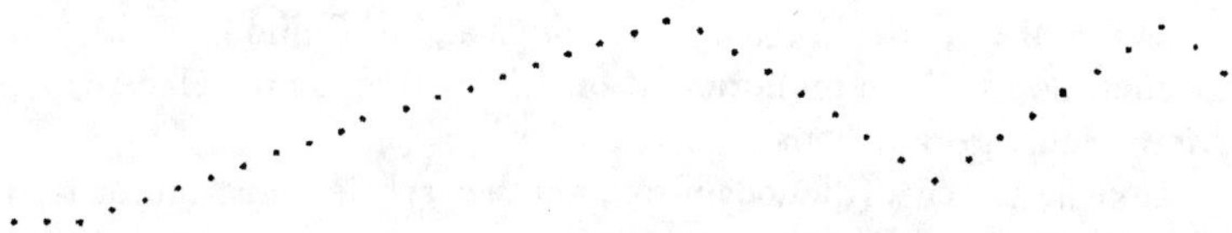

Telagoung is a middling-sized, dilapidated castle, in which it is settled the first blood is to be shed in the forthcoming contest, it is occupied by the old Deb's men. Up to its walls, thickets abound, and the fragrant rose was very conspicuous.

Its elevation is about 5,600 feet, yet a Ficus may be seen planted by the side of Cupressus pendula, and Punica thrives. The change in temperature was very great. Birds abounded throughout ; a new sombre-coloured dove was shot by P. : the most common birds were the orange-billed shrike of towards Tumashoo.

May 10*th*.—We left Telagoung at 7 A. M. and descended instantly to a small nullah, from which we re-ascended. The ascent continued without intermission, occasionally gradually, but generally rather steep for three or four hours. The descent occupied about as long, and about three-fifths the distance, following nearly throughout a small nullah. Woollakkoo, our halting place, is a good-sized village, and fourteen and a half miles from Telagoung.

To the nullah I observed Stellaria cana, Berberis asiatica, which has re-appeared, Erythrina, Rubus deltoid, which is very common all over these parts and whose fruit is palatable, Uvularia, Swertia plantaginifolia, Cæsalpinia, Mimulus, and Urtica foliis apice erosis.

The ascent commenced through woods of Q. robur, the shrubs consisting of Gaultheria fragrans and arborea, a Myrsinea, Thibaudia serrata, whose inferior limit is here, Rhododendron minus, but not very common. A good deal of wheat cultivation and of better quality occurred at 6,500 feet, assuming Telagoung as 5,600 feet, Pteris aquilina common throughout and up to 10,000 feet.

At 8,000 feet, Taxus re-appears, with Baptisia in flower, Thibaudia orbicularis, Luzula of Chindupjee, Smilax gaultherifolia, Thibaudia obovata, Fragaria vesca, which continues throughout, and has a range of between 3 to 10,000 feet, Bambusa microphylla, and Acer sterculiacea appear, woods of Q. ilecifolia, up to 7,200 feet, chiefly of Q. robur, Gaultheriæ two common ones, occur commonly.

At 8,500 feet, the woods composed chiefly of Q. castaneoides and glaucum, Q. ilecifolia less common. No Q. robur, path-like glades and rather open, Pythonium ecaudata, up to 9,000 feet, Primula pulcherrima very common.

At 8,500 feet, Saxifraga of Khegumpa and of Chindupjee, Mitella! Luzula, Carex, Viola reniformis, Lomaria of Khegumpa, Hedera, Ilex, Mercurialis, grey lichens.

Taxus, Quercus, Rhododendron, another species foliis subtus ferrugineo-argenteis floribus rosaceis.

Smilacina, Ophiopogon, Urtica carnosa decumbens, Limonia laureola, Pythonium ecaudatum.

At the same elevation and indeed below us, but on other ridges, cedars were seen in abundance: Hydrangea and Hydrangeacea calyptrata, Epilobium sp. withered.

At 7,800 feet, Aristolochia novum genus, Tritium glaucum, Thlaspi, Arabis cordata, Loranthus, Symplocos sessiliflora.

At 7,900 feet, Lardizabalea.

At 8,000 feet, Hamiltonia?

At 9,000 feet, Crucifera floribus amplis albis, on mossy banks, with Mitella, Spiræa densa.

Acer sterculiacea in forests, Cerasi sp. common.

Betula, Ribes, Arenaria, Lilium giganteum, Laurinea, Chimaphila, Acer.

At 9,300 feet, Rhododendron hispida and rosaceum, Taxus, Pythonium filiformia, Trillium album, Salvia of Royle, Rhododendron ferrugineo and obovata, Smilacinia densiflora, Sarcococea, Daphne cannabinum, here in flower, Anemone, Prunella, Hemiphragma, Cedar, but rare.

At 9,700 feet, Primula Stuartii in flower lower down, but here quite past, Corydalis linetta, Viola, Juniperus, Viburnum floribus magnis albis, Rhododendron deflexa, in flower. Acer: 1, vel. 2, Cerasi sp. altera, Paris polyphylla, and from 7,000 feet, Iris foliis angustis, Cerasus apetalus gathered below here a shrub, very common, Osmundia alia, Berberis ilecifolia and integrifolia, Rosa microphylla, Spinis latis, Baptisia, Corydalis altior floribus luteis, Aconiti sp., Papaveracea succo aqueo, ferrugineo hispida, capsula siliquosa, 3-valvis, replis totidem, stigmata radiata, 5-lobo. Prunella, Betula, Ranunculus minimus, Carex, Mimulus! Sambucus of below, Salvia of Royle, Polytrichum rubescens.

From the ridge the view to the south is pretty, the country undulated, either naked and swardy, or clothed with firs.

Abies spinulosa commences: and is soon succeeded by Pinus pendula, which, as we proceeded lower, soon became the chief tree; Rhododendron obovata finely in flower, Lilium giganteum common, Trillium atratum, Ribes lacineat.

Q. ilecifolia re-appears 500 or 600 feet below the ridge, Pinus spinulosa common, with a Salix, grey pendulous lichens.

At 6,000 feet, P. pendula, Mespilus microphyllus, Larix, Rumex, which has occurred throughout, Salvia alia viscosa foliis subhastatis trilobis, Cycnium, Astragaloides! bracteis subvaginant magnis, Rosa latispina becomes very common.

At 8,800 feet, Hedera, Hamiltonia re-appears, Galium sp., Juncus, Oxlip, Clematis, Salix, very common.

At 8,500 feet, a village is seen to the right; Q. ilecifolia is the chief tree, with P. pendula, Azalea, Baptisia, Pomacea of Rydang, Rhododendron arbor. minus. Red-legged crow, pine chatterers.

At 8,000 feet, Baptisia continues; all alpine vegetation ceased; Rhododendron minus continues, Q. ilecifolia, but no Corydalis, Anemone, Iris, etc. although Oxlip does; Salix continues.

The descent to the halting place is marked by return to the old vegetation indicated by re-appearance of Elæagnus fragrans and Rosa tetrapetala, Valeriana violifolia.

Baptisia rotundifolia and oblonga, this last a tree very common, Pinus pendula chief tree, Pomacea celastufolia, Elæagnus fragrans, Rosa tetrapetala, very common along the nullah, Baptisia continues low down, as Oxlip, Stauntonia alba, Viburnum, *Asteroides*, Jasminum luteum, Tussilago, Spiræa bella, found about the level of this.

All the monocotyledons have a defined elevation; Smilacina cordifolia is the lowest, except Uvularia, Lilacineæ and Trillium, are the highest, not being found much under 10,000 feet. There is an Osmundia likewise on the ridge, the fronds below are not contracted, it is ferrugineo-tomentosa. Hemiphragma has a wide range, between 6 and 10,000 feet: Salvia nubigena of Royle, confined to 10,000 feet, Aconitum, Corydalis lutea, lenella and cærulea, Prunus penduliflora, Papaveracea, Juniperus, Rhododendron obovata, Silacinea, Cerasus apetala, Ribes 2, are sure signs of elevation.

If the Mimulus be the same as that from Punukha, it has a very wide-range, as also Lilium giganteum, Pythonium filiformeis, limited, as well as ecaudata, Crucifera, Anemone, Laurinea, Polytrichium, were all definite. Mitella ranges between 9 and 9,500 feet, it is strange that the chief variety in vegetation occurred on the Telagoung side, on which springs are rare. No Thibaudias occurred on the other side, Euphorbia was confined to the Woollakkoo side, as also Primula, etc. etc. The chief cultivation about Woollakkoo is of wheat, but from the mode of cultivation the plant is evidently adapted for irrigation; rice is also cultivated. This is perhaps its maximum height. The hills around are covered here and there with snow, and must therefore be above 10,000 feet high. The highest were to the north-west.

The river is of moderate size, fordable in most places, but still well supplied with wooden bridges. Fish, in shoals too, were seen here and there.

May 11*th*.—Our march continued down this river throughout: we left its banks once or twice owing to ascending some hundred feet above its bed, occasionally it spread out, but generally was confined between the rocks. Its banks in some places were planted with weeping willows. The vegetation throughout was much the same. The most common plants were Rosa, this literally abounds, Pinus pendula, Viburnum grandiflora, a Symphoria! Cratægus 2 species, Mespilus microphyllus, Lantonea, Jasminum luteum, Berberis asiatica and obovata, Plectranthus canus, Elæagnus fragrans, Stellaria cana, Colquhounia, *Indigofera* sp. altera, Baptisia did not re-appear, Euphorbia continues, as does the Celastrus noticed yesterday, which commences at 8,500 feet.

Cycnium re-appears, it is in fruit, the cotyledons are not conduplicate. In the fields Stachys, Potentilla (common), Brumus, Lamium of Khegumpa, Cynoglossum, Thlaspi, Datura in waste places, Conaria, rare, Imperata! Scabiosa of Bulphai.

A low shrub abounded on the road sides and walls, having all the characters of Plumbago, a Lantonea likewise abounded, Fragaria, Swertia, Taxaxacum, Cardamina lilacina, Herminu sp., Marchantia, Astragalus, Ranunculus, Carex, Potentilla supina, Potamogeton, Clematis grata, Poplars were seen; of these, Taxaxacum very common. Quercus robur re-appears towards Lamnoo, as well as Juglans and Populus.

Weeping cypresses about villages, Hordeum hexastichum is commonly cultivated, A. Buddlæa floribus lilacinis noticed yesterday was found, its range is 8,500 to 7,500 feet, Zanthoxyla here.

A cuckoo was shot; this bird would seem to be as in Europe attended by the Yunx, at least a cry very similar to that of that bird was heard. Lysimachia of Punukha, Campanula re-appears.

The most common bird is Lanuis. The sombre-coloured dove too is rather common. The wheat cultivated here is poor, a good deal of the Bromus occurs with it. Astragalus is common on the borders of the fields, and in some of them Ervum, Lamium and Vicia.

The whole upper surface of the column of Aristolochia of Telagoung, is viscid and stigmatic, and likewise the margins of the depressions in which the anthers are lodged, it is certainly akin to Rafflesiaceæ.

May 12*th*.—Proceeded to Chupcha, our march to, and indeed beyond Panga, seven miles from Lamnoo, was through exactly similar country. The hills naked or clothed with firs, the path lay along the river Teemboo chiefly, but occasionally we met with one or two stiff ascents. On reaching Panga it was determined to push on to Chupcha, which was said to be but a short way off; we started, and descended after sometime to the river, above which Panga is elevated about 1,000 feet. We continued along the river, until we commenced to ascend towards Chupcha, this ascent was very long and rather steep, the road tolerably good. We found Chupcha to be ten miles from Panga, and 8,000 feet high, the greatest height we crossed being 8,600 feet, and this day we were told, that all our climbings had ceased. The road was generally bad, and well furnished with rocks: in one place we passed from 100 yards along the perpendicular face of a cliff, the Teemboo roaring underneath, the road was built up with slippery slabs of stone. The country was generally very pretty, the scenery along the river being very picturesque. We passed a waterfall of considerable size, which is Turner's Minzapeeza. After leaving Panga we came on an uninhabited country, nor did we see more than one village, until we reached the ridge immediately above Chupcha, 1,000 feet above this, there is a very large village inhabited by Gylongs, the bare summit of the hill rising an equal height above it: snow visible to the south. The greatest distance we descended was 6,500 feet, the greatest height 8,500 feet. The distance seventeen miles, the longest march we have yet had.

The vegetation was nearly the same up to the time we turned off towards Chupcha, it was characterized by a profusion of Rosa, among which the Cratæga, Symphorema, (which is less common than towards Woollakkoo,) Rhamnus, Viburnum grandiflorum, Pinus pendula, Thymus, Cycnium.

In grassy banks of fields between Panga and Lamnoo, Astragalus, Ervum, Vicia, Aster major, Rumex, Agrostia, in fields Hieraciæ sp., Caricia sp., Lactuca, Bromus.

Salix pendula about villages. After leaving Panga we came on to a place called Minzapeeza, here Adiantum, Aspidium? Hamamelidea, Cedrela? Rhus, Galium, Tussilago, Saxifraga ligularis, Valeriana violifolia, Smilax flexuosa, Aruncus, Sarcococca, Azalea.

Rhododendron minus recommenced after leaving the river towards Panga, a straggling cedar or two occurred, Populus rotundifol. very common, Gaultheria arborea.

About Panga, Lithospermum, Oxalis corniculata, Umbellifera, from the flowers of which *moud* is made, Rubus, Arabis, Taxacum, Dipsacus.

Beyond the waterfall the Quercus robur became common, forming beautiful woods, it continued throughout until we re-descended to the river, range 7 to 7,500 feet. In these woods formed likewise by Pinus pendula, Convallaria cirrhosa appeared, Rubia cordifolia, hispida, Paris polyphylla, Aralia cissifolia, Mitella, Ribes! Spiræa, Asparagus, Epipactis, Avularia, Houttuynia! Arum viviparum on rocks, Duchesmium, Populus oblonga occurred also, Coriaria! Hedera common, Benthamia common.

On rocks along the river, Peperomia, 4-phylla, Populus oblonga, Acer sterculiacea! Symphoria alia! Indigofera, Salix, Cedrela, Sassafras, arbor facie, Gordonia, Vitis, Syringa, Serissa, Buddlæa, Sedum on rocks, Eriophon ditto, Campanula cana, Pinus pendula, Rosa, Convallarium cirrhosa, Polygonum robustum, foliis cordatis.

The ascent up to 7,500 feet, was marked by similar vegetation: up to this point the prevailing shrubs gradually disappeared, they were never so common as about Panga. Quercus robur having ceased, was succeeded by Quercus ferriuginea, which is much like Quercus ilecifolia, and has very coriaceous leaves, this again at 7,500 feet, was succeeded by Quercus ilecifolia, Dipsacus up to this, Pteris aquilina, Gaultheria arborea.

At 7,600 feet, Rhododendron oblonga, a most beautiful species, Calyce discoideo commenced, as also Rhodora deflexa and Rhodoracea ochrolenea, which is, I think, that I before noticed as R. elliptica, foliis basi cordatis subtus argenteis et punctatis, Euphorbia occurs also here, as also the Rosa, Berberis asiatica.

At 8,000 feet, the trees were covered with grey lichens, and assumed the usual highly picturesque appearance: noticed Primula Stuartii in flower (Symphoria! ceased), Euphorbia, Gaultheria nummularifolia commences, Artemisia major, Cratægus odoratus continues, Saxifraga ligularis common up to this, Ribes commences,

Gaultheria of Bulphai, Galum, Hyperici sp., Lilium giganteum, Clematis grata, Populus species, do not ascend above this.

At 8,500 feet, Rhododendron minus, Rhododendron oblonga, ochroleucum, Coccineum appears, Ribes, Smilax sanguinea, Gaultheria of Bulphai very common, arborea stunted, Limonia major, Clematis grata! Rhododendron hispida, Potentilla, Pteris aquilina, Berberis asiatica, Mespilus microphyllus, Gnaphalium, Swertia, Viola, Patrinum! Elæagnus fragrans! Thymus, which ranges from 6 to 10,000 feet, Euphorbia, Pedicularis, Cycnii sp., Mimulus, Rhodora deflexa, Pinus pendula, Quercus ilecifolia, both stunted, Pteris aquilina.

The descent to the village was about 500 feet, Arenarium on rocks, Mimulus viola, Rumex, Juncus, Acorus veronica, Anagallis, Pythonium of Blake, Euphorbia, Pedicularis, Carex, Mespilus microphyllus: pine chatterers throughout, at least above 7,000 feet.

The summit, which was certainly 9,500 feet, was completely bare: Pinus pendula ascends a long way.

Chupcha—Hordeum hexastichor in beautiful order, the chief cultivation. Red-legged crow; larger dove. The form of the country traversed is as follows:—

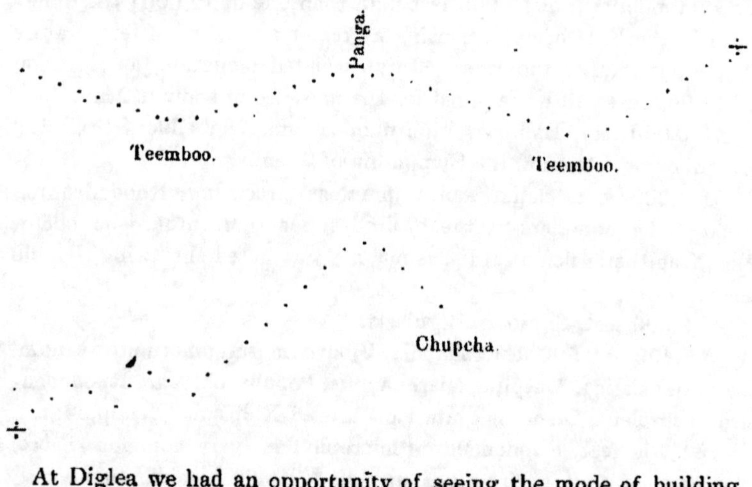

At Diglea we had an opportunity of seeing the mode of building in this part of Bootan; the houses are made of mud, which is trampled and beat down by men, who perform sundry strange evolutions while so employed; the mud is beat down in a frame-work; it is from the different layers formed that the lines seen outside finished houses result. The mode is slow, but must give great firmness.

May 14*th*.—Ascended to the Gylong village, above Chupcha, and then to the naked ridge. The village may be estimated as being 8,700 or 8,800 feet above the sea, and that part of the ridge to which I ascended as 9,800 or 10,000 feet. The ascent is uninterrupted up to the village; it winds through a fine fir wood, after diverging from the road to Panga, after that it is quite open, scarcely a shrub being met with until the ridge is surmounted. On turning to its northern face, woody vegetation becomes pretty abundant, and 500 feet below, woods occur. This is contrary to what usually happens; the south faces of mountains being supposed to be better wooded than the others, but in Bootan the difference would seem to be due to the piercing winds blowing from south, or up the ravine of the Teemboo. The scenery was very pretty, both in the woods before reaching the village, and from the ridge: vast quantities of snow visible to the north and north-east. I ascended to within 1,000 feet of snow, and I think that at this season, an elevation of 11,000 feet is required *in open places* to secure the presence of snow: it is obvious that local circumstances, such as shelter, etc. may cause it to descend nearly to 9,000 feet, and it is as obvious that snow will descend lower down a mountain of 15,000 feet high than one of 12,000; the difference in the beds of snow causing a greater reduction of temperature in the one than in the other. In an isolated mountain, an elevation of 11,000 feet will be required for the presence of snow in May.

At 8,000 feet, Baptisia, Viburnum canum, Umbellifera toxicaria, Colquhounia, Deutzia, the Symphoria of Teemboo.

At 8,200 feet, Salix, Abies spinulosa straggling, Rhododendron microphylla commences, the bruised has a terebenthaceous odour, Ilex, Gaultheria flexuosa, Parus major: variegated shortwing, Papilio machaonires.

At 8,300 feet, Saxifraga ligularis.

At 8,400 to 8,500 feet, Limonia, Viburnum grandiflorum or canum, Berberis asiatica, Mespilus microphyllus, Populus oblonga, Rhododendron ochrolena, Clematis grata viola lutea,* Epipactis, Hemiphragma.

At 8,700 feet, Rhododendron microphyllum very common, Ribes, Bupleuri sp.,* Rosa fructibus hispidis,* Rubia hispida, Sambucus, Berberis integrifolia, an vero distincta.

At 8,800 feet, Viola pusilla, Fragaria vesca and lutea, Baptisia, Rosa, Sphærostemma, Clematis grata, Pinus pendula, etc.

At 9,000 feet, commencement of sward, no trees, except stunted shrubs of Pinus pendula, Mespilus microphyllus, Baptisia, Gnaphalium

Pedicularis,* Rosa, Bistorta,* leaves with margins not united to the margins of pitchers of Nepenthes and Cephalotus, Pteris aquilina, Prunella, Rhododendron microphyllum, Euphorbia, Taxaxacum, Potentilla, Thymus, Primula Stuartii.

At 9,100 feet, Hyperica brachiata of Moflong.

At 9,300 feet, Morina Wallichiana, Osmundioid, Dipsacus, Scabiosa? capitulo nutanta, Verbascum, Juncus, Epilobia sp.

At 9,400 feet, Salix shrubby, Cyperus fuscescens of Tassangsee, dwarfed Larix.

At 9,500 feet, Anemona aurea commences, covering in some places the sward; it straggles down in favourable places with Iris angustifolia, to 9,300 feet, Primula Stuartii, Rhododendron microphyllum, Gnaphalia, Euphrasia.

At 9,800 feet, southern face of ridge bare, northern thickety, consisting of Rhododendron fruticosum, foliis ellipticis basi cordatis punctato lepidotis, Salix, Berberis, Pyrus aria, Bambusa, Tetranthera.

In wet sheltered spots, Iris angustifolia, Aconitum, foliis aconitoideum, on the sward Euphorbia radians. Below this a little, woods commence chiefly of Bogh Pata, Cerasus, Salix, Rosa fructibus hispidis, Acers, Abelia? Viburnum niveum, Hydrangea arbuscula, non-scandens, Berberis integrifolia. The woods are open, the open spaces occupied by remains of last summer's vegetation, as Compositæ, Umbelliferæ, Aquilegium, a plant five or six feet high, folii aconitoidie, etc. Epilobium.

Among these in the woods, Trillia sp., Saxifraga reniformis, Liliacea Brodidoid, Viola, Primula purpurea, a lovely species, Aconiti sp., Papaveracea hirsuta foliis, Aconitoid very common, Orchideæ, Ribes sanguina, Composita penduliflora, Arenaria pusilla of above Telagoung, Polygoni sp., pusilla repens hirsuit foliis cordata ovatis, vel reniformibus subtus purpurescent, Salvia nubicola? Euphorbia coccinea.

Abies densa appears, as also close to the Gylong village, from this elevation upwards, it is common.

Abies spinulosa common on north face at 9,000 feet, Abies pendula ascends on south side as high as 9,300 feet, but is stunted beyond 9,000 feet, it does not exist on north face.

Primula Stuartii throughout, very abundant.

The plants most limited were Papaveracea, Aconitum folium aconitoideum, Saxif. reniformis, Primula purpuria, Euphorbia radians, Rhododendron cereum, mentioned above, and another at 9,800 feet with similar leaves, but normal flowers, Abelia, Cerasus, Trillii sp., Anemona, Iris, Bistorta, Ribes, A. densa.

The most dispersed are Euphorbia coccinea, Salix, Bogh Pata, Mespilus microphyllus, Cyperus fuscus, Primula Stuartii, Rhododendron microphyllum.

Hordeum hexastichum gives fine produce here; nothing can exceed it in appearance, oats also occur mixed with it, but is not sown, at least, it occurs rarely on walls, Arabis, Magus stolonifer, Juglans in villages, (Ribes Juniperus in the Gylong village), Acorus, Carex, Stellaria cana, Media, Caltha, and Thlaspi.

The temperature is delightful, thermometer 46° at 7 A. M., 52° in the middle of the day.

May 15*th*.—Left Chupcha for Chuka, distant seventeen miles. Our march commenced by a very steep and indeed almost precipitous descent to the nullah, at the foot of Chupcha, of 1,800 feet. Thence we ascended gradually until we reached a temple visible from Chupcha, at which place we returned to the course along the Teemboo. The remainder of the road undulating, varying in level from 6,000 to 6,500 feet, until we commenced the descent to Chuka, which was long and tedious: we reached this at 5½ P. M. The road latterly was very bad, we passed Punukha, a small village, about 300 feet below our path. The mountains closing in the Teemboo continue lofty, at least 9,000 feet. Iris, cedars, and Abies densa, were common on the loftier parts.

We passed some beautiful places, indeed the march throughout was pretty. The vegetation was beautiful, owing to the quantity of water on the road, a stream occupying each hollow, round many of which we wound. Glades and pieces of green sward were not uncommon.

The Lamium of Bulphai is found about Chupcha. On the descent to the nullah the following plants were found.

At 7,000 feet, Iris commences, with a species of Lychnis, ground bare and rocky, Umbellifera cana, Umb., from which *moud* is prepared, common.

At 6,800 feet, Quercus ferruginea commences, on rocks here Stemodium ruderalis, Lantonica of Panga, etc., Convallaria cirrhosa.

At 6,500 feet, Hedera common, Aristolochia tetrarima, Berberis obovata, Viburnum cærulescens, Filix ferrugineo tomentosa, Pteris dealbata.

Iris common to 6,500 feet, continues lower down, but scarce. Along the nullah, which is a middling-sized torrent, Rhus, Cederela toone, Acer sterculiacea, Hamamelis, Fici sp., scandens, Rhus, Juglandifolia! Populus oblonga, Sassafras, on the ascent to the temple, Populus of very large size, and the above trees. Fraxinus floribunda, Osmundia in profusion, Aristolochia tetrarima, Scabiosa, of Bulphai, Prunella, Fragaria vesca, Duchesnum, Sarcococca, Elæagnus fragrans, Galium of Panga cascade, Corydalis, which continues to Chuka, but is scarce below 5,000 feet, Deutzia, Lilium giganteum, Uvularia very common, Primula Stuartii, Woodwardia (scarce), Pythonium pallidium, Campanula cana, Panax herbacieæ 2 species, Rhododendron agaleoides of ridge above Chupcha, Buddlæa cana, Ranunculus of Taseeling, Benthamia, Anemona ranunculacea, Buxus, Delphinum sp.? common, Gaultheria nummularifolia, Jasminum lutium, Conaria. This ascent was about 500 feet. Long-tailed pie seen here, red-billed shrikelet, first met with towards Tumashoo, common now as far down as 4,500 feet.

On passing the temple, or rather before coming to it, we changed the vegetation which became of the ordinary *dry* character. Woods of Q. ferruginea mixed with Pinus pendula, Benthamia, Pteris aquilina, Viburnum cærulescens, Conaria, Polygonum of Teemboo, Rhododendron minus, Gaultheria arborea.

The remainder of the march consisted of a series of winding round spurs: at about an average elevation of 6,000 feet found a Pythonium foliis pedalis, spad. apice filiformo recurvo, vel erecto, spathe viridi, Didymocarpea odora contuso terebinthaceo, Solanum nigrum, Succulent urticeæ, Scabiosa of Bulphai, Gnaphalium, Polygonum globiferum, Scirpus eriophorus, Hippocratia angulata, Mitella, in damp spots, Cycnium, but rare, Sarcococca, Impatiens two species, one at 6,500 feet, with a creeping plant, foliis ranunculaceis floribus solitariis hypocrateriform albis. No Buxus or Delphinum was observed, in any other glens than the first crossed. Alnus became common soon, the pines disappeared, Osmundia common, Primula rotundifolia, Paris polyphylla, Bletia as of Churra at Punukha, Sphæropteris.

In some places Rhododendron minus common, and with it Quercus ferruginea, Rubia hirsuta, not uncommon throughout as far as 15,000 feet, Thalictroides majus, Houttuynia, Betula.

In glades, Smilax gaultherifolia, in a wood round the marsh a Pomaceous tree: on the march, Swertia, Peloria, Carex stricta, and of Chupcha, Spiranthes rubriflora, Berberis pinnata, Saxifraga of Bulphai occur here.

Still further on, the forest assumed the appearance of those towards Khegumpa. Q. robur, recommences, cedars straggle down;

Pinus pendula, more common, Arenariæ sp., Lomaria of Khegumpa, Hottoneoides ranunculofolia common, Luzula, Sedi sp., Sambucus common throughout in shady spots, Radsuræ sp., Daphne papyracea, rare, Acer sterculiacea common, Sabia, Hydrangencea calyptrata, Hamiltonia, this last common to 4,500 feet.

On wet rocks Hutchinsia, Arenaria, succulent Urticea. In woods Cucurbitacea cessifolia, Ajugæ sp., Polygonum rheoides. On open spots, Benthamium in flower, Gaultheria arborea, here of large size, pines cease without changing the elevation, Q. ferruginea ceased, this is limited to dry spots.

The first change indicated by the appearance of Laurineæ, and Symplocos among oaks and chesnuts. The woods continued thick for some time, but on commencing the descent, which is gradual, especially at first, Q. robur is common, Gaultheria arborea, Rhododendron minus.

At 5,500 feet Hottonia, Rubia hirsuta, Hydrangeacea calyptrata, Phytolacea, also at 6,500 feet, and as low as 4,000 feet, Senecio scandens, Verbenacea of Dgin appears, Uvularia, Duchesnia, Polygonum rheoides.

Umbellifera gigantea, Potentilla supina appear, Pythonium recurvum, Rhus, Dipsacus of Churra, Alnus, Pomacea macrophylla, Stauntonia angustifolia, Photinea parviflora, Benthamea disappears, in flower at least, Didymocarpea, Rhamnus, and also at 5,000 feet, Fragaria vesca, in fruit! Paris, Curculigo pygmæa appears, Sedum continues and ceases at 4,500 feet, Ranunculus of Taseeling found also as low as 3,600 feet, Daphne nutans appears. This found first near Taseeling, found as low as 4,000 feet, Primula Stuartii, Rhododendron minus, Viburnum cærulescens continue, Thibaudia myrtifolia, Rubus deltoideus appears.

At 4,500 feet, a Malvaceæ Sidoides, Erythrina, Rosa fragrans, Pythonium sp. majus, spadicis apice filiformi 2-pedali, Incerta of Taseeling, Ribesioides, Quercus ferruginoides, Indigofera major, Berberis obovata, in fruit.

At 4,400 feet, Cuscuta, Hamiltonia, Hottoneoides, Daphne pendula vel nutans, Impatiens, Mimosa, Menispermum tropæolifolia, Celastrinia sp., Panax crucifolia, Hypericum japonicum.

At 4,300 feet, Conyza nivea, Q. robur, Indigofera major, of Tassgoung, etc. Gaultheria arborea, Hedychium appears! Buddlæa of Nulka, Mæsa salicifolia!

At 4,200 feet, Thibaudia lanceolata appears, ranges between 4,200 and 2,000 feet, Sanicula, Cynoglossum, Zyziphi sp.

Along the bed of the river, Zizyphus arborea, Urtica, foliis apicæ erosis, Berberis obovata, Erythrina, Artemisia major, Elæagnus fragrans, and Stellaria cana, occur, the last ranges between 3 and 6,000 feet, Thlaspi, Polygonum globifera, Dendrobium pictum, Verbenacea of Dgin, Clematis, petiolis basi connatis demum induratus majus, Magnolia, Randia of Punukha, Liriodendron tulipif., Apocynum nerufolium.

At Chuka, Ficus elastica, but not flourishing, Musa, Salix pendula, Phytolacea, Buckwheat, Crucifera cordifructus, Sanicula, Stellaria cana, Thibaudia lanceolata, Cynoglossum, Vandea, Parkioides common.

The most limited plants are Iris, Silene, Aristolochia tetrarima vix infra 6,000 feet, Buxus, Delphinioid, Fraxinus non infra 6,000 feet, Epipactis ditto, Hutchinsia, Lomaria of Khegumpa, Mitella, Carex stricta of Chupcha, *Peloria*, Smilax gaultherifolia, Osmundia non infra 5,500 feet, Hydrangeacea ditto, Cucurbitacea cissifolia, found about Sudya, etc.

The most diffused, Hottonia, Q. robur, Gaultheria arborea, 5 to 3,500 feet, Corydalis.

The subtropical forms, Mimosa, Impatiens, occurrence of fleshy Urticea, Ficus elastica, but not flourishing, Musa, Salix pendula, Buckwheat, Urtica urens, peaches, Stellaria cana, Crucifera cordifructus, Panax curcifolia, Andropogon arbusculoid, Rubia cordata.

May 16*th*.—The fort of Chuka not being whitewashed, is not conspicuous: its situation is strong, and against Bhooteas would be impregnable. It occupies a low hill arising from the centre of the valley, one side of which is washed by the Teemboo or Tchien-chiw. The room we were lodged in was a good one. The village is a mean one, and consisting of three or four houses.

We crossed the river by a suspension bridge much inferior to that of Benka, and then rose gradually and inconsiderably, following the Teemboo. To this we subsequently descended by a most precipitous road built for the most part on the face of a huge cliff: we reached the Teemboo at its junction with a small torrent; the tongue of land here was strewn with huge rocks, and bore evidences of the power of the torrents, for it evidently had been once a hill, such as that we had just descended. Thence we continued ascending, following the river, from which however we soon diverged to our right, but not far. The road was rugged beyond description. As we approached Murichom, it improved somewhat, but was still very bad.

We reached this place which is visible for some distance at 5 P. M.; the march being one of eighteen miles. No villages occurred en route. The hills were densely wooded to the summits and much lowered in height than those to which we had been accustomed. Passed two waterfalls, one less high, but more voluminous than the other, is the Minzapeeza of Turner; both these occurred on the left bank of the river. Minzapeeza, is a fall of great height, but the body of water is small.

The vegetation to-day partook much of the subtropical character, almost all boreal plants being left behind. We ascended and descended between 3,000 to 4,500 feet near Chuka, Parkioides, Mimosa arborea! and M. frutex. Magnolia! Rubia munjista, Impatiens! Cucurbitacea!

Oxyspora latifola! Rosa fragrans, Incerta ribesioides, Piper! Urtica heterophylla! Wendlandia! Phytolacea, Daphne nutans, Rottleria! Curculigo orchediflora, Acer, Eurya pubescens, Rhus, Alnus! Adamia, Gordonia! Q. robur reappears at a lower elevation than before seen: Dipterocarpioides arbor vasta trunco ramoso! Smilax auriculata! Pothos pinnatifid! Briedlia oblonga! Corydalis, Dipsacus, Acanthaceæ common, Rubiaceæ of a tropical character, such as Ophiorhizæ; Celastrus! Pythonium majus, Tetranthera macrophylla! Quercus coriacea! Gaultheria arborea scarce, Deutzia on the descent to the Teemboo, Macrocapnos, Sterculia platanifolia, Melica latifolia! Arundo! Achyranthes densa! Labiata spinosa of Khegumpa or Phlomis, Labiata, Quercoides. The rocks on the river side are covered with Epiphytical Orchideæ; Saurauja sterculifolia, Pythonium pallidum, Elæagnus fragrans.

Along the banks of the Teemboo, Pandanus! Rhododendron azaleoides, R. pulchrum, Lyellia, Begonia picta, Composita arborea! Ficus! on ascent above its banks, Dioscorea! Elæocarpus! Acrosticum atratum! Convallarium oppositifolia, Thibaudia loranthiflora! Pogostemon of Dgin! Leea! The only northern plant a species of Viola; Otochilus linearis! Entada! Kydia! Mussænda! Macrocapnos altera of Yen, Callicarpa arborea! Panax aculeato palmiformis supra decompositæ of Dgin! Solanum farinacium! Urena lobata! Marlea, Panicum plicatum! Before ascending to Murichom we made two descents to two streams, crossed by common wooden bridges: that nearer Murichom being the largest; elevation at 2,500 feet. Here tree-fern; Pythonium majus, Duchesnia, Lysimacha, Begonia of Punukha! Caryophyllea scandens, Urtica gigas! Modeceoides exembryonata! Commelina! Conbreta sp.! Bæhmeriæ! Piper spica caudata pendula and another species!! Euphorbia! Galina of Panga, Croton malvifolius! Bambusa major! Bauhinia! Engeldhaardtii!

Although we subsequently ascended 1500 feet, very little change occurred: no re-appearance of tropical forms, Sterculiacea novum of Moosmai, Adamia, Volkameria! serrata, Triumfetta mollis! Briedlia avalis of Chilleeri! Gortnera! Corydalis! Hydrangeacæ! Melastoma malabathrica!

The march was very tiresome, some of the ranges passed were high and well clothed with firs. Those marked thus* are subtropical or tropical, and one glance will show their predominance: only Corydalis straggles down. The woods were in many places damp, in others dry: it was obvious that less rain had fallen between Chupcha and Chuka, than in other situations: a large proportion of Laurineæ and Acanthaceæ appeared in the woods, with Gordonia: the oaks and chesnuts when they did present themselves bore a tropical form, pointed out by their coriaceous undivided or merely serrated leaves. I certainly never saw such a predominance of tropical forms, at such an elevation as 3,500 or 4,000 feet.

For Lyellia I had been hunting for three years, but never thought of looking for it at low elevations; as it was I believe given out to be a native of high places. Of birds, Bucco, Picus intermedius, green pigeon, azure shrikelet, occurred.

May 17*th*.—Murichom is a small village of eight or nine thatched: houses, it is well and prettily situated: about it maize and wheat are in cultivation, Ficus, Hoya, Dendrobium, Croton malvæfolius, Meliacea, Cedrela Toona, orange, Verbesina, Datura, Artemisia major, Echites, in fact it would be difficult to point out an elevational plant. The same remark applies to the march to Gygoogoo, distant twelve miles, and situated 500 feet below the road, but still it is about the same level as Murichom. The march commenced with a steep descent, followed by a steeper ascent, then winding along, in and out, at an average elevation of 5,000 feet. The road was very bad, rocky and rugged as usual, P. and B. passed the village, and pushed on to Buxa, a distance of twenty miles, which place they reached at 7 P. M. At Murichom, Ficus cordata, fructibus pyriformibus, Clerodendron infortunata, Adamia, Spilanthes, Melastoma malabathrica, Bignonia, Pentaptera. The Oollook or Simia Hylobates, of Upper Assam.

Scarcely any thing worth noticing occurred; the vegetation being precisely the same. No oaks or chesnuts, at least comparatively few:

Elæocarpus, Rhus, Gordonia are the most common trees; Pythonium common, Hoya rotundifolia. Gygoogoo, a small village of two or three houses, was passed.

May 18*th*.—Marched to Buxa, ascending from Gygoogoo over a wretched rocky road, winding in and out. No water was to be had until we reached a ridge from which to Buxa is one continued descent. This ridge is between 5 and 6,000 feet, and yet there is scarcely a change in the vegetation. Pythonium abounded, especially P. majus, which literally occurred in profusion. The trees towards the top of the ridge were covered with moss, but all appeared subtropical; a few chesnuts, E. spinosissima occurred, Bambusa nodosis, verticillatis, and spinosis.

En route thither, Pholidota imbricata, Thib. loranthiflora, Aralia terebinthacea, Rottleria foliis peltatis, Ranunculus of Taseeling, Meniscum majus, Byttneria ferox, Caladium foliis medio discoloratis sæpius atratis, Gnetum, Ixora, Choulmoogra, Phlogacanthi sp., Corisanthes of Sudya, Acer platanifolia, Croton foliis oblongis irregularis dentato-lobatis occurred before, between 2,500 to 3,500 feet, Calamus, wild plantains as before, Gordonia, Rhus, Mimosa, Rottleria, Wallichia, Sida cuneata, Tradescantia cordata, Æschynanthus fulgens, et altera, Tupistra, Lobelia baccifera, Costus, tree-fern, as high as 5,000 feet, Bambusa fasciculata; of birds, the large Bucco.

At 5,000 feet, Thibaudia serrata, and on this side, as low as 2,500 feet, myrtifolia, Gordonia, Pythonium majus and medium, cinnamon, Piper, Acer platanifolia, Mucuna, Angiopteris, Saurauja ferruginea.

At 5,300 feet, Polygonia pinnatifolia, Hookeria macrophylla, Aralia scandens, etc. as before.

On descent nothing remarkable, except steepness: same vegetation. Pythonium majus not below 3,000 feet, Guttiferæ at 3,000 feet, Acanthaceæ, Carduaceus 2,800 feet.

At 2,500 feet, Buchanania undulata, Hyalostemma undulatum, Roydsia.

What can be the cause of this tropical elevation at such altitudes? Buxa is hot enough for any tropical plants, as jacks, mangoes, Cactus, etc. are found in fine order. It is not attributable to a gradual rise, as the ascent from this to 5,500 feet, is excessively steep. It must be owing to local causes modifying the climate: at 5,000 feet on the Dgin route, there are many elevational plants, indeed more than of subtropical.

It must not be forgotten that no Pinus longifolia exists on this route after leaving Telagoung.

Buxa is a rather pretty place, but as usual poor: the Doompa's house is the only decent one in the place, the others amounting to eight or ten, are common huts. The big house occupies an elevation in the centre of the pass, being cut off from the neighbouring hill, on either side by a ravine, one of which is now quite dry, the other affords a scanty supply of water. The hills are covered with jungle, the only clearing being about Buxa, and this, except the flat summit of the hill, is overrun with bushes, Capparis modecea, Croton malvæfolia, Menisperma tropæolifolia, Bergeræ 2 species, Ixora, Brucea same as of the plains, Atriplex, Tournefortia of plains, Mæsa macrophylla, Mimosa scandens, Ficus elastica in good order, jacks, mangoes, oranges, plantains, Tabernamontana, Calamus, Cedrela Toona, are found.

Black pheasants, Bulbuls, Drongoles, Ooroos, Bucco, green pigeons. Long-tailed blue-crested shrike, etc. are found here. The Doompa, or Chong Soobah, is a man of no rank, and the place itself is of no importance, except as the pass or entrance between the mountains of Bootan and the plains of Bengal.

The descent from Buxa is gradual at first and not unpicturesque: after passing a small chokey about half a mile from Buxa, sandstone of a coarse nature commences. The descent is very steep, and continues so until within a short distance of a place called Minagoung, at which the bullocks are unladen at least of heavy baggage. The remaining descent is very gradual, and continues so for several miles. The march throughout and until the level of the plains is reached, was through tree jungle. The underwood being either scanty or consisting of grass.

On reaching the plains, the usual Assamese features presented themselves, viz. vast expanses of grass, intersected here and there with strips of jungle. Reached Chichacootta about 3 P. M.: distance eighteen miles, of which about fifteen were over either level or very gradually sloping ground. No villages occurred, and only one path struck off from the Buxa one. We passed two or three halting places.

The vegetation throughout was subtropical. At the same elevation as Buxa, noticed Cassia lanceolata, Torenia the common Leucas, Bheir, Solanum quercifolia, Banyan, Alstonia, Styrax, Caryota, Elephantopus, Osbeckia linearis, Herminioides, Wedelia scandens.

At 1,500 feet, Celastrus guttiferoid, Malvacea digyna, of which I found flowers on the path, Kœmpfera terminal, Antidesma, Anthericum, Echites arborea, Careya, Mimosa scandens, Pavetta, Rubiacea alia, Lepidostachys, Lagerstrœmia grandiflora, Leea crispa, Costus, Thunbergia grandiflora, Gordonia, Commelina, Phyllanthus, Briedlia, Dioscorea, Cassia fistula.

As we approached a lower level, the same plants continued; a Dillenia very common, Urena lobata, Hedera terebenthacea: the root is in some cases like figs, Spathodea, Nauclea, Sterculia carnosa, foliis palmatis, Dalbergia, Panax, Semicarpus, Rhaphis trivialis, Cymbid. alvifolium, Sarcanthus guttatus common, Apocynea fauce, 10-glandulata, Ixora, etc.

Saul was not common, nor did I see one tree of any size; it commenced about the margin of the Toorai.

Among the grasses forming the underwood of the Toorai and the grassy masses clothing the plains, Sacchara were the most common and the most conspicuous: next to these a species of Rottboellia. Sciurus Bengmoria occurred, Hemarthria, Greweia edulis, Leea crispa, Crinum in the Toorai, Viburnum of Sudya, Millingtonia pinnata, Volkameria serrata, Labiata Sudyensis, Mussænda erecta, humilis, Cinchona, Premna herbacea, Phœnix pumila.

Arrived at Chichacootta, a small village, situated in an open grassy plain, miserably stockaded; and lodged in a good well elevated house.

The following day started and reached Cooch Behar territory, after crossing a considerable but fordable stream. The contrast between the desolate territories of Bootan, and the sheet of cultivation presented by Cooch Behar was striking.

The same contrast continued until we reached the Company's territories, and its less cultivated portions along the bed of the Brahmapootra. The only plant worth notice on the route, was a species of Swertia; the vegetation being almost precisely the same as in Upper Assam.

Rangamutty, Bhooruwa.

Date.	Station.	Temperature of the air.	Water Boils.					Elevation.		Remarks.
			Large thermometer.	Small metal ditto.	Wooden ditto.	Centigrade ditto	Woollaston's Ther. Bar.	Determined by the temperature of boiling point.	By Barometer.	
Jan. 27th,	Sassee, ...	62	204⅓	198	205½	96	6.22.4	4,225	4,325	
,,	Giri Nuddee, lower station, ...	64	206⅓	..	..	..	6.4.3	3,184		
,,	Ditto, upper station,	70	205¾	..	..	..	..	3,450		
29th,	Bailfa, ...	45	200¾	..	201	94	5.9.2			Value of each degree of Centigrade, deduced from difference between this and Sasee, ... 810 ft. Ditto ditto between this and Bailfa, 1,060 ,, Ditto ditto between Sasee and Bailfa, 1,247 ,, 3)3,111 ft. Mean, ... 1,037 ft. But as Sasee and this are correct or nearly so, 810 to be assumed as the right value.

Date.	Station.	Temperature of the air.	Temp. of Boiling point Fahr.	Altitude.		Remarks.
				Det. by Boiling point.	By Bar.	
Jan. 30th,	Bailfa, ...	53	194	....	6804	Each degree is according to this equal to 358 feet 4 inches.
"	....	45	195	6,764	..	Equivalent each degree to 377 feet 9 inches.
31st,	....	36	195			
"	Roongdong, ...	..	199	5,175	..	True value of a degree of large Thermometer 398.6 = 398.6.
Feb. 1st,	....	46	199			
"	Benka, ...	64	204	....	..	Assuming 204 as the mean.
2nd,	....	..	204	....	..	

Value of each degree, deduced from differences in the Barometrical height—

Bulfai and Roongdong,	..	408 feet 3 inches.
Bulfai and Benka, ..	..	402 " 9 "
Roongdong and Benka,	..	398 " 7 "
Mean of the three, ..	..	403 feet 2 inches.

Value of each degree, deduced from differences in the Thermometer height—

Bulfai and Roongdong,	..	387 feet 6 inches.
Bulfai and Benka, ..	..	398 " 0 "
Roongdong and Benka,	..	406 " 5 "
		3)1191 feet 11 inches.
Mean, ...	..	397 feet 3 inches.
Mean of both series,	..	403 " 2 "
		2)800 feet 5 inches.
True value, ..	..	400 " 2 "

According to this, this Thermometer will boil at the level of the sea at $211\frac{8}{10}$.

Date.	Station.	Temperature of the air.	Temperature of Boiling point.			Altitude.		Barometer.
			Cent.	Fah.	Wooll.	By Ther.	By Bar.	
2nd,	.. ..	8 P. M. 50	97½	..	627	3,182		
,,	.. ..	4 P. M. 66	..	..	627	....		
,,	.. ..	8½ P. M. 58	..	..	629	....		
,,	.. ..	8 A. M. 52	..	..	630	....		
3rd,	.. ..	9 P. M. 60	..	..	630	....		
4th,	.. ..	8 A. M. 55	..	..	631	....		
,,	.. ..	12 P. M.	..	..	629	....	.. ..	The cause of the variation in Woollaston's instrument is, I find, the presence of air within the instrument, occupying when the tube is inverted about 2 lines of the tube itself, otherwise it is visible in the bulb. I have therefore taken out the tube and put in a tube from a Centigrade thermometer.

Date.	Station.	Temp.	Boiling point Wooll.	Alt. by Boiling point.	Bar. Alt.	Difference.	Remarks.
Feb. 4th,	Benka, 9 P. M. ..	60	755	.. .. ..	3,182		
5th,	,, 7 A. M. ..	..	755				
,,	Monass R., N. Bridge, ..	62	768	1,988 6	1,960	28 6	1,222 feet below Tassgong.
,,	Nulka, ...	68					
,,	Nulka, ...	66	759				
6th,	,, 7 A. M. ..	62	759	2,814 8	2,776	38 8	8 P. M., 8,262 feet above Monass bridge.
,,	Ghoomkuna, ..	..	760				
,,	Bridge over Koollong, ..	..	757	.. .. ..	2,430		
,,	Khumna, ..	..	742				
,,	.. .. ..	..	$742\frac{5}{10}$	4,360 1	4,292	68 1	1,557-6, above Nulka; 2,386-8, above Monass bridge.
7th,	Phoollong, ..	..	$736\frac{5}{10}$	5,830	5,929	99 0	4 P. M. The scale is now fastened so that the Vernier corresponds to the lower mark and to the first division above Zero, hence to equalize them, it must be subtracted from all, after to-day.
8th,	,, in doors 47, ,, out 39,	47 39	$736\frac{5}{10}$	Mean, 737			
,,	,, ...	..	738				

Date.	Station.	Temp.	Ther.	Altitude.	Bar. Alt.	Difference.	Remarks.
Feb. 9th,	Phoollong, ..	35	$736\frac{5}{10}$				
,,	,, 9 P. M. ..	46	741				
10th,	Tassyassa, $4\frac{1}{2}$ P. M.	60	742	.. ..	.. ..	.. ..	Mean deduced from 4 series $91\frac{5}{10}$ (P.)
,,	,, 9 P. M. ..	52	743 5	Mean from comparisons with all,			$91\frac{3}{10}$
11th,	,, 9 A. M. ..	42	744				
,,	,, 12 P. M. ..	56	743 5	5,206	5,272	.. ..	743·8 is the mean.
,,	,, 4 P. M. ..	60	743				
,,	,, 9 P. M. ..	50	745	....	.. .	.. ..	
12th,	,, 10 A. M. ..	48	745	....	.. ..	.. ..	
,,	,, 12 P. M. ..	54	743	....	.. ..	.. ..	
,,	,, 4 P. M. ..	51	744 5	....	.. ..	.. ..	
,,	,, 9 P. M. ..	49	745	....	.. ..	.. ..	
13th,	,, $10\frac{3}{4}$ A. M. ..	48	744 5	....	.. ..	.. ..	
,,	,, $12\frac{1}{2}$ P. M. ..	57	742 5	....	.. ..	.. ..	
14th,	,, 7 A. M. ..	43					
,,	Sanah, 4 P. M ..	51	716 5				
,,	,, 9 P. M. ..	50	719	7,845	7,983	138	Storm threatening.
15th,	,, 6 A. M. ..	46	717 5				
,,	1st Hill, ...	..	705	9,078			
,,	2nd Ditto, ...	39	681	11,269			
,,	Summit, ...	..	667 5	12,477			
16th,	Halt, ...	..	699	....	9,602		
,,	Linjai, ...	51	734				
17th,	,, 10 A. M. ..	54	735	6,385	6,335	50	
,,	,, 12 P. M. ..	55	734 5				
,,	,, $4\frac{1}{2}$ P. M. ..	54	734				
18th,	Kooree, ...	$1\frac{1}{4}$	760 5				
,,	,, Bridge, ..	$1\frac{1}{2}$	761	3,878 5			
19th,	Ling-ling, $11\frac{1}{2}$ A M.	52	752 5				
,,	,, 1 P. M. ..	53 5	752 5	4,601	4,522	79	Cloudy, threatening day.
,,	,, 4 P. M. ..	53 5	752 5				
20th,	,, 10 A. M. ..	54	755	....	....	....	Fine.
,,	,, ,, ..	55	753 5				

,,	,, 4 P. M. ..	57	753 5				
21st,	,, 11 A. M.	56	754 5	....	....	....	Cloudy, raw day, especially towards evening.
,,	,, 4 P. M. ..	55	753	....	....	....	
22nd,	,, 10½ A. M.	54	754 5	....	....	....	Cloudy, and apparently snowing all around; same raw weather.
,,	,, 4 P. M. ..	55	754	....	....	....	
23rd,	Greatest height, ..	..	734	6,211			
,,	Tumashoo, 4 P. M.	55	747	....	....	....	Cloudy, raw, threatening day.
,,	,, 8½ A. M.	56	749	5,022	5,012		
24th,	,, 7 A. M.	54	749	.... ..			
,,	1st Ravine, ...	65	749 5	4,886	4,807	....	Fine day, thunder at 3 P. M., Rain in evening; snow falling on heights around.
,,	Gratst. ht. 2½ P.M.	58	724 5	7,169	7,272	....	
,,	Oongar, 5 P. M...	58	734	6,256	6,371	....	Rainy and threatening, ditto ditto.
25th,	,, 9 P. M...	54	735				
,,	Oongar Brg. 12¼ P. M.	..	744	5,366	5,381	....	Rainy, cloudy weather.
,,	Ascent 1st Stat...	..	717	7,853	... .	....	Cloudy with showers.
,,	Pémee, 8 P. M...	..	702 5				
26th,	,, 8 A. M. ..	..	702	9,197	9,692	....	Cloudy and misty.
,,	Rodoola Peak, ..	..	672	1,200 3	12,335	....	Ditto ditto.
,,	Bhoomlung-tung, 8 P. M.	..	713				
27th,	,, 11 A. M. ..	46	713	8,570 3	8,668	8,668	Sunny.
,,	,, 4 P. M. ..	..	709				Cloudy occasionally.
28th,	,, 11 A. M. ..	51	711 5				Sunny.
,,	,, 4 P. M. ..	53	711				
,,	Ridge above Byagur,	..	....	....	9,947	....	Broken.
March 2nd,	Byagur, 4 P. M...	50	569 5		8,149	8,149	New tube, 54 5 8=558
3rd,	,, 9 A. M. ..	45	569	569 2 5	.. ....	....	Tassgong, ... 658=3,182
,,	,, 10 A. M. ..	60	569		.. ....	....	Byagur, ... 569=8,149
,,	,, 9 P. M. ..	45	569 5				89=4,967= 55 8
4th,	Summit, ...	48	539	1,114 9	11,035	11,099	Tassangsee, 623, ... 59 7
,,	Nullah, ...	49	552	987	9,642	9,810	Mean, ... 57 7
,,	Jaisa, ...	..	556				
,,	,, ...	..	555 5	555 8 1	9,410	9,444	Byagur and Tongsa.
5th,	,, 7 A. M. ..	..	556				

Date.	Station.	Temp.	Ther.	Altitude.	Bar. Alt.	Difference.	Remarks.
March 5th,	Summit, 12½ P.M.	..	538	....	10,931	11,204	Byagur, Jaisa, and Tongsa.
,,	Ravine, 3 P.M. ..	..	562 5	....	8,473	8,737	Ditto ditto ditto.
6th,	Tongsa, 10 A.M.	53	585 5	....			
,,	,, 4 P.M. ..	58 5	585	....			Sunny day with passing clouds.
7th,	,, 11 A.M. ..	53	585	....	6,527	6,588	Sunny day, deduced from Jaisa and Byagur.
,,	,, 4 P.M. ..	..	585	....			Cloudy.
8th,	,, 10 A.M. ..	53	586	....			
9th,	,, 11 A.M. ..	55	585				
,,	,, 4½ P.M. ..	60	585 5				
10th,	,, 10½ A.M.	53	585 5				
,,	,, 4 P.M. ..	53	583	....	....	....	Raw, cloudy day.
11th,	,, 11 A.M. ..	51 5	584 5	....	....	.... ..	Fine weather, snow around at night.
,,	,, 4 P.M. ..	59	583 5				
12th,	,, 11 A.M. ..	52	584				
13th,	,, 10½ A.M.	53	584 5				
,,	,, 4 P.M. ..	58	584				
14th,	,, 10½ A.M.	52	585	....	....	....	Fine.
,,	,, 4 P.M. ..	62	583 5				
15th,	,, 10½ A.M.	55	585	....	.... .	....	Fine.
,,	,, 4 P.M. ..	60	584 5	....	... .	... .	Cloudy.
16th,	,, ...	56	585				
17th,	,, 10 A.M. ..	55 5	585				Fine.
,,	,, 4 P.M. ..	59	583 5				Cloudy, rain throughout night.
18th,	,, 10½ A.M. ..	55	586				Cloudy.
,,	,, 11 A.M. ..	58	586				Fine.
19th,	,, 10 A.M. ..	54	587	584 9	6,588	6,527	Cloudy, threatening.
,,	,, 4 P.M. ..	58	585				Cloudy, slight rain.
20th,	,, 10 A.M. ..	54	587				Ditto.
,,	,, 4 P.M. ..	62	584 5				Fine.
21st,	,, 10 A.M. ..	55	586				Cloudy, rain in the morning.
,,	,, 4 P.M. ..	57	585				
23rd,	,, Bridge, ..	63	599	5	5,154	5,417	— 263. Rain.
,,	Taseeling, 4 P.M.	..	576	576 7 5	7,358	7,233	+ 125.
24th,	,, 7½ P.M. ..	.	577				

,,	Pagoda, 2½ P. M.	..	572	....	.. ....	7,829	7,602	+ 227.
25th,	Chindupj. 10 A.M.	51	571		571 5	7,875	7,863	+ 122.
,,	,, 4 P. M. ..	59	572	....	.. ....	....	....	Confluence of Gnee and Roogoon, 8,213.
26th,	Summit, ...	48	540 5	....	.. ....	10,955	10,873	+ 82.
,,	Rydang, 4½ P. M.	58	579	} ..	579 2 5	7,110	6,965	+ 145.
27th,	,, 8 A. M. ..	59	579 5					
,,	Ridge, 12½ P. M.	..	566 5	....	.. ....	8,374	8,308	— 66.
,,	Santagong, 9 P.M.	..	587	....	.. ....	6,276	6,325	— 49.
28th,	Thain, 4 P. M. ..	..	599					
30th,	,, 10 A. M...	62	599 5		598 4	5,213	5,279	Cloudy, — 66.
,,	,, 4 P. M...	61	598	....	.. ....	....	....	Cloudy, windy.
31st,	,, 10 A. M...	60 5	597	....	.. ....	....	....	Fine.
April 2nd,	Punukha, 10 A.M.	68	617 5					
,,	,, 4 P. M. ..	73	614 5	....	.. ....	....	3,640	— 617-5, windy.
,,	,, 12 P. M. ..	..	615		3,654			
3rd,	,, 10 A. M. ..	69	617	....	.. ....	....	....	Fine.
,,	,, 12 P. M. ..	75	615 5					
,,	,, 4 P. M. ..	78	613					
4th,	,, 10½ A. M.	72	614 5	....	.. ....	....	....	Cloudy, windy. Thermometer at 2½ P. M. 82°.
,,	,, 4 P. M. ..	77	612	....	.. ....	....	....	Fine.
5th,	,, 10½ A. M.	71	615	....	.. ....	3,789	....	Cloudy, windy.
,,	,, 4 P. M. ..	72	611 5	....	.. ....	....	....	Cloudy, calm.
6th,	,, 10½ A. M...	66 5	614 5	....	.. ....	....	....	Stormy, slight rain, violent wind SW., 9 P.M. 68° 5′.
,,	,, 12 P. M...	68	614	....	.. ....	....	....	Calm, fine, 8 A. M. 63°.
,,	,, 4 P. M. .	70	614	....	.. ....	....	....	Ditto ditto.
7th,	,, 10 A. M.	65	615	....	.. ....	....	....	Cloudy, rain at 2½ P. M., 9 P. M. 65°.
,,	,, 12 P. M. ..	73	613	....	.. ....	....	....	Calm and fine, 8 A. M. 63° 5′.
,,	,, 4 P. M. ..	70 5	613	....	.. ....	....	....	Windy.
8th,	,, 11 A. M. ..	66	614	....	.. ....	....	....	Windy and cloudy, 9¼ P. M. 68°.
,,	,, 4 P. M. ..	68 5	612	....	.. ....	....	....	8 A. M. 64°, hazy, calm.
9th,	,, 10 A. M. ..	64	615	....	.. ....	....	....	Windy, rain—rain at night.
,,	,, 12¼ P. M.	70	614	....	.. ....	....	....	8 A. M. 61° 5′, fine, very clear.
,,	,, 4 P. M. ..	71	613 5	....	.. ....	....	....	Fine and calm.
10th,	,, 4 P. M. ..	66	....	....	.. ....	....	....	Rain, windy, 9 P. M. 68°, cloudy.
11th,	,, 10½ A. M.	65	614 5	....	.. ....	....	....	Overcast, rain during night, 8 A.M. 63°, 9 P.M. 43° 5′.
,,	,, 12 P. M. ..	66	614	....	.. ....	....	....	Cloudy, calm, showers, drizzling yesterday.
,,	,, 4 P. M. ..	67	612	....	.. ....	....	....	Ditto ditto.
								Ditto ditto, 9 P. M. 66°, very cloudy.

Date.	Station.	Temp.	Ther.	Altitude.	Bar. Alt.	Difference.	Remarks.
April 12th,	Punukha, 10 A. M.	66	613	....	....	....	8 A. M. 62°, calm and fine, very cloudy.
„	„ 4 P. M. ..	72 5	611 5	....	....	....	Cloudy, windy, 9½ P. M. 68° 5', cloudy.
13th,	„ 10½ A. M.	70	614	....	....	....	8 A. M. 68°, fine ditto ditto.
„	„ 12 P. M. ..	76	611	....	....	....	Wind getting up.
„	„ 4 P. M. ..	79 8	612	....	....	....	Cloudy, windy, violent wind from NW. at 5 P. M.
14th,	„ 10 A. M. ..	67 5	615	....	....	....	8 A. M. 65°, rather cloudy, ditto ditto.
„	„ 12 P. M. ..	69 8	612	....	....	....	Cloudy, close.
„	„ 4 P. M. ..	74	611	....	....	....	Violent wind, thermometer 3½ P. M. 67° 8'.
15th,	„ 10½ A. M.	66	614 5	....	....	....	8 A. M. 62°, fine and calm, ditto.
„	„ 12 P. M. ..	76	612 5	....	....	....	Cloudy, but calm, strong wind from usual direction [at 1.
„	„ 4 P. M. ..	71 5	613 5				
16th,	„ 10 A. M. ..	66	614	....	....	....	Fine.
„	„ 4 P. M. ..	72	612	....	....	....	Cloudy, calm, strong W. wind at 1-3.
17th,	„ 10 A. M. ..	65	....	....	....	....	Broken.
„	„ 12 P. M. ..	71 5	....	....	....	....	Cloudy, calm, slight shower at 6 A. M.
„	„ 8 P. M. ..	66					
18th,	„ 8 A. M. ..	64	....	3,739			
„	„ 10 A. M. ..	67	....				
„	„ 12 P. M. ..	74	....	....	....	....	Windy, rather cloudy.
„	„ 4 P. M. ..	75	....	....	....	....	Ditto ditto ditto.
19th,	„ 8 A. M. ..	67	....	....	....	....	Cloudy.
„	„ 10 A. M. ..	69	....	....	....	....	Ditto
„	„ 12 P. M. ..	73	....	....	....	....	Clouds and sun, wind rising.
„	„ 4 P. M. ..	74	....	....	....	....	Cloudy, very windy.
„	„ 9½ P. M.	70	....	....	....	....	Very bright, clouds as usual from N.
20th,	„ 8 A. M. ..	69	....	....	....	....	Fine.
„	„ 10 A. M. ..	72	....	....	....	....	Passing clouds.
„	„ 12 P. M. ..	74	....	....	....	....	Cloudy and windy.
„	„ 4 P. M. ..	76	....	....	....	....	Ditto.
„	„ 9½ P. M. ..	70	....	....	....	....	Cloudy.
21st,	„ 8 A. M. ..	69	....	....	....	....	Fine and cloudy.

Date.	Time.	Temp.	Remarks.
April 21st,	10 A. M. ..	72	Fine, some clouds.
,,	12 P. M. ..	78	Fine, windy.
,,	4 P. M. ..	80	Cloudy, very windy.
,,	10 P. M. ..	73	Rather cloudy.
22nd,	8 A. M. ..	71	Fine, sultry.
,,	12 P. M. ..	80	Rather cloudy, gusts of wind.
,,	4 P. M. ..	78	Slight rain, windy, at 7½ P. M.
23rd,	8 A. M. ..	72	Fine.
,,	10 A. M. ..	73	
,,	4 P. M. ..	81	Windy and cloudy.
,,	11 P. M. ..	71	Rain at 9 P. M.
24th,	8 A. M. ..	68	
,,	10 A. M. ..	70	Fine and calm.
,,	4 P. M. ..	82	Fine, windy.
,,	11 P. M. ..	73	
25th,	8 A. M. ..	70	
,,	10 A. M. ..	72	Calm.
,,	12 P. M. ..	79	Wind getting up.
,,	4 P. M. ..	82	Windy.
,,	8 P. M. ..	75	Windy, hazy.
26th,	8 A. M. ..	70	Hazy.
,,	10 A. M. ..	72	Calm, sultry.
,,	4 P. M. ..	81	Windy.
,,	8 P. M. ..	78	Windy, till 9 or 9½ P. M.
27th,	8 A. M. ..	73	Sultry, hazy.
,,	10 A. M. ..	74	Ditto ditto.
,,	12½ P.M...	82	Ditto ditto.
,,	4 P. M. ..	83	Ditto ditto, windy.
,,	11 P. M. ..	76	Ditto ditto, fine.
28th,	8 A. M. ..	72	Sultry.
,,	10½ A. M.	75	Ditto.
,,	4 P. M. ..	83	Wind violent.
,,	10 P. M. ..	75	Cloudy.
29th,	8 A. M. ..	70	Cloudy, hazy, sultry.
,,	10 A. M. ..	75	
,,	12 P. M. ..	79	
,,	4 P. M. ..	78	Hazy, less windy.
,,	10 P. M. ..	73	Cloudy, rain at 8 P. M.
30th,	8 A. M. ..	70	Cloudy.
,,	10 A. M. ..	71	Cloudy and hazy.
,,	12 P. M. ..	74	Close.
,,	4 P. M. ..	76	Windy, very hazy.
,,	9 P. M. ..	73	
,,	10 P. M. ..	73	Cloudy.
May 1st,	8 A. M. ..	71	Hazy, sultry.
,,	10 A. M. ..	71	Cool, cloudy.
,,	12 P. M. ..	72	Ditto ditto.
,,	4 P. M. ..	75	No wind to 6½ P. M.
,,	8 P. M. ..	73	Cloudy.
,,	10½ P. M.	73	Ditto.
2nd,	8 A. M. ..	70	Cloudy and hazy.
,,	10 A. M. ..	73	
,,	12 P. M. ..	75	
,,	4 P. M. ..	75	Usual wind about 5 P. M.
,,	10 P. M. ..	73	Much less violent.
3rd,	8 A. M. ..	71	Cloudy.
,,	10 A. M. ..	73	Fine, cloudy and windy since 12 P. M.
,,	12 P. M. ..	75 5	
,,	4 P. M. ..	79	

Date.	Time.	Temp.	Remarks.
May 3rd,	10 P. M. ..	73	Cloudy.
4th,	8 A. M. ..	71	Cloudy, rain at night.
„	10 A. M. ..	73	Cloudy, wind getting up.
„	4 P. M. ..	75	Cloudy, rather windy.
5th,	8 A. M. ..	71	Cloudy, rain.
„	10 A. M. ..	72	Ditto ditto.
„	12 P. M. ..	72	Cloudy, close.
„	4 P. M. ..	76	Fine, rather windy.
„	8½ P. M.	71	Cloudy.
6th,	8 A. M. ..	72	Fine, sultry.
„	10 A. M. ..	73	Ditto ditto.
„	12½ P. M.	80	Windy, fine.
„	4 P. M. ..	76	Windy, clouds flying.
„	.. ..	..	Clouds.
7th,	8 A. M. ..	72	Fine.
„	10 A. M. ..	74	Ditto.
„	„	79	Violent gusts from west with dust.
11th,	7 A. M. ..	51	

CHAPTER XIV.

Journey with the Army of the Indus. From Loodianah to Candahar through the Bolan Pass.

I reached Loodianah on the 10th December 1838, after a dâwk journey of fourteen and a half days. After passing the Rajemahal Hills, the country presents an uniform aspect, but becoming more sandy as one proceeds to the northward. The hills alluded to, form a low range, the only one of any height being that called Pursunath. They are well wooded, the under-vegetation being grassy. Undulating ground bare of trees, but provided with shrubs, is passed before coming on the wooded tracts, the vegetation of these present much similarity with that of even 31° N. The ***Dhak***, Pommereulla, Zizzyphus, occurring. The ***Mahooa*** occurs in abundance on the hills, but does not reach much beyond Cawnpore. The country from the hills upwards, is almost entirely cultivated; very few trees occurring, and those that do, are almost entirely mango. The Borassus does not extend in abundance much beyond Benares, but the ***Khujoor*** is found everywhere in sandy soil.

Loodianah is situated about five miles south of the Sutledge, in the midst of a sandy country, very bare of trees. The fort and Capt. Wade's house are situated on a rising ground, at the base of which runs a nullah, a tributary of the Sutledge. There is much cultivation about the place, chiefly of grain, barley and wheat, bajerow, cotton, the latter bad, but there is much land uncultivated. The surface is often flat and somewhat broken; in such places there is much of a low prickly ***Bheir***, much used for making fences. This and ***Dhak*** jungle, which occurs in strips, form two marked features, the ***Dhak*** occurs in patches. The grasses, which occasionally form patches, are Andropogoneous; Anathericum, Pommereulla, and Eleusine occur.

Sugar-cane occurs; it is cultivated in thick masses, it is poor, and always fenced with the ***Bheir***.

The most common trees are the mango, Parkinsonia, ***Babool***, Acacia altera babooloides, a Leguminous Mimosoid tree, Tamarisk, a middling sized tree and very pretty, Ficus.

The hedges about the cantonments, etc. are formed by prickly pear; much Ricinus occurs in waste places, and it appears to me to be different from that to the south.

The most varied vegetation occurs along the nullah, but consists entirely of aquatic or sub-aquatic plants; among these the most common are two or three Scirpi, particularly a large rush-like one, a large Sparganium, a very narrow leaved Typha, Hydrocharis ! a pointed leaved Villarsia, Potomogetons three or four, one only natant; Chara, Naias, Ceratophyllum, Ulva, Valisneria, Marsilea, Herpestes, Jussieua repens, Fumaria common in fields.

The town is a large bustling place : the houses low and regular, and of a somewhat picturesque style, built of brick, the streets are wide and regular, having been laid out by our officers. There is a good deal of trade, and the place is filled with Cashmereans, who may be seen working their peculiar shawls, and producing very beautiful dyes.

January 22nd and 23rd.—Violent south-east winds during the day; abating at night.

February 4th.—Arrived at Hurreekee, having halted on the previous day at Mokhoo, a small village, with the usual style of mud fort. The marches were as follows: from Loodianah to Ghosepoora is eight miles; to Boondree, eight miles; Tiraia, ten miles; to Durrumkote, ten miles; to Futtygurh, ten miles; to Hurreekee, ten miles. Thus Hurreekee is at least eighteen miles from Durrumkote, although we had been told it was only five. The country near Loodianah, and perhaps as far as Durrumkote, is occasionally very sandy, but beyond that it is easily traversed by hackeries. Being much less cultivated and overrun with grasses, among which Andropogons are the most numerous and conspicuous, these grasses are either coarse and stout or wiry and fine, should afford excellent cover for game, which however, does not seem to be very abundant. Very few trees are visible in any direction, and although neither very much cultivation nor many villages are visible, it would appear from charts that the country is very populous. The most interesting plant was a species of Fagonia.

Durrumkote is the largest of the villages we passed, and has a respectable looking mud and brick fort. Inside the village is filthy; the houses wretchedly small, and the streets very narrow. It is much the same sort of village as other Seikh ones. In the bazars cocoanuts were noticed. All the Seikhs eat opium, and very often in a particular way by infusing the poppy-heads, from which the seeds have been extracted by a hole in the side; great numbers of these are found in the bazars.

Hurreekee is on Runjeet's side. I crossed the Sutledge, which is between 400 to 500 yards broad with a sufficiently rapid stream, by a bridge of boats built by the Seikhs, under the superintendence of Mr. Roobalee. It contained 65 boats, placed alternately up and down the river; the boats were moored to posts: over them were placed, both lengthwise and across, timbers, then grass, then soil; many elephants passed over, until it gave in, but was quickly repaired, and since many more hundreds of camels, horses, and thousands of people have passed. The right bank is thirty feet high, the left low and sandy. The country where uncultivated, is clothed with grasses, and the only trees visible are perhaps the Pipul; the *Jhow* occurs but not the Parhass; a few Bukeens are visible, Ricinus, Salvadora, which is occasionally a climber, especially at Tiraia. The river rose suddenly on the night of the 6th and carried away the bridge. The Himalayas had been seen very distinctly throughout the day, so that the rain must have been local: the height of the rise was three feet.

We left Hurreekee on the 8th at 10 A. M., the river up to this time (9th) presents the same monotonous appearance—sandy banks clothed with grasses, intermixed with *Jhow* here and there, and occasionally Æschynomene, and Typha. Very few villages have been passed, nor does the rare occurrence of topes indicate that there are many near it. The channel has been throughout much subdivided, and flats are of frequent occurrence. Yesterday we passed two busy ferries, at which two or three boats were unceasingly employed, and there was an obvious demand for more. Black partridges were heard frequently, black-bellied tern, herons, cormorants, etc. The stream averages three miles an hour. Parkinsonia was seen near Hurreekee. Reached Ferozepore at 12½ on the 9th; it is a very busy ghat, more so than that of Hurreekee: two large godowns were passed on the Company's side. The river is wider by 100 yards than at Hurreekee.

10th.—Reached Mamdot at 9½ A. M. The fort appears of good size, with high walls: it is about half a mile from the river. The country continues the same. Some wheat cultivation, in which Fumaria, Anagallis, Medicago are abundant; Calotropis Hamiltonii common; some grapes; *doob* grass wherever there is or has been cultivation. The only trees I see are Babooloid, but not the true *Babool*, which has very odorous flowers, and is always an arbuscula, a shrubby *Bheir*, spina una erecta, altera recurvo also occurs; among the fields, Lathyrus, Aphaca, and a Compositæ which has the leaves of a thistle, are common.

Halted at Buggeekee, which is, I imagine, the Pajarkee of Tassin's Map.

11*th.*—Continued passing down; breakfasting at Attaree: few signs of villages, but a good deal of cultivation. Persian wheels not unfrequently employed in raising water from the river: a short channel having first been cut in the bank, and the banks, when loose, propped up. Wheat, radishes, etc. Grasses appear to be much less common, while the *Jhow* is increasing much. The river is much subdivided, and the actual banks are scarcely discernible owing to the want of trees. The soil and current remain the same: no impediments have been met with by our boats, nor have I yet observed any to tracking, the grass jungle being easily overcome, and very unlike that of the Brahmapootra, and the *Jhow* not reaching that height necessary to make it troublesome. The Nawab of Mamdot visited the Envoy to-day, accompanied by a small party of horsemen. Only two alligators have been seen thus far: no game even to be heard, and but few living creatures visible.

12*th.*—The river becomes even less interesting than before; the channel is occasionally much narrowed by sands, over one of which we found yesterday evening some difficulty in passing; it is much more spread out and subdivided, and from this circumstance, will occasion difficulty in tracking up. The banks are low and generally within reach of inundation: scarcely a village is to be seen; and *Jhow* is the most uniform feature. Yesterday evening saltpetre was visible in abundance on some of the higher banks, and on these *Phulahi*, *Jhow*, a Composita, and Salsola? or Chenopodium were observed. Since the 10th, the few boats seen are of different structure from those to which we had been accustomed; they are flat, less wide, and much better fastened together, elevated at both ends; they are propelled as well as guided by the rudder, which is curved, so as to bring it within reach of the helmsman, who is on a level with the bottom of the boat. Very little cultivation: Tassin's Map of but little use, as few of the names are recognised by the boatmen or villagers.

Paukputtea was passed to-day; it is the shrine of a *fakeer*, and one in great repute, as passing through a particular gate is supposed to authorize one to claim admittance into Paradise. The Moulavee consequently has proceeded there in full faith and extravagant joy: with natives of the east such absurdities are to the full as much believed by the educated as by the uneducated; indeed the former are much the more bigotted of the two. The *fakeer* alluded to, not only lived for years on a block of wood carved into the likeness of a loaf, but subsequently suspended himself for several years in a well, without even the wooden loaf. He is then said to have disappeared, and is no doubt now enjoying all the pleasures of a Mohammedan paradise. We were detained by strong winds at a small village opposite Paukputtea, which is situated on rather high ground, as far as could be judged from the distance.

13*th*.—The cultivation round this village consists of wheat, radishes, a sort of mustard cultivated for its oily seeds, and the Mehta of Hindoostan. Among the fields I picked up a Melilotus, a Melilotoid, and a genuine Medicago, which is also found at Loodianah, both these last are wild, and their occurrence is as curious as it is interesting; the latter being a decidedly boreal form. In connection with these annuals I have to observe, that most flower about January or February, at which time the mornings and nights are the coldest: also observed Lathyrus cultivated, a Chenopodium was also found, Calotropis, a large Saccharoid, Amaranthaceæ, were the most common plants, Gnaphalium, Lippia; *Purwas*, occurs scantily.

14*th*.—Detained till 12 P. M. by bad weather. Sissoo not uncommon but small, *Babool*, the true sweet scented sort. The Colocynth seen in fruit much like an apple, not ribbed; it has the usual structure of the order, viz. 3-carpellary with revolute placentæ, so much so, that they are placed near the circumference; seeds very numerous, surrounded with pulp, not arillate: no separation taking place; oval, brown, smooth. In fields here, a wild strong smelling Umbellifera occurs, called *Dhunnea*, used as a potherb, and esteemed very fragrant by the natives. Besides the absence of an arillus, there is another anomaly about the above Colycynth, which is, that between each placenta a broad partition projects from the wall of the fruit, usually provided with 3-septa, so as to be divided into two chambers, these contain seeds, the funiculi passing completely through them; seeds are also contained between the outermost septa and the placentæ themselves.

Passed two or three villages. The Persian wheels continue in vogue; their site is always on a sufficiently high and tenacious bank. I observed some wells, communicating with the river by an archway in the bank. Most of the cattle are blinded by the conical blinkers or hoods over the eyes.

15*th*.—Halted at a village partly washed away, surrounded by a good deal of wheat and radish cultivation. The mango tree and Moringa also occur here with the larger *Babool*, which invariably has long white thorns. The small Sissoo still occurs. Snake bird seen, black crowned tern.

The river remains most uninteresting; the banks are low and covered chiefly with *Jhow*. In many places recent shells are very abundant, but do not appear to be composed of more than three species. Reseda, Oligandra in fields.

16*th.*—No change in the country. Heavy fog yesterday morning; to-day strongish north-east winds. Grass and *Jhow* about equal.

17*th.*—Cloudy, drizzling, raw weather; river more sluggish; more villages and more cultivation: Phascum, and Gymnostomum common on tenacious sand banks.

18*th.*—Weather unsettled, windy and rainy. *Jhow* and grass jungle continue, Tamarisk, *Furas* fine specimens, Fumaria continues in fields, Capparis aphylla, which has something of a Cactoid habit, and whose branches abound with stomata, Reseda.

19*th.*—Weather finer but still cloudy, north-east wind still prevalent, and impeding our progress in some of the reaches very much. Salvadora, Capparis aphylla, *Phulahi, Bheir,* large *Babool, Furas,* Ranunculus sceleratus: *Jhow* and grass jungle are the prevailing features. Current much the same, only occasionally sluggish. Pelicans, black-headed adjutants, (Ardea capita,) wild geese, ducks very numerous in the jheels formed by alteration in the course of the river; the country is more cultivated, but as dreary looking as imaginable. Phœnix becoming more frequent and finer, P. acaulis ? likewise occurs occasionally, rather young *Khujoors*. We passed Khyrpore about 3 P. M., it seems a straggling place, stretching along the bank of the Sutledge; there are a great many *Khujoor* trees about it, and indeed about all the villages near it. A little below this large tract, the banks were covered with a thick *Sofaida* shrubby jungle, which looked at a distance like dwarf Sissoo. The country is much improved, and there is a great deal of cultivation, especially on the left bank.

20*th.*—Continued—the river is very winding, and its banks present the same features: the immediate ones being covered with short *Jhow* or grass, or both intermixed; the extreme ones well wooded, and well peopled. *Khujoor* very common. Yesterday near Khanpore, caught a glimpse of the descent, and to-day again the ground appears uneven, and almost entirely barren. It must be within a mile of the Sutledge. The left bank continues well cultivated. In some of the fields I noticed Medicago vera, Anagallis, Fumaria, Chenopodium cnicoideus, Prenanthoid, the *Furas*, larger *Babool*, and Calotropis Hamiltonii continue. Radishes very common, as also *Teera Meera*.

21*st*.—Halted about 8 coss from Bahawulpore. The Khan's son, a boy of 8 years, came to see Mr. Macnaghten, and saluted him with "good night," he was attended by about twelve indifferent pony *suwars*, or horsemen. The river is very tortuous, both banks a good deal cultivated; there appear to be a good many canals, which have high banks owing to the excavated soil being piled up: they are 8 or 10 feet deep, and about 20 feet wide, at this season they are nearly dry, becoming filled during the rains. The same plants continue—*Furas*, *Jhow*, Chenopodia 2, Reseda, Linaria, Malva, Boraginea, Lactucoidea. The wheat throughout these countries is sown broad-cast. Irrigation is effected by means of small ditches, and squares formed in the fields —each partition being banked in, so as to prevent communication; when one is filled, the water is allowed to pass off into its neighbour, and so on. Irrigation is entirely effected by Persian wheels; the cattle are hoodwinked in order to keep them quiet: besides from not seeing, they are led to imagine that the driver is always at his post, which is immediately behind the oxen and on the curved flat timber which puts the whole apparatus in motion. Saw a man cross the river by means of a *mushuk* or inflated skin. The very common bushy plant with thorns and ligulate leaves which commences to appear about Hazaribagh and continues in abundance throughout the sandy north-west, is, judging from its fruit, which is a moniliform legume—a Papilionacea; the fruit are borne by the short spine-terminated branches: the stalk of the pod is surrounded for the most part by a cupuliform membranous calyx. I have only seen however withered specimens. Reached Bahawul ghat at 1 P. M. The Khan visited Mr. Macnaghten in the afternoon, his visit was preceded by one from his Hindoo minister, and another man, Imaam Shah, who is a very fat ruffianly-looking fellow. The Khan was attended by numerous *suwarries*; he is a portly looking, middle-aged man.

22*nd*.—We returned the visit to-day, the Khan having provided us with one horse and two bullock *rhuts*: we traversed the sandy bank of the river for about a mile before we reached the town, the suburbs of which are extensive, but very straggling, and thinly peopled. The inner town seemed to be of some extent, the streets narrow, the houses very poor, and almost entirely of mud; there were a number of shops, and the streets were lined with men and a few old women. There is very little distinction in appearance between the Khan's residence and any other portion of the town, and I did not see a defence of any kind. The Khan received us on some irregular terraces; near his house, the street leading to the private entrance was lined with his troops, as well as that leading to the terrace, and this was surrounded with his adherents, variously and well-dressed. The troops, for such appeared, were decent, and those forming one side were dressed in white, in imitation of our Sepoys, and the other side were in red and blue, *more proprio* I imagine: they were armed with muskets; the red ones for the most part having muskets of native workmanship. A royal salute was fired when the meeting took place, which was on the terrace, and as we proceeded up the *street*, a band made a rude and noisy attempt at 'God save the King.' Having had a private consultation, Mr. Macnaghten withdrew with similar honours, presenting arms, etc. The presents were a handsome native rifle, with a flint lock, and the fabrics of the city, some of which called Kharse, were very creditable.

There are a good many trees about the place, indeed these form the chief mark when seen from the ghat: the principal are mangoes, *Khujoors*, Moringas, oranges. The natives are rather a fine race, but dirty: some of the women wore the *Patani* veils, or hoods, with net-work over the eyes.

Continued down the river; though much delayed by strong south-east winds. The vegetation, etc. continue the same, Potentilla sp. in flower, Phascum very common.

23*rd.*—Nothing new has occurred: the current is stronger than above Bahawulpore: the channel continues very winding, and sand banks very frequent. *Furas*, Salvadora, *Phulahi* very common. The boats accidentally separated, and we went without dinner in consequence: came into the Pungnud. The mouths of the Chenab seem to be two, both apparently of no great size, yet the Pungnud is a noble river, and although much subdivided by sand banks, is a striking stream, the waters are very muddy, and when agitated by a strong wind become almost reddish. The jungle continues much the same: the Sissoid jungle again occurred to-day, the natives call it *Sofaida;* it has a very curious habit, and is gemmiferous, the gemmæ abounding in gum. Quail, black-grey partridge, hares, continue; a goat-sucker (Caprimulgus,) was seen.

24*th.*—The boats joined early this morning: we were delayed the whole day by strong north-east winds; the whole country was obscured by the dust.

26th.—The wind abated towards evening, and occurred again in gusts during the night. This morning we came in sight of the southerly portion of the Soliman range, by which name however, these mountains do not appear to be known hereabouts; their distance must be forty miles at least, yet they appear to be of considerable height: the range runs north and south nearly. Wheat is here sown in rows. *Khujoor*, large *Babool*, Fagonia, continue, *Jhow* very common. Towards evening we came to a subdivision of the stream: following the smaller one in which the current was very strong; in some places, apparently six knots an hour. We came to for the evening at a village on the limits of the Bahawul territory.

27th.—We came on the Indus early in the morning and stopped opposite Mittunkote until 2 P. M., awaiting the arrival of Mr. Mackeson. The mouths of the Attock river are scarcely more striking than those of the Chenab; neither is the combined river immediately opposite Mittunkote of any great size: certainly the stream we followed was not more than 800 or 900 yards wide, the extreme banks are at a considerable distance; and half a mile below Mittunkote the surface of the water must be one and a half to two miles in breadth; the river is much subdivided by banks, and shallows are frequent, yet some of the reaches are of great extent.

The banks are low and rather bluff, the vegetation continues the same, but *Jhow* is far the most common plant. *Bheir*, *Babool*, and the *Seerkee* Saccharum continue; the cultivation is the same; Calotropis Hamiltonii. Mittunkote appears, from a distance of two coss, a place of some size, with a somewhat conspicuous dome. Immediately behind it are the Soliman Hills, of no great altitude; and, except at the bases, which are covered with black patches of forest, they appear uniformly brown, otherwise there is nothing to vary the monotony of the scene, scarcely any trees being visible. On stopping for breakfast, a general scene of embracing among the dhandies or boatmen and their friends occurred; women were also embraced in the usual way, but with apparently less tenderness or warmth than the men. The boats tracking up, have masts, but the goon or rope is seized with both hands, a plan far less advantageous than that adopted on the Ganges and Bramahpootra, where the principal tracking is exercised by a bamboo placed over the shoulder, farthest from the goon.

28th.—No change worth noticing. The current continues rapid. The hills visible, running parallel to the river, and ending very gradually. Typha is very common, and in some places Arundo.

29th.—We remain in sight of, and generally continuing in the same direction as the hills, which run out very gradually indeed. Scarcely a tree is to be seen, and very few villages. The country continues to have some vegetation. The *Sofaida* is now found in flower, it is the *Ban* of the natives of these parts; the former name indicates in Persian, a tree, said to be wild Poplar, with which this has on obvious affinity. Saccharum *Seerkee* very common, growing in tufts and covering extensive tracts. Scarcely any cultivation is to be seen along the river, and altogether a very small proportion is rendered available. River very much subdivided: towards evening the sky is obscured to leeward by the smoke arising from burning jungle. Water-fowl are very common along the Indus; especially wild geese, which frequent open streams, whereas ducks, etc. haunt places which only communicate with the main streams during floods: myriads of *Bogulas*, (the general name for herons,) were seen yesterday in a compact body. The Soliman mountains are by no means rugged, and this only in one or two places, where they become peaked. In Mr. Elphinstone's account of a Journey to Cabul, the limestone said to be found in the desert contains shells; it would be most interesting to compare this with the limestone of Churra more especially. Mr. E. also mentions a wild rue as forming part of the very scanty vegetation of the desert; the chief plants being *Kureel*, which is a Capparis; Phoke ———— and *Bheir*. Mr. E. also says that the material of which the tope of Manikyalah is built, resembles petrified vegetable matter, an observation to be kept in view. The mottled king-fisher occurs throughout, but is commoner in southern latitudes of India.

Alligators abounded to-day, and it was curious to see them basking in the sun with flocks of herons so close, that at a little distance they appeared to be perching on the backs of the alligators, or rather crocodiles. Again saw a man swim the Indus by means of a *mus-huk* or inflated skin: he swam very rapidly, and with great ease; half his body nearly being out of the water; he reclined on the skin and kept the aperture by which it is inflated in his mouth, carrying his clothes on his head. Passed Chuck about 4½ P. M. The country appears populous hereabouts.

30th.—We have seen a good many boats to-day employed in carrying grain to the camp; the smaller ones are not unlike Bengal boats, having a high stern: all on the Indus however have square bows and flat bottoms.

The *Jhow* has increased in size in some places as has *Sofaida*, which is occasionally a moderate tree, and it is now more advanced in flowering: the temperature having visibly increased. The river puts on the same features and is much subdivided; the channels by which we have come, are not above 400 to 500 yards in breadth, yet there is often seen to be a waste of low sand banks stretching to a great extent, and the extreme banks are very remote, so as generally not to be visible.

31st.—Arrived at Uzeeypore about 9 A. M. Here we found horses and camels for our conveyance to Skikarpore. Uzeeypore appears to be a well frequented passage of the river, although we did not see any ferry boats. Bukkur is visible from it, apparently occupying a hill almost to the extreme right of a low range running south-west; it is seven or eight coss distant. We left for Shikarpore about 2½ P. M. and reached about 7 P. M.: the distance is said to be twenty-four miles; the road is generally very sandy, although the sand is not very deep; the substratum being solid. We passed some cultivation and a few villages, at one of which (Khye) there is a neat sort of fortification; here we changed horses. The jungle throughout consisted of Furas, Tamarisk, Salvadora, *Phulahi* parva, the prickly Leguminosa, with the habit of Fagonia, Calotropis Hamiltonii, Saccharum.

Shikarpore is not visible until one reaches the clearing around the town; in the twilight it appears to be a very large place.

February 2nd.—We do not proceed to Larkhanu, as daily news from Hyderabad is expected. I see nothing likely to interest me about this place; there is absolutely not a flower to be got any where. The jungles consist of *Jhow*, small *Furas*, *Rairoo*, a small arbusculoid Mimosa, *Kureel*, and Ukko, Calotropis Hamiltonii, *Bheirs* shrubby; one of the most abundant plants is the *Joussa* or prickly Leguminosa, with the habit of Fagonia; some of the saline loving Compositæ, No. 51, frutex 2-3 pedalis, foliis carnosis lanceolato-spathulatis, sessilibus. Corymbis et Cymi axillaribus et terminalibus pauci capitat. Floscules inconspicuis, also occurs. Near the Shah's tents there is a grove of *Phulahi*, all more or less demolished, and a good many *Khujoors*. Hares and grey partridges appear common. The changes of temperature are very great; in the mornings and evenings it is cold; in the afternoon the thermometer reaches as high as 82°.

9th.—Shikarpore is getting hotter every day: thermometer ranges from 40° to 85°.

15th.—The heat continued to increase until the 12th; the range of thermometer being from 50° to 95°; the evenings gradually became hotter, and the night although cool, had the peculiar thrilling coolness of tropical nights.

On the 12th, the barometer commenced falling, and has since continued to do so. The visible signs of rain have been confined to cloudy mornings; the fall of the mercury is perhaps connected with the occasional strong northerly winds, which at times, as last night, blow nearly half gales. The range of thermometer is now from 55° to 85°. The change was sudden on the 9th or 10th; the nights were cold, thermometer at 5 A. M. 34° 36′; and the days were only moderately warm. The weather now is pleasant. Shikarpore is disagreeable *inter alia* from its dust, every thing becoming covered with it.

The suburbs of the city are well wooded, and all such portions are well provided with gardens. The *Khujoor* is the most common tree, the Moringa, mango, *Jamun*, *Bheir*, *Neem*, Cassia fistula, Sissoo, *Peepul*, *Furas*, *Phulahi*, another Mimosa and Agati, occur; oranges in gardens, and a Pomaceous tree from Cashmere, which appears to thrive very well. The cultivation consists chiefly of wheat, *Mahta*, mustard, radishes, *Soonf*, coriander, beet, *Bagree*.

In these fields Phascum, Plantago, Ispaghula, Singee, Chenopodiaceæ 1-2, Salsola lanata, and Bœhmeria, may be found; Composita salinaria, stocks and wall-flowers in the gardens.

The vegetation elsewhere is very scanty; consisting of *Jhow*, *Bheir*, *Furas*, *Ukko*, *Joussa*, Andropogon *Seerkee*, *Rairoo*, *Kureel*, a low bush called ———, and a Lycium ? Bœhmeria albida.

The town is miserably defended: the streets are very irregular and very narrow: the houses all of mud, of the usual Scindian form, and completely irregular. The bazaars or arcades, are mere ordinary streets, covered in with timbers, over which tattered mats are placed: in these are situated the Hindoo shops, and in some places darkness is completely visible. These Hindoos have a peculiar elongated Jewish aspect, and are reported to be very wealthy. Grain and cloth are the principal articles in which they deal, and they say the streets are covered in order that the purchaser may buy with his eyes half shut. The city is a large rambling place, and each house deposits its own filth before it. The inhabitants, especially the Hindoo portion, have a peculiar complexion, and by no means a healthy one. No one seems to have deserted the town on account of our approach, neither has fear hitherto prevented them from bringing their merchandise into camp.

The weather has continued cool: yesterday we had a good deal of rain; to-day it is very cloudy. The range of the thermometers from 46° and 48° to 82° outside.

Artificers are not uncommon, as carpenters and blacksmiths, but their tools are miserable: and there is no such thing as a large saw to be seen. Wages are high, and from the slowness with which they work, it is ruinous to employ them.

Left Shikarpore on the 21st and marched to Jargon, 13½ miles, one of the usual fortified villages of *kucha* or unburnt brick. Houses surrounded also with *Jhow* fences. The jungle and country precisely the same as that round Shikarpore, road at first bad, but subsequently good enough: water is to be had very good: at no great depth.

22*th.*—To Janidaira, 11½ miles: road excellent throughout. Country less covered with jungle: features mostly the same: a curious looking plant occurred plentifully, but to a limited extent near Jargon: and subsequently, as the country became more sandy, we had abundance of Salicornia, of which camels are excessively fond, otherwise *Jhow, Furas*, very common, *Rairoo, Kureel, Ukko* throughout; near Jargon, Elrua very common, Chenopodium cymbifolium throughout.

The soil at first is very fine, finely pulverized, brownish as we proceeded onwards, becoming more and more sandy. Hills of some height, apparently very distant, are seen ahead due north, and to the west. We passed one village to the left, two canals of small size, and some *Bagree* cultivation. A small ridge with a hillock occurred after passing the village, otherwise all was flat. And about this the jungle was thin, entirely of patches *Kureel, Rairoo,* and *Furas*, Peepul.

We had a violent north wind yesterday evening with some rain.

23*rd.*—To Rogan, distance 11 to 12 miles: country generally flat, presenting here and there sandy undulations, generally bare of vegetation. Salvadora, *Jhow, Furas, Kureel, Rairoo*, continue; *Furas* and *Rairoo* most common; a new Chenopodium and a Salsola, or a plant of the same genus as that met with yesterday, swarming in some places, both species were common in some parts, in others one of the two only occurred. Road generally excellent, level and unbroken. Two small ghurrees or forts occurred, with a large patch of cotton, and still larger of *Bagree:* a small Sedoid. looking plant with yellow flowers, and one or two other (to me) novelties occurred: Heliotropium, Fagonia, *Joussa, Bheir.* In those parts in which loose sand had become accumulated, it not only formed banks, but every bush was submerjed in it. The fresh sand must be derived from decomposition of the hard level plain by the action of the air : yet there should be a regular gradation in size of the waves; those nearest the windward side of the desert ought to be the smallest. Rock pigeon of Loodianah seen.

There are two ghurrees or forts at the halting place, both small; the water is tolerable. The chief trees are Salvadora and *Rairoo*.

24th and 25th.—Left in the evening and marched all night through the desert, which commences within two miles of Rogan, and towards which place vegetation gradually becomes more scarce until it disappears entirely. This sandy waste is upwards of twenty miles in extent: in the direction we traversed it, NW. or NNW., it is almost totally deprived of vegetation; one or two plants, such as Salsoloid, being alone observable near its borders. The surface is generally quite flat, in some places cut up by beds of small streams: the surface is firm, and bears marks of inundation: tracks of camels, etc. being indented. We reached Bushore at 5½ A. M.; the camels performed twenty-six miles in ten hours. We halted for four hours in the centre of the desert and tried to sleep but the cold was too great, striking up as it were from the ground. The camels marched through without halting, and we suffered only one loss amongst them next day. The occurrence of this peculiar desert is unaccountable, especially its almost absolute privation of vegetation; for many other places, equally dry, have their peculiar plants, such as Salsola, Chenopodium, *Furas, Rairo, Ukkoo, Kureel.*

25th.—Bushore is a miserable place, consisting of the usual mud houses and defences: the adjacent nullah does not invite attention; it is however the only seat of wells, which, as in all this country since leaving Rogan, are of small diameter, from thirty to forty feet deep, and contain very little water, which also is rather brackish and well impregnated with sand. The surrounding country is so barren that it may be called a desert, while the desert itself may be called the desert of deserts. I should mention that this ceases first to the west, in which direction shrubs encroach on it. *Phulahi*, Evolvulus acanthoides, Tribulus, *Kureel*, etc. are found about Bushore, but the prevailing plant is Chenopodium cymbifolium.

26th.—Leaving Bushore, we proceeded to Joke, which we reached late, it being nineteen miles: we lost the road however, which is in a direct line only sixteen miles. We soon came on a nullah, or canal, which we followed to Meerpore, a rather large double village, with a nice grove of *Furas*, situated on the dry river Naree, which is as contemptible in size as deficient in water, this is only procurable by digging wells of thirty feet deep, and even then in small quantity. Before reaching it, we passed several villages, mostly deserted and ruined.

The country is frightfully bare of wood: the chief plant is Chenopodium cymbifolium, and along the canal lemon grass, *Kureel*, *Rairoo*, *Joussa*, *Ukko*, *Bheir*, etc.; near Meerpore a Centaurea, and Evolvulus acanthaceus. But along the nullah some wood may be found, stunted though it be, it is chiefly *Rairoo*. We left Meerpore and proceeded about one and a half mile from Joke, following the nullah until we came on a canal in which, from a bund having been thrown across, there was a puddle or two of water. Here we halted. Much remains of cultivation is presented about this, chiefly *Bagree*, which is perennial. Durand tells me that the sprouts of the second year are poisonous to cattle, i. e. horses; but this report may have been given out purposely by the natives. Along the river, *Jhow* and *Furas* occur, in the naked plains, Chenopodium cymbifolium, *Rairoo*, and a few *Kureel*, but they are so naked as to afford little fodder for the camels: there is a little cultivation of mustard, and *Taira meera*. The hills are about twenty miles off, and appear about 4,000 feet high, they are precipitous, but the outline is not rugged: they appear perfectly barren. Those to the north which run nearly east and west are more distant. No new birds were seen; rock pigeons occur. The soil would be rich if water were abundant: in the *Bagree* fields it is of a cloddy kind.

Reseda, Euphorbia, Salsola lanata, Chenopodium cymbifolium, Evolvulus, Panicum, and Andropogon occur here. *Jowaree* sells at twelve seers a rupee, and *Khurbee* is very dear. A large plain occurs here covered with Gramen Panicum, which is in tufts, and has the appearance of being cultivated.

27*th*.—Halted at our camp near Joke. The Naree runs one and a half mile to the westward: its bed is fifty yards wide and about ten feet deep; the banks are well clothed with *Furas*. There is a good deal of *Bagree* cultivation.

28*th*.—To *Oostadkote*, nine and a half miles. The road is not a made one for the latter one-third. Crossed the Naree about two miles from our encampment: the country appeared the same On arriving near our halting place, green wheat fields, intermixed with much fresh Chenopodium, Gramen Panicum, Reseda were most abundant,

Chloroideum, Sinapis, Raphanus cultivated with *Taira meera,* two Cruciferous plants common, Salsola lanata also occurs. Water abundant in a channel of fifteen yards wide and three feet deep, clear and tasteless. *Furas* the most common shrub. No grass occurs but the remains of Panicum. Wheat is here sown in drills, in some places the crop is promising. The country is evidently occasionally overflowed, witness the indurated surface and the fissures, which away from the road, renders it bad for camels, being full of holes.

There are several villages visible round our camp, all of the usual miserable description, and there is a good deal of *Bagree* cultivation. The water does not extend more than a mile; it is eight feet deep, and about twenty yards wide towards the head, where the bund is thrown across.

March 1*st.*—To Bagh nine and a half miles. The country is quite similar: the chief plants continue to be Chenopodium cymbifolium, *Kureel,* a *Rairoo, Ukko, Joussa,* and Salsola robusta, but occur in no great plenty, they and all the face of the country exhibit marks of inundation. Bagh is visible a long way off from its being ornamented with a gamboge, or ochre-wash, otherwise its aspect is poor and muddy. We came on the Naree about three miles from the town, and as it has been bunded, it is full of clearish blue water, to a good depth. We encamped about one and a half mile on the south side of the town. About the head of the bund there is a good deal of wheat cultivation, and some mustard. In these *khets* Reseda is very abundant, Heliotrope is also common; I picked up a Matthiola and a Pommereulla. The banks of the Naree are clothed with small *Furas,* which in these parts are always encrusted with saline matter, or, as it would seem, pure salt. Rock pigeons both sorts, Loodianah rats, etc.

Bagh is celebrated for gunpowder; it is a largish, straggling, but poor place, though thickly tenanted. Its latitude is 29° 1′ 20″, and is placed thirty miles too far south in Tassin's last map. Sugar-candy from Bussorah and cloth, are the principal articles sold.

4*th.*—Marched sixteen miles to Mysoor: direction at first NNW. and latterly west, close to the Brahorck hills. Water is plentiful in bunds and river, but the country is very very bare, Salicornia robusta uncommon, Plantago canescens, Poa, Cynodon, *Ukko* is very common, otherwise *Kureel* is the predominant plant. A good deal of wheat cultivation, every thing depends on water: the wheat along water-courses is luxuriant, but where water is less plentiful, stunted: soil the same, a tenacious sandy clay when wet: fields very free from weeds. Reseda very common, but very small, Heliotropium ditto, Crucifera hispida ditto. Green wheat a maund for a rupee. The road or rather country, is intersected here and there by ravines.

5th.—Halted. The nearest range of hills are six miles off, they have a very peculiar irregular brown appearance. The higher ones also have a similar appearance; these appear quite precipitous, and have in some parts a curious crenated outline. The chief vegetation about this place is *Kureel*, especially along the river and towards the bund, which last is well filled with water. *Kureel*, *Furas*, *Ukko*, very common, Cynodon, Prenanthoid, Poa minima, *Joussa*, Fagonia, Saccharum, Nerioid. In the water Scirpus, Cyperaceus, Charæ two species, Potomogeton two species, Valisnaria, Typha. On banks, Plantago cana, a curious *Sileneacea*, a splendid Orobanche, and a Brassicacea.

The birds continue the same: there is abundance of Fulica, swarms of waterfowl, herons, plovers, etc.; starlings re-appear.

Some wheat fields well irrigated; most luxuriant *Khujoors*, radishes.

6th.—Marched to Nowshera, sixteen miles: five first miles across a plain scantily furnished with *Kureel*. Sturt tells me the country looks quite a desert to the eastward from one of the hills. Thence we came on the hills, through which and the dividing valleys we proceeded for two miles, thence emerging into a narrow valley in which Nowshera is situated, drained by the river of Mysoor, which is an insignificant running stream.

The hills are very curious, totally bare of vegetation, not more than two or three stunted Chenopodium cymbifolium being seen on or about them. They do not exceed 300 feet in height; their composition is various; they are much worn by rain, and the outline although generally sharp, is often rounded. They present great variety, but chiefly are of a soft clayish looking substance, distinctly enough stratified, the uppermost strata being indurated and often quite smooth, and of a sub-ochreous appearance. The outer ridges on each side of the range slope gradually outwards, and the surface in these slopes is smooth. Inside, or towards the inner part of the range, they are generally precipitous, but beyond the uppermost strata, the exposed face is not indurated, hence this can scarcely arise from exposure to the weather. In these places they look much like sandstone, the fragments at the base of the cliffs are clayey, mixed with brown angular masses, occasionally shingle, and indeed, a low ridge near the north side of the range is chiefly of shingle. The direction is NNE., the angle of inclination of the slopes say 30°. The hills are highest towards the centre, and here some of the strata are curved.

The plain between this and the main range is much broken by ravines caused by rain; it is thinly covered with *Kureel*, Salsola robusta, Chenopodium, etc. The vegetation along the river is the same as at Mysoor. Durand finds nummulites, but thinks them brought down by the river. The strata or rather debris of slips often intersected by nearly erect projecting lines of a fibrous dyke. There is some wheat cultivation in the fields, a new Plantago, a Ruta, Silenacea, a curious Composita, two Boragineæ, Phalaris, Phleum, Avena, two or three Crucifera, Trigonella, and Melilotus are to be found. The vegetation elsewhere is much the same, *Rairoo, Kureel, Ukko*, Chenopodium, Lycium albidum re-occurs.

7th.—Proceeded to Dadur, a distance of seven and a half miles, nearly north. The country is a good deal cut up by water: within two and a half miles of Dadur we crossed the Naree, a running stream, with small boulders, and high clayey banks. The country improves towards Dadur, topes becoming more frequent. Salsola lanata abundant: a good deal of cultivation occurs along the river.

10th.—Dadur is a good sized, and more orderly looking place than Bagh, and is ornamented with well wooded gardens, among which the *Khujoor* holds a conspicuous place. An elegant and large *Bheir* and a Mimosa, are two other trees of the place; it is situated on the left bank of the Bolan river. The bed of this river until the Levee bund was cut, had been dry, but there is now plenty of water in it. It is in some places much choked by bulrushes, etc., it is eighty yards broad, and is shingly. Dadur stands nearly on the end of a good sized plain, surrounded on all sides by hills, of which those traversed to Nowshera, run NNE. and are lowest. The main range is four or five miles off. The greater part of this plain is uncultivated and covered with *Rairoo, Kureel, Joussa*, Sal. lanata, and Chenopodium; but along the sides of the river, as well as near that crossed en route to this place from Nowshera, there is a highly luxuriant cultivation of wheat, bearded and beardless, and barley. In some places near the town, are rich gardens of *sonff*, coriander, *Mola*, cress, onions, carrots, beet, among which a few poppies and Canabis occur. These, as well as the fields, are protected with loose *Bheir* fences. There are a few small villages around, all of the same *kucha* or temporary construction, together with some remains of cotton, which in these parts is perennial.

There are no wild trees to be found, excepting perhaps an elegant species of willow. The vegetation of the fields is highly interesting, consisting of many European forms, similar to those at Nowshera —Avena, Phleum, Polygonium, Zanthoxyloid, Erodium! Anagallis in abundance, Plantago, *Pecagee*, Cynodon two species, Andropogon, Melilotus, Medicago, Boraginea, Malva, Tetragonolotus, Astragaloides, Sperguloides, Cruciferæ.

In the bed of the river Nerium, Pæderioides, Crotalaria, etc. of which the former is common every where: Fagonia, Viola found in the bed of the river crossed en route hither, a very curious plant. Antirrhenoid was brought from the hills by Capt. Sanders, singular in the inequality of the calyx and the great development of the posticous sepal.

Altogether this spot is curious in regard to vegetation, for the mean annual temperature must be high, and the winter temperature by no means low enough to account for the appearance presented.

The only novel birds are a jackdaw, with the voice and manners of the red-billed Himalayan species, and which I have only seen at a distance, and a different sort of Pterocles.

11th.—Proceeded to Drubbee, eight miles from Dadur, and about three within the range of hills, the plain towards which is rather elevated, and generally covered with boulders and shingle. The vegetation of this shingly plain is much the same, Chenopodium *Ukko*, Salsola, *Kureel, Rairoo;* the most common shrubby plant, however, is an elegant Mimosa, much like the *Babool*, with white thorns; Nerium oleander is also very common along cuts.

In some wheat fields I procured Imperata, a new Plantago, and a curious Gnaphalium. The entrance to the pass is gradual; the hills almost entirely bare. I noticed *Rairoo*, Salvadora, *Kureel*. The most novel plant is a curious, erect, bushy, thorny Convolvulus, which is one of the most common plants farther in. The pass to Drubbee is wide, say 300 yards; the only obstacle exists in the shingle, which renders the road heavy. No abutments are present, jutting out from the hills, the stream is considerable but easily fordable, and abounds with fish, the Mahaseer, and two or three species of Gonorhynchus. The hills about Drubbee are not more than 500 feet high. They are generally of a coarse breccia, the component parts principally limestone; abundance of nummulites. The chief vegetation of the pass is one or two Andropogoneous grasses, and Apocynum nerioides. There is absolutely no fodder for camels, which however, take readily to grass. Towards the mouth of the pass, Pæderia involucrata, Villarsia, Lycioid, Stenophyllum and *Ukko* are common, but they are rare inside, although the last continues some distance up the hills and attains a large size, becoming quite arboreous. A Crucifera, a rhubarby sorrel, a Goodyera, and one or two grasses, were the only additional novelties met with.

12*th.*—Marched on eight miles, after five of which we turned to the right, and the pass became and continued narrow, until we reached our halting place, which is something like what we may suppose to be the remains of a mountain, still a good deal elevated above the bed of river. The mountains continued the same in the gorge, until we came to limestone cliffs, which afforded a peculiar vegetation, Linaria retephioides, Linaria alia pusilla foliis 5-gonis cordatis, floribus luteis minutis pubescens, specimen lost, one or two Rubiaceæ, a Salvia, several very interesting grasses, among which is a Stipa, a Composita, Santanoides, a curious Capparidea, Cassia, etc. etc.

The hills have increased in height, in many places they were extremely picturesque, split and divided in every direction. The valley running off to south on our entrance into the gorge: river diminished somewhat in size. Jheely spots, with very deep water common, surrounded with thick Andropogon, Typha and Scirpus jungle. Few fish were seen and none taken. Can the Mahaseer not reach this? Gonorhynchus continue, but they never take a fly; Ophiocephalus, *Sowlee;* turtle caught by bearers, Silurus. No less than twenty-three plants novel to me were gathered on the limestone, which looks as bare as the breccia; all its plants grew in small tufts or singly, and all adhered firmly to the rock. The only tree which continues is *Phulahi* or *Rairoo*, Convolvulus spinosus very common, a very curious Chenopodioid, Reseda with Cruciferous qualities.

13*th.*—Proceeded to Gurmab, eight and a half miles. Country continues the same. The defile after crossing some rather broad water three feet deep, opened out into a rather large valley, near the south end of which Gurmab is situated, and it is *ornamented* with a good many *Rairoo* trees, of indifferent size and appearance. No change whatever in the vegetation; Salsola prima occurs sparingly.

14*th.*—Halted at Gurmab. The hills close to our encampment are of limestone, which is in many places very angular. Oolite found by Durand in a low range, standing by itself in the valley, it generally bears a vast quantity of nummulites and madrepores. A flat discoid organized remain occurs in abundance, and probably belongs to the same group. *Ukko, Rairoo, Kureel* rare, Convolvulus spinosus, Frankenioides, Stipaceum gramen, Euphorbia, Polygonum rheoides, Salvadora, may be found. Along the water Andropogonoides 2, Typha, Arundo, Juncus, Scirpus juncinus in abundance. In the water, a new Naias, and Conferveæ. In a ravine near our camp, I found a Cynoglossum and a curious Periploceous plant, in habit approaching to certain Aphyllous, true Asclepiads.

A few stunted dates are visible near Gurmab, which is three miles from Kirtah, and towards the deep water there is a ruin of a single house. *Rairoo,* Nerioid, and Lycium albidum are the most common ground plants. There is only *Rairoo* for camels, who do not thrive on harsh grasses, although compelled by hunger to eat them. Large flocks of Doombah sheep and goats belonging to Khelat men were met with. Mahaseer in abundance, and very greedy after a red hackle of fish, Macrognathus and Opheocephalus occur also. Of birds the white vulture, Alauda cristata et alia, with a notched beak, a partridge which I had not previously seen, Motacilla alia.

15th.—Proceeded to Beebee Nanee, nine and a half miles up the valley in which Gurmab is situated. The road tolerably level and good; boulders not however common. The village of Kuttah, is one mile to the right, consisting of one ruined house; near the exit from the valley a burial ground occurs, having flags, or banners, pointing out the graves, which are covered with heap of stones. The exit from the valley is by a narrow pass through a low range of angular limestone, thence up another narrow shingly valley or narrowish gorge, and over a small stream of water of ordinary temperature, where we encamped: in the second valley two spots were observed covered with graves. Immense flocks of birds were seen on the range to the west of the valley. In the first valley Pæderia involucrata and Salsola prima, are the most common plants. On the limestone hills, Convolvulus spinosus, Frankeniacea, Plantago villosa, and a curious Composita, subacaulis, involucro foliaceo, of which the single specimen has been lost, a few *Bheirs*.

Encamped in a small valley or pass leading to Khelat, a marked one only a few hundred yards wide. To the west, the hills continue very barren. Gurmab—this takes its name from the warmth of the water, which apparently rises in several sedgy spots; the united waters form a small stream abounding with Mahaseer, Barbus, etc. and falling into another stream, again meets the main river, which runs off to the eastward from the place where it is crossed towards Gurmab. There is no sign of bubbling in the springs, although the water commences to run visibly from within a few yards. The temperature of one did not vary from 76°, which must be about the mean temperature of the place, but the temperature of a deep body of water after the confluence of several springs was 82°, so that some of them must hence be of considerable temperature: the highest examined was 81°.

Of three springs examined—the first of these had a temperature of 82° Fahr.—the second of 77°, these unite to form the streamlet that runs towards the east—the third spring had a temperature of 77°: this is crossed on entering the valley from the south, it runs under a limestone range, and then bends off to the south-east to unite with the main stream. Cyprinus fulgens and C. bimaculatus were found in the 82° spring. From the variation in the temperature of the three, it is obvious that neither represents the mean temperature of the place.

16th.—To Abigoom, eight and a quarter miles, through a similar country up a valley in a NNW. direction; the valley is narrowed towards the middle, and is a plain of considerable inclination, the chief rocks passed are limestones. No fodder for camels, and little enough on the road for horses; the chief vegetation consisting of Nerioides, Pæderia involucrata, and small tufts of *Kuss-kuss* grass; Ruwash is common, Lycium album; Salsola prima are not common, and the *Bheir* is rare. A new and curious plant looking like *Kureel* was found, male flowers with large semi-antheriferous bearing disc. Apocynum viminale not uncommon, and not ruined by cattle, Prenanthoid albiflora, Echinopsides, a fine Begonia, B. punicoides, arbuscula; Salvadora also occurred. The inclined valleys are very shingly and bouldery. The mountains as barren as ever.

There is at Beebee Nanee a running streamlet, in which small Mahaseer, Nepuroid, Gonorhynchus and Barbus may be found; also a species of Cancer. We were encamped close to the cliffy termination of a limestone range, in which Linaria, Trichodesma, Cynoglossum, Ruwash, Labiata, and a most singular Telepheoid polygalous looking plant were found. There is some fodder along the water for horses, but for camels scarcely any: we accordingly lose six to ten camels now daily. There was a curious echo from the cliff.

17*th.*—To-day we halt at Abigoom, which is at the extremity of an inclined plain, and 2,500 feet above the sea; some of the boundary hills are considerably higher, the valley is shingly and bouldery, covered with the usual plants, but more scantily: Nerioid, Pæderia involucrata, Lycium albidium, Apocynum viminale.

I went to some wheat cultivation yesterday afternoon about two and a half miles off, in a small valley to the south-east. The wheat was fine, all bearded, most of the Dadur plant occurred in it with some curious novelties, Boraginea, Cynoglossum, Compositæ, Cuscuta, and a new Reseda. The Melilotus and red Anchusoid were not found, Plantago, were among the most abundant. A single *Furas* tree and some *Kureel* were seen near the wheat. The weather unsettled; cloudy; rain fell at night and early this morning. A *cafilah* or caravan from Candahar with figs and raisins passed us. Rock pigeon of Loodianah and the small partridge were observed. There is a streamlet here.

18*th.*—Detained by bad weather, which threatened the whole of yesterday. The river came down during the night, flooded, and upset some of the tents, damaging many things, but not carrying off much. It rained smartly almost the whole night: we moved this morning to rather higher ground, but not so high as to preclude all danger should the river rise again. A dawk man arrived last night, bringing a handful of tulips which he said came from Shal; it is a small species, foliis subtortis undulatis caule 1-flora, flore amplo aureo subodora.

19*th.*—Advanced to Sirekhugoor, distance nineteen miles, ascent throughout on a considerably inclined plain up the bed of a river, shingly and bouldery; the pass is not much contracted, but a short distance from Abigoom we parted from every thing like valleys. The vegetation continues much the same: *Kureel,* Salsola prima re-occurred near Abigoom but sparingly, chief vegetation consists of clumps of withered coarse Andropogons, Nerioides, Pæderia, and Lycium, but less common than before, while Apocynum viminale, and Convolvulus spinosus have increased. The bed of the streamlet is until near Sirekhugoor, chiefly occupied by a large Arundo just past flowering, in which Typha also occurs sparingly: within 300 feet of the halting place, a solitary *Khujoor,* and some wheat cultivation occurs, the latter much behind that of Abigoom. In the fields Polygala occurred with a Galium; the most common plant being a Sinapis found at Dadur: some *Bheir* trees also occur here; a few Compositæ, Labiatæ, and Cruciferæ, similar to those at Abigoom, are also found: the novelties were *Peganum* which continues throughout the pass, Hyoscyamoid, and one or two Compositæ; while in water-courses close to it the first dripping rocks occurred covered with Adiantum and fructiferous mosses, and a curious Primuloid plant out of flower, with a curious Clematis.

The halting place is at the head of the stream, which gushes copiously out of a rock; the bed of the river or defile is 100 yards wide: the mountains immediately adjoining not exceeding 1,000 feet in height, but the second range is much higher, that to our north being plentifully sprinkled with snow. These mountains are barren, chiefly covered with Convolvulus spinosus, which has a different aspect, with a Sytisoid, handsome silvery shrub, a species of Caragana and Apocynum viminale: about the spring and in other places there are thick patches of a very dwarf palm, and a solitary fig tree, a Lycium album continues: the bed occupied by tufts of coarse Andropogons and Apocynum viminale; about the spring Adiantum, a small Boraginia, white flowered small Compositæ, a withered Hepaticum, two or three efructiferous mosses, and the Primuloid plant. In the stream Chara, Conferva, Peppermint, *Beccabunga*, Convolvulus, like C. reptans, Arundo left behind nearly. On the mountains fragrant Labiatæ, Compositæ, and Umbelliferæ are commencing. The barometer stood at 25.669; thermometer 64° at 11 A. M. Many soft rocks occurred: passed a clayey looking one, with very elevated strata, containing veins of transverse crystals: the sides of the defile are often precipitous, these are generally formed of conglomerate.

20*th.*—Continued up the same defile, a gradual ascent, and about two miles from Sirekhugoor entered the pass by pre-eminence; very much narrowed, precipitous cliffs on both sides: this continues for some time. The road good, shingly, but not very bouldery; very winding, and generally capable of strong defence; much cover exists from the rugged margins of cliffs, and windings of the road. The mountains, after four or five miles were passed, gradually receded and became less precipitous: at length we came to gradually rounded more distant mountains; then to a small valley; then ascended say 100 feet, over a low rocky range, and descended into a fine valley, surrounded by usual barren looking mountains: high ranges to the north and south covered with snow presenting a beautiful view—and now entered Khorassan. We were accompanied by several bands of a gypsyish-looking people, forming parts of a *cafilah.* They were accompanied with numerous goats: and camels ornamented with trappings.

Throughout the very narrow portion of the pass the vegetation continues the same: at Sirekhugoor a Xanthoxylon appears and continues nearly throughout: this and an oleinous looking small tree are the only arborescent plants: Apocynum viminale and the other plants of Sirekhugoor continue, nor did I notice any new ones further than a Sedum, and Tortula. However fragrant Labiatæ and Compositæ increase in number, but none are in flower.

As soon as we opened out from the pass, the vegetation almost entirely changed; the hills assumed a rounded form, covered with low bushes, and were much less rocky. Umbelliferæ, Labiatæ, and Compositæ abound, some of them deliciously fragrant: an Astragaloid spinosus very common, a shrubby Cerasus, Thalictrum, Hypoxis, and small Cruciferæ abundant. The chief vegetation consists of grasses in low round tufts; Anemone, Tulipa, etc. all small. After crossing a low range we came into the valley, which is almost entirely covered with an Artemisioid odoriferous plant; no verdure was visible, even on the snowy ranges. We encamped close under a ridge about two and a half miles to the north of the summit of the pass.

21*st*—Halted: there being some water collected in attempts to form a nullah from the last rain, it is quite brownish and opaque, but deposits no sediment, and makes good tea, although disagreeable to drink in any other form. I walked out in the afternoon into a valley to the west, close to our encampment, and thence ascended a hill 600 feet high at least.

This valley like the one in which we are encamped is covered entirely by an Artemisioid, a very fragrant plant, each shrub of which is distinct; mixed with it are tulips, several small Cruciferæ, and a Fritillarioides.

The same Artemisioid is also the chief plant on all the hills: it is mixed, but in small quantities with Cerasus pygmæus, Equisetoid, Caragana, and one or two shrubby Labiatæ; and also especially above, with a curious Astragaloid looking plant. The herbaceous plants are numerous, consisting of very fragrant Umbelliferæ, bursting into leaf; tulips, Fritillarioides, Trichostema, Erodium, Iris, Thalictrum, Senecio, Boragineæ 2, Gilenacea, several tufted Gramineæ, Berberideæ, Ranunculoides, Myosotis, Anemone cracea, Asphodeloid, Mesembryanthoids; of mosses Tortula, Grimmia.

22*nd*.—Proceeded to Sinab, a distance of fifteen and three quarter miles, up two valleys, no ascents. These valleys are elevated towards the mountains and generally depressed in the centre: in some they stretch out a long way from the mountain to which they may be imagined to belong. The mountains seen from a distance jutting out from perhaps the centre of a plain, look curious. The vegetation is generally Artemisioid, and very fragrant: the first valley in its depressed portions was covered with a Salsoloid looking plant, to the exclusion of Compositæ, but these last recurred in the higher parts.

With the Compositæ, swarms of small Cruciferæ occur; that with purple flowers and pinnatisect leaves being the most common. Very rugged hills are visible to the north-east and north of our route, presenting a very different appearance from the usual aspect: they are steep to the east, and present inclined slopes to the west.

Sunday, 24th.—Halted this day. Little new occurs in the valley, except a few trees out of leaf and flower, which, though trees here, yet the species are not so elsewhere. At this place are the heads of the river of Pisheen, which appear to arise more artificially than naturally from *Kahreezes*, or wells dug in a rude way, and communicating by subterranean channels; those nearest the natural outlet of the water being the shallowest. The vegetation is the same; there is a little cultivation, but nothing to indicate any descent. The amount of population is not great; and the hills to the west are covered with snow. The chief vegetation is *Santonica.* In cornfields Fumariaceæ, Adonis, Cruciferæ, Pulmonaria, Arenaria, Hordei sp., Tulipa lutea, and Hyacinthus? may be found.

The vegetation of the plains, inclusive of Santonica, consists generally of three or four small Cruciferæ, Tulipa lutea.

I went to the west towards the snow, and found in the river here an aquatic Ranunculus, foliis omnibus immersis, floribus albis, Chara is common; gravelly slopes commence some distance from hills, covered with Santonica, Astragaloid spinosus, Leguminosæ, a spinous Statice, Cytisus argenteis, Composita floribunda carnosa.

The mountains are covered with masses of rock. One tree occurs with a Fraxinus? a Thymeleous looking shrub, Cytisus, Caragana. The herbaceous plants are very numerous, Compositæ, Cruciferæ, small Leguminosæ, Berberideæ, Isopyroides, Crocus? Gentiana, Onosma, and other Boragineæ, Umbelliferæ, Silenaceæ, especially small Arenariæ; Cupressus commences about 6,500 feet, near the Cypress an Arctium occurred, at least it has the habit of that genus, Onosma, a curious Boraginea calyce sinubus bidentigeris, demum plano! ampliato bilabiato! clauso, quasi hastato lobato, nucibus compressis,

2, Sedums 4, Arenariæ, a fine Gentiana, Crocoides, Iris, Ornithogaloides or Trichonema occurred, with many others. The greatest elevation attained was about 1,200 feet above the camp. Chikor and the smaller partridge were seen.

25th.—Marched to Quettah, eight and a half miles up the valley over a delightful road. The valley is cultivated, and many villages are visible with their orchards, consisting of mulberry trees, cherries, and apricots, surrounded with mud walls; the houses miserable, and all trees out of leaf: the crops under cultivation are more advanced, but depend on irrigation, some salad-bearing plant occurred cultivated in trenches like asparagus: the fields are clean, and sometimes well manured. A Veronica allied to V. agrestis, 2 or 3 Euphorbiaceæ, a very well defined Plantago, Hyacinthus, and a pretty Muscari, were among the novelties; Juncus, Chara, Carex, occurred in some marshy spots. I was most struck with the occurrence of at least two species of Lucerne, or Trefoil: wells are common, and water abundant. The climate is delightful, temperature 49° at 9 P. M. in a tent.

26th.—I ascended towards a snowy range to the ESE. of our camp, crossing a cultivated portion of the valley extending to the gradual slopes so universal between the level portion and the bases of the mountains, and which are always covered with shingle, and occasionally much cut up by watercourses. Turning a ridge I ascended up a ravine, rather wide and easy at first, but becoming gradually narrow, and at last difficult. On coming to its head I rambled some distance higher among precipitous rocks, the ground generally covered with loose shingle, giving bad footing. The rocks too were treacherous, often giving way under the feet. I was still 1,000 feet from the summit, which is the second range between our camp and the snow, but which is not visible from the camp. From it I saw the camp, and the valley of Pisheen beyond the termination of the Tuckatoo range. Water boiled at 196° 7′, making the height about 8,300 feet, in my (new) Woollaston instrument at 686; temperature of the air 46° 5′. Nothing occurred to repay me for the fatigue of the excursion. Junipers or cypress form the chief arbusculous vegetation, but even these are scanty; they commence at 6,500 feet, and continue to the snow: Fraxinus occurred about 7,000 feet, and another tree of which I could make nothing, it being out of flower and leaf. Compositæ were the prevailing vegetation; but of these, only the remains were found, which were very fragrant. A large thorny Leguminous shrub out of leaf, etc. looking much like a Rosa,

Equisetoides, etc.; of mosses, Weissia Templetonii, and Tortula, so that in these there is very little variety; the debris of one Hepatica occurred.

At the foot of the mountains, the only place out of the valley where any vegetation is to be found, Asphodelus, radicibus luteis, foliis triangularibus, a fine plant coming into flower, Cytisus, Caragana, Narcissus? Cruciferæ, among them a small Draba, Cerasus pygmæus, Peganum, Salsoloid of Mumzil, Trichonema, Myosotis, Gentiana of Chiltera, Buddlæa, Carex; indeed the vegetation is precisely the same as at Chiltera. The only novelty was Bardana in flower, and it proves to be a cruciferous plant of large size.

On the stony slopes, a shrubby spinous Centauroid, foliis pinnatifidis glaucis, Cytisus, Caragana, Asphodelus and Cheiranthus are the prevailing plants. No Santonica is found about here.

A new Iris occurs in abundance: near this in wettish parts of the valley a Vicia, Muscari, Hyacinthus and others as before. The chief cultivation is wheat, irrigated in plots: the soil when saturated with water, forming a clayish, adhesive, finely pulverulent mass, which cakes on drying. A watermill for flour, having a horizontal wheel acted on by the stream as in Bootan occurs; the grain drops in from a pyramidal cone fixed over the two horizontal stones, in the upper of which there is a hole. The apparatus is very rude.

The height attained by me on the eastern ridge being about 8,300 feet; that of the 2nd range, will be 9,300 feet at least, and the height of the peak or highest ridge, cannot be less than 11,000 feet.

30*th.*—Continue to halt. There is a good deal of cultivation about this place, but the crops will not be ripe before August: it is principally wheat; munjit is also cultivated on trenched ground: the young sprouts have a good salad-like flavour. The Suddozye Lora runs through the valley, about two miles from the town: it is a small stream, crowded here and there with bulrushes, sedges, etc. Towards its banks there is a good deal of Santonica, but elsewhere there is no good fodder, and wherever this is the case the camels eat Iris, and destroy themselves. The valley is sprinkled over with villages and orchards, and is picturesque enough. In one spot, where water runs over the surface, it is delightfully green and velvety, covered with short grass and trefoil, Carex, etc.

In cornfields in this direction, Berberidea ranunculiflora is very common, Muscari, Hyacinthus, Taraxacum, Plantago. Of animals the Jerboa, sent to Macleod by Mr. Mackenzie, of the Artillery, several specimens having been caught here : presenting affinities obviously with the hare, and analogies with the Kangaroo. Macleod has just given me, from his namesake of the 3rd Cavalry, a tadpole-like animal, very similar to one from the Khasiya Hills. I fear it is a tadpole, but I keep the specimen lest it should be a Lepidosiren.

The orchards here consist of cherry, and a pomaceous tree which also is cultivated at Shikarpore, and on the skirts occasionally of willows, which, were they unmutilated, would be handsome trees. The Punjabi name of the pomaceous one is *Sai-oo*, of the cherry or plum *Aloochah.*

Senecionoid glauca is extremely common towards the river, but is not eaten by camels. In the streams arising from springs a Myriophylloides is very common ; as also in some places, Ranunculus aquaticus, Beccabunga, Mentha piperitioid, a Sicyoid, Juncus, Coniferæ, and Cariceæ, all small.

Along the banks of the river, there is a good deal of a small thorny shrub with white bark and fleshy clavato-spathulate leaves. Themopsis is extremely common, Crucifera glauca ditto, Peganum less so, Achilleoides is very common. In damp spots a Lotus (out of flower occurs). The ground is covered in many places with an efflorescence of saltpetre.

Quettah.—The country was so disturbed throughout the greater part of the line, and attacks on followers so frequent, that I did not go out so much during the last few days as I otherwise would. The only plant that seems to a considerable extent local, is the larger Asphodel, which is however found occasionally towards Kuchlak. Within the last few days vegetation has rapidly progressed; the orchards bursting into leaf, and the whole plain, where uncultivated, is assuming a greenish tint. I have nothing to add respecting the botany, except having found Ceratophyllum and two species of Chara, one a very interesting species from having the joints furnished with semi-reflexed, very narrow leaves, it is apparently Dioeceous, there is also a Naiad, much like that found at Dadur. No Lemnæ occur among the vegetation : there is some sort of pea cultivated : but the chief object is wheat, then next to it in extent is Lucerne, which is cultivated in plots; the ground being laid out as in wheat, so as to allow of irrigation.

The climate is variable; rain generally falls every four or five days, before this happens it becomes hot and hazy, afterwards it is very cold and clear : the alternations are hence very great. From the thermometer immersed in the fount of a spring gushing out from a *Kabreeza*, the mean temperature would appear to be 56°. Water running in cuts close to it, was 66°. A Tauschia occurs in abundance near the spot, and is remarkable for illustrating the nature of the leaves of the upper parts; it is curious that all such have a peculiar aspect. (For other plants of this neighbourhood, see Cat. and Icones.)

The town although the third in Khorassan, is a miserable place and has a deserted aspect, the houses are of the most temporary construction, and the hill is crowned by a poor half-ruined *kucha* fort; the gates of the town are ornamented with wild goats' horns and heads. There is no trade, and the place is stated to be plundered often by Caukers. Orchards—apricots of large size, and very large cherry trees, a pomaceous plant with the habit of poplar, occurs; the Ulmus of this place is one of the largest sized trees; no walnuts.

April 6th.—Left Quettah for Kuchlak. We traversed the sandy plain, and then ascended the gravelly slope to the pass traversed before reaching Kuchlak, the ascent and descent were about equal, but the former was long and gradual, the latter rapid and short. The features of the country are precisely the same; the pass is short, the descent to the ravine, which in the rains is evidently a watercourse, short and steep, not 100 feet. The mountains forming the sides are steep; and those to the left, bold and romantic, with here and there a small tree. The plain of Kuchlak is like that of Quettah, well supplied with water-cuts and one small canal, but miserably cultivated, and with very few villages. The hills forming its west boundary are low, rugged, and curiously variegated with red and white. Tuckatoo forms part of its eastern boundary: no snow is visible on its face towards Kuchlak: a few low rounded hillocks occur in the centre of the valley. The chief vegetation round the camp, is Santonica. We encamped close to the western boundary of the valley, about two miles from the grand camp: total distance of the march thirteen and a half miles. The climate is very hot and variable; thermometer ranged to-day from 40° to 86°.

The chief vegetation of the gravelly slopes is as marked as ever, and differs entirely from that of the sandy tillable portion; it consists of Centaurea fruticosa, C. spinosa, Anthylloides or Ononoides, Astragalus spinosus, and Staticoides, another thorny Composita occurs, but is not common, the herbaceous plants are Cruciferæ in large numbers, as well as Compositæ; of Boragineæ, a good many, some Labiatæ, a large Salvia: towards the tillable lands or where gravelly places occur among these. Asphodelus is common with Cheiranthus; one or more fruticose Dianthi occur in these places, and a curious shrubby Polygonum.

In dry watercourses Cytisus is common, with a host of small Cruciferæ, Boragineæ, and Compositæ; Papaveraceæ are very common with Glaucium.

The novelties in the pass were Ficus, Lycium, some grasses, Onosma. (See Cat. from Nos. 411 to 430,) Marchantiaceæ.

7th.—Proceeded to Hydogee, distance eight miles. The country is very barren, diversified by curious low hills, of a red, white, or yellowish colour, divided by small bits of plain, which in some cases were a good deal cut up by ravines. Passed immediately on starting, the Sudoozye Lora, here a sluggish muddy stream, knee-deep, twenty yards wide, and in addition to a bad dry cut, we passed likewise another little stream with a pebbly bottom and rapid current.

The crops composing the very little cultivation seen before arriving, were backward and scanty: so were those at Hydogee.. The chief vegetation is Santonica; here and there are gravelly spots with Centaurea fruticosa, spinosa; Statice, Salvia, etc. re-occur. The commonest shrub along the watercourses is Lycium, with another Lycioid thorny plant.

The low hills were in some cases stratified, the strata in others and perhaps in most were indistinct: most were rounded, but the outlines at a distance were very diversified. The novelties today were a fine vesicular calyxed Astragalus, an Isatidea, tuilip of red, orange, and yellow, indiscriminately mixed, Papaver Rheas, Cheiranthus lapidium, Asphodels both sorts, but the second and larger one is uncommon, Iris *Stacyana* very common in sandy places, Iris agrestis, most common about Suddozye, Adonis, and Ranunculus Anemoides occurs. Snow on north side of Tuckatoo mountain as heavy as on Chiltera; the valley of Pisheen is here a miserable place, narrower than that of Quettah.

9th.—Advanced to Hykulzyea, distance twelve miles to the town, about eleven through a similar country with that previously noted, and until the expanded part of the valley of Pisheen is entered the aspect is very barren; the road extends between low rounded hills. After crossing the valley of Hydozyea, three streams are passed, none of any size. Botanical features continue the same, Santonica being still the prevailing plant. The curious frutex pluvinatus of Sinab reoccurred, together with an additional subspiny Astragaloid shrub and a small Ruta. The hills are covered with distinct small shrubs, never coalescing into patches. Peganum continues in addition to the other plants: Glaucioides has aqueous juice, Papaver Rheas ditto, the other smooth-leaved one has it slightly milky.

Lycium and Tamarisk 4-fida is rather common: Hykulzyea is a far larger place than Quettah, but miserably defended. The houses are very inferior, consisting of thatch and mud. The cultivation of wheat is rather extensive around. Many villages are seen towards the hills to the north and NNE.; also one or two forts, but not a tree is to be seen in the valley which is comparatively very large and very level. The hills to the north have the ordinary appearance; those separating us from the valley of Hydozyea, more especially the lower ranges, are so confused that they look like a chopping sea, and present a red and white colour. The rock pigeon of Loodianah is common about Hydozyea. A few novelties occurred in the vegetation, the chief of which being a large Salvoid Labiata, a plant which is very common throughout Khorassan from Sinab in gravelly spots. Leguminosæ, Boragineæ, Compositæ, Cruciferæ, and Labiatæ, are the prevailing plants; Salsola tertia not uncommon. Birds as before, Alauda cristata, and Sylvioides being the most common; no red legged crows were seen. Rock pigeons are abundant.

10th.—March to Berumby, distance thirteen miles, the road very bad in one or two places: the first difficulty being a rather deep ravine, the second a nullah, with water knee-deep, and very high precipitous banks, yet both these had to be passed. Much of the baggage was not up at the encampment until 5 P. M., although we started at 3 A. M., but the nullah was literally choked up with camels. No change in the vegetation has appeared, except in the occurrence of large tracts of Tamarisk, which tree reaches to nearly the same size as the *Jhow*. Very little cultivation is to be seen; the villages are tolerably numerous, especially near the hills forming the north boundary of the valley.

11th.—Entered the pass which is at first wide, with a gradual ascent, but which soon becomes narrowish, with a good though gradual and easy ascent: the mountains are of no height, and they are not generally precipitous: no limestone, but much clay slate occurs. The ravine up which we passed, or rather watercourse, was well stocked with Xanthoxylon, some of large size as to the diameter of trunk, but very stumpy: water is found not far from the entrance: some cultivation also occurs and one large walled village, Dera Abdoollah Khan, lay to our left. Not much change in the vegetation: Xanthoxylon is almost entirely confined to ravines, Cerasus common, and one or two other prickly shrubs, and a Ruta, Onosma, Linarea, coming into flower, are among the novelties.

We encamped where the pass becomes narrow, and the ascent steep, and where water is plentiful, but the stream being soon absorbed does not appear to run down the main ravine at this season.

12th.—Halted, to make the road where the main ascent commences about 400 yards from our camp, and which is about 300 feet high; thence there is a descent, and afterwards an ascent to about 600 feet above the camp, whence the *low* plains of Candahar are visible, as well as the range to the north of which Candahar stands. The road is good compared with places elsewhere to be seen, and for common traffic on camels may be easy enough; but for guns, it is steep and difficult. The way it has been made by the Engineers is admirable and rapid; three other passes without roads, and in their rude natural state are as yet to be crossed. The pass here is narrow, none of the hills rise more than 1,000 feet above it, they are easily accessible, and are composed chiefly of clay slate. Chikores are frequent. The cuckoo was heard to-day, as well as a beautifully melodious titmouse, with a black crown: a fine eagle, or falcon was seen.

The hills are as usual barren, all the shrubs are thorny, and all the plants unsocial, never coalescing into any thing like groups. The Xanthoxylon is found throughout in ravines up to nearly 7,000 feet, the utmost height of the pass. Fraxinus of Chiltera also occurs, Cerasus primus, in abundance, Cerasus alius, tertius, not uncommon, Berberis! here and there in ravines, Equisetoides, Caraganoides altera; the most common shrubs of any size are Cerasus primus. The other shrubs consist of the low customary Compositæ, and Astragaleæ, Umbelliferæ are common, among which last the Nari, a species of Assafœtida occurs? A beautiful Iris is common, as well as tufts of Berberideæ, Asphodelus major, and which is much eaten when cooked as a *turkaree* by our hungry followers, Eryngioides, Aconitoides, a Valeriana, three new small Veronicæ, small Cruciferæ, Silenaceæ, Boragineæ, and Labiatæ, form the bulk of the herbaceous vegetation. An Arenarioid, Muscoid, Cruciferæ, common at the head of the pass. A large Acanthoid leaved Umbellifera, a Rheoides papillis verrucosum, this is a true Rheum, and when cultivated becomes the *Ruwash* of the Affghanistans; it is very common on the Candahar face of the pass, particularly about Chokey, where it is in flower.

13*th*.—Proceeded to Chokey, not quite four miles. The top of the pass may be reached by three or four passes. I went by one to the right, which is easy enough, and the descent from which is much better adapted for camels than the made road, which is very steep, with two sharp turns, but soft. The descent thence is gradual, down one of the ordinary ravines, well clothed with the usual shrubs and Xanthoxylon: our camels were a good deal fagged, but more from the halt at the pass, where some cathartic plant abounds and weakens them very much, than fatigue. The view from the top of the pass is very extensive: the plains are seen to have nearly the same level, and are divided here and there very frequently to north-east and north, by the ordinary mountains.

14*th*.—Halt; water here is not abundant, and is obtained from driblets and pools; around these, the surface is covered with a rich sward, which affords fine fodder for a small number of horses. In the swampy spots, *Beccabunga*, Anagallis, Mentha, Carex, Glaux, apparently identical (so far as a memory of 7 years may be trusted,) with the English plant, the small variety of Leontodon, Medicaginoides, Phleum, and the very small Amaranthoid, Polygonea, occur.

The hills around Chokey, and below it are rounded, those towards the pass being more steep. They are covered with Centaurea fruticosa, and C. spinosa, a favourite food of camels when it has young shoots, Santonica, Statice, all of which grow precisely as before, Boragineæ, Compositæ, Labiatæ, and Papilionaceæ, are the predominant forms, and mostly of the same type: I observe a tendency among Boragineæ to have cup-shaped nuts. Generally speaking, the plants are the same as those before found. Rheas, Papaver, Glaucium purpureum, especially the two last are common, Labiata salvoides, Iris persica, and crocifolia (rare), Trichonema, Gentiana, Alyssoides.

The novelties were Rheum, Silena fruticosa, Linaria, Ruta, Astragalina, 2 small Silenaceæ, Iris, Glaucium aureo-croceum, a beautiful Boragineæ with cup-shaped nut, Lotoides, an Hippophaoid looking shrub, Scrophularia sp. singulous, Malthioloids spiralis, Allium, Glaux, Nitella, etc. (See Catalogue 482 to 516.) Graminea very common, Rottboellia and Anthistiria, 2 curious forms, the other more northern, Umbelliferæ common, Nari much less so than on the south face.

The vegetation of the summit which is nearly 7,000 feet, and of peaks which rise 600 to 700 feet above the pass, has no change, except the abundance of Cruciferæ and Muscoides; Cerasus is the chief shrub; Thymelæus frutex occurs at 6,500 feet. The prevailing rock is clay slate.

16*th*.—Marched to Dund-i-Golai, distance fifteen miles, we first descended gradually to the plain, and then traversed this until we skirted some low hills, about one and a half mile, from which a pool of water was situated, where we halted, and which was fed by a small cut coming from some distance. The road was very good throughout, the water-cuts although not unfrequent, being either shallow or skirting the left of the road. The vegetation continued the same as about Chokey, until the plains were reached, but the prickly shrub, habitu Berberidioides, became more common in the water-cuts below than I had seen it before, while Santonica, Centaurea spinosa, and the plants of Chokey, disappeared as we reached the plain, except some few herbaceous forms, which continued throughout. I was much indisposed during this march, and for the time we halted at Dund-i-Golai, a period of four days, was unable to go out, but Capt. Sanders and my people brought me many novelties, which I have not yet noted down. The chief vegetation of the plain is Salsola tertia, the surface is level and firm, clothed with scattered Salsola and a few stunted herbaceous plants, among which a yellow Centaureoid, a Crucifera siliquis junioribus clavati 4-gonis, were the most common, there was also a curious Thiscoid looking plant. A considerable change commenced about the low hills, a Thymelæus shrub, some curious grasses, an Erodium, a Santonica, occupying the places of the former shrubs, and Dipsacus or Scabiosa becoming very common. The height of this place is about 4,040 feet, the climate most variable. Fahr. thermometer 48° to 105° in single roofed tents. No cultivation seen, a pool of water is situated near the hill, and a little is reported as situated half-way between this place and Chokey, this however I did not see. The country is much parched up, and bears every appearance of always having been so; no remains of tanks, villages, etc. visible. Painted partridges were seen; and the eggs of a large bird like a plover? The wind inclining to be hot, but it is cool up to 7½ or 8 A. M.

Alaudo cristata? and an Alauda with the form of Sylvia.

Sunday, 21*st*.—Proceeded to Killa Pootoollah, a distance of ten miles. The road was good over an open, dry, level country, but intersected with small cuts: some cultivation was passed, but no villages. Some little improvement was observed close to the Garrah hills, which are of the usual description, and of no great height: a curious slip of the strata exhibited itself, in which the upper strata are cut away in the centre as if there had been a watercourse there. Vegetation continues the same. The Thymelæous shrub and Iris, still occur in sandy spots, Allium and a second species; Centaureoides, yellow and pink, Thesioides, a curious sand-binding grass, Salsola tertia most common, and in some open firm places *Joussa* reappears as it did at Dund-i-Golai: Anthemis occurs, Rheas, Salvioides in stony places, otherwise few of the plants of the Pisheen side are seen; grapes abundant about old and new cultivation, Hordeum, Bromus several species, Triticoides, etc., in profusion. Passed a deep well of considerable diameter, which had an open communication with a widish and deep canal, the only place I have seen that would hold a good deal of water; it was cut throughout in shingle, and was perhaps fifty feet in its deepest part.

22*nd*.—Left Pootoollah for Mailmandah, and on our arrival found some of the troops and the cavalry had passed through and made a double march to the river Lora, a distance in all of twenty-four miles. There is a good deal of pure water at Mailmandah running in a cut by the side of that, which is in the rains a considerable stream, also one or two *Kabreezes* about two miles further on, producing excellent water. The road first led up a ravine of some width, and swardy, and then over low hills, until we surmounted these to descend into the valley in which part of the army halted. The country continues mostly the same; although if possible it is still more barren than before: the mountains generally are more rugged: the ridges frequently toothed, and the sides precipitous; not a tree to be seen, except a willow near some water, and a small arbusculoid fig. After passing the halting place we re-ascended an inclined plane, entered a gorge, and again issued out of it: after a short time again we entered into another valley drained by an actual river, *really containing water*, and bounded to the west and north-west by curious red low hills, not unlike an embankment. The vegetation continues much the same: Salsola tertia very common in some sandy places, Centaurea spinosa, Statice, Santonica, etc. re-assuming their places on all gravelly slopes: some novelties occurred as (See Catalogue, Nos. 543 to 574 inclusive,) one or two new shrubs, Cytisus, etc. The heat continues great; 102° Fahr. in tents in the middle of the day. We encamped on a flat ground about 200 yards from the river, which contains a good deal of water, and has a sluggish stream running to the north, surrounded by mountains, none of any height. Wheat cultivation, Arundo, Vitex, Prunus or Cerasus abundant in the pass to the river, and yet the former does not indicate water as it ought to do, Lycium, Tamarisk, Arundo on the banks of the river, and Tamarisk in profusion in its bed.

The cultivation on the opposite side of the river is remarkably clear of weeds, as compared with the cultivation at Quettah, etc. Achilleoides, Veronica, Iris crocifolia, Phalaris, Chenopodium, Rottboellioides, Hordeum vulgare, being the only or the chief plants cultivated.

Proceeded next to Dai Hap, thirteen miles, over a similar but even more barren country, the hills being destitute of all vegetation, except a few stunted small shrubs, such as Statice. The usual plants recur with shingle and in sand, the chief is a *Santonica,** a few novelties occurred, among which is a curious plant, with large vesiculate petaloid connectiva. See Catalogue, No. 576, et sequent.

The hills continue with toothed ridges, near Dai Hap, where water is abundant, but not in the form of a river. Thymelæa occurs in abundance, with a Mimosea fruticosa humilis: a curious hairy-fruited Polygonum et Peganum, is among the most common plants.

25*th.*—To Khoshab, distance twelves miles, over a large level plain, either sandy, and then generally cultivated, or gravelly, and then uncultivated: road open: passed two dry beds of rivers: one must be of large size, but is very shallow. A new Tamarisk occurs along it; no trees are visible until we approach Candahar: vegetation continues much the same. *Santonica,** Centaurea spinosa, Astragalina (Ononoides recurs), Staticoid, Asphodelus, Mesembryanthoid, Peganum, are the chief plants, especially on gravel; most of the small Cruciferæ have disappeared, Labiata-Salvioides continues; a curious subaphyllous Composita occurs, Iris persica is not uncommon; another Iris is found here and there in profusion, with Gnidia in sandy spots, Compositæ, Monocotyledons of Abigoon are common in shingle. New rock pigeons. Fine madder cultivation in *khets*. Of birds the yellow hammer occurs. Villages numerous, poor, and though built of mud and straw yet present abundance of small domes.

In these dry hot plains the prevailing wind is westerly, blowing very strong in the heat of the day, and having a tendency to become hot: the thermometer is here 98°. The cultivation of wheat is very general around our present encampment which is within four miles of Candahar, the wheat is fine; Lolioides occurs in it.

* Referred to by the Author as an Anthemidioid, and on one occasion as *Santonica achilleoidea*.

26th.—Halted: Candahar is hid from us by some low hills, on the surmounting of which a large straggling place is obscurely visible, interspersed with trees, the valley is much smaller than that in which we are now, which is very extensive. Munjit cultivation is conducted by deep trenches, it is a different species I think from that of the Himalayas. The bed of the Turnuk is now dry and very shallow: and the hills near us are extremely barren, the chief vegetation being Pæderioides vestila and Staticoides cymosa, Cheiranthus continues. The vegetation is very poor as indeed it has been since leaving the Khojeb Amrah, nor is there any appearance to be seen of a better autumnal vegetation.

Candahar is visible at a distance of six miles, from some low hills to the north of our camp.

27th.—Moved to Candahar, skirting the low hills just mentioned and passed through two villages, a mile from Candahar in a fine open plain.

Candahar has rather a pleasing aspect; it is situated close to a picturesque range of hills, and is well diversified with trees, barley and wheat fields. The slope on which the town stands is a parallelogram; towers occur frequently along the wall, which is however, of mud, and not strong; it is surrounded by a ditch utterly insignificant on account of its narrowness and shelving banks, this ditch is crossed by an insignificant causeway. The gate at which I entered is oblique, and is defended by a tower: it leads into the main street which is rather wide and not very dirty: towards the centre of this you pass under a middling dome, a street branching off to the right and left; the continuation of the main street or bazar leads to the *topekhanah*, or artillery ground, a small space quite disorderly, containing eight or ten guns, most of them melted at the mouth; one Sheik 18-pounder of cast iron, another of English make, 140 years old. From the end of this space you pass over another similar ditch into the fort, the entrance to which is covered, affording two or three angles capable of good hand to hand defence. Passing thence through some spaces occupied by low buildings, you reach Khoondil Khan's house, an extremely rude looking place outside, but very different within. It consists of two houses, one looking into a small square with a delicious reservoir of water, and some fine and very green mulberry trees; the ground being laid out as a garden with sweet-william, etc.; the water is supplied by a small cut, and is seven or eight feet deep. The garden fronts of both houses are prettily ornamented, one has a *tharkhanah,* delightfully cool; generally the rooms are small, coated with a pretty sort of stucco. The remaining sides of the square are occupied by offices; small rooms opening into the garden by lattice-work evidently denote a portion of the *zenana.* Altogether the Khan must be a man of taste.

The bazars of the city are well thronged, but the shops are by no means equal to those of Buhawulpoor, and the manufactures, except those of earthenware, are utterly insignificant.

Tobacco, *atta, musallahs,* dried fruits, *aloo-bokhara,* figs, apricots, raisins, salt, sugar, a green fruit something between a plum and greengage, meat, onions, salads, *dhie, sherbets, kubabs,* wicker-work, singing birds, are offered for sale: also abundance of Lucerne and some *bhoosee.* Altogether it is a busy place, but not so busy as the road near the gate, which is thronged by followers, and dismounted Europeans, who are forbidden access to the city without a pass. Tea from Khiva of good quality is procurable in small quantities. No women but old ones to be seen. The dress of the inhabitants very often, and in some cases very completely, approximates to that of the Chinese. The features too of most are evidently of Tartar cast, and some wear two tails of plaited hair. Blue seems to be a favourite colour of dress.

The chief trees about the city are mulberry, a few *Khunjucks,* which is the Xanthoxylon of Bootan and the Kojhlak passes, occur outside; willows are frequent, and generally appear to be cultivated, among these a weeping species here and there occurs.

May 3rd.—The resources of the city are evidently small, the only things indeed that appear plentiful are earthenware and milk: grain is excessively dear, but is reported to exist in considerable quantities. Khoondil Khan having ordered all those out of the city, who had not provided themselves with six months' provisions. *Atta* or flour is now selling at two seers a rupee, or 6*d* per pound, and every thing is proportionally dear: wood excessively so, the chief fuel is derived from the *Santonica,* which in some form or other appears to constitute a principal feature of the vegetation of Central Asia, and there is some other wood apparently derived from some tree I have not yet seen.

Some discontent prevails in the town owing to the high price of provisions, which is, no doubt, severely felt. The established price of grain is at the rate of eight seers the rupee, a rate established by the king, but on occasions like the present there can be no rule. Water is very abundant, it is to be found within four feet of the surface, and some regiments have already supplied themselves from this source by means of temporary wells. The water is excellent.

Asses, ponies, and horses are common, the former are excellent, 150 rupees is a good price for one; they carry heavy loads with the additional weight of an Affghan on their back; the ponies or tattoes are less valuable, but still they are strong.

The horses are indifferent; good, generally speaking, but heavy, and with little spirit. Excellent milch cows have been procured for twenty-five rupees, including the calf. Goats are not easily procurable. Sheep *(Doombas)* are common, and afford excellent mutton, they vary in price from two to three rupees.

Tea from Bokhara is procurable in small quantities; its quality is decent: it was originally eight rupees a seer but is now thirty. Coarse Russian cloths, and very inferior silks are also procurable.

The great drawbacks are the want of wood, and above all want of inhabitants; from what I have seen of the cultivation, the soil appears to be very capable, and well adapted to barley and wheat; rice might also be raised as a summer crop. With regard to water, if there is a scarcity of this element, it is due to the indolence of the people. I have not yet seen any vestiges of buildings, topes, etc. to indicate that Candahar has ever been a very populous place, the want of trees considering the ease with which they may be cultivated, is a strong evidence of the extreme laziness of the Affghans, who appear to me remarkably low in the scale of civilization; and in personal habits, very generally inexpressibly filthy.

Poplars, mulberries, and willows are the principal trees: the poplar is very much akin to the *Sofaida* of the Sutledge, it is a handsome tree, with a fine roundish crown. The fruit trees generally appear small in gardens; lettuces and onions are commonly cultivated, especially the latter, fields of Lucerne are very abundant, and I believe clover also; a pony load of the former now costs five annas, but it is sufficient for a day's consumption of two or three horses. The pomegranate attains the ordinary size. In gardens two or three Ranunculaceæ, Jasminum, pinks, sweet-williams, marigolds, stocks, and wall-flowers, are common, with a broad-leaved species of flag, the flowers of which I have not seen.

The crops vary according to the mode in which they have been watered; if this has been properly done, they are rich. Some of the fields are tolerably clean, others filled with weeds, among which a Dipsacea, and one or two Centaureæ are very common.

The villages are not generally defended: each house has its own straggling direction, is built of mud, and the roof is generally dome-shaped, and it has its own enclosure within a mud-wall. The houses are very low, and indicate poverty, and want of ingenuity. The better order appear always with arched roofs, and none are without picturesque ribs and recesses.

The vineries here are so well enclosed, that there is no way of access except by scaling the mud-wall: the vines are planted in trenches; a row on each side, and allowed to run over the elevated spaces between the trenches. In one garden pomegranates, a pomaceous tree, and mulberries, whose fruit is now ripe but quite devoid of flavour, occurred. A Zygophyllum, a beautiful Capparis, an Anthemis, Marrubium, Centaureoides 2, occurred as weeds, with Plantago, Phalaris, Cichorium.

For an excellent register of the thermometer at this place, I am indebted to the kindness of Dr. Henderson; the range in the open air is from 60° to 110°!!!

The variations in the wet bulb are due to the currents of air, which beginning about 11 A. M., pass into a rather constant strongish west wind about 1½ or 2 P. M., and even almost become hot. The climate is excessively dry, as indicated by the effects it has on furniture, etc.

The difference of temperature between a tent, even with two flies or double roof, and the open air in free situations, is by no means great; thus when the thermometer was 105° in part of my tent, it was scarcely 110° in the sun; in Capt. Thomson's large tent 102°; placed against the outer *kunnat*, it rose to 105°. Hanging free with black cloth round the bulb, 112°. But to shew the great heating powers of the sun, the thermometer with the bulb, placed on the ground and covered with the loose sand of the surface of the soil, rose to 141°.

Black partridges occur in the cornfields here, but in no great numbers. Much of the cultivation of barley, wheat, and rye, is very luxuriant, but the proportion of waste, to cultivated land is too considerable to argue either a large population or active agricultural habits. Pastor roseus occurs in flocks; it is evidently nearly allied to the *mina*. The capabilities of this valley are considerable, more particularly when the extreme readiness with which water is obtained in wells is considered, as well as the nature of the soil, which is well adapted to husbandry. Candahar, viewed from about a mile to the west of our camp, backed by the picturesque hills (one bluff one in particular), the numbers and verdure of the trees, the break in the mountains on the Herat road, presents a pretty scene.

8th.—The installation of the Shah, which took place to-day on the plain to the north of the city, was a spectacle worth seeing on account of the grand display of troops; but there were very few of the inhabitants of Candahar or surrounding villages present. Mulberries and apricots are now ripening. Rats, a Viverra with a long body and short legs, tawny with brown patches, face broad, blackish-brown, white band across the forehead, and white margins to the ears which are large; storks were seen when alarmed. Pastor roseus occurs in flocks; magpies, swallows, swifts, and starlings. There is a garden with some religious buildings, to which an avenue of young trees leads in a north-east direction from one of the Cabul gates, for there are two on this face. The buildings are not remarkable; nor are the trees, which are small; a few planes (Platanus) occur, the most common is the *Benowsh*, a species of ash, (Fraxinus) of no great size or beauty. The elegant palmate leaved Pomacea likewise occurs, with the mulberry: the marigold is a great favourite.

The fields are now ripening, this being the harvest-moon. Wild oats occur commonly, although they are not made any use of; the seed is large, and ripens sooner than any of the others; from the size of the uncultivated specimens, I am sure that oats would form an excellent crop.

In the fields Cichorium is very common, and Carduacea, Centaurea cyanea, Dipsaceæ, and in certain low places an Arundo, are the most common weeds; two or three Silenaceæ, and Umbelliferæ also occur. In the ditches Typha, Butomus, watercresses, Alomioides, Ceratophyllum, Lemna *gibba?* Confervæ, Gramineæ two or three, Ranunculus, Potamogeton, one species immersa; Mentha, Sium.

On the *Chummuns*, which are of no extent, but which are pleasing from their verdure and soft sward chiefly consisting of Carex, Trifolium, Juncus rigidus, Santalacea, and Gentiana likewise prevail.

The fields of lucerne are luxuriant, but require much water, the price of which is very dear; one ass-load costs eight annas!!

Iris crocifolia is common in old cultivations.

The city is situated at the termination of one of the shingly slopes, which are universal between the bases of the hills, and the cultivated portion of the valley. The ditch is hence shingly, whereas an equal depth in the cultivated parts would meet nothing but a sandy, light, easily pulverizable brownish-yellow soil, tenacious, and very slippery when wet. The tobacco crop is excellent.

CHAPTER XV.

Candahar to Cabul.

The good old *Moolla* of a mosque, to which we resort daily, gives me the following information about the vegetable products of this country, from which it would seem, that every thing not producing food, is looked upon with contempt. The fruit trees, are—

1. *Sha-aloo, Aloo-bookhara,* (damson), which has ripe fruit in August, the same time as figs; *Zurd-aloo,* (apricot), *Aloocha*-apricot, *Shuft-aloo,* another kind of apricot; *Unar,* (pomegranate); *Ungoor,* (grapes); *Unjeer,* (guava); *Bihee,* (figs); *Umroot, Toot,* (mulberry); *Aloogoordaigoo, Shuft-aloo,* all these *Aloos* being Pomaceous.

The Elæagnus is called Sinjit: it produces a small red fruit, used in medicine as an astringent, it ripens in August, and sells at eight or nine seers the rupee; it is exported in small quantities; but the plant is not much esteemed.

The *Munjit* is an article of much consequence; it is exported chiefly to China and Bombay, some goes to Persia; the roots are occasionally dug up after two years, but the better practise is to allow them five to seven: the price is six Hindostanee maunds for a rupee. The herb is used for camel fodder. The Affghan name is *Dlwurrung.*

The common Artemisia of this place is called *Turk;* the camels are not so fond of it, as they were of the Sinab and Quettah sort; perhaps this is due to their preferring Joussa, which is found in abundance.

The carrot is called *Zurduk;* it is dug in the cold months, and sown in July; three seers are sold for a pice: both men and cattle use it.

Turbooj, (watermelon,) ripens in June; it is not watered after springing up; four seers are sold for a pice. But I have not seen much of this fruit.

The wheat is watered according to the quality of the soil, the better the soil the less water is required, and this varies from four to eight repetitions of water. *Jhow* requires two waterings less. Wheat is considered dear if less than one maund is sold for the rupee. One year ago, three maunds of barley, and four of wheat were sold for a rupee.

Iris odora, *Soosumbur;* (the two kinds, and *Datura* has the same name) is indigenous.

The timber trees, or rather trees not producing fruit, and which the *Moolla* thinks very lightly of, are the *Chenar*, (plane) *Pudda*, (Poplar ?), Baid, *Sofaida*.

The fig trees are often planted in rows, they are very umbrageous, and look very healthy. These, and the mulberry, are the most common; next are the bullace and damson. Neither are worth introducing to India, nor have I seen any thing yet in the country that is so.

It is certainly the interest of the inhabitants to keep the army here as long as our commissariat places so many rupees in their hands. It may indeed be questionable whether with an overpowering army, the rates paid for grain and other supplies for the troops should not be established by authority rather than advancing money for grain at exorbitant rates, when the crops are entirely within the command of foraging parties. *Atta* now sells at two and three-quarter seers the rupee, a mere nominal fall, for the dealers will only give fifteen annas for a Company's rupee.

There is a curious *hazy* appearance of the atmosphere over the city in the evening, occasioned by fine dusty particles from cattle, suspended in air; which, from their fineness, are long in subsiding.

This curious hazy weather increases daily, yesterday evening was very cloudy, and this morning the wind rather strong and southerly up to 8 A. M.: and at 5½ P. M. the sun is either quite obscured, or the light so diminished, that the eye rests without inconvenience on his image. In the morning the wind strengthens as the sun attains height and power.

The old *Moolla* says that this weather commences in Khorassan with the setting in of the periodical rains in the north-western provinces of India, and continues with them. From the direction of the wind it is probably connected with the commencement of the south-west monsoon at Bombay, for the rains at Delhi do not commence before June.

The haze is so strong at times that hills within three to five miles are quite obscured; it tends to diminish the temperature considerably, especially between seven and eight of a morning: curious gusts of hot winds are observed, even when the general nature of the wind is cool.

21*st.*—A fine and clear cold morning; thermometer 56° at 7 A. M. in the tent. Air fresh; thermometer 75° at 9 P. M. A few drops of rain at 12; *cloudy generally.*

22*nd.*—Thermometer 48° at 5 A. M. Similar weather, clear and elastic: south winds continue but of less strength.

Easterly wind prevails in the morning up to 9 A. M., after which hour the westerly hot wind, variable in strength, sets in: the range of the thermometer is then somewhat increased, although in the house it does not rise above 90°.

The *Moolla* tells me, that snow is of rare occurrence at Candahar; he mentions one fall in about four or five years. The rains last for three months, and happen in winter. During the winter all occupations out of doors are suspended, and people wrap themselves up, and sit over fires.

Clouds are of very rare occurrence, and then only partial.

The clouds, if resulting from the south-west monsoon, ought to be intercepted by the Paropamisus and Hindoo Koosh, and rain ought to fall along these and about Ghuznee at this time. In the evening a cool wind sets in, indicating a fall of rain somewhere.

Rarity of dews in Khorassan: as dews depend on a certain amount of moisture either in the soil or atmosphere, it follows that in a very dry climate no dews will occur. The occurrence of the dews here at this period, is another proof that rain must have fallen somewhere (to the southward), to which the coolness of the weather is attributable. Yesterday and to-day, the thermometer at 5 A. M. stood at 48°, 49°; at 8 P. M. 75°, 72°, the daily range in the mosque is from 70° to 80°. Capt. Thomson suggests that the dews observed here are either confined to, or much greater in the *Chummuns,* in which the water is very close to the surface, as indicated *inter alia* by the green turf.

The kinds of grapes are numerous; those earliest ripe are the black, and a small red kind called *Roucha;* which will be ripe in the latter end of this moon. *Kismiss* another sort, comes in July. The *Tahibee* is the best kind produced here, and the dearest.

Tobacco is cultivated chiefly along the Arghandab; it is planted about this season, and gathered in two or three months, and requires to be watered ten or twelve times.

The barley is now fully ripe, and is generally cut and thrashed in some places. Pears in gardens are now ripe.

Candahar valley is of great extent to the westward, or south-west, and SSW.

The wasps, with large femora, I observe build their mud nests in houses. The rarity of Lepidoptera, except perhaps some nocturnal moths, is curious; Coleoptera are more common, but inconspicuous. Ants are abundant in the mud walls. A small gnat with large noiseless wings, is very annoying, and the bite very painful and irritating. Doves, and wild pigeons are tolerably common, as also crested larks, and swifts. Abundance of lizards; a venomous snake of brown colour, having an abruptly attenuated tail.

Every thing that happens shows how credulous, and how unenquiring we are; and in all cases out of our particular sphere, how extremely apt most are to give excessive credit, where a moderate only is due. It is a generous failing which it is difficult to condemn, particularly with regard to our travellers in this direction. Instance Connolly, and certainly Gerard whose acquaintance with Burnes and its results demands attention. It is singular that his name scarcely occurs in Burnes' book, although his scientific knowledge and MSS. submitted to Government, entitle him to be considered an observant, and well-informed traveller. Pottinger is another instance of what I have said above.

The general opinion is, and it is one which I have not discarded entirely, that he threw himself into Herat, that he was throughout the siege daily employed in the front of the garrison, and that it is owing to his personal exertions that Herat was saved. I hear however on good authority that he was at Herat accidentally, and wished to leave it when the besiegers appeared, but was prevented by want of funds. So anxious was he however to get away, as his leave of absence had expired, that he was obliged to discover himself to Yar Mahommed, and request loans to enable him to rejoin India. The Vizier at once secured him, took him to Kamran, and hindered him from leaving, forcing him indeed to the dangerous elevation of British Agent at Herat. His merits, if this be true, rest on very different grounds from those generally supposed; his courage however has been proved of a high moral cast.

The *Joussa*, the *Moolla* tells me, is the *Kan Shootur* or *Shootur Kan*. Burnes' account of the *Turunjbeen* or manna is correct, except perhaps in the limits he assigns to its production. It is at any rate produced here and sold in the bazar, its production while the plant is in flower is curious, and worthy of examination; it may however be deposited by an insect, in which case the probable period of its production would be that of inflorescence.

There is some cultivation of Indian corn here, the plants have now attained one-third of their growth.

Except in the immediate vicinity of the town, nothing can exceed the sterility of the valley, or rather its desolation: scarcely a plant, beyond the Peganum and *Joussa*, is to be found.

Khaisee, an excellent smooth skinned apricot, is now ripe, and is of light yellowish colour, sometimes faintly spotted; it is a product from grafts, the seeds are useless, as they do not continue the good qualities of the fruit: it is here grafted on *zurd-aloo, thulk*, Potentilla quinquefolia.

Melons and grapes are now coming in; the former, at least those I have seen, have pale pulp, and are not superior. The grapes first ripe are the ordinary black sort: we tasted yesterday some very good ones in the *Moolla's* garden. The *Kismiss* are especially delicate, and another large sort of very fine rich flavour, both were rather unripe. Those for packing are still unripe. The trenches in this garden are very deep: the vines are planted on the northern face only.

Gardens are very common to the south-west of the town. The valley of the Arghandab is the most fertile part of Khorassan I have yet seen. A strip of cultivation extends along the banks of the river, and from these last not being high, the stream is easily diverted into channels for irrigation. Seen from any of the neighbouring hills, the valley presents one uniform belt of verdure, almost as far as the eye can reach, and the view up and down is of some extent. The chief cultivation is wheat, barley, and lucerne; *Chummuns* also occur. Gardens abound, together with fine groves of mulberry trees, the former are walled in, and are verdant to a degree.

There is a bluff mountain to the north of Candahar, the disintegration of which is so rapid, that it is evident from the slope of the debris, it will in time bury the original structures.

The hills forming the ridge separating Arghandab from Candahar, as well as all those rugged looking ones about Candahar, are of limestone, they are much worn by the weather, and full of holes. They are very barren, the only shrubby vegetation of any size being Ficus, which may be the stock of the *Ungoor*, as it resembles it a good deal, Centaurea spinosa, Pæderiæ 2, Echinops, Pommereulla, one to two, other Graminæ, lemon-grass, Dianthus, Peganum, Cheiranthus as before, Sedum rosaceum, Gnaphalium, *Hyoceyamus, Didymocarpeæ*, Gnidia, etc.

The Arghandab is a good sized river, with channel subdivided: its stream is rapid and fordable; no large boulders occur in its bed; the temperature of its water is moderate.

The fish are a Cyprinus and a Barbus, or Oreinus with small scales, thick leathery mouth, and cirrhi; a Loach of largish size, flat head, reddish, with conspicuous brownish mottlings, and a Silurus.

The hills forming the northern boundary of the valley are picturesque, and of several series, and perhaps the subordinate valleys are not so large and fruitful in this direction.

Between Arghandab and Candahar, two ranges occur; one interrupted: the other nearer Candahar has first to be surmounted at a low pass; the pass is short, rugged and impassable for guns. The inner ridge is much closer to the cultivated part of the valley than the northern range.

Between it and the Arghandab, at least six cuts occur: these are met with generally in threes, and are at different elevations; the inner one being close at the foot of the hills; great labour must have been required to make them. Numerous villages, some with flat roofed houses occur.

Arundo, Salsola, Plantago, P. coronopoid, Cnicus, Juncus, Veronica exallata, Santalacea, Mentha, Lactucoides, Chenopod. 2-3, Panicum, Samolus, Ceratophyllum; Salix occurs near the river; apricots, apples, pomegranates, damsons or plums, bullaces, pears, mulberries and raspberries in the gardens.

The shingle found about all the hills in Khorassan, can scarcely be derived from any source but disintegration, it slopes too gradually and uniformly for upheavement. If my idea is correct, the mountains will at some period be buried in their own debris, of course inspection of the shingle will at once point out whether this is true or not, more especially *in all those places where the rocks are of uniform structure.* There is a curious desert to the south and south-west of Candahar, elevated a good deal above the valley, quite bare, and stretching a long way to the westward: it is seen for forty miles along the Girishk road.

Curious reflection.—Observed in ghee used as lamp-oil, a bubble ascending from the surface of the water on which it floated, met by another descending; the deception of this is perfect. That it is due to reflection, is apparent from the variation of the length of the descent, according to the angle under which it is viewed. When viewed from beneath at a very oblique angle, the descent is complete, but if viewed parallel to the surface, no appearance of the sort occurs. The reflection is due to the surface of the ghee which appears to be more dense than the rest, probably more oily; this mathematical reflection may suggest others of a moral nature, touching our liability to mistaken views of things, from observing only one side.

Old Candahar is about three miles to west of the new town; it is immediately under a steep limestone range, running about south-west, and not exceeding 500 feet in height. It bears marks of having been fortified, and at either extremity remains of forts are still visible. The fort of forty steps is at the north end of the range. The town is in complete ruins; indeed none of the edifices are visible except those that occupy the mound of stones, (with which they are partly built) probably the site of the citadel. On three sides, the town is fenced by two respectable ditches, the outer one about 50 yards wide; both are now, especially the outer, beds of marshes; they were supplied by cuts from the Arghandab river. Wells exist however. There is one white mosque in good preservation. The works were strong, and much better than the very indifferent ones of new Candahar; and the walls of the town were prolonged up the face of the hills.

About Candahar, conical houses occur, probably for granaries. A curious mosque cut out of the rock in situ, is seen on the Girishk road, with a flight of steps leading to it, cut in like manner out of the rock. There is also in the same quarter the fort of Chuhulzeenat, or forty steps; a work not of very considerable extent; and as in other Asiatic countries I have visited, troughs are cut in rocks for separating grain from the husk. But there is no work to be seen indicating vast labour or any genius.

Some remains of good pottery may be picked up; and the earth of which the works, etc. were made, is filled with remains of coarse pottery.

27th.—Moved four miles to Shorundab, the country is very barren: not much *Joussa:* the water is brackish at our present encampment, which is within sight of Babawallee.

28th—Proceeded to Kileeyazim, ten and a quarter miles, marched at 2 P. M. and reached the place at 6 P. M., the camels arriving one hour afterwards: the ground is generally good, throughout stony, difficult in places and undulated, particularly in two situations occasioned from cuts. There is a square fort, situated at the halting place with a tower at each corner, and on north face two; as well as towers at the gate: but without windows. *Joussa* is abundant, as also grass along the cuts. Salsola rotundifolia, a Chenopodia, and a curious prickly, leafless Composita and *Joussa* occur, the latter most common, Artemisiæ sp. Also rock pigeons and the raven. Halted one mile to the east of the fort.

29*th*.—Proceeded to the Turnuk, near Khet-i-Ahkoond, distance fifteen and a half miles. The country continues the same, no cultivation to be seen before reaching the Turnuk. The road tolerable, over gravelly or shingly ground: it was at first level, until we reached a mountain gorge, when it became undulated. Passed the dry beds of two streams, the second the larger: its banks were clothed with Vitex instead of Tamarisk. At the entrance of gorge a fort similar to that of yesterday was passed. Scarcely any change in vegetation. Artemisiæ one or two, Centaurea spinosa, Salsola cordifolia and aphylla? are the most common plants, Euonymus and Malpighiacea? Polygonoides, occurred along the nullah, a pretty species of the plant, Antheris globosis petaloideo-terminalis, in profusion in some places, literally colouring the ground: close to it another very distinct species, foliis connatis, floribus albis, a Rubiaceous crystalline looking plant, another novelty; all the plants about the hills at Candahar continue: Dianthoid, Statice, Pæderia villosa. Cultivation along the Turnuk, melons in small trenches, the crops are now cut, *Jhow* or *gaz* along the bank: but there is not much water. The hills around are apparently of limestone, very picturesque, and presenting very fine cliffs. The valley of the Turnuk is here very narrow, and the country very arid looking, completely burnt up. *Joussa* rather scarce, *doob* grass occurs along the river, the water of which is discoloured.

30*th*.—Proceeded to Shair-i-Suffa, ten miles and six furlongs. The country continues the same. The road extending along the right bank of the Turnuk, over undulating ground for one and a half or two miles, is bad, very narrow, and over-hanging the steep bank of the river, scarcely passable for wheel carriages without preparation. Vegetation continues precisely the same: little verdure to be seen even along the Turnuk: the hills desperately barren; a high mound occurs in middle of the valley near our halting place, well adapted for a fort, but unoccupied. Small fields of cultivation are now seen. A small species of mullet occurs in the river: thermometer 101° at 1 P. M. in the tent.

Nothing can exceed the barren aspect of this valley, which is near Khet-i-Ahkoond, but at several miles distance, a few trees are visible in nooks: the only green along the banks of the river, is occasioned apparently by Tamarisk: the hills are picturesque, rugged, varied with bold cliffs, the valleys are changed in structure, being now occupied by rounded undulated ground, instead of hollow basins.

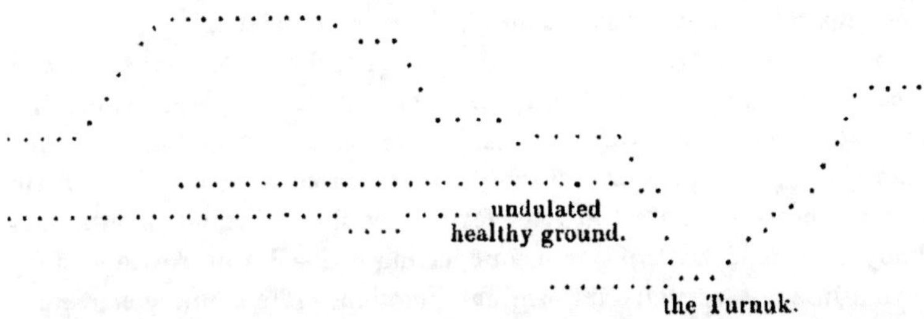

July 1*st*.—Proceeded ten miles, and halted on the Turnuk within one mile of the tower of Tirandaz. The country continues precisely the same: the road at first is bad, owing to the inhabitants having tried to flood it. At a distance of six miles we ascended a small defile without any difficulty; the remainder of the march being over undulating stony ground: the valley then becomes narrow, and we again enter into the arable part, which is especially narrow. The hills present the same aspect. *Joussa* very abundant, and also Artemisia, and a Salsoloides flore ochroleuço. No villages are visible. We are unable to judge of the extent of cultivation, because the country, which seems uniformly dried up, is rugged and bouldery: on the right is the old bed of the river, consisting of dry sand. We crossed one small nullah, when an old fort became visible on a hill, in the centre of the valley.

2*nd*.—Proceeded to Toot, a distance of eleven miles, through a similar country; the road dividing at the low hills approaching the river and forming its banks, which are in places precipitous; the greater part of the difficulties were avoided by taking the lower route, that along the hills being impassable for guns owing to the large rocks scattered in every direction, and detached from conglomerate hills. Two or three nullahs were passed, one with a little water. The ground was besides a good deal cut up towards the centre of the valley, and a water-cut was crossed several times. Owing to the delay in making the road, the troops did not reach the encamping ground before 8 or 8½ P. M., the camels in some instances not before 12 P. M. An attack is reported to have been made on the baggage at the river where the road ascends the cliff: it was prevented by a party of the 13th, who shot two of the marauders. *Joussa* is plentiful, and Mentha in flower.

The Turnuk river is 20 feet broad, the current rapid, and the water discoloured; the banks are sandy, 15 feet high: coarse grass, Clematis scandens fol. ternatisectis pinnatis. *Jhow* is abundant.

3rd.—From Toot to ———, nine miles and four furlongs. Road decent, over the usual sort of ground, except in one place, where the bank approaches the river; this defile is much shorter and much easier than that at Tirandaz or rather Jillongeer: a small river with a little water is crossed: here the road for a very short distance bends suddenly to a little west of north, but having crossed a narrow and deep ravine-like cut, resumes its original direction. The country continues precisely the same, the valley however becomes narrow and more undulating, while the peculiar limestone ranges appear to be fewer. Reached the encamping ground in very good time, the vegetation almost precisely the same as before, but with some willow trees. Many of the ravines are however, actually covered with thickets, apparently of the prickly yellow flowered Dioica shrub of *Chummun;* trees and these shrubs occupied by thousands of a hymenopterous insect or fly. *Joussa* very abundant: a village, the lights of one were visible *en route*. The water of the Turnuk is still very much discoloured, its bed shingly, and the ground near it much cut up; a mill was passed on the river; the valley here not being 500 yards wide: the climate is more agreeable, though still very hot in the middle of the day; in the shade, the air continues pleasant up to 10 A. M. Thunder not heavy, was succeeded by a squall from the ENE.; little rain fell, but there were clouds of dust.

4th.—Reached Khilat-i-Gilzee, distance thirteen and a half miles, from our last encampment, direction NE. by E. as before: the aspect of the country is unchanged, the road became somewhat difficult about one and a half mile from camp, where a defile exists along the hills forming the bank of the river; it was however much easier than that of Botee. Thence we continued over undulating ground, leaving the Turnuk river to the right, but reverting to it beyond the fort. Half-way the deep and steep channel of a river presented a serious obstacle; the country gradually rises until Khilat-i-Gilzee fort is passed, from thence it descends somewhat. At this place there is a considerable expanse of irregular valleys: and to south curious low undulated ground occurs: to the south-east is a patch of table land, which is not an uncommon form in these parts; some cultivation here exists along the Turnuk, which runs half a mile below the fort, which is in ruins, occupying a hill not commanded by any near ones. This is of no great height, and has two ramifications, and in the centre the remains of a tower.

In the valley extending NNE. two villages with castles occur, together with a good many low trees. Vegetation the same: a curious Antirrhinoid plant occurs out of flower, Echinops, Carduacea, and a curious Centaurea. Wet places abound in Rumex and Tamarisk along the river. Horsemen were seen after passing the fort: two or three willow trees about the villages. *Jhow* or barley is selling for ten seers the rupee, *atta* or flour at eight.

5th.—Khilat-i-Gilzee is a very uninteresting place, with little appearance of cultivation. The vegetation of the undulated ground continues the same, Asphodelus, Mesembryanthemoides, remains of Tauschia, and the former Cruciferæ. The Turnuk discharges a good deal of water much discoloured, and forming a series of constant rapids. The most common plants are Artemisiæ two or three species, Centaurea spinosa, Salsola luteiflora, Almond groves, Iris crocifolia? vel sp. affinis, Asphodelus, Mesemb., Salvioides, Thermopsis, Cichorium, *Joussa*, and Mentha recur, the two last in abundance. The new plants are a Chenopodium, Polygonum, Lotoides, Triticum, Astragalus, Scirpus, Cæsalpinioides, Centaurea micrantha, and Eryngioides: a spring occurs in the old fort of Khilat-i-Gilzee.

Indian-corn is just sprouting up, barley and other crops ripe. Latitude of Khilat-i-Gilzee 32° 7′ 30″; altitude, Bar. 24·740: the climate is disagreeable from the violent sudden extremes to which it is exposed. West winds during day, and east winds of a morning.

6th.—Proceeded to Sir Tasp, ten miles, north-east, road good over an open undulating country, the only difficulty in the way arising from a cut with deep holes in it. Vegetation continues precisely the same: limestone hills less frequent, or at any rate much less rugged, and the country assumes a much more open character. Artemisia most abundant, of large size, Cæsalpinia, Euonymus dioica, Centaurea spinosa, Echinops, new plants two Linariæ, Eryngium, Verbascum. Altitude 24·505, latitude 32° 12′ 22″ north. *Atta* has risen in price to seven seers a rupee.

7th.—Arrived at Nooroock after a march of nine miles; still extending up the valley in a direction north-east—direct on the star Capella.

The country is undulated; vegetation still the same. Artemisia most abundant and of a larger size ; road good : no fodder for horses, except along the river : the valley open, distant hills on either side with a fine range to the north of the camp, apparently composed of limestone, with abundance of junipers, and the Iris of Dund-i-Golai very common. Hares, rock pigeons, Alauda. Myriads of Cycada, and the Jerboa rat. The Turnuk river is again occasionally in sight, valley apparently little cultivated. Stipa very common, as well as Iris, Festuca vivipara, Astragali sp., and Artemisia. Cloudy evening, followed by a stormy night ; wind southerly.

8th.—Reached Tazee, eight miles seven furlongs from Nooroock : direction still the same, no change : the road good, extending over an undulated country, except one or two small nullahs with rather steep banks. A range of mountains seen to the north, called Kohi-Soork, continue forming a long line, the southern boundary of which is broken : we are encamped opposite a valley running east, presenting much cultivation : several villages indicated by distant *smoke:* some trees are seen here and there : the face of the valley is rather green, indicating more water than usual. Vegetation is precisely the same ; no *Joussa* or other fodder for camels than Artemisia and spinous Compositæ. Morning very cloudy and cold at 12 P. M. The plants met with are Chara, Naiad, Polygoni 3, Malva fl. amplis lilacinis, on banks of river.

9th.—*Shuftul,* five miles : the direction lay towards the star Capella : road bad, requiring to be made over three difficult ravines, all forming beds of torrents descending from the Koh-i-Soork. The country otherwise presents the same features. The Turnuk runs close under the southern boundary of the valley, and is here a pretty stream of considerable body. *Joussa* grows abundantly on its immediate banks, together with excellent grass and some clover, one or two new Compositæ, one of them a Matthiola, otherwise Artemisiæ, Stipa, Centaurea spinaceis herb. Astragalus, and Peganum, are the most common ; Muscoides, Plantaginacea reoccur, a curious *leaved* Composita ?

10th.—Halted yesterday, and went out along the banks of the Turnuk : where I found twenty-six species not obtained before. Some cultivation was observed, but as usual weedy, abounding with two species of Centaurea. In ditches two species of Epilobium, Sparganium, Mentha, Polygonum natans, Ranunculus aquaticus, Lotus, Carex, Astragaloid on swards, on the sandy moist banks of the Turnuk : Epilobium, two Veronicæ, several Cyperaceæ, 2 or 3 Junci,

Cyperus fuscus. Alisma abundant in swamps: small partridges: no chakor: hares, swifts, rock-pigeons. Springs of beautiful clear water: temperature not changeable, 59°; two small platiceroid fishes in it; tadpoles. Temperature of the river 78°. The fish of this river are the same as those of the Arghandab, the large Cyprinus takes Cicada greedily. The vegetation of the hills is the same: Cerasus pygmæus and canus, common; the novelties were a fine Composita, Plectranthus, Ephedra in fruit, Artemisia, and Astragal., formed the chief bulk; *Joussa* is common on the river sides.

This place is 150 feet above the last, yet the increased elevation is not appreciable to the sight: the tents of the army at the Tazee encampment are distinctly visible. *Atta* sold at eight seers yesterday, barley sixteen seers for the rupee. Where the sellers come from I know not. *Atta* was fifteen seers, but it was soon made eight by the approach of the army, and to-day it has risen to four and a half.

11*th.*—Proceeded to Chushm-i-Shadee, ten miles six furlongs, direction the same: road good, not requiring any repairs; it continues up the valley but at a greater distance from the river than before; the valley is enclosed in hills on both sides. Koh-i-Soork, the northern one, is not very high, but bold and cliffy, with very little cultivation: the country is less undulated. Chushm-i-Shadee is a beautiful spring, not deep, but extending some distance under ground: large-sized fish are found in it: apparently Ophiocephali, but only parts of their bodies can be seen. Indian-corn and madder are cultivated: a new Asteraceous flower was found. Passed a small eminence in the centre of the valley, about three miles from Chushm-i-Shadee. *Joussa* very abundant. Temperature of spring 59°.

12*th.*—Reached Chushm-i-Pinjup, six and a half miles, direction more northerly; keeping Capella a little to the right: the country is precisely the same, the road good, one or two easy ravines; one with water in it.

The valley is rather wider, soil much less shingly, and capable of cultivation; several patches of trees are visible in many directions, indicating villages. We encamped opposite the entrance or gap between the mountains forming hitherto the southern boundary, and a more lofty range is seen running parallel with them, about east and west. This range is of considerable height; presenting a *peculiar slope* rising almost half-way up, and very conspicuous: four forts are seen in this direction; together with several patches of trees, and a good deal of cultivation, but nothing to what might exist. Artemisia is the chief shrub; several good springs occur: clover, and good grass are both adundant for a small party; *Joussa* in cultivation. The mountain range to the north is very fine, and apparently of different formation from the others; here and there whitish patches occur. There is a very evident slope, which is very gradual from the northern range to the *peculiar slope* of the southern.

Several springs of fine water occur: the temperature of which is 60°. Fish are abundant about the mouths of these springs, which are like caves; their waters form one of the heads of the Turnuk, along them Mentha, Gramineæ 2, Plantago major, Centaurea magnispina, Compositæ, Trifolium. In the spring Polygonum natans, and P. graminifol., Chara, Cyperacæ.

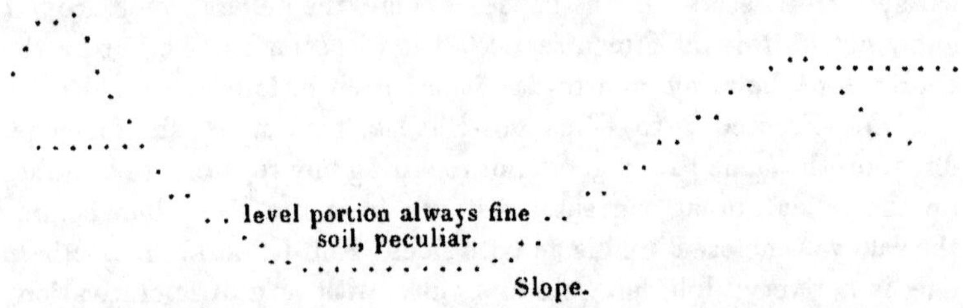

13*th.*—Gojhan, the distance to this place is 12 miles 6 furlongs: it is not within sight of the Turnuk, though still up the valley of that river, with the same boundaries: a few ravines were crossed but they were not difficult: the road, otherwise level, turning most of them, and capable of easy transit. One small stream was passed, when we encamped on a small cut with excellent water: the banks as usual clovery and grassy; opposite this are two villages on either side of a gorge in the northern boundary, both apparently fortified; the one to the north of the gorge is of large size. The country is not shingly, but the soil is mixed with small pebbles; to our right is a bold hill; vegetation the same. *Bicornigera* planta is very common, and a good deal of madder cultivation occurs; wheat and barley all cut and thrashed or trodden out: *atta* selling eight and a half seers the rupee. Thermometer at day break 49°, the west winds continue strong: they arise about 11 A. M. and continue till sunset, sometimes even a little later; they are not hot.

This place, and its environs, is one of the most promising looking I have seen; the whole face of the country being perhaps capable of cultivation. No *Joussa* seen except perhaps among the cultivated fields; grass is plentiful enough for a small force, and *Boosee* likewise.

Quails were seen on the march at some distance: it seems to be a great country for potash, and perhaps for camphor, which is evidently abundant in one species of Artemisia.

14*th.*—Proceeded to Mookhloor or *Chushm-i-Turnuk*, twelve and a half miles; direction about NNE. The country is the same, but the road is more raviny: certain passes occur about three miles from Gojhan, presenting a fine defile, and some smaller ones afterwards. Vegetation continues the same. Artemisiæ, Astragali, and Peganum, are most common; observed a new Astragalus. The valley is much wider after passing Gojhan; the southern boundary is not so distinct, owing to the haze: there is not much cultivation which appears to be confined to the slopes under the hills. Mookhloor is situated under a fine limestone cliff; and an excellent stream of water occurs here, and abundance of fine grass along the humid banks: along this water villages are abundant, they are all fortified. Trees are plentiful, indeed after Candahar and Arghandab, this is the best looking place we have seen: the view is not distinct however, owing to the haze above alluded to: beyond the water, lies a vast and barren plain. Fish are abundant in the stream, and vegetation luxuriant along its margins. This stream divides into two or three branches, which are all soon choked up with sedges, etc., a cut carries off the greater part of the water, the slope is to the south, or a little to the west of south.

Typha angustifolia occurs in profusion, Mentha, Cochlearia, Epilobiæ 2, Calamus abundant, Cyperaceæ in profusion, Ranuncul. aquatic. Alisma ditto. The vegetation of the plain where we are encamped is chiefly Artemisia.

15*th.*—Halted: and I here ascended the hills overhanging the heads of Turnuk where many villages are visible along its branches, fifty may be counted, but it is not known how many of these are in ruins, the villages occur at little distances from each other; the valley is very broad. These hills, which are of conglomerate limestone, except about the upper one-third, which is simple limestone, have no peculiar vegetation. Ficus is the only moderate sized shrub, Asphodelus, Lameoides, Salvia alia, which must be a beautiful species, Labiatæ cæspitosa, Bæhmerioides, Pommereulla, and several grasses, Compositæ, Linaria, Senecionoides glaucescens of Quettah, Dianthoides frutex alius congener, Staticoides alia, Composita Eryngifolia, Eryngium, Astragali 2, Umbelliferæ 2-3, Hibiscus vel Althæi, Rutæ sp., Frutex pistacioides, Sedoides rosaceus, Onosma, Verbascum, Dipsacea,

Cerasus pygmæus, canus, Scrophularia tertia, Compositæ, Labiatæ, and grasses, are all the most common plants.

The novelties along the water are a pretty species of Astragalus, in turf a Triglochin and Typha in flower, Potamogetons 3-4, and Ecratophyllum occur: barley is now selling at sixteen seers, wheat at eight seers for a rupee.

16th.—Reached Oba-kahreeze, the distance of which from the last encampment being fourteen miles. The country is open, but very uninteresting; the boundary hills are scarcely discernible owing to haze: the road is good, and a few small hills occur here and there. Vegetation is comparatively scanty; Astragalus novus, common; the chief plants, however, is another Artemisia of much more medicated qualities than those previously met with, that is, less fragrant, Peganum common. Water is plentiful enough, but fodder is scarce, and scarcely any *Joussa* occurs; but a good deal of cultivation was passed, consisting of madder, barley, and wheat. A few trees were observed here and there marking the sites of villages. The country is much poorer than that at Mookhloor, but almost the whole expanse of plain is capable of good cultivation: soil pebbly. Fowls a good many are procurable. Apricots are also brought for sale, but very inferior: a striking boundary hill to the north presents a rugged, lofty aspect, not less in the peaks than 4,000 above the plain; several ranges occur, but those to the south are low, rounded, and small; rounded clumps of Astragali are seen.

17th.—Proceeded to Jumrat, 12 miles and 2 furlongs, our direction lying to the north of the star Capella. The country continues to present a similar aspect: valley expanded, road tolerable, several ravines and beds of dry watercourses, with sandy bottoms; indeed as compared with yesterday, the soil is much more sandy and less pebbly. Vegetation is the same, no more dense aggregations of Artemisia fruticosa are seen, but the plants consisting of scattered Artemisia of yesterday, barely suffruticose, Peganum, Astragalus, Astragaloid Muscoideus, and Senecio glaucescens. A good deal of cultivation occurs on both sides of the slope towards the southern boundary, which is here lofty, presenting the usual limestone characters. Many villages are seen, all fortified, and about Jumrat there is the appearance of much population. Jerboas, ravens, rock pigeons, and wild pigeons, are common: hares are uncommon. Very few trees are to be seen, but there is abundance of good water and grass along the margins of the cut. Sheep are also to be had, but they are small, and goats for one rupee each, large sheep two rupees: *dhal*, *atta*, barley procurable; and Herat rugs.

To-day the native troops were put on short rations of twelve *chatacs*; servants, etc. on eight. Horsemen to the number of 100? came to meet the Shah, all mounted on decent ponies, but quite incapable of coping with our irregular horse. Barometer 23·305, thermometer 87°. Wooll. new thermometrical barometer 697·6, old 595·8.

From 11 P. M. to 12 P. M. heavy rain; very heavy for about twenty minutes, with a threatening aspect in the horizon at 7 A. M. to south by east, from which direction the rain came: thunder and lightning; latter very frequent.

18th.—Entered the district of Karabagh, distance to our present place of encampment from that we had left eight and a half miles. The road decent, traversing several watercuts, one or two ravines, and a small stream, indeed water becomes more abundant to-day than in almost any other march: our direction lay the same as before, but as we approached the low hills, separating us from Ghuznee plain, we proceeded more east in order to turn them. The features of the country are the same, together with the vegetation, the only novelty being a genuine Statice and a Cruciferous plant, which I observed at Mookhloor, and a Composita, Echinops spinis radiantibus continued. The medicated suffruticose Artemisia: *Joussa* in old cultivation, and Peganum are the most common plants.

Grass abundant along the cuts and streamlets, mixed with a pretty new Astragalus, and the Astragalus of Mookhloor, *Composita depressa*, etc.

The valley narrowing, we halted at the foot of low hills, which we are yet to traverse; the ground about our camp stony and barren, producing Astragalus, thorny Staticoides, Centaurea spinosa, Verbascum, and Thapsus.

The soil of the plain good and deep, as instanced by ravines, and the deep beds of streamlets. Cultivation is abundant, villages numerous, and, as usual, all walled; their form generally square, with a bastion at each corner, and often two at each face, in which there is a gate. The people are very confident of their own security in these parts, crowding to our camp with merchandise. The country continues bare of trees, except about some of the villages; northern boundary hills lofty; a curious snow-like appearance is occasionally produced from denudation of land slips, like a long wall running along one of the ridges: southern hills distant, presenting limestone characters.

The articles sold in camp yesterday, were *atta* (wheat) eight seers, barley sixteen *chenna*, sugar three to four seers. Lucerne abundant, at one rupee four annas a bullock load, *soorais, kismiss*, three to four seers, *zurd-aloo* twelve seers, dried *toot* or mulberry one and a half seers for a rupee, but these are insipid, very sweet, but also very dirty, *pistacio* nuts one seer: crops not yet cut, but ripe.

Kupra, cloth of common quality, as well as a black kind called *soosee*.

Barometer, mean of three observations (12 P. M., 1 P. M., 2 P. M.) 23·433, thermometer 85° 6′. Wooll. new therm. bar. mean of two observations, 699·1, old, 597·5. Lichens abundant on black *lime-stone?* rocks. On hills about camp, Labiata nova, and a curious tomentose plant were the only novelties.

19*th.*—Proceeded to Argutto, distance nine miles, direction easterly, the country continues unchanged until we ascended gradually the end of the low ridge between us and Ghuznee. The slope was very gradual: the road towards the foot generally sandy, and in some places very bouldery: on surmounting the ridge, which was not 300 feet above the plain, we descended a trifle, and encamped in an open space with hills to the north; this place slopes to the south into the valley up which we have come for some marches. The valley in this upper portion is not so fertile as the lower parts we have seen lately, still there are a good many forts, and some cultivation: one or two cuts were passed, and water is abundant at our halting place in cuts, or *Kahrezes*, as well as in a small torrent with a shallow bed. Several forts were seen on the north side, situated in the small ravines of the hills, they are however, mostly ruined. No change in the vegetation. Jerboas not uncommon. An Accipitrine bird, the same as that obtained at Shair-i-Suffer.

Horsemen, about thirty, were seen on the hills; they descended thence and skirted the base in number; when they were pursued by our cavalry, but escaped through a ravine which Sturt says, leads into a fine plain with many forts. The 4th brigade joined with the Shah's force. I observed to-day a curious monstrosity of an Umbelliferous plant, in which the rays of the umbellules are soldered together; forming an involucre round the immersed central solitary female, the male flowers forming the extreme teeth of the involucre.

Datached thermometer 83° 3′, attached ditto 83° 3′; barometer 23·262, mean of three observations: old therm. bar. 597·2, new ditto 696·9. Abundance of villages throughout the part of the valley running east, and then north, and many trees.

made on the spot by W Griffith

M & N

20th.—Proceeded to Nanee, distance eight to ten miles, bearing north-east; after descending slightly from the ground we encamped on, and turning the east extremity of its slope, the road is good, sandy and shingly, running close to low undulated hills. No change in vegetation. Encamped on undulated shingly ground formed from low hills to the north, about half a mile off: Ghuznee is thence visible, situated close under a range of hills, the walls high, having many bastions, and one angle on the south face. Abundance of villages and topes or groves about the valley closing up with irregular barren mountains. Picquets were seen about five miles from our camp, but no appearance of an army about Ghuznee.

The valley up which we have come since leaving Mookhloor, runs opposite this place, from nearly east to north, and apparently, terminates beyond Ghuznee; it is highly capable, is well inhabited and much cultivated. So are all the valleys that we have seen on surmounting the boundary ridges: the villages occupy each *indentation* of the valley, as well as its general level.

Barometer at 1 P. M. 23·336, thermometer 91°: new thermometric bar. 697·1, old 597·2. Latitude mean of three observations 33° 24′ 26″ North.

21st.—Moved to Ghuznee, ten miles six furlongs. Cavalry in very regular columns on the left; infantry to the right, and the artillery in the centre; the park bringing up the rear: to the last moment we were not aware whether the place would hold out or not. The Commander-in-Chief and staff moved far in advance to reconnoitre until we entered a road between some gardens, at the exit of which we were almost within range of the town; here we halted; a fire was soon set up against us from gardens to our left, and somewhat in advance, but all the shots fell far short. On the arrival of the infantry, the light companies of the 16th, the 48th were sent to clear the gardens, which they easily did, although from being trenched vineyards, walled and *treed*, their defence might have been very obstinate. In the mean time the guns on the south face of the fortress opened on us, and our artillery forming line at about 800 yards range, opened their fire of spherical case and round shot in return; other guns in the fort then opened, and a sharp fire was kept up on those in the gardens by *jhinjals* and *pigadas*, who when hard pressed took refuge in an outwork or round tower. The fire from the south-east extremity was soon silenced *pro tempore*, the shrapnel practice being very effective. The howitzer battery on the extreme left of the artillery line was too great a range, and with the exception of one gun, all the shells fell short. In the *mélee,* the Zuburjur 48-pounder, was dismounted, and carried with it a considerable portion of the wall of the citadel where it is built upon a scarp in the east face. After some further firing, the troops were withdrawn almost without range, but sheltered by gardens and broken ground. From 9 A. M. the engineers with an escort reconnoitred the place, and having ascertained that the only practicable point of attack *with our means* was the Cabul gate, we were moved off, and marched to the new ground in the evening. Owing to the difficulty of crossing a river and several cuts which intercepted the way, and formed the worst road for camels and guns I have yet seen, much of the baggage was not up till twelve next (i. e. this) morning.

One European was killed, accompanying the escort. Graves severely, and Von Homrig slightly wounded, a *golundauz* lost his leg, and a few others were wounded. Their gun practise in the fortress improved much towards the end, and against the reconnoitring party, was said to be good.

22*nd.*—The ground we now occupy is the mouth of the valley, up which the Cabul road runs: our camp stretches obliquely across this; the Shah's camp taking a curve and resting by its left on the river. On our (i. e. the sappers) right, is a range of hills, from the extremity of which the town is commanded; between us and the range in question, the 4th brigade is stationed, and on the other side, the remainder of the infantry. We are it seems within reach of the long gun, which has been remounted, and occasionally directs its energies against the Shah's camp. The night was quiet, the troops completely knocked up by the fatigues of the day, the distance we came (to the right) was certainly six miles, and that by which the infantry moved to the left, was still more.

The gardens between us and the town are occupied by the enemy, but the village of Zenrot on the ridge, is not. Large numbers of cavalry are seen on the other boundary range of the valley, opposite our encampment, certainly 2,000; this is probably the other son of Dost Mahommud, who left the fort with the Gilzee cavalry on the night of our march to Ghuznee, for the purpose of attacking our baggage; they were easily driven from the ridge, which is now occupied by our horse.

23*rd.*—Ghuznee was taken this morning by a coup-de-main, the whole affair was over in half an hour from the time the gate was blown open; there was, however, a good deal of firing afterwards, and some of the inhabitants even held out throughout the day, and caused almost as much loss as that which occurred in the storm. The affair took place as follows: the guns moved into position between 12½ and 2½ P. M., and about 3 P. M. commenced firing at the defences over the gate: under cover of this fire the bags of powder, to the amount of 800lbs. were placed against the gate by Captain Peat, the hose being fired by Lieut. Durand. In the mean time the road to the gate was occupied by the storming party, the advance of which was composed of the flank companies of all the European Regiments. The head of the advance was once driven back by a resolute party of Affghans, who fought desperately hand to hand, but a jam taking place, the check was only momentary. After clearing the gate, the enemy must have become paralysed, and both town and citadel were gained with an unprecedentedly trifling loss. None of the engineers, or of the party who placed the bags, were touched, although from the enemy burning blue lights they must have been seen distinctly: two, of a few Europeans who accompanied Capt. Peat were shot; one killed. During the day a great number of prisoners were taken, among whom was Dost Mahommud's son; a great number of horses also fell into our hands.

24th.—Ghuznee: by this morning at 9 o'clock every thing was quiet, and the last holders out have been taken; strict watch is kept at the gate to prevent plunder, dead horses are now dragged out, and dead men buried: the place looks desolate, but the inhabitants are beginning to return. It appears to me a very strong, though very irregular place, the stronger for being so: the streets are very narrow, and dirty enough, houses poor, some said to be good inside, it is a place of considerable size, perhaps one-third less than Candahar. It is surrounded by a wet ditch, of no great width, the walls are tall and strong, weakest on the north-east angle immediately under the citadel; parapets, etc. are in good repair. The loop holes are however absurd, and even when large are carefully screened. The ditch is crossed at the Cabul gate by a stone bridge. The Zuburjur is a very large gun, but almost useless to Affghans, who are no soldiers. Every side of the town might have been stoutly defended.

The view from the citadel is extensive and fine, the mountains to the north and north-west extremely so, and seem crowded in the view, while the river and its cultivation add novelty to an Affghan landscape; many villages are visible in every direction, surrounded with gardens and orchards.

There is a good deal of cultivation all round the town, which is situated on a sloping mound, separated by the ditch from the ridge forming the northern boundary of the valley, up which the Cabul road runs; there is a small mosque on this ridge, and below it, within 400 yards of the ramparts, a small village, from which the attack was best seen. The gardens are as usual walled, and are all capable of irrigation, the plots being covered with fine grass or clover. Apples, apricots, pears, and plums much like the Orlean's plum, a sort of half greengage, bullace, Elæagnus, and mulberries, are the principal fruit trees; of these the pear is the best, it is small but well flavoured; the others are indifferent. There are many vineyards dug into shallow trenches: the plum is allied to the egg-plum, but altogether there are four kinds.

The chief vegetation of the uncultivated ground is a small Salsola, Salsola luteola, this is mixed with Peganum, Santalaceæ, Senecionoides glaucescens, Umbelliferoid bicornigera, Composita, having the decurrent part of the leaves dislocated and hanging down. Centaurea spinescens, Linaria, *Joussa*, and one or two Astragali.

The vegetation, with the exception of an Artemisia indicæ similis, a Malvacea, and an Orobanche growing on Cucumis sp., is precisely the same as that met with from Mookhloor hither, Cichorium, Polygonum graminifolium natans, and two others, Rumex, Mentha, Epilobium micranthum, Dandelion, Plantago major, Panicum.

There are two kinds of willow trees; Thermopsis is not uncommon, Centaurea magnispina and Zygophyllum of Candahar are very common, Sisymbrium, Lophia, Hyoscyamus, Centaurea cyanea, Tauschia. Magpies, Hooppoes, Pastor roseus. Corvus corax, etc., along the water-cuts.

Some fine Poplars occur at a village, or rather a *Fuqeer's* residence; about one and a half mile to the south-west of the town on the road to Candahar, and about it, one or two Carduaceæ, one a fine one, to be called C. zamufolia, Pomacea acerifolia, also in gardens: among the cultivated plants are maize, fennel, aniseed? Solanum, Bangun! Madder, the beautiful clover of Mookhloor, lucerne, melons, water-melons, cresses, L. sativum, radishes, onions, beet root.

There are no ruins indicating a very extensive old city. About our camp are the remains of bunds and old mud walls; near us, and between us and the city, are two minars, with square tall pedestals, of burnt brick, about 100 feet high, and 600 paces apart: there is nothing striking about them, although they bear evidences of greater architectural skill than any thing I have seen in the country, excepting the interior of Ahmed Shah's tomb. The base is angular, fluted, and equals the capital, which is but little thicker towards it base. They are brick, and derive their beauty from the diversity in the situation of the bricks. The one nearest the city is the smaller, and appears perfect, it is likewise provided with a staircase: the larger one is broken at the top of the capital.

26th.—I went to see Mahmoud of Ghuznee's tomb, which is situated in a largish and better than ordinarily built village, about two miles from the Cabul gate, on the road to Cabul, at a portion of the valley densely occupied with gardens. The situation is bad, and the building which appears irregular, quite unworthy of notice; it is situated among the crowded houses of the village, and to be found, must be enquired for.

At the entrance of the obscure court-yard which leads to it, there is a fine rivulet that comes gushing from under some houses, shaded by fine mulberry trees; in this court are some remains of Hindoo sculpture in marble; the way there leads past an ordinary room under some narrow cloisters to the right, then turning to the left one enters another court, on the north side of which is the entrance to the tomb; there is no architectural ornament at all about it, either inside or out. The room is an ordinary one, occupied towards the centre by a common old looking tomb of white marble, overhung by lettered tapestry, and decorated with a tiger skin: over the entrance, hang three eggs of the ostrich, for which the natives have the very appropriate name of camel bird, and two shells, like the Hindoo conches, but smaller. The roof is in bad order, and appears to have been carved. The doors appear old; they are much carved, but the carvings are effaced; they are not remarkable for size, beauty, or mass; and appear to be cut from some fir wood, although the people say they are sandal wood. The tomb strikingly confirms the idea that the Putans became improved through their connection with Hindoostanees, rather than the reverse; the tomb is unworthy of a great conqueror.

I then ascended the ridge, and descended along it to the picquets on the flank of our camp. This ridge, like all the low ones from Mookhloor to this place, is rounded, very shingly, and generally on the northern face, is partly covered with rocks, apparently limestone. The vegetation presents nothing unusual, with the exception of a very large Cnicus, Cnicoideus zamiafolius, capitulis parvis, an Umbellifera, a Scutellaria, Dipsacus; otherwise they are thinly scattered with two or three Astragali, two or three Artemisiæ, among which A. gossypifera is the most common, Labiata fragrans of Karabagh, Senecio glaucescens, Compositæ, Eryngioides, Centaurea alia, magnispinæ affinis, Santalacea, Leucades, Onosma major, et alia, foliis angustis, Echinops prima, Sedoides, Cerasus, Canus pygmæus, Dianthoides alia.

The view from this ridge is beautiful, it shows that three vallies enter the Karabagh one about Ghuznee, the largest to the eastward; then the Cabul one, then that of the Ghuznee river. The slope of this valley from the mountains to the river, presents a very undulated appearance. The cultivation is confined to the immediate banks of the river, which is thickly inhabited, and to most of the ravines of the mountains, shewing that water is generally plentiful. The river is to be traced a long way by means of the line of villages and orchards which follow its banks.

The mountains are very barren, much varied in the sculpture of their outlines, and are by no means so rugged as those of limestone in the Turnuk valley. The lofty one which presents the appearance of a wall near its ridge, and of snow, alluded to during the march hither on the 18th ultimo, is still visible. Considerable as is the cultivation, it bears a very small proportion to the great extent of waste, and probably untillable land, untillable from the extreme thinness of the soil and its superabundant stones. Cratœgus occurred near Mahmoud's tomb, also Centaurea cyanea.

29*th.*—Halted: nothing new; botany very poor; poorer than ordinary.

30*th.*—Moved to Shusgao, distance thirteen and three-quarter miles, direction still the same, or, to the north of the star Capella. The road extends over undulating ground, is cut up by ravines, but easily traversed, ascending and descending; then crossing a small valley, at the north-east corner of which the ghat is visible: the ascent to the mouth of this gorge equals apparently the height attained before descending into the valley. The pass is narrow, the sides steep but not precipitous; the hills are not very rugged, and they are generally thinly clothed with scattered tufted plants; the pass gradually widens, and has a ruin or remains of a small fort-like building as at the entrance. This ruin, or fort, looks down into a poorly inhabited, poorly cultivated, Khorassan valley: road good, with a gradual ascent for one and a half mile from the exit of the pass, where we encamped, about five miles on the Cabul side.

The Botany is rather interesting, the general features are the same as those of the hills round Ghuznee; the most common plants Senecionoides glaucus, Plectranthus of Mookhloor in profusion, a new densely tufted Statice very common, Verbascum, Thapsioides, Linaria, Artemisia very common, Cnici, two or three of large stature, Astragali, two or three, Asphodelus luteus, Labiata of Mookhloor, Santalacea, Dipsacus, *Thymus*, Lotoides, Staticoides major.

In the undulated ground before reaching the valley preceding the pass, a fine tall Cnicus occurs, also Plectranthus; Peganum is very common.

About our halting place the same small Artemisia and Composita dislocata occur in profusion; Cnicus zamiafolius, Dianthus aglaucine, *Astragalus*, a peculiar prim-looking species. Leguminosæ, Muscoides two or three, very large Cnici, Plectranthus, Iris out of flower, Astragali alii, 2-3.

Cultivation consisting of mustard and very poor crops, of which wheat is the principal: a few ordinary villages are seen with good and abundant supplies of water; the country notwithstanding is inferior, as compared with that about Ghuznee. The soil coarse and gravelly, or pebbly. Thermometer 47° at 5 A. M.

After descending from the gorge, the summit of which may be estimated at 400 to 500 feet, the ascent is considerable: barometer standing at 1½ P. M. at 22·323; thermometer 86°; so that the extreme ascent since leaving Ghuznee has certainly been between 1,100 to 1,200 feet.

The inhabitants are coming into camp with articles for sale, as lucerne, clover, coarse rugs, and sheep.

31*st.*—Proceeded to Huftasya, eight and a quarter miles, direction about the same, continuing down a narrow valley with a well marked and tolerable road, extending over undulating ground, having a slight descent throughout: the centre of the valley is cultivated, villages extend up the ravines of the northern side. We halted near several villages, with a good deal of cultivation around, consisting of beans and mustard. But few trees are seen about the villages, and there is no change in vegetation: water abundant from covered *kahreezes* or wells, which generally flow into small tanks.

The slope of the southern boundary is undulated, that of the northern though generally flat and uninteresting, yet near us becomes very bold and rugged, but its ravines and passes are easily accessible.

Shusgao—The plants found here about the cultivation, are Achillæoides, Asteroides, Plantago major, Hyoscyamus, Tanacetoides,

Artemisia, Trifolium, Taraxacum, Mentha, Phalaris, Rumex, the small swardy Carex of Chiltera, Astragalus, calycibus non-inflatis, tomentoso villoso, this last with Composita dislocata is common on shingly plains.

On slopes of hills Leucades, Cerasus canus, pygmæus rare, Dianthoides, Plectranthus very common, Cnici 3 or 4, Labiata of Mookhloor, Senecionoides glaucescens common, Artemisia, sp. very common, Staticoides of Dhun-i-Shere, Anthylloides, Verbascum.

Hyoscyamus. The circumcision of the capsule of this genus is apparently in connection with the peculiar induration of the calyx of the fruit; its relations to the capsule is so obvious that its dehiscence is the only one compatible with the free dissemination of the seeds, *the calyx remaining entire. Hence?* the induration of the calyx should be the most permanent if *it is the* cause, but to obviate all doubts, both calyx, fructus induratus, and capsula circumscissa, should enter into the generic character; the unilaterality of capsules, and their invariable tendency to look downwards, or rather the inferior unilaterality, may likewise reasonably be considered connected with the same structure of calyx, as well as the expanded limb of the calyx.

The indurated calyx is the cause, because although circumscissa capsula is by no means uncommon, and in others has no relation to the calyx, yet in this genus it has such, and should have in every other similar case.

August 1st.—Hyderkhet, distance ten and a half miles down the same valley; the road is bad, and after crossing the undulating terminations of the southern slope, very stony and bouldery; in several places it is narrow and uneven. The country is well inhabited, and very well cultivated, particularly towards the bed of the river, which is here and there ornamented with trees. Numbers of villagers are seen on the road as spectators. Beans very abundant, mustard less so, excellent crops of wheat; the fields are well tilled, and very cleanly kept: this portion of the valley, though small, is perhaps the best populated and cultivated place we have yet seen: the descent throughout is gradual: the boundary hills, at least lower ranges present a very barren character, covered with angular slaty fragments. Some tobacco cultivation.

2nd—Shekhabad, nine miles and six furlongs, direction north-east by east. The road throughout is rather bad, particularly in places near the Schneesh river, which has a very rapid current. We left this on its turning abruptly through a narrow ravine to the south: towards this, the valley narrows much; we then ascended a rising ground, and descended as much or perhaps less until we reached the Logur, a river as large almost as the Arghandab, this we crossed by a bridge composed of stout timbers, laid on two piers composed of stones and bushes, and tied together by beams: the cavalry and artillery forded below, and above the bridge. Crossing the bed which is low and well cultivated, chiefly with rice, we ascended perhaps 100 feet, and encamped on undulating shingly ground; we then passed much cultivation on the road: villages are plentiful, and often placed in very narrow gorges unusually picturesque for Affghanistan; one scene was especially pretty, enclosed by the high barren mountains of the southern boundary, in the distance a village or two, and the Schneesh, with banks well wooded, and willows in the foreground.

The aspect of the hills, except some of the distant ranges, is however changed; quartz has become very common among the shingle, with reddish, generally micaceous, slate: the mountains are rounded, and easy of access: very poorly clothed with vegetation. The course of the Logur is nearly north and south.

There are some villages about this place, with lucerne, clover and bearded rice of small stature.

The elevation of the country is here about 100 feet below our camp, which is about half a mile from the river. Barometer 182, 23·362; thermometer 95°; latitude 34° 5′ 30″.

3rd.—Halted: the Logur river discharges much water; the whole of the tillable portions of adjacent banks are not under cultivation, the rocky sides to the south composed of micaceous slate, are very precipitous; these mountains were originally rounded, but are now formed into cliffs; willows and poplars are abundant along the river. But the vegetation of the cliffy sides scarcely presents any change, except in a Salvia, a Ruta, a small withered Leguminosa; the other plants are Polygonacea frutex uncommon, Senecionoides, Salvia Horminum common, Artemisia two: the usual one very common, Asphodelus, Mesembryanthoides, and luteus, several Compositæ, two or three Cnicoidei, a Pulicaria, etc. of the same section, Cuscuta, Linaria angustifolia, Stipa, several withered grasses, Dianthoides, Scrophularia, Allium, Cerasus canus, pygmæus uncommon, Sedoides, Boragineæ, Boraginis facie common, Leucades, Astragali, three or four, Onosmæ 2, angustifolia and majus, Scutellaria, Equisetoides, Ephedra.

Anthylloides, Plectranthus common, Peganum uncommon, Staticoides major, Compositæ dislocata common.

In the swardy and wet spots, along river, the usual plants occur; the novelty being a Hippuris out of flower, Plantago, Glaux, Chara, Alisma, Tamarisk, Salix, Trifolium fragiferum, Thermopsis, Cyperacea, Triglochim, Equisetum. The *Nuthatch* found in the cliffs, cultivation occurs.

To-day news arrived of the flight of Dost Mahommud to Bameean, with 3,000 Affghan Horse. Captain Outram sent in pursuit. The Shah joined us, attended by perhaps 2,000 Horse, and people are said to be flocking into our camp from Cabul.

4th.—Proceeded to Killa-Sir-i-Mahommud, distance ten and a half miles, direction north by east, the park of artillery, etc. remaining behind, the road for the first half extending over undulating ground to the head of the valley, then becoming level and good with some inferior cultivation: the valley is dry and barren. We encamped on stony ground forming a slight eminence under a beautiful peak, certainly 4,000 to 5,000 feet above the plain, and hence 12,000 to 13,000 feet above the sea. The valley at the base of the hills is occupied by a few villages, but generally speaking little population exists in these parts. No change in vegetation; at the level part of the march the Chenopodiaceæ of Karabagh is very common.

The 2,000 Dooranees who joined the Shah yesterday dwindled down to 300 by the evening, and the camp was fired into at night. There is some cultivation about this, chiefly of mustard, carrots, millet and Panicum, Setaria.

5th.—To Maidan, distance eight miles? direction at first as before, but after crossing the river due north, we continued down the valley, passing some villages and cultivation consisting of beans, etc.; water being abundant about three miles from camp, forming a small brook, which falls into the Cabul river at the end of the valley. Before reaching this we crossed a low spur, and then descended into Maidan valley: which presented a beautiful view; much cultivation, and trees abundant along the Cabul river.

Crossing this which is a rapid current one foot deep, twenty yards wide, running south, or in the contrary direction to that which is given in Tassin's Map, we ascended an eminence on which a ruinous stone fort is built, we crossed this eminence between the fort and main ridge and descended into a valley again, keeping above the cultivation at the foot of the east boundary range, for about a mile, when we halted. The ruins of a stone bridge exist over the river, one arch remaining on the left bank.

The valley is the prettiest we have seen, the hills to the west and north being lofty and picturesque; one to the latter direction presenting an appearance exactly like that of snow on its ridge, quite white, but not changing even at noon, nor occupying such places, as it would do if it were snow. The mountains, except those to the west, are not boldly peaked, the valley is prettily diversified with wood, all of the usual sombre cypress-like appearance, from the trees, especially poplars, being clipped. Cultivation and water both plentiful: villages and small forts numerous, with very barren mountains. This was the place where Dost Mahommud was to have fought; he could not have selected a better, the ridge entering the valley, and the passage of the river, as well as that of the fort would have afforded good positions: a road however runs round the base of the eminence on the river side. By swamping the valley, or cutting a canal, and entrenching himself he might have caused great difficulties. Apples are abundant here, rosy and sweet.

Cultivation of the valley consists of wheat, barley, Cicer, not *chunna*, maize, rice, carrots, beans, peas.

The river side is well furnished with willows and poplars, Salix viminea also occurs; the villages are generally square, with a bastion at each corner, and loopholes. Cyprinus microsquamatus,* common.

6th.—Arghundee, distance eight miles, direction for the first fourth of the way NE., then considerably to the eastward, when we soon left the valley and commenced with an ascent over a low ridge by a vile stony road over undulating ground. On reaching the ridge a similar descent took place, where the road becomes less stony, but much intersected by ravines. We encamped about three miles from the ridge, in a rather barren narrow valley. Nothing of interest occurred on the road, except Dost Mohammud's guns, which are the best I have seen in the country. The hills to our north crowded closely together, the inner ranges are very high, with the appearance of snow.

Hindoo-koosh is dimly seen in the distance to the eastward. In some streams water birds, particularly the small kingfisher of India are seen. The Hoopoe is common, Merops, Pastor, and ravens. New

* Schizothorax Edeniana, Cal. Journ. Nat. Hist. Vol. II. p. 579.

plants a Boragineæ floribus infundibuliformis, tubiformibus, lœta cæruleis, venosa roseis, melons. Snow on the Hindoo-koosh : rain in the afternoon, and at night a heavy thunderstorm to the north.

7th.—Kilah-i-Kajee, lies one mile to the eastward: distance of to-day's march, nine miles ? one continued but gradual descent over a bad, frequently very stony road, not much water. Direction at first ENE., then on descending into the first valley, due east or even to the south of east; we encamped in the centre of a well cultivated valley, near dense gardens, having good apples; apricots indifferent. Hindoo-koosh is here more distinctly visible with several ranges interposed ; the outline is rugged, highest point presenting a fine conical irregular peak towards the south-east.

8th.—Halted : encamped close to gardens and rich cultivation. The fields are separated by rows of poplars, willows, and Elæagnus ; scenery pretty from abundance of trees with rice fields interspersed among woods ; the umbrageous banks of the rocky river of Cabul, are quite of unusual beauty for Affghanistan : extensive fields of cultivation lie in this direction, as well as across the valley in the direction of Cabul, consisting of rice in great quantities, mixed with much of a Panicum stagninum, lucerne, carrots, peas, quantities of safflower, which appears to me to be of a different species, wheat and barley both cut, the rice is just in flower.

In orchards, hazel-nuts, apples, pears, etc. some of the fruit excellent, particularly pears, but generally they are coarse ; apples beautiful to look at, but poor to the taste, excellent but too luscious plums, good grapes, excellent and fine sized peaches, melons as good as those of Candahar, water melons, cherries of very dark colour.

Some change is to be observed in the vegetation, see Catalogue, two or three Labiata, an Ononis, an Aconite, Tussilago ? etc. among the most striking, Ammannia and Bergioides, remarkable as tropical forms, but it is now hot enough for any plant : rice fields crowded with Cyperaceæ and Alisma.

Cratægus oxycantha, or one very like it. The poplar here grows like the Lombardy one, either from cropping or crowding ; its leaves (when young) are much smaller ! and at this stage it might easily be taken for another species.

Heliotropium canus common. The large poplar when young, or even when matured, has its younger branches with terminal leaves like the sycamore. The pomaceæ-foliis palmatis subtus niveis of Quettah and Candahar are nothing but this poplar in its young state!! Nothing can exceed the difference between the two, both in shape and tomentum.

12*th*.—Halted since 10th at Baber's tomb, situated at some fine gardens, or rather groves very near the summer-house of Shah Zumaun, and to the right of the entrance into the town. It is a delightful residence, and for Affghanistan, a paradise. There are some tanks of small size, around one of which our tents are pitched under the shade of sycamores and fine poplars; the tank is fed by a fall from a cut above its level, and which skirts the range of hills at an elevation of fifty feet in some places from its base. The tomb of Baber is poor, as also is the so-called splendid mosque of Shah Jehan, a small ordinary open edifice of coarse white marble. In the gardens, one finds beautiful sycamores, and several fine poplars both round the tank and in avenues. Below them a Bauhinioid fruit was found, together with abundance of hawthorn, roses, and jasmines.

The view from this spot is beautiful, as fine as most woodland scenery. The view from Shah Zumaun's summer-house is also extensive, and not to be exceeded as a cultivated woodland scene; it is variegated with green swardy commons, presenting all sorts of cultivation; with water, villages, abundance of trees, willows, poplars, hedgerows, and by the grand but barren mountains surrounding it, the Pughman hills, which must be at least 13,000 feet above the sea.

The entrance to Cabul on this side, is through a gorge flanked by hills; these to the left are low, those to the right reaching 1,000 feet, through which the Maidan river, here called the Cabul river, runs; it may be 100 yards wide. The river is subdivided, and crossed by a ruined stone bridge of many arches, one parapet of which (the outer) is continuous with the wall before mentioned. The gorge is occupied by cultivation of several kinds, having the city wall at its termination, running irregularly across the valley. A village is situated between the entrance of the gorge and the wall. There are no defences to the city worth mentioning: one enters immediately into narrow dirty streets, with here and there a fever-breeding stagnant sewer; while the streets are narrow, the bazars are good, of good breadth, well covered in by flat ornamented roofs: the shops are clean, and well laid out. Shoemakers and leather-workers, and fruiterers, are the most common: there are armourers, blacksmiths, drapers and bakers. Hindoos and Mussulmen intermixed, form the population. There is great bustle and activity, everywhere profusion of fine fruit, especially melons, grapes, and apples are presented.

13th.—I ascended this morning the ridge above us, up which the wall runs; the ascent is, after surmounting the summer-house of Shah Zumaun, considerably steep, and very rugged. The highest position of the wall is 1,150 feet above the city. It is eight feet high, and six or seven thick, composed of slabs of the micaceous slaty stone of the place, cemented by mud, with a parapet of two feet, generally of *kucha,* or mud, with loopholes, and bad embrasures. It is furnished with bastions, but is now in a ruinous state. It is a work completely thrown away. To the south, the wall bends eastward, and is continuous with the outworks of the upper citadel; to the north it dips into the gorge, and re-ascends the hills on the opposite side.

From the peak, (which is not the highest point of the ridge, there being two higher to the south, on the nearest of which is a mound, and a small pillar) a beautiful view is obtained of Cabul, its valley, and its mountains, together with the far more beautiful valley in which the army is encamped.

The town itself presents an irregular outline, and is, with the exception of some gardens towards its northern side, some lucerne fields near its centre, and one or two open spots of small size, densely crowded with the usual terraced-roofed, *kucha,* or mud houses, which are so close, as to show no streets whatever.

There is not a single conspicuous building in it, with the exception of the lower Bala Hissar and a mosque of small size on the right bank of the river, occupying an open space near a garden, which alone renders it distinct.

The Bala Hissar occupies the eastern corner: its outworks are regular enough. It is surrounded by the remains of a wet ditch; its works have been lately improved. Excepting the part occupied by the Shah, etc. the space is crowded by houses exactly like the town. The fort to its south and commanding it completely, is the upper citadel, and is altogether out of repair; this continues the defence formed by the wall. The walls of the city themselves are not distinguishable, excepting those of the nearest quarter, occupied by Kuzzilbashes. The river intersects the town, it is crossed by two, three, or perhaps more small stone bridges, and runs nearly due east, and may be traced almost to the foot of the eastern boundary range. From near the mosque a fine straight road runs NNE. or thereabouts, with avenues of trees of small size near the town. Two other roads are visible on the east side; one is continuous with that which runs along the north face of the lower citadel, it runs due east; and the other slopes towards this, and meets it about two or three miles from the city at the end of a low range of hills.

The valley is not so well cultivated as ours, (i. e. the one in which the army is encamped) nor by any means so well wooded; it appears bare some way from the city, but this may arise from the stubble of the prevailing cultivation of wheat and barley. There is abundance of water, the only distinct *Chummun* is to the south of the citadel, it is now under water.

Some low isolated hills or ranges are interspersed in the valley; of these the largest is that running nearly parallel to the central road; the next is due north of the city, and midway between it and the saltwater lake which stretches several miles along the north of the valley, and which appears to be a large body of water.

The boundary hills are generally fine; to the east is a high scarped bold range, running nearly due north and south, its terminations being plainly visible; near its southern end commences the ridge that forms the oblique south boundary of the valley, and which runs up towards the south into a fine broadly conical peak, very conspicuous from Arghandab. To the north are the fine Pughman mountains; these run east and west: they are of great elevation, and of fine outline, presenting here and there appearances of snow. To the west is the walled ridge, not exceeding 1,300 feet in its highest point above the general level; this is interrupted by the Cabul river, and never reaches such elevations again; before ending to the north, it sends off a spur to the east.

Beyond the eastern boundary, glimpses of the Hindoo-koosh are obtainable.

To the west, there are no very high hills visible, excepting the western part of the Pughmans; those of our valley are not exceeding 2,000 feet in height, and are low to the south, in which direction the Maidan river flows into the valley. Beyond the highest point of the walled ridge, are several crowded high mountains.

The vegetation of the western hills is not peculiar, Echinops, a tallish Carduacea, Carduacea alia, Senecionoides, Astragali, Artemisiæ 2, Statice of Dhuni pass.

Leucades, Labiata of Karabagh, Gramineæ, several small Compositæ, foliis dislocatis, Leguminosa, fructu echinatis, Santalacea, Asphodelus luteus, Ruta angustifolia, Umbellifera, foliis maximis of Chiltera, a very stout plant, with a very medicinal gum, a new Polanisioid, a Centaureoid, and a fine Carduacea, are to be found in it.

A Marmot, the size of a large rat, is also found here, the large specimens are of a reddish tinge, the small ones of a blackish.

The bazars are crowded all day, and in the morning are obstructed from asses loaded with wood. Most things are procurable; the cloths seen are mostly the indifferent common kind of cloth related to the Seikh Puttoo; camel hair *chogas*, posteens or coarse blankets; these last indicating very cold winters: there are not many other things peculiar—long knives, and the shoes and boots are among the most so, and wretched silk handkerchiefs.

The most common grapes are the *kismiss*, a long coarse grape which answers for packing, a round, very sweet, purple grape, with large seeds, and small seedless ones intermixed, are all capable of being much improved by thinning, and a huge, tough-skinned, coarse, purple grape, of good flavour.

The best peaches have a green appearance, even when ripe; the ordinary ones are coarse, and not well-flavoured; but the Affghans are quite ignorant of the art of packing fruit, and hence most are bruised.

Two sorts of apples are common, both rosy; one very much so, but much inferior to the other.

Pears principally of two kinds, both allied to the common pear in shape; the large ones are very coarse, but well adapted for stewing.

Aloocha excellent for jellies, as also the cherries: most kinds of plums are now out of season.

The melons vary much in quality, the watermelons are generally better, and vary less: the muskmelons I have here seen, are ruined by inattention to the time of gathering; some are very fine, the pulp is never very deep coloured; it is very rarely green; some of the Kundah sort are very good; this and the *turbooj* are both excessively common. The usual Cucurbita is cultivated, as well as the other common cucumber, pumpkin, Luffa fœtida, and L. acutangula.

Cabbages common, beet root ditto, *bangun* ditto, excellent spinage (Spinaceæ).

All sorts of spices procurable, but they are generally old: sugar very good, is sold in flat candied cakes, one and a half inch thick; *koorool* in small cakes resembling chunam.

CHAPTER XVI.

From Cabul to Bamean—The Helmund, and Oxus rivers.

24th August, 1839.—Left Cabul for Bamean, and marched to Urghundee.

25th.—To the Cabul river, distance twelve and a half miles; diverged from the Cabul road at Urghundee Chokey, striking obliquely across a ravine that debouches into the main valley at this point. The course of the river ENE. or thereabouts, then we entered a ravine to the west side of the river, and commenced ascending the pass, which is not difficult, and although rather steep at first, subsequently it becomes merely undulated, the surrounding hills of the pass have the usual character, but are separated by mere ravines. Vegetation very scanty; Senecioniodes very common, as also *Joussa* and Statice of Dund-i-sheer; here I noticed the Solora found in the wood at Kilatkajee. The Barometer at the summit of the pass, 22·148: thermometer 60°. An extensive view is had from it, up the Cabul river, the valley of which is well cultivated, but presents nothing very striking in its neighbouring mountains. Great numbers of sheep passed us going towards Cabul, also numbers of Patans with their families, all on camels, than some of which last nothing could be finer. The women's dress consists of loose gowns, generally bluish, with short waists coming almost up under the arms, and leggings of folded cloths; they are a gipsey-like, sun-burnt, good looking people. Numbers of asses laden with grain were also passed. At the halting place indifferent apples only were to be had. Slight rain fell in the afternoon from east, then it became heavier from west.

26th.—Distance eight miles, the road lay along the Cabul river up a gentle ascent, over undulated ground; features of country the same, villages, etc., abundant. Heavy rain set in from the west after our arrival at the encamping ground at 4 P. M., with thunder. Night hazy, heavy dew.

27th.—To Sir-i-Chushme, distance ten miles, direction continues easterly up the Cabul river valley: features the same; road generally good, here and there stony, crossed a large tributary falling into the Cabul river, from the north at Juljaily, a large village, the largest in the valley, and very pretty. Poplars and willows in plenty along river. Near Sir-i-Chushme the valley becomes narrow; the river passing through a gorge, on the left side of which on rugged rocky ground, are the remains of a tower. The rocks here are mica slate, reposing at a considerable angle, occasionally nearly vertical. The surface is thinly vegetated, Silenacea, two or three *Muscoides* (981), Scrophulariæ sp., common, etc. (see Catal. 971, etc.) Beyond, the valley again widens, presenting similar features to those just mentioned. To the right side of the valley there is a beautiful narrow ravine, bounded on the south with springs, to the north by a noble bleak rugged ridge, with much snow; it has the usual features, namely, a shingly inclined plane between huge hills. The village of Sir-i-Chushme is built on a rising ground or small spur, surrounded by numerous springs which supply the source of the Cabul river; the bed of which above them is nearly dry. The springs abound with the usual water plants, a Cinclidotoid moss in abundance, a Celtoid tree stands over one spring; Peganum continues. A shallow circular pool occurs at the foot of the hills, on which the village is built; it is crowded with the peculiar Cyprinidæ of these parts,* some of which attain three pounds in weight, as also a small loach.†

The cultivation throughout this valley is good. The soil is however heavy, but in places it gives way to a brown mould : rice is cultivated up to Julraiz, but not beyond, millet (Setaria), Indian-corn, lucerne, mustard, beet root; beans and peas are very common.

Great pains are taken with watercuts, which are led off into each ravine that debouches into the valley, at elevations of sixty to eighty feet above the river; opposite each, the river where led off is bunded across. The watercuts or courses are in some places built up with stones. Apricot trees continue, also mulberries near Julraiz, but they are not productive.

Timber is cut in good quantities, and is floated down in the spring to Cabul. We continue to meet flocks of sheep and camels with Patans, Momums, and Ghilzees going to Cabul, thence to Julallabad; after selling their produce at Cabul, they return in the summer to the same pasturages.

The oxen used to tread out corn are muzzled: grain is winnowed as in Europe by throwing it up in the wind, the corn falls nearest the wind, the coarse chaff next, then the fine chaff. Sir-i-Chushme is about the same height as the pass into the valley of the Cabul river.

* Schizothoracinæ.

† Cobitis marmorata, see Calcutta Journal of Nat. Hist. Vol. II, p. 560, where the Fishes collected by Mr. Griffith in these parts are described.

English Scrophularia were observed to-day at Julraiz. We obtained all provisions cheap at this place, but of very inferior quality compared to Cabul.

The most common plants are Senecionoides and Plectranthus; Artemisiæ one or two, some Carduaceæ. Very few novelties occur: hedges of Hippophae and roses, Salvia very common to-day; asses were seen laden with dried *Ruwash* leaves.

28*th*.—To Yonutt, twelve miles, continued for a short distance up the Sir-i-Chushme valley, then we diverged to the north-west, still following the principal streamlet up an easy defile; on reaching a beautiful *kila*, differently ornamented from the usual form, we diverged along the same ravine much more to the west. We continued doing so for five or six miles, passing a little cultivation in every possible spot capable of it, and four or five forts. The ascent then commenced to be steeper, still continuing up the watercourse which was very small; this we soon left, passing over five ridges of easy access, the third being the highest. Barometer 20·365: thermometer 80° at 10½ A.M.; after this we descended the 5th ridge or kotal, 200 or 300 feet, which is very steep, having a watercourse at its bottom; direction of stream lies to the north, thence ascending we again descended gradually over an open stony ridge, until we reached the fort of Yonutt, where we encamped near a green wet spot, visible for some distance.

The road here and there was bad owing to stones; except at the last kotal, or ascent, it was nowhere very steep, but difficult enough for camels, especially up the ascent of the 1st kotal. It lay up a ravine not unlike others we have seen, the ascent being considerable, but gradual, when we left the watercourse, however, we came on a different country, very elevated (1st kotal not under 10,000 feet), longly *undulated*, the mountains generally massive, rounded, here and there rising into peaks, especially to the south, near Yonutt, where there is a fine ridge not under 14,000 or 15,000 feet, rugged with spots of snow; the mountains to north of this are more rounded; slate and limestone abundant, but not a tree from the base of the 1st ascent. The ascent is very practicable, the road is made, or artificial in many places, soil soft and broken: there is water at seven miles from Sir-i-Chushme, and even at the foot of the 1st kotal, at least there are two or three of the usual villages; there is one with its wall demolished. Many granite blocks are strewed on the road. For ponies and horses, even laden, the road is very easy, but for draft it is difficult. We experienced a cold cutting west wind from 11 A. M. Grass is plentiful along all the moist spots, but it is useless as the camels prefer the Carduacea of this place, though a bad fodder for them.

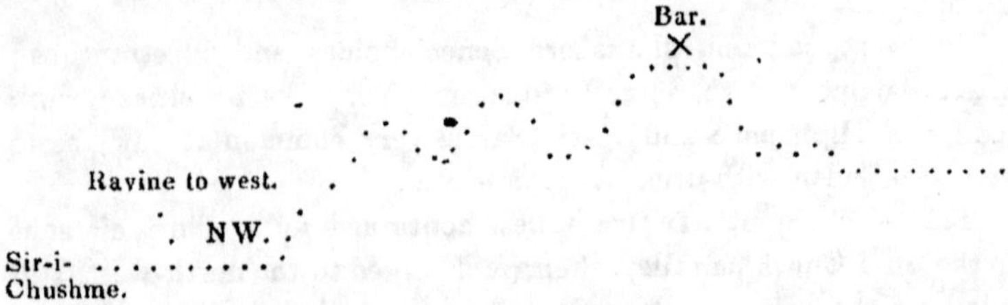

Not much change was observed in the vegetation for half-way up the 1st kotal or ascent; willows and poplars continue to nearly one mile from the last village. Here and there along the ravine or streamlet, Salvia is very common, Senecionoides, Bubonoides on rocky ground, Sinapis, Verbascum decurrens used in the Himalayas for German tinder, Statice of Dund-i-Shere, Muscoides of yesterday, Urtica of Cabul, Malva rotundifolia, Hyoscyamus 1-labiat., Polygonum prostratum of shingly spots, Composita dislocata, Leucades, Boraginea, Boraginis fasciæ *of before*. About Kila Moostaffur Khan a coarse tufted grass, Centaurea oligantha common throughout, first found at Khilat-i-Gilzee; Onosma major, Cochlearia, Dianthoides, Chenopodium diclinum, villosa, Astragali 2-3, Cichorum, Linaria angustifolia, Euphorbia angustifolia, Marrabium, Hyoscyamus of Quettah, Testucoides annua appears about here, Epilobium minus, Rumex, Lactuca fol. cost. subtus spinosis, Melilotus, Silene angulata, Arenaria, calyce globoso inflato, Echinops of Cabul. The water plants are precisely the same as those of Cabul.

For new plants see Catalogue 980, etc.

Summit of 1st kotal Statice of Dund-i-Shere, Statice grandiflora, Dianthoides, several Astragali, one with the pinnulæ dentato serratis, petiola spinosa, a tufted Monocotyledonous plant with terete canaliculate subulate leaves, *Salvia*, Gramen alterum, Composita dislocata, Carduacea, this is the most common plant on the open rounded parts, while the others occupy the rocky sides of the hills. The vegetation is however very poor.

Cultivation various, as seen in different stages along the gorge up to the ascent. Thus, people are seen ploughing for the next year's crops amidst stubble fields, and lucerne; but above and throughout the ascent, no crops are cut, while the wheat and barley on the descent are in the ear: mustard very common. Several encampments of what are badly called black tents, and paths are to be seen very frequently over the hills in most directions, together with flocks of sheep. A large road leading off to the south-west from the summit is seen; from this our road is well-marked.

29*th.*—Halted: every tillable spot is made use of about Yonutt, where there is a fort with forty families. The crops are chiefly wheat and a four-awned barley, the grain is fine though scanty, and the plants are of stunted growth. Ravens the same, round-tailed eagle as at Urghundee, and Percnopterus, wagtails, three kinds of Conirostres, and an Alauda are found here, one or two Sylviæ. The sward about this place is abundant, affords good pasturage for a few horses, and water is plentiful. This sward is chiefly occupied by a Leguminous Caraganoid shrub, rather thorny, and not unlike some species of Barberry in habit, this is abundant, and is first met with in the ravines beyond the Oonnoo pass, Cyperaceæ, viz. 2-3, Carices, small grasses, Leontodon, Astragaloid cærulens, Trifolium album, Composita corona, Cnicus acaulis, and Gentiana pusilla, compose the sward chiefly; in the drier parts of it there is a very fine Carduacea, which appears very local.

The hills about are all either clay slate, pure slate, or micaceous slate, the strata generally vertical.

Descended the ravine which the rivulet passes down, to where it joins the Helmund, the hills bounding it are of no great height, but the slips are sometimes bold. The Helmund runs between rocky cliffs, its bed not much broader than the stream, the water is clear, rapid, and the column considerable.

This gorge is picturesque, the sides being generally precipitous.

The plants of these hills are, Umbelliferæ very common, Statice 2, Carduacea, Ephedra, Labiatæ of Karabagh vel similia, Arenarioid out of flower in the crevices, a large Mattheoloid, Leucades, Dianthoides foliis undulatis, Artemisiæ two or three, one a peculiar one, No.—a shrubby Astragalus, stunted scraggy Polanisia of Cabul? Campanula of Karabagh in the bed of the stream, Cnicus of Kot-i-Ashruf, and Salvia are excessively common, Artemisia pyramidalis, two or three: mosses occur on the banks, and several Gramineæ, see Catalogue 1,005, etc. Cnicus alius, Verbascum.

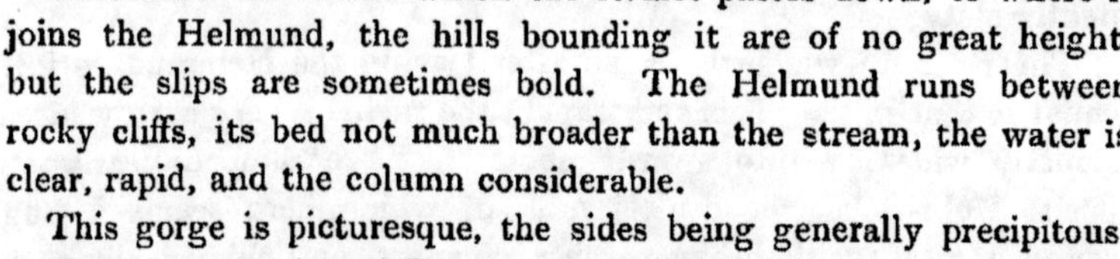

30th.—We continued ascending gradually, crossing a low ridge covered with sward, and then descended to surmount another ridge, which appeared to me to be as high as the top of the Oonnoo. We thence descended, crossing several small ridges; and, at about the distance of five miles from the commencement of the day's journey, suddenly turned north, entering a gorge of the usual structure, drained by a small stream, and thence came on the Helmund, not much increased in size as compared with the point at which we had seen it first, but in a comparatively wide and partly cultivated ravine, containing three or four ruined forts. We continued a quarter of a mile down the Helmund, then ascended up a considerable stream through a similar gorge, until we reached an encamping spot, after performing thirteen and a half miles. The barometer at the Helmund stood at 21·206, thermometer 63° in sun.

Kohi-Baba is first seen from the first ridge, but it is seen beautifully from the second, and still better from some distance beneath this; it is a noble three-peaked ridge, the eastern peak is the largest, and of angular, conical shape. The other two are rugged; the central one is perhaps the highest; the lower portions cliffy, evidently slaty.

The river up which we came after leaving the Helmund, is fully equal to that in size; it is very rapid: the ravine is very narrow, occasionally widening into swardy spots. We encamped nearly opposite Kohi-Baba, the conical peak of which here seems a huge rounded mass, with heavy patches of snow, particularly along the northern ridge: the second range to the south is very precipitous and cliffy: at this place a small streamlet falls into the river from the direction of Kohi-Baba.

No particular change in vegetation is observed: two or three Umbelliferæ, a Scrophularia, Geranium, Ranunculus aquaticus, Herba immersa, foliis anguste loratis, Potentilla, ***Panserina***, a new Graminea.

The most common plants are still Carduaceæ and Salvia; Rosa occurs also, (Senecionoides ceased sometime before) Statice, Scutellaria common, Verbascum, Euphorbia linearifolia, Linaria ditto, Mentha: no change in water plants, or in those of the sward, Chenopod. fæmin. villos, coarse grass, No. 998, common; the chief new feature is *Ruwash*, the dead red leaves of which are abundant. Two villages were passed after leaving the Helmund, both ruined, yet all spots cultivated, several with Cicer. Watercourses as high up cliffs and hills as 100 feet above the river.

A dreadfully cutting dry wind blows down the ravine, and in our faces all the way. Limestone cliffs occurred, about which the vegetation became rich, more especially near a bridge consisting of trees thrown across a narrow portion of the river, at a point where the stream is very deep; near this are two willow trees of a different species. A fine Rosa, a new Epilobium, Aconitum, Salisburifolium, a small Crucifera, one or two Compositæ, a curious Polygonum, a Rumex, a Dianthus, Silene, three or four Umbelliferæ, among which is the yellow Ferula ? of the Kojhuk pass, two or three new Leguminosæ, Saponaria, Silenacea inflata, Cerastium may be found among them, or in the fields close by.

31*st.*—We ascended the high bank or cliff over the bridge, and continued up the ravine which lies over the river, but whose bed is too narrow for a road: we passed two or three villages, the road undulating over ground covered with granite boulders, or rather small masses, rounded only when exposed to weather; the bottom of each undulation is covered with sward and giving exit to a small stream; sometimes we came on the bed of the river. At six and a half miles we came on a fort, used as a custom house, and diverged again to the east up a ravine; the Arak road continuing along the river. We passed another fort, and then commenced the main ascent of Hajeeguk. In a ravine to the left, 100 feet above us, was a large mass of half frozen snow: barometer at the foot of main ascent 20·320, thermometer 80°. The ascent is rather steep, but easy enough: barometer 19·755, thermometer 80°. Thence the descent was steep for about 800 feet, and then gradual for four or five more, when we encamped on sward. From the top of the pass we had a beautiful view of the *ridge* of Kohi-Baba, running about WNW., presenting a succession of fine bold rugged peaks, the conical mass was not seen well, as there is heavy snow on it, and on some other parts of the ridge.

Water is plentiful in all ravines, the lower parts of which are covered with swardy grass. Cultivation is less advanced than at Yonutt, consisting chiefly of barley; every capable spot is made use of. Boulders of antimony, also a large mountain close to, and on the right of our camp composed of this ore, which is very heavy; a ruined fort on the hill near us, shewing again how some of these ridges become disintegrated. A *cafila* passed with huge loads of cloths of various sorts, carried on asses, going to Bamean: they paid toll I observed at Choky fort.

The vegetation in the snow ravine was rich, and varied in the swardy spots: Ranunculi 2, Swertia 2-3, Gentiana a fine one, Junci, Carices, Euphrasia, Triglochin, Veronica as before, Cardaminoides; near the snow in sward, a pretty Primula in flower; two other Pediculares. A Brynum on the dry parts of the ravine, two Astragali in flower 2-3, Cruciferæ, Echinops, Carduaceæ, Silene pusilla, Stellaria, Campanula odorata, Rutacea about springs, Parnassia? Astragali 3-4, in flower, long past this elsewhere, Thalictrioides, Secaloides.

See Catalogue Nos. —— of exposed face; Staticoides of Yonutt, Graminæ 998, Carduaceæ very common, Statice aliæ rare.

The hill over which the pass runs, is chiefly covered with a herbaceous Carduacea out of flower in profusion, one or two Astragali, an Artemisioid, small Compositæ, and the abundant Carduaceæ of Yonutt, Astragaloid pinnulis on the west side, *Koollah hujareel*, Statice, Macrantha dentatis; a spinous leaved Carduacea, different from the Zamea leaved ones out of flower, Gramin. 998 common, Chenopodioid? Arenaria spinosa, Onosma, Carduacea alia, two or three Astragalus primus. Altogether the vegetation is different from that of Oonnoo, in the comparative absence of Statice, Dianthoid, and Astragali.

Similar swardy spots occur on the west of the pass, a large Swertia, Caraganoid, Carices, etc. as before, Gentiana of Yonutt, a new Potentilla, Salix fruticosa; here also occurs the first Orchidea I have seen in Khorassan: it belongs to the tribe Orchis, but is out of flower. On the 1st of Sept., I re-crossed Hajeeguk, directing my way again into the snow ravine from the top of the pass, and found a number of plants, for which see Catalogue. A Campanula abundant about springs at 12,400 feet. The vegetation of the ravine close by the little fort is rich, and would repay two or three days' halt, as it runs a long way up the antimony hill, Swertia in profusion, Geranium also, Stellaria, a fine Conyzoidia.

I had here an opportunity of observing the curious effect of a patch of snow in retarding vegetation, all the plants about, being as it were a spring flora, even such as at similar elevations elsewhere, were all past seed; such as Astragalus primus. Again, why do some plants flower sooner at such elevations than at other lower places? such as Cardamine, here past flower, but not commencing at Cabul; is it because this plant will flower in the winter in Cabul? so there may be a law requiring such plants to flower in wintery situations by a certain time? The idea is perhaps absurd, as their growth depends exclusively on the power of the sun.

September 1st.—After re-crossing Hajeeguk we continued our march to Sohkta, five and a half miles. The road continued along a considerable descent throughout, at first down the valley in which we had halted to the west, thence down the large Kulloo valley in a northerly direction; towards the mouth of first ravine or valley it is bad, passing across a land slip, then it crosses the bed of a huge torrent falling at a great rate, and obstructed with boulders; the right bank, a high almost precipitous mountain, the left a high aggregate of granitic and other boulders. Water abundant, divided into three streams or so: this torrent comes direct from the nearest portion of Kohi-Baba, which appears of easy descent, presenting beautiful peaks. The road then keeps along left bank, undulating over the ravines, down which water flows from the hills on the eastern side; some of these are very steep, and the road itself is infamous, as may be supposed, crowded with boulders, and impracticable for wheeled carriages: one precipitous ravine we passed through, the rocks consisted of blackish, curiously laminated, and metallic looking stone. On descending one steep ravine, we then came on the road leading up to the Kulloo mountain, where we halted.

A good many villages, with forts, as usual were passed; the cultivation more advanced than at our last halt, crops consisting chiefly of barley. One good fort was observed close to our halting place opposite the direction of the small Kulloo ravine; across the valley a well marked road is seen running up a part of Kulloo ridge, at a lower elevation than that which we crossed.

Poplars and willows occur in the large valley, particularly towards Sohkta, a small orchard of stunted mulberry trees. Cultivation consisting of peas; barley of fine grain, resembling wheat when freed from the husk.

The plants of the valley of Kulloo were badly observed, as I was greatly tired and fatigued. Polygonum fruticosum re-occurs, Silene, Clematis erecta, Tragogopon, Salvia but less common, a curious Cruciferous plant, Lactucacea purpurea of Cabul, Chenopodium villosum fœmin. Dianthus, Saponaria, Lychnis inflata, oats common in fields, the common thistle, Urtica, Caragana abundant along the bed of the river, Papaver. On rocks about camp, 2 Salsolæ, Glaucum, Umbelliferæ of the Yonutt ravine, Artemisiæ, Rosa *Ribes!* Scrophularia alia.

The valley is very narrow at camp, the river running between precipices, in some parts passable without wetting the feet.

2nd.—From Sohkta Kullar-Rood to Topehee, eight and a half miles. The road lay in a northerly direction for a quarter of a mile, then turning up a steep ravine, with an ascent for 800 feet; then small descent, then levellish, until we came to a black cliff, over which another steeper but longer ascent extended, then it became levellish for some distance; two other moderate, extended, longish ascents, led us to the summit, which is 500 feet higher than that of Hajeeguk. The descent continued steep and most tedious on reaching the precipitous ravine of Topehee, the road wound over small spurs, until we came to a grove of willows near the village. The road although steep is not bad, the soil being soft, that of the upper parts and of the descent, even annoying from the sand, both might with little trouble be made easy, but especially the descent.

The mercury of the Barometer on the summit at 11 A. M., stood at 19·513, at 11½ A. M., 19·506, Thermometer 66°.

The camels all came up but one, though very slowly; to them as to us, the descent was more tiring than the ascent.

From the summit a fine view of Kohi-Baba was obtained, running to NW. by N. To the NE., another high range, but not so marked as Kohi-Baba, was seen running in a similar direction; on this, two considerable peaks present themselves, but only visible when lower down.

A splendid view of the Bamean valley is here obtained. We have now obviously passed the highest ranges: to west where the country is low and flat; to the north, the mountains indistinctly visible, are beautifully varied, presenting rugged outlines 10,000 feet above Bamean, also a view of an unearthly looking mountain, most variedly sculptured, is obtained, with here and there rich ravines and columnar sided vallies, presenting tints very varied; in those of the lower ranges, rich rosy tints are predominant; also niches in which gigantic idols are plainly seen: also a view of Goolghoolla, looking as it is in reality, a ruined city: a fine gorge apparently beyond the Bamean river, and a large ravine due north, by which I expect the Bamean river reaches the Oxus; not a tree is to be seen, except a few about Bamean. The whole view is indescribably volcanic, barren yet rich, requiring much colouring to convey an idea of it.

To the top of the pass it is three and a half miles; the character of Kulloo mountain is different from that above described, it is rounded, and composed of a curious compact slate, towards the summit well covered with plants, large tufts of Statice, two or three

From a Sketch made on the spot by W Griffith

M & N Hanhart, lith Printers

kinds, two undescribed; immense quantities of Artemisia, coarse tufted grasses, Onosma, Carduacea herbacea of Hajeeguk, uncommon; Triticoides 998, not common; Alium fusco purpurea common. A few exposed rocks occur on the summit. The ravines are all dry, there being no water or very little in them, and no cultivation; thus the contrast visible on both sides of the Kulloo river which runs round the foot of the mountain, is remarkable. Vegetation being distinct on either side.

Yet the ravine of Topehee shows, that when exposed to the action of water, this rock becomes very precipitous, cliffy, easily dislocated: the latter part of the road winds over a portion of this. Chakor, Ptarmigan a fine bird, voice somewhat like that of a vulture, to which it is perhaps anologous.

About Sohkta or in ravines, Euphorbia linearifolia, Ephedra, Asteroides, Rosa Ribes, Composita dislocata, Artemisiæ, Aster pyramidalis, Chenopodium villosum fæm., Senecionoides.

Scutellaria, Scrophularia, Santonicoides, Polygonum fruticosum, Salvia, Artemisia linearifolia, Centaurea angustifolia, Cochlearia, Umbelliferæ of Yonutt, Stellaria, Glaucium, Labiata nova, Hyoscyamus minor, Lactucacea, Linaria, Salsola elegans, Marrubium, common thistle, Rumex, Potentilla anserina, Sinapis of Siah-Sung ravine, Berberis, Secaloides, Statice, *Marmots*, Statice glauca pedunculata, Stipha of Nakhood, Aconiti sp., Ferula? Spiræa facie frutex, Ribes, Muscoides.

First ridge Dianthoides, Statice three to two glaucous species, one sessile the other pedunculate, Ferula, Scutellaria, Labiata trumpet-shaped calyces, Astragali, Diacanthus, Stipa, Ribes, Arenaria spinosa, Triticum carneo pubescens, Pulmonaria corolla trumpet-shaped, Salvia sparingly, Pommereulla, Artemisia in profusion, Spiræoides, Chenopodium villos., fæmin. parvus, Leguminosæ two or three, *Ruwash* sparingly.

Not much change beyond, 12,000 feet, at that height Glaucium in abundance, with a few Hyoscyamus parvus, Borago.

Labiatifol, inciso dentatis occurs throughout, Sinapis of Siah-Sung straggles to 12,000 feet.

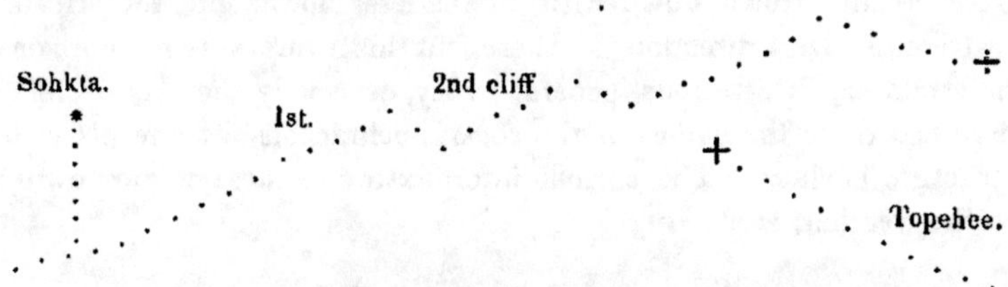

The same vegetation continues down to Topehee; on the red hills over its ravine, the plants are different. Portulacea cana, several pretty Salsolæ, a Polanisia occurs, with Statice two or three, a straggling Astragalus, Ferula, Peganum re-appears! Cerasus canus, Carduacea Frutex of Mailmandah, fructibus combretiformibus, Muscoides which .is a Sedum, Polygon. fruticosum common, the usual plants of cultivation, etc. etc.

3rd.—We proceeded from Topehee to Bamean, a distance of twelve miles, for two and a half miles down Topehee ravine. The road is a decent descent, although steepish: from thence turning abruptly at the Bamean valley, we cross the river, which is of considerable size, but fordable, although rapid. The road then extends along the left bank, not in the valley which is occupied by cultivation, but winding over and round the bases of low hills and cliffs, forming a northern boundary; throughout this part the road is villainous, often impeded by huge blocks. After a distance of about ten miles it improves, the valley expanding into a cultivated plain.

Topehee valley narrows towards its mouth or exit, which is walled in by high, red, raviny cliffs; above, in its upper parts it is well cultivated with beans, barley, wheat, and oats, and contains two villages: it opens into the Bamean valley at a village also called Topehee, there the Bamean valley is well cultivated, with oats intermixed with barley or wheat, trefoil, etc., it then narrows, forming the bed of a ravine occupied by Hippophae, Tamarisk, etc., then it widens again.

The structure of the hills is curious, and generally exhibiting the appearance of having been much acted on by water. They are often cliffy, composed either of limestone or a soil of red clay, with which salt occurs in abundance, conspicuous from the white appearance, or springs. Crystals of carbonate of lime are frequent, limestone, or coarse conglomerate with large rounded stones, occurs; together with a curious laminated clayey rock, with white and ochraceous layers intermixed. The tints most various, as well as the sculpture of the mountains: here ravines representing tracery occur: there, columnar curiously carved cliffs, exhibiting all sorts of fantastic forms: here, as it were, a hill thrown down with numberless blocks into the stream, scattered in every direction; and here, but this is rare, very red horizontal strata, colours various, generally rosy, especially the clayey cliffs: here and there the colour of the rock is ochraceous, at one place its structure is slaty. The curious intermixture of these colours owing to the weather, is striking.

From the head of two of the ravines by which considerable torrents flow into Bamean river, beautiful views are obtained of the Kohi-Baba, whose peaks according to native authority, stretch sixty miles to the westward of Bamean, without much diminution in height. The scenery, however, is less beautiful after emerging into the widened part of the valley, where the hills are less varied both in form and tints, than they are in lower parts: fine views however of Kohi-Baba are occasionally had.

Salsolæ are the prevailing plants of the rocky sides of the valley, Clematis erecta common, here and there a small Statice.

Caves occur throughout the wide portion of the valley, but chiefly on the northern side; they also extend a little way into the narrow portion, where they seem to be excavated into clayey-looking, red, earthy limestone, or more commonly conglomerate, of coarse grey, or reddish colour.

The caves are most common in two cliffs composed of conglomerate mixed with transverse strata of the same rock, 3,400 feet high, presenting a rugged outline; and between the two, which are 800 yards apart, large idols are carved. These cliffs in some places have suffered little from the action of the elements, as testified by the perfect nature of the opening of the caves, and the corners, &c. of the niches enclosing idols; in others they are furrowed by the action of water; in others again slips have taken place to such extent in some, as to cause the fall of all their caves, or of their greater portion, thus exposing the galleries, etc.

The base of the cliffs is irregular, formed of the same conglomerate and clay, but covered more or less by boulders, evidently brought down by the river; by these many caves are choked up, so that originally the cliff might have been perpendicular to the edge of the base, and if so, the caves in the cliffs, and the idols, are of later date than those of the rugged base. But more probably the cliffs, and the caves, are much as they were originally, the boulders having been a subsequent deposit.

The western corner of the cliff beyond the large idol, is much destroyed; on this, the force of the current would have acted: a breakwater occurring along the returning face.

The caves are very numerous, but are confined chiefly towards the base of the cliffs, not scattered over them as I believe Burnes represents. These are of no size, finish, or elegance, and it is only their number, and the extreme obscurity of their history, that makes them interesting; the roofs are usually arched, and the walls are often supplied with niches, and covered with a coating of tar of some thickness, and intense blackness. The galleries are low, arched, and admit one person at a time, or a line of persons with ease; they often form the ascent to the upper caves now inhabited, but originally they were enclosed in the rock, they are defended in such cases by a parapet.

The largest caves are those about the idols, but I see none of any size. They are often domed, the spring of the dome is ornamented with a projecting frieze, some of these are parallelogramic, in one instance with an ornamented border thus.

Some of the caves are situated as high as, or even above the tops of the idols; all parts within the rock are lighted by small apertures.

Access to the large idol is destroyed; the smaller one is gained by a spiral staircase of rude construction, and by galleries. The floor of the galleries is rugged, the steps and the cement of the conglomerate having worn out from between the masses of rock. The images all occupy niches in the face of the hill: two are gigantic, the rest not very large. They are generally in the usual sitting posture, and rather high up, while the larger ones are erect, and reach the base of the cliffy portion of the rock. They are all male, and all obviously Boodhistical; witness the breadth, proportion, and shape of the head, and the drapery; both are damaged, but the smaller is the more perfect, the face of the large one being removed above the lower lip; the arms are broken off, showing they were occupied by galleries. The drapery is composed of plaster, and was fixed on by bolts which have fallen out, leaving the holes. The arms in the smaller one are supported by the falling drapery. The height of the large image in the niche is 135 feet.

The pictures are much damaged, the plaster on which they were painted being mostly very deficient, all the faces are damaged by bullets or other missiles: their execution is indifferent, not superior to modern Burmese paintings; the colours however are good, the figures are either grouped or single, and one is in the style of the time of Henry VIII, with a hat and plume, others represent groups flying —one a golden bird, another a man with a hemispherical helmet, all are much damaged. The hair in some is dressed as in the modern Burmese top-knot, often surrounded by a circle.

Otherwise the niches are not ornamented, except in one instance, as above alluded to; the head of the smaller figure was formerly covered by the roof, as evident from holes or troughs for timbers in the gallery. These holes are now inhabited by pigeons, and the lower ones by cows, donkeys, fowls, kids, dogs; some are filthy apertures blocked up by stone and mud walls; the doors irregular, and guarded between two giants.

An old tope occurs near some small figures, it is composed of stones very much disintegrated, with curious blocks of *kucha* work, and large Babylonish bricks; the smaller figures are much destroyed, some completely; all are in alto-relievo.

The plants about Topehee valley, are Cichorium, Centaurea lutea, Berberis common, Salvia, Cicer cultivated, Lucerne, Centaurea angustifolia, Cnicus of Koti-Ashruf, ditto of Karabagh hills, Triticum, Asteroides, Avena, Centaurea glauca, the common thistle, Ephedra, Mentha, Rumex, Melilotus, Medicago, Artemisia pyramidalis, Lychnis inflata, Saponaria, Bromus, Verbascum, Cerasus canus, Ferula, Statice, Salsola, Astragalus, Polygonum fruticosum, Composita dislocata, Clematis erecta, Clematis alia, Echinops, Leucades, Pulicaria fragrans, Hyoscyamus parvus, rare; Geranium, Rosa, Fabago of Maidan, fructi echinatis, Arundo, Hippophae.

Halted at Bamean till the 6th, and inspected Ghoolghoola or Bheiran, which presents extensive ruins: those of the city are almost destroyed; but those of the citadel are more perfect, and situated on a mound 300 feet high, which still stands with steep banks or fortifications, apparently of Kafir origin, generally *kucha*, with bases formed of boulders. Three lines of defences remain on the valley side; and the remains of a ditch 50 feet broad at the mound on the east side. *Pucka*, or burnt bricks are common among the debris, also pottery, but this is of the ordinary sort: I observed but few *pucka* bricks in the fortification on the west side. Great masses of rocks have been thrown about near the building of the fort, and some of the lower bastions were built on these masses. The mound is chiefly occupied by Salsolaceæ, some of which exist in profusion. Nothing seems to be known about the history of the place, except that it was built by *Julal*, to whom the Mahommedans fix *Ud-deen*.

Quails are abundant in the fields about Bamean; it is a curious thing that in many of these fields oats far preponderate over other grain; yet they are not cut, although all the seeds have fallen out of the ear! Can it be cultivated solely for the straw?

Fine groves of poplars occur about certain portions of the valley; from beyond this to the south, a beautiful view is obtained, embodying the cliffs with the large image, and the back hills whose varied surface and tints it is impossible to describe, so as to convey a correct idea of their fine effect. The poplar grove contains some ordinary Mahomedan *tombs*. The trees are the P. heterophylla, but the leaves are much smaller and more silvery underneath than usual; a beautiful poplar of large size and unencumbered growth, of the same sort occurs in the ravine beyond the small image. Abundance of wild sheep's heads are preserved about all the sanctified buildings, together with a few of those of the ibex, and fewer of the wild goat. The plants of Bamean require no specification, the hills are very barren, chiefly occupied by Salsoleæ, of which 6 or 7 species occur.

The water plants continue the same as at Cabul; Hippurus and Triglochin, Mentha, Cochlearia., Naiad? Potamogeton of Siah-Sung, Polypogon.

The other plants are those found in cultivation, and present no change, Anchusoides alba, abundant. Choughs very abundant; wild pigeons, ravens, Laurus; the nuthatch, a noisy but not unmusical bird, Chakor, together with small partridges, but these are rare; several Conirostres.

The greatest curiosity is a genuine trout,* this appears rare, the spots are very bright, the largest caught was only six pounds in weight. I could not take any even with the fly; but I caught with this, Schizothorax, or one of the universal Khorassan Cyprins.

The range of the thermometer is great; before sunrise it varies from 28° to 30°! in the sun in midday it is 100°! when there is no wind, and the mornings are delightful.

* Salmo orientalis, Calcutta, Journ. Nat. Hist. Vol. III. p. 283.

Throughout Southern Asia, including the Punjab, and both plains and peninsula of India properly so called, no species exists of the trout family or Salmonidæ. Their discovery in the streams descending from the northern declivity of the Hindoo-koosh distinguishes that chain as the southern boundary or limit of the family. It is also remarkable that the Hindoo-koosh should likewise be the exclusive province of a numerous group of small scaled Cyprinidæ, met with only in the rivers of Affghanistan, consisting of the genera, Schizothorax, Racoma, and Oreinus, of which one or two species only have been found to extend south along the plateau of the Himalaya, as far as 27° N., while the bulk of the family is confined to 34° N. See Calcutta Journ. Nat. Hist. Vol. II. p. 560 t. xv.

One of the long-tailed clumsy Brachypodiums occurs in the fields: bears also are found here.

Joussa, Mentha, Tanacetoid, Polypogonum, Cichorium, Plantago, common thistle, Potamogeton longifolium, Labiata arvensis of Yonutt, Centaurea lutea, Cyanea angustifolia, Cochlearia, Hippuris, Ranunculus, Potamogeton pectinata, Triglochin, Convolvulus arvensis, acaulis, Glaux, Capparis of Arghandab, Centranthera pinnatifida, Malva rotundifolia, Asteroides, Lactuca purpurea.

Salt is obtained in some places from the red earth, as also alum an earthy substance of a whitish or brown colour, and irregular surface, sent in quantities to Mindosh, called Zak.

6th.—To Zohawk, down the valley two miles beyond the mouth of Topehee ravine, or embouchure of the Kulloo-Rood. The angle is occupied by a Kafir fort called Kojhuk, of very large size, situated on a precipitous dusky-red and very high rock, facing towards both rivers; the defences reach down the eastern face of rock to the Kulloo bed, and are in good preservation, more ornamented than the modern fort, and better proportioned. A pretty grass sward occurs here, with Tamarisk.

The fort must have been of great size, and is chiefly weak, *i. e.* to a native army, from depending on the river for supplies of water, for it is commanded from the opposite sides of either ravine. The bed of the river under the east face, presents the remains of outworks to protect the supply of water, which is perhaps a sign of its being a recent structure?

The works are good, much better than those of the Affghans, the view of the fort from half a mile down the Bamean river, with the sun gilding the ruined battlements, while the precipice contrasts with it its dusky-red colour, is beautiful.

The Bamean river, especially after receiving the Kulloo-Rood, is of considerable size, but fordable at the head of most of the rapids, its course is rapid, and its waters greyish, while those of the Kulloo are quite colourless; its bed is of some width, presenting a capital road over green sward, with plenty of willows, Lycium, Hippophae, Berberis, and Tamarisk.

About one mile east of our camp, its ravine turns to the south. Wild ducks, quails, chakor, and trout occur whose haunts are in holes, and taking the worm are easily caught.

This fort of Kojhuk is as well worth examining as any place we have seen, the dusky-red rocks are coarse conglomerate. A violent wind prevails up the ravine, commencing about 2 P. M. A curious staircase situated at the corner towards Bamean, ascends through rock, the bottom of which is defended by a bastion and round wall; near, or close to this a slip has occurred, destroying part of the wall and blocking up one exit.

Ascended the cliff by the gateway of the Kulloo valley, and found the line of fortifications, with good loop-holes and parapets extend two and a half miles up, a few houses likewise occur. The path leads through the face of the solid rock: abundant defences, with arched buildings occur above: this cliff is almost totally separated from the upper citadel by a ravine: the citadel has four lines of defences surmounting a steep ridge with outworks on the Kulloo river, the bed of which is 60 yards broad.

7th.—Proceeded to Erak, six miles. We crossed the Kulloo-Rood, and immediately ascended its right bank, 100 feet high; then descended into the ravine up which we continued, then leaving it we struck over the spur of a high mountain; the ascent being about 1,000 feet, thence we commenced a steep descent, of 5,600 feet into the Erak valley, up which we proceeded for two miles distance and encamped. From the top of the pass, a fine view is obtained of Kojhuk, and the valley of the Bamean river, presenting a rich and varied surface beyond description, with beautifully sculptured rocks, of purplish-red colour, which are seen up the Kulloo, close to Kojhuk.

The hills and ravines are however very barren, nothing but Salsola occurs. At the top of the pass a section is partly laid open, shewing a mass of conglomerate, twenty to thirty feet thick, resting on red clay. This conglomerate being less acted on by water than the clay, the rocks often assume curious shapes, and are occasionally even fungiform.

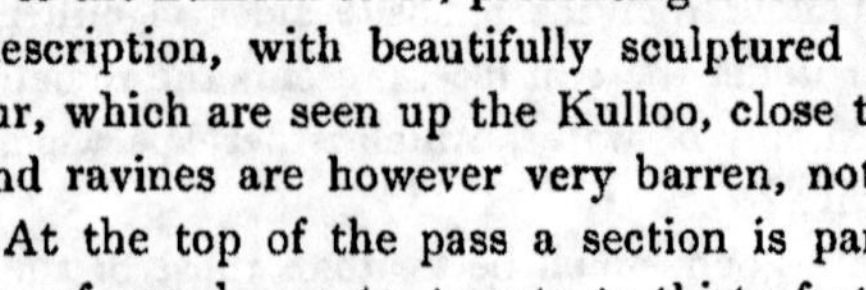

a, Conglomerate. *b*, Clay.

We observed here a new partridge, at least one to which we were not accustomed; it is almost the size of chakor, black on the back, with a grey neck, and very shy; chakors abundant here in coveys. The valley of the Erak is very narrow, but well cultivated, and with a good many villages.

All the mountains in this direction have rounded shapes or outlines, the precipices variously curved, the surfaces are thus formed by the action of water on the outer strata; when this is once exposed, the changes appear often rapid, as may be imagined in a country of such low winter temperature. Caves occur in the Erak valley, chiefly situated in a dirty white conglomerate.

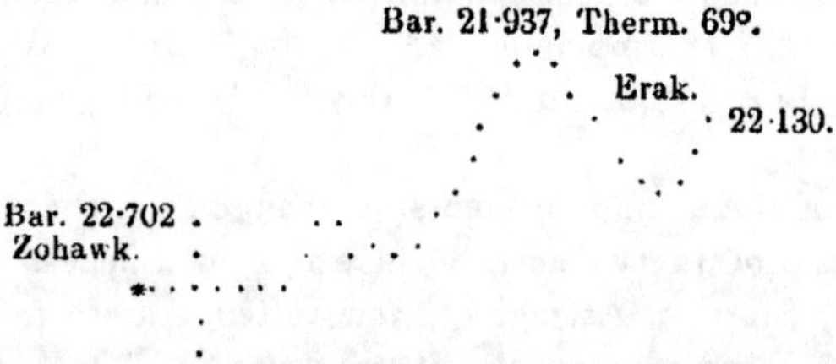

8*th.*—Halted and encamped eight miles up the Erak ravine on a swardy spot: the road easy, ascent bad in some places, but generally good, particularly for the latter part of the march: the rocks in some places rising in abrupt rugged cliffs, generally rounded, slaty. We passed one mass of snow about two miles from camp, botany good, especially about the snow; so much so, that it employed me all day.

Caragana appears at about 10,000 feet, a Tamerioid of large stature in abundance, Asphodelus, not as I thought a Mesembryanthemum, but a beautiful and very distinct species; see Catalogue for other plants.

Our camp is within one and a half mile of the head of the Erak ravine, where snow occurs in two large masses; patches of snow also occur on the ridge or a little below it; these ridges rise about 1,200 to 1,500 feet above us.

Unsettled evening, snow during night on all the ridges about us; with frozen sleet in camp. Thermometer at 6 A. M. 31°.

Large round-tailed eagle seen.

Barometer 20·164, thermometer 61°; boiling point of Wollast. new thermometer; barometer 650, old ditto 555·3.

Swardy plants. Parnassia, Swertia, Gentiana, Carices, Composita coronata, Primula, Labiata, Menthoides, Caprifoliacea! Pedicularis, Umbelliferæ.

Plants of hill sides Asphodelus, Leguminosæ alter, a Nakhood Moschata, Nakhood Labaria violacea, Mulgedioid, Euphorbia, Astragalus prior, alter., Pedicularis, Onosma versicolor, Boraginea, stamens exserted.

9*th.*—Proceeded to Kurzar, eight miles up a ravine to the left or eastward, about one and a half mile, then the steep ascent of the pass;

thence the descent was as steep for 800 feet, then gradually down a swardy ravine until we came to the Kurzar ravine, which we followed till we reached the Choky. The road good; the acsent for 1,000 feet is very steep, the soil good, hills rounded, here and there slate rocks outcropping. No change in vegetation. Passed a mass of snow: abundance of snow on the summit where the mercury in the Bar. stood at 19·200; thermometer 58°; boiling point of Wollast. new thermometer; Bar. 648.5, old 539·1, this being the highest spot we have visited.

The vegetation of the summit presents no change from that of the rocks and hill sides 1,500 feet below. There is a good deal of vegetation, Carduaceæ, Statices, Astragali, a few tufted grasses forming the great bulk, *Nukhood* rare on the Kurzar side, 500 feet down, Statice becomes most abundant, it is curious that on the sward of this side, neither Fumariaceæ, nor Campanula were observed, Silene fimbriata one species.

Caragana all about, even at Kurzar in ravines; Primula abundant, also Swertiæ, generally all four plants are found at the Hajeeguk snow ravine, and may be found between this and Erak, with some interesting novelties. The distance to Bamean by both routes is within two miles of the same, the Kulloo-Rood being the shorter, but Hajeeguk the best road. That of the Kulloo river is followed to Zohawk. The weather unsettled with showers of hail, clouds and sunshine: and heavy gusts of wind occasionally from Kohi-Baba, whose eastern extremity comes in sight after entering the *Kurzar* ravine. No view from the summit of the pass.

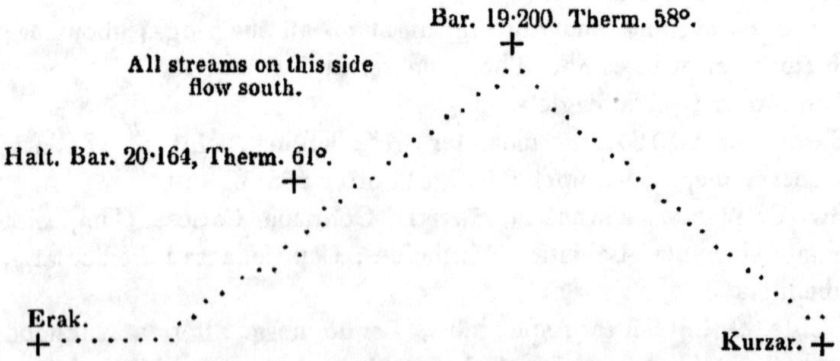

Pedicularis, Campanula, Rubiaceæ, Hippuris in flower, Phleum, Carduacea of Yonutt, Cnicus of Koti-Ashruf, Pulmonaria, corolla tubiform, Euphorbia linearifolia, Composita dislocata, Cardamina lutea.

10*th*.—Proceeded to the Helmund, thirteen and a half miles; the only novelty met with is a curious spring about half-way between

Siah-Sung halting place, and the Helmund consisting of limpid water emitting a copious ebullition of gas, not water, as the overflow is very small; a copious deposition of fine red earth is formed all round, which looks especially bright in the springs themselves. The water possesses a peculiar acid taste.

Quails abundant, especially about this place, the water of the Helmund is very clear and affords excellent fishing with worms which are greedily taken, and also with the fly, particularly towards evening, by a species of Gonorhynchus.

11*th.*—Returned to the foot of the ascent of the Oonnoo, nine miles: nothing new having been met with, except that Kohi-Baba is seen to great advantage from the higher ridges of this pass. On going to Bamean we saw it for the first time from the ridges beyond Yonutt, badly from the first, but beautifully from the second ridge. The weather continues as usual threatening in the evening, clearing up after sunset: there is less snow on Kohi-Baba now than when we went.

12*th.*—Proceeded to Sir-i-Chushme, eight miles, which was one continued descent. Passed Killa Moostaffur Khan, built by a Kuzzilbash; it is the prettiest fort in the country. The common Carduacea disappears below 9,500 feet, Cnicus of Koti-Ashruf commences here.

Temperature of the spring at Sir-i-Chushme, 55° (1½ P. M.); that at Kallo, on the other side of Hajeeguk, 45°.

All crops are cut, and the ground ploughed or preparing; in one place the young wheat is springing up; but the country generally looks very brown, and the hills small. Abundance of black teal. Plectranthus reappears at the foot of Oonnoo, Verbascum rare, if any, on the Tartary side of the Hindoo-koosh. Abundance of Loaches or Balitora in the streamlets arising from the springs.

13*th.*—Proceeded to Julraiz, eight and a half miles, having passed a waterfall, as well as abundance of people going to Jallalabad. Bar. 22·760 at noon; Ther. 75°.

14*th.*—Proceeded to Koti-Ashruf, where there is excellent fishing with worms, the fish however did not take a fly, though they often appeared at the surface: a large headed Silurus occurs, but I was unable to procure a specimen.

15*th.*—Proceeded to Arghundee, where we met the Bamean force.

16*th.*—Proceeded to Topehee Bashee.

17*th.*—Returned to Cabul. Eryngium is rare between the foot of Oonnoo and Moostaffur Khan's fort.

CHAPTER XVII.

From Cabul to Jallalabad and Peshawur.

October 7th.—Proceeded to Bhootkhak, nine and a half miles from Cabul, and seven from our camp: the direction lay easterly. A canal and a river were both crossed by bridges, the latter of stone, but much needing repairs: the country generally marshy: the marshes were crossed by a causeway of stones, rough and broken here and there. The road is one apparent continued slope to this, but the Barometer gives no indication of any difference of level. The march proving uninteresting, and the country an uniform brown and barren tract.

8th.—Proceeded to Koord Cabul valley, the distance of which from the place we left being eleven miles: first having rounded a spur extending from the south boundary of Cabul valley, we then entered a narrow ravine, chiefly occupied by a small stream, which we crossed several times. The mountains being chiefly of limestone, then becoming slaty, very precipitous, rugged, and barren; on emerging from this very tedious ravine, we entered on some sward with plenty of Tamarisk, and Salix vimenea. Koord Cabul valley is a frightfully barren, and very stony place; the chief vegetation of the valley, as also of the ravine, being Artemisiæ, in which there is abundance of Carduacea subspicata from Baber's tomb.

The road throughout is indifferent, but only so from the stones, the largest of which would require removal, and there are not more than two or three difficult rocks in the way; these however might be avoided by keeping in the bed of the stream. There are two ruined stone walls thrown across the ravine, the *remains* merely of the very few villages of Koord Cabul. A high truncated mountain stands to the south, on which some patches of snow are visible.

The mountain forming the east wall of the ravine is the subconical one, seen to such advantage from Arghundee, it is of limestone, quite precipitous, with a few large bushes of, I do not know what; none of them being within reach,—Ilex, and *Cupressus.*

9th.—To Tazeen, the road for seven miles extends over somewhat undulated ground, generally good; but here and there stony, with a gradual but almost imperceptible ascent, until the top of the pass is reached; from this, the view of Tazeen valley, and the summit of the Sofaid-Koh is good.

Thence the road extends over ascents and descents, three of which have considerable, and stony inclinations, then it enters the ravine drained by a small stream, and continues down it until we enter Tazeen valley.

Two streams are passed in the ascent; the first, near the former halting place, flowing, where it is crossed, between slaty cliffs of no height; the second one, small, frozen, and not sufficient to supply a large party: there is however a spring a short way below the summit, although very small. Temperature 58°. The rocks forming the narrow ravine are very rough and slaty: limestones presenting the usual characters.

This march has been said to present a very bad road, but it is not the case, at least in comparison with many of the Affghan roads, distance twelve and a half miles, the time it takes for camels to perform the journey is six hours. The road, where not stony, is very well beaten.

No change is observed in the features of the country until the opposite side of Tazeen valley is seen, and the summit of the Sofaid-Koh: here, wonderful to relate! are abundance of firs extending down and along the ridge to some distance, but not forming forests.

Otherwise the vegetation consists of Senecionoides, *Astragali, Rosa,* Statice 2-3, Artemisiæ, and Plectranthus, which last is very common in the ravine leading to Tazeen valley, which is drained by a small stream. Here also Carduacea, and Onosmoid angustifolia occur!

In this ravine, Xanthoxylon of Kojhuk, a willow, Rosa, and a distinct Ilex, occur, forming chiefly a shrubby vegetation. Ilex is also, so far as can be judged from appearance, the bushy thing seen on the limestone hill at our last halt, also Cupressus, a fine specimen of which I found on limestone at about the height of the top of the pass, (22·76 Bar.) Ther. 60°, with a very small Spiræa.

The large-winged vultures of Arghundee are common here. Some ruined villages were past, a mosque stood near one of these, two and a half miles from last halt, little cultivation in the Tazeen valley, and in the centre of this, two villages with orchards are visible.

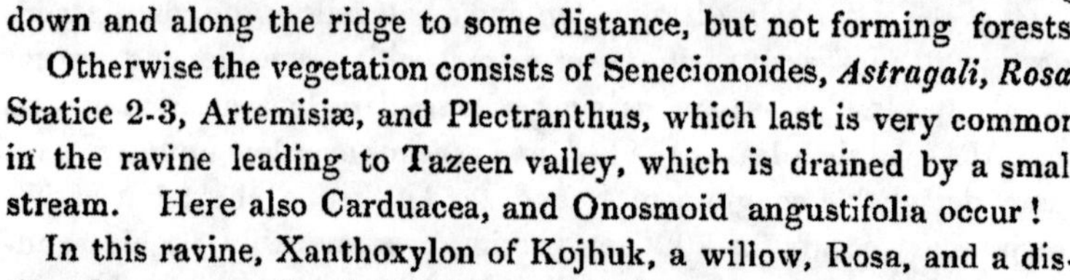

9th.—Tried to get to the firs, but failed.

The lower hills, and indeed the range between the valley and the fir range, are conglomerate, easily disintegrated, then limestone, which often occurs quite vertical. Some of the hills are red, others brown, in one instance the coloured substance is interposed between strata of limestone, which last have alone withstood the effects of climate, this range is as high as the Koord Cabul pass.

Ilex very common, and much used for charcoal, the trunk being eight to ten inches in diameter; almost all are pollarded. Pomacea common at 500 feet above this, Plectranthus, Senecionoides.

Artemisiæ, Astragali, Statices, Rosa, bastard indigo, Cerasus. The orchards are now assuming their autumnal tint, Salvia pinnata, Canus aliusque, *Ruwash*. Chough, ravens, nuthatch, and chakor here occur.

Heavy snow is observed on the eastern portions of Hindoo-koosh, which are quite barren. The best way to the fir tract I find on enquiry will be to follow the bed of the stream up to it. Fields are being now ploughed and sown. Thermopsides very common here in old cultivation: it affords decent fodder for camels.

10th.—To Barikab, distance ten and a half miles; the road extending down the Tazeen ravine, over a tract with a considerable descent for about nine miles; on passing a long dark looking rock and its spur, the road then leaves the bed, and ascends over low undulations of easily detachable conglomerate, and sand; then a short but rather steep ascent occurs for 200 feet, passing over an easily friable sandstone, either existing as grains slightly adherent, or caked; thence the descent passes over the preceding sort of conglomerate, to an abominably barren ravine, drained by a very small stream.

The road only once leaves the bed of this ravine, but soon rejoins it before finally turning off.

The mountains present the same features; where no outcrop of strata occurs, they are rounded, brown, and very barren, with here and there an Ilex; towards the end of the raviny part in one or two places, more wood than usual occurs, forming scattered thickets. Fraxinus, the older branches of which have much smaller leaves, Thymelia of Chiltera, Cerasus canus, and alius, Senecionoides, Compositæ, Artemisiæ, Polygonum frutescens, which last is not uncommon throughout. Equisetoides becomes common towards the black rock.

Where the road turns off from the ravine, a *Khubar* or tope occurs, shaded with two or three large Xanthoxyleæ now in fruit, called *Khinjuk*.

Snow visible from Barikab to the north, but generally in ravines. The country continues abominably barren, we passed the entrance of the Lutabund pass, near the black rock, but without seeing it: no difficulty occurs on the road, except from the jolting of stones. There is however no forage to be had at the halt, and but little fodder. A sprinkling of holly-looking bushes are seen extending over the lower ranges of Hindoo-koosh.

11*th.*—Jugdulluck, ten and a half miles from our last encampment; on leaving Barikab we commenced ascending, winding over undulating ground for a short distance, until we reached the main ascent, which is short, but moderately steep: thence we descended steeply for perhaps 500 feet, hitherto the road extended over sand hills, with quantities of stones. On reaching the foot of the steep descent, we then descended gradually over a long stony inclined plane, then entered undulating ground, descending from which the road took us over a small stream, which we followed up, soon entering a gorge, up which we continued till we reached Jugdulluck. This gorge is the finest and boldest we have seen, the rocks forming precipitous cliffs 2,400 feet high, which often hem in the road, and confine it to a breadth of a few feet, sufficient merely for a gun to pass.

On emerging from this we reached the tope of Jugdulluck, now a grove of mulberry trees, surrounded by the remains of a wall.

The country, until we entered the gorge, presented the same features as before, being frightfully barren. Passed a spring of water at the foot of the main descent where there is level ground sufficient for a small party, afterwards we passed a smaller spring containing less water, but situated in much better ground than Barikab.

The vegetation of undulated ground continues unchanged, very poor and stunted; in ravines below the main descent, Stipa is very common; in others, a large Andropogon occurs near the mouth of the gorge along the bed of the river, also *Jhow* in patches, and one patch of Donax.

The vegetation of the gorge is more varied; two small trees occur, one the *Khinjuk*, and it is the commonest, the other a Terebinthacea; Thymelæa of Chiltera is common, Ephedra, Ilex occurs but is less common than on hills.

Along the water to which it gives exit, and which is abundant, the usual Cyperaceæ, Junceæ, Gnaphalium, Potentilla, and Epilobium occur as at Cabul; the place is chiefly remarkable for two or three

Saccharoid grasses, Stipa common, Polypogon, Donax, Dracocephala of Quettah and the Bolan pass, Spireæa, Typha, young Tamarisks.

Chakor, large vulture, ravens; a woodcock rose from a dripping rock, covered with a tropical Andropogon in dense patches. Adiantum, Rubus, Erythrea, Labiatæ two, common; Salix.

The gorge appears to be a distinct formation of sandstone, slate, and limestone: on the way to it, we continued over the sand and conglomerate hills, which again recur at Jugdulluck, with plenty of Holly.

The Sofaid-Koh is visible from the main ridge: it is a ridge running perhaps SW. to NE., tolerably covered with snow, as barren as any others: a few fir trees are found in the direction of Tazeen: are these confined to the sandstone formation? little grass, a few rice fields, bad forage.

```
        Sandstone or conglomerate.
     Ilex . · · .      Ilex.
Thymelæa .          · .
          .  .     .
        .  .  .      .  very stony.
     .   .   .    .    .
Bar. 25·1.  .          .
Barikab .   .             .   Andropogon,
                        .    Tamarisk,          Xanthoxylon,   . . Bar. 25·04.
                      · . .   Donax.            Terebinthacea, · Jugdulluck.
           Artemisiæ.  · . .  Stony             Ephedra, . . ·
           Senecionoides.  · · · .                         . . .
                                 . . .   Gorge . . .
                                       . · . · ·
                                       .    .
                                            .
```

12*th*.—Halted at Jugdulluck. Small partridges are common: observed a curious Certhioid creeper, whose flight is like that of the Hoopoe; it is scandent over rocks.

13*th*.—To Soorkhab, twelve and a half miles over a similar country: region of Hollys continues; we first passed up a ravine, then over undulating ground, until the summit of the pass is reached. From this a fine view of Sofaid-Koh is obtained, the lower ranges in some places being black with firs; thence a continued descent, varied here and there by small ascents over undulating ground, we at length came to a ravine filled with bulrushes: we followed this, leaving it near the halting place, and winding over rocky ground and a bad road, we descended to the bed of the river. The road good, though stony here and there, but nowhere so, to such an extent, as the previous marches.

Hills precisely similar to those already passed, either sandy, easily friable, or conglomerate, held together by sandy cement. Vegetation continues the same; *Baloot*, or oak, is said to be abundant though I did not see it; Daphne, and Xanthoxylon, compose the chief shrubby vegetation; Saccharum here and there. Small partridge very common. The greatest ascent is 5,600 feet. No grass for forage; several very small streamlets were passed en route, so that a small party might halt anywhere.

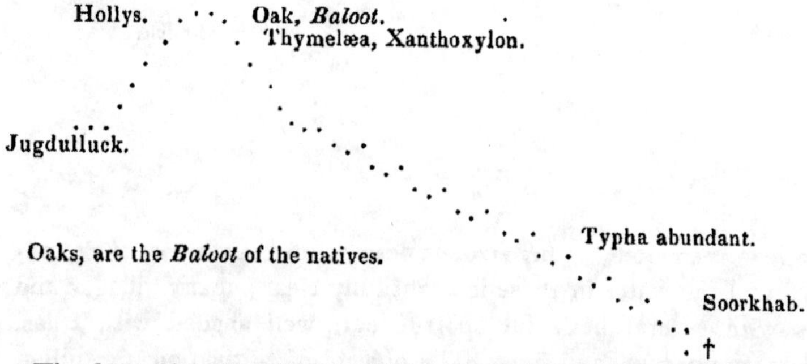

The beautiful Himalaya looking range Sofaid-Koh, runs east and west; it is very high, in the back ranges with very heavy snow on both ridges, and peaks. The view from the pass shows a rapid fall in the country to the eastward, which still continues hilly, and very very bare. Large coarse grapes are had here, also pomegranates: some *seedless* rice cultivation occurs since we descended to Jugdulluck.

14*th*.—We proceeded nine and a quarter miles, throughout until reaching a grove near Gundamuck: the road lay over undulating ground, is more sandy than stony, and in two or three places it is raviny, and requires to be made. Then the road emerges into a fine sort of valley, dipping down to a small stream with many sedges. In the bed of the stream, willows occur, and mulberries about it: we then ascended and halted just beyond the ascent. Water and *dhoob* grass are both plentiful, as well as supplies of grain, pomegranates, and grapes, as yesterday; *Bajree*.

A fine view is obtained of Sofaid-Koh, which forms the southern boundary of the valley; many villages, with cultivation in a very sandy soil. Small partridge very abundant. A fox observed. The ravines wherever there is water, crowded with Typha, and Saccharum; oaks are seen in abundance on the mountain to the south; left the Soorkhab river after fording it near yesterday's camp; the bridge is quite useless for cattle, as the ground is rocky and broken on this side, no pains having been taken to carry the work to the road.

cypresses, planes and mulberry trees in the gardens: Cannabis, also one patch of cotton cultivation was passed.

No descent, but rather small ascent on the whole, say 200 feet, the ascent from the principal nullah crossed being equal, though much shorter than the descent to it.

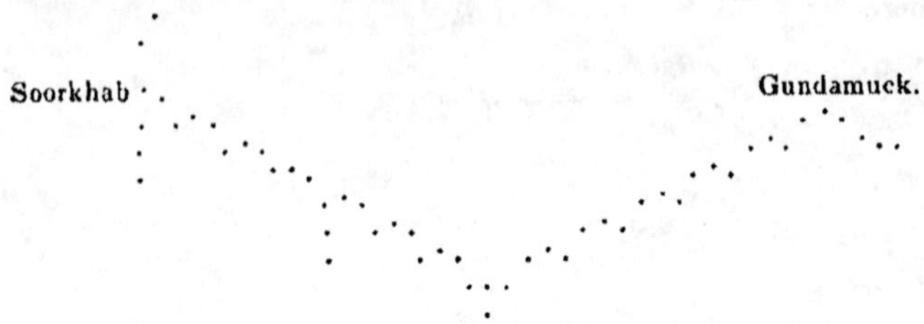

15*th*.—We halted: many rivulets descend near us from the Sofaid-Koh; and the water in these is beautifully clear; many villages and mills with several beautiful spots occur, well shaded with trees, poplars, mulberries, and figs. The objects of cultivation are millet, Indian-corn, rice, and wheat; this last just sprung up: many *bedanah* pomegranates, but none I think of superior quality.

All the low hills here, and indeed between us and the boundary ranges of the valley, are of sandstone, generally very slightly held together, here and there more firm, and distinctly stratified towards the upper surface. The surface consists of conglomerate, formed of boulders imbedded in the same kind of sandstone as that below; often very friable, occasionally it is as hard as flint. In the sandstone below, a few stones occur here and there; but I saw no fossils. The upper surface of these hills is remarkably stony, all the stones being more or less rounded.

Several new plants were found in these ravines, a Lythrum, a very aromatic species of Compositæ, Samolus in some of the swamps with Typha, which swarms in every ravine and ravinelet, Rubus, Clematis, Bergia, Ammannia, Lythraria, Chara, Xanthium.

The plants of tropical forms are, Celosia of Digera! Polanisia, Andropogons, two or three.

The tropical cultivation consists of cotton, the usual annual sort; Indian-corn, Pennisetum, and rice.

The fish are, four kinds of Cyprinidæ, including one Oreinus, and one loach.

16*th*.—Proceeded to Futtehabad, eleven and a half miles. The road leaves the valley after crossing a stream with a ruined bridge, like that at Soorkhab, but of two arches, and ascending a little way, then winding along over undulating very stony ground; this continues until we descend steeply and along the Neemla valley, a mere ravine, historically interesting, as the field on which Shah Soojah lost his kingdom in 1809, and for a fine tope of trees: then crossing a streamlet, we ascend a little way over sandstone, then another stream, which we follow for 500 yards, and ascending a little, we proceed thence to camp, along a slight slope of very stony, generally *very level* ground, where we halted on a rivulet with a wide grassy bed, Lythrum growing around.

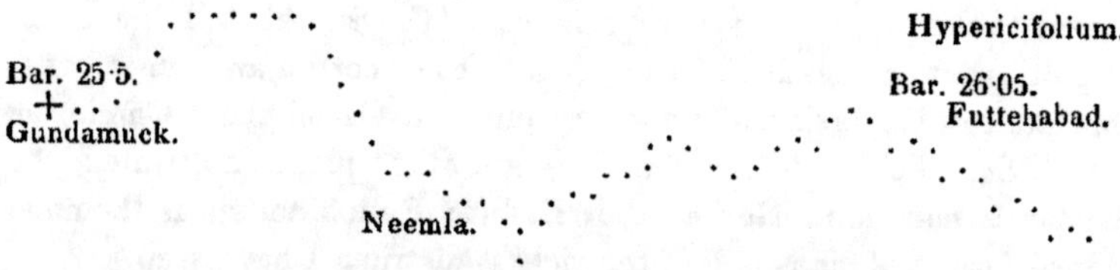

No change appears in the vegetation: the surface very barren in stony parts, chiefly Artemisia, Saccharum, Andropogon albus, in ravines, Capparis common, also Ærua and Lycionoides.

The northern boundary of the valley is comparatively low, and from Sofaid-Koh to this is an uniform slope, broken by ravines; here and there by small hills; ravines occasionally dilating into small valleys, the only parts in which cultivation is to be seen. This is so far different from the usual formation where the valleys occupy the level tract between the slopes from either boundary range. Neemla is a very confined space for any thing like the battle said to have taken place here, the rising grounds inclosing the small space being too much broken for cavalry.

The rocks consist of conglomerate at top, below sandstone, layers of both alternating near the surface: a break occurs (nearly opposite) in the hills, this break is minutely undulated.* Rock pigeons were seen on the march by Thomson, and small partridges. I find that though to our senses there was comparatively but little descent, that the barometer and thermometer indicate one of 1,500 feet. The Neemla river must be the boundary between the hot and cold countries alluded to by Burnes.

In spite of this descent, and our small altitude, about 3,000 feet, but little change if any occurs in the vegetation, and none in the

* This alludes to a sketch of the valley.

general features of the country; the Apocynea of Dadur and Bolai (Nerioides) has re-appeared.

At this season (October), throughout the way we came from Cabul, there is a curious white efflorescence covering the Shootur Kari, I do not know what it is, but it is not Conferva. A good deal of forest is seen on some of the ranges to the north of this, bearing from camp about NNE., certainly not firs, perhaps oaks.

19*th.*—Yesterday we went to the Soorkhab, which runs east and west along the northern boundary of the valley; half the distance down the bed of this stream the ground is strewed with boulders, thence to the hills, and excepting the bed of the Soorkhab, is one sheet of cultivation, consisting of large quantities of cotton and sugar-cane, this latter of small size, and not very juicy, castor-oil plant, Corchorus *(Pat)*, *Sun*, Tel., radish, and among the other plants cultivated, the Mudar is common: Nerioides of Dadur; Epilobium sp. is the chief Boreal form. This is one of the richest districts I have seen.

Trees—Bukkhien,* *Furas*, Ficus, Cupressus, with much rice cultivation.

The vines are trained on mulberries, as Burnes says, or the Lilyoak. Pomegranates are also to be mentioned among the fruits of this place.

The Soorkhab river is not seen after leaving the place of the same name; after it crosses the road, it runs due north through the mountains, in a narrow, almost inaccessible bed; its waters are of a reddish colour.

The villages here are larger, and not so fortified as those about Cabul. Balabagh stands on a high bank of conglomerate, overhanging the Soorkhab, and is in danger of being cut away by the river. The peasantry are civil, and unarmed. Ravens, quails, *minas*, sparrows, and a beautiful swallow were seen about the Soorkhab river; the latter, with metallic blue on the back of the head, crown of head tawny, tail short, two exterior feathers elongated into beautiful almost setaceous bodies, exceeding the length of the bird. This swallow, or one with a similar tail, was seen by Sanders on the Helmund, at Girishk.

20*th.*—We proceeded to Sultanpore, eight and a half miles, passed Futtehabad, thence a gradual descent over a very stony slope to the halting place, where the valley becomes narrow, and water plentiful in

* Melia.

a small stream. Willows, mulberries, ashes. Two large pollards at Futtehabad.

The vegetation consists of Gramineæ in patches, Ærua Nerioides, and Mudar.

Sultanpore, is a village of some size, situated about a mile north from the road, and contains many Hindoos. All villages here crowded with highish two or three-storied houses, something like Shikarpore: they are surrounded with gardens and mud walls, apricots, mulberries, greengages, pomegranates in profusion; the cultivation very rich as yesterday, and there is an air of repose about the villages unusual in this country. Tobacco. The rice-pounder or *dekhee* I observe is here lifted by treading on it with the foot, as in Hindoostan. The country hereabout, has the advantage of being well watered. *Isain*, Dolichos sp. occurs.

Trees as before: the plane flourishes, fine ones were seen growing around a Hindoo Zearut, where there is a double spring of water with a copious ebullition of gas. The temperature of this is said to be hot in winter. Salsola common, *Joussa*, a curious Ericoid plant was observed, Typha angustifolia, latifolia ceased since we left Gundamuck; Isachne, Pulicaria, Epilobium, Sagittaria, Cyperaceæ, Marsilea! Polygonum, Ranunculus sceleratus, Lythrum, Lemna, Alisma, Menthoid, a Cuscuta common on cotton plants, as at Futtehabad, several tropical grasses, Aristida, Poa, and Andropogon appear.

Descent though almost unappreciable, yet amounts to 1,000 feet. Bulbul and Parus common, as well as doves and ravens; quails are scarce.

21*st.*—To Jallalabad, eight and a half miles, the road keeping along the southern edge of the valley, occasionally extending over small undulations sometimes stony, more often sandy.

Typha latifolia occurs in profusion along parts of Futtehabad nullah, general features the same otherwise, Ærua and Nerioid are common on stony parts, and fewer coarse grasses.

Cypresses in gardens, also *khujoors*. Starlings.

The entrance to Jallalabad, or rather to its suburbs, presents the usual desolate, disorderly appearance, of such places in this country; the ruined walls to the city; the sandy barren soil, and the odious looking low hills between it and the Sofaid-Koh, present as sad and melancholy a picture as could well be met with. The same desolate, disorderly, dirty appearance is to be met with in most Asiatic capitals, particularly those that have been subjected to independent misrule:

while the more distant surrounding villages look cheerful, and as clean as can be expected: the appearances immediately around the chief towns are always bad. To what is this owing? is it to their being more completely under the thumb of a rapacious governor? to the insecurity of property, or to defect in the laws? or to all these causes together?

At Cabul it was just the same, particularly on the Peshawur side, where stagnant pools, half destroyed mosques, and mutilated trees present a total contrast to the smiling valley of Kilah-i-Kajee.

At Shikarpore the same.

The most common fruit tree in the gardens here is a sweet lime: grapes are brought in from the villages of Sofaid-Koh, they are the same sort as those at Gundamuck: Narcissus, Rosa, Cerasi sp., Mirabilis, stock, Cupressus, mulberry also in gardens, *Bheir* of waste places, Salsola, Artemisiæ, two or three: Kochia villosa, Peganum, Ærua, Croton of Candahar, Ricinus, *Joussa* of wet places, Lippia, Typha latifolia, angustif., Azolla, Riccia, Cyperaceæ, several Lythrarieæ, Potamogeton, three species. The fish here will not take a fly, and the bottoms are too foul and stony for worm-fishing, the largest sort of fish is somewhat like a Barbel. Jackdaws and Corvus, alter atratus, dorso ventre griseo: very few quails. *Furas* common.

27*th*.—To Ali-Baghan, distance six and a half miles, road winding, generally good: after it crossed the dry bed of the nullah, it then becomes rather undulated extending over raviny ground; it then crosses the broad bed of the stream, in which there are swarms of bulrushes, then the same sort of sandy ground leads to camp, which is near the village Ali-Baghan.

The river here is much increased, much more deep; banks alluvial, steep; soil deep. Chenopodium sp., very common, but too much eaten up to be recognized, also Salsolæ sp.

Nothing new observed. We passed the break above-mentioned in the northern hills, whence issues the Coomur Nuddee. Serratuloides very common in sandy undulations. Porcupines and foxes. Beds of grass in islands of the river Barikab.

28*th*.—We proceeded to Bankok, twelve and a half miles from the encamping ground, having turned nearly due south, in order to avoid the slope, which is seen in this direction from Jallalabad; then a valley, with low hills on either side, is passed; then the road ascends over undulating ground, until 500 feet is gained; then a long and gradual descent is traversed over a very stony plateau.

No water nor cultivation on the road, nothing can exceed its barrenness. Ærua Nerioides, Lycioides, Andropogon albus, are the principal plants on the plateau; Kochia common, and a few straggling *Bheirs*, small rock pigeons. Geology unchanged, sandstone and conglomerate, with enormous boulders.

We passed the gorge through which the Cabul river runs. The road, by this is said to be only six miles, but is only passable by pedestrians and horsemen.

One village of some size is situated in the south towards Sofaid-Koh; from the plateau as well as from our camp, a curious and characteristic scene is visible to the north, showing a barren lofty range with peculiar undulations at the base, as well as the isolated hills jutting up above its surface: the trees and villages being confined to the course of the river which may be thus traced by its fertility. In this last direction there is a good deal of *Abadi*, but nothing comparable to that about Jallalabad.

At camp Serratuloid australasicus, very common, as indeed it was yesterday; *foliis verticalibus* in consequence of both surfaces being stomatose, the base of the leaf is so twisted as to present each surface equally to the light. It is curious that all such leaves have the veins prominent on both surfaces, showing a relation between the veins and the stomata, the more stomata the larger veins.

29th.—To Bassoollah, eight and a half miles, the road for guns is good throughout; better perhaps than any yet met with, from the soil being sandy. We came by a straiter road, and a very bad one, instead of diverging to the south, and rounding a range of hills, we entered these, and passing through a gorge coming upon marshy ground, running for some distance along the Cabul river, to which we were here quite close. Passed several villages about the mouth of the gorge, which is a short one.

The general features of the country continue the same; we crossed a nullah near the camp, and another near the gorge, six miles from camp, towards this last, grass covers the plains, though of a coarse kind; Ærua Nerioides most common on the barren ground.

We observed on the way a new Pterocles, and passed an old tope situated on a low ridge.

The gorge is rather pretty; the Cabul river runs close, along the foot of a range, forming the northern boundary of the place, where Bassoollah is situated, this is also a pretty place, with much good grassy ground for encamping on.

The country under Sofaid-Koh presents a long strip of cultivation, with many villages: hills barrener than ever, chiefly limestone. Very little snow here observed as on the eastern face of the high peaks of Sofaid-Koh, compared with the quantity visible on the face towards Jallalabad.

About half-past two, a slight shock of an earthquake was felt, presenting a rumbling noise, very audible, proceeding from east to west.

Between the village and the river, an extensive strip of level land occurs, with sandy soil well adapted to rice, of which quantities are grown. The crops are now ready for the sickle, and some partly cut: much of this land is occupied by a marsh choked with bulrushes of both sorts, Typha latifolia being the most common; Cyperaceæ abound, Marsilea in profusion, Azolla, Mentha, Epilobii sp. as before, Lemna, Valisneria *verticillata?* Sium., Sagittaria, Pulicaria, Chara, Lippia, Monniera, *Jhow*.

The river runs close under the hills, which are very barren, its course is rapid, cataracts also are of frequent occurrence transmitting a great body of water; no fish are visible. Some cotton and maize and *Toot* cultivation. *Furas* the only trees.

The mountains slope off from Sofaid-Koh in distinct groups, and are seen to advantage, broken in some places into undulations: about the centre of the slope an irregular strip of village forts and cultivation is extended. The course of the Cabul river in many places is curious; flowing between singularly round ranges. Snipe common; quail rare. Erythræa common on moist sward.

30th.—Proceeded to Lalpore, the country undulating, the road skirting the stony portions of the plain is bad to Hizarnow, three miles from thence it is very stony, thence continuing on the skirts of the hills, which are principally slate, and passing through a small ravine, it then extends over sandy or stony ground, until the Chota Khyber is reached: this is a narrow, but short, and not very steep pass; slate rocks compose the upper parts, and are entirely disintegrated, thence they descend at once into the plain opposite Lalpore; the distance of the march is eleven miles, the road generally decent.

Much rice cultivation occurs, and much land, it must be confessed, also occupied by marshy ground, Typha, etc. The same plants continue; Butomus trigonifolius not uncommon.

On the slate rocks of Buttencote Kochia recurs, Heliotropium luteum, Nerioides, and Lycioides of Shikarpore are found.

Near Hizarnow, Serissa, Acaciæ sp., which is the black wood of Madras; Sissoo, and *Bheirs*. Hizarnow is a large place, curiously occupying receding slopes of the base of a low range of hills, but it must be dreadfully hot. We passed several *Kaburistans* with pollarded, stunted, excavated *Furas* trees. One mile before Hizarnow, a curious hill of slate occurred, covered with boulders.

The road is very winding in consequence of its following the bases of the hills forming the southern boundary of the valley. The Cabul river is visible almost throughout the whole march.

All houses in the villages are now roofed in this part of the country with straw. Starlings observed in swarms.

31*st*.—Halted at Lalpore, this is a very busy large place: the houses are one-storied, and flat-roofed. The only peculiarity being occasional square towers. The river is here quite open for commerce downwards, and is well adapted to small canoes: the stream is rapid and crossed by a ferry.

On rocks under which the river flows near this, a species of Fissidens occurs, where the rocky surface has passed into sand. Glycyrrhiza, Rubus, Artemisia, Asparagus, Pommereulla, Andropogon albus, Arundo, Cyrthandracea, an Hyoscyamus of the Bolan Pass, Beebee Nanee, Heliotropium flavum.

It would be curious to enquire why the powers of variation change so completely in the different families? Thus for instance in Orchideæ, no character can be taken from the vegetation with some limitations, and none from the fruit or seeds; two products in most orders very fruitful in discriminating marks. This leads one to the idea that in monocotyledonous plants, the fruit is very generally of limited powers of variation; witness Orchideæ, Gramineæ, Smilacineæ, etc. this idea deserves to be followed out as much as possible. The river at the ferry is 100 yards wide, and twelve feet in the deepest part, the current five miles an hour, but confined to one and a half towards its centre.

November 1*st*.—Marched ten miles: the road from the camp extended up an acclivity, the ground becoming more broken than usual to the mouth of the ghat, which is four miles distant; thence up to the ghat which resembles much the Bolan Pass, it extends up an inclined plane over a shingly road. The ghat is rather wide throughout, and all the features are the same as the Bolan Pass, slate rocks most common. We passed on the way a large and a deep but dry well, ascribed to the *kafirs;* and near it the ruins of a fort built half-way up a small mountain, the top of which is level with the ghat.

Vegetation to the ghat unchanged. In the ghat Capparis as before, Lycioides, Chamærops, Andropog. albus, Schænanthus, *Bheir*, Nerioides, Pommereullioid, Andropogonea, appear at once, Ærua, Asparagus.

At 300 feet up, Mimosæ sp., foliis tomentosis, occurring here and there. Heliotropium flavum, Plectranthus lavandulosus, Scrophulariæ sp.

At 500 feet, Dodonæa : this is very common, and being very green, gives the ghat a pretty appearance.

At 600 feet, a curious pomaceous looking Rhamnaceous plant is found.

The most common plants are Nerioides, Andropogon albus, *Bheir*, Chamærops, Dodonæa.

The bed of the ghat is formed of debris from the boundary hills, this bed is very thick, and the particles have the appearance of being carried to their present situation by water.

Our halting place is a confined irregular piece of ground, water abundant, but no grass, except coarse Andropogon ; no fodder, except *Bheir* and Mimosa.

I ascended in the evening the ridge to the south, and which is 1,200 feet above the road, to the ruins that run along the summit. The ridge, like all others in this neighbourhood, is rugged and much distorted, the top is limestone, much varied and weathered ; then slate : masses of greenstone occur towards the base.

The vegetation is chiefly at the summit. Schænanthus, Periploca, Dodonæa, an arbuscula nova, Euonymus, Chenopodiaceæ. Below this, (but the elevation is scarcely sufficient to form any difference,) and along the water, Euonymus, Adhatoda, Buddlæa cana or Syringia, Rhamnacea, Periplocea, Linaria, Labiatæ, 2-3, Pistacea, Roylea, Acanthoides, *Urticea !* habitu, U. pendulifloræ, Vitex, Convolvulus spinosus of Bolan, Sempervivum, Stapelioides used as a vegetable, and for fever by Hindoos, Artemisiæ, Solanum sp.

Along water, Adiantum, Mentha, Epilobium, Verbena officinalis, Solanum nigrum, Jacquinifol. pinnatif. spinosus about cultivation.

On slaty rocks which form the bed of the ravine or ghat, Dodonæa, Hyoscyamus, and Cyrthandracea are found.

The building consists of a wall near the edge of a ridge, which terminates some twenty feet from the steep precipice of 300 to 500

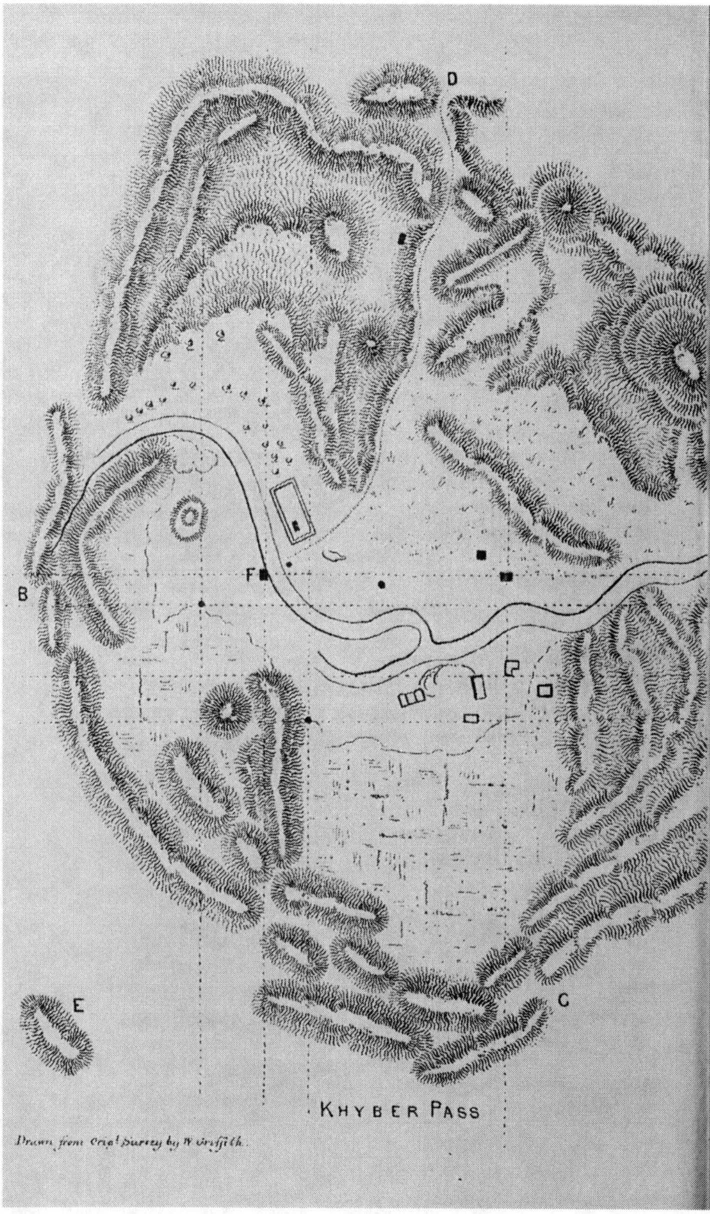
D
B
F
E
C
KHYBER PASS
Drawn from Orig¹ Survey by W Griffith.

feet: it is 200 to 300 yards in length, and is terminated at either end by two towers, both of which are ruinous, it is built of slabs and rough blocks of limestone, between which are layers of slate, much like the Bactrian pillar, and very superior to modern buildings: what its use was, it would be difficult to conjecture as it is out of musket shot of the ghat, which it only commands by being above it. There is no water on the top, nor is there any well marked path up to it: curious mortar-like excavations were observed in a mass of limestone just below, probably for pounding rice. Up the ravine are remains of terraces formerly used for cultivation, but now mostly disused. At 700 to 800 feet above the ghat the ravine abounds with the Ficus of Gundamuck; this and the Adhatoda or *Rooss* are perhaps cultivated: the ravine is pretty well entangled with Ficus and brushwood. It consists of metamorphosed rocks and excavated limestone; some mosses occur, and Adiantum abounding.

From the ridge, a rather extensive view to the south is obtained, extending to the Khyber fort, which is of the ordinary square form, and just below it, a tower and house. To the east, and all around a good deal of cultivation occurs; also several high ridges, say 7,000 feet; one terminating 4,000 feet above us, presents a very rugged outline with the appearance of rather large trees. The road up to the ghat is visible, as well as the *Choky* and a fort, with a small sheet of cultivation to the eastward. Beyond this a ravine, then two other ridges, of which the nearer one is high. The Cabul river passes to the NNW., and Lalpoor lies to the north. One peak and a small piece of ridge of Hindoo-koosh, white with snow, is seen very distinctly though distant, it must therefore be very lofty; far more so than any part we have seen to the westward.

The general character of the hills in every direction except the snowy range, is bluffly rounded, very bare, and brown, with here and there a shrub.

That which Burnes calls Noorgil, is the range of Kareaz, and is distinct from Koonur. Kashgur lies beyond the snowy range.

The inhabitants of the mountains, like those of Lalpoor, wear sandals made of the fibres of Chamærops, which is common: one plant of Ephedra used *for snuff?*

3rd.—Proceeded to one mile beyond Ali-Musjid. The ascent commences immediately where the *Choky* is seen from the camp, by a very good road cut out of slate rock; the rocks are steep on both sides, and very zig-zag; a short partial descent in one place occurs to a small pool of water. From the *Choky*, a descent takes place by a similar road for perhaps two miles, until the ravine which we left at camp is turned; this is thence followed, occasionally leaving it where the road is bad and runs through low rugged hills. The road then after passing some of the old ruins opens, out into a space with cultivation. Close to this is the highest spot of the pass, surrounded by low hills, none higher than 500 feet. Cultivation occurs especially at Lal-Ghurry Beg, a space of some size, containing several villages, of the usual Khyberry form, namely, surrounded by low, quadrangular walls, with a thin square tower and very broadly projecting eaves. A short distance from its summit, just after passing the villages, and before entering the ravine which leads us to our present camp is a Khyberry tower, built on a fine Bactrian tope, which is nearly half ruined; on the top of this a dome of good proportions is built on a double-terraced foundation.

This gives a rude idea of what the tope was originally, now half the dome has fallen down.

The entrance to the ravine gradually becomes narrower, the bed is stony, very winding, and narrow. Bold precipices of limestone cliffs ascend on either side of Sir-i-Chushme; then a little below, very copious springs issue from limestone. The temperature of the principal spring is 75°; it contains abundance of fish—a loach and cyprinoid. Passed some ruined fortifications on the right, leading down to water, evidently *kafir* works; then we enter a narrow but short gorge, occupied by the stream; a few more turns and you come on Ali-Musjid. No change occurs in the vegetation, bare rocks at the summit of which the Bar. stood at 26·72. Andropogons and Artemisiæ are the chief plants.

In the gorge downwards, Acacia occurs in abundance, with Adhatoda, and otherwise the shrubs of Lundyakhana occur in abundance, and Adiantum about the spring.

After passing the fort, the rocks open out into a ravine, with low undulated hills on every side, covered with the usual vegetation; Astragalus one species.

At Lal-Ghurry Beg, one Khinjuck tree, Elæagnus, occurred; and grass in very small stacks, well pressed and covered with a thatch of bushes and a layer of dirt.

There is excellent fishing in the stream. Loaches, Perilamps, and especially an Oreinus? swarming at Sir-i-Chushme, and taking worms very greedily.

Description of the annexed map of the Khyber Pass.

A. Kumdhukta. By this is Abkhanah route.

B. Little Khyber ghat, on Peshawur side.

C. Khyber ghat, entrance on the Jallalabad side.

D. Kurraha route.

E. Direction of Sofaid-Koh in the distance.

F. Flagstaff in the middle of the Pass.

The ground between the dotted lines and river, on the south, is, or has been cultivated. The ground near the river on the north side is covered here and there with brown grass. About the Flagstaff, sand and short dried up grass occur.

No forests whatever visible in this direction; the arborescent vegetation being confined to scattered and small trees.

5th.—We halted near Jumrood, after a march of ten miles and one furlong. This place is situated at the mouth of the pass, within sight of the Seikh camp at Jumrood. Marched down to the ghat, which is generally speaking narrow and very strong, opening out here and there, into easier parts extending down the stream all the way; this stream loses itself suddenly, but after a little distance it is replaced by another from the right, where ravines enter: here the pass is well adapted for pillage, elsewhere the sides are so steep, that robbers could not dispose of their plunder. At the mouth, the pass opens out into a good breadth, with an even, small, shingly bottom. At Kuddun the Seikh troops were drawn up to compliment the C. in C., one regiment met us shortly before to protect the baggage. Maize cultivated. At the mouth, the Khyber is more difficult than any other pass, except the Bolan: perhaps it is much narrower than that, except just above Sir-i-Bolan.

No change in vegetation, one or two new plants occurred, viz. a Labiata, and a treelet, foliis linearibus oppositis, Jasminacea aspectu, Baloot, Vitex common, Salix, and shrubs as before, Veronica, etc.

The Khyber mountains viewed from the mouth of the pass are brown, and dotted with peculiar looking trees.

6th.—Proceeded six and a half miles to near the ruins of an old tope; first, down the nullah, then by the fort of Futtygurh, a Hindoostanee mud fort with high parapets, two lines of works, and a *pucka* citadel with embrasures for guns on a commanding mound : thence we passed over a gentle slope with a good many scattered *Bheirs, Kureels,* Ærua, Mudar, etc. to camp, where the ground is very rough and stony, abundant water obtained from a cut with sheets of maize cultivation. Fossil shells, Pterocles, found in arenaceous limestone (Durand).

7th.—To Peshawur, eight and a half miles, over a sandy plain; road bad, intersected with cuts and ravines; three canals had to be crossed by small bridges which occasioned a good deal of delay to the camels. Passed the Seikh lines, between the fort and north face of town, and encamped on east face opposite the Governor's house: three gibbets were passed, with twelve persons hanging from them, some of old date.

In the evening we had a gay party at M. Avitabili's, who is a fine looking man, with an intelligent Italian countenance.

In a room gaudily decorated and painted, was the following very appropriate motto—

> Donec eris felix multos numerabis amicos.
> Tempora si fuerunt nubila, solus eris.

If this was true in Rome, and is true in Europe, to what extent does its truth not reach in this country. In the evening we were entertained with dancing and fireworks; excellent dinner and admirable bread.

14th.—To-day the atmosphere is hazy, but the snowy range is not topped with clouds. It is curious enough that the part which is most exposed to our view, and which bears about north-east, is generally clouded throughout the hotter parts of the day, while apparently equally high peaks in other directions remain clear.

It is curious that in Khorassan remarkably few climbing plants occur, and of these, the chief form is Cuscuta.

Botany here at this season is a non-entity, in the marsh close to the fort, there occur some few plants, the chief European forms being Veronica. Ranunculus sceleratus is now coming into flower, Typha angustifolia abounds, with Arundo, also Sparganium, Sium, Butomus trigonifolius common; otherwise Cyperaceæ, *Epilobium out of season!* Ranunculus aquaticus is most abundant; two species of Chara, or rather 1 Chara, and 1 Nitella, the last a beautiful species, Marsilea in profusion, Azolla common, Lemna two or three species, one *new*, a floating Marchantiacia, Nelumbium occurs, but only as a cultivated plant.

Of two Boreal, or European forms found in sub-tropical countries, that form is the most northern which flowers, etc. in the coldest season, hence Veronica and Ranunculus are more northern than *Epilobium* in this particular district. The most elevational plant at Cabul is Cardaminoidea, floribus luteis, this flowers at high altitudes in August and September, and at Cabul shows no symptom of flowering even in October; it is there a winter plant? The same is true of Hippuris, which to flower at Cabul requires a greater degree of cold than is obtainable during the summer months.

What I have said of Epilobium above, is true of Typha and Arundo, both now passed flowering, and both found in India, to a considerable extent.

Royle's idea of the comparatively greater extent of distribution of water plants is not I think correct, in the sense he seems to entertain it; to be so, the species should be the same, which they are certainly not. It is only with pre-eminently aquatic forms that the annual temperature can be more equalised than obtains with strictly terrestrial plants. The humidity which may appear connected with the rapid evoporation in these countries, and which obtains? in the vicinity of all bodies of water, may account for the appearance here of Arundo, etc. All genuine aquatic types have leaves involute in vernation?

The least valuable of all northern forms, are those associated with cultivation, especially if they be annuals, because in the first place they may be acclimated species, a circumstance of great importance; and in the second, because if annual, they are confined to the cold season. All such forms have probably migrated into these countries, they have come from the westward: this shows us why at almost equal elevations they are most common, the nearer we approach to the elevated regions towards the west, because it is self-evident that the nearer we approach the regions whence they have migrated, the more abundant and diversified will the migrating plants be, only particular species having the power of extending the range of migration.

When all the Indian plants hitherto met with, have been tabulated; when all their respective heights at which they have been found have been determined; when their more strictly geographical sites have been fixed; when we have some data as to the quantity of humidity pervading their localities; then, and not till then, shall we be able to legislate for the geography of Indian botany.

The Botanist who travels without the means of determining these points, destroys half the value of his collections.

December 16*th*.—Yesterday was very raw and cloudy, to-day clear as usual, towards 1 P. M. a strong north-east wind occurred for a short time as usual, because once or twice before, it occurred after threatening weather.

Rationale.—It blows from the *nearest* snow to supply the rarified air in the valley heated by the sun, even now tolerably powerful; it blows for some days so long as a vacuum is formed, and discontinues when clouds again appear; hardly so, as it before only blew for three or four days, although several more elapsed before clouds re-appeared: it may however be dependent on each fresh fall of snow in the hills.

26*th*.—Cloudy morning, forenoon fine, clear and calm.

Mosses are the analogues of Zoophytes; these analogies are to be looked for in the most striking and most constant parts of the organization of the divisions of nature.

Marchantiaceæ are the representatives of radiate animals, another reason why Jungermanniaceæ are to be separated from them.

Hence, Radiata, = Marchantiaceæ.

,, Zoophyta, = Musci.

I am quite convinced that the true subordinate groups of Acotyledones are far from being discovered.

Are the sheaths found on certain radicles strictly confined to monocotyledonous plants. There is this certain about them, that they depend on the presence of vascular tissue, from which the radicles or the divisions of each root originate: see young Hyacinth roots, grown in water.

Although the sheaths cannot exist without a positive cuticle, their existence does not depend so much on its presence as on the direction of the adhesive powers of its component parts: witness certain forms of Marchantiaceæ, and the vaginate forms, as Azolla, Lemna, etc. Also the sheath may not have adhesive powers at its apex to prevent the escape of the radical at that point: witness Hyacinth roots? We may imagine a case in which the primary radicle may be without a sheath, while its divisions shall have them, this depending on the want of adhesion of the cuticle over the original one.

The emerged and immersed leaves of plants are well worthy of examination, since Microphytum proves that stomata do not depend on the presence of a cuticle as Brongniart supposes: their presence is united with, or allied to an amount of density in the cellular tissue, sufficient to prevent the due aeration of the inner cellules, without direct communication with the atmosphere. Vide Musci ! ! Hence the inner tubes of the leaves of the generality of aquatic plants, (exception Eriocaulon fluitans.)

What is the cause of the plurality of radicles in certain species of Lemna, and their blank in others ? It will be necessary on this point to examine well the sheaths of Azolla, and to look at the Mergui Æschynanthus.

The formation of Affghanistan is very curious : it consists of a wide extent of country, variously elevated steppes being separated by ridges usually very accessible, generally isolated. The mountainous part varies as to its formation, but there is no variety in the declivities and acclivities forming the lower elevations, which are composed of conglomerate ; nor is there much in the usually narrow strip at the lowest portion of each steppe or valley, which is very generally the only cultivatable portion.

In the Khyber ghat the ridges are either of limestone or slaty rocks, between which conglomerate occurs of various thicknesses ; this being dependent on the angle of the mountains forming the sides of the ghat : it is from this conglomerate in such places consisting usually of a loose texture that the very excellent roads (for mountainous passes) are naturally made by the draining streams, which are only periodical. The conglomerate consists of water-worn stones of all sizes, even boulders are not unfrequent, yet the wearing is such as occurs in courses now filling the beds of torrents. The conglomerate increases in density and adhesion towards Lalpoor, and in many places is exceedingly hard.

Whatever the country may have been previously, one might explain its present appearance by supposing it to have consisted of a tolerably level extent of conglomerate, with here and there a strip of soil in the lowest part of each portion, and that the elevation of the mountain ridges was of subsequent occurrence : this would account for the formation of the lower slopes, and the frequent isolation of small eminences of the same character as the neighbouring mountains. It will account for the appearance of the conglomerate in every ravine until the top of the culminating point is reached.

As the mountains were elevated, portions of conglomerate would be detached, and these resting again on all suitable places, would account for the existence of conglomerate on certain parts which are flatter than usual.

Whirlwinds are common about Cabul, commencing as soon as the sun has attained a certain degree of power.

In all cases they assume the shape of a cone, the point of which being a tangent on the earth's surface: the cone varies in shape, is generally of a good diameter, occasionally much pulled out, some being 2,300 feet in height, the currents are most violent at the apex.

They come and go in all directions, even after starting, not always preserving the original direction. They are less common on days in which winds prevail from any given direction, and vary much in intensity from a mere breeze, lightly laden with dust and with no tortuosity, to a violent cone of wind, capable of throwing down a *soldari.*

Northerly winds are prevalent here from 1 or 2 P. M. untill 8 or 9 P. M., occasionally they only commence in the evening, when they are obviously due to the rarefaction of the air of the vallies by the great heat of the sun, amounting now to 100° at 3 P. M., and the vacuum being supplied by gusts from the high mountains to the north and north-east.

CHAPTER XVIII.

From Peshawur to Pushut.

January 8*th.*—At Ichardeh. Between Busoollah and Lalpoor are three curious low ridges, none above sixty feet high, and all of small extent; they are covered with fractured masses of rock of the same size as those strewn so liberally about the shingly slopes; but they are much cleaner or fresher looking, and appear to me less worn. Whence do they derive their singular situation? They occur in such numbers, that one would at first think they originated from a mass of ruins, but the ridges present scarcely any surface for buildings to stand upon, certainly not to such extent as would account for the abundance of these fragments.

About Huzarnow and on both sides, low ridges of sand occur. In this sand graves are usually dug, and in some places to an extent indicating dreadful devastations from disease, each grave is headed by a stone, and about every ramification of the irregular size of the burial ground, there is a building of the usual mud structure, designed for a mosque, but not domed as is customary in Mussulman cemeteries, but ornamented with flagstaffs bearing white bits of cloth. These low sand ridges are often very much undulated; they consist of a very fine powder, and at Huzarnow are evidently of the same nature as the cultivated soil: they are neither in attachment as it were to the neighbouring hills, nor distinct from them, but always have some communication with the shingly slopes, to which they are evidently inferior.

So that the base of Khorassan may be taken to be the tillable portions, over which occur, to a vast extent, the shingly very barren slopes, which every section shows to be nothing but a mass of debris, resting on the mountain rocks.

9*th.*—Ali-Baghan. To this the road is good, along the right bank of the river, wherever it does not wind along over the spurs forming a considerable part of the march. To the first point where this occurs, it extends over the same sort of plain as that about Ichardeh; keeping rather close to the bank of the river, it is good; also through the valley of Gundikuss, and from near the *Choky*, to Ali-Baghan.

The first rocky ridge is about three-quarters of a mile in length, and is not very difficult; at the end near Gundikuss, is a curious ruin built into the stream, where the latter runs with violence on the rocky bank:

it consists of a broadish pathway, with a wall on the river side, breast high ; the masonry is good and solid, of the usual Bactrian materials, but well cemented ; it has mostly been ruined by the river, only one end being perfect. Although the materials are *Bactrian*, the contour is Mussulman, and I was told by some people that it was a Mussulman erection : originally it perhaps extended all along this part, as slight traces here and there are discernible ; for what use the original structure was intended I know not, as there are no remains visible of a fort.

The inlet of Gundikuss is well cultivated, the village itself a large straggling one, built close under a ridge.

From this to the *Choky* the path is rocky, and in many places very bad, consisting of a series of ascents and descents, and winding round spurs ; in the worst place, the path almost overhangs the river 200 feet above its bed, and it is very hard and very rocky. The distance between ten or eleven miles, the road is impracticable for guns, etc. nor could our camels with loads well get over it.

10*th.*—To Camp at the Bussout river, nothing remarkable occurred ; immense quantities of Serratuloides on the sandy raviny parts of the road. Crossed the river on the usual *mussuck* rafts, the animals forded it, at the quiet head of a rapid, water breast deep : this river is smaller than that from Kooner.

11*th.*—To Bussout, five miles. A village passed about one and quarter mile up Kooner ghat, here a mile broad. No change in the features of the country, which throughout is well cultivated ; here and there abundance of sedges, in the low ground ; plenty of watercuts, but none of any great size : road worse at the entrance of the ghat rounding the east boundary, but guns might avoid this ground by keeping towards centre of the ghat.

12*th.*—To Sha-i-wa, distance 8 miles. The road after turning the angle of Bussout ghat, passed entirely through cultivation, villages, trees and inhabitants more numerous than in any other place, cuts numerous, but the road altogether from this cause and the cultivated fields very bad. Rubus found along cuts at Chunar-Bukkeen. *Toot, Phœnix.* Vines numerous, of large size, running up mulberry trees ; forests seen on Kooner mountain ? *Umlook* and *Julghogal,* very common grain, very dear. The women are generally clothed in dark blue *Noorgul.* The road now extends up a gorge to our front, named Durrah.

Gooraiek fort on the opposite side.

13*th.*—Halted. River much clearer than that of Jallalabad ; its bed affords abundance of large grass.

14th.—Rejoined camp, keeping on the north bank of river. The road passed over tillable recesses among the hills forming the north boundary of Kooner valley, and over the spurs dividing these, of which the first is short but bad, the last is a mile long, road infamous, narrow, rocky, and in some places overhanging the river. I was attacked about a mile and a half from camp, my servant Abdool Boyak, the bravest and most trustworthy Asiatic I ever saw, wounded, losing the two first fingers of his right hand; this was opposite the old Fort, Noorgul, which is a dilapidated *kafir* ruin on a low island in the centre of the valley and river, a strong position.* Other ruins occur on the road, one near Sek-Syud, the spur being covered with its remains.

After leaving Deh-Syud, the valley becomes contracted; the river occupying almost all its level portion, being much spread out, and with numerous grassy islands: the cultivation occurring in the recesses between the banks of the rivers and the glacis slopes.

15th.—To Kooner, the road passes to Noorgul, an old *kafir* fort, done up and occupied by Kooneriles, to its south-west, three-quarters of a mile a hostile fort is situated. The ferry is about two miles from Noorgul, and is with difficulty fordable: the streams, three in number, the last almost brim full, and very rapid; thence to Kooner is over a cultivated country.

Noorgul is on a commanding position, the ground rising gradually on all sides to it; the valley here is very narrow. Observed Cnicus, Fumaria, Lotus, Anagallis cærulea, and Veronica agrestis, springing up: trees continue the same to about Kooner: some fine plane trees observed.

All the mountains are wooded at a certain height, and in greater quantities, very different however from Himalayan forests, being dotted in parts, rather than uniformly clothed with forest, Andropogon one of the ordinary spring forms: the *churs* or islands in the river are also covered with Andropogoneous vegetation.

16th.—To Pushut, or rather to within one mile of it, rain throughout the day accompanied by an unpleasant wind down the valley. Road except for the first mile, during which it passed through cultivation, troublesome, otherwise with the exception of two ravines, at one of which the horses were taken out of the guns, very good: valley narrow, say three miles, the boundary ridges to the north presenting

* For the particulars of this attack in which Mr. Griffith nearly lost his life, the reader is referred to extracts from private correspondence.

as it were, truncate faces to the valley, all the mountains at certain heights are well wooded.

17*th.*—Rain continued since, almost without intermission, very dirty weather, but no wind.

Snow on the hills around, almost within 1,500 to 2,000 feet of this, the mountains to the south are well wooded, the woods occurring here and there in forests; snow is said to fall here occasionally.

18*th.*—The attack took place this morning, and failed on account of the weather, which was sufficient to damp any thing, and which prevented the powder bags from exploding, as well as a second cask of cartridges. The men were withdrawn about twelve, rain pouring down, ammunition of the guns being expended, and that for musquetry quite useless; a few more rounds would have demolished the entrance gateway and brought it down bodily; loss severe, twenty-five men killed, thirty-two wounded, several dangerously. The fort was well defended, and evidently by a mere handful of people.

19*th.*—Last night the fort was evacuated as well as that on the opposite side, and the Syud has made off into the hills. It cleared up in the morning but is now as threatening as ever, the ditch of the fort is twelve or fifteen feet deep, but like all Affghan ditches it is narrow. The parapets were very slight, so that a more powerful battery would have kept down their fire completely; no injury had occurred to the inner gate except its being off one of its hinges, or rather out of one of its sockets. The entrance *was thus round the gate*, not through the gateway: it was protected by a thick screen of brushwood and mud, all of the shots from the second position had lodged in the wall close to the side of the gate; every thing was carried off, except a little grain, and some gunpowder.

20*th.*—Continued rain.

21*st.*—Snow within 500 feet.

22*nd.*—Moved camp.

23*rd.*—Continued rain and sleet, almost passing into snow.

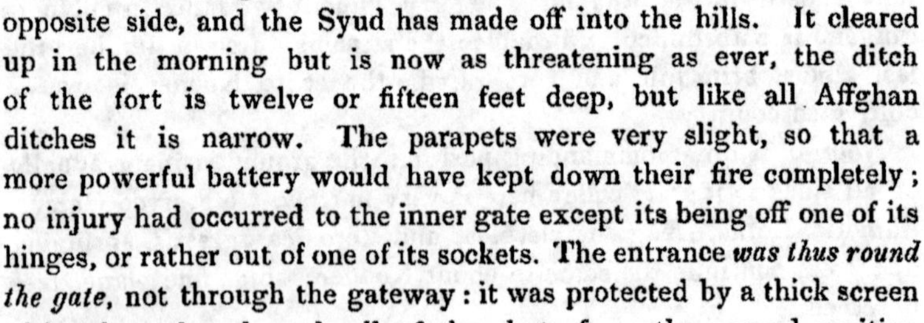

Desideratum.—Required to ascertain positively whether the shingle and boulders are in all cases not derived from the boundary mountains: that they are not in many cases is clear, witness the declivities of slate rocks, totally incapable of assuming the form of boulders. The proportions of the cultivated to the uncultivatable land is previously given rather in favour of the tillable portion, this is always a light, almost impalpable powder, consistent when wetted: generally the soil owes any fertile qualities it has here, to the presence of water; thus the Dusht-i-Bedowlut produces nothing beyond its indigenous plants from having no water.

The transition from the extremely bare mountains of the Hindoo-koosh as seen on the road to Bamean, to the well wooded ones of the Himalaya, takes place at Jugdulluck, the hills, round which, produce plenty of Baloot: in this direction, the forests become much thicker as we proceed to the eastward. There is a mountain near Jallalabad, which at once arrests the attention from its being wooded. Nothing like it occurring between this and Cabul, on any part of the chain of mountains distinctly referrable to the Himalayas. Wooded as this is, it is nothing to the woods on the mountains about Pushut, the size of these has been well demonstrated by the late snows: some bare places occur, which appearances, Abdool says are from cultivation of Kohistanes. Baloot abounds, Dodonea also is now coming into flower! a curious fact pointing out its northern qualifications, although in form it is very like a Mergui Dodonea.

24th.—A clear day after a night of heavy rain, still no appearance of settled weather; walked in the afternoon towards the Dhurrah at the south side of the valley. The bouldery slope presented an abrupt bank of a considerable angle, and its limits were most marked from that of the tillable soil; as we approached the foot of the ghat, the fragments became larger, they are angular, and have been little if at all worn; thence I walked eastwards to a small isolated ridge of limestone, perhaps a mile from the foot of the boundary chain, and returned to camp. In this direction, which is that of the torrents, occasionally rushing out of the Dhurrah, the transition between the mountain slope, and the tillable soil, was gradual, the action of water carrying farther down small fragments, and turning some of the fields into a sandy shingly soil: the depth of the beds of these torrents here, is perhaps four feet, the section being a mass of very unequal fragments.

I am not certain whether these fragments are derived from the mountains or not, they seem to be too varied, and too widely spread for that, although the course of the occasional torrents must vary very much.

Another puzzling thing is, that in the section afforded by the ditch of the fort, and which is seventeen feet deep, the shingle underlies the tillable soil.

The vegetation of the slopes here partakes of the nature of the Khyber pass, the prevailing feature consists in coarse tufts of Andropogonous grasses, Lycioides occurs, also Periplocea, also Cryptandoid, Euonymus, these are on the cliffy ridge of limestone alluded to, 2 sp. of Astragalus, Solanum jacquini? Schænanthus, Sedoides pictum very common, a small fern, apparently a Cryptogramma, Grimonia, Tortula, a Bryum, three or four lichens, one Marchantiacea found under boulders or in crevices of rocks, one Salsola, Fagonia, Dianthoid, Statice common, Onosma, Artemisiæ one or two, a large Cnicoid.

The only new feature is a shrubby dwarf fragrant Composita, foliis albis subobovatis, dentatis grossiusculi margine revolutis.

24th.—A break after a very wet night, cloudy throughout the day.

25th.—A fine day, particularly towards evening, beautifully clear.

26th.—No rain, but very cloudy, cold north-east wind.

27th.—Rain very threatening, a disgusting country in which it is impossible to take exercise without a strong guard: no means of access to the beautiful forests visible in several directions, and the natives are so intractable that it is impossible to induce them to bring in specimens of their various trees, the only things about which I am anxious.

In the meantime I have begun to use the theodolite, and getting approximations to the height of those peaks remarkable for their features of vegetation.

It is curious that no pines are visible on any range south of the Kooner river, until we reach those heights on the opposite side of a very conspicuous ravine, up which the Bajore road runs. To the north, on all the ranges of sufficient height, fine forests are visible, especially of firs, other large-crowned trees exist, forming the bulk of the forests, below the limit of the pines, but never grouped as those are, but occurring isolatedly, these I call generally, *Baloot* woods, i. e. Quercus *Baloot*.

The only means I have of gaining any idea of the composition of these forests, are derived from the twigs and branches, which are used by the natives as pads for the loads of *wood* which they bring into for sale, and which almost consequently are from the lowermost limits of woody vegetation. To go among the woods unguarded, is impossible, and secondly, the weather is very bad.

Memoranda.—That it cannot always be deficiency of soil which causes the extreme barrenness of the usual Khorassan mountains, because on the Kalo Pass to Bamean, nearly 13,000 feet high, the soil is abundant; but in this case, height may interfere.

It is obvious between Kooner and Cabul, that the transition from absolutely treeless mountains to well-wooded ones occurs nearer to Kooner than Cabul, because the Hindoo-koosh about Cabul, and to the eastward, is said to be treeless.

How interesting will the examination of these woods be, how different will be their flora from that of Khorassan proper!

To define the Khorassan Province also, by its being destitute of wood or trees. Note its passing off from this character between Ghuzni and Quettah, see Marryott's letter about Kooner, compare with *Mazenderam forests.* Fine plane trees occur here, all the vines are trained on mulberries. What is Burnes' holly oak, or lily oak?

Rubus occurs, Ranunculus stolonifolia, a cold season plant, Euphorbia ditto, and the usual Peshawur forms.

28*th.*—Fine weather, clouds however, still flying about.

29*th.*—A fine morning; in the afternoon threatening, night cloudy, all the clouds come down the ravine! except when the wind occasionally shifts to west.

30*th.*—Fine weather, although still unsettled. I procured the other day a few specimens of trees from the hills to the south of this, among these which amount only to a few, are one Myrtus, an Olenia, both of which bear me out in assuming that the woody vegetations of these hills will present a curious transition between the genuine Australio-European and the Himalayan forms.

31*st.*—Almost every isolated rock in this country is covered with ruins which vary much in extent, and are often barely perceptible, but careful looking will detect them in all situations about gorges, and such places. From the rivers running under rocks, the paths which must be resorted to, at least at this season, are very difficult. It would be curious to speculate on the different state of preservation of these ruins, and the singular people to whom they are due.

The soil of this valley is very deep in places: in one place on the opposite side of the river, it is twenty-five feet at least, the depth obviously diminishing towards the bed of the river, or the lowest part of the valley.

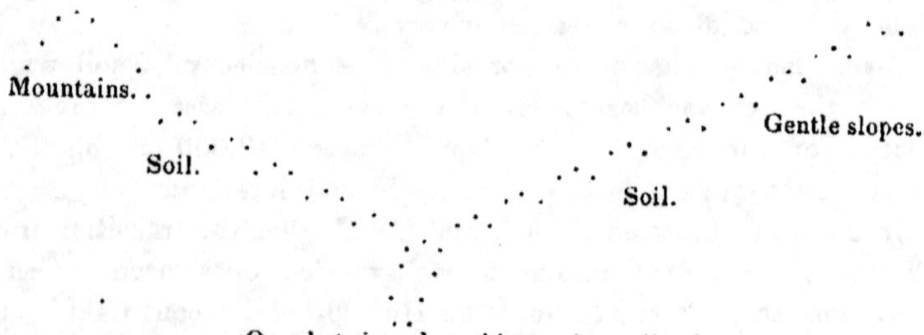

On what river does this rest immediately ?

In this valley, at least about here, curious round thatched huts are visible about villages, intended for religious females, they are closed except at a small door.

Cotton much cultivated.

The *Jala*, or float skins used for crossing rivers, are inflated by *bellows* of the usual description, this causes delay as some require to be inflated very often owing to the eagerness of those who want to be ferried over, and who rush indiscriminately on the *Jala* which, from the rafts being few and far apart, occasion delay; such ferries were not intended for impatient travellers; nothing can show the want of intelligence of the people more than this abominably slow method of crossing rivers; here, there is little excuse for it, as wood is abundant.

The Culminating peak to the west of the north Dhurrah, shows that here, as elsewhere, snow lies longer on the north than south sides: it also affords a curious instance of the various disposition of snow: those angles of its faces presented to the south having none, or little snow; or does this depend upon the faces having different declivities.

February 1*st*.—First part of last night clear: but the wind shifting from west to north-east, has again thoroughly clouded the sky, night beautifully clear, no rain, and no wind during the day.

2*nd*.—A windy but clear night, succeeded by a beautiful morning, wind as usual, north-east or thereabouts, i. e. down the river.

I have seen it mentioned somewhere, that in arid climates the only support of vegetable life exists in the dews, which are hence, at least in the cases alluded to, supposed to be providential adaptations to supply certain deficiences. But considering that dews consist of nothing but a deposition of moisture: it follows that in very arid climates, as there is no moisture, so there can be no dews. For the deposition of a dew, the first essential thing, is moisture, either in the ground or in the air, this last may have been derived from the ground. If neither the ground nor the air contain moisture, no dews can exist, this is the case in Khorassan.

Throughout the whole campaign no dews were noticed, although the nights were almost uniformly serene. and calm, and the time chosen for marching, would have certainly brought us in contact with them had they been deposited. Dews therefore do not form in Khorassan, *with these exceptions*, that wherever from the nature, and the level of the soil, water was found very near the surface, dews were deposited; as on the *Chummums* or low marshy pasturages at Candahar, Cabul, etc.

But even these were trifling, the aridity of the air being too great as compared with the small extent of Chummums, to allow the deposit of any considerable portion of the moisture it had derived from the ground.

So that aridity, instead of being adapted to dews, is a serious obstacle to their ever appearing. With the rarity of dew, that of hoarfrost which is nothing but frozen dew, may be associated; nor does hoar frost often occur, because in Khorassan it rains in the winter too freely, particularly in all such places whose elevation is not sufficient to cause the formation of snow, and hence where other circumstances are favourable for hoarfrosts, *they are too much watered* as it were, and seldom occur. With extreme aridity, Khorassan unites extreme electricity, the casual friction of woollen cloths, especially those of camels' hair being accompanied by discharges sufficiently startling. The same thing happens when caressing dogs or horses. I could never fill the barometer without experiencing a shock as the mercury approached the *bottom end* of the tube, which (when nervous) used to endanger it.

It is this extreme aridity that gives Khorassan so rich a spring flora, this season being that of rain, of melting of snow, and the ground being well moistened.

It is this extreme aridity that necessitates the abundance of bulbous plants in Khorassan, these deposits of nutrition existing even in several of its Compositæ.

Query—Why are Carduaceæ, (Artemisia) so adapted to aridity?

The region of Carduaceæ, commences about Ghuzni, and extends to *Maidan* or Cabul, it is at its maximum about Shaikabad and Huftasya. The abundance of Carduaceæ on the higher grounds, as for instance towards Bamean, belong rather to a vernal flora.

I hope to be particular in hereafter comparing the floras of all the deserts ? and to notice the absurd remarks of some travellers in Khoristhan, on the domesticated parasitic nature of the watermelon plant, on the Hedysarum Alhagi, *Shooturkari*.

3rd.—Fine moderate north-east wind, very clear.

4th.—Over-clouded.

5th.—Rain.

6th.—Unsettled.

7th.—Rain, thunder, distant lightning occasionally last night.

8th.—Fine : ice in the morning, thermometer five feet from the ground 35° at 7 A. M.

9th.—Fine diffused clouds last night, succeeded by a strong north-east wind.

10th.—Fine.

11th.—Fine in the morning, then threatening.

12th.—Quite over-clouded, north-east wind. The inferior level of snow is now several hundred feet above that which it was at first.

Oxalis corniculata in abundance, what an universal plant this is.

All the natives of these parts wear sandals, those about the Khyber being made of the leaves of a small Chamærops, which is common on the rocks of those mountains.

A proof of the extreme want of useful plants is seen in the fact, that baskets are scarcely ever seen, all the loads of flour, etc. being invariably carried in skins.

Leopards' skins for the purpose are obtained from Chugur Serai, Pullung and also Sofaid-Koh.

16th.—The troops marched on their return. A lark very much like the English species occurs in flocks; it is a stupid bird, although obviously aware of its resemblance to clods of earth, which it makes use of on every occasion when a little frightened. The Gypaëtos is also found here; it feeds principally on carrion. I observed Trichrodroma for the first time here to-day, this bird is by no means a powerful climber; indeed the individual seen to-day could only cling, he was employed about sand banks of the irrigating canals, etc. hopping from one likely spot to another, clinging here and there momentarily, and always aiding himself in his inclined position by a flutter of his wings; holes seemed always to attract him. It is by no means a shy bird. I should observe however that I have seen this species running up and down cliffs, so that perhaps the rather loose sand would not give firm hold to his claws.

As I mentioned elsewhere, this bird is allied, at least in analogy to Upupa, it has its precise habit of flight and a good deal of its habits in looking for food, although the Hoopoe pokes about in the ground, or rather hammers the ground alone. It is however fond of building in holes of walls, it breeds at Punukka, in April.

I observed, and shot a weasel, or a *mungoose* to-day, whilst it was employed feeding on the cast away skin of a goat or sheep, so that some of these creatures evidently feed occasionally on carrion, although they are said to live upon live prey.

CHAPTER XIX.

On the Reproductive Organs of Acotyledonous plants.

17*th*.—Fine weather, the sun daily increasing in power, is having a remarkable effect on the peculiar spring vegetation, but this is not sufficiently developed to bring in the corresponding birds and insects. Gypaëtos is common now about the dead camels.

On the low east ridge, along the path that leads over the river, ruins of ancient times are discernible, this only adds another to the many proofs of similarly situated ruins, that the people who built them have been located about Cabul, Jallalabad, and Peshawur, certainly not about Candahar.

In the soil between the rocks, and in their crevices saturated with moisture, most of the plants are just sprouting. Trichonema, Crocus, and one or two other monocotylydons, Labiatæ? Sedum three or four species, exclusive of Sedoides foliis deltoides sphathulatis, and a Stapelioid Asclepias, are to be found. I also got a new fern, the fourth species out of 1,300 sp. it is a Ceterach or Grammitis, a curious stalked snuff-ball, and one or two other Fungi, with an inverted cap, were met with.

In the fields a young Ranunculus in profusion, Veronica agrestis, Euphorbia, Festuca annua?

Kochia spinosa, and a curious Mathioloid are among the few *wild* plants to be found about Pushut.

It would be a curious circumstance if all indusiate ferns were to be found reducible to a *marginal production* of the reproductive apparatus. I will bear this in mind, as certain forms of Pteris or its affinities lead me to suspect that in these tribes the indusium may be a long way from the margin, and yet be, quoad origin, marginal; this section illustrates my meaning.

The transition to this might reasonably be suspected. The philosophy of ferns is most ill understood, the higher points connected with them have been quite neglected, and botanists in this as in other departments of the science have been contented to confer names on certain external forms, without sufficient regard to structure.

To-day I commenced examining Adiantum, with the view of determining if possible the nature of its reproductive organs, and the mode in which they are impregnated, if they are impregnated at all.

As I had long been aware that the fructification of each frond is a thing to be determined at a very early period, and that if not determined then, it is never likely to be determined afterwards, my attention was directed more strongly, if possible, than it would have been otherwise, to examining the subject at the earliest possible stage of its development.

The first piece examined gave me the idea that I had trouvé le nœud de l' affairé; the second made me doubt this; the subsequent ones went far to disprove it.

I was immediately struck with the resemblance of those organs, called ramenta, to what are fairly assumed to be the male bodies, in certain other families of the same grand division; and I at once came to the conclusion, that the barren fronds, were barren, because almost destitute of these ramenta; and that as these ramenta were confined to the base of the stalk, that is, to the part below its first ramification, an obvious necessity existed for the peculiar nature of the vernation.

Further examination of the thing, especially of the base of the stipes and the adjoining part of the rhizoma, threw me back almost into my original difficulties. I find that the rhizoma is entirely covered with ramenta, which are brown, much detached at the base, and obviously represent a low form of leaf, i. e. in appearance, perhaps partly in function, but not in structure. Among these, mature ramenta at the punctas of prolongation, which appear to be very irregular, are concealed, others much smaller, and much narrower, (which bear as obvious a resemblance, or even more so to the male organs of certain other orders,) than the ramenta on the stipes. These are never entirely brown, the end cell alone is coloured, but though occasionally tinged with brown, they are filled with some fluid (even this is not so at first,) but do not appear to open. I believe that subsequently all become highly tinged with brown, but what increase of growth they subsequently undergo, I know not. The terminal cell is always solitary, very often attached to the one next it, which is generally single, obliquely placed, occasionally looking like the dimidiate calyptra capping a young seta. The number of cells forming the base, or dilated part varies, but is always small in proportion to the larger ramenta, or protecting scales:

these last have a single terminal cell, which in fact must be the same in every really cellular growth *sooner or later*, the last degree of formative power being the production of a single cell.

At a subsequent period, still an early one, the terminal cell is fuscous-brown, and this colour then extends to the next in various degrees, but if it reaches the basilar ones at all, it does so at late periods. The base of the terminal cell, and parts of the parietes of the next and next, present a coagulated appearance, precisely as in certain mosses.

No such thing as a petiolate leaf occurs in acrogens, all are attached by a broad base? Of acrogenous leaves, those only are leaves whose attachment is at right angles with the stem; the rest are divisions of a frond. Thus far with the ramenta. The divisions of the frond, are, I find, not gyrate, but rather cochleariform involate. The future reproductiveness is settled at a very early period, and is distinguishable under the microscope by a sort of *margination* of the frondlets. In the earliest stage I have looked at, the margin is greenish, striated by narrow cells, and passes into the body of the leaf gradually; the greater development is perhaps central; even now the bulk of the cells of the leaflet have green granules, and are opaque from air. The vessels are marked out, or at least their future course, and along them the opacity from air does not exist, so that the veins appear depressed.

The next stage presented a greater development of an isolation of the margin, but no other change. The next presented an isolation of the margin, which remains almost white, the other part being green, but more so because of a thickening as it were along the base of the marginal part, and an evident deposit of grumous matter, from which, under every circumstance new tissue seems always to be developed. Pressure causes its discharge, its contents were unappreciated by my poor instruments; after this the leaflets revert to the appearance of the second stage. Here I ceased for the day, having I think ascertained that ferns are endorhizal, and that the primary divisions of the roots hence have sheaths, which adhere to the apex of the root itself.—What a strange union of roots, that of monocotyledons in the main divisions, and of pure acrogens in the minor!!

I cannot help thinking that the secret is hidden in these ramenta, which, as is known, are so universal as obviously to have higher functions than those of mere covering scales. The appearance of those I have described as existing about the points of growth, are exactly the same as the processes mixed with the anthers of mosses, and of which the anthers are nothing but more developed growths; this would point out, as indeed appears to me otherwise evident, (especially from consideration of the theca, and its want of style,) that ferns are lower organised as sexual beings than mosses and Hepaticæ. I know nothing of Lycopodineæ, more than they are the highest of all acrogens; and are not to be included in the same category with ferns.

The objection to the ramenta being anthers, will be the closed nature *(apparently)* of the terminal cell, and although the anthers of mosses do burst, and most especially those of Hepaticæ, yet the argument is not conclusive—inasmuch as *boyaux*, to which they are analogous *do not open?*

These ramenta explain fully the nature of those confervoid organs found in some Neckeræ, and perhaps in other mosses, and it becomes paramount to prove whether these Neckeræ have also the usual anthers, or if they are confined to these, in which case a presumptive proof will thus be afforded of their functions: if they have both forms, they will nevertheless constitute an analogous passage between the two orders: if they have only *these*, such Neckeræ will form, as indeed they do, a very distinct genus.

The nature of the barren fronds requires distinct analysis. Are they barren from mere deficiency in supplies, such as may result from many circumstances; or are the antheriform ramenta deficient? They are barren from defective growth. I am aware how readily objection may be taken to these views, some will say these young ramenta are nothing but young scales as the older ones evidently are scales; but this amounts to nothing, because we may expect simplicity in the sexual organs of this division, and it will be only a proof of the uniformity of nature in making so great a difference in a function depend on, or be associated with so small a one in form. My view I think explains their uniformly brown colour—analogous to Brown's sphacelation in mutatis mutandis.

Others will say how absurd the idea is, when you cannot show the place to which the impregnating influence is to be applied. But the consideration of mosses does away with this objection partly, and that of Anthoceros, entirely; because in mosses, the *ovule*, or preexisting cell, ready to receive the male influence becomes an empty cell, terminating the seta; and the sporula become developed at its opposite end, the first growth appearing to be quite unconnected with that of the future reproductive organs: and in Anthoceros there is no fixed punctum ready for the application of the male organs, but these have to form a communication with the lower, or inferior cellular tissue of the frond, before even the growth of seta can commence.

Besides a case in point exists in Viscum, or Loranthus, in which no point is ready prepared for the reception of the male influence; showing how universal the law is, that in no one point or place is there an absolute want of gradation.

As in mosses the influence of the male *disregarding the ovule,* is thrown into the development of the seta, and then of the theca at the apex of this; there can be no conclusive reason why in ferns the same influence should be thrown into the development of the frond, and then into that of the theca.

While Anthoceros proves that in these orders the male influence may exert its effects upon any point.

As there is no styliform production in Anthoceros, so there is none in ferns. If the ramenta be anthers, they will not be dubious ones, because as they remain fixed, people cannot say, that possibly they are also reproductive bodies, which by the bye is no objection at all, after instances of anthers bearing *ovules* instead of pollen!

Why the peculiar distribution of the male influence (on which we determine our genera,) takes place, is another question, and one that cannot be fairly asked?

Why it is confined to the under surface perhaps can, it being a law that in all cases it is the under surface of the leaf, or its modification, from which new growths originate, and as nature has closed indusia, how could the under surface be interior if this rule were not regularly adhered to?

That the indusium is a *special* organ, i. e. not an eruption of the cuticle, I am sure; hence it is essential to examine extensively both indusiate and other forms, the precise extension of their veins, &c. at an early period to ascertain if their most diversified situations cannot be reduced to some one type.

Query. Is the gyrate vernation of any ferns comparable to the form of certain shells, to which (at least Mollusca) ferns are supposed to be analogous.

Memo. To ascertain the most peculiar, and most universal points of Mollusca and Pseudo cotyledonea, it is in this way that we may hope to extend our views. Some there are indeed who, while the whole course of their studies has been to neglect structure, deny the applicability of presumptive evidence in favour of doctrines, the subjects of which are barely susceptible of direct proof. Thus Greville and Arnott, angrily ask, what do persons mean by saying that mosses have pistilla, etc.? they protest against such community of application in the use of terms. Many more deny sexuality because it has not been proved. Considering the invisible nature of the fluid of the anthers of mosses, etc. how do they expect that we are to demonstrate its application to the pistil, and the subsequent steps? As well might they doubt the necessity of the application of the boyau to an ovule, (or the existence of the boyau itself,) because the derivation of the embryo cannot be proved.

One word more; in all cases the appearance of the reproductive body after impregnation, is of late date; that date becomes later as we descend the scale. The embryonary sac of Phænogams does not always exist at the time of application of the boyau, and the appearance of the embryo is always posterior to this.

Again, ferns are superior to mosses in this, that in many cases the male influence is exerted directly on the parts that become the thecæ, which is not the case in mosses.

18*th.*—Continued examining ferns, and to-day completes my knowledge of the ramenta of three different genera.

In the first which is Cryptogamma, the resemblance of the young ramenta to the anthers of Jungermannia is evident enough, they are capital, and the head is at one period filled with granular matter: so are the cells throughout, to a greater or less extent. They are to be seen in all stages of development on the pinnæ of a very young frond, those near its base having perhaps effected their purpose, while those at the apex of the pinna, or the prolonging part of pinnula, may be formed of only one cell. It is curious that the terminal cell does not become spherical for some time: in its earlier stages it is cylindrical like the rest.

The appearances of the old ones are, if possible, more markedly in favour of my hypothesis; there is the same aggregation of grumous *congealed* matter about the ends of each cell, the same curious communication between these masses which hide the septa from view, evincing a greater or less tendency to assume the peculiar fuscescent or fusco-brown appearance. I observed in two instances what appeared to me decided irregular openings in the terminal cell, from one of which grumous filaments projected; these appeared to communicate with the mass in the terminal cell, which like that in all the others, is congealed; but it assumes a different and very undefined form.

People may object and say, why were not more met with *opened?* This is no objection, because it is obvious that a spherical body may be opened in part of its surface, and yet unless this portion happens to be on the *edge* as it were of the sphere, it may escape detection with a microscope of poor penetration.

In this the ramenta are confined, or nearly so, to the under surface of the fronds. Most occupy that which is called the costa. In this the first change as in Adiantum is in the definition of the margin. But this point I have not paid much attention to, as with my present means here, it would be absurd to attempt *proving* how the fecundation takes place; all that I can attempt is, to ascertain from structure and analogy, the male nature of these curious bodies.

See Plate *B* for the various sketches.*

The next genus examined, is perhaps the instance in which these ramenta have the strongest resemblance to ordinary simple hairs, both in their young, when they represent succulent, tinged, grumous molecular-containing hairs, and in the old, when they represent long, flattened, coriaceous hairs, still there is abundant evidence to prove that, however different these bodies are in appearance from those of Cryptogamma, that they undergo the same changes, excepting perhaps as to dehiscence. We have a tendency to fuscous colouring, a tendency to the aggregation of congealed matter about the septæ, precisely the places where it is to be expected. The same appearance of a canal of communication, the same irregular *constriction* of certain cells; in this too the first change in the pinnæ, or its component lobes, is the definition of the margin. In this genus the under surface of the frond is covered with these *hairy-form* bodies (which have been figured over and over again in Hooker and Greville's ferns): on the upper face, a few exist, but incomparably less developed.

From the examination of this genus alone, I do not think the idea I have been so diffuse upon, would have struck me.

To-morrow I examine Ceterach, assured that the scales of its under face are reducible to the same type. In a matter of such interest

* These sketches, together with the author's further views on the subject, will be more appropriately incorporated in the second part of his Posthumous Papers, entitled 'Icones Plantarum Asiaticarum,' and 'Notulæ ad plantas Asiaticas.'

and importance as this, many will, and with reason, dislike so important an assumption on such inconclusive evidence. But with our present means, it appears to me probable that no evidence to demonstration can be looked for, and for this reason, that the contents of these peculiar cells are so subtile as to escape definition even while in their cells, (or under the most favourable circumstance for a concentration of attention.) How much more so will this be the case, when we attempt to examine the steps of the application of the fecundatory matter, applied over a surface without any prominent points, and probably opaque.

When direct evidence is not to be had, we are justified in using presumptive evidence. As in human law, so in the laws of nature, presumptive evidence to a practised eye carries with it conviction. We have no direct evidence how the embryo is formed, yet no one doubts but that it is brought about by the agency of the boyau, which is a cell containing grumous molecular matter. However different a boyau may seem to many, yet when viewed in conjunction with Cycadeæ, the graduation to the present case becomes natural, and even the resemblance may be perfect, because in Cycas the grains of pollen get into the nucleus bodily, although they would still seem to throw out short tails.

Wonderful is the simplicity of nature! The male organ in its essence, consists of a single cell containing molecular matter.

The female in its essence consists of a single cell, likewise containing similar matter. The influence of the male is exerted, and so another cell is formed in the female cell, and this either becomes the embryo, or gives origin to another cell, and so on, until the terminal one becomes the embryo.

I believe from examination of the most developed scaly ramenta, that these have at an earlier period been fecundating organs, the same peculiarities are to be detected towards their ends, where in fact they retain their original structure, the dilated base being a subsequent development.

In reference to this, the examination of young ferns on their arrival at the age of puberty is indispensable. A curious question arises, what is the frond of a fern? Is it a mass of foliaceous growth containing certain lines of reproductive matter, or is it a distinct development from the axis, in which the reproductive organs are situated? Is it, or is it not, subservient to reproduction? Here again extensive examination is necessary.

If it is altogether subordinate to reproduction, we may expect the occurrence of far more simply constituted ferns than we are yet acquainted with. In fact we may expect a form reduced to an axis, a few ramenta, a frondose dilatation, and one punctum of reproductive organs.

With respect to duration, each frond is analogous to a single seta of a moss, it has definite limits, and is unlike the fronds of certain Hepaticæ, which are capable of compound growth; or if this is the case in ferns, as it is in viviparous ferns, the new formation becomes separated from the frond, as a Phænogamous gemma does. This is a question of importance, as perhaps it may prove that all the foliaceous forms, except Lycopodium, Equisetum, and Chara, are frondose; the dorsal situation is in favour of this assumption, since in all the genuine frondose forms, the reproductive organs of both kinds originate immediately from the under surface, although they may protrude through the upper.

I here ask, is there not *primâ facie* evidence that these organs have peculiar functions; a peculiar form, attended with peculiar changes, must have peculiar functions; and will any one show me in any single instance, like circumstances to the like extent, in any of those organs called hairs? By the bye, ferns themselves may prove that however like these are to certain forms of hair, yet that their functions are different, because the glandular hairs of ferns do not undergo the same alterations, and are evidently nothing but hairs, probably secretory.

19*th.*—In Ceterach the same thing occurs precisely, with this difference, that the *capita* of the ramenta are highly developed; and still more, that the terminations of each pinnula of the young frond, are mere scales without a terminal *head.*

So that almost all the scales of the under surface of the lobes of the mature frond, are mere scales. The peculiar ramenta are to be looked for along the insertion of each pinna, and along the rachis, in which all have the peculiar structure.

At the time that these scales are commencing their development, the peculiar ones are at the age of mature perfection, so far as function goes. No one can look at a young pinnula at this epoch and observe the evident capitation of each ramentum, the inflexion of its apex, so that the head is brought into contact with the frond, without suspecting that they have the same relation of *cause* to the appearance subsequently of the thecæ or capsules. It is curious that the colour of the scales is the same as that of the ramenta, in which the colour is developed from above *downwards*, a peculiarity as it appears to me.

The frond of Ceterach is very frondose-looking, it has stomata on its under surface, and the cells of the cuticle very sinuate. There can be no doubt of the propriety of including the nature of these ramenta and scales in its generic character.

I can see nothing peculiar in the situation of the scales or ramenta to suggest the reason of the situation of the capsules.

In several cases, each pinna appears to have scales only which become barren lobes? the scales and ramenta have the same imbricate situation. In this country it will be useless to expect more proofs. But the four genera alluded to afford evidence enough, and sufficient to show that these ramenta are formed with reference to some important function, that their universality is incompatible with any functions of such minor degree as are attributed to them by those who represent them to be scales or hairs.

To those who require proof of the existence of the complex male organ of Phænogams, or of a male of that form with which only they are familiar, I do not address myself; but to the philosophic botanist, who expects to meet with in the lower orders of plants, a lower organization, one with a tendency of reduction to the essential elements, and who bears in mind the comparative anatomy and structure of similar bodies in adjoining, or not very distant groups, I beg leave to suggest the intimate study of the ramenta of Ferns.

Various as the situation of the fructification is, in three out of the above four genera, yet the initial arrangements are precisely the same. The various forms therefore may not depend proximately on fructification itself, but on the peculiar growth given to the species, in the same way in fact as we have the numerous modifications of the theca in mosses, etc. and the infinite modifications of the carpels in Phænogams.

[Attention is particularly pointed to those ferns which have general capsules or involucres.

Above all to the Cyatheoid forms.

To Ophioglossum.

To naked Thecæ.

To indusiate as Asplenia, etc.]

But however erroneous these views may be, they will still have been of service if general attention is directed by them to plants, in consequence of the suggestions they make. The time now thrown away on isolated species, the station of which, still does not become fixed, when devoted to the philosophical examination of ferns, will rescue botany from one of its numerous reproaches. It is strange that such should exist to the greatest degree in all those families stamped by nature as most distinct. Those chaoses Polypodium, Aspidium, Davallia, would then undergo distinct creation, and the primary divisions of the family would become fixed; and we should then be spared the reproach of drawing characters from organs, of the nature and functions of which we are quite ignorant of, and of the importance of which in a science of demonstration like that of botany, it is impossible to judge, without a true knowledge of structure.

Vide Lindley's Introd. ed. 2, 407, for the protest of Greville and Arnott.

What is the most comprehensive definition of a pistil. A case in which the future organs of reproduction are developed; and here is a most curious circumstance, namely, that though the calyptra, which is a genuine pistillum containing an *ovulum*, becomes torn up from its base, yet it remains in contact with that part of the seta in which the sporules are developed until these make their appearance, or even later!! so that one might as well deny a pistillum to a Reseda, or Leontice, as deny it to these plants on the strength of its being torn from its attachments. Sprengel's objections are worthy only of being noticed from their having been quoted by Lindley. The vagueness of his statement destroys all weight.

His objections in all cases amount to the fact, that the *stellulæ* or *buds* containing the anthers are capable of growth. So is the prolongation of an axis of Ananassa.

A Gemma has a general character in its formation as well as an anther, or as pollen; one is a congeries of cellular tissue, with or without vessels, the other a sac consisting of a single cell containing active molecular matter. As an anther producing a single grain of pollen is not inconsistent with our notions of structure, so neither is an anther consisting of a single grain of pollen.

Will any one show me an instance of a proved gemma taking upon itself the form of one of these anthers? Will any show an instance of a sac containing fluid matter capable of growth *after dehiscence*. The real gemmæ of the Hepaticæ puts the question of gemmæ out of doubt. Is there any plant existing with two sorts of gemmæ, so differently constituted? Many phænogams have gemma in addition to sexes, so have Hepaticæ. Which is the most probable? That they should have no sexes, reproductive organs, and two sorts of gemmæ, or sexes, reproductive organs, or gemmæ of one evident kind?

I cannot adopt the belief of any one having seen the germination of the powder in the axillary bodies, that is, if applicable to the organs I take for anthers.

[*Memorandum.*—To draw up a parallel between the two sets of organs, and the steps followed in the development of each.]

CHAPTER XX.

From Pushut to Kettore and Barowl in Kaffiristan, and return to Pushut and Cabul.

February 20th.—Fumaria found.

23*rd.*—Cloudy, threatening rain. Swallows coming in, also Fringillaria, with blackish cheek-streaks, also Pyrgita alia, starlings uncommon up to this day about the site of the camp, where there is much straw, and camels are lying. Flocks of *rooks,* genuine rooks, flocks of daws, *minas,* pigeons, and many carrion crows have been daily resorting to camp, all very wild from being constantly fired at, as in this country every man almost, has a matchlock. No Gypaëtos seen for several days.

26*th.*—Fine weather after two days uncertain, in which the large-headed lark has just come in abundance, this and the *English* one frequent fields; the crystal one is found almost exclusively on certain stony cultivated places: swallows have likewise arrived with many wild fowl. Four raptorial birds are now seen about this, or rather three, for Gypaëtos has gone, viz. the common kite, or one which looks much like it, a beautiful white slaty-blue and black *harrier,* at least it comes about constantly, and looks much like an Indian species, and much like one I shot high up in Bootan, together with a large blackish and white one, with a *distinct collar.* The fishing hawk, I saw it yesterday catch a large fish, making a strong rapid plunge boldly into the water, and emerging again from it without much difficulty; its habits except while fishing, are very sedentary, and it seems to prefer *one spot,* viz. the top of some particular tree, near perhaps its favourite feeding place.

27*th.*—Another new bird has come in. A *Fringillina,* with curious Flycatcher habits, I have only seen two individuals, they perch towards the top of trees, and thence sally out after winged insects. I examined the contents of its stomach, and found only seeds, gravel, and soft insects.

The sun is increasing wonderfully in power, but the trees are not as yet budded. Shrubby Polygoneæ, with flagellate branches and leaves, in which the petiole is as much developed as the lamina, form a curious feature of Affghan Flora; Euphorbia linifolia common, the herbaceous one in profusion.

28*th.*—Spring coming on rapidly, snow not within 2,000 feet of where it was twenty days back, and the sun oppressively hot; winged ants in abundance: whenever this happens it proves the perfection of the crows, which are on all such occasions to be seen acting the part of flycatchers in addition to their various other callings, soaring and sweeping round after these insects, but not returning as Merops or real flycatchers to a fixed station. I have hitherto seen only the jackdaws at this spot in Calcutta, but here the real crow mingles in it.

In Calcutta, the common kite often acts a similar part, but catches only *with its feet.*

A small kingfisher is to be found here *rarely*, it is much like the Indian blue and reddish one, the white and black kingfisher is not seen here, although found at Jallalabad.

The species of *sub*-wader, with a stout upturned beak, is a true Grallator, yet is not always about water, but often in the driest places; the genus has a flight strongly resembling that of certain Anatidæ.

A *Monaul* pheasant, or some similar splendid bird is found in the snows of Kaffiristan, all I have seen of it are a few feathers.

Merula more common, *Anthus, Timalia,* observed.

To-day one good specimen of a splendid pinus, allied to P. longifolia, was brought from the mountains, where it is found *among snow:* this makes the third species; one cultivated at Candahar near a mosque; the short-leaved *Julghozeh*, from Tazeen; and this one which has as fine a cone as can be wished.

Where did the profusion of Justicia Adhatoda which I find here come from, is it not a distinct species?

March 2nd.—Proceeded to Chugur Serai, started from the other side of the ferry at 11-30 A. M., and reached at 4 P. M. No halt of any consequence on the road. Passed Nachung at 12-50: the first rocky ground occurred at the narrow part of the north side of the valley 2-25.

15*th.*—And thence to Chugur 4 P. M., distance certainly thirteen miles.

Road decent, good about half-way, where it extends over cultivation on firm ground, then over rocky, stony, raviny ground. From the 12-50 station, the valley becomes much narrower, and the river confined to one bed: cultivation scanty, between this and Chugur, where, about 400 yards of excessively difficult ground occurred, commanded by the precipice under which the path, which is execrable, runs. It is quite impassable for guns.

After this the country traversed seemed to be well cultivated: and even picturesque.

The fort is nothing particular; it is placed on the right bank of the river, which is deep, narrow and raviny: descent to the river abrupt. The bridge very richly ornamented, and of curious and simple Bootan timber construction.

Town small, and the people very civil: I lodged in Meer Alum's own house.

Iris crocifolia abundant, towards Chugur, a Mazus or Stemodia.

Mimosa that of the Khyber, common, Polygoni in abundance on the rocks, Dodonæa.

The hills about Pushut are here only recognisable in two instances, the central one presenting three peaks, next to it the barren cliff, and the three mountains south-west of Dhurrah.

3rd.—Proceeded to Bala Chugur Serai, which is not more than six miles up the river, occasionally passing along the stony bank under hills, otherwise over cultivation, which is conducted in terraces.

The scenery pretty, reminding me of low parts of Bootan, although much more barren; watercourses well made: two *kafir* ruins passed; valley very narrow, but rather straight. Both chakor and small partridges common. Vegetation is here the same as elsewhere. Zaitoon trees, Mimosa, Euonymus, Dodonæa, Amygdalus in abundance, Polygonum of yesterday.

The stony slopes of hills, covered with Andropogoneous grasses.

Rice, beans, wheat, oranges, *toot, chanra.* Narcissus in swarms, brought in from the *kafirs.*

Another bridge was here crossed, the same as at lower Chugur Serai. No tributaries passed, the river fordable at rapids, but the road is not passable for guns.

Aquila, Enicurus, Alcedo bengalensis common, as well as jack snipe.

Red-billed crow, chakor, yellow wagtail, Fringilla, Muscicapa in flocks, feeding in the fields, and from trees on insects.

The blackbird of the Himalayas, wild pigeons. Narcissus in abundance in sandy fields, Cryptandrioid, Clematis, Rubus, Euonymus, Pteris!

We had an interview with the *kafirs* or infidels about a mile below Katoor, they seemed at first much alarmed, our retinue not being small or unarmed, and their reliance on Mussulman faith not very strong. They took up their post at the foot of a hill where a deputation of the Khan of Chugur Serai, (who has married a Chief's daughter) met them ; they received the deputation with a *feu de joie* from one or two firelocks, and then accompanied him to us, preceded by two drums, one of ordinary, the other of an hour-glass shape, and two pipes of gramineous culm, with three or four holes, and apparently oblique mouth-pieces, but of ordinary sound. The Chiefs, the head of whom is Hussin Ali's father-in-law, having been introduced, advanced, and commenced turning and stamping round a circle.

The usual formalities then took place; the followers, although a fine bodied people, and very active, were excessively dirty, and not very fair; most were dressed in skins, having the hair inside, armed with bows, either straight or like cow's horns, and daggers.

The Chiefs were much fairer than their followers, and in the expression of face and eyes European; but in all cases the forehead was very slanting, and head generally badly developed.

Their dress consisted of cotton frocks, with slashed sleeves, embroidered thickly with worsted network: they wear short *pyjamas*, and skin shoes, with thick skin soles; one had short boots with hair inside: most were ornamented with the blue and yellow *longhys* of Pushut, etc. The hair is cut short except that of the Chiefs, who had fillets left round their heads, adorned with cowries, in radiated shapes, with a red, worsted, pendant tassel. The headman had a pendant wire chain with ornaments, and from the centre of the tassel, the *Monaul* pheasant feathers, and his back hair was plaited into many little tails.

Almost all had necklaces of beads, the better sort silver earrings (plain rings), and some pendant silver ornaments; many had bracelets, ornamented with brass; *kumurbunds* of plain white cloths: the poor ones have their heads naked, or with bits of cloth wrapped round.

They had no swords, but Hindoostany ones, and of these very few.

Even their archery, Macgregor says is bad; one or two had spears, the Chief's spear was provided with a very long head, and ornamented with cowrie shells at the top of the *haft;* two women came afterwards, their necks loaded with cowries and bits of bones, but otherwise well clothed with the usual gowns, the outer one without sleeves and very wide arm holes. They were decorated with very coarse, large, circular earrings. They approached the rest singing in chorus, not unmelodiously, but with very little variation in notes. Then a whistle, general and loud from the whole party, representing their rejoicing over a slaughtered Mussulman.

On the whole these people present nothing peculiar as compared with other hill people : like them they are vindictive, savage, poor, dirty, remarkable for great cupidity, fond of red cloth, beads, etc. They are a mixed race, some are like Indians, some like Europeans, but in all the forehead is low, Tartar eyes, often light brown or grey, hair often light. Put them among the Nagas, etc. of the Assam frontier, and none would notice them.

The Chief's son wore a black, narrow band round his head, ornamented behind with a few cowries and bone ornaments.

They are independent, appear to delight in talking of their victories over the Mussulmans, but the oddest peculiarity as compared with Asiatics, is their shaking hands, which was certainly done with us in the European custom.

The limits of the firs, are as strict as those of Baloot, etc., of the latter it may be stated as between 3,500 to 5,600 feet, of the firs between 5,500 and 8,000; what makes me say this is, that at Katoor the mountains are covered with heavy snow, and are naked above, but with heavy pine forest below, and then with forests of Baloot.

5th.—Ascended the hills to about 200 feet above the limits of inferior snow, which may be estimated at about 4,500 feet.

These hills from 3,500 feet and upwards, are well wooded, presenting no peculiarity in the distribution of the woods, which are thin, or thickish only in sheltered parts, down ravines, etc. but presenting a great peculiarity in the small variety of forms, for there are not more than three kinds of trees, and not more than a dozen shrubs : the trees are Baloot, which commence at the base, and ascend to the pines, say a height of 4,000 feet; Zaitoon, which commences at the base, and scarcely extends beyond 5,000 feet, Xanthoxylon, which has a wider range than Zaitoon, is comparatively rare.

The inclination of these hills is steep, but the ascent is not more extraordinarily difficult, they are covered with masses and blocks of rock, which are plentifully clothed with lichens and mosses, but of small variety of species. The more open parts are covered with Andropogoneous grasses; the lemon-grass occurs below.

The shrubs and trees are as follow; with their Pushtoo names—

Zanthoxylon, *Schneæ khinfuch,*
Quercus Baloot, *Ichairraye.*
Olea, *Khoo-unn Zaitoon.*
Amygdalus, *Budam, Junglee Tulk.*
Nanus,——*Naguhn.*

Celtis, *Tanghuh.*
Cyrtisoid of Bolan, *Wooraijoa.*
Periploca, *Burrara*, *Banduk.*
Cotoneaster of Tazeen, *Khurrowa.*
Euonymus, *Churroghzye.*
Dodonæa, *Wroolarskye.*
Artemisia, *Tuhakar.*
Rubus, *Khusuhurra.*

The higher ridges are crowned with beautiful pines; the most common on this side is called *Nukhtur*, and has not eatable seeds, its timber is in general use—and it is in much vogue for torches.

The *Julghozeh* also is met with, but rarely. Abundance of firewood.

Ixioides very common, and now in flower, Amygdalus, *Budam*, also, this is common, and a curious. Irideous plant, allied to Crocus; one Arum likewise occurs. Pigeons very wary, mostly of the green sort with whitish wing-coverts; a pretty small-sized Jay occurs, with a jerking bobtailed flight, a strong-billed Parus, of the climbing sub-genus, Chakors common.

March 6th.—Rain almost all day.

7th.—Unsettled weather continues. To-day the *kafirs* came in with plants of a decided Himalayan nature, a beautiful Iris, the flowers of which are of a deep indigo-blue, a Viburnum, Euonymus, Valeriana, Juniperus, Spiræacea, Adiantum, Asplenium, Pteris, etc.

How strangely intelligent all hill people are, and how they are urged by an insatiable love of money. I never expected any thing to be brought in, judging of the *kafirs* as I have learnt to do of Affghans and Indians, and here they have in one day, without even a lesson, brought in excellent specimens, including mosses, etc. I went out to-day to the end of Meer Alum's territory, this boundary being about one and a quarter miles beyond Shingan. The valley up to this is beautifully cultivated, and begins to look green. Saw and shot another Myophonus, a Saxicola and an Alcedo, the common one of India; this species has strengthening splints, as it were on both mandibles: and the feet, etc. have no scales, being very different from those of the generality of birds.

Myophonus I take to be the large beautiful metallic-blue blackbird, with obscure and elegant white markings. I have observed common to all hills I have seen, and is always found in damp wet places, this bird is very wary, and in carriage much like the English blackbird, on alighting from its short flight, flirting its tail about, etc. This bird leads me to remark how widely the river chats are distributed. The beautiful white-crowned black and red species, and the grey, with a red tail, are found about all hill streams in the north-eastern parts of India; the latter is a curious bird, radiating its tail out constantly. Enicurus is also widely distributed.

I also got to-day a beautiful male Lophophorus, the plumage of which surpasses description; it is a heavy bird, with brown irides, and a brownish-chesnut tail; it came from Daiwag.

I met with five *kafirs*, when out to-day, only one would come to me; he was a very tall man, with a savage face, light keen eyes, returning from a forage on the Safis: he was an *Arunsha* man, and a *Tor kafir*, who are represented as very different from the *Espheen* or white ones, who are found in the mountains adjacent to Balk, etc. Arunsha is three days journey from this, and has a lame, or one-*legged* chief, *Dheemoo;* my friend's name was *Bazaar*, he was armed with a matchlock taller than himself, and the usual dagger. How they compete with the Mussulmans I cannot imagine, as they can only fight in close quarters, and for which they have daggers about six inches long in the blade.

The *Kafir* names of the plants brought in are as follows:—

* *Praitsoo*, Hedera.
Akrumah, Iris.
* *Kreemapotak*, Melanthium.
Daisoo, Urtica urens?.
* *Joh*, Laricoides.
Wheeree, Ephedroides.
* *Amarr*, Rhamnea.
Whishtur, Juniperus.
* *Traih*, Quercus.
* *Unzoomal*, Spireæa.
Gutsuttur, Viola.

of these, those marked with an asterisk have no affinity at all with the Khorassan Flora: nothing can show the change in the Flora of Katoor better than this, that two *kafirs* bring in one day, without having their attention directed to ferns, as many species as I have obtained in all that part of Khorassan I have visited, amounting to 1,000 miles in different latitudes and at very various elevations. The following are the *kafir* names for the corresponding words:—

Darr, Mounatin. *Wussut*, Goat.
Trimm, Snow. *Wemmi*, Doomba sheep.

Trosse, Ice.
Wishin, Rain.
Earr, Clouds.
Populass, Lightning.
Doodoowunn, Thunder.
Tsaih, Sun.
Mass, Moon.
Tarah, Star.
Geutte, Jungul.
Julla, Tree.
Poutte, Leaf.
Pushe, Flower.
Bhee, Seed.
Tat, Father.
Zfee, Mother.
Porottr, Boy, Son.
Jhoo, Girl, Daughter.
Moochook, a little Girl.
Oorutur, a large ditto.
Birra, Brother.
Soose, Sister.
Tsoon, Dog.
Pishash, Cat.
Goh, Cow.
Ghora, Horse.
Sovurr, Hog.
Kookoor, a Fowl.
Melli, Bread.
Ow, Water.
Undah, Meat.
Ornachoa, Skin.
Haddi, Bone.
Jeet, Body.
Shai, Head.
Ash, Face.
Uchain, Eyes.
Jibb, Tongue.
Mass, Nose.
Dhermurr, Neck.
Kaitss, Hair.
Deh, Beard.
Troh, Chest.
Booh, Arm.
Ungree, Hand.
Sichupput, Fingers.
Noach, Nail.
Dust oungree, Thumb.
Koorr, Leg.
Papoa, Foot.

The mixture of Hindoostanee names is very curious indeed, particularly those names of things which, from being indigenous, one would suppose would have indigenous names.

7th.—Went up to Bharowl and returned to-day, March 9th, first went to Loongurze, the Barometer at which stood 24·758. Therm. in sun 85°. Bharowl is a small plain, but still three or four times larger than Loongurze, and perhaps 100 feet below it: this place is up the ravine leading to the fourth peak of the west side, which same peak must be between 9,000 to 10,000 feet high. Loongurze is visible from this, and is more to the south.

The villages consist of several houses forming a sort of wall; outside, the houses are of one story, with terraced roof, supported by timbers, they are built of stones, slabs of micaceous slate, which is the prevailing rock, and timbers interposed as ties; the rooms are very dark, and very dirty, with no outlet for the smoke. The only part of the furniture worth noticing consists of an inverted conical basket, made out of the stems of some large grass, coated with mud, and truncated at the top, used to keep grain in. The under, or ground floor appears to be used for the domestic animals which are cows, goats, fowls, etc. The inhabitants of Bharowl, *Bhawiolis*, are a *kafir* race with a Mussulman cast of countenance, but fair, of an unhealthy look, with in many cases light hair, and generally light eyes, they are a rather large tribe, and appear to have but few wants, are very poor, and very dirty; the better part of the men are clothed in Cashgar, *chargas*, and ordinary cotton under-garments; the women dress in blue. Both villages are on the limit of inferior snow at this season; there is enough of cultivation about to supply their wants, chiefly wheat and barley, and a sort of pea. Loongurze is infested with a villainous midge, of the same genus as that of the Naga Hills, but few are to be found at Bharowl.

At Loongurze I met a Khungurlye slave, of the caste Krungurlye, the head-quarters of which are at a mountain village, about eight *cos* off, in a north-west direction. The chief of Koorungul is Ahmed Khan, he is independent: his village having 400 men, well armed.

The man wore a goat skin jacket without sleeves, a skull cap of camel hair netted, and leggings to the ancle of the same, to keep off the midges; these leggings are likewise used at Bharowl for the same purpose. The following is a specimen of the Krungurlye dialect.

Baba, Father.	*Wurrik*, Water.
Aiee, Mother.	*Soourr*, Hog.
Lohideck, Brother.	*Kookoor*, Fowl.
Trizzai, Sister.	*Ow*, Bread.
Khleck, Woman.	*Trull*, Jungul.
Gillor, Horse.	*Psan-sa*, Cat.

The Krungurlies are said to have been *kafirs*, converted *long ago*. They are now quite Mussulman in appearance. They were doubtless originally a mixture of European and Tartar races driven by persecution to the hills, to which they are still perhaps restricted by the cause which led to their original isolation.

I tried to ascend the ridge, but the snow was impracticable even within 700 feet of the village. The *Nakhtur*, or Pinus, which is the prevailing feature above Bharowl, is the same as the Tazeen one, and is a Cedrus or *Abils*, leaves very short, cones erect and elegant, but only broken ones could be found. The ridge and its face is quite covered with them, they grow singly. Huge masses of micaceous rocks are scattered here and there, some are of gigantic size.

The Baloot is the next most common tree, but I fancy it does not extend beyond 7,500 feet; this is in general use for firewood, many of the trees, especially below, are much damaged, and on these the leaves are generally very thorny. Next is the Zaitoon, but it is not common in this direction, although common a mile to the south on the ridge first ascended. The soil is now saturated with snow water, and appears good and plentiful. The want of soil is another reason why the lower ranges are so barren, but this is just the contrary of what would be expected.

In spite of the beauty and fineness of these forests, there is still the Khorassan paucity of forms. Many herbaceous plants are doubtless hid under the snow, but few shrubs were to be seen: the Mespilus of Tazeen being the most common at 6,000 to 7,000 feet, a Thymus, Labiata, Olea fragrans, Ocymoidea, two or three Crucifera; Sedum pictum observed, and Melanthaceæ which has fragrant flowers, is very common. The rocks are covered with mosses, Grimmia pulvinaloides, every where in profusion. New forms consist of a fine Tortula and an Anictangioid, with leaves white, and membranous from the middle upwards.

Birds, a black and white Erythaca, eyes fuscous-brown; the wood pigeon; a jay, which is a beautiful bird, irides light brown; a small woodpecker, with a greenish subcrest; the *Parus;* a thrush not obtained; Parus cœrulens; a pretty red-crowned small Fringilla, eyes light brown; common crow, chakor, bearded vulture; a wren, not obtained, with irides light brown, but with exactly the manners of Troglodytis. Chamærops, *Maizurrye* used for netting ropes for bedsteads, Viscum of Baloot, used for food of domestic animals.

Wild goats, sheep, an ass-like animal *(Goomasht)*, and a fox which is handsome, of large size, and common.

8th.—Returned.

The *Kafirs* have a game exactly the same as the English leap-frog, called by them *Shutruck*. They were very much astonished at my understanding it. They are miserable marksmen, and were even at small distances unable to strike a large object, as for instance a hat at twenty yards, although offered a handsome reward; nor can they shoot at all at long distances. They are in this respect quite below Khasyas and Booteas.

Nakhtur
and Baloot . Colchicum .
. Andropogoneæ .
. Thymus, Ocymum, .
Celtis
Zanthoxylon mispilus . Cystoides
. Schœnanthus
Amygdalus, wild Budam.
Spærioides, . Edgeworthia
Dodonæa, . Pæriploca, Euonymus, Cryptondioid, Arum
Rubus, . Nerium.

March 9th.—Yesterday evening a female of Lophophorus, was brought in, and a beautiful pheasant, having claret-coloured neck. Body otherwise fuscous and blackish-brown, having a blackish-green head, white cheeks and fine transverse crest, as large as a middle-sized fowl. Apparently a new subgenus of Phasianus.

11*th.*—Swallows have now come in here. They are apparently a different species from the Pushut kind.

12*th.*—The large-headed lark has also come in, so that there is a difference of twelve or fourteen days between this part of the country and Pushut, where it was first seen, although this is only 500 feet higher, and about thirteen miles farther north.

The universality of the common crow is curious, especially when contrasted with the circumscribed locality of Jackdaws. The Indian Jackdaw is never found in hills.

A common plover was brought in yesterday, the wing-quills had been taken out, and its gestures on being liberated were most absurd, and although originating from fright, were much allied to pride, its head reclining on its neck, the latter curved, and the feet lifted high into a stately walk, while the crest was disposed in a most supercilious manner.

I have got into great request here as a physician, entirely I apprehend owing to the people's faith in *vilayuti daroo*, or English medicine, especially calomel and cream of tartar, a combination of which has proved an universal panacea.

Goitre is common here, and the place in the hot months is said to be very unhealthy, fever and jaundice carry off numbers of people. The Affghans, strange to say, have no popular medicines, but they are an unintelligent race in many other points. They are aware of blood-letting, which they practise most indiscriminately.

13th.—Unsettled weather. Heavy thunderstorm in the evening with clouds over the western range.

14th.—Beautifully clear, a genuine spring beauty on all sides.

The common *Maina* of these parts is a gregarious bird, which feeds generally on the ground, but is rarely associated with cattle, to which the Indian species are so addicted: this is an intelligent bird, although from its nature not unnecessarily shy.

It is fond of singing; its notes are very varied, but not very musical, including all sorts of intonations.

While so employed, the bird every now and then bobs his head suddenly down three or four times, much for the same purpose perhaps, as our public singers in the production of certain notes. I do not know whether these actions of the bird are really associated with particular notes, although they generally seem to accompany certain very flat and very base notes, not unlike the clerk of a coachman.

The snow is rapidly disappearing, rain having a most powerful effect even at the summit of the pine ridges: it is fast melting, and no new snow has fallen, although it has been raining occasionally during the last three days, and the sun has been altogether obscured.

Generally on the high Kuttoor range, fresh snow has fallen, a proof of the great height of that range.

Two species of Corydalis, the first Iris and Colchicum I had found in Kaffiristan. Corydalis is another analogy with the genuine Himalayan Flora.

Jackals were heard here for the first time, although they were heard many days ago at Pushut.

15th.—The antilopoid animal called Suja, has horns both on the male and female, it occurs in small herds fifteen to twenty in the wooded mountains, its hair is of the same structure as in the Moschiferus antilope; colour brown. Height to the shoulder two feet six inches; its height does not increase or decrease perceptibly behind; length of neck seven inches. Length of back from root of tail to nape of neck two feet eight inches.

The Lophophorus is called *Moorghi Zureem*, it is a very gorgeously coloured bird, but of heavy make; the tail is always carried erect. Length of body two feet one inch; the girth of the body at the shoulder including wings, seventeen to eighteen inches. Length of neck from commencement of the crest to the base of the under mandible, five to six inches.

The bird is not uncommon, being found on all the hills about here, and apparently at no great elevations.

16*th.*—The *Ungoor,* Ficus cordifolia is the first tree that buds. The Platanus, *Thagur;* Morus coming into flower, vegetation being very rapid.

A captive fox brought in, a fine and a handsome animal, with greyish fur inclining to fuscous on the back, and with blackish points at the back of ears, which are large, and dark-brown; eyes light yellowish-brown.

Measured as follows from shoulder to base of tail, 1 feet 3 inches.

„ „ to tip of nose	1	„	0	„
Height at shoulder, ...	1	„	4	„
„ at loins, ...	1	„	6½	„
Total length, ...	3	„	8	„
Length of tail, ...	1	„	7	„

There is also a nocturnal beast here which has a voice something like a jackal, but more of a bark. Shot one of the small grey, white-rumped water robins, which was examining a wall for insects, and fluttering about the holes in it. I saw two Carbos (cormorants), distinct from any I had hitherto seen, very black, with some white marks. The common black one also occurs.

17*th.*—Proceeded to Chugur Pair; the time occupied by the journey, excluding stoppages, was two hours and four minutes, at the rate of three and a quarter miles an hour.

Tulipa in abundance in fields, a beautiful species, external sepals rosy outside, odour faint but sweet.

On a ridge near Chugur Pair is a curious ruin, viz. a long wall.

The mountain is too high to enable me to say what it is like. The tulip has a tendency to produce double flowers: one specimen seen with a regular three-leaved perianth, eight stamina, and four carpellary ovary, angles opposite the outer perianth leaves; the upper leaf or bract has a tendency to become petaloid. If the anthers are pulled, the filaments are separated from them and remain as subulate white pointed processes.

19*th.*—Labiata, Ocymoidea, Salvia! erect, ramose, foliis rugosis, verticillatis; spicatis racemosis. *Cal.* bilabiata supra planisculis, medio carinatus, *Cor.* pallida, cærulea, bilabiata, labio superiora subfornicata: lateralibus subrevolutis. See Catalogue No. 52, in fields Chugur Pair, common on grassy banks.

A curious tendency is observed in Pomaceæ, Ceraseæ to have the stamina of the same colour as the petals, thereby *showing their origin ?* How is it explained that in some transformations of this, the anthers alone are petaliformed, while in others both filament and anther are equally and primarily affected.

The female Lophophorus has been living on nothing for at least a week; its voice is various, sometimes not unlike that of a large hawk, at others a cackle, or low chuckle; occasionally it runs forward, erecting its crest, and spreading out its tail like a fan, the *tail being depressed.* I fancy it roosts in trees not unlike certain pigeons, Hæmatornis one species come in, this genus I think represents Parus: it has the same fluttering clinging habits, it often sallies forth like Merops after insects, the genus is remarkable for the yellow or red colour of the under tail-covers, it is a noisy bird, and not wary until so taught by experience. I doubt its power of singing. The so called Bulbul, *hazari dastar,* the famous songster, is not a real *bulbul,* but either Alaudina or a stonechat.

With Hæmatornis has appeared a fine Merops, of which I have not yet got a specimen; its habits were quite those of Merops, and it made the same noise: it occurred with Hæmatornis.

Chugur is a large extent of ruins, traces of paths are visible leading to the houses, mere huts built of slabs of slate. There is one square part remaining much like the base of one of the topes to which it assimilates; the building, is of slabs of wood and stone, intervening. What could have induced the Mussulmans to build on such horridly hard barren and hot places, with no water near? or did they occupy places taken from the *Kafirs.* The latter I should think most likely from the names, which are evidently *Kafir.*

20*th.*—The bird alluded to yesterday, was again seen to-day. I remember shooting the same species at elevations of 8,000 feet in Bootan, in oak forests. It has the habits of Merops, with its voice or chirp, and is very gregarious, so that one part of the flock will not separate from the rest. It perches in a very erect manner making swoops and sallies after insects precisely as Merops. Plumage sombre, general colour slaty, quills and crest blackish, bill and feet orange, tail forked.

Is this bird of the sub-family Brachypodinæ, or is it a Fissirostral bird; the wings, although graduated as to the two first quills (the first being half spurious) are still long, and may be called pointed. It obviously has much analogy? with the Drongo shrikes in habits, and in forked tail: as well as in lengthened body? Both it and

Hæmatornes are very local, none being found here but just around a village called Pillipote, a favourite station—Zaitoon trees, or naked Bakkeins. Hæmatornis I have seen feeding on the ground, this species has the same voice as that of the genus generally.

The yellowish *Bunting-like* water-wagtail, is very common just now: it occurs in wheat fields; flight, chirp, and mode of getting up when disturbed just as in the Buntings.

Weather very unsettled, heavy rain and thunder last night, and now threatening a gale.

21*st.*—Returned towards Pushut: a Lanius, but not the one shot, was seen near the road in bushes.

22*nd.*—Of the four red-billed Shrikes, two are male and female, sexes alike, stomach fleshy like that of Hæmatornis, but food entirely vegetable: the two female stomachs contained each a seed of the *Bukkein* (Melia): the two males contained fragments of buds, perhaps of a willow, but not a vestige of an insect, so their swooping and sallying is a mere analogical representation of Merops. In Hæmatornis contents of stomach chiefly vegetable, partly of insects.

26*th.*—Very rainy and unsettled weather, thunder and lightning.

27*th.*—Clearing up: heavy rain in some parts of the night, otherwise fine.

28*th.*—A beautiful morning. Went to Kooner, distance twelve to thirteen miles: for three miles the road was dangerous but tolerably decent, no defiles being passed, in which murderers were likely to lurk, very little difference in seasons between this and Pushut.

29*th.*—Returned again to Pushut. The country about Pushut is one sheet of cultivation, studded with trees; so thick are these that few villages are discernible in consequence. Nothing particularly notable occurred, except that a tulip is common in the fields about Kooner, but not found in those about Pushut: it occurs also with Amaryllideæ, which is likewise a stranger to Pushut. What is the reason of the ruined forts so common in this country? One would think that it were useless to pull down or destroy a good fort, when it is the intention of building another, so that they are scarcely to be accounted for from a succession of conquerors.

The country has, and always will be, a distracted one. I observe that in all parts approaching mountains, in which the chief danger of robbery exists, that there are generally people and especially boys tending cattle, so that they must probably be familiar with robberies and murders, and seeing these done so openly, so easily, and so securely, they may well be imagined to become ready scholars. So even if the stock already existing in the robbers' sons, etc., were deficient, others would be found ready to take up the profession. The Kooner Dhurrah, or valley, is a very fine one, it is a good instance of the peculiar kind of slope or *talus*, so common in this country. The soil in such places being so stony as to be useless for cultivation. Low parts entering into the valley become useful for wheat, that is, if rain falls early, these Dhurrahs are formed or filled by debris from the surrounding hills, carried down by torrents, which are constantly changing their beds, the outline of the edge is circular, such as that of a sand bank at the mouth of a river, the finer particles being of course carried furthest down.

The Kooner valley may be considered as the second; the Shaiwa distinct forming the first; it continues as far as the bend to Chugur Pair; its beginning is close to Kooner village, near the ferry where the valley is much contracted.

31*st*.—The beautiful Smyrna kingfisher of India, with metallic plumage, chocolate-brown underneath, occurs at Kooner.

The common kite is very expert in seizing objects with its claws while flying: as is the Pondicherry falcon. They are often seen about standing water, fishing I fancy with their claws for shells, etc. on the surface.

The late rain has caused a torrent down Dhurrah Bader, and the fields and low grounds about Choke have been inundated; about these spots, birds have collected in numbers, the common crow taking advantage of the circumstance had turned as it were, kingfisher, swooping about like the kite. There were two species of Laridæ, neither of which I had seen before, several small Tringæ, the very long red shanked bird, Hematopus? the metallic Tantalus, common, jack-snipe, and hosts of Budytes, which were busily employed flying and flitting about after insects. Edolius occurs at Kooner as well as here. The number of birds is small certainly, although the trees, etc. are now in full leaf: no new birds seem to have come in, except the dove, and Edolius; neither Hæmatornis nor Brachypus yet observed, one or two fresh species of Alaudina, and stonechats have made their appearance. It is curious that the larks do not remain above a few days, none are to be seen now, that the crops are barely a foot high.

The female Monaul is going on well, though obliged to be crammed, for though it takes water voluntarily it will not take food. It is a very domestic bird, and fond of notice, its voice on such occasions is pleasing, on some others very harsh and hawk or eagle-like. Its manners are curious, depressing its tail, and arching its neck, and pecking at imaginary objects in a curious way. From the expressive manner in which it looks up at sunset on surrounding objects, especially trees, it is obviously accustomed to roost.

April 1st.—Pushut Fort.

4th.—Weather unsettled: a slight rumbling sound of an earthquake was felt yesterday evening, the atmosphere at the time being very close: this was succeeded by a squall. Strong winds are prevalent, generally easterly: clear sunshine is evidently of rare continuance at Pushut: little snow remains except towards Bharawul.

I was much struck this morning with the entire disappearance of a green mantle of Confervoid scum from the surface of a foul pool close to my quarters. Yesterday the pool was quite green, now there is no green, nor any traces of the scum except such portion as was not in the water but round the margins.

6th.—Proceeded to Chugur-Serai, which place was reached after marching 3 h. 10 m. at three miles an hour. Ocharrye one of the peaks near this is deep in snow; it is much higher than Speencas. The season here is now nearly as forward as it is at Kooner, although on my last visit sixteen days ago, it was fifteen days behind, but the narrowness of the valley must increase the heat much.

Great delay occurred in crossing the Pushut river, which is much swollen from the heavy rain on the 4th. Thunder and hailstone common, clear days decidedly rare in the spring of these parts.

Edolius occurs here, another stonechat has come in.

7th.—Proceeded to Otipore, which took 8 h. 9 m. to perform the journey; very unsettled weather. Yesterday several thunderstorms, and heavy rain.

10th.—Clearing up, went to Bharawul; and returned on the 12th. I was much disappointed at the paucity of forms, for I did not get ten species, not met with before. The flora of the fir woods amounts to almost nothing, Colchicum straggles up now and then, this and a grass or Carex, a Caprifoliaceous shrub, and Cotoneaster of Tazeen, and Fragaria are the only forms. The oak as it gets to higher altitudes assumes a different form, probably it is a different species, for the leaves are much less coriaceous, and are not glaucous underneath, otherwise there is little difference between it and the common Baloot, the chief plants found occurred in the clearings, which surround Bharawul to some extent. Alliaria is very common; also Tulipa. In this variety the dehiscence of the anthers continues until, from a single simple pore, a line reaching nearly the whole length of the anther is formed: a very pretty and sweet smelling Anemone common, Viola, Rumex, Thalictrum a rather fine species, Hedera, Rubia cordifolia, Valeriana, Corydalis, Fragaria, Thlaspidea, Sambucus, Ebulus adonis, Berberis, Equisetum, Clematis, Urtica urens, were noticed, either in cultivation or on the edge of the clearings. Poor as the flora is, I see no chance of its promising much variety, for I observe few other plants showing themselves: several ferns were met with in moist places, and under rocks, two Asplenia, one undetermined; Aspidioides very common in some places, but of last year.

The soil is deepish and good, when wet it is subtenacious. The *Nukhtur* is a large tree, seventy to eighty feet high; one of an average size measured fourteen feet in girth, four feet from the base. The slopes of the mountain are steep, and the ravines very rocky: on the ridges between these, the ground is covered with soil. Colchicum observed as high as 7,500 feet. I returned another way, keeping along the large ravine that drains the mountain to the north, and which falls into the Otipore river, below Shinegam.

Buddlea was noticed at 5,800 feet, Hyacinthus throughout from this to Bharawul, *Nurgiss* 5,800, feet Impatiens the same as the species below 5,000, Myrsinea ditto, Fraxinus is very common about 4,000 feet, it is very easily mistaken for the Xanthoxylon, which appears common over most parts of Khorassan. The range of the Cytisus, which is a beautiful sweet smelling shrub, is extensive, it may be included here between 3,000 and 7,000 feet: associated with it between 4,000 to 4,500 feet is a Caragana, and about this occurs a fine Salveoideo-Dracocephalum.

The limit of the Baloot may be taken at 4,000 feet, but in sheltered ravines it descends lower.

Euonymus *Moamunna,* Periplocea, scarcely extend above 4,000 feet, neither do the spirescent Astragali, these are succeeded by two or three espinous species, one the same as the Astragalus stipulis magnis of the river towards Pironi. Amygdalus ranges between 3,500 and 7,000 feet, the pretty Cerasus does not extend above 4,000 feet. There appears to be another Amygdalus above.

The chief vegetation of the mountain below 6,000 feet appears to be a tufted coarse Andropogoneous grass, and in such situations as this occupies, little soil is to be found; the Baloot, and Zaitoon, are confined to sheltered places. Above they occur indiscriminately on all faces, but Zaitoon is rare at such elevations; few birds were observed, the most common about Bharawul are an Emberizoid and a Certhia? Muscicapa flammea was seen at 7,000 feet in pine forests with several Sittæ: in these forests and about Bharawul, only one Garrulus was heard, and few woodpigeons were seen. The Picus is still common, Myophorus now extends up to Bharawul. Parus cæruleus still continues. Another female Nemorrhædus is brought in with young: the breeding time probably takes place two months later. The Merula before found below, now occurs in flocks about Bharawul.

According to the natives there is only about twenty days difference in the seasons of cutting wheat and barley; this is probably not true, yet it is borne out by the Tulip, Cytisus and Hyacinth.

The village has been founded five years since, and contains 180 souls. The burial ground contains sixteen graves, which will give the annual percentage of mortality. At Otipore the mortality is said to be great. Whence do these people get their curious grey eyes, and light hair?

Daphne extends to Bharawul.

14th.—The kingcrow is now in here, also Columba, and Lanius; this last has an unceasing jarring chirp, it has however considerable powers of voice.

Sitta feeds on seeds as well as on insects, but the structure of its stomach is insectivorous.

The female Monaul died yesterday. I heard some of these birds in the pine forests of Bharawul, their voice being very loud and grating; the female was a good tempered bird, capable of attachment, when caressed its notes were pleasing.

15th.—The Hoopoe seen; another fish brought in to-day, the usual mountainous form, but with a very rough nose.

The Edolius is here the earliest and the latest daily bird. I observed several to-day on a tree making a great noise with their harsh chirp, at each chirp the tail was for the instant jerked out like a fan.

17th.—A single parrot seen flying overhead.

19th.—What is the bodily strength of man to that of insects! I have just been watching an ant dragging the body of a hornet, many times larger than itself, up a door with the greatest ease; so much so, that after dragging it up three feet, it came down to alter its position, carrying it up a second time by its wing: the ant was of a large species.

23rd.—Pastor came in to-day, an elegant bird, eyes nearly white, tinged with grey, legs and beak yellow, base of gape leaden-blue, junction of yellow and blue parts greenish!

26th.—Mango bird first seen to-day, another dove came in about the 23rd. Quail coming in, Pastor roseus.

Every plant from the Kafir hills convinces me that they are Himalayan in their features, and that about this the transition between the American and genuine European forms takes place. Thus I have seen Asperula, two and three European looking Ranunculi.

Cratœgus, etc. in addition to the other forms, before alluded to.

There is a rather fine *sissoo* near Sheargar, it is curious that it is later in coming into leaf than any other tree. Does this indicate its being of a more tropical nature than the others? on the contrary, the Bukkeim is now in flower, also Citrus.

The Affghans are fond of Amaryllideæ, *Gratool, Goolab,* and Lonicera, in the season of the two former, every one met has a bunch placed over each ear.

Observed to-day a curious monstrosity of the ovula of the Lonicera of this place, from which it is evident, that the ovule represents a bud; the funicle the *stalk;* the teguments convolute leaves, and the nucleus the punctum of growth.

Every variation was observed, generally the more leafy the outer tegument the greater was the degree of straightness of the funicle, and the abortion of the nucleus.

29th.—To Chugur-Serai.

June 5th.—Arrived at Cabul.

The whole country betweeen Khuggur and Koord Cabul, even including the high ground of this, or Huft-Kotul, presents the same formation, but from Khuggur it rises gradually, and beyond Gundamuck loses all characters of tabularity, it consists of sand, overlying which is a bed of blocks or often of boulders; in this sand, which is here and there easily pulverised, (in other places it is pressed as it were into slabs of no great thickness;) layers or beds of conglomerate frequently occur, either regularly or irregularly; in one case two conglomerated beds approached at an angle and then united.

The framework or base of the country is generally limestone, sometimes slate which presents every variety of distortion, the strata being often vertical and wavy, no dykes were observed. The older rocks are generally completely covered by sand and shingle, or stones; but as we approach the boundaries of the vallies, they protrude into ridges, often of considerable size and height. The vallies however are not entirely bounded by these to the west, for as I have said, the plain of Koord Cabul is reached by crossing undulations of this same formation. From Khuggur to Gundamuck, about five stony steppes are crossed, each rising in height above the last, and each separated by deep ravines, with one or both banks generally precipitous, affording exit to streamlets from the Sofaid-Koh. It is curious that the streamlets, and streams about Gundamuck have not worn themselves half as deep channels as those about Khuggur, although no appreciable difference is apparent in the strata.

The surface is often rendered rugged in places by the occurrence of loose slabs, which give the appearance of stratification to the rocks.

It appears to me that the whole of the extreme eastern Khorassan originally was a bed of stones or boulders, overlying a formation of pure sand, and that its irregular surface is due to the subsequent upheavement of the foundation ridges. The good soil is in such case necessarily confined to the immediate neighbourhood of the streams, etc. descending from those ridges.

The following is a section exposed on the north boundary of the valley, not far from Jugdulluck:—

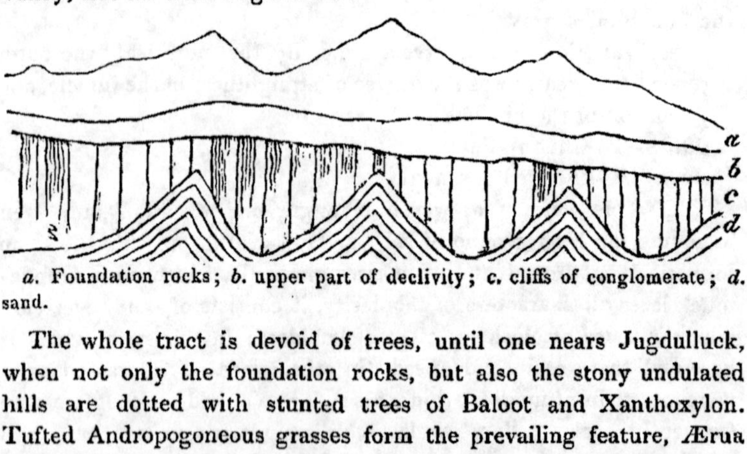

a. Foundation rocks; *b.* upper part of declivity; *c.* cliffs of conglomerate; *d.* sand.

The whole tract is devoid of trees, until one nears Jugdulluck, when not only the foundation rocks, but also the stony undulated hills are dotted with stunted trees of Baloot and Xanthoxylon. Tufted Andropogoneous grasses form the prevailing feature, Ærua also is common along the streams: and wherever the ground retains moisture, Typha latifolia abounds with the usual frequenters of watery spots. The road to Gundamuck, especially the ascent of the two last steppes, is infamous; but the regular Jallalabad road is good, having only one descent to Neemla, and an easy ascent from that place, and thence it is over a gentle declivity to Futtehabad.

The spurs from the Sofaid-Koh are very numerous, and the ravines they form show the great quantity of water derived from this ridge, their direction is N. 45, E. The direction of the streams after emerging from the lower ridges continues about the same.

The Cabul and Soorkhab rivers debouche at a much greater angle. Their direction being 95, E. The waters of both are turbid, but those of the latter are reddish.

Throughout the valley of Jallalabad cultivation extends alone along the streams, many of which are entirely consumed by agricultural processes; in no place does it bear any proportion to the uncultivated portion, which is invariably densely strewed with stones, the smaller of which are generally water-worn; the larger, masses of angular rock.

White mulberries ripen in perfection at Gundamuck in the early part of July. There is more cultivation about Khuggur occurring in a continuous and broadish tract, than in almost any other place.

I observed a curious tendency to anastomosis, or self-grafting in the roots of Morus: this in its young state often has pinnatifid artacarpoid leaves. Query, is this a sign of the greater development of Morus? or is it in any way analogous to that progressive development existing during the growth of every animated being?

At Gundamuck observed Oriolus; it differs in plumage and voice from the Indian Mango bird, which is a far more beautiful bird, with only one note: Edolius also seen.

Pastor and the other common birds. Merops was seen soaring over stones, and stooping at insects; in such situations it remains long on the wing; it does not appear to perch on any thing but withered branches.

Composita Senecionoides occurs about Soorkhab, Reaumuria occurs half-way between it and Gundamuck. Capparis continues to Soorkhab. Statices common, also Campanula; and about Jugdulluck a striking Boragineous plant, Boraginiæ sp., and on the sandy pass above Barkhab, a Salvia is found in profusion, one of the commonest grasses is Poa *cynosuroides?*

The stem of Hippuris is worth examination, inasmuch as it consists of a central easily separable axis, and a vertical system of great thickness, highly cellular, so that judging *a priori*, as these cells (which are compound) occupy the whole space between the ligneous system and the cutis, no longitudinal vessels can exist in that part which represents the bark.

15*th*.—Cabul. Glycyrrhiza thermopsoides frequently presents on the non-flowering stems, a pod-like transformation of the uppermost leaves.

In Centaurea *cyanea*, the disposition of the limb of the ray is such that the incomplete part or the fissure is outside. This is exactly opposite to the disposition of the same part in true Ligulatæ.

Judging from Centaurea, the smaller lip of the bilabiate species of Compositæ ought to be situated outside.

Erythræoides, Glauca floribus albidis occurs on the *Chummums*.

16*th*.—Regaled with a library: "Calumny and detraction," says Boerhaave, "are sparks, which if you do not blow them, will go out of themselves."—*Murphy's Johnston*, Vol. IX. p. 34.

In Johnston's Life of Drake, p. 99 to 100, are some admirable remarks on those minds, that disapprove of every strikingly novel scheme, and from which a good motto might be chosen, should any national system be proposed in Botany.

What were Sir Thomas Browne's five sorts of vegetables, and what were his remarks on the form of plants and laws of vegetation? —*See Johnston's Works*, Vol. IX. p. 296.

CHAPTER XXI.

From Cabul to Kohi-Baba.

July 17th.—Proceeded from Cabul to Shah Bagh; cloudy weather, occasionally a very slight shower during the last few days, depending probably on the Punjab rains. To-day, observed a small green caterpillar, climbing up a fine thread, like a spider's web, which hung from the fly of the tent; its motions were precisely those of climbing, the thread over which it had passed was accumulated between its third pairs of legs; it did not use its mouth.

I did not ascertain whether the thread was its own production or not; if it was, it must have come out of its tail.

24th.—The fish in the Cabul river here are, a Loach, an Oreinus, and a Barbel; none of these grow to any size, as there is but little water left in the river in consequence of the drain for extensive cultivation on both the east and west sides of the city.

Small specimens of these fish, especially the Loach and Oreinus, are found in the canals or larger watercuts, in which the current is slow and regular. It is curious that in the canal near the Shah Bagh, which has been lately turned off above the Cantonment, all the specimens of the Loach left in the pools of water were dead, while the Oreinus did not appear to have suffered.

This Loach is a Cobitis propria, it has the usual form of that genus, the spots are disposed irregularly, rarely becoming banded. The shape of the head is curious, the forehead being prominent, this gives the mouth an appearance of unusual depression.*

The country both on the east and west sides of Cabul may have been formerly a lake. Such indeed would seem to have been the origin of all the valleys in which there is an expanse of tillable ground, and not mere strips confined to the banks of the draining streams.

The eastern valley is indeed partly occupied by the large sheet of water to the north, and the west is very marshy. The eastern one is interspersed with low detached ranges of hills.

The birds are a magpie, a dove, Oriolus, Pastor roseus, Pastor alter, sparrow, water-wagtail, Hirundo, Hoopoe, Lanius, Sylvia sp., water-

* Nearly allied to *Cobitis chlorosoma*, As. Res. Vol. xix, pl. 52, f. 3.

hen, wild ducks on the lake, and Merops; almost all these as at Khujgal, but no *minas*, or Edolia.

At Urghundy occurs Potentilla quinquifolia, repens radicans pubescens, stipulis oblongis.

28*th*.—Halted at Koti-Ashruf. The most common plants on the Khak-i-Sofaid pass are two or three of the small pulvinate Statices, Senecionoides glaucescens. The yellow Asphodelus is very common, and I also saw A. mesembryanthemifolia. At the foot of the pass, I saw Scabiosa, which also occurred on the summit.

First march on the Cabul side of Ghuznee. Whole tracts blue with the Labiata Plectranthoides; at Urghundy, along a watercut, are planted several willows of the common large-leaved kind, the bark of these on all the older parts is cracked longitudinally, and the trunk has the appearance of being twisted, which I have no doubt is the natural state, the spire is from left to right. The prevailing winds are easterly.

Bean cultivation is very common in the valley of the Cabul river to the west beyond the Khak-i-Sofaid pass; I suspect it requires a greater altitude than most of the other cultivated plants of Affghanistan, it abounds in the high ground about Shaikhabad.

29*th*.—Proceeded in the morning from Julraize to Sir-i-Chushme. The fish of the place are the same, the Silurus being common. The two sorts of Oreinus vary much in the length of the intestinal canal,—the yellowish and large one having it five times: the small and less yellowish, three and a half lengths of the body. Both these species come close to Barbus, showing that the spinosity of the dorsal fin is a more valuable character than that of the form of the mouth.

The cartilaginous disc of Oreinus is a reflection outwards of the osseo-cartilaginous part of the mouth, the fleshy part alone is the lips. Oriolus, Upupa, and Percnopterus, continue with Columba. Grapes and apricots *khar see*, and the common ones reach as far as this, but are very inferior to those of Cabul; rice cultivated here and there. The chief trees are Populus lombardensis, Salix magnifolia, and S. pendula, Hippophae.

At Koti-Ashruf Salix angustissima is found, and on it Cuscuta gigantea; on to-day's march Hippophae, but this is found also at Maidan: Merops was heard at Koti-Ashruf. In the spring of Sir-i-Chushme, a Typhoid plant occurs in profusion, Veronicæ 2, alta et repens rotundifolia, Nasturtium aquatica, Scrophularia of Julraize, Juncus, Triglochin, and Plantago of the green sward, everywhere between 6,000 and 11,000 feet.

Trees end at the foot of Oonnye.

30*th.*—Girdun Dewar. Salvia swarms up the ascent and on the descent, but less so than before, and on the Yonutt platform it is almost absent; Cnicus also in profusion both up and down, and on the platform Festuca triticoides begins about half-way up; Statice are common over the whole pass. Caragana in the grassy swardy ravines. On the highest point Astragalus arbuscula, the fields studded with yellow buttons of tansy, and white flowers of Stellaria; Arabidea glauca siliculosa, also common; this is rare on the west side of Hindoo-koosh, as is also Stellaria. Tansy continues in some places.

31*st.*—To Kurzar. Proceeded up the Siah-Sung; along the river, green sward with patches of Caragana, Campanula, and Geraniums occurred in profusion in some places. Salvia not uncommon; at the first part, or perhaps for three miles from camp a large Hingoid is common, smaller and whiter than the species so common on the lower hills, and which is the large-leaved species of Quettah and the Kojhuk pass. Potamogeton cylindrifolia common; Senicionoides.

On the stony part, or beyond Siah-Sung, when one leaves the bed of the river, Astragali two or three species, Salvia, and Blitum. Two sorts of fish are found in the river, and perhaps a third in the black hammer-headed Silurus.* Of the two caught, one is an Oreinus, but passing close into Barbus. Beneath the glandular line, white, above fuscous-brownish, with irregular black spots, fins fusco-reddish.

The other is a loach, Cobitis propria, shape shark-like, colour yellowish-brown, almost tawny, sides irregularly spotted with brownish-black spots, arranged on the back in broad irregular, generally complete bands. Head not banded, fins tawny, with oblong black spots, eyes prominent, irides reddish-orange: this is a very abundant species.

Poplar trees, (P. lombardensis): these from being planted close, grow together, the union generally taking place near the base. I have not seen a section of the wood.

August 2*nd.*—Kaloo. So far as I can judge, the flora of this side of the pass does not differ, but in a few unimportant instances from that of the Kurzar side. The summit however has a much colder climate, probably from being exposed on the Kurzar side to an

* This is an undescribed species if not an undescribed genus, and was by some mischance lost from the collections; it may properly, when described, receive the name of the author, who was the first to notice so remarkable a form.

extremely cold and piercing wind from the Kohi-Baba range. Cnici 2, and Festuca triticoides are the most common plants, with Arenaria fruticosa, Composita No. 152, Asphodelus of Erak now nearly passed flower, and some Astragali. But on this side, Cnici cease almost entirely, although they re-appear lower down, but only partially, and the top of the pass is covered with the Statice of Kurzar, and Astragali, among which, that with the flat pod, winged on the dorsal suture, is the most common. Lower down the same, or similar features continue, and the only plants limited to this side are a curious Astragalus, Crotalarioid, Polygonum fruticosa, microphyllum, and spinosum, a Boraginea like that of Jugdulluck, but much smaller and decumbent, a Papaveraceæ, petalis Papaveris Rhœadis, with a siliquose fruit, and Clematis erecta: willow trees (the broad leaved species) occur here, a large Agrostic grass, Ribes and Symphorema of Erak.

The Affghans appear to cut every plant almost of any size for winter fodder, even thistles, docks, etc. The purple Lactucoid of Cabul re-appears, and the curious flat fruit calyxed Boraginea of Shawl both in abundance. The crops here are not more forward than those at Kurzar; the fields are *crowded* with Stellaria, but there is much less Tanacetum; Geraniums occur in profusion.

Silene fimbriata, is a night flower, withering by 9 A. M.

I found no snow up the left Hajeeguk ravine, and the effect was marked, namely, that none of the alpine plants are so abundant about it as last season, when they were in flower, or had passed.

There is on the hills about this ravine, a large burrowing animal, probably a marmot; it is of a dark colour with tawny rump: when on the alert it sits on its rump, or rather perhaps raised on the hind legs, and has the voice of an ordinary Rodentia.

I heard several of these, but saw only one.

Rich botanising is to be had on the swampy ground at the mouth of the right ravine. Pediculares 2, Silenaceæ 3 or 4, Veroniceæ 2, Orchis 1, Ranunculi 2, Junci 2, Carices several, Swertiæ 2, one the larger Solidago, Geranium, Gramineæ several, Parnassia of Erak, Campanula, Ruta odora, etc.

3rd.—To Topehee. The vegetation of Kaloo is far less varied than that of Hajeeguk, for it presents no such swampy ravines at such elevations.

The plants of the hills around Kaloo villages continue half-way up, on the road over the ravine Corvisartia is plentiful, with a Labiata,

Calyce Royleæ, in profusion; this and Cnici form the chief vegetation; Papaveraceæ also continue.

Up the 1st ascent Hingoid tenuifolia, Ephedra stricta, Ribes commence, Ephedra continuing throughout wherever the bare rocks project through the loose soil; one-third way up, Statice long and short-peduncled commence with an Astragalus. The bulk of the vegetation is an Artemisia; Royleoid and Chenopodium villosum continue, and do so for half-way up.

At the black rock half-way up, Dianthus, Astragalus, Crotalarioid, Rosæ sp., Statice pulvinata, are common, this last and Artemisia are the chief features: Scutellaria, Stellaria dichotoma, Umbellifera of Yonutt, Corvisartia, wild Gramineæ of Yonutt, Arenaria fruticosa, Festuca triticoides continues. Borago of upper Kaloo, and the Glauci of Kaloo occur. Astragali 2 or 3 sp., Silene sp., but the chief vegetation is Artemisia.

On the summit, Corvisartia, Boragineæ, Gramineæ, several; a straggling Plectranthus cœruleus, Arenaria fruticosa, Allium rubrum, Cnici 2, the yellow Erigeronoid of Hajeeguk summit, occur on the descent just below the ridge, and on this side the Statice pulvinata is in profusion, and of large size. Large marmot, with teeth like those of a rat.

4th.—Proceeded to Bamean. At Topehee was found a curious succulent Hypericum, it is odd that the leaves, etc. of these succulent saline plants are cold; strikingly so. Connected with this low temperature, is the fact, that if shut up in a box with other plants, and water thrown in, that even though they be at the top, they cause the deposit of all the water that passes up in the shape of vapour, while the ordinary plants remain quite dry! A wonderful provision of nature adapting them the more to extremely dry stations. About Topehee, Cichorium is common; Salvia of Oonnye, Geranium, Artemisia exaltata of Sir-i-Chushme, and Pulmonaria, so common everywhere, occur; Glaucum swarms in saline marshy places. Triglochin is also found, also Ranunculus stoloniferæ trilobata of Kaloo, Hippuris. The flat-calyxed Boraginea, Melilotus officinalis, also found; Potamogeton cylindrifolia, Centaurea lutea.

There also occurs along the barren slopes of the hills a glaucus shrub, much like that between Chunni and Dund-i-Goolai, decumbens, subspinos: glauco alb. fruct. baccato drupaceis, oblongis, purpuris, basi calyce parvo, 5-fido, stylo brevi apiculatis, putamina osseo-crasso oblongo ovato, Sem. immatur.

8th.—Bamean. The fish, so far as I have caught any, seem to be one trout, and two barbels. Of 5 species, one of these takes the worm greedily, the length of the intestines varied in every instance, and of three the relative lengths of body and canal were as follows:—

Inches.	Canal.		
Body 6	Times longer than the body.	$2\frac{1}{8}$	Of three since captured and about 8 inches long, all nearly the same size, the length of the canal was three times longer than the body.
,, 7		$2\frac{1}{2}$	
,, $10\frac{1}{2}$		$3\frac{1}{2}$	

The intestines as usual taper almost gradually from the stomach and œsophagus, and are gorged with greenish pulp.

This is worth following up. It is scarcely credible, but that the species are really different; or if not, the variety in the length will considerably diminish the value of the length of canal as a principle of arrangement.*

The glaucous long-peduncled, large-flowered Statice is limited to the east side of Kaloo. On this side another species occupies similar elevations, viz., 9,500 to 10,500 feet; it is a good deal like the one met with towards Ghuzni. These species are less alpine than the short-pedunculed species with large flowers, which continues all over Kaloo, being in great perfection on the west side, near the summit. Another short-peduncled species appears on the descent, close to upper Topehee. Towards this Royleoid occurs but sparingly, and the first change takes place in the abundance of Salicornia or Kochia. Also about this, Peganum and Salvia reoccur, both kinds not being uncommon about Bamean.

Lactuca dislocata occurs throughout.

The vegetation of Bamean is that of Topehee, but the small flowered Tamarisk is scarce—Potentilla anserina is common, Hyoscyamus spinosus of Kaloo occurs.

The Bamean river divides the Kohi-Baba from the Hindoo-koosh, but both are obviously of the same system, i. e. they divide the ranges to the north. To the east their offsets are divided by the Kaloo river. The direction of the Hindoo-koosh and that of the Kohi-Baba, is about 115 west. The space to the west consists of a low, rather flat plateau, (as it appears from the top of Kaloo,) this flat belongs to the Kohi-Baba range; the offsets of the Hindoo-

* It is chiefly important as a generic, not as a specific character, see page 500.

koosh to the east and north are ordinarily shaped. All the hills on the north side of the valley disintegrate on their south faces, forming cliffs of partial extent.

13*th*.—Proceeded to Akrobat, ascending the Bamean river, and then diverging up a *kotul* or acclivity of considerable height, but gradual ascent. Then descending at once steeply to Akrobat, which is about 9,500 feet above the sea. Along the river, Rosa, Hippophae, and Salix occur, the two former being abundant. Scarcely any change in vegetation occurs: an Ephedra, very common up the *kotul* and abundantly in fruit. The hills are very barren, and nothing remarkable is observable about Syghan. Apricot constitutes the only fruit tree. Salix, Populus, and Sinjit occur.

All the valleys are narrow, and the hills very barren, the chief vegetation being Salsolaceæ. The vegetation of the valleys is the same as that of Bamean; on the north of Akrobat two Statice occur, one with spathulate leaves scapigerous, the other a tall straggling plant.

22*nd*.—Erak. The vegetation of Kurzar consists of Hypericum, Salsolaceæ, Carduacea, and Hyoscyamus spinosus, but Salsolaceæ occur in profusion and several species.

Hypericum enjoys to perfection, the faculty of condensing water on its leaves, much more so than Salsolaceæ; it presents an obvious affinity to Rutaceæ, capsula radiata 5-valvis, loculicida: valvis linea centrali notatis, septis solutis imo apice exceptis. Seminibus basi locul. affixis, apice villosis; the tobacco is different from the Nicot. tobaccum, cor. virida tubo calyce, duplo longiore lamina brevi plicato: apricots in sheltered places.

24*th*.—Kurzar. The Erak *kotul* is thickly covered with Festuca triticoides, two Carduaceæ, Salvia, Artemisiæ, and Statices on the south side. On the north Statices, Onosma, and Carduaceæ are most common, and the vegetation is scantier. Ribes is common up the Erak ravine; with it, Rosa and Symphorema are the chief shrubs. Ephedra ceases about 10,000 feet. A snake found of general grey colour, with black-brown marking.

26*th*.—Ascended Kohi-Baba from upper Kaloo, the ascent occupied about five hours, the ridge was surmounted but no view of Baissoat was obtained, except that the crest surmounted, as well as the still loftier culminating one belong to ridges running 30° north from a main ridge, the passes of which, although apparently the same height as the peak surmounted, are much more heavily covered with snow. These passes do not appear very difficult.

At 2 P. M. set up the barometer on the ridge, the mercury stood 17.354. Therm. in cistern, 79.5. Detached Therm. in sun 85°—on the ground 105°.

September 2nd.—At 2½ P. M. the barometer stood 17.356.

Assuming this to give about 15,000 feet, none of the peaks will be found to be higher than 16,500. The culminating point was close by, and did not appear more than 1,000 feet above me. The different ridges are separated by deep spaces in which snow lies to a considerable extent.

Having descended a considerable way I again set up the barometer. Time 4-45 P. M.

The mercury stood at 18.889.

Therm. in the Cistern.............. 63°
Ditto in the air.................... 68°

The vegetation continues unaltered, the same as that of Kaloo kotul.

Carduaceæ, Astragali, Nardoid, Bromoid, Hordeoid pubescens, and Statices. And up to this, which may be assumed as 13,500 feet, the hills present the same features, rounded with a good deal of soil, and large granitic masses.

But above this the disintegration of the ridge has reached a great extent; for 1,500 to 2,000 feet the ascent is steep, passing over a profusion of blocks and slabs of granite, generally externally of a dark brown colour; here and there there is some coarse granular soil, and towards the second station, say at an altitude of 14,000 feet, a marshy spot occurred, crowded with Primula, together with Arenaria, Fumaria of Erak, Ranunculus of Hajeeguk, Carex, etc. From within 1,000 feet of the summit the ascent was easier, over ground composed entirely of small angular bits of granite, which rock protrudes to the north, forming the south wall of a huge amphitheatre, heavily snowed in places.

This granite varies much; being below a coarse quartzose grey rock, above a very compact brown rock, except perhaps in its lowest outcrop, where it has a slaty structure.

The second station may be assumed as the lowest limit of the inferior snow line, but this so much depends on casual circumstances that even many places at 15,000 feet are uncovered by snow, which as might be expected is always heaviest in the higher valleys which are least exposed to the sun's rays. The surface of the snow in many places was picturesque, being in the shape of crowded pinnacled ridges, the interstices from 4 to 5 feet deep, holding water or ice. I saw from the summit a flock of the large grouse, and at 14,000 feet, a large hare.

The peak surmounted is the lowest, and the nearest to Upper Kaloo. The granite on the west side formed a precipitous cliff of 200 to 300 feet deep.

The vegetation of the slope with small fragments, say between 14 to 15,000 feet was very scanty, a Cheiranthus, Polygonum scariosum, Papaveraceæ, Phloxoides and Statice, being the only plants; and perhaps this may be assumed as having no particular plant, all those enumerated being found below.

The vegetation of the steep rugged portion, which contained many patches of snow and better soil, was more varied; in the upper parts of this a Carex, two or three Graminæ, Cheiranthus, Plectranthus, Sedoides, Arenaria, Potentilla, Primula, Draboides and Brassicacea occurred. A Tanacetoid was perhaps the most common.

The most alpine forms of these were Carex, Holcoides, Sedoides, Statice densissima, and Papaveracea; but of these Papaveracea, Phloxoid, Statice densissima, Cheiranthus, and Polygonum are alone found above. Here again the effect of the proximity of a bed of snow in retarding vegetation was most evident. Phloxoides elsewhere partly in flower, being found in full flower near one of the beds of snow.

It is curious that no green spots are found above, all the water passing down under the soil, the swardy ravines scarcely extend beyond an elevation of 1,500 feet above the camp on Upper Kaloo.

The limit of the grey shrubby Salix may be taken as 1,000 feet above that, the other plants are precisely the same as those of other swards; Abelia extends higher than Salix.

The limit of crops is about the same, the issue of the water obviously being in relation to the extent of cultivation by irrigation. The associated plants present no change.

23rd.—Cabul. Curious transformation in Carthamus was observed, either affecting the involucrum alone, when those branches that would have become flowers become clavate, covered with very dense aristate leaves, or affecting the florets which become more or less converted in the branches. In these the involucre is little altered, and the receptacle is attacked by larva. In certain of these the florets are submitted to very curious metamorphoses, each envelope remaining, but quite green, the stamina being little changed, the pistillum changed into a leaf-bearing branch, the stigmata, etc. into two leaves.

This is chiefly remarkable because of the general tardiness of change in the stamina, since it shows that the binary formation of the pistillum is a primary effect: it may be asked, if the number should be 5, why has it not reverted to its original or typical state? The calyx is not reducible to 5. The permanency of the character of aggregate flowers is here shown, as well as in Echinops, so that it is scarcely probable we shall ever meet a compositious flower solitary in the axil of an ordinary leaf.

To be examined hereafter in detail.

If wood is a descending formation, produced by leaves, how are woody tendrils to be accounted for. In the vine the ancient tendrils are perfectly woody, although this may not be true wood, yet it is truly fibrous, and I ask, from what is it formed?

The growth of young shoots is at once a proof that the whole system may be formed from ascending growth, for in many we find woody fibre complete, though not indurated, and all the leaves from which wood is said to be formed are only in a rudimentary state.

October 2nd.—Seh-Baba. Spiræa belloides, commonish on limestone rocks in the ravine near the road which leads from Tazeen valley to Khubur-i-Jubbur. This limestone is in thin strata; the strata are subdivided by quartzose veins, they occur generally at a dip of from 15 to 20 degrees, but are occasionally quite vertical or highly wavey, presenting evidence of concentrated force upwards. The outcrop wears an uniform aspect, and occurs to the north of the ravine. The south here and there presents sheets of rock, the overlying strata having slipped off. The strike of the strata is north and south.

Coal is said by Hatchet to be formed chiefly from the resinous principles of plants,—this would account for its appearance when burnt, which is the same as that of burnt bitumen. But resinous principles are, even when they exist, of partial extent only in plants. In good coal the whole of the vegetable substance seems to be transformed, a supposition barely compatible with Hatchet's idea.

To study this, extensive examination of coal in all degrees of formation would be necessary, beginning with the wood so curiously changed by the Brahmapootra, i. e. brown coal occurring in its sand banks, and which has a very peculiar and disagreeable odour when burning. It would also be necessary to examine how far the coal-plants exhibit vegetable structure, are they mere impressions or are they the plants themselves changed? To what extent do these agree with coal? What particular plants and what parts of these appear to have formed coal? Its fibrous structure would hint at formation from the woody system, and it is not incompatible with the *deliquescence* of a thick layer of drift.

The plants of coal fields having been drifted, can only give us an idea of the vegetation along the natural drains of the then country, such may by no means have had *one universal character*.

The plants of the open surface of modern tropical countries being generally different from those along the beds of streams, in which situations now-a-days Equiseteæ, Lycopods and Filicis are chiefly found. Coal being drift, it follows that the plants of the coal fields can give us no information on the distribution of vegetables in those days; to gain information on this, the fossils should be in their original situation. And there again an obstacle may exist in our not being able to ascertain the height or level of that situation.

If the plants of coal fields are found to be converted into coal, then the only difference between coal shale, and coal will consist in the very small proportion of vegetable matter in the former.

The small number of coal plants, i. e. the small number of species, at once points to the supposition that fossil plants are confined to those of the most indestructible nature: here again is another sign of this in the preponderance of Ferns, which Lindley finds to be the most permanent.

Hence the preponderance of Ferns, is by no means explainable by their greatest simplicity of form, and consequent priority of formation.

CHAPTER XXII.

From Peshawur to Lahore.

October 14*th.*—Peshawur.—Cucurbitaceæ. The petals of cucurbita were observed in one instance united along two of the corollal sinuses to the staminal column, alternating with the smaller stamina ; the processes were produced upwards into petaloid appendages.

17*th.*—Proceeded to Nowshera. As far as Pubbe the road extended chiefly through a cultivated country, thence as far as could be judged at night, over a plain country covered with coarse grass, and here and there (whenever a sufficiently gravelly surface occurred) among the thick of *Bheir*, which is here used for fences ; Mudar, Ærua, Nerioides and Adhatoda occurred ; *Furas* a common tree.

18*th.*—Reached Khairabad. The same kind of country as about Nowshera, stony or sandy, with extensive tracts covered with *Bheir*, Mudar, and Ærua as before, Mimosa common towards Geedur Gulli, and on it also Kureel, which appears for the first time as it was not seen about Jumrood. On to-day's march many grasses are apparent, the pale Saccharoid grass of Jugdulluck common, a species of Cynodon (given to me by Dr. Ritchie at Dhukk) very common, a Pommereullioid, a curious Schœnanthus, a Poa, all are coarse and cover a large tract towards Geedur Gulli : Barleria spinosa appears.

Geedur Gulli is a ravine winding in and out in a curious manner among low hills at the north-west end of what is called the Afredi Spur. Mimosa very common, Kureel, Dodonæa and Edgeworthia, neither very common, but Moarcurra and Euonymus are both rather common. *Mudar* common ; some Andropogons, of which one is the same as that of the Khybur. *Bheir* very common, also a Mimosa like the common *Babool*, but flowers unscented. Chokeys, or police stations are situated along the whole line of road to Peshawur. Adhatoda common at the entrance to Geedur Gulli where the scenery is rather pretty ; Adiantum common on banks near the water ; the hills of Geedur Gulli are rather thickly sprinkled with wood.

The Cabul river is here a large stream, with a moderate confined bed between high banks on which Akora and Khairabad are situated. The view of the Indus from Geedur Gulli presents a desolate look of sand, which extends over a large space visible through a break in the hills to the north. The passage of the Indus through the Attock range seen from the same point is curious; but general remarks on scenery can be of no use, except when they are founded on an intimate acquaintance with the country. The most natural course, i. e. one less impeded by mountains, would seem to be to the east instead of south.

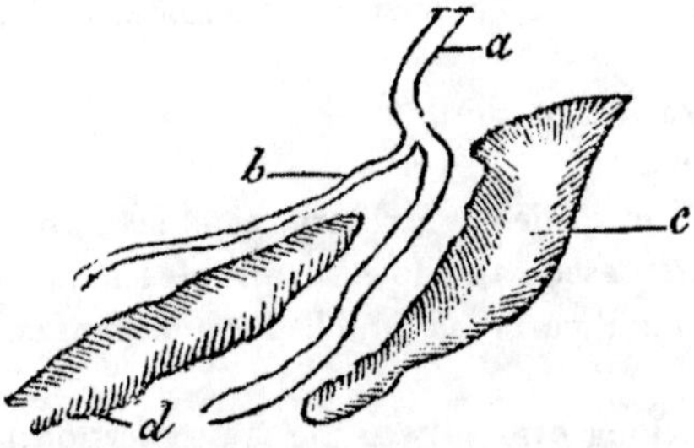

a. Indus.
b. Cabul river.
c. Attock range.
d. Afredi Spur.

Mulberry, Salix angustifolia, or willow, and *Buckein*, were seen at Attock. The scenery is not however bold, but on the contrary very poor compared with the defiles of the Irrawadi. The hills are low, rounded, and present no precipices of striking dimensions. An old fort situated near the junction of the rivers is a handsome looking building, but completely commanded. A large Serai or place for travellers is situated near it to the north. The water of the Indus is muddy, but presents nothing remarkable in temperature. The analogous points between the Indus and Irrawadi consist in defiles and the want of branches for a long way above their mouths. Jackdaws were the first old acquaintances I met with on entering Peshawur; and the common kite, the Affghan one not having the same thrilling cry that the Indian one has; grey partridges are found about Nowshera; as also Kuchaloo or Yams.

19*th*.—Proceeded over the plain to Chuch and Khot-bha, winding along the Attock hill round to the fort, and passing the Serai, and another smaller one in ruins near the plains, thence over level ground to within two miles of Bhowli, where conspicuous trees were observed, otherwise the plain is rather barren, a few *Bheirs* and some Phœnix only occurring about villages on hills. The vegetation is the same. Chuch plain, where not cultivated, is covered with short coarse grasses, Andropogoneæ. Among these a large-leaved Salvia occurs. The forms presented by the vegetation are however very little diversified. Mudar, a small-fruited Kochia, like that of Jallalabad; Bœrhaavia very common.

Cultivation is conducted in *Bheir* fences, and consists of Indian-corn, *Bajra*, and cotton.

From the Attock hills, the Indus is seen much divided by beds of sand, and churs or islands covered with a large purple Saccharum. Peganum continues to Attock and even extends beyond.

Water plants of Chuch, Trapa, Valisneria verticillata, and Nymphæa.

Shumshbad.—This town lies to the left of the road, one mile in the rear of my encampment.

The spines of Barleria are evidently axillary, as is seen in young branches, probably they represent the lower pair of leaves of the lateral branches, the terminal parts of which have a tendency to develope.

The spines of Mimosa belong evidently to the same exertion as the leaf; they are connate at the base, and from the centre of this hardened part, arises the leaf; they may be either the lower pinnæ, or they may be *spurious* stipulæ. The leaves developed within the true ones belong to an ill-developed branch. True stipulæ are leaves with a distinct origin. Spurious stipulæ belong to their leaves, as is evident from their not having a distinct origin.

20th.—Hussun Abdul. Until we came near the Boorhan valley, the road passed over a high, dry, sandy plain, with no cultivation, and no water, then the descent took place through picturesque raviny ground with a few isolated mounds, to a fine clear stream. The remaining part extended either along the cultivation of the Boorhan valley, or through similar raviny ground. Two streams were passed, the last is the Hussun Abdul river.

The vegetation of the high plain continues the same. *Bheir*, Mimosa, *Kureel*, Ærua, Mudar, Andropogoneæ, Pommereullia, Œgilops, Salvia, and Crotalaria aphylla.

Among the ravines and thence to Hussun Abdul, a new feature presents itself in the frequency of a largish Mimosa, probably that of the Khybur pass. This forms prettily wooded scenery, the white thorned Mimosa also occurs, Moacurra none, Euonymus, *Bheir*.

About Boorhan a Ficus becomes very common, Achyranthes, Kochia fructibus parvis, Salvia, Serratuloid of Ali-Baghan and Ichardeh. Paganum common—Adhatoda and Vitex. In scenery the country is pretty, particularly after passing the last river: a dampish spot was passed at Bhowli: a lage Acacia, Melanoxylon and Pteris were found on the river banks. Dodonæa seen on low hills near Bhowli, as also

Adiantum. Started at 5 hours 40 minutes and reached at 11-30; distance at least eighteen miles.

Hussun Abdul, is a pretty place, particularly the broken ground about the sacred stream, and the tank, in which Mahaseers abound; the water beautiful, many trees occur, especially Morus, Salix and Ficus.

Zyziphus is a fine tree here, Phœnix, Khuggur, Bukkein, Ficus, and Cupressus occur.

The jackdaw, *mina*, blue and chesnut kingfisher, a noisy bird. The small kingfisher, black and white kingfisher common: Myophonus, Pomatorrhinus.

21*st*.—The chief cultivation here is *bajra*, and Zea maize. The former produces a second crop from branches; hence it is left standing after the top spike, which is the largest, is picked; vegetation chiefly Indian, very few Affghan forms remaining, those of the hills are Mimosa, Adhatoda, and Euonymus.

The water plants are all decidedly tropical; no Epilobium seen since leaving Peshawur: Eclipta, Cyperaceæ.

Trichodesma, Cannabis.

Fish have few engaging habits, the tame Mahaseers take no notice of any one until food is thrown to them.

Tagetes, *Sud Buruk*, is a curious genus, on account of its simple tubular involucrum, very entire and pappus florets, conduplicate in œstivation, all florets fæminine are ligulate; are the folded up ones representations of the males?

22*nd*.—To Janika Sung, seventeen miles: the country continues much the same. The road passes out of *Hussun Abdul* over a low stony elevation, and enters another valley, the exit from which is through the Maha Gullah: a large Serai is passed about two and a half miles from the Boorgi; in the Gullah near this, is a portion of a formed road. Janika Sung is a small village, about five miles from the Boorgi.

The face of the country is undulated, intersected by ravines, rather thickly covered with the large Mimosa and *Bheir*: the same may be seen in every direction.

Affghan plants have nearly ended, Moacurra and Euonymus alone continuing. At the Maha Gullah a Carissa, and a *Zaitoon*, Ehretioides. This defile is picturesque, the wood prettily contrasted with bits of grassy ground. Adhatoda in abundance.

The Maha Gullah was formerly a notorious place for robbers, but is now quite safe, which says much for the Seikh rule.

There was not much cultivation passed to-day, although most of the surface is fit for it: water is near the surface. The Maha Gullah range is composed of limestone.

The white-spined Mimosa and crooked-spined one change places, the former occupies uncultivated plains, the latter stony, undulated, or hilly ground.

Carissa certainly represents Jasminum.

On the Kaliki Serai plain the chief plant is Mimosa albispina, then *Bheir*—here and there patches of Leguminosa, like the Cytisoides, so common in Affghanistan. In the *Bheir* thickets Schœnanthus is common; Andropogon and Pommereullioid also occur.

In the Hussun Abdul river there is a species of Perilampus approaching to Leuciscus, but with faint bars. In the sacred stream there is a small Cyprinoid, probably a Systomus, with a conspicuous spot on either side near the tail: there is also a small loach.

The Mahaseer in the water is a handsome fish, the edges of the scales being then blackish, as is also the longitudinal line.

It is curious that all plants hitherto found parasitical on roots, have no green leaves; to this, marked exceptions exists in Cuscuta and Cassytha, such true-leaved parasites being found only on the ascending axis; this rule is so permanent, that species of certain genera, such as Burmannia, the bulk of which are not parasitical, have no leaves. The mode of attachment of all parasitical plants is I think the same, otherwise I should suspect the above difference to point to a marked one in the nature of the fluid derived from the stock: thus leafless plants might be supposed to induce no particular change in the fluid they imbibe, while the others might be supposed to elaborate their own from that of the stock.

There is another very remarkable circumstance connected with the most typical leafless parasites, in their very frequent limitation to the genus Cissus, on which perhaps all Rafflesiaceæ and Cynomorieæ are exclusively found.

My chief reason for supposing Sarcocodon to be Monocotyledonous, or rather Endogenous, is the ternary division of its parts, and if my supposition be correct, it tends to establish, if indeed other ample evidence did not exist, the great permanence and consequent value of this numerical character.

And with respect to Sarcocoidalis I shall adopt the same opinion, if I find on enquiry that a binary number, and imperfection of the female as compared with the male, are more characteristic of Endogenous than of Exogenous growth. This same genus I consider in both these characters to allude to some analogy with one or more Acrogenous divisions.

The establishment of the order of Rhizanths, as well as that of Gymnosperms, I consider as a retrograde step in Botanical science. It is totally opposed to all sound principles of classification, and is a proof that, in the nineteenth century, arbitrary characters are still sought for, and when found are obstinately maintained.

Even in the arbitrary character, which is considered as destructive of all their other claims to ordinary vegetable rank, there is no unison whatever, for Rafflesiaceæ have ordinary ovula, while Sarcocoidalis very extraordinary.

The amount of testimony proving their analogy in germination to be with Acrogens, must be very strong before I am convinced that plants with perfect ovula as Rafflesia, etc. germinate from an indeterminate point, the existence of an aperture in the coats, points in the most marked manner to some part representing a radicle. With the exception perhaps of Sarcocoidalis, these plants differ in no respect whatever from other Phænogamous vegetables; we have instances of the same parasitical growth, and instances of the same apparent want of a radicle or homogeneousness of embryo, and in the structure of the parts of the flower there is tolerably absolute general identity.

It may be worthy of remark, as tending to prove the soundness of Mr. Brown's views with regard to the affinity of Rafflesia with Aristolochia, that a certain large and fleshy flowered species of the latter genus has the same putrescent smelling flowers.

In Rhizantheæ, as proposed by Endlicher, we have an assemblage of discordant characters; we have plants associated, differing in the number of their parts; we have some of comparatively simple roots associated with others of decidedly complex organization; we have Rafflesia in which highly complex female parts exist, associated with Sarcocoidalis, in which these are very simple. But besides the objection of combining discrepancies on the strength of one agreement, the establishment of divisions upon such pretexts is objectionable in another point of view; viz., that of making a transition of structure on one point, instead of in several.

We might as well form into one division all the ternarily formed Dicotyledons, and into another all those Monocotyledonous plants with evident distinction between the calyx and corolla.

But in addition to reasons founded on structure, I have this theoretical one, that it is as requisite that Endogens should establish a similar relation with Acrogens; otherwise a gradation exists between the first and third classes, and none between the second and third, between which, gradations ought to be the more frequent.

As Rafflesia approaches Aristolochia, so does Sarcocodon, Taccaceæ.

23rd.—Rawil Pendi. The country continues much the same to within five or six miles of this place, viz. high raviny ground, well covered with Mimosa, *Bheir*, etc.

Thence to Pendi, the country is open, bare, and much cultivated. From high ground near Pendi a considerable tract is visible, consisting of low ridges running nearly due south, interrupted here and there, and apparently quite bare.

24th.—To Manikyala, distance nineteen miles, over an elevated country, with not much cultivation; broken ground occurs here and there, especially near the river Hoomook, now a small stream, the road winding through Mimosa jungle. *Moacurra, Bheir*, Euonymus.

At a place about three miles from Manikyala, are the remains of a Serai now in ruins. From this to Metope, the road extends over an open country capable of cultivation, but neglected. Water in wells is thirty feet perhaps below the surface: the country about Tope very bare of trees.

A curious low chain of sandstone rocks here occurs, and occasionally protrudes in places from below the soil, seldom rising above five feet and occasionally dilated into undulated tracts.

Drill husbandry, (i. e. seeds sown after the plough,) seems much in practice here. The late noise about improving pasture grasses has been made with little reference to the nature of an Indian climate, or the genius of the Indian people. Pasture grasses only excel in countries where there is no division of climate into hot, rainy, and cold seasons; but not in those in which rain is equally, or nearly so distributed throughout the year. So far as I know, no place in India is calculated for pasture grass cultivation, because as none of excellent kinds can succeed without irrigation, this element of Indian agriculture is applied to more profitable cultures, such as artificial grasses. In the cold season and the rains, nature supplies *dhoob* grass bountifully, leaving the natives to apply their agricultural labour to other objects, and in such seasons the condition of cattle is decidedly good.

Manikyala Tope, seen from near Rowil Pendi, is an insignificant building, and presents the same architecture as other topes, and as the Cabul tower, although it is not of the same materials. The lower part of the base is of pure sandstone, the upper of a stalactital conglomerate of small pebbles, often perforated. The terraces at the base are now almost hid by rubbish, so that the whole looks like an overgrown dome or a low mound. There are three stone ledges below, with flat pilasters between the middle and lower ledge on the sides. The dome is much damaged. The stones of which the building was erected, were not hewn inside, but I do not know whether they have not been cemented together. Access is easy to the top partly by means of broken steps, otherwise the stones gave good footing. The top of the ruin is now open and discloses a square *funnel*, penetrating half the height of building; thence modern handiwork has caused a broken irregular perforation. The building is not remarkable for great size, nor are any of the stones large, still as a piece of achitecture it is far superior to any thing in modern Affghanistan. The country around is very bare and sufficiently open. It is curious that there are many Indian plants found on or about the building, all indicating a decided approach to Hindoostan. A Sida, Euonymus, Bheir, Lantana, and a Menispermum, are common shrubs on the building, also Solanum quercifolium, spinis albis floribus cœruleo purpureis.

25th.—To Puttiana, seventeen to eighteen miles; the country much the same, little wood but bushes of the old trees: it is tolerably open until Pukkee Serai is approached, when it becomes very much broken and intersected by ravines in every direction, showing most forcibly the action of water, many of the cliffs thus formed are picturesque. At Pukkee a small river is forded, thence to near Puttiana the country then becomes almost as raviny as before.

Ærua, Bheir, Mudar, a Kochia, much like one of the Cutch ones, and the before-mentioned plants continue.

26th.—To Bukriala, twenty-two miles. From Puttiana the road is good, extended over a high open country, except where it crosses two ravines; the first of these containing a stream of water, about ten miles from Puttiana. From Tammuch the road descends steeply into the Bukriala Kakhudd ravine, which takes you to Bukriala.

This ravine runs through a system of sandstone hills, of a blueish muddy aspect, and red clayey earth, often conglomerate. In colours not unlike the Bamean district. Water is plentiful in pools throughout the lower half of the road, which is all descent. Bukriala stands on the right bank of the Khudd river towards its mouth, the vegetation about this place resembles that of the open country, and is unchanged in the Khudd river, consisting of Kochia, *Phulahi,* and Mimosa albispina, Euonymus, *Bheir,* Adhatoda, Barleria, *Kureel,* and Capparis of Gundamuck; also Pommereullioid, Andropogon, Schœnanthus, Holcus, and Stipa of Kuta Sung, Carallunia, Grewia and Menispermum of Manikyala.

Also two plants not before seen, and neither common, one is a Butea, leguminous velutino pubescent arbor, it is the *Chuchra* of the natives, and is used for paper. The other is a curious, leafless, scandent, monocotyledon. Asparaginea, and an Apocynea.

Alhaji Maurorum is not found between this and Hussun Abdul, which is a curious thing.

27*th.*—To Rotas. The country to Mittian is very much broken and consequently difficult, consisting entirely of ups and downs: the road is only practicable for cattle; the bad part of it commences with an abrupt ascent. About Puttiana, four miles from Bukriala, it becomes better, but it continues partially raviny until within four miles of Rotas, when the country becomes open, and the road good.

Vegetation continues precisely the same, being still in the region of *Phulahi:* observed the Asparaginea again, Euonymus continues, also Astragalus, a Kochia, and an Affghan Chenopodium.

A beautiful *bhowli* or spring is passed on the way two miles from Rotas, it is covered with masonry, and the descent is by means of steps; the water passes under large arches, a work worthy of the Mogul emperors. Sissoo, Peroplocea of Bolan, common. Rotas is an immense irregular fortress, with the usual faults: it is much too large, and situated on a rocky plain partially commanded. It must have once contained a large number of inhabitants. Nelumbium, Potamogeton: half a mile from Rotas towards Peshawur, a square Serai, enclosing a garden, is passed.

The country immediately about it on the west is open: and well cultivated: there is but little water in the river. The town or village is of no size.

Butea not uncommon.

28*th.*—Proceeded to Jhilun. The road is at first steep, as it passes down along the Rotas river, about three miles from thence it is good, extending over a plain to the Jhilun. Fine cultivation observed on all sides, and of various sorts, chiefly *Bajra* and *Kureel.* Dhah abundant, but not arborescent, Euonymus, Peganum, *Bheir,* and *Phulahi,* the latter very dwarfish. Mimosa albispina and Adhatoda very common. The commonest tree in these countries is *Bheir*, and a very handsome tree it is; *Nihi-joari* cultivated.

Sun and *Tel* occur, the last is very common. Yesterday a new cultivation presented of a Composite plant called *Kalizeen*, used as a spice or *musala* for horses. The birds observed were Hæmatornis, Crateropod, Sylvia, Alauda cristata, Alauda alia in flocks.

The town of Jhilun stands immediately on the right bank of the river of that name, it is a large and flourishing place. The river is about 200 yards broad, not rapid, but here and there deep, and the bed at this place forms one undivided channel. The right bank on which the town stands has a stony sloping shore, the left is sandy.

It is a mistake to suppose that the hilly country ceases here, on the contrary, it crosses the Jhilun. At the ferry this river runs through a large valley, bounded to the west by hills like those to which we have been accustomed; to the east it is bounded by a low chain, which runs parallel with the general course of the river. The valley is open only to the north and south.

Otters, tortoises, and Mahaseer were seen in the river.

29th.—To Sera, twenty-four miles, half the distance extended over the uncultivated base of the hills, and then over the low range itself, from which at two points, fine views are obtained of the vast plain of the Punjab. Throughout this vast surface the vegetation is exactly the same—Euonymus continuing, Peganum and *Phulahi* forming chief vegetation; numbers of white partridge occur.

In the plains *Dhah* is found in profusion, especially where the cultivation is not extensive. A new Acacia appears, the *Kikkur*, forming groves about most of the villages. Noticed the Physaloides of Lundykhanah. Encamped under a fine Mimosa and *Bheir* near an old Serai which forms part of the village, with a splendid view of the Himalayas stretching away from east to west. It appears from this direction as if there was only one low range between the plains and the culminating range of the Himalayas. Nothing like these mountains has been seen in Khorassan. The chief cultivation about here is *Nihi-joari*, then *Bajra*—why is the former always bent?

Prickly pear common from where we crossed the Jhilun river.

A curious metamorphosis of Sesamum is of common occurrence: the calyx being unchanged, while the corolla preserves somewhat its shape, but is foliaceous, the other organs are much transformed, the ovary less so than the stamina, but generally much enlarged; *ovules in leaves* inside. This is worthy of examination, as it shows very plainly the origin of the stigmata from the placentæ.

30th.—Halted owing to having been robbed of two horses.

31st.—Wuzerabad, twenty-four miles. Ten miles from Wuzerabad the road extended through a highly cultivated country, and crossed the Chenab, on the left bank of which river Wuzerabad is situated. The Chenab is a fine river, the stream 150 yards wide, but on either side extensive beds of sand show that the river during some seasons is of great width.

Wuzerabad is a nice well built town, having a fine straight bazaar, with paved street. The chief gateways and residences built by General Avitabile.

Chilodia occurs in abundance, Eleusine sp., E. coracana; *Bajra* and *Joari Nihi* being the prevailing cultivation.

It is curious that in Phulahi major of Sera and the *Kikkur*, the young branches only are armed with thorns, so that the spines must be deciduous in certain species of Mimosa.

Cactus is an instance of a calyx composed of a congeries of adherent leaves, which leaves produce from their axilla, tufts of white hair and thorns; or is it not an instance of an axis hollowed out towards the apex, to the sides of which the ovary finally adheres, in this case the outermost series of the perianth will be calyx; one reason for adopting this supposition, besides the axillary bodies, is that there is no gradation between the small concave leaves of the calyx, and the outer series of the perianth.

November 1st.—Halted for fishing: Cyprinus Mrigala, is the *Mhoori* of these parts; it grows to a large size, is a handsome fish, and is indeed considered the king of fishes by the Punjabees. The intestines are in longitudinal folds of extremely small comparative diameter, and enormous length; in a large specimen it is twenty-three times the length of the body. The intestines of the *Mahaseer* are on the other hand only two and a quarter times the length of the body!

Of the fish obtained, two are Perilamps, here called *Rohi*,

5 or 6 Cyprinides,
4 or 5 Siluri,
2 Ophiocephali,
1 Esox.

Indeed I obtained a list of twenty-four species.

2nd.—To Goograuwala, twenty-four and a half miles, over a fine populous generally cultivated country. Goograuwala is a large town, having the streets paved with brick like those of Wuzeerabad. Cactus very common; *Kikkur* (Mimosa) is the chief tree here about the *Fukeer's* abodes. The Banyan also occurs.

Peganum and Kochia of Jallalabad continue. There is a fort of some size close to this town, built of mud; the ditch is unfinished, and not deep, it has a fausse-braie, with bastions like those at Peshawur and Jumrood. The surface of the ground is much broken close up to it, the earth being taken away for bricks.

3rd.—Proceeded to Koori, an inconspicuous village, belonging to M. Court; it is surrounded by extensive plains, on which a tall grass occurs to a great extent. Distance twenty-eight and a half miles, the time taken for to-day's journey was six and a quarter hours.

The country is precisely similar to that previously noticed, the only new feature being the grassy plains, in which at some little distance from Koori, deer, partridge, hares, etc. are said to abound.

A sissoo-like tree is not uncommon.

4th.—To Shah Durrah, twenty-three and a half miles at Nunzul, eight miles from Shah Durrah, a fort with ditch out of repair was passed, at Koori ten miles from Shah Durrah, passed a deep Nullah called Baghbuchah, with high banks, thence entered on a tract of country covered with Saccharum, *(Moong)*, from which ropes are made; (this is the same as the Chuch species,) we next entered on cultivation close to Shah Durrah, which place is well wooded.

Mangoe trees, *Ams*, Eugenia Jambolana, *Jams*, *Bheirs*, Phœnix, *Kikkur*, and Ficus, are the principal trees.

The grassy tracts of the Punjab represent probably the original vegetation, existing now only here and there owing to the extension of cultivation.

From Shah Durrah Lahore is visible, particularly the buildings of the Mogul emperor's, consisting of a conspicuous dome in ruins, and some minarets, a large Serai likewise going to ruin, standing in the immediate vicinity of the Royal Gardens. Lahore is decidedly a handsome looking city viewed from Shah Durrah.

So great is the tendency in palms to throw out roots towards the base, that these roots exist in the common *Khujoor*, although they have to get rid of the indurated bases of the petioles before they can make their exit. They are so extremely short and indurate that it is difficult to imagine the function they perform; at first they are capable probably of absorbing from the air.

5th.—Proceeded to General Court's house at Lahore, distance six miles, the road after crossing the Ravee river near a royal summer house of no extraordinary merits, passes on to the town, and then winds round under the Simon Boorge, a very striking part, at least exteriorly of the city, for the buildings, works, etc. are in good repair. Besides this the ground outside is swardy and prettily wooded.

CHAPTER XXIII.

From Lahore to Simla.

Lahore is surrounded by a ditch and wall, the work of former emperors' of Delhi; the environs of the city, particularly towards M. Court's residence, are studded with mosques, etc. mostly half ruined, and the ground is literally strewn with old bricks, so that the city must at one time have been an enormous one.

Seikh troops in large numbers are cantoned round to the east and south-east skirts of the town, in low pucka barracks.

Several low mounds apparently unconnected with ruins, occur in this direction.

I arrived to hear of the death of Kurruck Sing, who was burned the same day with five women; after the ceremony a scaffolding fell down, wounding Nehal Sing dangerously in the head, and killing the son of Goolab Sing. Late in the evening the Maharajah was senseless.

It is a curious thing, that the prince who this day ascended the *guddee,* and Goolab Sing, had been active intriguers against Kurruck Sing, who is said to have had his death hastened through chagrin at witnessing Nehal Sing's usurpation of power.

6*th.*—Not much cultivation was observed on the road to-day, which extended over a naked marshy saline plain, or through a *Kureel,* and small *Jundy* and *Phulahi* district.

To Kanah, seventeen miles—*Jundy, Kureel* and *Bheir* occur extensively. *Jundy* is a low prickly shrub, Mimosa. There is something curious both in the surface of the cavity enclosing the seed, and in that of the seed itself of Acacia serissa. The former presents the distinct appearance of a straight line, originating in the same spot as the funicle, and terminating in a very well marked, circular depression; it is formed by the funicle as far as the cells of the legume. If a section be made through the seed longitudinally and its cell parallel with the plane of the legume, this mark will be found on both sides of the cell, but more distinct on one than the other.

The mark on the seed by no means relates to this, at least it does not correspond with it, for it consists of a somewhat reniform elevated ridge, the ends of which do not meet, but one of which originates from an elevation to which the depression would seem to respond. The straight line does not correspond with the funicle, which is not straight, but is pushed up in a curved form against the upper edge of the cell.

It corresponds, however, with a straight subclavated line running from the hilum to the elevation whence the curved line originates, although this correspondence is not always well marked.

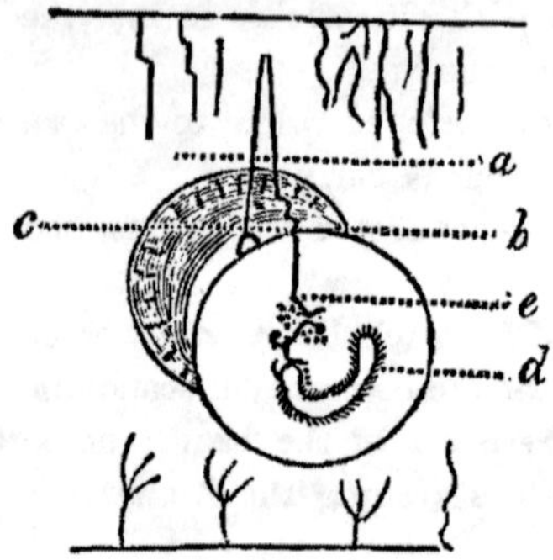

a. funicle.
b. cell.
c. line and depression.
d. seed.
e. line on seed, ending in a boss from which an elevated curved line originates.

The above marking, corresponding as it does in the flat part of the legume with the funicle, evidently points to a peculiarity in the distribution of the vascular system; probably it consists of the testa, and if so, it is worthy of remark, as the main vessels ordinarily a single one, run along the edge, and not on the flat surface of the fruit.

I know of no similar instance; in this plant the vessels of the testa are distributed primarily at right angles with the placenta, and not in parallel lines with that organ. If the seed were depressed instead of compressed, it would not present this peculiarity, although even then the two primary vessels would be remarkable. From this instance it may be assumed that the hilum may only be defined correctly as the spot of union between the body of the seed and the funiculus. The leaflets of the plumula are pinnate.

It is also curious that the distribution of green parenchyma is along the course of the veins of the legume, and that there is a more minute reticulation, and a greater development of the green colour on the faces of the cells, than on any other part of the surface of the legume. There is no difference appreciable by the naked eye between the placental and dorsal sutures, with the exception of the sutural line of union, which has the usual relation with the axis of the head of the flowers—Euphorbia occurs here.

The affinity of Cacteæ with Grossulaceæ is questionable, the systems of organization being very different. Query—What instances are there of affinity between inferior ovary plants, with distinct definite envelopes and stamina, and plants with a perhaps similar ovary, but with indefinite envelopes and definite stamina with a want of correspondence in the structure of the fruit?

7th.—To Kussoor, twenty miles. The road extended generally through a *Jendy* country: about half-way Salvadora appears in abundance. Kussoor is a large well-built town, consisting of three separate parts, each surrounded by a *pucka* wall furnished with bastions: these three parts are at some distance from each other. *Furas* tree common.

8th.—Ferozepore. About this place two species of Kochia occur, and Artemisia is not uncommon. The Serratuloides of Alli-Baghan and Ichardeh in profusion, affording cover for game.

16th to *21st.*—Loodianah. In the Nullah, Butomus begonifolius occurs.

The following are the fish of Loodianah taken both from the Nullah and the Sutledge.

Roh.—Cyprinus (Cirrhinus), a large, very handsome, excellent, orange-brown fish, takes a bait but is capricious.

Rohoo.—A sombre black-brown fish, intestines several times the length of the body, said to be the young of the above. Both these are different from the Roh or Ruee of the Ganges.

Coorsah.—Labeo Cursis, a definite scaled sombre fish, it is good food, and attains the size of two to three seers; intestines twice the length of the body, very narrow.

Khul Bhans.—Cirrhinus Calbasu, a sombre looking breamoid-shaped fish, attains the same size as the above, and is reputed to be excellent food.

Mhirgh.—Gobio Mrigala, a handsome fish, particularly when young; form very elegant, intestines fourteen times the length of the body; excellent food.

Bura Raiwah.—Gobio Rewah, a very handsome, eight-cornered, scaled fish, with orange fins and golden sides: takes no bait?

Chota Raiwah.—Gobio occurs in shoals—either occupied in busily turning up its silvery sides against the bottom, or at the surface, above which it may be seen protruding its head.

Bhangun.—Gobio, a handsome fish, not esteemed.

Potea.—Systomus, takes bait—worms; affords good sport and reaches to one seer, but is not esteemed; colours ordinary.

Systomus, a beautiful fish, back shining green, sides yellow, scales beautifully striate, with a spot near the tail; mostly found in still water.

Gonorrhynchus.—Snout rough, colours sombre, belly somewhat protuberant; found with Systomus. The intestines are of the usual form of the genus.

Gonorrhynchus, a sombre smaller fish, found in still water.

Bura Chalwa.—Much esteemed as food in the districts of the Sutledge.

Perilampus.—Intestines shorter than the body, having at the lower end a short curve; above green, from lateral line downwards silvery.

Moh.—A *Siluroid* fish, does not attain the size of the real Moh, which is a higher or deeper formed fish.

Tengrei.—Silurus platycephalus. Attains a very large size.

Gudha.—A Percoid. Colour irregular brown, mouth very protractile.

Gughal.—Ophiocephalus, a handsome fish, back rich greenish, mottled brown, with 3 or 4 black spots on the sides, which are yellow; passing off into white, and a peacock spot on the tail. Fins spotted with white: it reaches a large size.

Bham.—Macrognathus, body eel-shaped, with a row of movable spines along the back.

About Loodianah, the Naiad of Affghanistan, Monandra, stigmatibus reniformibus, is common in the Nullah, so also is Butomus begonifolius, but this may be a leafless form of Sagittaria.

Towards Roopur, Sissoo becomes more and more common. Roopur is a largish town, with a Seikh pucka fort on a mound. The fort is surrounded by a dry ditch. The town is situated on a low, rather rugged ground, forming the first elevations of the surface towards the Himalayas; beyond it to the north-east is a low spur, also to the west a similar spur, very barren, rugged, clayey rock forming the immediate bank of the river. Every thing assimilates to the Bukriala and Jhilun ranges. Saccharum, *Moong*, as before, *Bheir* likewise occurs.

Phœnix, Dalbergia sissoo, Ficus, Adhatoda, Boerhaavia scandens, Hyperanthera, Morus, Apluda, Tamarisk, Riccia, Ammannia, Euphorbia antiquorum, Cactus, and Dodonæa, form the chief vegetation.

Some rapids occur near the Bungalow: the strongest is under a cliff on the opposite side; no fish rose to red or black hackle or orange flies, all which were tried in vain in the deep still water close under Bungalow. The plants of this place are Guilandina, Grewia arbuscula in fruit, Justicia, *Bheir*, *Neem*, Mango, Parkinsonia, the latter rare.

Fish caught in net are Mullet, this fish is very active, and escapes by jumping over. Silurus, Mahaseer, several of the latter taken at a haul, the largest 10 lbs., it is a beautiful fish with golden sides, scales black, with the anterior half bluish-black, posterior half tawny-yellow, fins orange, lips very thick and leathery; it lives half or three-quarters of an hour after it is taken out of its element.

The *Nepura* of the natives, Gobio malacostoma, or Rock Carp of Gray, Hardwicke's Illustrations, is the *puhar-ka muchee* of these parts: it has the base and edges of the scales dull greenish-blue, fins dusky, a transverse pink line across the scales; the length of the intestines is twenty-two and a half times that of the body, filled with mud and coloured pulp, stomach continuous with the intestine, and more fleshy, filled with green and whitish pulp, and disposed in longitudinal folds.

The *Bangun*, Roh, (Gobio) is a splendid fish, base and edges of the scales dusky brown, otherwise refulgent gilded, belly white, fins dusky, head greenish-brown, less gilding about the dorsal scales. This fish I have not seen elsewhere. Length of intestines disposed in longitudinal folds, the posterior of which are nearly as long as abdominal cavity, the whole twenty-seven and a half times the length of the body. Organization and contents as in *Nepura*. The breadth or depth of this fish immediately behind the opercule three inches, across the body, opposite the first ray of dorsal fin, five inches, first ray of anal three inches, length twenty-two inches.

Query—In which part of a fish intestines like that of the Mahaseer, is the chief digestion carried on?

27*th*.—To Nalighur Bungalow, the distance rather less than sixteen, but over fourteen miles through a similar country to that round Roopur. The road passes a large village called Canowli; at rather less than about half-way it extended across a sandy dry river bed of some extent, on the right bank of which, at the highest part, is a Seikh brick fort. The road subsequently passes the Sursa, a small shallow rapid stream. The dry bed of which turns up on the south side of the low range to the south of Nalighur valley. No change in vegetation takes place, except the occurrence of a Croton, much like that of the Pagoda near Canowli.

Trees observed—Eugenia Jambolana, Mangifera indica, Ficus, *Bheir*, *Neem* or Melia Azadarach, Parkinsonia about the bungalow. Toon, Cordia, Bauhinia, Bambusa, Emblica, Morus, Plumeria, Mudar, Saccharum, *Moong*, Bheir fruticos and Kikkur are the most common indigenous forms. Dhak in patches here and there: Cassia also occurs.

Nalighur consists of a village and fort, the latter situated to the north-east half-way up a range of hills, the country about very barren. Indeed the aspect of the country is much like that between Hussun Abdul and the Jhilun, except in the rarity of *Phulahi*.

A great affinity exists in foliation between Terebinthaceæ and Sapindaceæ. Also both in foliation, flowers, and habit, between Myrtaceæ and Guttiferæ, the only material differences being in aroma, and adherent ovary.

The plants observed about Nalighur Bungalow, exclusive of species collected, were Cassia lanceolatoid, this is the common Indian *Tora*, Acacia, *Rairoo*, Achyranthes aspera, Digera arvensis, Polanisia viscosa, Carissa, Carandas, Bheir frutex, Coccinea communis, Cucurbita, Sida multilocularis, Amaranthus? spicatus, Cassia fistula.

Eleusine *echinata*; Poa very common, as well as *Dhoob*.

In gardens—Tabernamontana coronaria, *Bhee*, Chrysanthemum double and ligulate. Of Birds, *Pica vagans*.

28th.—From Nalighur to Ramgurh, a good ten miles. The road first ascends through and above the town, then follows a short twisting descent, and soon after a very long but not very steep ascent, until it comes over the ravine of the Ramgurh river, and the descent to that torrent; thence an uninterrupted steep ascent about as much as the descent to Ramgurh. There is no bungalow at this stage, merely a few shops and sheds. The fort is situated to the left of and 600 feet above the town.

From Ramgurh to Sahee Bungalow, the distance is eight miles, there is a steep descent to Sursa torrent, which contains very little water, then a rather long and gradual ascent, then descend to the Gumbur river. The road then extends up this ascent for one and a half mile, and continues ascending on the right bank until within half a mile of the bungalow, to which there is a slight descent. There is no made road along the Gumbur, and I missed or did not observe the Soorog river. The Gumbur is a clear, good-sized stream, fordable about the rapids, bed narrow confined.

The hills traversed were comparatively barren, and decidedly uninteresting. However much in appearance they may here and there assimilate to the Khorassan hills, no identity in vegetation exists except perhaps in the Apocynum found at Attock.

The country is cultivated with great labour, and the villages though small are numerous, and present a look of plenty, like English white-washed cottages.

There is a difference between the vegetation of the hills near the plains and those in the interior. On the former there are scarcely any trees, and Adhatoda occurs in greater profusion than elsewhere. The Himalayan provinces here present an extreme affinity with the same range to the eastward, as Bootan and Mussoorie, but the forms are by no means so frequent—i. e. species are not so numerous. Throughout the above twenty-eight miles the vegetation is tropical: a few European forms occur as one gets into the hills, but they are of no great value. The chief arboreous vegetation consists of Rubiaceæ, Mimoseæ, Cassiaceæ *(Bauhinia)*, Bignoniaceæ, and Myrtaceæ. These are much the most common between Ramgurh and the ridge over Naligurh. Here also Nyctanthes is very common; Zanthoxylon also occurs here and there like an Ash.

On the ridge above Ramgurh, Adhatoda is very common; Carandas likewise occurs, but is not very common; Eranthemoides is rather common, but this occurs in profusion on the descent; Cassia tora, C. lanceolata, and Peristrophe occur.

On the descent from the above ridge, Porana appears. Lemon-grass, Bambusifolia, Cryptogramæ calamelanos, Adiantum flagelliformis.

On the long ascent Grislea, Acacia, Bheir, Zanthoxylon, Cordia, Nyctanthes, Myrtaceæ 1-2, Wendlandia, Bignonia, Randia, and two or three other trees about houses, a species of Ficus; Euphorbia antiquorum common on the drier parts.

On the ascent from the torrent, the vegetation is thick. Bauhinia scandens, Carandas, Butea, Erythrina, neither common, others as before: Loranthus.

At Ramgurh, Peepul, Erythrina, Rhus planted; Euphorbia antiquorum very common, Cassia tora, C. lanceolata, Carandas common, Kalanchœ integrifolia, Adhatoda not rare, scarcely a single wild tree.

Scutellaria occurs on the descent. Rubus, Berberis, Gnaphalium. On the ascent from Sursa, Geranium, Clematis, Asparagus, Trichodesma of the plains, Bombax (young), Bambusa, Hirœa, Dioscorea, Fragaria, Adiantum flagelliformis, Calomelanos, Saccharum, *Moong*, Acacia, Adhatoda, Vitex, etc. as before, but trees are not common, except Ficus and *Bheir* in profusion.

Descent to the Gumbur the same. Pyrus pomum appears, Carandas, Anatherum muricatum, Briedleioides common. Along the Gumbur river, Pyrus, Adhatoda, Mimosa, Dalbergia sissoo, Myrtaceæ, Euphorbia, etc. continue as before.

Between Nalighur and the commencement of the descent to the Gumbur, and especially between the Sursa and that descent, the chief vegetation is tropical grasses, such as Andropogons. Along the Gumbur, the hills are well covered with tall bushes. Carandas common, but little if any grass.

Fossil shells are found along the Gumbur. Of birds Pica vagans, Hœmatornis, and several Sylviæ were observed.

About Sahi, young Pinus longifolia ; all around, the hills are of the same aspect. No fish were seen in the Gumbur, although I crossed it several times. The view of the plains shows the commencement of the great chain stretching out in low, very much undulated hillocks, precisely as in Khorassan.

29th.—Proceeded from Syree to Konyar : this I think the longest of the marches to Loodianah, and is nothing but one series of ascents and descents chiefly along the Gumbur ravine : at the foot of ascent to the Konyar, the road crosses a considerable stream, and nearly at the summit of the ascent, branches off to Soobathoo.

Konyar is a rather large village, well ornamented with trees, in rather a fine sort of valley, every inch of which is cultivated. The tank adjacent to the village is well stocked with Nelumbium.

To Syree, the distance is eight and a half to nine miles. The road crosses the Konyar village and valley, then ascends to the south-east, and continues ascending gradually by an excellent road for a considerable way, then it skirts a ridge and comes on the grand Soobathoo road. From this a short but steep ascent, followed by a descent of a mile and a quarter, conducts you to the bungalow.

No change occurs in the vegetation. The hills are more grassy and more bare of trees, especially near Syree, but this is partly owing to cultivation. The principal woody feature is Euphorbia antiquorum.

The plants before noticed occur throughout, except about Syree, where scarcely a shrub is to be seen, nothing but burnt up grasses.

At Sahee, Roylea appears, also an odd-looking Modeeca and a Deeringia. Near these is also an Asplenium, Echites. At Konyar, Prinsepia appears, and continues becoming more and more frequent up to Syree. Towards this place V. reniformis is seen, not a single northern grass, althôugh Syree must be nearly 5,000 feet high.

At Sahi, Pinus longifolia, Phœnix, Salix, and Polygonum of Chugur-Serai; this is common as far as Konyar. Acacia, Carandas, Urtica nivea. Rice cultivated.

About three miles beyond it, there is a beautiful ravine with dense jungle and fine trees, chiefly Laurinea, and I think a Rhus; this is the only spot I have seen reminding me of the Himalaya to the eastward.

At Konyar—Toon, Morus, Musa, Deeringia, Berberis, Briedleia.

The hills are as usual marked with wavy parallel lines, on which nothing appears to grow. These lines are united by smaller oblique ones, whence their origin?

30*th*.—To Simla. The road extends over undulated ground along ridges until the foot of the great ascent is reached; this is long and steep, especially steep at the first, or Buttiara pass, where it turns to the face of the mountain, and extends through beautiful woods. The ground frozen, with some snow; from this to Simla the road is tolerably level, and defended on the *Khudd*, or precipice side by a railing. It then passes through fir woods, etc. in which the exceedingly pretty Jay of Bharowli is common.

The vegetation to the foot of the ascent, and nearly half-way up, is unchanged. Andropogoneous grasses forming the prevailing feature; but little arboreus or shrubby vegetation occurs. About half-way between Syree and this an ascent takes place, on which Daphne, Hypericum, and Echinops occur.

Near Syree—Bombax, Ruta albiflora, Daphne, Pteris aquilina, Clutia, Aspidium, Polytrichum nanum and aloides, Hypericum, Berberis, Rubus, Prinsepia, Rosa, Jubrung, Grislea, (rare,) Clematis, Cerasus, *Datura*, *Bukhein*, Citrus, Spermacoce, Pœderia azurea, and Andropogon bambusifolia were observed. Ficus two species, Ficus repens, Pommereullioid spicis longis, Rubia Mungista, Galium, Polygonum of Chugur, Carissa, (rare,) Amaranthaceæ, Conyza.

The great ascent is very instructive; half-way up observed Gaultheria, conspicuous from its blood-coloured leaves; an oak occurs commonly but stunted, and a few stunted Pinus longifolia.

Buddlæoides occurs two-thirds of the way up, with Mespilus microphyllus, Alpina, Labiata and Pyrus.

The oaks and Gaultheria increase in number and size towards Bithuria, Conaria.

The first to cease is Euphorbia.

At the summit Berberis, Polygonum of Chugur, Rubus deltoideus, Conyza and Prinsepia may be found, but to no extent. From this to Simla the vegetation is chiefly northern.

Nothing definite is observable with regard to the distribution of forests about Simla. The principal secondary ranges, including the Choor, which is quite void of shrubby vegetation, is about north-east and south-west; generally the southern aspects of those ridges on which forests occur is bare; of this, there is a notable instance—Muhassoo.

Mount Jacka, which looks east and west by its broad faces, has both densely enough wooded with oak, Euonymus, Rhododendron, Gaultheria, and Ilex, but the ridge which looks to the plains is bare.

Some ridges again are quite bare, as that lowish one between Mounts Jacka and Muhassoo.

The thicket and moist humid woods decidedly occur on the northern faces of the ridges; and all about Simla instances of this occur. Such spots are at Simla so much sheltered from the sun, that the snow which fell on the 23rd November is scarcely diminished.

Even in these there is no comparison in luxuriance and variety of vegetation with the Mishmee or Bootan portions of the same stupendous chain.

The trees are few in number as regards species, the only ones I have observed are a species of oak which is very common, forming the chief vegetation of the northern faces, and of both those of mount Jacka.

The scarlet Rhododendron which occurs in the highest parts of the woods, an occasional Pyrus, Benthamia, Euonymus, Gaultheria very common, also Pinus Deodara, longifolia, and excelsa; of these the Deodar is most common. Ilex, a pretty tree, occurring on Mount Jacka.

The following forms also I have noticed—Saxifraga ciliata, Berberis asiatica, and Gnaphalia three or four species, which are chiefly confined to grassy naked ridges. Thymus is also confined to these.

Ruta albiflora is very common in woods; Dipsacea and Artemisia on exposed grassy spots; Swertia is common in damp places; Spireæa bella, Ledum, Stemodia, Epilobium, Viola, Saccharum rubrum, Valeriana, Fragaria, Galium, Clematis, Rosa, Rubus, Rumex, Leguminosæ, Coronilloid, Smilax.

Acanthaceæ, Androsaceæ, particularly a Gnaphalioides common on the exposed ridge of Mount Jacka; Myrsinea frutex, Parnassia common, Salix fruticosa; on Prospect Point, Lycopodium, Herminioid, Epipactis, Orchideæ aliæ, 2 Scitamineæ.

Elæagnus, Mespilus microphyllus, Polygonum of Chugur; 2 or 3 Amaranthaceæ; Prinsepia, rare; very little variety in ferns; Pteris chrysocarpa, Aspidium pungens, and another are the most common; nor is there any variety in Epiphytous ferns, and very few Jungermannias. The Mosses are Bartramia, Catharinea, Polytrichum aloides on banks with Fissidens, otherwise Hypna are the most prevalent. A Neckera hangs from every tree, and a Pterogonio Neckeroid covers almost every trunk, a Brachymenium is likewise common.

Altogether, though numerous, there is no great variety in form.

On the summit of Chaka, Quercus, Gaultheria, and Rhododendron are common; with here and there a Deodar.

On the east face of that mountain consisting of a long ridge, grasses form the chief vegetation, among which Andropogons and Schœnanthus are not uncommon, Gnaphalia and Artemisia occur; Thymus, Androsace gnaphalioides, Potentilla, Coronilloid, Labiata frutex, Jasminum, Rosa, Mespilus microphyllus, Clematis, Cnicus, Rubus, Labiata alia, Galium, Swertia, Salvia were noticed.

Of the tropical forms, Andropogoneous grasses are most common, Saccharum rubrum of the Khasyah Mountains, Desmodium, Acanthaceæ, and Elæagnus, which last occurs on Prospect Point.

Saccharum rubrum extends up to 8,000 feet.

The woods generally on the surface are matted down with grasses or Carexes, so that there is no variety of surface for the lower orders; in such places, Ophiopogon is very common.

Regarding the Coniferæ, Pinus excelsa is the rarest, Deodar is the most common; longifolia occurs principally on a southern projection from Chaka, and on the south face of the Mall ridge.

December 5th, 1840.—Went to Mount Fagoo. After passing Mount Jacka, or Chaka, you come on a bare country which continues at least on all the southern aspects until you reach the ascent to Muhassoo, which is at first steep, then gradual and long; the vegetation remains unchanged until the Muhassoo ascent is begun upon; then Rhododendron, Quercus and Gaultheria soon cease, and their places are occupied by a Quercus much like Q. semecarpifolius, Pinus excelsa also occurs rather abundantly, and of good size, the other vegetation continues.

The first part of Muhassoo, along which the road runs for some hundred yards under its crest, is occupied by grassy vegetation, chiefly Andropogon and Schœnanthus; Gnaphalia, Buddlæa, Labiata, Polygonum of Chugur, Thymus, etc., and the crest of the same is chiefly occupied by the undescribed oak.

But where the ridge takes a north and south direction, the west face becomes almost exclusively occupied by Deodars, among which as one proceeds up, Pinus Smithiana occurs; after turning again close to the little Bazar on the north face, the road continues on this side to Fagoo, extending through a heavy and magnificent forest of Pinus Smithiana and Quercus semecarpifolius, the Deodar almost ceasing to appear; occasional knolls are passed, on which grasses, Gnaphalium, etc. occur, the scenery is very beautiful, the trees being ornamented with the grey pendulous lichen, and with Neckeræ, particularly the dark Neckera pendula. The underwood consists here and there of shrubs, but generally herbaceous vegetation, as grasses, Gnaphalia, etc.

In fact Muhassoo is genuinely Himalayan.

From Fagoo eastward the country is bare, except at great elevations; near Muttiara to the north, forest-clad mountains occur, also at Huttoo, and far away to the eastward other fir-clad ridges appear.

It may be said that the really fine forests are restricted above, within 8,000 feet.

The Smithia pine is a really fine tree, often 100 feet high, and three to five feet in diameter, known by its downward curved branches, pendulous branchlets, and pendulous oblong cones: many dead trees from the effects of barking were observed. It is worthy of remark, that potatoes are now cultivated in these woods.

The Deodar is not so large as Smithia, and is known by its tabular branches and ovoid erect cones.

Andropogoneous grasses occur high up; even at the summit Acanthaceæ occur, scarcely any change in the terrestrial ferns, among which Adiantum is found in profusion along the road, little change in Mosses, a Polytrichum occurs at the higher elevations, also a Dicranum on dead trunks of trees.

The only new arboreous vegetation consists in an Acer, which is a small tree, also a small Poplar and Quercus semecarpifolius, this varies greatly, Pinus Smithiana, Limonia laureola, a shrubby Rhododendron.

Fagoo is only 5,600 feet above the adjacent heights.

On the edge of the forest, the following genera, etc. were noticed—Spiræa bella and S. aruncus,* Berberis asiatica, Swertia, grasses common, Gnaphalium, Senecio., Epilobium, Pteris chysocarpa, P. aquilina, Adiantum, Aspidium, Rumex, the Labiata fruticosa of Jacka, Potentilla sanguinea, Artemisia, Coronilloid, Androsacea, Gnaphalioid, Epipactis, Carex, Cnicus, Viola, Valerianum, Jasminum,* Viburnum,* V. aliud, Populus,* Silene, Mespilus microphyllus, Verbascum, Thapsia, Ilex, Euonymus, Loniceroid, Acer,* Eriogonoid,* Geranium scandens.*

Bupleuroid, Polytrichum, Rosa, Rubus, Salex fruticosa,* Fragaria, Cratægus,* Saxifraga crassifolia, Viscum, Rubia cordifolia.

Viscum has one attachment, but from this many branches spring after the form of the primary one. Muhassoo is of great extent, because an arm of the mountain extends to the south, and there assumes a considerable height, equal to that of Muhassoo itself, and equally well wooded. It is of all other situations about Simla the proper place for collecting. The succession of the pines in these regions is as follows :—

P. longifolia, dry barren spots, from 5,000 to 7,500 feet, as Rhododendrum arboreum.

P. excelsa, from 7,500 to 8,500 feet, no groups occur.

P. Deodars, from 7,500 to 9,000 feet, especially on southern faces.

P. Smithiana, from 9,000 to 10,000 feet, and is in the highest perfection on north faces.

One thing remarkable is the wide ranges of the above forms, for excepting those marked with an asterisk, all are found about Simla.

The most common herbaceous family on Muhassoo is Compositæ, and very strange to say, most of its forms, as indeed the others, excepting some of the trees, are found on the Khasyah Mountains at much lower elevations, and much lower latitudes. Of birds the *Cone-eater* of Bootan occurs.

7th.—To Annandale, a pretty level spot, some 2,000 feet below Simla, remarkable for its beautiful grove of Deodars.

Of the wild grasses they are almost all exclusively tropical forms, Paniceous or Andropogoneous. The chief cultivation of the hills, Atriplex sanguinea, *bhatoo vena,* some fine walnut trees, mulberries, also Celtoidea ? *Kirrack ven,* Zanthoxylon.

Passed a herd of red-rumped monkeys ; the crooked-tailed *Lungoor* is also found here.

Rich vegetation extends down the southern slope, where there is a waterfall. It is curious that both here and in Annandale the Deo-

* Means altitudinal.

dar grows to a large size, although naturally its range does not extend so low as this slope. Passed a beautiful temple, surrounded with fine Deodars.

Ferns occur in more abundance, thence downwards Woodwardia, Dicksonia ? Cyatheoides, and Adiantum. Mosses also occur on the dripping rocks.

An Alnus also occurs.

No fish were visible in the streamlet. Peristrophe occurs throughout from Roopur to Simla.

Epiphytous or at least *Epirupous* Scitaminia. Hedychium is found on rocks on this slope, which would give an elevation of about 5,500 feet.

On the sunny sides of hills about Simla, Dicerma is found, this is one of the most tropical forms.

No Epiphytous Orchidea are seen. And of birds Enicurus, the redstart of torrents, and Myophonus were observed.

CHAPTER XXIV.

*Heights and Latitudes of the Stations visited in Affghanistan.**

"The subjoined Table contains the latitudes and the altitudes of the principal stations passed through by the late Dr. Griffith during the Cabul campaign in 1838-40, from his original observations. The altitudes for the latitudes were taken with the sextant and the artificial horizon, and the results throughout are so nearly coincident, that it may be relied on the latitudes herein given are correct to within half a minute in space.

The altitudes determined by the barometer are on the principle, that the temperature and the altitude of the barometer as observed at any station on the preceding day would be the same, could the observations be made at it and the present station at the same instant of time. The formula from whence the altitudes have been deduced on this principle, is $60345.51 \{1 + 001111 (t + t'-64°)$ $\times \log. \text{of} \frac{\beta,}{\beta'} \left\{ \frac{1}{1 + 0001 (r-r')} \right\} \times (1 + 002695 \cos. 2\phi)$ where β, t, and r are the altitude of the barometer the temperature of the air and of the mercury at the lower station; and the same letters accented, the corresponding quantities at the upper station, being the latitude of the place."

Latitudes, and Elevations above the Sea, of the various localities visited in Affghanistan.

STATION.	No. of observations.	Latitude of Station.			Its elevation by barometer.
		°	′	″	
Loodianah, ...	12	30	53	22	....
Hureeky Ghat, ...	2	31	7	34	....
Shevalee (on Indus), ...	4	28	29	9	....
Shikarpore, ...	9	27	56	53	255
Bagh (Town), ...	6	29	2	20	....
Mysoor, ...	6	..	10	45	....

* The Editor is indebted to the kindness of Mr. Curnin, not only for the above note with which this table of heights and latitudes is introduced, but also for the construction of the table itself from the results of 437 observations for latitudes alone, and an equal number almost for altitudes.

Station.	No. of observations.	Latitude of Station.			Its elevation by barometer.
		°	′	″	
Nowshera,	4	29	22	16	....
Dadur,	4	..	28	31	744
Drubbee,	2	..	28	52	....
Kohinlai,	3	..	27	45	904
Gurmab,	5	..	35	14	1,081
Beebee Nanee,	2	..	41	28	1,700
Abigoom,	2	..	48	20	2,541
Sir-i-Bolan,	3	..	..	..	4,494
Mouzil,	3	..	55	10	....
Sinab,	1	30	6	0	....
Quettah,	9	..	12	53	5,537
Hydozye,	2	..	29	6	5,259
Hykulzye,	2	..	37	24	5,063
Kojhuk Pass,	2	..	50	40	7,492
Choky on descent to Candahar,	2	..	52	0	5,756
Dund-i-Goolai,	1	..	58	15	4,036
Candahar,	60	31	35	30	3,484
Kelat-i-Azim,	2	..	38	19	3,946
Turnuk river, Khet-i-Akhoond,	2	..	43	21	4,418
Shau-i-Suffer,	2	..	48	8	4,618
Zirandaz,	2	..	51	51	4,829
Zoot,	2	..	56	16	....
Julduck,	..	..	..	..	5,396
Khilat-i-Gilzee,	5	32	7	25	5,773
Sir-i-Asp,	3	..	12	22	5,973
Shuftul,	2	..	24	58	6,514
Chushar-i-Shadee,	3	..	31	17	6,668
Ghosan,	2	..	44	16	7,068
Mookhloor,	4	32	51	21	7,091
Oba,	2	33	0	47	7,325
Jumrat,	2	..	8	13	7,426
Karabagh,	2	..	13	13	....
Nanee Wells,	3	..	24	27	7,502
Ghuznee,	6	..	34	3	7,726
Hyderkail,	2	..	58	19	7,671
Shurgar,	..	..	..	..	8,697
Shaikhabad,	3	34	5	30	7,473
Kila Sir Mahomed,	..	..	..	..	8,051
Urgundee,	..	..	..	..	7,628
Kilah-i-Kazee,	..	..	..	..	6,522
Cabul,	23	..	30	31	6,393
Shak-i-Sofaid Pass,	..	..	..	..	8,670
Koti-i-Ashruf, Mydan valley,	..	..	..	..	7,749
Seer-i-Chushm,	..	..	..	..	8,836
Oonnoo Pass,	..	..	..	..	11,320
Yonutt,	4	..	28	29	10,618
Siah-Sing,	2	..	28	29	10,488
Foot of ascent (Hajeeguk,)	..	..	..	..	11,370
Top of ditto,	..	..	..	..	12,190
Kulloo Pass,	2	..	39	41	12,481
Kulloo-Ka-Rood,	2	..	42	40	....
Topchee,	2	..	47	6	9,085
Bamean,	14	..	49	51	8,496
Zohawk,	2	..	50	1	8,186
Kotul Erak,	..	..	..	..	9,155
Erak,	1	..	49	44	8,914
Erak Ravine,	..	..	..	..	11,545

STATION.	No. of observations.	Latitude of Station. °	′	″	Its elevation by barometer.
Summit of Erak Pass, ...	..	..	..	..	12,909
Kurzar, ...	2	34	39	24	10,939
Helmund, ...	1	34	30	56	10,076
,, ravine, ...	..	..	..	..	10,522
Seer-i-Chushme, ...	2	..	26	39	8,836
Julraiz, ...	1	..	28	36	8,082
Koti-Ashruf, ...	1	..	27	1	7,749
Shak Sofaid Pass or Urghundee, ..	3	..	28	44	8,670
Topchee Bashee, ...	2	..	30	39	7,628
Cabul, ...	19	..	30	37	6,396
Bootkah, ...	1	..	30	30	6,248
Koord Cabul, ...	1	..	24	6	7,466
Taizeen, ...	4	..	24	32	6,488
Barikab, ...	5	..	31	2	5,313
Jugdulluck, ...	6	..	26	25	5,375
Soorkhab, ...	4	..	20	42	4,373
Gundamuk, ...	5	..	17	37	4,616
Futtehabad, ...	7	..	21	12	3,098
Sultanpore, ...	4	..	24	38	2,286
Jallalabad, ...	24	..	25	4	1,964
Ali Baghan, ...	5	..	22	19	1,911
Barikab, ...	2	..	19	15	1,822
Bussoolah, ...	4	..	15	11	1,509
Lalpore, ...	8	..	13	25	1,405
Lundye Khannah, ...	4	..	6	34	2,488
Khyber Pass, ...	..	..	..	..	3,373
Ali Musjid, ...	1	..	00	41	2,433
Jumrood, ...	..	..	..	..	1,670
Mouth of Khyber Pass, ...	2	33	58	35	1,236
Peshawur, ...	6	34	00	3	1,068
Bussout, ...	3	34	28	38	....
Shauva, ...	3	..	34	9	....
Pushut Fort, ...	12	..	43	2	....
Chugur-Sari Paieen, ...	5	..	51	44	....
——— Ootipore, ...	19	..	54	38	....
Kooner, ...	4	..	37	38	....

Index.

END OF VOL. I.

BISHOP'S COLLEGE PRESS.